MW01254008

The Spirit of Creativity

Basic Mechanisms of Creative Achievements

Gottlieb Guntern

GUELPH HUMBER LIBRARY
205 Humber College Blvd
Toronto, ON   M9W 5L7

UNIVERSITY PRESS OF AMERICA,® INC.
Lanham • Boulder • New York • Toronto • Plymouth, UK

Copyright © 2010 by University Press of America,® Inc.

4501 Forbes Boulevard
Suite 200
Lanham, Maryland 20706
UPA Acquisitions Department (301) 459-3366

Estover Road
Plymouth PL6 7PY
United Kingdom

All rights reserved.
Printed in the United States of America
British Library Cataloging in Publication Information Available

Library of Congress Control Number: 2010921949
ISBN: 978-0-7618-5051-9 (clothbound : alk. paper)
ISBN: 978-0-7618-5052-6 (paperback : alk. paper)
eISBN: 978-0-7618-5053-3

∞™ The paper used in this publication meets the minimum requirements of American
National Standard for Information Sciences—Permanence of Paper for Printed Library
Materials, ANSI Z39.48-1992

To my wife, Greta, visual artist and highly inspiring and supportive
companion on the many trails of exploration and adventure
we have walked together.

Contents

Preface

Stepping-stones on the path leading to the present book:

Famous Persian polymath Ibn Sina (980-1037 AD), known in the Occident under the name of Avicenna, wryly stated: "The world is divided into men who have wit and no religion and men who have religion and no wit."

The town of Brigue, at the foot of the Southern Swiss Alps that separate Switzerland from Italy, boasts of an impressive castle. The *Stockalper Schloss* (Castle Stockalper) was named after its original owner Kaspar Jodok von Stockalper (1609-1691). He was a man obviously able to combine wit and religion. In the course of his life, the big-time entrepreneur and banker amassed so much wealth that admirers called him "the Fugger of the Alps." Popes, emperors, and kings showered him with honors. Ferdinand III, Emperor of the Holy Roman Empire, appointed him Chevalier of the Order of the Golden Spur. French ruler Louis XIV, the Sun King, bestowed upon him the Order of St. Michael.

Why was this man blessed with so much prestige, prosperity, and influence, enabling him to rub shoulders with the mightiest figures of his time? Three main factors were responsible for his breathtaking rise to power: he held the monopoly for the salt import over the Simplon Pass; he possessed mines and exported iron ores to various countries; and he was a ruthless human trafficker, selling thousands of mercenaries to the highest bidders in Europe.

During the Thirty Years War (1618-1648), a bitter religious feud involving all major European powers, two commodities were very much in demand: warriors and gunpowder. Mughal Emperor Shah Jahan of India supplied the warring nations with tons of saltpeter needed for the fabrication of gunpowder; von Stockalper alias, "King of the Simplon," provided them with scores of warriors. These resources helped to stage a mega-massacre resulting in a ruined landscape and, according to moderate estimates, the deaths of about seven million people who fell victim to war activities, famine, and epidemics.

With the money made in that war, Emperor Shah Jahan built in Agra, northern India, the Taj Mahal—a monument of love. He created the extremely expensive mausoleum in white marble for his favorite wife Mumtaz Mahal; it is considered to be the most magnificent embodiment of Mughal architecture. Kaspar Jodok von Stockalper invested his profits made in the Thirty Years War and in his other business ventures in two different building projects— both monuments to his ability to straddle Avicenna's dichotomy between men with wit and men with religion.

He commissioned an Italian architect to construct an imposing castle with an inner courtyard spacious enough to accommodate his multiple trade caravans with their precious cargo. That square was surrounded with rows of archways two and three stories high. Mighty towers marked three corners of the courtyard, their massive granite blocks promised to withstand the ravages of time. He named these towers after his three sons whom he had christened (oh modesty where is thy whisper?!) Kaspar, Melchior, and Balthassar in a grandiose salute to the Three Magi, or Three Wise Men, mentioned in the New Testament. The Three Wise Men had trekked from the orient to the cradle in Bethlehem to offer three precious gifts to baby Jesus: gold, frankincense, and myrrh.

In order to have God on his side, von Stockalper had a church built with an adjacent Kollegium Spiritus Sanctus consisting of a boarding school and a teaching facility catering to boarders and day-pupils. To foster excellence in performance, he put a group of Jesuits in charge of the educational program for his boys-only school. Often considered to be the intellectual elite of the Roman Catholic Church, the Jesuits' mission was to imbue the boys with a spirit of rigorous discipline and assorted values fitting the official ideology, intellectual aspirations, and moral code of conduct of the Roman Catholic Church.

The castle still stands today, so do church and Kollegium; yet the Jesuits didn't last. It is interesting to notice that in the seventeenth century, when they began to play a crucial role in von Stockalper's Kollegium, Jesuits—christened "Soldiers of God" and "Foot Soldiers of the Pope" —were involved in strategically important activities all over the planet.

In 1541, Francis Xavier, founder of the religious order Society of Jesus, began his missionary activities in Goa, the capital of Portuguese Indian colonies. In 1580, Jesuits were put in charge of the feudal fiefdom of Nagasaki, Japan; seven years later they lost that privilege because the Tenno of the Empire of the Rising Sun was alarmed at their growing influence. In the sixteenth century, Jesuits also began to invest their missionary zeal in China and by the seventeenth century, they established a strong foothold at the court of the emperors of the Manchu Qing Dynasty. Emperor Kangxi (1654-1722), one of the most powerful rulers China ever had, expanded his territories to the southeast by conquering Taiwan, to the northeast by defeating Czarist Russia, and to the northwest. Jesuits surveyed and mapped the territories he subjugated. His grandson Emperor Qianlong (1711-1799) twice invaded the Turkic domains around the Tarim Basin in the northwest of the Chinese Empire and took control of the Gurkha state of Nepal. To celebrate his victories, Jesuits had massive engravings produced in Paris.

In other words, in the seventeenth century, when they began to program the brains of country boys in von Stockalper's Kollegium Spiritus Sanctus, Jesuits were successful global players. Yet it was their keen interest in secular power that eventually sealed their fate in Switzerland. In 1847, after having been accused of meddling in national political affairs, Jesuits were expelled from the country.

In the 1950s, I attended Kollegium Spiritus Sanctus boarding school for eight years, then managed by priests of the Roman Catholic Church. They tried to maintain the spirit of the founding fathers although many of them didn't particularly impress us with their intellectual capabilities. Nevertheless, they provided me with two major lessons for which I shall be grateful forever.

The first lesson was that sheer tedium may, quite unexpectedly, turn out to be a blessing in disguise. I was bored stiff by the daily routine, which mercilessly stuck to the ecclesiastic maxim *ora et labora*—pray and work. In order to escape that monotony, I turned into an avid reader of books that inspired my imagination. As time went by, I read all the classics—historiographers, philosophers and writers from ancient Greece and Rome, some biographies on great scientists and artists living in the time span between the Italian Renaissance and the end of the nineteenth century, and major literature created by the great European and American writers of past centuries. The very last book I read in boarding school was Hemingway's novella *The Old Man and the Sea*. Devouring all these books allowed me to catch a first glimpse of the mystery of human creativity and kindled my life-long interest in that topic.

The second lesson was that rigorous rational thinking begins with a precise definition of basic terms; they constitute the building blocks of a conceptual framework, and if their inner structure is not solid, the whole construction will crumble. That lesson turned out to be of great value in shaping my scientific activities.

When I left boarding school, I attended university in order to study medicine. There I systematically began to read biographies on, and autobiographies by, great personalities—writers, painters, composers, scientists, discoverers, inventors, emperors, generals, and whatever else. Here I caught yet another glimpse of the enigma of human creativity.

Having finished medical school, I entered a special professional training in psychiatry, an endeavor requiring seven years of post-graduate studies in Switzerland and the United States. All in all, I worked for twenty years as a psychiatrist, ten years of it as the medical director of an in-patient and out-patient treatment facility. During these two decades, I practiced systems therapy and was involved in research in systems science. In my spare time I continued to study autobiographies by, and biographies of, great creative minds that had excelled in all kinds of professional domains. All of these experiences added to my understanding of the emotional and social life of human beings, and it also increased my interest in the riddle of creativity.

In 1989, I quit the field of psychiatry in order to fully dedicate my time and energies to the scientific investigation of human creativity. Three main motifs prompted my decision to enter the field of creativity research.

First, while offering supportive therapy to individuals at the brink of death—mostly victims of terminal diseases or terrible accidents—I discovered that, in the face of impending death, they usually regretted two errors committed in the course of their life. They were full of remorse for having spent too much time trying to impress people they had not liked or had even despised, and for not having spent enough quality time with those individuals for whom they had really cared. Moreover, they were sad because they had never mobilized their own precious dormant resources—specific talents that could be channeled into artistic expression.

Second, doing therapies with couples and families, I observed time and again that while people are quite clever in hurting, disqualifying, and degrading each other, often they are unable to show the same degree of cleverness to inspire and motivate each other to excel in their pursuits—the very essence of leadership. Moreover, in a negative and stereotypical way, they keep on making the same strategic choices that never brought them any success in the past, yet they neither show any gumption nor inventiveness to adopt different coping mechanisms to deal with problems they face.

Third, thirty years of reading of autobiographies and biographies had opened the windows to the life and work of great creative minds and had convinced me that creativity was a sphere I found more fascinating than any other subject in the world. In my travel on that joyous path, I realized that creativity is the fountainhead of all precious natural resources and makes our life worth living every single moment.

In the course of my scientific investigations on human creativity, I wrote a series of books on creativity and creative leadership. I also met, talked with, and interviewed (sometimes for hours, sometimes for several days in a row) a number of creative leaders working in various professional fields. Creativity is closely linked to productivity. During a time span of fifteen years, I served as a special advisor for boards and top managements of multinational corporations interested in developing creativity and creative leadership in teams for which they were responsible.

In 1979, my wife Greta and I established the *International CREANDO Foundation for Creativity and Leadership* (www.creando.org). Over the years, we have organized twenty international symposia on the topic of creativity and leadership in economics, arts, and science. Being the chairman of these symposia, I studied curricula and creative achievements of the speakers invited, had the opportunity to meet them personally, and learned a lot from them about the nature of creativity and creative leadership. Therefore, I'm deeply indebted to the following creative personalities:

Nobel laureates in literature Gabriel Gárcia Márquez, Joseph Brodsky, Wole Soyinka, Derek Wallcott; writers Maya Angelou, Edna O'Brien, Llosa Mario Vargas; critic of African-American literature Eleanor W. Traylor; author and dean of Berkeley School of Journalism Orville Shell.

Nobel laureates in physics Gerd Binnig, Donald A. Glaser, Samuel C. C. Ting, Arno Penzias, Charles H. Townes, Leo Esaki; physicists Mitchell Feigenbaum, Leo P. Kadanoff, Antonino Zichichi, Edward Teller, Alexander Migdal.

Nobel laureates in medicine Gerald M. Edelmann (immunologist), Günter Blobel (molecular biologist), Paul Greengard (neuroscientist); ethologist Jane Goodall; molecular biologist Zhangliang Chen.

Nobel laureates in economics Myron B. Scholes, Michael Spence; entrepreneurs and top managers Helmuth Maucher, Lothar Späth, Kazuhiko Nishi, Tom Alexander, Heinz Dürr, Angelo Gaja, Eberhard von Koerber, Peter Schneider; inventors and entrepreneurs Franco Sbarro, Kumar Patel, Sam Pitroda, Burt Rutan; expert in computer animation Nadia Magnenat-Thalmann; expert on intellectual capital Leif Edvinsson.

Mathematicians Anatol Rapoport, Benoit B. Mandelbrot, John B. Gage.

Film producers Saul Zaentz, Yuan Zhang, Diane Summers; film directors Werner Herzog, Eric Valli; film actress Liv Ullmann; TV producer Caryn Mandabach; theater directors Luc Bondy, Robert Wilson.

Architects Mario Botta, Zaha M. Hadid; curator and art historian Harald Szeeman; visual artists and designers Eiko Ishioka, Paul Scott Makela, Josh Greenberg; photographers Oliviero Toscani, Lucien Clergue; cartoonists Guillermo Mordillo, Tomi Ungerer.

Conductor and director of Bayerische Staatsoper Kent Nagano; composer Franghiz Ali-Zadeh; composer and jazz trumpeter Clark Terry; composer

and jazz pianist Abdullah Ibrahim; composer and jazz vocalist Betty
Carter; composer and rock musician Jon Lord; flamenco choreographer
and dancer Antonio Márquez; virtuoso percussionist Evelyn Glennie; composer and pipa virtuoso Jing Yang.

Master chef-de-cuisine Ferran Adrià; pioneer of esthetic surgery Ivo Pitanguy;
creator of perfumes Sophia Chodosz-Grojsman; high-wire artist Philippe Pe-
tit, rock climber Catherine Destivelle; politician Ziad Abu Amr; NASA astro-
naut Mae C. Jemison; head monk of Buddhist monastery T. Ryugen Oga-
sawara; design expert on Indian jewels and textiles Meera Kumar.

The cumulative experiences made in the course of forty years of my professional activities have shaped my scientific approach in the realm of general
systems theory and its practical applications. They also inspired and motivated me to write the present book.

The reader of this volume will find a great number of quotes from biographies on great creative leaders and, to a lesser extent, from autobiographies
by creative leaders. The rationale for these quotes and cases illustrating how
highly creative people achieve their goals is obvious. If you want to become
an expert free-style climber, it is wiser to learn the basics of that craft from
leaders in that field rather than from novices. And if you desire to understand
how human creativity functions, then it makes sense to learn your lessons
from true masters rather than from amateurs whose hobbies will never result
in outstanding creative achievement.

Let me emphasize that concrete examples discussed in the first half of
this book illustrate specific aspects of the creative process and stem mostly,
although not exclusively, from the realm of western developed societies.
There is no ethnic prejudice involved in the choice of authors and data materials quoted and discussed in some detail. The criteria for my preferences
were simply the following: First, I'm a European and therefore better acquainted with Western culture than with other cultures and their creative
accomplishments throughout the ages. Second, the sheer quantity of research materials I had to cope with in the course of my scientific investigations did not allow me to add yet another decade of supplementary data
collection before I could start to write this book. Third, I'm fairly confident
that the basic mechanisms described and explained in the present book per-
tain to creative processes independent of particular ethnic groups, nations,
cultures, or civilizations. The reason for this last statement is evident: biological evolution has equipped human brains with the same basic structures
and functions. What pertains to creative achievements made by human beings living on a specific continent is therefore also valid for people producing creative breakthroughs on another continent.

Austrian-Hungarian writer Franz Kafka wrote: ". . . a book should serve as
the ax for the frozen sea within us." That image has a rather strong connota-
tion because it implies the impact of an aggressive force. Since my book deals
with the topic of human creativity, the only inexhaustible natural resource on
our planet plagued by rapidly dwindling natural resources, I prefer another
image. I do hope that the text I wrote will serve as a key to unlock the door
leading to the readers' own creative talents.

Brig/Switzerland, Summer 2009

Acknowledgments

My heartfelt thanks go to Dr. Franz Mattig, chairman of Mattig-Suter and Partners, one of the most renowned audit, tax and advisory services companies in
Central Switzerland. His company operates in Switzerland, Austria, Romania
and Bulgaria, specializing in corporate analysis, strategy, revenue and controlling consultancy (www.mattig.ch). Dr. Mattig is a Member of the Board of the
International CREANDO Foundation for Creativity and Leadership and a co-
organizer of the International CREANDO Symposia on Creative Leadership in
Economics, Arts and Science. Over the years he and his wife, Ursula, have
become close friends of my wife and me. Without their generous financial and
moral support I could never have written the present book.

I should like to extend special thanks to Mr. Ashok Kurien, brilliant business
strategist and today one of the most successful entrepreneurs of India. A charismatic creative leader able to combine vision, wisdom, personal charm and
achievement-oriented determination he generously accepted my request for an
in-depth interview on the development of his personal and professional career.
In the days we worked together in a London hotel, he answered all of my questions with a forthrightness I have rarely witnessed in my encounters with outstanding business leaders. The selected excerpts of our interview form a thread
weaving its way through the fabric of the entire book, linking creative accomplishments of times past with those of our contemporary world.

Over the years Mrs. Bettina Mattia, my personal assistant, has helped me
to get hold of books, articles and other research material necessary for writing
this book. Mrs. Mattia (www.mattia.info) is a licensed helicopter and para-
glider pilot whose passenger flights are the delight of countless happy clients.
Undoubtedly her professional training has helped to forge the qualities of the
valued collaborator that she has become. Once again her efficiency, meticu-

lousness in organizing details, intuitive ability to comprehend the pattern
connecting a host of apparently isolated details, and reliability – all of which
I highly appreciate – have proved to be priceless for my scientific investigations. May she find here the expression of my sincere gratitude.

The editing of my manuscript was done, for the greater part, by Mrs. Myrna
Farage, a professional translator and highly appreciated, longtime CREANDO
collaborator. In order to meet the deadline for submission, Indian journalist
Mrs. Sangmitra Paal graciously accepted to step in and lend a hand. To these
ladies I feel deeply indebted, for their imagination, linguistic skills and expertise in cutting out the superfluous and often suggesting formulations more
precise than my own, rendered my text more concise and easier to read.

My sincere thanks also to Mrs. Caroline Ruffener, who mastered the challenge of compiling the comprehensive bibliography with great care and accuracy. She supervised and checked the countless corrections and amend-
ments necessary to complete the book while managing to organize permission
from the publishers for the many quotes.

I am grateful to Mrs. Luisa Tonarelli for the fine job she accomplished in
targeting potential publishers and in preparing the manuscript for editing. Her
experience with publishing companies and her linguistic skills have made her
an asset to CREANDO.

For two decades visual artist Renato Jordan has helped me to improve the
visual design of my concepts and models of basic mechanisms. His intelligence and esthetic sensibilities have been a great help to me, and I express my
gratitude for his competence and skills.

Last but not least, I should like to thank Mr. Daniel Pianzola, a chemist and
computer expert, and Mr. Arben Hazbiu, a master in coping with the difficult
technological problems I encountered over the last four and-a-half years
while writing the text of The Spirit of Creativity.

Chapter One

Separating the Wheat from the Chaff

1.1 WEAVERS SITTING AT THE ENCHANTED LOOM

"So schaffe ich am sausenden Webstuhl der Zeit und wirke der Gottheit lebendiges Kleid."

Johann Wolfgang von Goethe

"We sit at the fleeting loom of time and weave the shimmering dress for the gods divine." In this statement, the great writer and poet Johann Wolfgang von Goethe offered a beautiful metaphor for the mysterious nature of the creative activity of human beings. The tapestry of our creation is woven on an enchanted loom. Usually, we do not at all understand the inner workings of our weaving process, yet we are able to see and admire the new tissues, formal patterns and colors emerging from our loom.

Human beings weaving the tapestry of creative performance play a great number of different roles simultaneously. What happens to those role players is sheer magic. Dreaming extensively and working intensively, they are weavers imagining, planning, and producing a tapestry of creation. They are gifted designers and, at the same time, a particular aspect of the design produced. They are an integral part of the enchanted loom: shuttles whisking back and forth in order to generate a coherent tissue, and threads woven into a complex dynamic pattern of continuously evolving new fabrics. They shape the intensities, frequencies, rhythms, and harmonies of the weaving procedures and are shaped by them in turn. In other words, the weavers sitting at the enchanted loom participate in a process that transcends who and what they are. They partake in a venture at whose true depth, dimensions, and implications they can only guess and whose final results they are rarely, if ever, able to predict.

1

Despite these complexities and uncertainties, the weavers at the enchanted loom seem to be addicted to their craft. Addiction generates both pleasure and pain beyond the limits of habitual experience. This specific form of addiction displays a unique quality not shared by other addictions: in principle, the gains produced by constructive forces outweigh by far the losses suffered by destructive forces.

In the following chapters, we shall try to shed some light on the mystery of human creativity. While the photons of our insight illuminate specific spots in the cavern of our exploration, we shall not overlook the shadows and dark recesses that await the generations of investigators yet to come.

Before embarking on our journey, I should like to address a widely held prejudice. There are individuals who firmly believe that human creativity is, as it were, a supernatural realm that should not be molested by the curiosity of mortals. They presume that the enigma of human creativity in no way lends itself to an investigation based upon scientific concepts and methods. Even worse, they hold that a scientific approach will go so far as to destroy what, in principle, it is unable ever to comprehend.

In my view these assumptions are unwarranted, and an example from the history of scientific discoveries may illustrate my point. More than 2,000 years ago, Leucippus and Democritus postulated, purely on the basis of intuitive insight, that the whole universe was composed of atoms; atoms are tiny, indivisible basic building blocks of spherical shape and identical size. The two Greek natural philosophers assumed that atoms were able to combine themselves in countless manners thus producing all the objects, living beings, and events observable in the universe.

In the middle of the nineteenth century, the suggestion that the hidden nature of atoms might lend itself to a rigorous scientific investigation would probably have been considered lunacy. By the end of the nineteenth century, a group of highly creative scientists began to investigate the mysterious domain and made rapid progress in their attempt to unravel the basic nature of atoms. In 1895, J. J. Thomson founded an atomic research unit at the Cavendish Laboratories in Cambridge. Together with his young collaborator Ernest Rutherford (Clark 1972, 57ff.), he was soon able to prove that the atom predicted by Democritus and Leucippus did indeed exist. He discovered, moreover, that Democritus and Leucippus had erred with respect to two points. First, atoms come in different sizes. Second, an atom is of a composite nature; it consists of a nucleus and of electrons orbiting at high speed around that nucleus.

Their ground-breaking discovery was immediately followed by an ingenious idea conceived by Niels Bohr (Clark 1972, 200ff.). On the basis of his investigations, he formulated the hypothesis that electrons orbit in stationary circles around the nucleus of an atom. Whenever an electron jumps from one of its orbits to an orbit nearer the nucleus, it emits a radiation visible in the form of spectral colors. In other words, these colors are like stained glass windowpanes offering a glance directly into the mysterious inner world of atoms. In 1927, Niels Bohr and Werner Heisenberg presented the so-called Copenhagen interpretation of quantum mechanics, a comprehensive theory describing and explaining what was then known about atoms. And in 1986, a little more than half a century later, Gerd Binnig (Binnig 1995a, 303ff.) and Heinrich Rohrer were awarded the Nobel Prize for their invention of a microscope enabling the observation of individual atoms, and for a method allowing the transfer of single atoms from one molecule to the next!

Today, the creative process in human beings seems to be as great a mystery as the atom once was. Yet if human ingenuity decides to investigate it, then many of its basic features will eventually be unveiled and understood. Of course, so-called creationists (*nomen est omen*, indeed) will completely disagree with my prediction. Religious fundamentalists tend to decry the presumed narrow-mindedness of the scientific approach, despite their apparently poor understanding of how it actually works. A solid scientific approach implies more than simple rational reasoning. Rational reasoning generates logical deductions from given premises and makes explicit what is already implicitly contained in those premises. For that very reason, rational reasoning in itself is productive but not creative. Creative scientific thinking must be rational, but it must also be combined with imagination and intuition, emotional engagement, and instinctive drive. Only by combining these mental faculties is creative thinking able to leap beyond the given premises. An authentic scientific approach to observable reality endeavors to describe, explain, and understand specific aspects of that reality by any conceptual and methodical means available. If one day we are able to properly describe and explain—and thus understand—the mystery of the creative process, such an accomplishment will by no means destroy the inherent mystery and beauty of human creativity. The fact that we are able to explain scientifically the exquisiteness of a dewdrop glittering in all the colors of the solar spectrum does not at all prevent us from being captivated by the wondrous natural phenomenon.

It is my sincere hope that the present book will offer joy and excitement to its readers. It is also my wish that it will inspire and motivate talented young individuals to embrace the domain of scientific research on the nature of the creative process. There is much need for such research. Human creativity is extremely important for the survival and sustainable development of mankind, for, together with wisdom, it is one of the most precious natural resources available to human beings. Like wisdom, it is also, alas, a resource that is often poorly or not at all mobilized and used in a goal-directed manner generating authentic values for mankind. Yet quite unlike other natural resources, human creativity is virtually inexhaustible because successful creative performance tends to inspire and motivate further creative performance.

Talking with Ashok Kurien, one of India's leading entrepreneurs

Every structure in the universe seems to have a resonant structure, a complementary twin structure as it were. Along the lines of this idea, every section of the present book will have a resonant structure consisting of excerpts from an in-depth interview by the author with Ashok Kurien, a leading, highly successful and visionary entrepreneur of India. The interview took place in March 2008 in London. But let us begin with a brief presentation of Ashok Kurien's career.

CV of Ashok Kurien

If recognizing opportunities is a basic skill of a successful entrepreneur, Ashok Mathai Kurien is, simply put, a visionary. If partnering successful business models from their incubation stage and converting them into throbbing revenue engines takes the acumen of an architect giving shape to his vision, then he is the person with the Midas touch. Born in 1950, Ashok Kurien has been in the business of building brands for over 35 years now, particularly in the fields of media and communications. An early bird, Ashok Kurien has the keen eye for driving start-ups in emerging businesses and guiding them to size and scale, be they TV, lottery, PR or dot-coms. His property investments have also been resounding success stories.

After graduating in the Arts, he launched his career with Advertising Concessionaries Pvt. Ltd., where he remained for two years. Moving on to Rediffusion Advertising, he worked there for 12 years, rapidly climbing the command chain in the organization. It was during this phenomenal phase that Ashok Kurien's passion to "go on his own" fired his ambition, resulting in the formation of Ambience Advertising in 1987. The most formidable creative powerhouse in its first decade, Ambience has since come a long way.

Ambience Advertising merged with D'Arcy in 1999 to form Ambience D'Arcy Advertising, which was later sold to the Publicis Groupe. Ashok Kurien is now chairman of Ambience Publicis, Publicis India and Solutions-Publicis India. As a special advisor to the US$ 5 billion Publicis Groupe, he leads their mergers and acquisitions for India.

A co-founder of Zee TV (under the leadership of Subhash Chandra), India's first private satellite channel, Ashok Kurien has been instrumental in bringing about the television revolution in his country. Launched in 1992, the Zee Network today is a household name, totalling annual revenues of INR

15.1 billion and over 500 million viewers with 20 channels worldwide. Ashok Kurien is associated with the media house as its Director.

Mr. Kurien is Director and Strategic Marketing Advisor to Playwin, India's first online lottery business, and also the Zee Group's Direct-to-Home service, Dish TV, which already has a market cap of over USD 1 billion. He was also a Founder Member and Chairman of Hanmer & Partners, a multi-disciplinary communications agency giving 360 degree communications solutions to over 150 clients including some of the largest Indian corporate houses and MNCs. Launched in 1999, Hanmer & Partners is one of India's top three communications agencies. It is now a fully owned subsidiary of the Publicis Groupe, and is known as Hanmer MS&L Communications Pvt.Ltd. A Founder Partner of Flora 2000, one of the leading global flower distribution services on the web, Mr. Kurien also helped to set up Remindo, a corporate social network and productivity website, as well as a few other internet ventures.

Despite the great heights he has achieved in his career, Ashok Kurien has his feet firmly rooted to the ground. He believes in his commitment to society and is involved with a number of charities, NGOs, and social service organizations.

An accomplished family man as well, he is a doting father to two grown daughters, 30-year-old Diya and Priyanka, 27.[1]

Excerpts from an interview with Ashok Kurien (1)

In this first excerpt from our interview, several topics are addressed, all of which have to do with what weavers on the enchanted loom experience, who and what they are, and what they do. It also deals with how and why they became who and what they are as adults. There is a trivalent logic of reaction that governs our life: we can react to input with total acceptance, total rejection, or critical selection.

Creative leadership is a process of mutual inspiration and motivation that eventually generates outstanding performance. Ashok Kurien describes how such a leadership process began in his own life and how positive feedback loops gradually brought about that precious shift from his former norm – the paralyzing self-image, "I'm a non-entity" – to the gradual construction of a self-image that confidently attested: "I'm an individual of value!"

Below is a key message of his on creative leadership:

"In any business you can be the main, strong, single horse, the leader of the pack.
Or you can be the leader of a team of two partners.
Or you can be the strong second horse for the chariot or buggy.

You have to know and choose which horse you can best be
and stick to playing that role. That is the secret of success in any business
partnership.
I have played each of these roles in various businesses; the lead in some,
and the partner horse in others, much like the role of an actor in a movie or
play.
In the Zee TV business I have been the "Best Supporting Actor," whereas
in some of the others I have played the lead "Starring Role."

GG: [2] A while back you said something very interesting, namely that you are not
a highly educated person. Yet you have a unique track record. Genuine creative
individuals are per definition autodidacts because they cannot learn the essence
of their creative breakthroughs from somebody else. Yet creative individuals
often tend to overestimate the value of concepts and methods taught in high
schools, business schools and universities.

AK: Not being a highly educated person, I operate a lot on instinct. I never sit
back and think, "Why did it happen?" or "How did it happen?" Now, actually
detailing these questions down forced me to think a process through that I had
never thought of in my life. So it was a bit alarming. To be honest, I don't think
I'm very intelligent; but going through this process had me suddenly wondering
if I weren't a highly intelligent person after all – although I'm quite sure I'm
not!

GG: It amazes me that you say, "I'm not a highly educated person." With all the
accomplishments that you have achieved, you have had an education that few
people on the globe can match. *This* is education! You learnt so much and you
taught yourself so many things!

AK: You're right. I suppose I am street smart; I can simplify and process problems to find practical solutions based on common sense.

GG: Even if it operated more on the intuitive level than on the analytical-verbal
level, I would consider yours a very particular and high-level education, which
I admire all the more because as I never had any business instinct in life, I considered myself rather uneducated in that realm. Achievement motivation begins
with the perception of an actual – or sometimes only a presumed – insufficiency.
Once we have perceived it, we strive to overcome that insufficiency, to compen-
sate for it. Complacency, on the other hand, breeds pretentious self-sufficiency
in the same manner in which ignorance causes arrogance.

AK: Very well, let's go back to learning and knowledge. When the education
system doesn't accept you, you have no choice but to battle and struggle through
it, and if you're a failure, then the education system rejects you. At that point
you can decide whether you're going to be a failure for life or whether, forced
by circumstances, you are going out into the world to observe and listen and

watch and learn for many years. This is a completely different system of educa-tion that our education system doesn't prepare us for.

GG: You are absolutely right.

AK: I believe that's what happened to me: because the system rejected me, I rejected the system. I was different, and they couldn't understand my difference. And because I was rejected, and because financially and economically I had to survive, I was forced to be what we call "street smart." That then becomes learn-ing, and the moment you taste that first success, you just keep learning and learning and learning. As you said, you also learn from mistakes. You learn not to make your same mistakes again, and you see where other people went wrong. The truth is you don't know what's right, but observation and listening and watching can tell you what's wrong.

GG: Probably only dogmatic priests and overbearing pundits know everything; everybody else oscillates between doubt and self-doubt. Earlier you stated that there came a point where you decided that you had to go out and do it on your own. The problem is that our educational system crushes the self-confidence of many children to a point where when they reach the age of sixteen or seventeen and have been told "You're stupid," they firmly believe it. They don't have that force of personality, the fortitude to say, "I don't believe your legends. I'll go out for myself. I'll discover the world." In your younger years were you really con-vinced of what your colleagues told you?

AK: Yes, pretty much. But I was a fighter because I was a boxer; I was a sports-man. Since I had a hand-eye-ball co-ordination problem, I couldn't play tennis or anything with a racket, but I could box, I could run, I could play rugby – on the wing. I couldn't do anything clever in the middle, but if I was in the wing and somebody gave me the ball, I'd go for a touchdown. I had that ability to battle and not give in. However, when it came to anything intellectual, I couldn't cope. So sometimes it just takes one person to give you a spark of confidence, and from that confidence, shortly thereafter a second person comes along.

GG: In discussing confidence you said that a client told you that you were ex-tremely good.

AK: Yes, it was Shilpa Shah of *Garden Sarees*. Then a second client, who came in within a year of my starting the agency, did likewise. Now these two clients were very large owner clients, but they weren't professional managers.

GG: They could decide on their own, because it was their own money that was at risk.

AK: They could decide, and they used their instinct and their gut feel too. The first one was the equivalent of Levi's. It was the biggest sari brand in India and the most expensive. They were my first client. A lady came to me and said, "I believe in you." The second was the soft drink king of India who sold a cola called *Thums Up*.

GG: That's another big company.

AK: I met him on an aeroplane and he asked me if I could simply go and give
him some advice, as Coca-Cola and Pepsi were going to come into India. So I
went to give him advice, and he gave me his biggest brand. That was like getting
the Coca-Cola and Levi's accounts, and I didn't have any staff.

GG: You were on your own.

AK: I was on my own with a secretary and a studio artist. After that I brought
in another person as a creative partner, and I went on. Suddenly I realised that I
could actually give sound marketing advice beyond advertising that actually
made the product successful.

GG: Can you give a concrete example of such advice?

AK: If we take the textile client, it was family-owned between the woman's
husband and his brothers. They made saris, but I predicted that as India was
changing, younger people would wear fabric that they would stitch into what is
called the *salwaar kameez*, a pant suit with a scarf similar to what is worn in
Pakistan. I told him that business would grow a lot faster because of the youth
of our country. So he set up a second unit, where he owned more than his brothers, and in a year that business was almost as big as the sari business.

GG: And the sari business was about a hundred years old.

AK: Yes, it was about a hundred years old in the family. When his brothers saw
him completely change everything –it was a joint company – they actually gave
him more equity in the mother company, so he controlled it as a whole. Now what
I gave him was not an advertising answer; it was a strategic business solution.

GG: Yes, I see.

AK: With the soft-drink person it was advice on how to run his brands. I still
work with him today, almost like a partner. He sold off *Thums Up* to Coca-Cola,
yet today it outsells both Coca-Cola and Pepsi, ten years after the brand was
bought in India! It's still the largest selling cola in the country. Such is the power
of that brand. Currently I help him market bottled water and mineral water; he
is the Water King of India. I have also launched three new products for him and
done things which do not require much advertising – just strategic decisions and
design innovation. This is giving him thirty percent growth month after month,
compared to all the *Kinleys* and *Aquafinas* and all the other brands.

GG: Let's move to the next question: what role does creativity play in the development of personality? If you compare individuals whom you classify as being
creative with others who are not, what do you think? What role does creativity
play in becoming a mature person?

AK: Is it the creativity that plays a role in the personality of the person or is it
the personality of the person that plays a role in his or her creativity?

GG: One does not exclude the other; it's not an either-or proposition. It's an and-and proposition, a maybe-maybe proposition.

AK: All the truly creative people I know have similar traits in common. One of them definitely is child-like simplicity. They have a spontaneous child-like reaction to things and a child-like fascination with things.

GG: What are other typical personality traits you find in creative individuals?

AK: Insecurity.

GG: Insecurity, yes. They are not imbued with self-satisfaction. They do not consider themselves perfect the way they are.

AK: They are dealing with an intangible, indefinable commodity. Your book deals with creativity, the one natural resource – not commodity – that the world will never run out of. Yet every creative person lives in the fear that they will run out of that resource.

GG: Yes, that is a fact.

AK: According to you, it's the one resource the world won't run out of. Yet each individual's greatest nightmare is writer's block, creative block. That the resource will run out, that it is exhaustible.

GG: For each single individual it is exhaustible, indeed. But for mankind as a whole it is inexhaustible, because the results of somebody's creative achievement always inspire and motivate somebody else to strive for another creative achievement.

AK: That is a powerful thought: there is something which every individual will run out of, but the world as an entity will never run out of, and it will keep running on that. Someone will develop an alternative for fuel; new methods for providing water will be discovered. The planet will see its stocks of petrol depleted, but somebody will come up with a substitute. What are the other natural resources we have?

GG: Air, water, gas, iron ores, wood, fish, corn, wheat, human intelligence, wood...

AK: Someone will come up with a method for producing oxygen and air. Oh, they will find replacements! They will plant more trees. And all this thanks to their creativity. But the amazing thing is that each person will run out of his own creativity.

GG: Yes, and often they run out at an early age. Arthur Rimbaud, one of the greatest French poets of the 19th century, stopped writing at the age of twenty. He became a construction supervisor on the island of Cyprus, then a trader of coffee and weapons in Abyssinia. Now, let's go back to personality traits often found in creative individuals. We have already mentioned child-like simplicity, child-like spontaneity, and insecurity—the absence of smug self-satisfaction.

AK: There is perseverance, intense perseverance, to the point of pain and suffering. There is passion, fear, insecurity.

GG: Insecurity, yes you mentioned it already. In one of my books I wrote, "Complacency kills the cat of creativity."

AK: There is obsession with an idea.

GG: Obsession to achieve one's goals, yes.

AK: Conscientiousness.

GG: Yes, a truly creative individual is a perfectionist.

AK: The will to win.

GG: This is always a strong motivation for achievement. I also find that every creative person enjoys humour. There are rarely really great creative people who don't cherish humour. I'm not talking about silly jokes but intelligent wit. In the course of my investigations on personality development and creativity I often asked myself, "What is the very essence of humour and wit?" In my view, it implies a specific kind of playfulness that employs two different levels of logical reasoning until suddenly a new meaning appears. The emergence of an unexpected meaning triggers our laughter. I give you an example. Leopold Stokowski, a famous conductor, gave a concert in Philadelphia. As he was leaving the concert hall, a lady clad in silk and a mink coat dropped to her knees in front of him and groaned: "Maestro, you are a god!" He nodded and quipped: "Yes, indeed, but what a responsibility!"

AK: (laughs)

GG: So you see, humour occurs when the meaning jumps from one logical category to another. In this case Stokowski was expected to reject the idea of being compared to a god, but actually (in fact, apparently) he accepted it. Humour is very much connected to playfulness. I think if a person loses his or her sense of humour, then creativity suffers. It suffers because creative imagination does not exist without playfulness. A hypochondriac or a fearful person does have imagination, but it is not playful; it is dead serious and has a paralysing effect. The opposite of delightful playfulness is pathetic pomposity. I've never met a highly creative person who was pompous, but I have met many a pompous fool who was not creative at all.

AK: I would say I'm child-like and playful. I am forced by society or the need to earn money, to do a job, and the only way I can do it is to be creative. When I'm doing my job, I am serious, intense because I need my client to invest a million dollars of his money, and to do so, he has to believe in what I say. During that period I am not myself.

GG: You are in a state of temporary alienation.

AK: I am playing a role. I am being Ashok Kurien, the marketing guru. That's not me at all. So every once in a while I need to make a little joke to remind myself who I really am. I come back and say, "I'm still me. Okay, now let me switch back to my act." And I get serious again. The moment I finish work, I go to a bar for some drinks and some laughs because I want to be myself, the real me. After working hours, you will never find me answering a serious question; I am not being paid for it!

GG: So you play around to find yourself and to overcome that split between your role in your profession and what your innermost needs really are in true life.

AK: Quite. Why should I be serious and give anyone a serious answer when I'm drinking and laughing and being myself? I am not being paid. From nine in the morning to nine at night someone is paying me, I'm making some money, so I will be the pretender. All day I am a pretender. But every chance I get, I come out of the meeting and with a very straight face, I joke with my people.

GG: You need that to recover from the burden of your official role.

AK: I need that because I need to tell myself I am me, I need to tell all these people I'm me. I am not the person who was in that office. I cure and heal myself.

GG: The bar is a temporary room, a sort of shelter for recovery.

AK: I want my friends and the people I am close to, to understand that I know who I am and that this is the "me" they like.

GG: Let me add a last question to this topic: what role did creativity play in the development of your personality, in becoming the Ashok Kurien you are today? You started out as a young man bursting with anger, even rage.

AK: Yes, I was full of hate. What role did creativity play? It changed everything.

GG: If I understand you correctly, you are saying that creativity gave you your true identity. It offered you that insight that today you know unmistakably: this is my authentic self.

AK: And even more so after talking to you for two days.

GG: Thank you. The same thing happened to me while listening and talking to you.

AK: Two days ago I wouldn't have been able to answer the question regarding what role creativity has played in my life. Now I can say creativity has changed everything. (Good God, how much do you charge by the hour? You are wonderful!)

GG: We learn from each other while talking to each other.

AK: You have given me great insight as to who I am, a deeper understanding of myself. I am not such a bad guy after all.

GG: It would be nice if we could meet once a year to discuss together what it means to be an authentic human being.

AK: Go and have a great meal together...

GG: We could enjoy a playful-serious exchange about what is meaningful in life and what is not. I used to work as a family therapist, and I met so many adolescents who believed what their teachers told them.

AK: You are right. The damage is compounded even more if their family tells them the same thing.

GG: Yes, in that worst of all possible scenarios they will be in a real fix.

AK: I come from a family of highly educated people. My mother was a University professor, the head of the English department. She produced thousands of brilliant graduates and one useless son. As she saw it, God had come down from the heavens and punished her personally with this monster.

GG: The undesired avatar. But what does she think of you today?

AK: (Chuckles) You must realise that because of that rejection, I was determined to be a failure at home, so I was beaten and whipped; but that wasn't going to teach me mathematics and science.

GG: What about your father?

AK: He was very quiet and partially deaf. But I think he learnt to be quiet and smiling to survive my mother. He was a very gentle, loving man. Today I realise how totally honest he was, so he is my hero. He worked for the government in the income tax department, which is a very corrupt place, and never rose to a senior position. He was a man of principles and values. If somebody brought him a box of fruit at home as a gift, he would say, "I shall accept ONE piece of fruit from the basket because you have brought it. Please take the rest back." At the time that hurt me deeply, for I did not understand his principles. He did not want favours; he wanted only to do his job honestly and was happy with his status in life. Today I realise that he has no enemies, no anger; he sees only the good in people, he wishes everybody well, and there are very few individuals in the world who are so completely at peace! He has no hate and no envy.

GG: He lives in a state of serenity.

AK: He has complete serenity! And if I can reach that, I shall have reached Nirvana. He has no jealousy, no envy, he's just happy for everyone. It's amazing! At any rate, to get back to my younger years, the dominating person was my mother. At home I was told I was doomed; at school I was told I was doomed. Then I started accepting failure before I even faced the problem. If I got an examination paper, I knew I couldn't do it even before the paper was in my hands! So of course I didn't understand the questions. Now things are very different. Now I face challenge because something changed in my life. But for many years I was completely useless and sort of wandering about. I got into advertising when I was about thirty-seven, and it took ONE person – the first person in my life – to tell me I was good to make me believe in myself. That was my client,

Shilpa. My colleagues were all MBAs from the best universities, and they told me I was an idiot.

GG: They, too, chimed in to the tune of "You are a non-entity"?

AK: Oh, all of them! They spoke in a language called *Managementeese Jargoneese* which I did not understand. When they said "delta," I though they were referring to an aeroplane – seriously!

GG: Oh, yes, I see.

AK: They made me feel a complete failure. Then this one client turned around and said, "You have a talent and an eye other people don't have. You're also very honest, and you will not sell me anything which you don't believe in and which you truly don't think is good. If you come out, I will support you and you start an agency." It took one person to believe in me, and I started that agency.

GG: After having been in somebody else's company for how many years?

AK: Ten. Before that I had spent ten years doing odd jobs, like sticking stamps.

1.2 ALL THAT HYPE ABOUT CREATIVITY

August 2007. One of the world's leading news magazines praising the "creative class" that is supposed to "make cities sexy" writes about Amsterdam, "The conformity of the creative people prevails here today: rigorous cubistic house façades, big glass windows and an Arne-Jacobsen chair in the living room." Conformity of the creative people? The statement is an oxymoron! Creative individuals shun the conformity of uniformed social classes; proud of their independence, they hate to be heifers in a herd. To put things into a proper perspective, the above quote should read, "For the time being, trendsetters of various professional domains boasting the costumes, customs and symbols of currently fashionable in-groups prefer to live in cities they consider to be attractive." Full stop.

Contemporary newspaper articles, books, radio broadcasts, movies, TV documentaries, and talk shows (as well as other forms of publication and debate about the nature of human creativity) keep increasing at a staggering rate and generate so much content that nobody is able to keep up with it anymore.

Most of the individuals professing statements about human creativity do not even bother to define their basic terms; that is like trying to build a house with brittle basic building blocks. The result is rickety foundations and wonky walls, ready to crumble beneath the slightest impact of environmental forces. There are indeed authors who propose some definitions, but they are too shaky to withstand the test of scrutiny. And then there are some authors who really know what they are talking about and who have something constructive to say on the subject.

We have entered the twenty-first century, and there is a lot of silly talk about "creative palm reading," "creative astrology," "creative kindergarten exercises," "creative skin care in puberty," "creative disco-dancing," "creative dishwashing," "creative breast implants," and "creative designs for lucid night dreams." In colloquial language, we say that somebody "creates" a lot of chaos on his desk, or that a machine "creates" a lot of noise. We watch the latest news on TV and fall upon an enthused speaker exulting over "a creative powerhouse emerging on the skyline of global business" and we wonder what he is so ecstatic about. Then, propelled by his excitement, he continues to stumble over his own words and we begin to get the message: the presumptive creative powerhouse has come into existence because two multinational companies have merged. We can't help thinking that the merger of two big business organizations will probably produce little else than the usual tactical in-fights and bureaucratic maneuvers, consisting mainly of massive cost-cutting procedures imposed by career-oriented managers, eager to fire whole series of 'redundant' collaborators in order to improve the bottom line on the balance sheets and their own income. It is also quite probable that the allegedly creative powerhouse will soon turn out to be too big to be run properly. Eventually, it will be dismantled while a lot of investors lose their money and a great number of employees their jobs.

As these examples suggest, creativity has become a hot topic. And since we have to keep up with the Joneses, it comes as no surprise that today so many individuals claim to be "highly creative." Obviously, they confuse unbridled imagination with creative accomplishments. They have fallen prey to an error of logical reasoning whereby they mistake their grandiose intentions for actual performance. Alas, many ambitious creatures reach for the stars, but only a few grasp the light of creative illumination. Under the circumstances, it seems a good idea to begin our discussion by defining a few basic terms connected with human creativity. After all, we are eager to differentiate between the shimmer of authentic pearls and the lackluster appearance of mere dross.

Before we go into the definitions, let me add a few critical remarks with respect to their operational range. By its very nature, every definition is arbitrary. However, if a majority of the professionals working in a specific field accept an arbitrary definition, then their consensus will offer three main advantages. First, the professionals will be able to develop a coherent and meaningful interpersonal dialogue on a specific topic. Second, shared definitions permit not only a logically founded acceptance or rejection of the statements made, but also a critical evaluation of the quality of productive performance and its results. Third, if we do not accept proposed definitions, we are free to propose better ones.

Excerpts from an interview with Ashok Kurien (2)

The hype about creativity is particularly shrill in the art market. Too many people believe that every visual representation or produced is the result of human creativity. They cling to the misconception thanks to slick art dealers and so-called art critics who convince them to do so—pointing to the large profits they see winking on the horizon. Ashok Kurien has a completely different attitude.

GG: In which fields of contemporary India is creativity highest today?

AK: As you know, we are influenced by the mass media. Indian art used to have very little commercial value. For reasons other than creativity, this value has increased. Art became a method for using black money. In India no one had demanded that all your paintings be registered till today. I can take ten million dollars in cash and buy art and put the ten million dollars of art on my wall and say, "I've had this for five years." Then the artist will write letters to whomever owns his art saying, "sold this to you in 1962 for two rupees." So it's a huge laundry, and because of it the value has gone up. I don't know whether it's the real value or whether it's "laundry" value of the artwork. Three and-a-half years ago someone told me, "If you can organize ten million dollars for me, then I will return fifteen million to you in six months." And all the people I know who did it got back fifteen million dollars. The media are always promoting art, art exhibitions; it's big business, everybody is investing in art. I don't know how many people are enjoying the artwork they have bought. I know people who have rooms stacked full of paintings.

GG: But here we are talking about buying art, just another form of investment. And most of art produced and traded today has nothing to do with creativity.

AK: A businessman friend of mine purchases art from an art supplier who comes to him, sits on the floor and shows him photographs of various artists' work, rating them in terms of which one will go up and which one won't. My friend buys them by the dozen!

GG: He buys items in a haberdashery.

AK: Yes. Then what does he do? He organizes an exhibition and puts the collection on sale stating that he owns the artist's entire collection – or most of it. He buys them all for one thousand rupees each then prices them at ten thousand, fifteen thousand, twenty thousand, twenty-five thousand, forty thousand has an exhibition sale. He puts a "Sold" sticker on the first three priced at sixty thousand each. So people walk into the exhibition and think that somebody has bought those for sixty thousand!

GG: It's completely perverse. The art market is horrible. The whole commercial society follows the same rules of the game.

AK: I think the whole thing is a joke. I own two paintings only because they appeal to me and because the person who was selling them needed the money. There was yet another reason for buying them. One painting represented Christ, the other one Krishna. My children are half-Hindu and I am a Christian. By buying these two paintings I also did something for my children. I do own a few inexpensive design pieces, but not paintings; nothing for the commercial value game.

1.3 DEFINITIONS OF BASIC TERMS

What is human creativity? Human creativity is the ability to generate a new form that meets four criteria of selection (Guntern 1991, 1993, 1994, 1995a, 1995b, 1996). The new form may be an industrial product, service, or marketing strategy. It may be a technological invention, a scientific concept or theory, a work of art or an art event, a choreography, a feature film, a musical composition, a therapeutic method, an educational technique, or any number of things.

The four criteria of selection are as follows:

- The new form is *unique*. The Venus de Milo, presumably produced by Alexandros of Antioch in the second century BC, is a unique sculpture. Unique also were Newton's law of gravity, Mozart's *Requiem*, Edison's light bulb, and van Gogh's painting of sunflowers. Yet if a contemporary sculptor takes a hammer and chisel and works day and night until a new Venus de Milo emerges from the marble, then he is not a creative performer but a copycat, although certainly a very skilful craftsman.
- The new form *functions properly*, it serves the purpose(s) for which it was intended. What is the purpose of an industrial marketing strategy? It is supposed to serve the image of an enterprise and help to promote and sell a specific product or service. What are we to think if one of those glib talkers who call themselves 'creative art directors' comes up with a design for a new and unique marketing strategy that harms the image of the enterprise and consequently the industrial product or service it is supposed to promote and sell? In this case, the new strategy is not the result of creative performance, but rather of wild imagination unfettered by the structural constraints of common sense and critical reasoning.
- The new form is *beautiful*. Beauty pleases our senses and stimulates our mind; it corresponds to our deep-seated and often unconscious aesthetic needs. Every great creative performer strives to polish the result of her or his performance until she or he is unable to improve its formal perfection

any further. If somebody is satisfied too quickly by the aesthetic aspect of the result of her or his performance, then she or he is a dabbler or even a pretender but not an authentic creator.[3]

• The new form *generates values for society*. It does not suffice that new forms generate profits for producers, sellers, and connected special interest groups. Apple computer's Mac, on which the present text was originally written, has not only brought wealth to its inventors, producers, and vendors; it has also produced values for countless individuals who use it for generating graphics and other visual representations or simply as a typewriter. Across the ages Homer's epic poems, *The Odyssey* and *The Iliad*, have produced great values not only for woodcutters, paper manufacturers, book printers, and sales persons, but also for scholars, poets, artists, students, and millions of other readers. Homer's timeless epics have produced those values from the dawn of Western culture, when the blind Greek poet sang his spellbinding songs, up to this very day; and they will continue to inspire and motivate future generations for outstanding performance.

Our definition of human creativity deserves a few comments:

• There exists no objective critical evaluation of the results of human creativity. Each and every evaluation is subjective. Usually, the creative performer is the first person to believe that her or his performance has resulted in a new form meeting the criteria of creativity outlined above. Then her or his partners and closest friends may begin to share that belief. Eventually, as time goes by, there emerges a more or less widely spread interpersonal consensus with regard to whether a particular new form is creative or not. The longer this consensus exists, the more comfortable people will feel with their shared evaluation because it generates the illusion that it is based on objective criteria and not on mutual consent and intersubjective agreement.

• Today, nobody doubts that the Palaeolithic rock paintings in the caves of Lascaux, Les Trois Frères and Altamira in France and Spain; the Inca citadel of Machu Picchu in Peru; the Taj Mahal in Agra; the Acropolis in Athens; the Alhambra in Granada; the sculptures of the Yoruba in Nigeria; the Great Sea Garden of Daisen-in in Kyoto; the Golden Gate bridge in San Francisco; the Pont du Gard near Nîmes; the Taoist philosophy of Lao-tse; the poetry of the Chinese Tang poet Li Bo; the Mahabharata of Hindu mythology; the music of Johann Sebastian Bach and Ludwig van Beethoven; the poetry of Shakespeare and Arthur Rimbaud; the plays of Molière and Eugene O'Neill; the drawings and paintings of the great Japanese Zen artists Hokusai and Hiroshige; the paintings of Claude Monet and Paul Klee; the sculptures of Henry Moore and Alberto Giacometti; Isaac Newton's

Principia Mathematica and Albert Einstein's General Theory of Relativity;
the Copenhagen interpretation of quantum physics produced by a group of
physicists headed by Niels Bohr and Werner Heisenberg; Charles Darwin's
theory of evolution; Jonas Edward Salk's discovery of a vaccine against
poliomyelitis; the invention of personal computers; and the iPod are the
result of great creative achievements.

- On a scale from 1 to100, a specific result of creative achievement and/or its
  creator may be placed anywhere. Accomplishments placed by general consensus near the top of the scale are the works of genius. At the bottom, we
  place accomplishments displaying at least a hint of creativity. All other
  creative forms and their creators are positioned somewhere between the two
  extremes.
- In the course of history, a specific position on the above scale may change—
  and it often does. The work of Johann Sebastian Bach and Wolfgang Amadeus Mozart was highly appreciated by their contemporaries. Then it was
  almost forgotten for about two centuries. Today, we are convinced that both
  composers were creative geniuses. To take another example, dramatist G.
  B. Shaw's contemporaries compared his work to that of Shakespeare. Today Shaw's plays seem rather dated, but who knows? They may climb up
  the scale anew, although it is hard to imagine that they should again be
  compared to the work of Shakespeare.

While most readers will probably more or less agree with the criteria of
human creativity proposed above and the comments made thereon, some may
have doubts with respect to the criteria of uniqueness and beauty for obvious
reasons—we are facing here two rather delicate issues. Other readers may
have difficulty as to the proper categorization of creative inventions versus
creative discoveries. And some of our readers may wonder whether artistic
activity and its results are always creative, as many an artist tends to claim. I
dare hope that these issues will become clearer as the reader moves through
the chapters and sections of the present book.

After having defined human creativity[4] let us briefly define creative performance and the creative process.

- Creative performance consists of a series of efforts whose end result meets
  the four criteria of creativity outlined above.
- The creative process is a complex, multistage, and multiphasic course of development leading from the very first unconscious stirrings of a hunch or new
  idea to the production of a new form meeting the criteria of creativity.
- In my view, logic suggests that in the future, artificial devices designed by
  man (for instance computers) may be able to achieve authentic creative

performance. If this happens, we will be faced with a new type of creative process.

By now we have defined creativity. What remains to be done is to define three terms often connected with the topic of creativity. These terms are *leadership, leader,* and *creative leadership.*

Traditionally, an individual—usually a man—who directed a group of workers was called a boss. As enterprises grew larger and professional language became more sophisticated, bosses were called managers; this happened between the end of the nineteenth and the beginning of the twentieth century. About two decades ago, management magazines and mass media discovered the term "leader," and all of a sudden the former bosses or managers mutated into leaders or business leaders. Due to this semantic somersault, we now seem to have an abundance of leaders despite the fact that in almost every single domain of our society we deplore a conspicuous lack of leadership! What looks like a paradox is simply the result of unwarranted, ill-applied terminology.

What is leadership? Who is a leader?

Leadership is a term as widely used and misused as the term *creativity.* To set the record straight let's state first what leadership is not:

- Leadership is not an individual personality trait.
- Leadership is not something a person can possess.
- Leadership is not something a person can usurp.
- Leadership is not something a person can impose on other people.

Now let's state what leadership is. To put it simply, leadership is a process of mutual inspiration and motivation generating outstanding performance and results. What does this definition imply?

Leadership (Guntern 1992, 1997, 1998, 2000, 2001, 2003) is a specific social phenomenon characterized by the following features:

- Two or more individuals, sometimes millions of them, are involved in organized, purposeful activities.
- They play specific roles.
- They play basically equivalent roles.
- They play functionally complementary roles.
- They inspire one another.
- They motivate one another.
- They produce extraordinary performance generating extraordinary results.

Each one of these seven criteria deserves some comments.

- Several persons are involved in organized purposeful activities. Let's imagine the commander of a medieval horde of marauding warriors giving the sign for an attack and then galloping towards the enemy, whose cavalry is waiting in battle formation 500 yards away. After a few seconds, the commander turns his head only to find that nobody is following him. Is he a leader? Certainly not. He is a buffoon who has fallen prey to his own delusion of grandeur. Now let's imagine another example. In a city square, a boisterous crowd is milling around in chaotic agitation. Is there leadership involved in this mass phenomenon? Obviously not. In a situation involving true leadership, there are goal-oriented, organized activities, whereas in a crowd aimlessly milling about, we witness a total lack of organized activities.

Let's now have a look at the specific form of the interpersonal organization of individuals involved in a leadership process.

- They play specific roles. In a leadership phenomenon, interpersonal relationships are organized and, therefore, highly ordered. This order implies, among other things, specific functional roles played by individuals or groups of individuals. Let's take the example of an excellent jazz combo. There is a specific role for a drummer, a bassist, a pianist, a singer, etc. The better each member plays her or his specific role, the better the group performance will be. If one of the role players fails to perform properly, the overall performance of the combo will suffer.
- They play basically equivalent roles. In an excellent jazz combo, the drummer, the bassist, the pianist, and the singer play equivalent roles. No single role is more important than any other role. If somebody tries to outshine and subdue the other players, then the group's performance will suffer.
- They play functionally complementary roles. In an excellent jazz combo, the various roles complement each other. Unless each one of the role players is a highly gifted, multitalented musician, an excellent bass player cannot replace an excellent pianist, nor can an excellent drummer replace an excellent singer.
- They inspire one another. In an excellent jazz combo, gifted musicians inspire each other. They stimulate each other, mutually giving and taking until they reach a state of mind in which they are able to generate more and better musical ideas per unit of time than they would in an uninspired state.
- They motivate one another. A state of motivation is characterized by three features: a) there is a goal; b) individuals attribute a value to this goal; c) they do what they are able to do in order to reach the goal they consider to be of value. In a great jazz combo, the musicians motivate each other for an extraordinary performance. They attribute high value to this goal, because

their reputation depends upon continuous extraordinary performances. Therefore, they will concentrate on their music and do everything else that needs to be done in order to achieve the desired performance.
• There is extraordinary performance with excellent results. Wherever we observe an average or below-standard group performance generating mediocre or even dismal results, there is no leadership but some other form of interpersonal collaboration. A true leadership process always produces an extraordinary performance that naturally entails extraordinary results.

Depending upon the results of extraordinary performance, leadership can be destructive, constructive, or creative. Hitler and his Nazi Party were involved in a destructive leadership process, as were Charles Manson and his satanic sect. A civil engineer heading a team who builds a well-functioning bridge over a river in record time is involved in a constructive leadership process. Nelson Mandela and his close collaborators were involved in a creative leadership process. After twenty-seven years of confinement on Robben Island, Mandela was elected president of the South African Nation when the Apartheid regime crumbled. He and his political party, the African National Congress, could have opted for an interracial war of retaliation. Yet Mandela had the vision and magnanimity to adopt a strategy of interracial reconciliation; this feat made him a charismatic[5] leader who was—and still is—a personality loved and admired the world over. The creative leadership process he headed generated performance and results which were unique, well-functioning, beautiful, and generated values not only for South African society, but for that of the whole world as well by setting a high benchmark for other political leaders. The future of South Africa will show whether Mandela's followers will succeed in sustaining the process he helped to initiate.

Who is a leader? Leaders—and leadership processes—come in all possible shapes and colors. There are destructive leaders, constructive leaders, and creative leaders. There are leaders who fail and those who come through. Bad leaders usually try to maximize their rights while neglecting their duties. Good leaders aim for a proper dynamic balance between their rights and their duties. If they are denied their rights, they cannot do their job. If they neglect their duties, they will soon be rejected as leaders.

Depending upon the specific type of leadership phenomenon, a leader usually displays specific mental abilities, skills, and personality traits.

• In *destructive leadership* these mental abilities, skills, and personality traits include: cunning; power of persuasion; power to dish out punishment and inflict harm; attempts to establish dominance-submission relationships; egocentricity, self-righteousness, pomposity, ruthlessness; a grandiose self;

a tendency towards histrionics; psychopathic, destructive aggressiveness; a total lack of care for other people's needs; and a parasitic exploitation of followers and other people.
- In *constructive leadership* these mental abilities, skills, and personality traits include: clear ideas about goals to be pursued and strategies to be chosen and implemented; power of persuasion; excellent professional knowledge and skills; credibility based on a solid track record; resilience; endurance; ability to respect and integrate other people's opinions; and the ability to successfully manage interpersonal conflicts.
- In *creative leadership* these mental abilities, skills, and personality traits include: the ability to generate a compelling vision; the ability to inspire and motivate others; the ability to be inspired and motivated by others; the ability to establish a set of shared values; the ability to align people for a common cause; authenticity; credibility and authority based upon moral integrity; altruism; high professional competence; and a profound life experience.

A leader is a person heading a group involved in a leadership process; a creative leader is a person heading a creative leadership process. The true source of a creative leader's authority is a track record of performance on the basis of which people attribute to her or him the aforementioned qualities, which are the hallmark of truly creative leaders. In other words, the true source of a leader's authority lies in the positive attitude the people working with him or her have towards him or her. And let there be no misunderstanding: creative leaders are not individuals endowed with superhuman talents and personality traits; they are no angels; they may have all kinds of negative personality traits and they may, at times, even indulge in attitudes and behaviors that other people don't appreciate at all. Still, they are able to establish a compelling vision and a shared set of values; align people for a common cause; and inspire and motivate them for extraordinary creative performance because their positive traits outshine their negative ones. Moreover, creative leaders may not inspire and motivate only their peers working in the same professional domain. The influence of great creative leaders transcends professional domains, generations, ethnic groups, nations, cultures and entire eras. Homer, Socrates, Sophocles, Galileo, Leonardo da Vinci, Michelangelo, Shakespeare, Molière, Goethe, Mozart, Duke Ellington, Thomas A. Edison, Marie Curie and Albert Einstein, Subrahmanyan Chandrasekhar, and Freeman John Dyson have inspired and motivated millions of women and men all over the globe to aim for extraordinary performance. Great creative leadership is a source of tremendous energy; and it is, as already stated, the only natural resource that is virtually inexhaustible because successful creative performance and its results stimulate further creative performance.

Excerpts from an interview with Ashok Kurien (3)

First we talk about the essence of creativity. Then Ashok Kurien cites three examples of genuine creative business leaders and their particular performances. He also speaks about his own creative contributions and is rather modest about it, although he is fully aware of what he has accomplished. His self-confidence is amazing, but he never succumbs to bragging about his achievements. He is quite candid, even with respect to rather delicate topics such as his humble beginnings and deals made in the twilight zone between the correct and the incorrect. He strikes the interviewer as a mature personality who may have been as cunning as he was courageous at times, but who has now reached a state of wisdom and serene detachment—like an eagle that has weathered a storm whose gales have killed weaker birds. He is open-minded and doesn't shy from recalling the meandering pathway that led to his current status and prestige: he honestly confesses that his beginnings in business were not necessarily governed by the ethical code of conduct he embraces today.

In a second round we speak about the essence of leadership in general and of creative leadership in particular. Ashok Kurien describes the trail of development that brought him to the position he holds today: where and how he learned the basics of business, how he opened the antennae of his perception to grasp the peculiarities of the Indian market and the expectations and needs of clients; how he understood that he needed the right partners to reach his strategic goals. He describes a trail leading from rags to riches, a trail full of hurdles and traps, a trail trod by merchants, pilgrims, good companions and lurking highwaymen alike.

Chance only favours the well-prepared mind. Ashok Kurien was equipped with solid instincts and boundless imagination; he trained his analytical powers, and as a keen observer able to watch and listen, he trained his intuition to be able to separate the wheat from the chaff within split seconds. An intuitive judgement is accurate if, and only if, it is fed by the subterranean aqueducts of accumulated experiences. If an experience made is thoroughly analysed in its manifold meanings and implications, it sinks into the subconscious mind where it connects with other experiences sunk into the ground of an individual's self. Woven together all these experiences eventually form a subliminal fabric, a solid inter-neuronal take-off base for rapid decisions.

Ashok Kurien also describes the personality traits he acquired while walking the trail of his development—from his days as a pre-school boy to adulthood. At the age of three he had a near-death experience that left him with a deaf ear. He was rejected and responded with rebellion because he was a strong boy. He was into drugs and indulged in habitual violent behaviour—

until he learned to curb his temper and mastered the handicraft of self-control. He had many near-death experiences but survived them all.

We talk about the challenges a leader faces while working with teams and about his method to cope with these challenges.

In the course of our interview emerges the self-portrait of a man who was able, eventually, to snatch success from the brink of impending failure.

Creativity

GG: If art per se is supposed to be creative, how creative is the Bollywood film machinery?

AK: Is it creative?

GG: That's my question.

AK: Or have they found a formula to make money? Whenever someone in Bollywood breaks the formula and still becomes a commercial success, I think there's creativity there. I personally do not find Bollywood creative.

GG: It simply generates products?

AK: It is product; it is understanding the pulse of the market. What they call *creative* is the ability to move one step further and introduce a tomorrow thing, but it is a formula: boy meets a girl, he is from a poor family, she is from a rich family; he had a brother who was lost at birth, he has a twin, he'll find himself, (imitates a songline) *na-na-na-na-na*, and they sing some songs. Bollywood is really creating formula music, they're looking for trends; in fact the whole game in Bollywood is to see a trend and leap at it first. Trends aren't permanent. Trends are temporary.

GG: As you said before, there are millions of people who think that art is, per definition, creative. I happen to think that this is not the case at all. If you take painting or any art form, more than half of it is reproduction or production. Most of it has nothing to do with creativity whatsoever. Similar things can be said with respect to science. Most people don't realize that the majority of scientific publications have nothing to do with creative performance: they are productions or reproductions. Many scientists just compile and reformulate what has been published before. They even cheat by stealing data or, in some cases, they invent their data. So there is a huge misunderstanding in the world since too many people presume that art or science per se are always creative. When I tell people that I'm a creativity researcher, they say, "Aha! Painting!" or "Aha! Sculpture!" and I say, "No." Now you said earlier that there is a whole domain in society, the business world, to which most people are reluctant to attribute the label "creativity." Could you please expand on that topic? What about creativity in the business world?

AK: To me, the ability to find a completely new solution to a problem is creative. If I am reproducing something, it's not a new solution; it's a twist on something that has been done before. I think one of the most classic examples of creativity in business is Starbucks. If I told you, "I am going to go into the coffee shop business" you would think I had one drink too many. There are already coffee shops everywhere! The creativity lay in producing – in a very short period of time – an environment, an ambience, a range, and a kind of coffee that offered a new experience in coffee drinking. Now that is extremely creative. Someone was able, conceptually, to create a mood around what coffee drinkers do every day and make them pay for it. They pay five dollars for a cup of coffee which they can get in McDonald's for two dollars, in a side-street cafe for one dollar, and make at home for fifty cents! That is incredibly creative! Howard Schultz founded Starbucks in 1971 and is recognized as a business success. But has he been recognized as a truly creative person?

GG: Probably not. You were talking earlier about the influence of drugs, and coffee is a drug. As a physician I consider every chemical substance influencing the mind to be a drug. One of my scientific concepts is that the effect of any drug on the human organism and mind depends upon four interconnected factors: quality, quantity, set and setting. Let me explain. First, quality: an excellent Columbian coffee is better than some watered-down coffee of doubtful origin. Second, quantity: two litres of coffee do not have the same impact as one cup has. Third, set: the current organismic state influences the effect of a coffee; being relaxed or tense, angry or happy influences the subjective taste experience one has while drinking a coffee. Fourth, setting: the physical and social environment – the ambience – influences the impact of coffee on the organism. When these four factors are in balance with one another, then you have a great time drinking a coffee.

AK: Now that Schultz is an orchestra conductor. And that's what the true businessman is: someone who can conduct an orchestra, recognize which instruments must be played and who plays them when and how. That's why, when you go to Starbucks, you spend fifteen minutes sitting there to have your cup of coffee alone, but when you go to another coffee shop, you leave after five minutes.

GG: That's exactly how it is. Can you give me other examples of great creativity in business?

AK: Virgin Airlines, look at it! Richard Branson understood men. The male is the business traveller. All aircraft look like traditional British or American clubs; yet Branson creates a hip nightclub. It has purple and mauve and blue lighting. The seats are red, and there's a little bar at the back, so you can go and sit at the bar and make friends. Virgin also has a masseur – or I should say *masseuse* – on board. When businessmen are under stress, tired and tense, they appreciate a pretty girl who can massage their shoulders, back and head. They love a nice backdrop and wonderful, clean service. What does Branson do? He gets all these girls, measures them and dresses them one size smaller so they look like the American airhostesses of the fifties.

GG: I see. The psychology of that procedure is quite evident.

AK: With Virgin Airlines Branson has orchestrated the entire experience. The food is neither typically French nor typically British. He serves *cuisine nouvelle*; his chefs are new. He addresses a different audience. Look at the lounge. You walk into the Virgin Airways lounge to find a hairdressing salon, a massage parlour, a shoeshine boy, video games… you are in a club furnished with elegant seats, tasteful music and chess sets lying around. You can sit and play chess or Scrabble. It's amazing what that man has created!

GG: That is indeed the work of a true creative leader. Do you have still another example for creativity in business that you admire?

AK: If I say *Apple*, it's very boring because everyone has talked and written about Apple.

GG: But you would agree that Steve Jobs came up with a creative performance?

AK: I have an *iTouch*. I use that *iTouch* for my music, I love it.

GG: I have an *iPod* and an *iPhone*. I've been working on Mac computers for at least twenty-five years, and I love the design of their laptops and notebooks. It is very beautiful and very functional.

AK: Steve Jobs positioned Mac as a tool for creative people. The Mac wasn't sold for commercial usage; initially it was sold for people who used it for art, so he made it artistic. He has a mantra that says, "I must be a creative leader in everything I do." So he breaks the product down into twenty items and asks himself, "How do I creatively improve every one of these twenty items?" In design, graphics, touch, feel, simplicity, ease, quality, sound, everything! And he does it again and again. He re-invents himself every time he launches something. That's creative leadership!

GG: Absolutely. I fully agree with you.

AK: So here are three examples for you.

GG: Now, I bring a fourth one: you have been called the Branson of India.

AK: No, that's a joke! I'm not the Branson of India, please. Some journalist must have written that.

GG: What is your most creative achievement? We might even talk about that creative venture you are still planning.

AK: Please don't listen to what journalists say. Richard Branson is a true creative leader because he does it alone, without partners. He brings teams together around him, he hires the best people and respects their freedom. He gives them direction.

He makes quick decisions; he doesn't want presentations and boards. He does it alone, I do not. I do different things with different people. Someone might have a germ of an idea that they want to pursue. I happen to be around, I have a relationship with that person, and he or she allows me to take the idea and run with it. Now how do you describe somebody like that? I take the idea, I give it form, I give it a direction, I shape it and mentor it, that's the role I play.

GG: It's certainly a leadership role.

AK: It is, because I take it upon myself. I take a risk, because if I fail, that partner will never deal with me again. Very often there's big money behind it. Now, to get back to those three creative examples, I think I talked about Zee, India's first private satellite chain: that simple thought of doing four hours of programming versus twelve or sixteen changed the mathematics of the business! It also made the going much easier. I didn't need a hundred people on the team; sixteen people were enough to get it started. I could oversee all of it personally. The ability to understand that there is an existing distribution system which you can cash in on, which will get you there very fast is important. So it's about getting there fast, getting there with good quality – and getting there with a difference. You can take such an opportunity only when there is one other player.

GG: So basically you team up with only one person per project?

AK: Right, with one.

GG: Whom you trust and…

AK: …who trusts me. Very often it's instant, it's instinctive. In fact I started a PR company with a man with whom I had briefly worked. I didn't know him too well but I instinctively liked him. I knew he was of great integrity, tremendous commitment, old school in many ways but a very big driver. When he fell apart with his partners and lost money, he came to me and said, "I'm sorry, I've let you down. I've just walked out; I'm no longer part of that business." I had associated with his company. So I said, "What are you going to do? Do you have a new job? Do you have plans?" And he said "No, nothing." I suggested, "Why don't you start up your own company?" He replied," I can't start one myself." I said, "I'll partner you. I'll finance you." The whole decision took thirty seconds; we shook hands and set it up. It turned out to become India's two largest independent PR companies – which I just sold off to the Publicis group for some pretty good money. In fact I had fifty-one percent of it, so he had forty-nine, but he did all the work. I felt guilty, so three years ago I turned around and said, "Look, I can't live with this; I just reached my hand out to help you and you have done so well, I can't take this kind of money from you, so take twenty-five percent back." I kept twenty-six just to be able to have some kind of say on the board.

There is another venture which was for a brand of water called *Bisleri*, a processed water in plastic bottles. It's not spring water, but it had about fifty percent of the Indian market share. Although it was a big brand, it wasn't getting anywhere because there was *Aquafina* from Coca Cola, *Kinley* from Pepsi, *Himalaya* and various other brands all over India. So something dramatic was required to change things. I became very close with Ramesh Chauhan, the chap who sold the soft drink companies. He was just sitting on this water, and I helped him. We kept playing little tricks which jumped to five percent, ten percent. All the bottles in India are coloured blue; they bear a standard, blue label. So I came up with a strategy which said: "You have to go and find a spring somewhere and launch a small quantity of water which is actually spring water from the Himalayas. Take all your advertising money and spend it on advertising the spring water. Change the shape of your existing bottle and give the same shape to the spring water bottle. On the spring water bottle put a mountain, and on the regular bottle, put a splash of water. Use the entire advertising budget to advertise the spring water." That was the first decision. The second decision was: change the colour of the bottle to aqua green. In India you can't make the bottle a different colour, you can only change the label and cap. So we changed them to aqua green. When you are one of the biggest brand leaders in the country, you don't change the packaging. So we changed the bottle and the colour, while retaining the same name for the water. And I thought, "I want to give the spring water a different name." Here again, in India the word "spring" refers to a spring in my ball-point pen, the spring in my bed, the spring with my motorcycle, and for the intelligent people spring is a season! Nobody understands the concept of a spring from which water comes. So I said, "Create a new definition for this water and call it mountain water." Now no one had ever called water "mountain water" in India. When you say "mountain water," you immediately think of the mountains of India, the Himalayas. And when you say "mountain" in India, "Himalayas" and "snow-capped," you speak of the abode of the Gods.

GG: Absolutely.

AK: So suddenly you've got spirituality in it. You've got holiness in it. You've got purity in it. You've got healing in it. You've got cure in it.

GG: Every possible mental association.

AK: You get all the associations by changing the colour to aqua green, a modern, new colour, which also says health and purity.

GG: It looks young, like the sprouts of plants.

AK: Yes, young... and then there is the "mountain water." Sales are increasing every month by thirty percent over what we sold during the same month last year. Thirty percent! Thus a simple strategy that helps you to leap from forty percent to sixty percent of India's market share can be called creative.

GG: Yes, it can.

AK: Of course the whole strategy also had to do with understanding Indians. The source of the Holy Ganges is Gangotri, which is the home of the Gods. It's holy water; all our rivers come down from the Gods. The Gods send it down and because of that water our crops grow, we live in health. It is pre-programmed in our souls that the concept of water coming from the home of the Gods must be pure and better.

GG: You have invented a very clever business strategy.

AK: What other creative achievements have I accomplished? I'll go back to that soft drink called *Thums Up*, a big-selling cola. It is interesting to note that we created an advertising campaign which is still running today, thirty years later. In fact, up until a few years ago, they even used the same actor that we had engaged twenty years ago! This was just before Coca-Cola and Pepsi came into India. We had a campaign line which said, *"Thums Up,* Taste the Thunder." That's not the kind of line you put onto a soft drink. Why would you say, "taste the thunder"? What does "taste the thunder" say to you?

GG: Something very fresh. I would think of the smell of two white silicate stones, which we call "fire-stones." When you crush them together, you produce a spark that gives off a characteristic smell. As a goatherd in the Swiss Alps every day I would pass by a certain place high up in the mountains. I used to throw at least twenty or twenty-five stones into an abyss because the friction caused as they tumbled on the rock generated a smell I liked very much. So when you mention "mountain" and "taste the thunder," it's that smell I associate with those terms.

AK: That's very interesting, because it is completely out of context with the soft drink, a dark cola! The logo, by the way, for "taste the thunder" had a bolt of lightning in it, because thunder and lightning belong together. But we used, in a strange way, my own life story to build into that campaign, because the basic meaning was "taste the thunder of victory." It all came out of my learning and experience with Indians. All Indians were insecure. We didn't know what lay ahead for the future or whether or not we would have jobs. Thanks to my own life experience I understood the state of mind of the eighteen-year-old Indian male – and mainly it's males who go out and drink colas. For him everything is a battle; everything is a struggle. We produce ten million graduates, but how many of them are going to get jobs? It's a very insecure world. So the interpretation of "taste the thunder" was "taste the thunder of achievement"; "taste the thunder of victory." When you win, you can taste that.

GG: You taste the thunder of triumph and you lose your fear. You feel strong, you are a winner, you experience triumph.

AK: It's triumph, it's tasting. If I close my eyes, I hear the thunder of applause. It's that sound, the roar of the crowd, that's like thunder. It's about tasting the thunder of victory. The ads always showed a guy who didn't have a good chance of winning, who went out and built something or achieved something. He was always a good guy who would battle the bad guys, the bullies, the policemen, the bus drivers and the taxi drivers. That campaign created such a strong bond between the

people and the product, that twenty years later, they're still running *"Thums Up,
Taste the Thunder."* It still speaks for all average Indians because we've been subdued, we've been kept down there at the bottom of the scale, we've been told we
don't have a chance. So all our dreams are about winning this; it's very male, very
macho. You were talking about "the heroes' journey"; somewhere it had that basic
intrinsic top: the suffering Indian with a lot of hardship.

GG: That ad must have touched a subliminal dream in those men. Now you have
basically defined what creativity means for you: generating unique solutions for
problems; producing something that functions, that serves its purpose; what you
produce must be beautiful: it must please the senses and stimulate the mind; and
it has to be something that generates values for society. Not only profits for the
producer because if these guys who "taste the thunder" feel better and have
positive associations while drinking that cola, it's of great value for them. They
feel strong, assertive, ready to do battle

Leadership

GG: What for you is the essence of leadership? Who is a leader, what is leadership?

AK: We talked about it a little earlier: you can have leadership with fear, or you
can have leadership with power. You can be a leader in sports. If you look at a
team leader in sports, he is very intelligent, very tactical, but he commands.

GG: How do you define leadership?

AK: You have to create a new idea; there has to be something new in it, otherwise why are you different? Why would people follow you? Then your followers must have faith in you; not necessarily blind faith, but at critical times when
they are not sure, they must follow you blindly.

GG: They must trust you.

AK: They must trust you! And that's a completely different kind of faith. When
I say, "We're going to get that piece of business" and they say, "No, we can't,"
I say, "It doesn't matter. I will lead from the front. Just follow me, we will go
out and get it." When I started my advertising agency, Elsie, who came in to be
my creative partner, was the art & creative head. I told her I was setting up an
agency, and I got the finest textile company as my client. I said I would get the
biggest soft drink company in India as my client, and I did. I said that I would
get the Taj Mahal Hotel chain – which is the best in India – as a client, and we
got that too. I said that I would get India's biggest cosmetic company, *Lakme*,
and we got it. I said I would get *Vadilal Ice Cream*, which is the finest ice cream
in India, and we got it. In six years I got all five clients that I had promised to
get from day one. Now, how did that come about? It came out of believing that
"That's the kind of brands I will go and win." I knew I already had one in my

pocket and the second one was close, so if I could do two, then I could also do the other three. Leadership is about continuously demonstrating that you're winning. You cannot be a great leader if you win once. It's about whether you won yesterday and whether you're going to win again today. Last year's success alone doesn't help. You have to constantly go out and demonstrate your leadership, either by creating new things, new businesses, new brands or come up with new achievements within the same business. The day you stop, I ask the question whether or not you're still a leader.

GG: As soon as you stop being inspiring...

AK: ... the faith goes. Trust goes.

GG: I do understand what you are saying. In my language I would say that the moment you don't inspire your people anymore, their motivation fades. In my view, motivation implies three things: first, you have a goal; second, you believe in the value of that goal; and third, you go after that goal until you achieve it. Now, if you no longer win, the members of your team will ask themselves, "Is there any value in that new goal he sets? Why should we go after it?" And then the motivation begins to waver, and if the motivation wavers, you're not a winner anymore, and your team will fail to reach the goal set.

AK: And then you are finished! In India we have a local train system, and I use that as a didactic example very often in my speeches at home. There is a slow train and a fast train. The slow train stops at every station. The fast train stops only at four major junctions. Now, do you want to be on the fast train or the slow train? Rupert Murdoch is on a fast train. So I created brands, whether it was my ad agency or whatever, that very quickly moved to No.1 position. I mean, if you aren't going to be No. 1, why are you doing it? You've got to do it differently, you've got to be first on the market, and you've got to be No.1 and stay No.1. So as long as you're on the fast train, everybody wants to be on the fast train. The moment your fast train slows down and starts stopping at every station, your employee might as well get off and board the other slow train because it's less crowded or it's got nicer cabins or it's got longer lunch breaks or it's got better bonuses; whereas if he is on the fast train, you pay him less because he has to pay you for being on your fast train. So your salaries are lower and you're far more profitable, and you can put that money back into learning. You can say, "We're taking the whole office on a holiday every year. We party and have no conference at all." That's what we did at our agency.

GG: Okay, I've grasped your view of what a leader is.

AK: But I think as a leader you also have to be flexible. You cannot predict what will happen the day after tomorrow. You might predict tomorrow, and as you approach tomorrow and you realize things are changing, you've got to be honest with your people and say, "Hey, we thought it was this way. It worked so far but now we've got to be flexible. We all have to sit together and think about how we can change. The final decision, I'll take; I carry the can."

GG: You are talking about the credibility of a leader that is based on achievement and integrity rather than on hierarchical position within an organization.
If you cheated at that moment and pretended, "I know exactly how it goes..."
then...

AK: You would fail. You have to say, "Hey, we got it a little wrong. Let's swing
left." Or "Let's go back a bit and go that way."

GG: Okay, beautiful! I like it very much. To return to Macaulay and his verdict
against the Earl of Galway[6]: a leader must find it more honourable to win by
means of flexibility and innovation rather than to lose by rigidly following rules
that were established a long time ago.

AK: If you are a leader, you write the rules! You change the rules! And then you
change the game. Your opponents are still playing the last game; you have created a whole new game. I mean, normally if you've changed the rules, you've
changed the game, you've changed the battleground, you've changed everything!

GG: That takes vision and courage.

A trail of development producing a creative business leader

AK: I created my agency at the right time; I wouldn't have been ready for it
before. If I had stayed longer in my former job as an employee, I might have
become very comfortable and not taken a chance. I left my job with a wife who
wasn't well, one daughter who had been very unwell and near death at one time,
and five thousand rupees in my bank account.

GG: Which corresponds to how many dollars?

AK: A hundred and eight US dollars. You have to be stupid – and everyone told
me I was really stupid to walk out of a job with a hundred dollars in the bank
and say I am going to start an advertising agency. That's why I didn't hire anyone! (chuckles) Now, I keep reminding myself that I am stupid. I am never
grandiose about what I do. I will always underestimate my potential because I
am insecure. I am not sure, but it is this wisdom of insecurity that keeps me
within control and makes me think the problem through a hundred times. I don't
sleep at night, or at least I sleep very little, but I will thrash it threadbare, I will
tear it apart, I will look for every single thing that can go wrong. You see, when
you are insecure, you only see the failure. So for everything that can go wrong,
I come up with a solution. I am actually filling all the holes, and it's not that you
can fill all of them, but if you fill most of them, you have a very good chance.
When you know your capability, you always find a partner. In the advertising
business I needed a partner who could actually aesthetically create and communicate. I could communicate strategically but not aesthetically. So I had a
partner there. In Zee TV, my partner was a big, powerful man who knew how to

walk the corridors of power – and the government. With him I later started the first lottery business in India.

Soon thereafter we launched the first directly-to-home business in India, which I still mentor; and I go in as a mentor, I never overstep my role. We began that venture without a CEO because that way the entrepreneurs can make entrepreneurial decisions. However, what we have now learnt is, don't wait too long to hire a good CEO, because we are not good managers. So I have learnt to mentor, to bring in a CEO once size and scale have been created, and to make sure that CEO has the strengths I don't have. So If I don't understand distribution and ground service, then he *must* know distribution and ground service. Subhash Chandra, the Zee TV boss, is strong with respect to finance, government, getting the big picture; he has got power and leverage and other things I don't know anything about. But he trusts me and leaves the strategic marketing decisions up to me, and this helps the business grow. So in every case there is a partner. Your partner's strengths must be your weakness, and his weakness must be your strength. The perfect team! Each time. In my Internet businesses I have a guy who is very strong in technology and has got great gumption; he keeps going, and going, and going. I only contribute into a direction, into an opportunity – which brings us back to opportunity. Opportunities go past us all the time. You can pick the wrong ones, and you are doomed. You have to use something within you to be able to pick the right ones.

GG: What is that something within you?

AK: That something is something that comes in a flash. It is the sum total of all my years of living a hard life, of watching people, of knowing how poor people react, of understanding what one cent means; nobody today understands the meaning of one cent. I understand because I lived in the villages of India for three years. And I ran away from home.

GG: At what age?

AK: I was eighteen or nineteen. In India people don't leave home at that age. I came back as a twenty-three year-old. But that experience taught me to understand how common people live. My family is from a fairly poor, lower middle class background. So one understands how they react and respond. One also hung around with very rich friends, because they paid for your food, for the bills and for everything. So one understood how the rich thought and how they functioned. One also understood how the super rich thought and behaved. I think it is that as I actually lived all those lives, I developed an ability to take any opportunity and say, "Hey, where does it fit, for whom, who will buy it, how do I make him buy it, what will convince him to do it and why will it work?" Because if a person doesn't need a product, he is not going to buy it.

GG: If I understand you well, intuition must be fed by experience. If not, it doesn't grasp the opportunity.

AK: Without experience, there is no intuition.

GG: What kind of experience did you gather in the few years you lived in that village?

AK: I understood the real India which is out there in the villages. I understood generosity: when a poor villager is sitting with just one plate of rice, and one crushed onion and one green chilli for his meal and he says, "You haven't eaten," and he puts his hand in the middle and says, "You eat this half and I'll eat this half," that is generosity. You also understand that the government is making him pay two rupees to have every acre of land crop sprayed with a helicopter while it subsidizes seven or eight rupees for every acre. The two rupees means a week's food for the villager, and when some government officer wants to cheat and dilute the chemical, it's not going to work for this guy. It made me very angry to see such things. So I understood reality, but I had to survive this job, which was effectively playing nursemaid to a pilot, an engineer, and a team who went from village to village to make sure that the government officer signed the certificate of the day's work. I was given money to bribe him every day. I had to bribe the government officer with the company's money to make sure he signed for so much acreage, so that the company could collect the money back from the government. So one understood the way the world worked.

I understood that because I wasn't a Hindu, I was untouchable. Of course, I had to get food for my team. If I was in a temple-town, which was run by Brahmins, they wouldn't let us set up a kitchen there. So I had to go to the only restaurant in the village and stand outside holding out my hands as though I were begging, and they would wrap the food in newspaper and drop it into my hand. They saw me as untouchable.

I had to take that food back to the helicopter crew. So it humbled me; it made me understand compassion; it made me understand hard work. I've slept in the back of a truck; I've slept under a truck because at times there was no place for me to stay. Villages of India are a sight to behold, and forty years ago they were still unsophisticated villages. I slept under a truck with snakes creeping around. The only water to be found was in a little ditch two feet wide on the side of the field, and you washed and did whatever you did there. In the morning the boy would fill the kettle from that same ditch and boil the water for tea! So you learn about hardship. I think those are the major learning experiences. You understood commercial dealings. You understood that the company gave you five hundred rupees to bribe the government officer. Now if you were charming and smart and you spent time with this government officer in the evening, you got away with four hundred rupees, which left a hundred rupees for you in your pocket! So I learnt great dishonesty. When I came back, something taught me to believe that you can actually run an honest business, as long as the part that you looked after was honest. The reality is you cannot do big business in a place like India honestly; but in my advertising business we were completely honest and above board. We led people through that honesty and taught them not to fear being honest. Many people are afraid of what other people will say. They don't dare admit, "I don't understand." They are frightened to ask questions, frightened of being regarded as stupid. A villager has no fear of saying, "What is that?" when the reply is, "This is the key that goes into the truck, and you turn it, and it starts the truck." He asks, "Why do you have a zip on your trousers?" He has no fear. And I don't think he is stupid. When I tell him what the zip is for, he says, "Ah, ah, wow!" and then explains it to all his fellow villagers. So he becomes the smart guy in the village. I think village life taught me to not fear.

GG: Ashok, you said earlier that often you don't sleep much at night, you analyse things back and forth: advantages versus disadvantages, probabilities of success versus probabilities of failure, and then comes a point where you take a leap into the unknown. For instance, when you dared to build up your own business when your wife was ill and one of your two daughters was ill, and you had only a hundred dollars in your account. Let's talk about courage. Where did you learn courage? There comes a moment when you have to jump; you have made up your mind and then it still takes courage.

AK: There is a thin line between courage and foolhardiness.

GG: Sometimes that's the case, indeed. I should like you to begin by giving me a general overview of the biggest challenges you have met and how you coped with failure. Let's start with your earliest memories, when you were four or five years old. How did you develop into the personality you are today?

AK: Oh, this is a crazy story! I had an accident when I was three years old. My mother, my elder brother and I had gone to visit an uncle who was an ex-army-major.

GG: That high up in the military hierarchy?

AK: Yes, so he had lots of decorative shells and ammunition. There was a hand-grenade somewhere. I don't have a clear recollection of it; my elder brother was five or six, my cousin was eight or nine. I think there were two or three other children there. At any rate, my elder brother was fair, intelligent, very bright. I was the second son who was dark, not so smart, etc. Now, what I am telling you is hearsay, as I don't remember very clearly. We were all playing with this hand-grenade. Apparently one of us stuck a compass in it, and it went off. My mother was sitting about ten feet away, and the explosion killed all the children. This was in the early fifties.

GG: Killed all the children but you?

AK: Yes, they thought I was dead, too. They put all the bodies on a handcart and were pushing the handcart to get to a hospital and apparently, somebody saw my finger move. In fact, I think it was the eldest sister of my cousin who died. She says, "We saw your finger move, so we put you on a handcart and took you to the hospital." My mother was pretty badly injured. Her left hand has a steel rod in it, and in those days they didn't fix things up too well. I had scars all over and bits of shrapnel, which I still have.

GG: You still have shrapnel pieces in your body?

AK: Yes, look here (shows his hand). Here is big one which I love playing with. It flips like that. That one must have entered from this direction. It's a nice big piece (chuckles).

GG: You are the proverbial man of iron!

AK: At any rate, I think my mother must have had a nervous breakdown, but in the fifties nobody understood this, and no one talked about this event.

GG: It was taboo.

AK: Yes, it was taboo. The accident happened in the house of my cousin who died in that event. Many years later his brother went to Germany to study medicine. When he started doing surgery, he couldn't bear the sight of blood, and he went unwell. He committed suicide many years later. His sister is the only one still alive, and she talks very little about it. But she was only twelve or thirteen at the time. So apparently we rushed off to hospital, and my mother must have had a breakdown. A few years ago, somebody mentioned she had gone mad and my father really looked after her and was very gentle with her. She didn't go back to work for a couple of years. She became very religious and spiritual after this incident.

GG: Your elder brother was the preferred son?

AK: Maybe I believed that. Undoubtedly in her mental agony, my mother must have said many unkind things to me. Now that accident left me partially deaf in this ear; I have a hearing aid. But that impairment was something I discovered much later; I didn't even know that I had a hearing problem. Of course this happened in India many years ago. We are not well-off people; we are lower middle class. So there was a lot of hate from my mother.

GG: She was full of hate against the fate of having lost her beloved son?

AK: Yes, and she and took it out on me, because she said many terrible things which I still remember. I believed I was the one with the compass. I was responsible for the deaths. I was a murderer.

GG: But you were only a little child!

AK: Yes, but she said things like, "Why did God take him and leave me to suffer with you?"

GG: Ah! You were the dark son.

AK: I was the evil one. By that time I had become rebellious at a very young age. I know that I broke neighbours' windows and flowerpots, and I used to run out of frustration. I would really push my body to run. Probably that's how I became such a good runner. It was just that frustration…

GG: You were like an athlete pushing his forces to the limit.

AK: I used to cry and run around on the streets just to take that frustration out somewhere. My learning disability, however mild it may have been, somehow got heightened because I certainly could never comprehend mathematics or science in any manner. I think I definitely had a memory problem. I would retain things in my head for a short while and then they'd vanish. Much later in life, in fact in my thirties, I learnt to write everything down. I always have a pen in my pocket and paper next to me, because if I don't write things down, it all disappears. My mind is like a bagatelle machine; it just keeps going. The ball of an idea pops up and then vanishes (snaps his fingers), just like that! So I have paper and a pen handy at all times. I also have an answering machine, and I call my own number and leave messages for myself – all the time. It's a method of coping with a problem. By the fifth standard in school I was at the bottom of the class; by the seventh standard I failed the first time and in the ninth, I failed again. But because I was such a superior sportsperson, they didn't throw me out of school. My rebellion, however, caused huge differences between my mother and me.

GG: Before we go on, just one question for my understanding: how old was a boy when he entered the first standard in India back then?

AK: Five.

GG: And how many standards were there?

AK: Eleven.

GG: So in the eleventh standard you would be sixteen years old.

AK: Yes, but because I failed twice, I was eighteen when I graduated.

GG: Under those circumstances you began your strong rebellion against your mother.

AK: Yes, and against society. My rebellion turned into physical violence; I would beat people up or constantly get into fights. I was hated and looked upon as a troublemaker in school, I was looked upon as a troublemaker at home. My mother and I really didn't communicate till I was forty-five. In fact we couldn't sit in the same room together for any period of time.

GG: You left home at eighteen? You ran off?

AK: Before that I was already staying with friends. I would go home, fight, go off for a few days, come back, and by eighteen I went off to the villages for three years with that job. Progressively my violence got worse. I was arrested a few times.

GG: Did you hurt anybody seriously in those fights?

AK: I was always compassionate. There was an incident with a hired hood, a guy with a knife who was hired by someone to stab me when I was in school. I remember disarming him, holding the knife to his throat and then saying, "I am letting you go." That attitude became part of me. But I did seriously hurt a number of people, and then during my school days, it became a game to beat up policemen. It was an inability to handle authority. I only beat up policemen and bus drivers, because bus drivers in India are very…

GG: Aggressive, powerful figures?

AK: Yes, indeed. They're bullying, they drive big buses and they're protected by the government. Taxi drivers also behave really badly in India. Every time a taxi driver tried cutting me, I would stop the car, pull his head out of the window and smash the door into his head. I was arrested a number of times including for car theft. Yes, I was in serious trouble. I got into drugs, I started drinking.

GG: What kind of drugs?

AK: It started with hashish and grass but it went on to Mandrax, speed and LSD, smack[7] and then heroin.

GG: Did you become dependent on it?

AK: The year after I finished school I was staying with this very rich friend who had an apartment to himself because his mother was a movie actress. The two of us were doing acid for two or three days, and the third day he got up and didn't recognise me and went completely crazy. That frightened me so much, I never touched chemicals again except maybe the occasional snort of cocaine now and then. But I was frightened. Much later, my wife was an alcoholic, and she drank herself to death. I lived with that alcoholic wife for fifteen years. That's why I am terrified of being out of control. But back then, before I was married, I was close to all the addictions, all the habits. I started drinking when I was very young. Physically, for an Indian, I was a very big boy; older kids used to take me in as their friend. Besides, I didn't fear anything, and I'd be ready to battle any time.

GG: You were a small king.

AK: I was a little street gang boy. These older boys encouraged me to smoke when I was seven years old. In India people didn't start smoking at seven. By ten or twelve I was carrying cigarettes around. In India people did that much later. Despite the prohibition in India I used to drink country liquor with my older chums when I was ten or twelve.

GG: Is country liquor something like brandy?

AK: No, it's homemade hooch.

GG: With a low or high concentration of alcohol?

AK: It's very strong alcohol made with fruit and vegetables and spirits. Distilling it is very illegal. Many people went blind drinking that stuff! Some even died. In order to get it, you sneaked into a little lane somewhere, had two shots and came out. So I got into this kind of extreme rebellious behaviour whereby I was violent and would hurt people. I know I must have hurt a lot of people with hockey sticks.

GG: What was the worst pain or hurt you inflicted? What was the peak of your violence?

AK: Officially it was probably in the boxing ring. I remember an opponent went deaf. Let's not discuss the unofficial ones. I used to lose my temper; today I don't lose my temper at all.

GG: You used to be very explosive, very impulsive.

AK: Yes, and the answer was always the fist.

GG: How old were you when you got married?

AK: I was twenty-seven.

GG: Had you had relationships with other girls before? I am not asking about sex. I'm interested in the quality of your relationships with women. When you have a rebellious sort of relationship with your Mum, there is a certain danger that you develop a specific mental map, a negative picture of the female gender. I wonder whether this was the case with you.

AK: Yes, I suspect there's some kind of revenge. My relationship with most women was one of conquest. I also remember the need to publicly humiliate women when I was seventeen or eighteen. I think there was lots of anger towards them. Moreover I didn't have money. So I went through a whole phase of using people who were attractive and well-off because I had no income, no money. For a bit I suppose I was something of a gigolo. Then I reached the stage where I was just sick of it and I finally got a degree and got a job in advertising.

GG: You went to college, then you dropped out, and then you went back again?

AK: I dropped out for three years and then went back to what we call morning college. You can go to class from 6:30 or 7:00 till 10:00 am. If you attended these morning classes, you could sit for your exam in October or June. We also have a system where you pass one subject at a time. So it took me seven years – or actually ten years from when I first started college – to finally get a degree and even then, I cheated.

GG: You got a Bachelor of Arts?

AK: Yes, but even that belonged to the guy who sat next to me. I cheated.

GG: Your Bachelor of Arts was in what branch?

AK: I did sociology because somebody had told me that it was the easiest sub-ject to pass. A second branch was required, and that was cultural history. You also had to pass Hindi, which is the national language. I had a big problem with that because being from the South, I spoke Malayalam, a language very close to Sanskrit and whose speakers are called Malayalees, though they come from the state of Kerala. No one in the South speaks Hindi, the language of the North. Despite the obstacles finally I got a degree, and I got my first job, at which point I decided that I really wanted to settle down with the first good woman I met. At last I had a salary to support a family. At a point you reach a stage where you are sick of yourself and you feel sort of cheap. It was about being able to live on one's own. It was all about pride. At the end of my career as a do-no-good there was a lot of hate and no pride in myself. But at least I had a job, and I met this very wonderful woman, whom I married two years later and we had a daughter. Actually we hadn't planned to have a child so soon, but due to some medical complication, we had to have our first daughter. This turn of events made my wife extremely angry because she had to sacrifice her career and much of her life in many ways because of the child.

GG: She felt cheated out of a beautiful future she had planned for herself?

AK: Right.

GG: What was her career?

AK: She was in garments and fashion. She used to export clothes. That was her career and her dream.

GG: How old was she when she had her first baby?

AK: I was twenty-nine and she was thirty-one—which in India is very old. In India people get married at eighteen; if they're educated, maybe twenty or twenty-one. You normally have your first child by twenty-two or twenty-three. But she was a career woman, and she wasn't going to just get into an arranged marriage. She wasn't going to settle for a habitual family life. She was a very strong, independent woman, which in those days was not very common.

GG: No parents were involved in arranging your marriage?

AK: No, no parents. She was a Hindu, I was a Christian. Two entirely different families; I came from the South, she came from the North.

NOTES

1. Diya = Lamp, The Light of my Life; Priyanka = The Beloved of my Life
2. (Abbreviations used: GG = Gottlieb Guntern, AK = Ashok Kurien).
3. A creator is simply a person who creates. Adherents of religious faiths speak of the Creator, a supernatural entity to whom they attribute the creation of the universe.

4. Human creativity occurs in cultural evolution. Yet geophysical evolution and biological evolution have also produced creative processes. The Grand Canyon and Mount Fujiyama correspond to the four criteria of creativity discussed before; so do the rain forests of the Amazon and the species of honeybees. As our book deals only with human creativity, from now on we shall omit the adjective "human" when speaking of creativity.

5. Greek: χάρισμα = gift, grace (bestowed by the gods), outstanding talent. A charismatic leader is a person attracting other human beings in a manner transcending the operational range of purely rational explanations. Charismatic leaders—a rather rare social phenomenon—occur in constructive, destructive, and creative leadership forms.

6. In 1707 in Almansa, the Earl of Galway, a general commanding British-Allied Forces, lost a decisive battle against his Franco-Spanish foes. Later statesman Macaulay scoffed, "He found it more honorable to lose according to the rules rather than to win by means of innovation."

7. Smack = a cheap adulterated form of cocaine

Chapter Two

On the Structure
of the Creative Process

2.1 ON THE NATURE OF THE CREATIVE PROCESS

Structural constraints give birth to spontaneity; spontaneity generates structural constraints.

Gottlieb Guntern

Human creativity manifests itself in a series of ideas, activities, and procedures whose goal-directed combination is called a creative process.

A process is a structure that changes its appearance and functions in the course of time. Major changes of structures and functions mark the beginning and end of what we call stages or phases. According to our predilection for splitting apart items or lumping them together, we may arbitrarily differentiate between a greater or smaller number of stages or phases within a given process.

Over the years, the international literature on creativity research has proposed various concepts of the creative process. The number of phases[1] indicated by these concepts varies from at least three to almost a dozen (Brown 1989, 5f.; Hadamard 1945, 43ff.; Mansfield and Busse 1981, 85ff.; Martindale 1989, 214; Preiser 1976, 42ff.; Schregenberger 1981, 159ff.). In my view, none of these concepts pass the test of critical scrutiny.

After twenty years of scientific research in the realm of creativity, I shall present in this book a systemic concept plus a visual model of the creative process that, to my way of thinking, fit observable facts. In the course of my investigations, I have made a great number of interviews and have had countless discussions with creative leaders in various professional domains. Since 1979, our International CREANDO Foundation (www.creando.org) has orga-

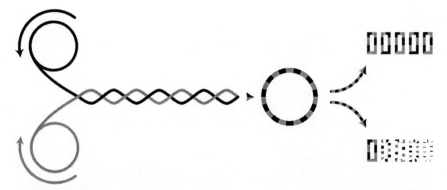

Figure 2.1.   The Four Stages of a Creative Process (general overview). Stage I = Chaos (grey colour) and Order (black colour) begin to interact. Stage II = Seven Phases of the Creative Process. Stage III = Cultural Evaluation. Stage IV = Morpho-Evolution and Morpho-Elimination.

nized twenty international symposia on creative leadership. In all of these encounters and events, I have discussed my model of the creative process and, by and large, most of my interviewees and invited speakers have agreed with my major findings.

As I see it, there are four major stages characterizing every single creative process, and the second stage is composed of seven phases.

I should like to emphasize that these stages and phases do not follow each other like Antarctic penguins marching along in single file. Their deployment resembles rather the behavior of a swarm of mosquitoes chaotically zigzagging through the air on a sweltering summer evening. To put it more abstractly, individual stages and phases of a creative process appear and disappear in what cyberneticists call a highly redundant[2] manner; that is, there is continuous repetition with variations. Moreover, several creative processes may occur simultaneously within the same individual, and they may continuously interact. Also, in teams or in whole professional domains and cultures, several creative processes may occur simultaneously and continuously interact. We should therefore constantly be aware of such mind-boggling dynamic complexity as we discuss, in a strictly linear manner, the various stages and phases of the creative process.

Nonlinear phenomena abound in nature while human language and analytical reasoning proceed in a strictly linear manner. Linear reasoning has its advantages and disadvantages. The main advantage is that it simplifies complexity. The main disadvantage is that simplification may turn the multidimensional reality of a living being into a lifeless skeleton. Yet there are ways to counteract this disadvantage. We may use metaphors and concrete historical examples to pack muscles, inner organs, blood, and nerves onto that skeleton. And we may use what General Systems Science calls *systemic perspectivism*: by adopting different viewpoints of observation, description, and explanation, we produce a great number of overlapping aspects of the same phenomenon or event, out of which a living organism will eventually emerge.

The model presented here was first published in 1991 (Guntern 1991a, 55) in a version that I have modified in the course of my ongoing investigations into the nature of the creative process. In the following chapters and sections, the specific stage or phase discussed in detail are always indicated by a hatched grid. That presentation helps the reader's orientation through the maze of creative performance.

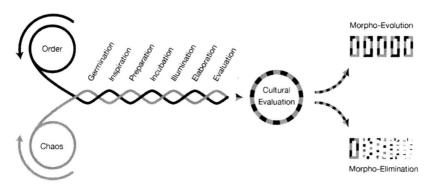

Figure 2.2.   The Four Stages of a Creative Process (details). Regarding figure 2.1 and figure 2.2, here are a few general remarks on the overall structure of the creative process; they will be specified in more detail later:
- The whole model should be read from left to right.
- Stage I: Chaos and order are twin forces whose interaction drives the four stages of every creative process. There incessant interplay does not only occur in the minds of creative individuals or teams, but also in their environment.
- Stage II: The seven phases of stage II occur in the minds of creative people.
- Stage III occurs in the social environment where critical minds judge the merits of creative achievements produced by individuals, teams, ethnic groups, nations, cultures and whole civilizations.
- Stage IV occurs in the social environment. Depending on the results of cultural evaluation new forms enter morpho-evolution —subsequent creative production inspired by the results of specific creative achievements—or morpho-elimination—the removal of results of achievements: they are forgotten or even destroyed physically.
- The continuous interplay of order and chaos is represented by the continuous convergence, divergence and juxtaposition of the colours black (order) and grey (chaos).

NOTES

1. To the best of my knowledge, no author has ever talked about stages in a creative process.

2. In colloquial language *redundant* means superfluous, unnecessary. In science *redundancy* implies repetition with modifications.

2.2 STAGE I: CHAOS AND ORDER BEGIN TO DANCE

Whenever the destroyer god Shiva stamps the world into a sea of flames, silence begins to reign. Then the creator god Vishnu falls once again into a visionary slumber, and thus, in a play of imagination, a new world emerges.

Ancient Hindu myth of creation.

Every single creative process begins with an intricate dance in which chaos and order interact continuously. Chaos implies—among other things—chance, random events, freedom, and instinctive, emotional, or intuitive spontaneity. Order implies—among other things—necessity, determined events, structural constraints, and rational calculation. While chaos implies unpredictability, order implies the predictability of future events.

Both chaos and order are vast fields of forces interweaving the internal mental world of the creative individual and the external world of the ecosystem where events of the physical and biosocial environments influence each other. These highly dynamic force fields have no beginning and no end, and they continuously change their form, combination, and impact.

Let us now explore this fascinating topic and breathe life into the abstract formulations just proposed. We shall begin our characterization of stage I with a short discussion of a few crucial aspects of specific creation myths. A myth is a prescientific narrative describing and explaining the origin and evolution of a specific world (for instance, a particular ethnic group, a nation, a culture.) Creation myths represent archetypical concepts of the creative process that has brought into existence living creatures and human beings and their environment. They have been produced by almost every culture on our planet and all of them relate, by and large, the same story, although it is usu-

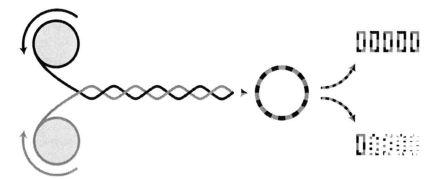

Figure 2.3.   The interaction of chaos and order.

ally formulated in different ways. The story is one of collective cultural imagination and, like every story imagined and well told, it generates a profound conviction of truth based on emotional belief rather than rational proof. But despite these apparent shortcomings, mythical tales confer to us the legacy of precious ancient knowledge generated by our ancestors. They contain an intuitive-empirical insight into the first stage (and often also into the subsequent stages) of a creative process generating a specific world. We shall briefly take a look at six creation myths, whose content corresponds to that of all the other creation myths we know today.

Creation Myth of the Old Testament

The Book of Genesis in the Old Testament (Ridler 1960, 7) opens as follows: "In the beginning God created the heaven and the earth. And the earth was without form, and void; and darkness was upon the face of the deep. And the Spirit of God moved upon the face of the waters. And God said, 'Let there be light': and there was light. And God saw the light, that it was good: and God divided the light from the darkness." And thus God continued to create and name things and living beings until eventually He created Adam, whose existence was soon complemented by the creation of Eve.

What are the basic ingredients of this mythical account of the beginnings of our world? There is a process of creation. It is initiated by a supernatural entity called God. The myth does not tell us where God comes from, nor what or who created Him. Him? The Jewish God was obviously that of a patriarchal society who decided that the first creator had to be a God rather than a Goddess. This male God obviously wills into existence the things, events, and organisms He creates. His will implies imagination, vision of a desired goal, planning, decision-making, and implementing effective, purposeful strategies. God begins with creating heaven and earth, and thus a duality comes into being. Nothing is said about the materials God uses in His creative process, although the official belief of the Roman Catholic Church holds that God produced a *creatio ex nihilo* (a creation out of nothing). God's process of creation results in a heaven whose appearance is not specified, although we may assume that it was somehow patterned, structured, or ordered. At the same time, the process of creation results in an earth whose appearance is characterized as being "without form, and void" and immersed in darkness. This seems to be a circumscription of chaos.

God creates a duality of heaven and earth and transforms the oneness of darkness into the duality of darkness and light. It is explicitly stated that God "divided the light from the darkness;" division is a hallmark of mental activities based upon analytical-dualistic thinking. Analytical-dualistic reasoning operates in the either/or mode, splitting apart oneness or unity and generating, with each step of reasoning, two opposites—for instance heaven versus earth, light versus darkness. In contradistinction to analytical-dualistic reasoning, the intuitive mind operates in a holistic-monistic manner; it thinks in terms of integrated wholeness, oneness, and unity.

We read in the creation myth of the Old Testament that God calls the light Day and the darkness Night. By splitting apart and subsequent labelling, He separates the land from the sea, the creatures dwelling on the earth from those living in the sea. After each act of creation and labelling, there comes an act of evaluation. The Supreme Creator is obviously satisfied with the results of his endeavors because each time he sees that "it was good".

It is only much later, after human beings have multiplied and turned out to be quite destructive creatures, that God has serious doubts as to the value of His creations. That is when He decides that chaos must intervene in the new order He has created; He resolves to send a great flood that will destroy all living beings on earth. All living beings? Not exactly, because in the sixth chapter of Genesis (Ridler 1960, 12), we read that God told Noah to build an ark, specifying: "But with thee will I establish my covenant; and thou shalt come into the ark; thou and thy sons, and thy wife, and thy sons' wives with thee. And of every living thing of all flesh, two of every sort shalt thou bring into the ark, to keep them alive with thee; they shall be male and female."

I should like to point out that the continuous interplay between chaos and order described by the Jewish creation myth is a topic running like a red thread through most of the creation myths we know.

Greek Creation Myth

About three centuries after the Book of Genesis was presumably written, a similar tale emerges on the Greek shores of the Mediterranean. In Hesiod's Theogony[1] we read about the beginnings of the earth: "Chaos was born first, then came *Gaia* the broad-breasted . . ." (Boorstin 1992, 35). The Greek term *chaos* corresponds to the Hebraic term *tohu-wa-bohu*[2] used in the Old Testament. Gaia, with her structure of two breasts, represents order. In the Old Testament we read about an act of *creatio ex nihilo*, creation out of nothing; Earth-Mother Gaia, in opposition, begins to procreate (first in a parthenogenetic manner, later with several lovers) until the Olympus, the earth and the sea are swarming with gods, goddesses, and human beings, but also hybrids endowed with both god-like and human-like features. All of these creatures soon begin to oscillate wildly between the two extreme poles of chaos[3] and cosmos.[4] While the god Dionysus is a top representative of chaos, Apollo is a representative of the ordered cosmos (Guntern 2001).

There is, however, an important difference between the creation myths of the Jewish-Hebraic and the Greek cultures. The creatures of the monotheistic worldview of the Old Testament are governed by one single God who is the embodiment of the principle of supreme order. The Greek world, however, is a pantheistic one, in which Olympians and human beings are continuously frolicking or suffering in whirlpools of chaotic turmoil. While the Hebraic-Jewish Lord is a rather austere rational thinker obsessed with order, the Greek gods are sensual, orgiastic creatures driven by lower instincts and emotions and therefore given to confusion and chaos.

Hindu Creation Myth

The Hindu myth of creation mentioned at the beginning of this chapter suggests that Shiva is the god of chaos, while Vishnu is the god of order. Their respective activities follow each other in a merry-go-round of repetitive destruction and construction whereby different worlds come and go. Although Vishnu is called the creator god, he could not be creative without Shiva's destructive dancing. Chaos is a sine qua non (indespensible) for creative processes, and so is order.

There are, by the way, many different versions of the Hindu myth of creation. One of them specifies how Vishnu delegates the actual work of creating the world to Brahma. Interestingly enough, in the Jewish/Christian creation myth, a serpent plays a central role seducing Eve to pluck an apple from the tree of wisdom. In one of the Hindu myths, a serpent plays also a central role. Therefore, we may assume that intercultural communication has influenced some of our creation myths.

Here is how the Hindu story goes.

Before the beginning of time there was no heaven, no earth, and no space in-between; just a vast, dark ocean whose waves rolled upon the shores of nothingness, licking the edges of the night. A giant cobra floated on the ocean, and in its endless coils slumbered Vishnu, well-protected and undisturbed in his dreams.

Eventually from the depths of the ocean, there rose a humming sound: vibrating Om, a primordial sound. It grew and grew, throbbing with energy. The night ended, and Vishnu awoke from his slumber. At dawn, a beautiful lotus flower sprang forth from Vishnu's navel, and in it's midst sat Vishnu's servant, Brahma. Vishnu ordered Brahma: "Create the world!" and then vanished with his serpent. Sitting on his lotus blossom tossing about in the sea, Brahma lifted his arms and calmed wind and waters. Splitting the lotus flower into three parts, he created the heavens, the earth, and the skies in-between. And then he proceeded to create all living beings.

Hopi Creation Myth

A similar story of repetitive creation and destruction is related in the creation myth of the Hopi Indians[5] of Arizona. It holds (Waters 1974, 3) that three worlds have already come and gone, and that today we live in the fourth world. In the beginning of the universe there existed but two entities: the creator god Taiowa and Topkela, the endless space devoid of form, time, and life. Taiowa seems to correspond to order, Topkela to chaos. Their interplay created all existing structures until out of those structures emerged *manas* (Bateson 1976, 458f.), the supreme pattern of order connecting all existing things, organisms, and events.

According to our present knowledge, the first Indians migrated from Siberia across the Bering Strait to Alaska during the last Ice Age (approximately 20,000 – 30,000 years ago). This fact may partly explain the amazing correspondence (Briggs and Peat 1990, 22) between the creation myth of the Hopi Indians and those of the Inuits and of Chinese Taoists.

Inuit Creation Myth

The Inuits, natives of Greenland, Canada, and Alaska, depend on seafood for their sustenance. That explains why one of their creation myths centers on the sea goddess, Sedna.

At the beginning of the world, giants roamed the earth, living off the fruits the land offered. One autumn day a baby girl was born to two of the giants, the creator god Anguta and his wife. They named the child Sedna.

As the sun grew smaller and weaker, Sedna grew bigger and stronger. She ate and ate and ate until there was nothing left to eat. One night, tortured by hunger pangs, she began to gnaw at her parents' legs. Outraged, Anguta and his wife decided to get rid of Sedna. After a long, hard struggle, they managed to subdue their voracious daughter, wrap her in a blanket, hoist her onto a canoe, and paddle out to sea. When they reached the middle of the ocean, they heaved her overboard into the icy waters.

Shivering in the cold night and plagued by feelings of remorse, they began to paddle back home in the pale light of a hazy moon. Suddenly the canoe came to a stop and for all the parents' paddling, it would not budge. Then, to their utter horror, they spied Sedna's hands firmly gripping their vessel and wildly rocking it from side to side. The huge girl caused the boat to heel, putting it in danger of capsizing and tossing her parents into the gelid Arctic, where they would certainly drown. In a desperate act of survival, Sedna's genitors pulled out their knives and began to cut off their child's fingers. One by one the digits fell into the deep, where they were immediately transformed into the swimming creatures that populate the oceans.

Fingerless, Sedna swam through newly-created shoals of fish down to the bottom of the sea. There she took possession of a tent erected by the fishes. High above her new abode a crust of ice formed, sealing Sedna in her glacial water-world. Whenever the Inuit suffer from a shortage of food, they call upon their sea goddess for help and Sedna provides the food they need, even in the midst of the Arctic winter.

In a nutshell, the Inuit creation myth holds that order (the creator god Anguta and his wife) gives birth to order (the baby Sedna). The order degenerates into chaos (voracious Sedna who, in her boundless bulimia, goes so far as to indulge in cannibalism). Anguta and his wife increase the ongoing chaos by chopping off Sedna's fingers. But out of this chaos grows new order (the creatures of the sea). Only after order and chaos are balanced (Sedna sealed away beneath a crust of ice in her underwater realm), does life on land and sea continue to pursue its normal course.

Chinese Creation Myth

According to the Chinese Taoist creation myth, the world began as a beam of pure light emerging from chaos. The beam, called Yang, brought forth the sky. Out of the remaining Yin, called "the heavy muddy" the earth appeared. The continuous interplay of Yin (dark, female) and Yang (bright, male) creates the 10,000 things, that is, whatever exists in the universe. Since both Yin and Yang emerged from chaos, they maintain their chaotic potential at all times. If Yin increases too much, it will give way to chaos; if Yang increases too much, it will also yield chaos. Only if the dynamic interplay between Yin and Yang is subtly balanced is the right order of existence maintained.

There are, by the way, various other Chinese creation myths, but we shall not go into their complexity, which is best summarized by the Taoist creation myth.

Amazing Parallels

Let us now compare the intuitive formulation of the creation myths with the scientific explanation of the origin of the universe offered by contemporary physics. About 13.6 billion years ago, there occurred what is known as the Big Bang. In a matter of seconds, out of a mathematical singularity—a non-dimensional, ultradense entity—an explosion created all the particles, forces and laws of nature governing the interactions between these particles and forces.

From that very instant, our present universe went on expanding. In the process, physical evolution eventually produced biological evolution, which in turn generated mankind and its cultural evolution. The universe is still expanding, but one day it will begin to draw in until it vanishes once again into a mathematical singularity. Then a new Big Bang will occur. The whole redundant process is governed by deterministic chaos, the continuous interplay of chance and necessity; by random events and events governed by natural laws; by freedom and structural constraints.

The above theory is the *manas*, the supreme pattern whereby all things are connected. This is the cosmic tapestry which contemporary science has woven on the loom of its rational explanation. The parallels between what are known as the 'primitive' creation myths and the sophisticated concepts of contemporary science are amazing indeed.

What may we learn from these creation myths? What do they have to do with the creative process of human beings?

As mentioned before, myths are prescientific conceptual frameworks that attempt to describe, explain, and therefore help us to understand specific aspects of the world and its events. From generation to generation, cultural myths transfer knowledge based upon intuitive-empirical insights into the mystery of the world and its manifold manifestations. Mythic tales about the creation of the world contain knowledge about the beginning of a very specific creative process. Myths about gods and their roles contain knowledge about human beings because, after all, gods are creatures invented by human beings; they are symbols of the grandiose self of man projected upon imaginary, superhuman beings.

In other words, since the dawn of mankind, human beings have known that every creative process begins with a continuous interplay of chaos and order and that this interplay runs through repetitive cycles of creation and destruction. But it took mankind a long time to formulate these ancient insights in rigorous scientific terms. Today, contemporary chaos theory offers us a theory of causality containing the core concept of *deterministic chaos*. It holds that all events in the universe are caused by the continuous interplay of chaos and order. That is why we cannot predict future events in terms of certainty (determinism) but only in terms of probability (uncertainty). That is why some short-term predictions of future events turn out to be reliable, while most long-term predictions are not.

There are a host of terms that are connected in one way or another with the two complementary entities of chaos and order. Let us mention a few which are of interest in the context of the present book.

Table 2.1.   Chaos and order and related terms and concepts.

Chaos	Order
random events	lawful events
chance	necessity
probabilistic events	determined events
unpredictability	predictability
uncertainty	certainty
lack of pattern	pattern
lack of structure	structure
lack of form	form
freedom	structural constraints
requisite variety	structural constraints
spontaneity	calculation
crisis	routine
turbulent stream of events	laminar stream of events
non-linear events	linear events

Great creative leaders have always been aware of the fact that creativity depends on the continuous interplay of the two complementary forces and factors listed in the table above. I should like to mention but three examples to illustrate my point.

The writer Schiller once wrote to his colleague Goethe: "My heart is contracted and the lights of my imagination are extinguished. I am in need of a crisis. Nature brings about destruction in order to bring forth anew" (Solomon 1988, 122). Schiller keenly perceived that his imagination was trapped by the rigor of too much logical-rational thinking and that he needed to burst that bubble in order to be creative again. He had to enter a crisis, a whirlpool of chaos whose forces would be able to catapult him into the realm of freedom.

The composer and virtuoso pianist Franz Liszt (Solomon 1988, 118) differentiated two types of music in Beethoven's work. Emphasizing that Beethoven's compositions mirrored a dialectic between freedom and necessity, he stated that in the compositions governed by freedom Beethoven's "thought stretches, breaks, recreates and fashions forms and style," whereas in the compositions governed by necessity, "conventional and traditional forms contain and govern the master's thought."

The great quantum physicist and Nobel laureate Richard Feynman (Gleick 1993, 324) held that scientific creativity is imagination in a straitjacket. This statement echoes an aphorism coined by the Bauhaus architect Walter Gropius, who held that "creativity is dancing in fetters." The terms "imagination" and "dancing" are circumscriptions of the freedom situated at the chaos pole, whereas the terms "straitjacket" and "fetters" illustrate the structural constraints situated at the order pole.

Chaos and Order in the Ecosystem – The Basic Unit Able to Produce a Creative Process

Now let us move from mythology and the scientific chaos theory to the realm of the creative process of individuals living in a specific physical and social environment.

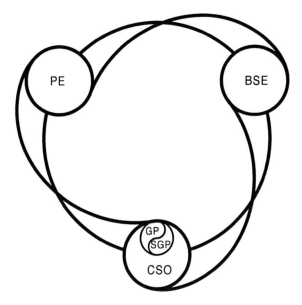

Figure 2.4. The ecosystem, the basic unit of survival and development. The three circles indicate the three structural components of an eco- system.

A reference system, the circle at the bottom of the above figure, is the entity observed or studied. In the context of the present book an individual, a team, or the population of a whole culture may constitute a reference system. In the above figure the reference system is the organism of an individual. Details about CSO (current state of organismic operation), GP (genetic programme) and SGP (syngenetic programme) will follow later.

A physical environment (PE) consists of the natural physical environment (for instance, geographical location and its surroundings with mountains, sea, lakes and rivers and with its climate and weather) and of the artificial, man-designed physical environment (for instance, roads and streets, houses and furniture, machines and tools, art objects, clothing, etc.)

A bio-social environment (BSE) consists of the natural bio-social environment (for instance, microbes, plants, animals, human beings) and the artificial, man-designed bio-social environment (for instance, myths, legends, traditions, values, rules, role expectations, costumes, religions, ideologies, scientific concepts and theories, concepts of art, etc.)

The geodesic lines between the three circles indicate the exchange of matter-energy and information signals between the three structural components of an ecosystem.

A creative individual lives and operates in concrete existential situations where chaos and order—and their various aspects mentioned in the above table—continuously interact. These interactions occur in the mind of creative individuals, as well as in their physical and social environment. Hence the implication is that the basic entity permitting the operation of an enchanted loom is not the individual or team, but the ecosystem.

• In the *creative individual's organism,* there are all kinds of events taking place, and all of them are governed by deterministic chaos. In the brain, single neurons and whole collections of neurons, called neuronal cell assemblies, fire in a random and therefore unpredictable fashion. Spontaneous ideas pop out of the unconscious mind and slip into the conscious mind, where they may be focused on and elaborated, taken seriously, neglected, or even rejected. Instincts, emotions, mental associations, and intuitive insights may enter the mind in a random and therefore unpredictable manner. Imagination may move on in a completely free, spontaneous way from one topic to the next. Yet, at the same time, there are all kinds of orders existing in the mind of an individual. If a person is very hungry, then predictably the thought of food will prevail. For a person full of vigor who has not had any sexual activity for quite some time, that issue will be predominant. If someone has high ambitions that have not yet been achieved, then time and again the question of success will occupy that person's thoughts. In the case of humiliation, there will be fantasies of obtaining justice or even taking revenge. In short, the mental life of an individual is governed by all kinds of structural constraints impinging on the freedom of imagination, perception, thinking, and emotions.

  In the course of one's life, a person undergoes a great number of experiences, and these experiences will predictably influence the activities in which that person engages and/or avoids. Countless things are learned during the twin processes of socialization[6] and acculturation[7], which last from birth to death. There are values, norms, prevailing ideas, beliefs, convictions, assumptions, hypotheses, concepts, theories, rules, taboos, motivations, purposes, and other items in the mental inventory of an individual, all of which impose structural constraints on the mind's ongoing activities. There is rigorous logical-rational reasoning restricting the freedom of spontaneously emerging instinctual needs, emotions, moods, and intuitions. A creative person is both a master teaching and a novice learning, incessantly exposed to the interplay of chaos and order, uncertainty and certainty, necessity and chance, guessing and knowing. These two complementary factors follow each other in continuously changing sequences. The cradles of mastery are rocked in the living room of uncertainty; and the cradles of uncertainty are rocked in the living room of mastery.

An individual has a brain, of course, but also a whole organism whose functions continuously influence the mind. A sudden thrombosis in a leg, on the one hand, will promptly inhibit a creative process; dreadful pain kills the mood necessary for imagination, inspiration, illumination, intuitive insight, and sharp rational reasoning; massive food poisoning will severely interfere with all higher mental activities. Pregnancy, on the other hand, may prompt the mind to think more deeply about the mystery of life, and if the pregnant mother—or the father who is aware of the pregnancy—is a writer then, quite predictably, the event will leave its traces in the new novel being written. If somebody is physically handicapped from early childhood (for instance paralysis of the leg, rachitic deformation of the thorax, hunchback), then this handicap may well inspire goal-oriented imagination and thus enhance the motivation for extraordinary performance and achievements. If somebody has inherited an unusual gift for mathematics and at the same time poor manual dexterity, then that person will be motivated to make creative contributions to mathematics while developing a tendency to avoid areas of creative endeavor demanding high manual dexterity.

Creative performance is influenced by the current state of operation (CSO) of an individual's organism. CSO comprehends content and form (or quality) of current perception, cognition, emotion, physiological functioning, and behavior, including verbal, paraverbal and nonverbal communication. An individual's creative performance during severe flu is seriously hampered, while it is enhanced after prolonged and very restful vacations.

An individual's creative performance is influenced by two organismic programs: the genetic program (GP) contains the results of phylogenetic learning by the species; the syngenetic program[8] (SGP) contains the results of ontogenetic (individual) learning (Guntern 1989, 77ff.). The genetic program (GP) determines a basic operational disposition, for instance the ability to produce sophisticated mental operations or a tendency towards high stress and frustration tolerance. The syngenetic program (SGP) determines the details of specific characteristics of an organism's operations and their purposeful fine-tuning, such as the ability to reduce complexity by means of well-trained analytical thinking or the choice and implementation of specific coping strategies while dealing with stress and frustration. Chance and necessity govern the current organismic operation as well as the formation and current functioning of the two organismic programs.

- As stated earlier, a human being lives in a *physical environment* governed by deterministic chaos, that is, by the continuous interplay of chaos and order, chance and necessity, freedom and structural constraints. There is the *natural physical environment*, which corresponds to a geographical region on the globe, (e.g., desert, tundra, savannah, or the basin of the Mediterranean Sea, the Alps, the Punjab valley, the Pampas, the Amazon). It comprises the climate with its temperature and humidity, ionization of the air, amount of light or darkness (e.g., the Arctic night), and quality and quantity of gases in the atmosphere (e.g., concentration of oxygen, carbonic acid, ozone, etc.). Geographical location and climate strongly influence mental activity and especially the sophisticated thinking involved in a creative process. Parallel to the natural physical environment, there is the *artificial physical environment*, or physical environment designed by man. It includes houses, bridges, and other buildings and constructions; machines and the noise they make; factories and the pollution they produce; furniture, appliances, and art objects in manifold shapes and colors; television sets, movies, photos, music, clothing in various styles and colors, perfumes, food, wines, and countless other objects conceived and realized by man. Last but not least, there are all the technological tools and devices such as microscopes, computers, painting equipment, cameras, etc., without which creative performance could not be achieved.

In both types of physical environments, there are random events and strictly determined events that generate chaos and order; there are freedom and structural constraints that foster or inhibit instinctual, emotional, and intuitive spontaneity as well as rational calculation. The creative process, therefore, is continuously subjected to outside influences.

Let us study a few examples in order to illustrate how chaos and order existing in the physical environment may influence a creative process. In a climate that is very hot and humid—like that of the virgin forests of the Amazon—it is very difficult, if not impossible, to begin and maintain a creative process because the human mind prefers a dry, cool climate for sophisticated thinking. The sweltering heat of July may well block the creative endeavors of a scientist at Rockefeller University in New York unless work can be done in an air-conditioned room. An artist of the Swiss Alps will have great difficulty in keeping focussed on a specific task in the sultriness of a gathering thunderstorm; mental concentration will suffer, irritation will grow, and errors in reasoning will increase while manual dexterity will falter. A sudden earthquake will interrupt an ongoing creative process—or trigger a new creative process in a film director working in the San Francisco area. An engineer operating in an environment of noisy machinery will be blocked in his imagination and intuition. He will also be inhibited in his inspiration and ongoing activity if the computer-aided design he has been working on for weeks suddenly falls prey to a virus. A beautifully decorated and well-furnished room inspires most people, while the contrary may block ideas and stifle the mood necessary for the productive output of a team in the R & D department of a multinational company. A dim environment has a tranquil-izing or even inhibiting effect and thus fosters meditation, whereas plenty of natural light helps to activate the arousal system in the instinct brain of a marketing specialist trying to come up with a new concept.

- A human being lives in a *bio-social environment* governed by deterministic chaos. There is the *natural bio-social environment* with microbes, plants, animals, and human beings, all of which have an impact on creative pro-cesses. And there is the *artificial bio-social environment designed by man* with its technological, demographical, economic, religious, political, and sociocultural characteristics.

  In a given area, the level of technology available (such as telegraph, cell phones, e-mail, radio, and television), produces all kinds of random or determined information that will influence an individual's creative process. The demographic situation of a society may also influence the creative process of individuals. Sociologist Emile Durkheim held that the *"densité morale"*—the density of population and therefore the number of interper-sonal interactions—necessarily produces innovation and thus social change. While his hypothesis is not quite convincing (Guntern 1979, 14ff.), it is true that up to a certain threshold, increasing social interactions tend to stimulate the minds of human beings; it is equally true that many creative individuals shy away from crowds because they possess low input thresh-olds and are thus highly responsive to sensory input overload. The means of communication offered by the technology of a globally interconnected world may offer all kinds of stimuli for a creative mind and at the same time distract individuals from their creative process (for instance the phone ringing or the noise of an incoming fax). Mass media may foster or hinder creative processes. The economic situation of a specific society may have a fostering or inhibiting effect on creative processes: poverty, for instance, may stimulate or block creative processes. Wealth may offer great oppor-tunities for creative endeavors, just as it may produce complacency and arrogance and thus inhibit creativity. An unexpected stock market crash produces chaos. This chaos will not only interrupt creative processes, it may wipe out all of the savings of some people and even seriously threaten their economic survival. Yet the very same crash may offer new opportuni-ties and trigger the flow of creative energy in other individuals. Ideological or religious convictions; prevailing ideas, norms, and values; traditions and customs; role prescriptions and role expectations; and similar sociocultural factors have an impact on human creativity. Religious and political zealots are notorious for not being creative at all. They are often in staunch opposi-tion to creative individuals and try to disqualify or even physically destroy their accomplishments. A same factor may offer both freedom (opportunities for choice), and structural constraints for creative processes. A same factor (such as dogmatic religious convictions, values, and beliefs), may stimulate the creative process in one person while blocking it in another. In short, for specific individuals, specific factors may at a given time foster their creativity, and at another point in time, block it.

In other words, nothing is as simple as it seems. The Taoist *T'ai-chi-tu* offers the best insight into how the dynamic complexity of events functions. It represents the interplay of two complementary forces governing all events in the universe.

The more the Yin increases, the higher the probability that in its very belly the Yang will begin to grow. And the more the Yang increases, the higher the probability that in its very belly the Yin will begin to grow. This self-regulatory mechanism influences all events in the universe.

Due to this continuous interplay between Yin and Yang, the bio-social environment seems to have an uncanny ability to know when the time has come to move from the chaos pole (irrational ideas and convictions based upon strong emotions and drives) towards the order pole (rational ideas based upon rigorous logical thinking and intuitive insights), or vice-versa. The dark Medieval Ages were enlightened by the emergence of the Renaissance. The rationalism of the Age of Enlightenment gave rise to the pathetic Sturm-und-

Figure 2.5.   T'ai-chi-tu. Diagram of the Supreme Ultimate.

Drang period and the genius cult of Romanticism. The Romantic Era provoked a sober scientific orientation in the twentieth century. Impressionism was a reaction against an academic art of painting fettered by the structural constraints of too many dogmatic rules. Cubism rebelled against the perfect beauty and harmony of the colorful paintings produced by the Impressionists. The representatives of Dadaism revolted against a bourgeois conception of art whose prevailing values had been questioned by the First World War. When modernist architecture reached a zenith of formal perfection, harmony, and purist homogeneity, deconstructivism began to reintroduce more irregularity, unpredictability, and heterogeneity.

To sum up, chaos and order exist in the creative individual and in her or his physical and bio-social environment and continuously interact, fostering or inhibiting specific creative processes. Chaos and order—and their many different aspects mentioned in the table above—are as ceaseless in their activity as are the waves of the sea. They superimpose and cancel each other. They produce countless patterns of combination. They weave in and out of creative processes to produce either spontaneous (and therefore unpredictable) impacts, or impacts that are determined and therefore, in principle, predictable. They may appear suddenly or emerge slowly, then vanish again as suddenly or as slowly as they had happened. The build-up of their impact may be gradual, incremental, or it may occur in discontinuous, catastrophic[9] leaps.

There is no static dichotomy separating chaos and order. There does exist, however, a complementary and highly dynamic functional relationship between these two entities of mutual influence. As mentioned above, if the Yin of chaos increases, then in its very center the Yang of order will emerge; if the Yang of order increases, then in its very center the Yin of chaos will emerge. The relationship between these two factors is governed by what the ancient Greek philosopher Heraclitus called *enantiodromía*[10]*:* functional opposites flow into each other, immerse themselves in each other, bring each other into existence. Chaos generates order and order generates chaos.

A good example of the above is the revival that an established form of art may undergo from the rebellion of newcomers (e.g., the representatives of Dadaism) eager to regenerate a petrified scene. Another example of how dogmatic order generates the chaos of rebellion is the geometric abstractionism developed by Kazimir Malevich in his revolt against the Soviet-Russian Marxist straitjacket conception that art had to serve but one purpose: educating the ignorant masses. Against so much finger wagging, Malevich postulated what he called the "suprematism" of pure feeling.

Another example of the multiphasic interactions of chaos and order is Giambattista Vico's well-known concept of *corso e ricorso*[11] in the course of history. He asserted that the development of a society runs through the following cycle: animal stage $\Rightarrow$ barbarian stage $\Rightarrow$ heroic stage $\Rightarrow$ civilized stage. His concept implied a gradually increasing order from the animal to the civilized stage. But if the civilized stage becomes too hemmed-in by structural constraints (rules and conventions), then there emerges a destructive rebellion that will throw society back into a chaotic animal stage. Then, according to Vico's concept, the whole cycle begins all over again. Observable reality, however, if we take the situation in contemporary Afghanistan and Iraq, is more complex than Vico's concept suggests. What we witness time and again in history is that societies and their cultures emerge, are maintained, transformed, and eventually vanish. But these four stages do not necessarily follow each other in single file. Sometimes specific stages (for instance the transformation towards more complexity and refinement) may not occur at all. The emergence of a society may almost immediately be followed by its destruction. A culture may vanish from the face of the earth never to be revived, as was the case with the unfortunate Rapa Nui of Easter Island.

A third example of how random (chaos) and determined (order) events interact is Marie Curie (Reid 1974), the first human being ever to have received two Nobel Prizes—and even today the only one to have received Nobel Prizes in two different sciences. In the last decade of the nineteenth century, Marie Curie and her husband Pierre were involved in the scientific investigation of radioactive radiation. One of their major problems was how to get pitchblende, the uranium ore from which radioactive uranium could be extracted. Buying tons of radioactive materials and transporting them from Czechoslovakia to Paris cost a huge amount of money. Since the heads of the physics department at the Sorbonne in Paris took a dim view of the couple's scientific interests, Marie and her husband Pierre could not expect any help from the administration. They racked their brains to find a solution to their basic problem, but to no avail.

The couple lived in pitiful conditions, investing all their money in their research. For years on end they gave up new clothes and good food. Each time Marie Curie went to the butcher, she would buy the cheapest meat she could get. One day, as she was standing at the counter, she couldn't make up her mind as to what kind of meat she could afford. The butcher, who pitied this poorly dressed, always polite woman with her care-worn face, did his best to recommend various alternatives, but all were too expensive for Madame Curie. Finally the good man lifted his arms in a gesture of helplessness and exclaimed, "Dear lady, I really don't dare to offer you my waste products!"

Waste products? Marie's eyes lit up. Unexpectedly a purely random event had shown her the way out of a seemingly inextricable situation: waste products! With the financial help of their friends, the couple organized the transport of pitchblende from Jáchimov to Paris by rail. Pitchblende being a waste product of the uranium mines, it cost nothing.

The moral of the story? A random event (the butcher's phrase "waste products") triggered an association in Madame Curie's well-prepared mind (determined event), enabling her to solve an urgent problem and allowing the couple to continue their scientific research, which eventually led to their discovery of radioactive radiation. In 1903, Marie Curie, her husband Pierre and their colleague, Henri Becquerel, were awarded the Nobel Prize in physics for their breakthrough. Marie Curie went on to discover two hitherto unknown chemical elements, radium and polonium. In 1911, she was awarded a Nobel Prize in Chemistry for these discoveries.

Many individuals have a specific mind-set, and there are all sorts of mind-sets: instability in goal-oriented operation; lack of endurance; intolerance of stress and frustration; the strange conviction that exact knowledge and learned skills impede spontaneous creative performance, to name a few. Such mental attitudes push individuals too close to the chaos pole, where they will be little or not at all creative. The conviction that exact knowledge and learned skills are a hindrance to spontaneous creative activity seems to be widespread, especially in individuals hedging romantic notions about the mental attitudes and lifestyle of creative artists. These chaos-adepts might profit from a statement made by the great Renaissance sculptor, Lorenzo Ghiberti (Pochat 1986, 224): "Talent without self-control or self-control without talent cannot lead to a perfect work of art." Self-control implies discipline and hard work while learning the basic know-how of the craft in which one desires to one day excel. It also demands a resolute attitude when it comes to separating the wheat from the chaff during the phase of evaluating one's own accomplishments.

Other individuals, on the contrary, lean too much towards the order pole. There are, for instance, people with a phobic-obsessive character that blocks their imagination by impulsively and immediately controlling every single idea that pops up in their mind before it has a chance to trigger an inspiration. To take but one example, in some representatives of what is broadly known as conceptual art we witness an amazing lack of imagination. Completely subdued by their more or less interesting concepts, *rigor mortis* seems to govern whatever they produce. They might profit from Henry Moore's (1964, 144) remark that an overdrawn conception "either weakens the desire to do the sculpture, or is likely to make the sculpture only a dead realization of the drawing." There are yet other individuals who are constantly in a frenetic action mode (i.e., very tense workaholics unable to relax), so their receptive mode is blocked. Accordingly, their antennae of perception are out of order, and the train of their imagination is glued to the narrow-gauge tracks of immediate goal attainment. In this state of operation, their creativity is barred by too much order of the wrong kind. They lack the touch of chaos necessary to be creative because, as Nietzsche's *Zarathustra* aptly put it, "I tell you: you need to have chaos to give birth to a dancing star."

There is a third category of individuals, in whom chaos and order form such an unhappy blend that their creativity is inhibited. This is the case, for instance, with individuals who lack autonomy and courage, two personality traits necessary for creative performance. To create a new form which is unique implies, per definition, the ability to quit the downtrodden paths of daily routine and habitual performance, to deviate from established norms and to venture into new territories. The same autonomy and courage is also necessary for dealing with the critical stance outsiders tend to take with respect to a new form. The public has to adapt to a new form. The more unique the form, the more adaptation is required. Such a demand for adaptation produces stress, and stressed people may feel angered with the author of the new form and respond with nasty critical remarks or even total rejection. It takes guts to deal with rejection, and to maintain the self-confidence necessary for future creative work. In the face of social attacks, a person devoid of autonomy and courage caves in and abandons the further pursuit of creative activities.

Requisite variety and structural constraints are a sine qua non for creative performance. Without requisite variety (diversity of ideas and concepts, methods, and techniques) individuals do not have the opportunity to choose from different alternatives. Without structural constraints (i.e., well-defined criteria and standards of quality) individuals do not know how to choose properly between available alternatives. Many authors publishing articles or books on creativity seem to assume—and so does the general public—that chaos provides human beings with requisite variety, while order provides them with structural constraints. While there is some truth in this belief, it is not the whole truth. In my view, it is the incessant interplay of chaos and order that provides human beings with both requisite variety and structural constraints. The exact knowledge of highly ordered concepts and methods, for instance, provides individuals with a requisite variety of ideas for thinking and doing things. But whatever is known exactly may also impose structural constraints upon the freedom of spontaneous thinking and acting. Quantum physicist Wolfgang Pauli once complained to his colleague Abraham Pais (Regis 1987, 195f.) that he was having a hard time finding a new physics problem to work on. "Perhaps," he ventured, "that is because I know too much."

The freedom of choice among spontaneous ideas provides us with chaos. But it also imposes structural constraints on us, because our mind tends to order ideas that emerge spontaneously into categories or typologies. The truth of the matter is: while purely abstract thinking is able to neatly separate opposite entities (for instance chaos and order, freedom and structural constraints, random events and lawful events, requisite variety and structural constraints) in an either/or fashion, concrete life prefers the hurly-burly of maybe-maybe or and-and entities. That is why we have to be careful that, in our need to set things in order, we do not oversimplify living complexity. Although at times oversimplification may be helpful, it is also able to kill the essence of our insights into the nature of reality.

Chaos and order exist elsewhere than in stage I of the creative process. Stage I is where their interplay begins (or rather, we arbitrarily begin our discussion of their interplay at that specific point), and then it continues throughout the whole creative process, even including stages III and IV which are, strictly speaking, outside the creative process itself—although connected with and influencing it. This continuous interplay of chaos and order makes the creative process, and the outcome of its stages and phases, unpredictable. Neither the creative person nor her or his social environment is able to predict with certainty: (a) whether, where, and when a creative process will begin; (b) how it will continue; (c) where and when and with what kinds of results it will end; and (d) what kind of impact and consequences the new creative form will produce encountering the mechanism of cultural selection. The weavers working at the enchanted loom of human creativity have to live with these uncertainties at all times, and so does their social environment.

As clearly shown in the preceding paragraphs, creative individuals must learn how to properly balance chaos and order and their various manifestations. They must become high-wire artists walking with grace, their center of gravity in constant adaptation, their destination always in mind, their sense of formal perfection ever intact, as subtly they balance along the hidden gradients of force fields governed by deterministic chaos. Following is an example that nicely illustrates my point. In 1992, at an International Zermatt Symposium organized by the International CREANDO Foundation, I wanted to know how the great writer Gabriel García Márquez (Guntern 1993, 216f.) dealt with deterministic chaos. For this purpose, I presented him with two examples of creative individuals, one who had leaned towards the order pole and the other, towards the chaos pole. I quoted Gustave Flaubert's (Sandblom 1987, 27) well-known dictum "I would rather die than to win a single second by accepting a sentence before it is perfect" and Picasso who once stated, "*Quand c'est fini c'est foutu*" (When a work is too perfect its value is ruined). Then I asked García Márquez where he would place himself with respect to Flaubert and Picasso. He hesitated for a second and replied, "I always work in chaos, but in rigorous chaos." That is a beautiful statement, welding order (rigor) and chaos (freedom) into a single entity. Great creative minds are indeed high-wire artists totally and wonderfully at ease with rigorous chaos.

The mix between chaos and order is not necessarily a fifty-fifty interplay. The two factors do combine in various proportions—for instance 10:90, 20:80, 30:70, 40:60,50:50, 60:40, 70:30, 80:20, 90:10. Still, generally there is more chaos than order at the beginning of a creative process; and there is more order at the end of a creative process. The same holds true, of course, for the interplay of freedom and structural constraints, chance and necessity, spontaneity and rational calculation. Billy Wilder (Karasek 1992a, 443), a great creative leader of film making, sums it up nicely when he states about the art of screen writing: "Chance events are only permitted at the beginning of a story. In the third act there is no place anymore for chance events."

Last but not least, I should like to point out that events governed by deterministic chaos are able to interrupt every single stage and phase of a creative process. Whoever embarks on the racetrack of creative performance must be aware of the fact that while many competitors enter the race, not all of them will reach the finish line; and even those who do cross it, will not always do so with a result satisfying their original ambitions and intentions.

Excerpts from an interview with Ashok Kurien (4)

In this part of the interview Ashok Kurien talks about his professional experience with the interplay of chaos and order, chance and necessity, freedom and structural constraints, spontaneity and rational calculation. He describes how that interplay impacts the whole process of organization of creative and habitual productive activities. He begins his report with the spontaneous idea his partner and he had while they were watching a CNN report about the Gulf War. That idea eventually led to the rationally planned and implemented creation of Zee TV, the first privately owned TV channel in India. Ashok Kurien also emphasizes how the interplay of freedom and structural constraints has influenced his childhood and the growth of his personality.

GG: Can you please give me an example of the interplay of chaos and order, chance and necessity, freedom and structural constraint, spontaneity and rational calculation that you have experienced in your creative business activities?

AK: A client of mine had an amusement park for which I did advertising work. One day we were sitting together watching a CNN report on the Gulf War. Quite spontaneously we said, "Hey, why can't we do this in India?" He asked, "What do you know about it?" I responded, "More than anyone else." The truth was I knew precious little – but to me it was more than what a lot of people knew. That advertising client of mine and I became partners to set up the first TV station. That is Zee TV today. He is the big partner, I am the small partner.

GG: If I understand correctly, your inspiration came from the CNN coverage of the Gulf War, and you spontaneously thought you could do a similar thing with your own company? You could do what Ted Turner had done with CNN?

AK: Yes, but I mustn't take credit for the thought, because Subhash is a visionary businessman. It was his thought, but I said I knew how to execute it, and how

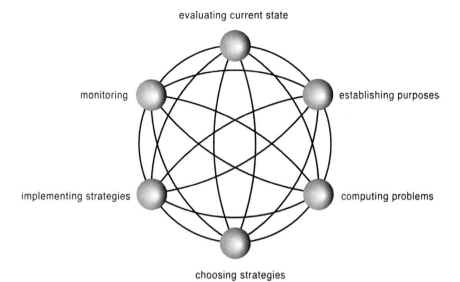

evaluating current state

monitoring

establishing purposes

implementing strategies

computing problems

choosing strategies

Figure 2.6. Process of organization of human activities. There are six phases in every single process of organization; every single phase is represented by a grey sphere. The continuous interaction of the six phases is represented by the lines.

to market it, and how to create it. His job was to find out which technology to apply because that is something I don't understand. We had never heard of satellites before. There was only one, government-controlled, terrestrial television station, which was very boring. So we actually established our enterprise and production facility in Hong Kong, and we sent our programmes via satellite to India. But I'll tell you what I think my greatest creative contribution here was. Subhash got a plan from somebody in the government who knew television and had been in the television business. It was about three hundred pages, and the investment would have been about a hundred million dollars. I did six handwritten pages, gave them to him and said, "We don't need more than seven million dollars to start off something like this"

GG: About fifteen times less than the sum habitually needed for such a project?

AK: Yes, and I told him that we could do cash break-even in the first year, and we did exactly that. There were two thoughts here. Everyone plans a TV station with twenty-four hours of programming, out of which at least ten to fifteen hours are original programming. So there is a huge cost for programming that you have to recover in advertising. I just asked, "Why do you need fifteen hours of programming? The whole of India watches one TV channel, and they watch it for four hours every evening. Why don't we just do four hours of programming and fill the rest up with music or repeat the programme in the afternoon and again in the middle of the night? You don't need to spend money on fifteen hours of programming, so that's a quarter of the cost. Moreover, I figured out how to do the programming at a much lower cost than what the government programming cósts were. So there were two radical shifts from the world's method of doing television. Interestingly enough, I hadn't read a single book on television, so I wasn't biased by that, and I was able to do something very different. We had a crude, illegal cable business in India. One million homes in India had been wired up by local cable operators, and they showed movies illegally because we had no rules at that time. They sent those movies into that small circle of a few hundred homes or whatever, and they spent money renting that movie or buying it, to show it on their TV. So I said, "All you need to do is give free dishes to all these cable operators; we are giving them a software free, we will show one movie every day, they will all connect, and within months you will have one million viewers, with only four hours of programming, so your cost is only one-tenth." And that's exactly what we did. But we could do it only because we were the first on the market. So it was that complete out-of-the-box thinking that actually offered the ability to create with very low cost. According to established opinion, you can't start a television station with twelve million dollars, but we did it, and today it's a multi-billion dollar company. So it is this confidence that just kept going and going and going, and that's it! Now you ask your questions.

GG: In Greek tragedy, the hero fails in his endeavour whenever he falls into one or both of two possible traps. One trap is set by *kairos*. Kairos is the god of the propitious moment for doing something or for refraining from doing something. If you come too early or too late, you are no hero, you will fail. Your story reminds me of god Kairos: it was the right moment to do what you did. You were the first; if you had come a little bit later or if you had come before these guys had cabled the surrounding houses, it wouldn't have worked.

AK: It wouldn't have worked. It was the Gift of Perfect Timing.

GG: The second reason why the hero fails in the ancient Greek tragedy is because he succumbs to *hybris*. He thinks he can accomplish much more than he is actually able to. He develops a grandiose self because he had a few successes. Hybris is the firm, irrational conviction that I am always better than anybody else, that I can achieve any goal I set for myself. So if you have an eye and an ear for the *kairos*, which is a very fleeting moment where everything is right, you'll be a successful strategist. And if you are able to avoid the trap of hybris, you'll be a successful strategist.

AK: When you win, it's courage; when you lose, it's foolhardiness. When you look back, what is it? Was it courage or was it foolhardiness? When you have nothing to lose, you have a lot more courage. In every one of these cases of my creative business ventures I've told you about, there was an opportunity to do something that no one had ever done before. If I look at almost everything I have done, I wonder: how can one person have been involved in five or six first-time ventures? This is difficult to explain. Maybe it's a good fortune of having met

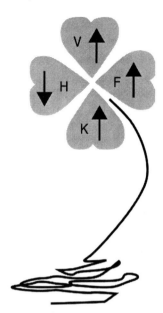

V virtù
F fortuna
K kairos
H hybris

**Figure 2.7. Four-leave clover of the successful strategist. The four factors are repre-
sented by clover leafs. Upwards directed arrows indicate what the strategist must strive
for. The downward directed arrow indicates what the strategist must avoid. The stem of
the cloverleaf represents the strong personality of the strategist who is solidly rooted in
her/his physical and bio-social environment.**

the right person at the right time, and I believe I have no control over the timing.
Common sense says the timing should be right but in the end I feel something
else decides that timing, because timing is something no one can know. The
stock market can crash tomorrow, and the timing changes. You can invest in real
estate today, and if real estate drops thirty percent like it has in London and
everywhere else, you are out! So timing is very difficult to explain. I honestly
believe there's a different power that grants you that timing.

GG: Years ago I had developed a basic concept about the difference between
a successful and an unsuccessful strategist. It consists of four factors that interact which each other. Two factors are *kairos* and *hybris*, which I have already mentioned. Two other factors I discovered while studying the ideas of
the Italian political philosopher and diplomat Niccolò Machiavelli, who was
born in the second half of the 15th century and worked as a secretary at the
Chancellery of the Republic of Florence. He wrote a book, *Il Principe* (Machiavelli: Il Principe), *The Prince*, in which he said that a successful political
leader must possess *fortuna* and *virtù. Fortuna* is the happy coincidence that
helps the strategist to be successful—and we know that chance only favours
the well-prepared mind. *Virtù* is actually the content of the well-prepared
mind. It is the sum of all the ideas, concepts, methods, techniques and skills

learned in the course of a lifetime. Putting these four factors together I said, a successful strategist must seek the *kairos*, avoid *hybris*, have *fortuna* and develop as much *virtù* as he possibly can.

He can control the avoidance of *hybris* and the acquisition of *virtù*. He can train his receptive mind to spot the emergence of *kairos*. And if he does these three things well, then he has a good chance that *fortuna*, the goddess of good fortune, will help him in his endeavours. In your case these four factors played so well together, that you were successful in your creative achievements.

AK: That's an interesting concept. I will have to think about it.

GG: Let's now talk a little more about the interplay of chaos and order. I sent you a few alternative terms for chaos and order.

AK: Yes, I saw that! There was chaos and order, chance and necessity, random events and determined events, freedom and structural constraints, spontaneity and rational calculation.

GG: Let me give you a concrete example so that the topic doesn't sound so abstract. A random event: tomorrow we intend to eat dinner in a Japanese restaurant. Let's assume that at the neighbouring table you overhear somebody saying something which exactly fits a problem you're just now dealing with. And all of a sudden, you begin to think how you will go about it. This would be a random event that starts a creative process in your head. Whereas a determined event would be: you have a meeting with a client, and...

AK: ...and he says, "Here is this concrete problem, this is what I want to do."

GG: Right; so this would be a determined event, an event governed by law, by a set of rules.

AK: Got it!

GG: Random is just like seeing or hearing something on TV or in a bar while you are not consciously dealing with the problem you want to solve. During this interview you have often said, "I hear. I listen." Up to now I have never heard you say, "I watch" or "I read." Is it fair to say that, as far as creative work is concerned, for you the acoustic contact to the reality you are interested in is more important than the visual contact? Is the spoken word is more important for you than the written word?

AK: The written word? Oh, very often it could be a document! It could be a written document, but basically it's the client's communication and information.

GG: When you speak with your client, it's oral. Do you write each other paper slips?

AK: He might. I might take notes. I make notes.

GG: Okay, because it struck me that very often you use the phrase "I listen."

AK: I listen and I make notes so that I don't forget. I write just about every word he's saying, and then sometimes he'll give me a document, and I'll read it and then put it away. So I do listen. But the reason may be my poor ability to read. I may see nothing in a document, but if the same thing is orally presented to me, with key slides, I often see what others cannot. The same is true with visuals; I manage to see stories in pictures. But what is it that makes that random event work?

GG: You tell me.

AK: You see, I am an "idea" addict, and I'm tuned in 24/7. I can be sitting in a bar, six whiskies down, and this guy makes a joke, and it's registered. Let me tell you, there's a product which I believe I invented. When I approached a partner with whom I wanted to develop, produce and market that invention, he said his technical chief had told him somebody else was doing it somewhere else in the world. Supposedly they were ahead of us because they already had a prototype, so we should forget about it. Do you know that today that product is still not in the market? And you know how I began to think of that invention, how I got the idea for it? It was a random event. More than four years ago, in 2005 people started putting videos on their mobile phones. One day I was sitting in a bar, and this guy was trying to show me a video on his mobile phone, but I couldn't see anything because it was so small. There was some little joke about "I'll hold it over here next to you, and it'll be this big." It was just somebody clowning around. I got up the next day and said, "This is going to be an extension of the human body, this mobile phone. It is the only device we carry around with us all the time." Maybe you don't, but most people do: women, men, adolescents, children. They carry it to the toilet and they take it into their beds. It is truly an extension of the human body. In the end everything has to converge onto this. We don't need anything else. Today people are putting videos on it, picking up their Internet messages on it, and most of the time the text or picture on the screen is too small to read or watch. I jotted down a little note that said, "Let's create a small projector the size of a matchbox that could be laser-driven."

GG: That you could project on a wall?

AK: Let me explain. Phase one: you plug it into your mobile, set it onto your lap or whatever, open your briefcase, put a blank sheet of white paper on it, and project it to the size of a computer screen. You can watch a movie on it, read presentations on it, look at a whole financial accounting statement on it, right? Phase two: you can take it to a meeting, project it to the size of a 30-inch TV screen, so there is no need to carry a projector or a big lap-top. It is plugged into the mobile phone, which is connected to wherever it is, downloaded, and projected onto a wall. Phase three: it's projected onto a big screen. Phase four: it is fed electronically into a roll screen and presented straight off from a lap-top.

GG: Stage five: project it on the firmament, the night sky.

AK: Who knows? Who knows? But it's simple! So I shared this with the same guy who owns the TV business, who by then had a chief technical officer who shot down the idea by saying, "Somebody else is doing this, and it's already been prototyped." I said, "Are you kidding? What's this about being prototyped? We can create it in India, manufacture it in Taiwan, and we'd probably be able to sell it at less than a hundred dollars. Why are you waiting for someone to sell it at four hundred dollars? Everybody should have one of these!" All of this happened two-and-a-half years ago, and I haven't seen it on the market as yet. I'll send you the original note I made back then, with the date on it.

GG: What a pity! Let us now talk about freedom and structural constraint. Many artists, or other individuals working in various professions, think that total freedom is a sine qua non for being creative. They believe that any structural constraints—for instance, what the market demands or rejects—would only block their creativity. What do you think of this?

AK: I understand that an artist or a poet or a writer would think so, because he's not doing what he does for any outside purpose; he's doing it for his own purpose. Nobody tells him what he has to do. If I'm doing something which is only for me, I can afford to have no bounds, and I can create a painting which is the ugliest thing in the world if it makes me happy. But if I have to show it to someone else...

GG: Couldn't one argue that if somebody—a painter, for instance—worked in total freedom, which means no structural constraints whatsoever, not even the constraints of his critical mind for the evaluation of his end-product, he might not do high quality work? There are some artists who believe that the slightest critical input would destroy their creativity or at least severely hamper it. But can they really be creative with such an attitude?

AK: I think they can. There are perfectionists who will keep trying and destroy, and keep trying and destroy, and keep trying and destroy till they get it right.

GG: I would agree with that. These perfectionists manage to balance freedom and structural constraints properly. They destroy their intermediate solutions because they have a critical mind.

AK: But the structural constraint is self-imposed.

GG: Yes, absolutely! But if they don't have a degree of freedom...

AK: Who defines that freedom?

GG: They themselves.

AK: They themselves? So I would type the first page of my book, tear it out because it doesn't start right, and write it again and again, and keep going until I'd finally say, "Voilà! This is it!" It's MINE!

GG: Yes, you have the freedom to do that, when the constraint of your critical mind tells you that it is no good. You know, Friedrich von Schiller was a good friend of Goethe's, and they are the most important classical German writers. Schiller was once asked by a young writer who suffered from total creative sterility, from writer's block, what he could do to overcome that obstacle. And Schiller actually gave him the following advice: "Don't jump at every idea that comes to your mind and try to have it immediately under total control. Play around with it; first let it move around a little." Then he used the example of a cat sitting in front of a mouse hole. If the cat jumps the very moment it sees the mouse's whiskers coming out of the hole, it will never catch that mouse. A good cat will feign not to see anything, wait until the mouse is out of the hole, and only then will it pounce and catch the mouse.

AK: I see what you mean.

GG: On the other hand if somebody who wants to produce creative work lacks the structural constraints and indulges in too much freedom, then she/he will never be creative. I can give you an example that illustrates what I just said. The top manager of a multinational corporation once asked me for advice. The situation, as he told it, was as follows: "We spend more than two billion dollars a year in internal and external communication. We are convinced that about eighty percent of the money we spend for advertising is thrown out the window and only twenty percent is well spent. But we don't know exactly what is good and what is not. One of our difficulties is to evaluate the quality of TV spots we produce all over the globe." To make a long story short, I spent weeks on end analyzing those TV spots, and most of them were in languages I didn't speak. So I had to focus on pictures, scenes and sounds—but not on the spoken word. I understood the overall story and I watched carefully how well or how badly the people in those spots acted. In my opinion more than two thirds of those TV spots were silly, boring, and the emotions expressed by the actors and actresses were about as credible and lively as cardboard masks. Yet despite those facts, there is a lot of word thrashing in advertising agencies about how creative they are. It seems to me, however, that most of the TV spots you can watch in various countries are not creative at all. They are *déjà-vu*, produced by copycats who pretend to be highly creative. These slick talkers persuade their clients that their advertising campaigns will hit the bull's eye. I'm really convinced that most of these TV spots do nothing more than the swindlers in *The Emperor's New Clothes:* they make people believe what they want to believe. I guess almost eighty percent of the TV spots would fit that category.

AK: Yes, I think so, too. But I also think that our schools impose too many wrong structural constraints on our children, and that process destroys creative potentials. Our education system is based on something somebody thought of twenty years ago to prepare people for – 1990? Not even 2000! Yet the world has changed! These youngsters are going to graduate in 2020! What do we know about 2020? Do we know what the world's going to be like then?

GG: We also destroy autonomy, independent thinking, in our educational system.

AK: And they destroy the children's imagination by demanding specific routine answers!

GG: What our traditional educational system demands is that you have to adapt – and even over-adapt – to whatever an authority wants from you. The faster you become a sheep trotting behind the bellwether, the better your grades will be. And if you are...

AK: ...imaginative, if you think out-of-the-box...

GG: ...then you are a misfit, you're punished non-stop in order to force you back into the herd.

AK: You fail!

GG: You, Ashok, were a very strong boy, so the fight as a rebellious misfit against the authorities made you stronger. But if you had not been such a strong person, the authorities would have bent and deformed your personality.

AK: I would have broken!

GG: Had you been a weak child, they would have broken you, because that is what fate does to weak individuals.

AK: I still remember how I had to fight them.

GG: Your social environment makes you stronger, it bends you, or it even breaks you— depending on what your basic disposition is. Now, I should like to return to your example about going to a bar and entertaining yourself with a bimbo. Obviously you're a very hard worker and a go-getter by nature, yet you also balance hard work with playfulness, and you seem to do that very consciously. One thing that certainly helps keep the flow of your creativity is that you take care of your playfulness. You know how to laugh, and the moment you laugh, you're relaxed. Ripples of laughter are like a good massage: they relax all the muscles of the face and the belly. If you're a boxer, you have a *défense musculaire*, a muscular defence shield here in your ventral region to protect you from blows. You produce that hard muscle shield instinctively every time you punch your opponent and you expect him to punch you.

AK: That's true.

GG: Now, some people are always in the action mode; they never relax their defence shield and get very rigid as years go by. To this physical rigidity there corresponds a mental rigidity that kills off not only all imagination but also all intuition. Imagination and intuition work best when you are in a relaxed mode of operation. Then you are playful. and you open a window of opportunity for your freedom and get rid of structural constraints.

AK: Yes, that's exactly how it is.

NOTES

1. Greek θέος = god, γίγνομαι = to become, to come into being, to be born; *theogonia* = birth of the Gods

2. Hebrew *tohu*= formlessness, confusion; *bohu* = emptiness

3. Greek χαός = primordial, not ordered matter or stuff; confused situation

4. Greek κόσμος = ordered, structured, patterned

5. Native American Hopi language: *hopitú* = peace-loving people

6. Socialization introduces an individual to the traditions, rituals, customs, beliefs, ideas, role expectations, norms, and values of the society to which the individual belongs.

7. Acculturation makes individuals acquainted with the traditions, rituals, customs, beliefs, ideas, role expectations, norms, and values of other societies.

8. Greek: συν = together; γίγνομαι = to become, to develop; συγγένεια = relationship; syngenetic = whatever has been learned during an individual's life in its manifold relationships with its own experiences, the physical, and the biosocial environment.

9. In colloquial language, the term 'catastrophic' implies an undesirable and destructive event. In mathematical language, the term 'catastrophic' implies a sudden, unpredictable, and major change of quality—completely independent of whether this change is desirable or undesirable, constructive or destructive.

10. Greek ἐνάντιος = to be opposed, to stand opposite; δρόμος = course, run

11. Ital. *corso* = run, course, evolution; *recorso* = return, repetition, revolution

2.3. STAGE II: SEVEN INTERCONNECTING
PHASES ON THE ENCHANTED LOOM

The process of human creation has been likened to the process of biological procreation. There are indeed some analogies. Both processes display a multiphasic structure; both are co-determined by a set of interacting intra-organismic and environmental random and determined events; both eventually generate a new form that has to face a test of selection. Beyond these similarities, the differences between the two processes prevail.

In the course of time, a variable number of phases have been proposed by investigators interested in problem solving. Not all of these hypotheses deal explicitly with creative problem solving, although usually the creative aspect is at least implied. For more about the history of phase concepts, the reader may refer to the following authors: Hadamard (1945, 43ff.), Preiser (1976, 42ff.), Schregenberger (1981, 159ff.), Mansfield and Busse (1981, 85ff.), and Brown (1989, 5f.).

Today we can state about these phase concepts what Preiser (1976, 48) wrote more than three decades ago: In the creative process there are distinct phases whose existence can be experimentally proved.

It is obvious that the number of phases characterizing a creative process is finite rather than infinite. According to our tendency towards analytical splitting or intuitive lumping, we may differentiate a higher or lower number of phases. On the basis of my own studies first published in 1991 (Guntern 1991b, 55ff.), I proposed a conceptual model containing four stages and seven phases. Each one of them seems to be a necessary condition for a creative process; their adequate interaction constitutes the sufficient condition for a creative process.

Now let us discuss the seven phases in a linear order, keeping in mind what was stated above: In a creative process the individual phases may sometimes follow each other in a linear fashion, but as a general rule they occur in redundant loops of continuously varying synchronic (simultaneous), diachronic (sequential), and hierarchical (priority, importance, impact) orders. After having discussed the seven phases of stage II, we will have more to say on this topic.

2.31 Phase of Germination

A seed takes its time to grow into a seedling.

Gottlieb Guntern

Architect Frank Lloyd Wright (Gill 1987, 393) was known to boast with respect to his designs, "I simply shake them out of my sleeve." This always

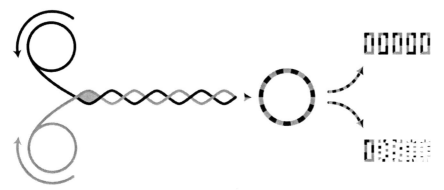

Figure 2.8.   Phase of germination.

impeccably dressed man used to cut a dashing figure eager to impress an audience. He also displayed an uncanny expertise in weaving the tapestry of his personal myth. Being the master gambler he was, he never revealed where his ideas had originated before they slipped out of his sleeve.

Creative ideas begin to germinate in the unconscious mind, and nobody is able to tell when, how, or why such germination begins. It seems reasonable to assume that germination may begin a long time before inspiration and the subsequent phases of the creative process occur. In his *Metaphysics,* Aristotle (Solomon 1988, 132) proposed the hypothesis that "the form of a work of art is present in the soul of the artist long before being translated into matter." That soul is the well of the unconscious mind to which Paul Valéry (Burnshaw 1970, 51) alluded when he wrote about "the depth where treasures are always buried."

Germination begins when chaos and order, chance and necessity, freedom and structural constraints, coalesce in the unconscious mind and trigger a process of fertilization generating the protoplasm of a new idea. How this coalescence of complementary forces of fertilization happens is an enigma even today—as was the fertilization of an ovum by a sperm cell before scientific investigation lifted the veil of that mystery.

By definition, the creative individual is not at all aware of what happens in her or his unconscious mind. Sometimes, when the phase of germination is almost completed and the phase of inspiration is about to begin, the creative person may perceive a vague inner tension searching for release and the desire to undertake "something," though without having the slightest notion of what this "something" might be. When asked where his work originated, playwright Arthur Miller (1987, 86) confessed he had no idea about where that could be. Then he added that there are "circumstances in which plays collect and form, like bacteria in a laboratory dish, later to kill or cure." The simile is an apt one. A petri dish is like a soil enriched with all the substances a plant needs to grow. Human experience is the laboratory dish of which Miller speaks, and that experience is more comprehensive than what a specific individual has lived through. Individual experience, also called ontogenetic experience, is rooted in the phylogenetic experience of the human species and even in that of our prehuman ancestors. Collective knowledge gathered during phylogenetic experience is coded into the genes of our chromosomes, and it contains the heritage of the life experiences living beings have encountered in the course of biological evolution. While there is nothing we can do to enhance our phylogenetic experience, we may find ways to facilitate access to its vast stores of knowledge. As poet John Keats (Rothbarth 1972, 52) wrote, "Heard melodies are sweet, but those unheard are sweeter." Heard melodies arise from a cavern filled with unheard ones. From that cavern emerges what flamenco singers call *cante jondo*, the song from the depths of our individual and collective unconscious mind.

Interestingly enough, Bernstein (1974, 169), one of Einstein's biographers, remarked that in physics the "really deep discoveries" never come from well-posed problems. A well-posed problem is couched in precise language that often suggests well-known methods for solving it. But the unconscious mind has no precise language. It poses problems and sets goals in a more hazy, protean, and (of course) nonverbal manner, which will often call for concepts, methods, and strategies of problem solution yet to be developed.

A mighty tree has got deep roots; tumbleweed has not. Without proper roots, an oak seedling cannot grow into a mighty tree; the wind will uproot it and blow it away. Without deep roots, only tumbleweed, but no oaks, will grow in the landscape of human ideas and performance. Thus a phase of germination beginning deep in the fertile soil of the unconscious mind will develop towards a better fate than a germination beginning just below the functional boundary separating the unconscious and the conscious mind. In other words, the better the content of a germinating idea connects to ancient life experience, the deeper it will be rooted and the more fertile it will usually turn out to be.

Poet Stephen Spender (1985, 119) must have alluded to the transition from germination to inspiration when he spoke of "something still vague, a dim cloud of an idea which I feel must be condensed into a shower of words." Perhaps he was aware of an observation made by John Steinbeck (Benson 1984, 784): ". . . in the back of my mind there is arising a structure like those great cumulus clouds you see over high mountains." It is a well-observed fact: germination saturates the unconscious mind as vapor saturates the atmosphere until, eventually, it condenses into clouds and rain will fall. But rain does not always fall, and then the process of germination begins to dissipate and even stops altogether.

Stated in other terms, germination begins in the atmosphere of an individual's unconscious mind, which is an integral part of one's personality. The humidity rising from this mind and condensing into a cumulus cloud hovering over the high mountain peak of creative intentions originally stems from the rills, brooks, and rivers carrying the water of all the experiences undergone during the course of an individual's life. This water, in turn, is fed by the deep-seated aquifers of the phylogenetic experiences of untold species in the course of biological evolution. If we are able to tap into those aquifers of collective phylogenetic experience, we are unable to change or enrich them in a purposeful manner. But we are able to enrich the waters of individual experience. To put it differently, whoever wishes to germinate creative ideas should try to increase the probabilities of success by growing into a mature, multidimensional personality saturated with individual life experiences. A good example to illustrate my point is, again, Gabriel García Márquez. Eight times during his student years, Gabriel (Guntern 1993, 229) boarded a ship and travelled up the Magdalena River to reach Bogotá where he attended a boarding school. The vivid experience of these journeys germinated in him until one day he was able to use that whole scenario along with his personal experiences, where observed reality and imagination had fused into a single entity. Thus he was able to describe in pictorial detail the journey of the protagonists in his novel, *Love in the Time of Cholera* (Garcia Marquez 1989).

Poetess Amy Lowell (Dias De Sousa Ribeiro and Bonboir 1985, 817) stated that she meets her poems in her conscious mind only ". . . after they have already covered a long distance on their way of development." In a letter written by Schiller (Burnshaw 1970, 55) to Goethe on March 27, 1801, the former stated that a poet's ideas begin in the unconscious mind and that a poet must consider himself lucky if, after a period of conscious work, he reaches a point where he is able "to rediscover undimmed the totality of his first dark ideas in the completed work." And the poet Wordsworth (1985, 82) suggested that poetry stems from "emotions recollected in tranquillity." All of these statements allude to a phase of unconscious germination of ideas.

Automobile constructor and technical inventor Franco Sbarro (Guntern 1991a, 166) reported at an International CREANDO Symposium[1] that he always wanted to create things he was lacking. He conceded that he did not know what these things could be and added, "I only know that I have, somewhere, an unsatisfied hunger and that I would like to appease it. I turn around in circles with this idea." In Sbarro's statement we get a glimpse of one of the many causes of germination: the desire to satisfy frustrated needs. The same cause is mentioned by Baines (1986, 130), a biographer of Joseph Conrad, who pointed out that the writer had once been without a particular occupation and had had plenty of free time, ". . . perhaps feeling restless and dissatisfied with the seeming emptiness of his existence, a state of mind which is often the prelude to creative activity."

Relaxation, silence, solitude, and a rather passive yet receptive mind are conducive to germination. Poet Paul Valéry (Burnshaw 1970, 61) wrote that a creative person is unable to prompt a creative process into existence: "We must simply wait until what we desire appears." Similarly, writer Rudyard Kipling (Burnshaw 1970, 54) admonished, "When your Daemon is in charge, do not try to think consciously. Drift, wait and obey." Rock musician Chuck Berry (1987, 126) reported in his autobiography that many of his songs had been conceived "during these solitudes, when plunking on the guitar and coming across an inspiring passage." Poetess and writer Maya Angelou (Elliot 1989, 12) said in an interview, "It's like knitting, where, after you knit a certain amount, there's one thread that begins to pull." The pulling thread, that is, the germinating idea holding the potential for developing into a phase of inspiration, may be a mental picture, the memory of a scene, a sensation of muscular movement, a word, a phrase, or a sentence. In a letter to French mathematician Jacques Hadamard, (Hadamard 1945, 142f.) Einstein wrote that to him, a new creative idea never came in terms of language or mathematical symbols, but rather in terms of elements of "visual and some of muscular type."

Germination is an organic process. No mental tricks, drugs, or fancy "creativity-enhancement" gimmicks are able to trigger or accelerate it. It happens all by itself. As Paul Cézanne (Bornstein 1985/86, 101) put it, "An artist . . . should create his work as an almond tree produces its blossoms." Although Cézanne must have had the whole creative process in mind, his characterization is a perfect metaphor for the mysterious working of germination. A tree takes its time to grow, and only when the moment is ripe will germination produce blossoms and, later, fruit.

Painter Wassily Kandinsky (Kandinsky and Marc 1974, 148) assumed that there is a "creative spirit" that "awakens a yearning, an inner urge." This creative spirit searches for a "spiritual value for materialization. Matter is a kind of larder from which the spirit chooses what is necessary for itself, much as a cook would." The larder is yet another metaphor for the realm of germination. It echoes Miller's laboratory dish, Spender's dim cloud, Steinbeck's cumulus clouds, and Cézanne's almond tree.

Let us now sum up the essential aspects of the phase of germination. In the privacy of the unconscious mind, protean fantasies float around until, at one point, they begin to condense into a primordial pap. The pulsations of life eventually transform this pap into a germinating idea. When the pregnancy of germination is completed, the mind gives birth to a phase of inspiration, and the "baby" glides into conscious existence. In other words, when the phase of germination reaches its natural state of maturity, the germinating idea is ready to break through the surface of the unconscious mind into the realm of the conscious mind.

Excerpts from an interview with Ashok Kurien (5)

It is difficult to say anything about one's own phases of germination and incubation, because both phases of the creative process occur in the unconscious mind. Yet Ashok Kurien remembers his first forays into the world of business. Those were days of unrest and inner tension, when he oscillated between weightless playfulness and deep frustration. Eventually when his first phase of germination was over, he had the idea of compiling a little book about the basics you need to know for running ads in the media. It was a success. As he concludes, "... there WAS something before." The enigmatic X that WAS before, was obviously a phase of germination that eventually paid off.

What he reports in this section of the interview also illustrates how open his mind was to all kinds of activities, from competitive sports to various art forms. It shows the imagination of his alarmed mind and his ability to anticipate future events. Haunted by the fear of turning into a complete failure in life, he was continuously working out plans to escape into a better future. One gets the impression that he ran through redundant loops of trial and error before his very first germination phase eventually gave birth to the idea of compiling a book and thus becoming an author.

GG: In the course of my investigations I have studied the biographies of great writers, painters, sculptors, and scientists; I have interviewed, or had discussions with, a great number of creative individuals. On the basis of my studies I have come to the conclusion that there are seven phases in every single creative process independent of the professional domain – science, arts, business, etc. – in which it occurs. Unless a client comes to them with a specific problem requiring a solution, creative individuals start off with a vague sort of feeling, a kind of foreboding that something is brooding in their unconscious mind. What can you tell me about this very first phase in the creative processes you have gone through?

AK: What happened in the very first phase was certainly not conscious. As a young man I didn't for a moment believe I was creative, although as a student, before I started my career, I was into theatre, classical music, modern music and started my own beat group. While in the theatre, I wanted to be a ballet dancer because I was a gymnast, but back in the sixties in India people would laugh when you told them you wanted to be a ballet dancer! Then, in keeping with all my failures, all my theatre dreams vanished because I couldn't memorize the lines. Maybe because of my impaired hearing in those days I wasn't able to pick up the words unless I read them. Although I sang in a church choir and various chorales for over a decade, I was never able to learn how to read music. The notes were just meaningless dancers all over the page. I would learn all the music by heart, and no one ever knew I couldn't read it! Since I couldn't do any of those things, they all vanished. At no stage did I think I was creative; I thought I was playfully inventive. Many years ago I saw an ad in a newspaper that read, "Executive Wanted. Must be creative and inventive." So as a joke, I applied, saying, "I'm very creative and inventive in the office. I know how to take a paper clip, bend the end like the shaft of an arrow, chew blotting paper and make a ball out of it, dip it in ink, make a catapult out of a rubber band, put it on my fingers, and splatter the inky ball onto the ceiling or onto somebody's head." This may have been a joke, but the employer still has that letter. He was a very successful businessman at the time. My application was a joke because in my life I couldn't do anything except joke! I didn't dream of money or wealth or cars or homes or success because I didn't have the guts to dream. Any dream like that was a nightmare because I knew it was impossible. I just didn't have the guts to dream of the things people dream and desire. I was happy to manage to get my next meal and lift my head up with some kind of pride. Perhaps all that sleeplessness I suffered during those years triggered something within me.

GG: This may have been the phase of germination, during which something was being prepared; that one day you would become an independent, for instance.

AK: I used to wake up with these terrible feelings of insecurity: my life is doomed, it's finished; everything is going wrong. Then I thought there was no point in sitting up at that hour of the morning and thinking about it because it kept me even more awake. So I started converting each of those worries into, "What would I do if it really happened?"

GG: I see. You were thinking about exit strategies, about how to turn impending failure into success.

AK: Or into solution strategies for whatever possible solution there was. Now if I thought of twenty things that could go wrong, I would think of twenty methods for preventing them from going wrong, or correcting them if they were. I found this worked in my job! When I was faced with a concrete problem regarding my job, I'd wake up at three in the morning and think of all the reasons why it could go wrong and fail. Then I'd start plugging up all the holes and end up with one solution that sounded like it was the right one. It was a way of making the insecurity work. In a strange manner I think I started connecting that to work. A while back I mentioned the wisdom of insecurity: you think of *everything* that can go wrong because you're so convinced it has to fail. If I do this, it's going to fail; if I price it like this, it's going to fail; if I sell it like this, it's going to fail; if I do it this way, it's going to fail. Then you start thinking about how to make it *not* fail. What could I do in each situation to make it go right? It's like a strange little game you play in your head, rather than lying there and feeling miserable about how everything is going wrong in your life. That's probably the closest I came to a foreboding, but I *never* woke up with a feeling that something was going to happen; never. I can't ever remember any sensation.

GG: Before my wife Greta begins a new line of work in her art—in photography, drawing or painting—she really doesn't know where she wants to go. Yet as soon as I find her cleaning up her studio—which takes about five days to do, because she puts every little paper, every tool in place and cleans every bit of it meticulously—then I know she's pregnant with a new idea, although she doesn't yet have the slightest idea what it might be. But I have learned never to make remarks about her cleaning up and putting order because...

AK: ...she feels something is coming.

GG: Yes, and sometimes order and cleanliness are not enough. She must put in some new lamps or a new table. God knows how many new neon lights we have already invested in her work. But then I know this is the germinating phase; she's completely unaware, but she feels, "I have to attack a new line of work," and she begins by putting order into the chaos of her work environment. On the basis of what you just told me, it seems to me that you put some order into your mental environment to escape the pain of expecting failure: "I'm analyzing solution strategies and preparing them and plugging up all the holes."

AK: Yes, but usually those things happened when I was already faced with a problem a client had put to me. Or sometimes it was an idea that filled a vacant hole. It might have been a personal problem of having no finances. So what was I to do? I started a little book to make some pocket money on the side to pay off my loans. When you run an ad in the media, you need to know the sizes of all the magazines and newspapers, what material they use, and what the rates are. All the media managers had these big piles of information which they looked through for the answers, and it took ages to find them. So I thought, "Why don't we just compile all that into a little book?" I told my media man, "Give me information on all the newspapers and magazines as to what type of printing they use, the size, their circulation, their rates, etc." I produced a booklet of about fifty pages entitled, *Adman's Ref.*, which means "Advertising man's reference." It was the first of its kind in India, and I wrote a letter to all the advertising agencies telling them about my book. I printed it on a Xerox machine and bound it, because that was the cheapest way to do it.

GG: And everybody bought it.

AK: Everybody bought it, and I made half a year's salary in two weeks. With that, I could pay off the loan on my house. The following year I gave it to my media chap to compile again, but with new instructions: "Now that it's been bought by every single guy in advertising and marketing, I want you to go to every newspaper whose details we're carrying in the book and ask them to give me an ad and charge them 1000 rupees per page." So I got eighty to a hundred ads, I made two years' salary in two weeks, and I gave the media chap fifteen percent. Now that gave me great confidence that a good idea like this, with no

money investment–because I took credit from the Xerox guy, saying, "I'll pay
you when I get the money back"–could earn me one year's salary in two weeks.
In fact the second time around I didn't do any work; I just told my media manager, "Duplicate it, sell the ads, I'll give you fifteen percent." He did all the
work. Since he was the media manager, everybody came to him and he would
say, "You want ads from my agency, you also put an ad in this book." Wow! That
same year I went to the government TV station. At the time there was no reference as to who was running which TV commercial, which day, how much they
spent, etc. So I went to them and asked, "Do you keep a ledger?" The reply was,
"Yes, I have to give my boss a monthly report; these are the people who run the
ads, we charge them so much, they run so many ads." So I asked him for a Xerox
copy of that. "How much do you earn?" He replied, "My salary is two thousand
rupees." So I said, "I'll pay you a thousand rupees a month. Every month just
give me a Xerox." So every month he gave me a Xerox, and I compiled it and
made a book out of it. Every advertising agency and every marketing company
and every client bought one copy of it, every month. I made three years' salary.
(My salary wasn't very good in any case.) Now this experience gave me the
confidence on that one day, when my client came and asked me to start an
agency, to think, "I'm not as stupid as everybody says I am." So there you are.
But always, there WAS something beforehand.

2.32 Phase of Inspiration

> *During a state of high inspiration our ideas flow like magma in a volcanic
> eruption.*

> Gottlieb Guntern

An inspiration appears suddenly and unexpectedly, like a flash of lightning out
of the blue. In the atmosphere, a lightning flash is due to the sudden electrical

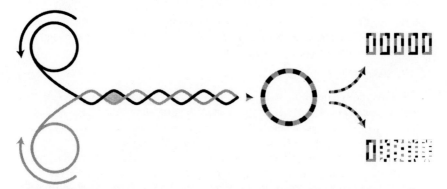

Figure 2.9. Phase of inspiration.

discharge of opposite charges occurring between two clouds, or between a cloud and the earth. Inspiration is due to a kind of mental short-circuit suddenly connecting the two force fields of the unconscious and the conscious mind. It is fair to assume that some form- or content-specific resonance between unconscious and conscious ideas is responsible for the short-circuiting that produces a flash of inspiration. In his autobiography, Frank Lloyd Wright (Gill 1987, 360) thusly described his state of inspiration: "The birds began singing again below the house of Taliesin; dry grass on the hillside turned green, and the hollyhocks went gaily into a second blooming . . . What a release of pent-up energy—the making of those plans! Ideas came tumbling up and out onto paper . . ."

From a neurobiological perspective, we may state that inspiration implies the sudden simultaneous firing of millions of interconnected neurons. In the course of repetitive unconscious and conscious learning, these neurons are connected by protein bridges or dendrites, forming synaptic clefts with the body or axon of other neurons. These bridges permit the mental associations between different ideas to occur. The synchronized bioelectrical discharge of neuronal cell assemblies is subjectively experienced as a jolt, as an arousing, startling event. That is why, in the nineteenth century, psychiatrist Cesare Lombroso (Lombroso 1988) erroneously assumed that inspiration was the functional equivalent of a focal epileptic attack.

The creative individual is almost always in a relaxed mode of operation when inspiration hits home. Inspiration is a state of grace requiring no effort; ideas gush out spontaneously from the well of our mind. Russian poet Alexander Pushkin (Briggs 1983, 45) wrote about ". . . that blessed state of spirit . . . when verses lie down before your pen and ringing rhymes run to meet up with a nicely turned thought." In contradistinction to this highly elegant formulation, Honoré de Balzac (Parini 1989), whose youth had been marked by Napoleon Bonaparte's grab for imperial power and international grandeur, offered a more pathetic, although equally dynamic, account of his states of inspiration, writing that ideas ". . . pour out like the regiments of the Grand Army over the battlefield, and the battle begins. Memories come charging in with flags flying; the light cavalry of comparison extends itself in a magnificent gallop; the artillery of logic hurries along with its ammunition train, and flashes of wit bob up like sharpshooters."

Sometimes the suddenly inspired individual is involved in activities that may have little or nothing to do with the content of inspiration. Amadeus Mozart (Ghiselin 1985a, 11) is supposed to have said that his ideas flowed best when he was "completely myself, entirely alone, and of good cheer—say, travelling in a carriage, or walking after a good meal, or during the night when I cannot sleep . . ." Although the historical source of this statement is questionable (Solomon 1988, 129), the quoted phrases fit not only a concept of inspiration fashionable in Mozart's time, but also many an individual's personal experience with respect to the phase of inspiration. Later, however, in the Romantic period, authors writing on creativity often took *pars pro toto*: they mistook the phase of inspiration (as well as the phase of illumination) for the whole creative process, as if the complex creative performance of an individual resembled the spontaneous activity of a silkworm spinning its thread in a self-generated and completely effortless manner.

A relaxed mood often favors the emergence of inspiration, but the sheer opposite of a relaxed mood may produce the same effect. Physical pain is rarely inspiring, but the pain of our soul is. Doubt, uncertainty, unhappiness, fear, anxiety, despair, a tortured state of mind are all able to trigger a strong inspiration. The blues was invented and sung by slaves treated worse than animals. Mozart composed his famous *Requiem* in a state of sheer despair. Many great paintings, and God knows how many plays and novels, have been inspired by mental suffering. On June 8, 1962, Bob Dylan's girlfriend Suze Rotolo boarded a ship and left for Perugia, Italy because she was young and beautiful and willing to get more out of life than the often harsh treatment Bob had in store for her. He was very unhappy about her departure. When she was in Italy, she was reluctant to take his phone calls, and wasn't eager to answer his letters either. He understood that she slipped away from him and he was so torn apart that he couldn't sleep anymore. Tortured by a mix of self-reproach, self-pity, misery, rebellion, and helpless anger, he began to write the lyrics to "Don't Think Twice, It's All Right." Then he composed the music for that song and performed it. The ambiguity of the lyrics, the power of expression, and the suggestive metaphors made the song an instant hit. Dylan entered a state of inspired frenzy—while Suze enjoyed Perugia and the attention of a young and attractive admirer named Enzo Bartoccioli and didn't waste her time with Dylan's pleadings for her to come home—and began to write one song after another. As his friend and fellow musician Mark Spoelstra (Sounes 2001, 121) remembers Dylan would sit in Gerde's Folk City and write on napkins while everybody else kept talking and drinking: "And you couldn't interrupt it. He was driven, and obviously enlightened." Dylan's reaction to his pain illustrates the Australian folk tale of the thorn-bird that will sing only one single song in its life: when the spikes of a thorn-bush pierce its body so that it can't move anymore and is about to die. In 1964, Suze had an abortion and after a long and bitter argument with Bob, she was practically thrown out of the apartment in which she lived with her sister Carla. Although he had been unfaithful to her and had indulged in a barely hidden on-off relationship with the singer and guitar player Joan Baez, he was very unhappy about the break-up with Suze. The pain of this loss inspired him to write the highly emotional, lamenting "Ballad in Plain D."

Happiness and unhappiness, relaxation and inner tension, are opposites. How can we explain that these opposites are equally helpful in bringing about a phase of inspiration? The following model helps us to understand the puzzle.

Let me add here something that will be of interest to persons in top management positions who would like to stimulate the creativity of individuals and teams under their guidance. In the course of my professional career, I have worked for fifteen years as a special advisor for boards and top management interested in developing creative leadership in multinational companies. Time and again I have observed that, in their attempt to be successful, these managers quite often followed a method that seemed to be governed by the motto of a Kentucky mule driver: "Take a two-by-four and hit it hard between its eyes!" In other words, they tried to put pressure on already overstressed teams. Their skewed approach had a reverse effect. They blocked the imagination and intuition of the teams and instead of inspiring and motivating their collaborators for a higher creative performance, they drove them into an even more stressful organismic state[2] than they suffered from before. In their zeal to be successful the go-getters and over-achievers of the *bel étages* (upper floors) of multinational companies not only failed to foster creativity, they actively blocked the most precious resources they were supposed to harness and mobilize towards a positive goal-orientation.

Let's now discuss to the impact a phase of inspiration has upon the creative individual.

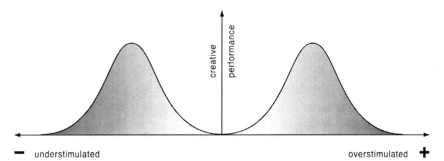

— understimulated   overstimulated **+**

Figure 2.10. Windows of creative opportunity. The horizontal line indicates the amount of mental stimulation. At the intersection of the vertical and horizontal black lines creative performance (indicated by the surface enclosed by camel-hump) is very low, almost non-existing. As stimulation grows (right half of the graph) creative performance increases until it reaches a top level. As soon as human beings reach as state of maximum over-stimulation it decreases again. Similarly, as stimulation decreases (left half of the graph) creative performance increases until it reaches a top level. As soon as human beings reach a state of maximum under-stimulation it begins to decrease again.

Inspiration has an arousing and energizing effect. All of a sudden, the inspired individual is wide-awake, tuned in, and ready for action, catapulted into euphoria and convinced that she or he has just given birth to a great idea. At times, this is indeed the case. Not always, though, because inspiration also gives birth to many a stillborn baby. The true quality of inspiration will become apparent only after the excitement it produces has been replaced by the labor of conscious work. The moment in which inspiration occurs is nonetheless a happy one; negative thoughts are swept away, and feelings of surprise, wonder, amazement, joy, pride, and gratitude prevail. Self-esteem is high, and the winds of imagined success swell the sails of the grandiose self. The inspired person is ready to steer the ship of strategic intentions out of the harbor of safety into the wide-open sea of adventure and uncertainty.

The energizing effect of inspiration may last for hours, days, or even longer. It sustains the creative process through periods of stress and frustration and helps motivation to overcome the obstacles that arise on the path towards the desired goal. A typical example of the sustaining power of inspiration was reported by Andalusian poet Federico García Llorca (Gibson 1989, 315). After having written a series of poems, he told a friend, "I've been like a fountain writing morning, noon and night. Sometimes I've been feverish, like the old Romantics, but without losing the immense conscious joy that creation gives."

Why is the phase of inspiration connected with emotions? Obviously the arousal produced in the reticular activating system of the brain stem, an integral part of the instinct brain, spreads up into the emotion brain (*limbic system*) and stimulates it. Although I shall not enter a comprehensive discussion of our brain's anatomy at this point, some general remarks are indicated.

The brainstem contains the *formatio reticularis*, also called reticular activating system, which connects the spinal cord with the thalamus and cortex. The *formatio reticularis* is a widespread network of neurons involved in regulating many organismic activities. It is considered to be the center of arousal focussing our attention, activating our neocortex for differentiated and adequate responses, alarming our consciousness, and co-regulating goal-oriented behavior. It plays a role in our states of wakefulness and sleep. It receives input from many sources including our facial nerves and neocortex, among others. That is why a phase of inspiration—a specific kind of mental activity—produces a general awakening: the conscious awareness of the content of inspiration and the ensuing activities exploring that content and its possible importance and implications. An imbalance in the neurotransmitter norepinephrine in the cells of the *formatio reticularis* is believed to play a significant role in disorders such as Alzheimer's disease in the elderly and attention deficit disorders in hyperactive children.

In states of relaxation (leisure, drowsiness, meditation, hypnosis, etc.), our *formatio reticularis* shows a low level of arousal. But when we are bombarded by external stimuli or exciting thoughts and emotions (anxiety, rage, inspiration), our *formatio reticularis* responds with a high arousal. The phase of inspiration abruptly switches the *formatio reticularis* from a state of low to a state of high arousal. A similar phenomenon occurs, by the way, during the phase of illumination, to be discussed later.

The thalamus, known as "deep soul" by the ancient anatomists, is the basic relay station for all sensory input, and has, therefore also been called "the brain's sensory gatekeeper" (Greenfield 1996, 114). It analyzes the form and content of sensory input, then sends portions of it to the centers of the neocortex (cerebral hemispheres) where the input information is further processed. The thalamus is moreover involved in the regulation of sleep, wakefulness, and consciousness—as well as in motor functions, although the latter activity is as yet only poorly understood.

The *amygdala* and *hippocampus, including* their nerve fibers surrounding the *thalamus* and *corpus callosum,* are integral parts of the *limbic system,* involved in the generation and self-regulation of memory, emotion, mood, motivation, and stress mechanisms (fight-flight response and helplessness response). The limbic system is strongly connected to various parts of the thalamus and the neocortex. The neuronal connections between the limbic system and the prefrontal neocortex, where purposeful thinking occurs, suggest that the pleasure we derive from goal pursuit and successful goal attainment is due to these inter-neuronal links.

The frontal lobe, parietal lobe, occipital lobe, and temporal lobe are integral parts of the neocortex. The two brain hemispheres of the neocortex, where all higher mental activities occur, are interconnected by a structure called the *corpus callosum.* It consists of 200 million nerve fibers and functions as a veritable data highway. Up to 2 billion information signals per second may flit back and forth over it. We shall have more to say about this amazing process later.

Let us now return to the question why inspiration is (a) linked to strong emotions and (b) these strong emotions are of an agreeable nature. A stimulated emotion brain (*limbic system*) generates, among other things, an egocentric value attribution to events witnessed and experiences made, which in turn generates emotions. A stimulated emotion brain also generates judgements based upon the question: What does this event or experience mean to me? What does it imply for me personally? At times, for instance when we are falling in love or feeling humiliated, these value judgements can be very rigid and absolutistic. In such situations, the logic of value judgements runs like this: no rational argument is able to influence my personal judgement; I know the whole truth and there is no other truth besides my own.

Why does inspiration provoke desirable rather than undesirable emotions?

The activated *corpora amygdale*[3] of the emotion brain trigger a physiological fight-flight stress response accompanied by a mental conviction of competence, an I-can-do-it attitude. In that mental state, an individual obviously assumes that the content of inspiration will increase and not diminish her or his chances of survival and proper development. Thus, ultimately, the joy and exuberance of inspiration are due to a gratification pattern connected with a rightly or wrongly expected favorable process of natural selection. In evolution, the process of natural selection favors species fitting environmental conditions because a proper fit increases the probability of survival and further development. Hence a phase of inspiration generating a new and conscious idea promises to provide the individual with an adaptive advantage in the struggle for survival.

In the inspired mental state, the number of mental associations per unit of time increases, and these ideas are of a better quality than those produced in an uninspired state. When meeting other people, the inspired individual tends to be very expressive in mimics and gesticulation and verbally as well. So much exuberance can be contagious, prompting the same surge of energy in others, who will also feel inspired. Inspired individuals are happy, and happiness attracts; unhappy individuals, on the contrary, tend to drive others away. If the environmental setting is right, and the feedback loops are positive—that is, if they amplify a deviation from habitual norms—then imagination is soaring, and out of mutual inspiration within a group, great ideas may be born. At her first encounter with poet Samuel Taylor Coleridge, Dorothy Woodsworth (Holmes 1997, 34-35) was reminded of Shakespeare's characterization of a poet, and she described Coleridge's revved-up, inspired and inspiring state as follows: "His eye ... speaks every emotion of his animated mind; it has more of the 'poet's eye in a fine frenzy rolling' than I ever witnessed."

The inspired human organism seems to be weightless, the pull of gravity suspended. The Pegasus of imagination swells into full gallop and soon takes flight over the meadows of sheer delight. Freedom prevails while structural constraints seemingly vanish. Everything appears possible. Ideas emerge with ease as emotional spontaneity has replaced rational calculation. Words, sounds, pictures, and other elements of creative composition are integrated as spontaneously as the threads of a spider spinning its web—though a good deal faster. There is often a strong rhythmical element involved in mental activities, suggesting rhythmical neuronal discharges in the brain. When inspired, one may drum one's fingers on the desk, hum, sing, dance, and walk up and down, animated and in high spirits.

The excitement of positive emotions (surprise, awe, joy, exuberance, fascination, enthusiasm, gratitude, pride, triumph, hope) may give rise to peculiar sensations in the organism and thus to the assumption—or even conviction—that inspiration is due to extra-mental or even extra-organismic events and forces. The poet Alfred Edward Housman (1985, 89f.) had the impression that the source of his ideas was in "the pit of the stomach." This sensation had to do with the fact that the neuron fibers of the *formatio reticularis* connect to the hypothalamus and thus to the autonomous, vegetative nervous system regulating visceral, cardiac, and respiratory activities. Isaac Bashevis Singer (Armbruster 1989, 179) spoke of "a feeling as if some little imp or devil is standing behind you and dictating to you." Novelist William Makepeace Thackeray (Martindale 1989, 215) spoke of a sensation as if "an occult power was moving the pen." The Eskimo poet Orpingalik (Burnshaw 1970, 53) described inspired thoughts as being "driven by a flowing force" and stated that those thoughts "can wash over him like a flood, making his breath come in gasps and his heart throb." All of these characterizations describe an altered state of consciousness in which perception, cognition, emotion, physiological functioning, and behavior are different from the operations of an organism in habitual states of consciousness.

Since the beginnings of our Western civilization, the state of an exulted mood provoked by a phase of inspiration (the same holds true for the phase of illumination[4]) has often been characterized as a divine possession. Socrates spoke of the *"daimonion"* while Plato used the term *"mania"* to describe a state of inspiration or illumination. Plato (Perkins 1981, 2) attributes to Socrates the statement that poets draw their inspiration in the gardens of the Muses ". . . for the poet is a light and winged thing, and holy, and never able to compose until he has become inspired, and is beside himself and reason is no longer in him . . . for not by art do they utter these, but by power divine . . ." In ancient Greek mythology, the nine Muses were the daughters of Zeus and Mnemonsyne, the goddess of memory, and they were the goddesses of the arts and sciences. Socrates' demon and his formulation "beside himself and reason is no longer in him" indeed allude to a state of altered consciousness characterizing inspiration (as well as illumination). So too does Plato's mania.

Arousal, accelerated thinking, exalted mood, high self-confidence, boundless energy, and the urge to be very active generate the subjective conviction that nothing is impossible for the inspired individual, endowed, as it were, with divine powers. The ancient Greeks characterized this organismic state as *enthousiasmos*[5] In Renaissance times, painter Zuccarò spoke of the *scintilla della divinità* (the divine spark). The Elizabethans used the term *frenzy* to emphasize the high arousal experienced during inspiration. William Blake (Pochat 1986, 528) wrote that he was "commanded by the spirits." The French still use the term *feu sacré* (the holy fire), obviously referring to the *scintilla della divinità*. Novalis, a philosopher and author of German Romanticism, described a germ of self-forming life ("Keim des selbstbildenden Lebens"); he held that nature was animated by an art instinct, and considered the artist to be an instrument of a higher power. Similarly, Paul Klee viewed his hand as being "completely an instrument of a faraway will" (Grohnmann 1977, 98).

All of these terms indicate the subjective experience of an altered state of consciousness that inspired people used to attribute to the intervention of a transcendental power, and they all betray the same implicit or explicit assumption: there is an Olympian (or other divine) forge with embers glowing; a spark flies through the air, hits the mind of a creative person living on earth and there it kindles the flames of fascination and high motivation. In reality, the sparks of inspiration stem from the smithy of the unconscious human mind, where synchronized neuronal assemblies fire at a high rate and intensity, thus provoking the sparks and the ensuing fire of alertness and conscious creative activity. In this sense the poet Percy B. Shelley (Burnshaw 1970, 58), using the language peculiar to the Romantic period, stated, "When my brain gets heated with a thought, it soon boils, and throws off images and words faster than I can skim them off."

In the realm of the Andalusian *flamenco,* a state of inspiration is known as *duende. Duende* is an inner spirit, a magic state of mind lending charm, magnetism, authenticity, and depth to a singer, dancer, or guitarist's performance. It connects a performer to her or his innermost unconscious mind and has a spellbinding, enchanting impact on an audience. *Duende* is an organismic state in which a singer, dancer, or guitar player is in an intuitive mode of mental operation, at peace with herself or himself and the world, and inspired to a point where creative performance is enhanced beyond the point of habitual performance. Paul Valéry (Burnshaw 1970, 52) alluded to a more subdued form of inspiration when he spoke of having been "charmed by those divine murmurings of the inner voice." But, whether inspiration is experienced in a more or less dramatic or discreet fashion, it always produces a revelation of something unique and deeply moving.

The idea of divine madness, introduced by Socrates and Plato, influences individuals speaking about their own creative process even today. To take but one example, in 1989 physicist and Nobel laureate Gerd Binning (1989, 130) wrote, "A person who is creative must be crazy." That is a manner of speaking. The kernel of truth in that statement has to do with the criterion of uniqueness that the result of a creative performance must meet. That criterion implies a deviation from habitual mental states paralleled with a deviation from habitual ideas, methods, and behaviors. In this sense, creative performance is norm-deviant; but this norm-deviance has nothing to do with the madness encountered in psychotic disorders. There is no pathology involved. It simply transcends our habitual standards and establishes a new type of norm, a hyper-normal state, so to speak.

Countless creative people have made revealing statements about their inspired states. But we have to be cautious in interpreting what they say in order to avoid the danger befallen by many presumed experts who even today throw inspiration and illumination into the same basket. The criteria I have established for differentiating between inspiration and illumination are as follows:

- A phase of inspiration often occurs without any prior conscious work on the issue suddenly projected into one's consciousness—save in a few cases. Illumination, however, always presupposes prior, often even prolonged, conscious work on a topic presenting apparently unsolvable problems.
- Inspiration, on the one hand, offers a new idea that the inspired persons finds fascinating because it promises great things to come. It sets the reels of mental associations in motion, thus opening new avenues of thinking and doing. Illumination, on the other hand, offers an unexpected and fascinating problem solution emerging after a given period of incubation (see phase of incubation) that has been preceded by a period of intense yet futile effort to solve a problem.

The new idea offered by a phase of inspiration and the problem solution offered by illumination have both been worked out in the unconscious mind— a phase of germination produces a phase of inspiration; a phase of incubation produces a phase of illumination.

The great scientist Louis Pasteur (Edwards and Sproull 1984, 175) stated that, "inspiration is the impact of a fact on a prepared mind." This may indeed be the case, but the same statement would better fit the phase of illumination. Often inspiration and illumination are not due to the impact of an external fact on a prepared mind; they are due rather to the inter-neuronal networking going on in the unconscious mind until that weaving process reaches a point where the sparks of a new idea are fired off into the conscious mind. Moreover, the impact of external facts on a prepared mind also invariably occurs in the phases of preparation, elaboration, and evaluation. And, although we are not yet certain, we believe it may even occur in the phases of germination and incubation.

A phase of inspiration cannot be forced into existence, although it may be facilitated by suitable conditions. Vladimir Nabokov (*New York Times Magazine* 1989) was once asked by a publisher how he found his inspiration. To his wife Vera he suggested that she write the rather sober answer: "It finds me."

Whatever the setting in which inspiration appears, it is always a sudden event, and creative individuals use its momentum to progress quickly. Bob Dylan (Shelton 1987, 125) said about his song writing: "Either the song comes fast, or it won't come at all." This amounts to stating that a phase of inspiration and its content thrown into the conscious mind serve as mental accelerators and are a sine qua non for each and every single creative process.

Creative individuals may indulge in all kinds of behaviors and rituals in order to facilitate inspiration. A few examples will illustrate this fact.

- As the Old Testament has it, the Jewish-Christian ancestral mother Eve was inspired by an apple plus the glib talking of a snake. Although her inspiration led to a loss of grace and exile from paradise, the mythological apple from the tree of knowledge seems to have retained its suggestive power.
- As legend has it, Isaac Newton (Rothbart 1972, 13) was inspired by the sound of an apple thudding to the ground as he sat in the moonlight in his mother's garden in Woolsthorpe, Lincolnshire. He promptly began to think about the mysterious force drawing a falling apple towards the ground. Suddenly, with a leap of imagination, he discovered an amazing analogy. The apple was attracted to the ground by the mass of the earth, and it was this same force of attraction—gravity—that drew the planets into their orbits around the sun! While the sound of the falling apple was the source of Newton's inspiration to think about gravity, the discovery of the analogy between a falling apple and an orbiting planet was due to a sudden illumination (see chapter on the phase of illumination).
- Friedrich Schiller (Spender 1985, 114) used to sniff rotting apples he kept in his desk drawer, as the smell inspired his fantasy.
- Dumas the Elder used to stand at seven o'clock each morning under the Arch of Triumph in Paris where he would eat an apple. Of course, the symbolism of the Arch of Triumph, which celebrates major French military victories, may have served his inspiration better than the actual eating of an apple. Still there might be more to an apple than its mythological power and agreeable form and taste. Years ago I came across an article whose bibliography I have unfortunately been unable to retrieve. Its author held that apples contain two acids, one of which is malonic acid, able to generate an activating effect on the arousal system (*formatio reticularis*) of our instinct brain.
- The industrialist and technological inventor Alfred Krupp (1989, 87) had a predilection for quite another kind of apple. He was a horse-lover, who had his inventor's lab installed right over the stables. Airshafts gave the scent of horse manure free access to his lab, and the smell (in German *Pferde-Äpfel*, meaning literally "horses' apples") inspired him.

- Dame Edith Sitwell (Ackerman 1989, 1), a poetess, used to lie every morning for half an hour in an open coffin in her studio. Obviously this ritual had an inspiring effect on her because it reminded her of the fact that human beings are mortal and therefore have but a limited time span for creative work. Dame Edith was a very ambitious person who wanted to leave a scratch on the wall of oblivion before she died.
- Some individuals use music to kindle the flames of inspiration. Mozart (Einstein 1983, 26) was not at all inspired by contemporary folk music, but rather by the classical music of other composers.
- In my own experiments with creativity, I have found that a piece of linear music repeated time and again (for instance on a CD player where I push the repeat button) inspires me. Among others, part one of "Tubular Bells" by Mike Oldfield; a "Mozart Lied" by the soprano Kathleen Battle; "The Photographer" by Philip Glass; part one of the "Köln Concert" by Keith Jarrett; the song "Snow in San Anselmo" by Van Morrison; "Nobody But You" by Lou Read & John Cale; or Bob Dylan's "Knocking on Heaven's Door" had this effect upon me. I suppose that the repetitive music synchronizes large numbers of neuronal cell assemblies in the human brain and thus facilitates inspiration. Interestingly enough, I also found that a specific song or other composition would work for a certain period of time then cease to inspire me. This fact suggests that there must exist a mutual fit between a specific external input and a specific mental state in order to produce a phase of inspiration. The unsolved questions are: What are the neurophysiological and neuropsychological characteristics of that mutual fit? Why does it change in the course of time?
- Charles Baudelaire (Pochat 1986, 558) likened nature to a "dictionary," but he warned against the "vice of banality" in which people who simply copy nature for want of imagination indulge. Yet nature has more in store for us than the vice of banality. A gorgeous landscape inspires most human beings. It turns on our imagination and sets ideas flowing. Whether in the living or non-living world, beauty, in all its multiple and multisensory manifestations, inspires most human beings. Ugliness, contrarily, tends to block our inspiration. In 1999, molecular biologist Günter Blobel was awarded the Nobel Prize for his discovery that proteins have a sort of zip code, consisting of a specific sequence of amino acids. The cell wall has the capacity to decode that zip code and therefore the ability to decide which of the millions of proteins produced by the cell can leave it, and which are to remain within. Professor Blobel told me that for years on end he would spend his holidays in gorgeous Italian hotels because their beauty inspired him, giving him food for thought for the rest of the year. While famous Belgian singer and songwriter Jacques Brel sang of "*la*

laideur des faubourgs," the ugliness of the suburbs and their depressive effect on human beings.

• Many individuals smoke because nicotine (Guntern 1990, 197) taken in moderate doses stimulates the postsynaptic membranes of the ganglia of the sympathetic and parasympathetic nervous system. Due to the mechanism of physiological counter-regulation, moderate doses of nicotine foster relaxation. First there occurs an arousal reaction in the brain accompanied by mental stimulation; then a biochemical counter-regulation sets in, putting the mind into a relaxed mood. In extreme doses, however, nicotine intoxication produces a massive inhibition of mental activities.

• Caffeine, a chemical substance contained in coffee and tea, has a similar effect. Honoré de Balzac (Parini 1989) used to drink huge amounts of strong Turkish coffee every day in order to keep his inspiration going, and eventually died of caffeine intoxication.

• Many creative individuals drink alcohol and/or combine various drugs either to kindle their inspiration or, on the contrary, in order to relax in the evening after a hard day's work. Turning off focused mental activity and turning on a dreamy mental state fosters relaxation and thus inspiration. The sculptor Alberto Giacometti (Lord 1985, 491) smoked up to eighty cigarettes per day; he drank huge quantities of coffee and quite a lot of alcohol, too. Charles Baudelaire and Jean Cocteau used to consume hashish and opium. Paul Valéry, Arthur Rimbaud, Maurice Utrillo, Sinclair Lewis, John Steinbeck, Ernest Hemingway, Eugene O'Neill, William Faulkner, F. Scott Fitzgerald and Tennessee Williams (who took other drugs as well) used to drink alcohol in considerable quantities. Quite a number of Jazz and Rock musicians (for instance Billie Holliday, Charlie Parker, John Coltrane, Miles Davis, Jimmy Hendrix, Janis Joplin and Jim Morrison) took alcohol, hashish, cocaine, heroin, or amphetamines in rather high doses. Although all of these individuals may have consumed these drugs also for anxiolytic (anxiety-reducing) and other purposes, it remains a fact that all of these drugs intervene in inter-neuronal connections, inhibit analytical rational thinking and habitual forms of mental operation, while facilitating the intuitive pictorial thinking and unusual mental associations that drive the wheels of imagination and thus enhance inspiration.

More often than not, inspiration comes unaided by any learned methods or techniques. It may appear during a state of well-being or be triggered by a totally opposite condition. Suffering is a well-known source of inspiration because pain can serve as fuel to fire up our imagination. Following is a telling example. One day, Russian poetess Anna Akhmatova (Bayley 1990, 9-10) was standing beside the Neva in St. Petersburg, in front of a prison where

Stalin had incarcerated her son. There she came upon another woman whose son had also been imprisoned. The woman recognized the poetess and, alluding to their shared suffering, pleaded with her, "Can you put this into your poetry?" Akhmatova replied that she could, and after that encounter began to write her famous "Requiem," a powerful dirge about grief, mental turmoil, loneliness, and sorrow.

Sometimes an unconscious threat to one's health may lead to the germination of an idea that eventually inspires and activates the imagination of creative individuals. I remember my discussions with a creative cabinetmaker and inventor who in old age became obsessed with the idea of inventing a new jet turbine engine that would be more effective than those available on the market at the time. He intended to construct a turbine with a smaller diameter in its water conduct so that the jet would hit the blades at an angle of exactly ninety degrees. Lacking the technological know-how in the field, I helped put the old man in touch with the engineering department of the best technical university of our country. Its representatives did not think that the idea was of any practical value whatsoever. They pointed out that the mechanisms of modern jet turbines were by then so sophisticated that no further improvement seemed possible. Perhaps they were right, perhaps not. Needless to say, the inventor was terribly discouraged by their response. A few days later, he was admitted to a hospital and the doctors discovered that there was a cancer growing in his bile duct. The patient's age and the advanced stage of his cancer forbade any surgery. He died soon thereafter. But I could not help thinking that his cancer had inspired first his unconscious and then his conscious mind to produce a new invention whose structural and functional properties where somewhat analogous to those of his gall bladder and bile conduct, which no longer functioned effectively.

Creative individuals with a competitive, aggressive streak may draw inspiration by watching a *corrida*, a boxing match, or another form of fierce competition by physically fighting themselves and even by getting hurt badly. A good case in point is Hemingway. Fascinated by the Spanish bullfight, he wrote the novel *Death in the Afternoon* (Hemingway, 1974) to celebrate its virtues. He liked to box and could really roughen it up—even when the opponent was his good friend, poet Ezra Pound. Hemingway never missed a fight if he could get one. He once stated (Hotchner 1967, 54f.): "That cut on the head, plus roughing up that lion, finally sprung me." What was he referring to? In Paris he had wrestled with a lion, and "feeling absolutely wonderful from the loss of all that blood," went to the bike races. After that catharsis he was ready to begin writing *A Farewell to Arms* (Hemingway, 1984).

Hemingway's (Astre 1961; Baker 1980, Gurko 1969; Hemingway 1976; Kert 1983; Lynn 1987; Hotchner 1967) obsession with aggressive, destructive action was rooted in his life experience and, particularly in the story of his own family. Strongly affected by his father's suicide, he accused his mother of having pushed the man to the brink of despair. His parents' marital relationship became not only an incentive for coping with his own aggressive, destructive tendencies, it also turned into a major source of inspiration. His novels and short stories are full of fighting, killing, suicides, insidious women, and weak men. Similarly, Eugene O'Neill's (Gelb and Gelb 1987, 9) parents were involved in a love/hate relationship, and their temperamental incompatibility gave rise to interminable fights and nasty rituals of mutual contempt and humiliation. Their marriage inspired, among others, O'Neill's masterwork *Long Day's Journey into the Night* (1956). His brother tried to commit suicide and was admitted to Bellevue Hospital in New York where the psychiatrists diagnosed a "death wish." One of his sons was an alcoholic, the other, a heroin addict; both committed suicide. In O'Neill's plays (Gelb and Gelb 1987, 189), seven protagonists commit suicide; twenty die cruelly, either electrocuted, drowned, burned alive, or publicly strangled. Joseph Conrad (Baines 1986, 75) was another writer who once made a suicide attempt and this experience, quite naturally, affected him deeply. It also inspired the fate dished out to the protagonists of his novels: nine of them kill themselves, one attempts to kill himself, and three sacrifice themselves in a quasi-suicidal manner. As the examples of these authors suggest, conflict is a sine qua non for drama. Without conflict, all drama collapses, and a narrative or play tends to become flat and boring. That is why early childhood experiences with the excitement of conflict and drama are a very important and inexhaustible source of inspiration for writers. In their famous study, *Cradles of Eminence,* Goertzel and Goertzel (1962, 152) report that one hundred percent of the actors and eighty-nine percent of the playwrights and novel writers they investigated came from disturbed family settings. In contradistinction, only twenty-five percent of the financiers and twenty percent of the inventors were reared in distressed households.

A well-known source of inspiration is the work of other creative individuals, especially of geniuses. Countless are the people who have been inspired by Homer, Aeschylus, Sophocles, Socrates, Plato, Praxiteles, the Tang poets Li Po (also called Li Bo or Li Bai) and Tu Fu, Galileo Galilei, Leonardo da Vinci, Michelangelo, Shakespeare, Goethe, Molière, Rembrandt, Monet, Einstein and Edison, the Muslim scientists Ibn Sina (Avicenna), Al-Tusi and Al-Buruni, and the Japanese painters Hokusai and Hiroshige, to name but a few. Gabriel García Márquez (Garcia Marquez 1993, 198) emphasized that his writing is strongly inspired by the work of Sophocles—and that he hoped that "this influence will last a whole life." Whoever reads his *Chronicle of a Death Foretold* (Garcia Marquez 1983) can recognize that the inhabitants of the village where an archaic vendetta is about to take place behave like the chorus in a Greek tragedy. García Márquez (Garcia Marquez 1993, 220) was a student in Bogotá when he read Kafka's *Metamorphosis* (Die Verwandlung), in which the main character, Gregor Samsara, wakes up one morning to find that he has been transformed into a bug. This story—and the fact that Kafka was able to make plausible such an absurd metamorphosis—impressed young Gabriel so much that he abandoned his law studies to become a writer. His imagination eventually created a whole new genre, the universe of magical realism—not to mention that of the countless more or less gifted imitators he in turn inspired. In a similar vein, the famous songwriter Bob Dylan (Shelton 1987, 13) confessed in an interview, "If it wasn't for Elvis and Hank Williams, I couldn't be doing what I do today." He could have added to his muses the folksinger Woody Guthrie, whose topics, singing style, and even physical appearance and behavior Dylan imitated in his younger years, before moving on to become a rock star with his very own brand of identity.

Creative individuals become inspired not only by social role models who work or have worked in the same professional field as they do. The sparks of inspiration jump easily from one domain to the other. To take but one example, Wassily Kandinsky (Lankheit 1974, 38) and his painter colleagues from *Der Blaue Reiter* movement were very much inspired by Goethe's statement that creativity in music composers was high, because there existed a coherent theory of composition. Goethe insisted that in painting "the knowledge of the thorough bass was missing." That statement set Kandinsky's imagination in motion. He initiated not only experiments with specific dark colors set as counterpoints to bright colors (one is tempted to say that he began to use double-bass colors), but also began to gather the basic building blocks for a theory of creative painting. Moreover, Kandinsky (1977) was strongly inspired by the word "structure" used in contemporary physics and the musical term "composition," as well as by children's drawings and the spontaneity in which they revealed "the inner sound of the subject." It is interesting to note that one of Paul Klee's paintings is entitled *Tiefer Klang* (Deep Sound). Klee and Kandinsky were friends and collaborators in the *Der Blaue Reiter* movement as well as colleagues in the Bauhaus in Dessau.

The success of a creative social role model is an inexhaustible source of inspiration. Paradoxically enough, the lack of success in role models, such as fathers who were failures professionally, may also prompt inspiration. In their study on 400 eminent individuals (eminent individuals are not necessarily creative!) Goertzel and Goertzel (1962, 73) reported that the fathers of Louis Armstrong, John Barrymore, Enrico Caruso, Charles Chaplin, Kahlil Gibran, James Joyce, Eleanor Roosevelt, and G. B. Shaw were alcoholics.

In the twenty years during which I worked in Switzerland and the United States as a systems scientist and family therapist, I discovered (Guntern 1989) that there exists a mechanism I call an *intergenerational delegation deal.* Children of parents, or grandchildren of grandparents, who have been failures receive the implicitly or even explicitly formulated task to become very successful in their own professions in order to redress the family's balance sheet. Besides the delegation deal, there are other mechanisms propelling individuals to outperform poor performers who are supposed to be figures of identification. Due to their talents and ambitions, creative individuals disdain mediocrity, banality, and failure, whether it occurs in their own work or in the work of colleagues or official role models. That is why mediocrity, banality, and failure inspire them to prove that they are able to avoid and outdo what they dislike and reject.

The revival of an ancient art form that has slumbered in oblivion for a long period of time is able to turn into a powerful source of inspiration. Creative vision is the prince kissing the Sleeping Beauty and bringing her back to life. In my view, creative vision implies looking far back into the future; hidden forces contained in forgotten masterworks are unleashed whenever our current Zeitgeist connects with them. Let us take two examples to illustrate this fact.

The Basilica di Santa Maria del Fiore in Florence had been standing for more than one hundred years and still it lacked a cupola. After many vain efforts to construct one, the wool merchants' guild of Florence held a competition in 1419 in which the designer, sculptor, goldsmith, architect, and writer Lorenzo Ghiberti and his former disciple Filippo Brunelleschi (Guntern 1998, 36ff.) were the main contenders. Brunelleschi won and was entrusted with the commission to build the dome. He was eager to take on the job and succeeded where the best master builders of Europe had failed time and again before him. From where had Brunelleschi drawn his inspiration for the construction of the cupola, whose diameter spans 41.5 meters? During the years when his offer to build the cupola had been rejected several times in a row by the magistrate of Florence, Brunelleschi had spent much time in Rome studying ancient architecture. One of the objects of his investigation had been the Pantheon, originally commissioned by Emperor Hadrian and built between 118 and 125 AD. Its huge domed structure spans a diameter of 43 meters, and from his careful observations Brunelleschi got an inkling of how the old master craftsmen had been able to erect the structure. His inspiration proved to be fertile, and in the years between 1418 and 1436, Brunelleschi built a cupola for Santa Maria del Fiore, a stupendous structure I once characterized (Guntern 1998 40) as ". . . a song frozen in mid-air. It has a theme, a melody line, a rhythm, and a harmony."

In 1912, Manuel de Falla, Miguel Cerón Rubia, and Federico García Llorca (Gibson 1989, 109f.) organized a flamenco festival in Granada. This festival prompted the rediscovery of an ancient Gypsy art form that had almost been forgotten. Llorca's imagination was greatly inspired by the primordial forces of flamenco rhythms and melody lines, and he stated, full of enthusiasm: "Inspiration, pure instinct, is the only raison d'être of the poet."

Inspiration and imitation are closely linked. Creative achievements are able to invite imitation that, in turn, will generate inspiration. A spiral of interaction is able to give birth to a strong up-stream current where imitation, emulation, and inspiration continuously influence each other. The results of this dynamic interplay may or may not turn out to be creative. An example of the creative impact of a Zeitgeist is the exalted, exaggerated, and even pathetic behavior—hairdos, clothing, emotional outbursts, and use of key phrases of the creative leaders and their epigones in the nineteenth century arts. Another example of the interaction of imitation and inspiration is the streamlining in the design of forms. First used in the design of trains, cars, and airplanes, streamlining soon began to spread to other areas in the 1930s. From whole buildings to household appliances (Gill 1987, 370f.), all kinds of objects were streamlined, even when streamlining made no functional sense at all. A third example for the inspiring force of Zeitgeist is the ideology, attitude, and styled behavior of the rock musicians in the 1960s, which rapidly generated a whole mass culture influencing creative leaders on the rock scene as well as millions of non-creative followers.

There are, by the way, fluid transitions between imitation and outright stealing. These transitions occur particularly in domains where copycats are the heroes of the day because they are celebrated by the hype of mass media, always on the outlook for new superlatives. When fashion designers talk glibly of having been "inspired" by, let us say, tsarist Russia or ancient Crete, more often than not their designs turn out to be the conspicuous results of mere cultural shoplifting rather than of an authentic creative process. But fashion is not the only realm where window dressing and pretension prevail. As the ethnomusicologist Charles Seeger (Shelton 1987, 164) writes, plagiarizing and plain stealing "are quite frequent in the domain of song writing." The same mechanisms occur in many other spheres as well.

Sometimes inspiration may stem from a rather highly individual experience connecting a random observation made much earlier with a specific current mood. A good case in point is Alberto Giacometti (Lord 1991, 4), who had once observed and been marked by the pitiful appearance of a lonely-looking Chinese dog trotting down the streets. One evening, Giacometti was walking down the rue de Vanves in pouring rain, brushing by the buildings, his head bowed in a state of extreme sadness, and feeling as forlorn as a stray dog. Suddenly the memory of the Chinese dog fused with his mood at the time, generating the inspiration to create his famous naturalistic sculpture of a dog.

In contradistinction to Giacometti who became inspired by means of intuitive identification, Chekhov (Troyat 1984, 57) was an inveterate onlooker. He was constantly visiting theater wings, tribunal halls, and coffeehouses where literary men enacted their debates and other scenes of social intercourse took place. Later, the enchanted loom of his mind transformed what he had seen and heard into words and scenes. That is why his biographer Troyat (1984) writes of the "mysterious alchemy" able to transform people, objects and events observed into words written on a page. Chekhov's short story "The Steppe" (Chekhov 1991) reveals that kind of alchemy as well as the admirably meticulous and highly precise descriptions of individuals and their behavior that only a keen observer of human beings is able to produce.

James Joyce (Ellman 1983, 3) was another author who drew his inspirations mainly from carefully watching and listening to people in private homes and public places. In his masterwork *Ulysses* (Joyce 1961), Joyce's alter ego Leopold Bloom takes the reader on a journey leading from his home into the streets of Dublin and back again. The reader is induced to actively participate in the rich, multisensory experience of perceptions inspiring the imagination of his cruising hero, whose curiosity and propensity for sensual pleasures knows no bounds. Joyce lived for a long time in voluntary exile in Trieste, Paris, and Zurich. There he sought and found inspiration not only by observing people, but also by reading the daily newspaper. The same source of inspiration fired the imagination of Vladimir Nabokov (Field 1986, 332), a fellow writer also living in self-imposed exile.

Since the dawn of mankind, love and erotic attraction have been known as powerful sources of inspiration. The playwright Ibsen (Meyer 1985, 50) had a predilection for frequenting young girls because, as he confessed, he needed them for his inspiration. William Faulkner (Oates 1988, 30) likewise sought the company of young women because they inspired him. He once referred (Oates 1988, 24) to his inspiration in rather crude terms: "When I have a case of the hots I can write like a streak." A subtler example of erotic inspiration is reported by the Greek legend of Zeuxis (Pochat 1986, 64). It illustrates how cumulated sensual excitement fosters inspiration. As legend has it, Zeuxis, an artist living in the fifth century BC, was offered to paint the goddess Hera Lakinia, whose portrait would then be placed in the temple of Hera in Kroton. In order to create the desired portrait, Zeuxis selected the five most beautiful maidens in the city as models. Each one possessed some characteristic beauty, but none was endowed with all it took to represent Hera in her perfect resplendence. Zeuxis painted the nose of one maiden, the neck of another, the bosom of a third, and so forth. By faithfully representing various body parts of different maidens, he succeeded in portraying the gorgeous goddess in a work that enthused his contemporaries.

Erotic imagination also seems to have inspired Lewis Carroll (Newman 1991, 100-128) to write his famous story, *Alice in Wonderland*. One summer day, the shy mathematician who felt strongly attracted by very young, beautiful girls, was rowing little Alice and her sisters up the Thames from Oxford to Godstow five miles away. They urged him to tell them an entertaining story. He complied with their request by spontaneously spinning a yarn. Later he confessed, "I had sent my heroine straight down the rabbit-hole . . . without the least idea what was to happen afterwards." Obviously the three sisters inspired him to invent what happened next, because little Alice went roaming around in the strange underworld of Carroll's imagination, a realm whose figures, dialogues, and mind-boggling events remind us of the surrealistic imagery usually occurring in dreams and on psychedelic trips.

Many creative individuals are convinced that there is nothing they can do to trigger or facilitate their inspiration. As we have already seen in the case of Nabokov, they often state that they have to simply wait and be ready for inspiration. To be ready for inspiration means to be in a receptive state of mind (Guntern 1992, 191ff.) and to take care of an inspiring idea immediately, whenever it appears, because inspirations tend to be of the fleeting kind—if they are not taken care of right away, it is likely they will vanish as quickly as they came. That is why experienced creators will always interrupt an ongoing activity to jot down a new idea that suddenly pops up in their mind. They have a pencil and notepad, or some other material, at hand on their night table, ready to record the content of an inspiration that might emerge during a dream as soon as they wake up. Indeed the moment when drowsiness slips into sleep (what is known as the *hypnagogic state*) and the moment when the sleeper slowly awakes from slumber (*hypnopompic state*) may be very conducive to inspiration. In both cases, a diminished rational control of mental operation facilitates the emergence of specific mental images and, with it, the transfer of unconscious ideas to the conscious mind. But, whatever the circumstances in which inspirations pop up, the creative individual must be ready to take them into account without delay because it is very difficult, if not impossible, to retrieve them even a short while after they have occurred.

The topic of mental images brings us to the topic of metaphors. Metaphors are linguistic formulations containing a picture. As linguistic devices, they address the dominant brain hemisphere that thinks in language. As pictorial devices, they address the visual cortex of both brain hemispheres. That is why well-formulated metaphors are able to generate inspiration. In the course of time, a great number of physicists have been inspired by the terms *field force*, *bubble universe, super-string*, and *bootstrap*. Biologists have been inspired by the terms *struggle for survival, nature red in blood and claws, natural selection*, and *cycle of metamorphosis*. Interestingly enough, analytical thinkers are often also inspired by abstract terms. During the latter half of the last century, many scientists of different disciplines were inspired by the terms *gradient, catastrophe, self-organization, autonomy, self-similarity, emergent qualities*, and *coping strategies*.

Let us sum up what has been stated so far. Any idea, object, living being, event, or experience may turn into a source of inspiration provided that it fires up strong emotions able to set the wheels of imagination spinning. Emotions stirred up by inspiration may be of a positive or negative nature—although the positive ones prevail. Emotions may be triggered by dramatic events but also by factors and circumstances an uninformed outsider might consider as utterly trivial. To take but one example, Joseph Conrad (Baines 1986, 168) declared that looking at an empty page of paper lying on his desk inspired him.

To close this section, we might ask: what happens to creative individuals if they have to wait in vain for an inspiration?

- Creative individuals suffer terribly during periods of mental drought when, in sweltering cerebral inertia and torpidity, the clouds of inner tension gather without being able to discharge their precious load into rain showers of inspiration. Let us take three examples to illustrate the inner tension due to a lack of inspiration, or the release of tension due to a sudden inspiration.
- In one of his poems Alexander Pushkin (Briggs 1983, 29) referred to the lack of inspiration in the following verses:
  "Drop by drop, slowly I swallow the poisoned drink of boredom.
  . . .
  . . . I shut the book,
  Take up my pen and sit there, violently wrenching
  Disjointed words from my nodding muse.
  The sounds won't come together. . . I lose all control
  Over rhyme, that strange handmaiden of mine.
  The verses drag out their sluggish way, cold and misty."
- In a letter which Vincent van Gogh (Ghiselin 1985a, 3) wrote to his brother Theo, he helplessly raged against his lack of inspiration describing himself as an anguished prisoner ". . . in an I-don't-know-what-for horrible, horrible, utterly horrible cage."
- Rainer Maria Rilke (Sandblom 1987, 117) once suffered a period of creative barrenness lasting for a whole seven years. But then, all of a sudden, inspiration as well as illumination struck, and within a couple of weeks he wrote the ten *Duino Elegies* (1974) plus the *Sonnets to Orpheus* (1952). He

marvelled, "Everything in only a few weeks, it was an indescribable storm, a hurricane in my spirit."

When inspiration is strong enough, it triggers a phase of preparation and with it the beginning of a conscious creative process. The next section describes how that phase of preparation functions.

Excerpts from an interview with Ashok Kurien (6)

A phase of inspiration implies a relaxed organismic state and a receptive mind where the antennae of all sensory organs are able to catch even the most fleeting signals emerging from one's body and mind. Ashok Kurien speaks of the process of emotional cutting-off (detachment) that is important to enter a relaxed mood. Once more he mentions his childlike open-mindedness and playfulness and regrets that our education systems kill most of these personality traits, thus squandering valuable creative resources. He also speaks about the importance of having the right partners in order to succeed in a difficult task. Quite obviously he is fully aware of the fact that there are two windows of opportunity for excellent achievements and that a creative leader must see to it that over-stimulation and under-stimulation in the leader and in the teams under one's tutelage are properly balanced in order to obtain the best possible results.

Ashok Kurien tells the interviewer how he was inspired to build what he calls a STORYEUM in order to make the whole population of India aware of their history, brighter side and darker moments included. His eyes sparkle, his facial expression and gesticulations become very vivid, and he speaks faster than usual: a telltale of the enthusiasm fired up by a great inspiration. As he tells the interviewer about his project, he is already describing how inspiration led to a phase of preparation, first mental and then physical, organizational preparation. He even mentions various aspects of that mega-project that has meanwhile entered the phase of elaboration.

GG: Do you go to certain places, do you do certain things to facilitate your inspiration and motivation?

AK: Yes! I visit bars – and (laughing) I want to go tonight! You have to cut off now and then. Nowadays it isn't as bad, but there was a time when I was running two businesses parallel, getting involved in some Internet project, diving into this and that. I would have to get into a noisy bar somewhere, so noisy that I couldn't hear myself think!

GG: The environmental noise served to drown out all the rest and calmed the waves of your mental activity.

AK: Yes, because I didn't want to think. I didn't want to be with an intelligent woman, I wanted to be with some dumb, giggly bimbo. If I sit around all by myself, I'll only think of another idea, and I don't want to think. But I suppose I've passed that phase now.

GG: When you say, "I wanted to be with some dumb, giggly bimbo," this statement implies that hard, focussed work must have a counter-pole, a complementary force in order to function in an optimal way. That counter-pole is playful relaxation.

AK: Because I'm a child.

GG: And a child can switch off his preoccupations by becoming completely absorbed in a game.

AK: I am a child, and I will remain a child! I think like a child. Every child is born a musician or a dancer or an artist. Give any child a pen and paper, give them coloured pencils, and they start drawing. Put some music on, they all start wiggling! They all sing with no embarrassment. Then what do we do? Our education system says, "That's not how you draw! Draw like this! That's out of tune! You dance badly!" We kill their creativity! We just kill it! And they don't draw or sing or dance for the rest of their lives.

GG: We kill it by imposing rigid rules and structural constraints where freedom and playful exploration should reign.

AK: When a child starts wriggling and moving around we say, "Stand still!" That child is hearing music in its head! That child is dancing! We kill our child's creativity with our education system.

GG: Absolutely. I fully agree.

AK: I didn't get educated, so nobody killed my creativity.

GG: What keeps a human being young?

AK: I'm young because I'm a child.

GG: What is the essence of a child?

AK: It's simplicity.

GG: Which mental faculty is the most vivid in a child?

AK: (Chuckles)

GG: Imagination.

AK: Imagination, okay! Of course! I'm an *imagineer*!

GG: I have seen children prematurely aged.

AK: Exactly!

GG: You see them on television in regions where catastrophic events occur, for instance in Afghanistan, Iraq or Darfour.

AK: I agree!

GG: What happens to them is a terrible fate which kills their imagination.

AK: Education kills children's imagination.

GG: It does, but war and political fights are even worse. Terrible hunger, loss of parents, loss of loved ones, abuse and violence kill the imagination of children and then they age prematurely. On the other hand, if you look at an older person who appears to be still very young, you'll always find that that person has a very lively imagination.

AK: I do! I'm going to be sixty years old, but I don't feel older than twenty-five or thirty. Do you know who my friends are? People my daughters' age; all my daughters' friends are my friends.

GG: Let's talk some more about the cutting-off mechanism.

AK: The important thing is to cut yourself away from all worries. Sometimes I drink a little too much, (chuckling) just to clear it out of my head! You've got to wipe it away, bring a curtain down, blank it out. You've got to give up! I think that is it. You have to surrender. My ego and my conscious mind always want to win, so I consciously cut off because if I don't, I'm going to lose my greatest power.

GG: Your cutting-off reminds me of the Zen concept of non-attachment. Sometimes, instead of clinging to the topic and greedily grasping it, you turn your back on it, cut it off and push it away as far as possible out of your conscious mind. And only if you have this attitude of total non-attachment – which is detachment actually – will your intuitive mind get a chance to gently work overnight – or however long it takes – to work out a solution which then one day (snaps fingers), when you wake up, hits you, and then you know: that's it!

AK: When you're too involved in a problem, you are *in* the bubble, and you're struggling to get out because you're part of the mess. When you're out, you see it from the outside, and you see it in a very simple manner, like somebody who doesn't know. From the outside you can see exactly where the problem lies.

GG: So when you're actually in the bubble, the antennae of your perception no longer work. If you're locked in, you're incapacitated, blocked, blinded, you no longer hear, you can no longer smell.

AK: Absolutely! Very often you'll find in a product or an organization that the team is overly involved in it. They think it, they live it, they breathe it, they are *in* it, and they cannot see it from the outside because they're looking from the inside out. An example came to me that illustrates this topic nicely. If I'm in the middle of a maze and am trying to find my way out, I don't know where to go: there's one wall, another wall, a turn, yet another turn, it's like walking around this building!

GG: However, if you're detached like a bird, like a kingfisher or kestrel, hovering high above the labyrinth...

AK: ...the moment I'm up there, I can look down and clearly see: this is the path!

GG: It's an excellent picture!

AK: If you've ever tried one of those puzzles where they give you a maze and say, "Find your way out," you can't do it. But if you start from the outside, you just follow whichever pathway and it takes you right in! It's very easy!

GG: Yes. It's easier to get lost in a maze than to find your way out of it.

AK: But if someone puts you outside and then says, "Go to the centre," you find that getting into the maze is easy. Getting out is the problem!

GG: Yes, you are right!

AK: Like I said, that is the closest I can get to trying to explain the phenomenon. But the process truly involves a cutting off – and the acceptance that everything you've done till then can only give you conventional answers. By the way, sometimes your subconscious answer could be the same as your conventional answer; but that doesn't make you always right.

GG: I'm just thinking about strategies for cutting off. In the first half of the last century, to be a writer in America was not a position of prestige. A businessman was respected, but not a writer; writers were looked down upon. It's interesting to note that eight of the greatest writers in America working in the first half of the last century—before they became famous and respected—were all heavy drinkers. The Nobel laureates Sinclair Lewis, Ernest Hemingway, William Faulkner and John Steinbeck were alcoholics. Playwright Eugene O'Neill, who won four Pulitzer Prizes and a Nobel Prize, was an alcoholic. Tennessee Williams, the great playwright, was an alcoholic; and so were F. Scott Fitzgerald, who wrote *The Great Gatsby*, and Thomas Wolfe. The struggle to create plots and a decent style of writing, the lack of prestige, the rejection slips from publishers pouring in for years on end, and the want of money to sustain themselves and their families or partners, all that stress and frustration was so unbearable that they needed an outlet, a relief, a kind of rescue mission in order to survive. Thus they all began to drink, some of them mainly in the late afternoons or evenings; others, like Eugene O'Neill and William Faulkner went on binges that sometimes lasted for weeks on end. This was their method of producing an emotional cut-off and escaping the tyranny of rational thinking tinged with a depressive mood. When they were sober again, they were able to find their way out of the maze in which they had been stuck. Okay, this was just a comment on your highly interesting concept of cutting-off.

AK: There's a parallel. However, you used the word "alcoholic" but actually you're saying they were addicts. All your pop singers and rock stars today are addicts; if it's not alcohol, it's drugs. You're *addicted* to something. Most businessmen are addicted to work…

GG: … and to institutional power.

AK: Workaholism, poweraholism, they're all different interpretations of the same disease! Godaholism! God-aholism: when you're willing to sacrifice everything to go after God, it's that escape. As for workaholism, look at business people: their families are destroyed!

GG: Absolutely. I observed that phenomenon often during the fifteen years I worked as a special adviser to boards and top-management of multinational corporations.

AK: They don't care about anyone. They will completely give in to their addiction to that power, that success!

GG: Look at leading politicians; there we have the same syndrome. They are not only addicted to power but to the limelight of the mass media. They want to be in show business.

AK: That's it! At the cost of everything else; like those writers.

GG: But there is an important difference between those writers who drank too much and the drug-addicted rock stars; and there is a great difference between those writers and the politicians and top managers addicted to power. Unless they were on a binge, writers would not drink before a day's work was done. Hemingway started to dip into daiquiris only at around four o'clock in the afternoon. He was an early riser and worked with high concentration and utter discipline until around four in the afternoon. In that respect the title of his book on the Spanish *corrida—Death in the Afternoon*—is rather revealing. While these writers were in the process of creating a novel or a play, they would never drink in the morning. Once they had finished their day's work, they began to drink till late into the night or even go on a binge lasting for days or weeks. Whereas addicted power gamblers and drug-addicted rock stars who are not at all creative— or creative only on a very modest level—are rarely sober. Their minds are clouded at all times by their chronic intoxication. They lose their rational control over their interpersonal relationships, their own personality, their thoughts, because they never stop indulging in their addiction.

AK: Yes, you're right.

GG: An alcoholic can be a consumer, and the consumer still has control because he sticks to the same quantity of alcohol per unit of time. An addict, however, has lost all control; addicts must continuously increase the quantity of their intake to get the kick they are after.

So, cutting-off is a precondition for getting an inspiration. Now, can you give me an example of a phase of great inspiration you once had? A state of mind where your imagination got all fired up?

AK: Yes I can, and there was a trigger to that inspiration. Pramod Kapoor, whom you met at the Frankfurt Book Fair, a good friend of mine, calls me up one day and says, "Ashok, I'm just calling to see if you'd like to help. I have a friend who's in the University of Jamia Islamia, and he says he can give us a little space to put up photographs to commemorate our Indian independence. It might cost some money, but I'll pay from my pocket. I'm willing to give five or ten lakhs, but it may cost more. Would you be willing to help?" And I said, "Of course, I'll help you! It sounds like a good cause, so I'll give you another five or ten lakhs if you need them; I'll match your contribution." It's a good thing to give something back to your own country.

GG: What is a lakh worth?

AK: A lakh is one hundred thousand rupees. Divide that by sixty, roughly, and you'll get Euros. So he was going to put in the equivalent of about two thousand Euros and wanted me to put in the rest, which of course I agreed to do. But when I said "Yes," there was a flash, and I thought: "Why are we creating a room full of photographs? It's dusty, it's old, it's yesterday's generation." What we're doing here is letting people know what happened during independence, which is a full sixty years of struggle. And because Pramod is in the publishing business and has access to photographs, he's thinking of working with that. But I thought, "There's an opportunity here."

Now the trigger for my idea was Pramod. Sixty years after independence no one had thought of creating something to tell the story. They had built monuments – a tower, a gateway – but what does that have to do with independence? Sixty years later half the population of our country is under eighteen, and they don't know a thing about independence! They don't know who struggled, who gave their lives, that there were freedom fighters. They know there was a Mahatma Gandhi somewhere; they studied a little bit about him one year in school when they were twelve years old; after that, nothing. And they're the new India! So I thought, "Hey, there's a story to be told! A great story, a heroic story! It's also a story of great tragedy because during partition, there was the largest single movement of people across countries, and one or two million people died!" So just look at it! It's not about putting photographs up! How do I get children from the age of fifteen and adults aged twenty-five or thirty to get to this place and enjoy it? So I said, "I don't want to build a museum. I want to build a STORYEUM."

GG: And what is a story-eum?

AK: A STORYEUM is a place where I tell a story!

GG: Aha! Instead of building a mute monument…

AK: I don't want them in a museum in a collection of items.

GG: Is "storyeum" a neologism or does the word already exist?

AK: I thought I made it up!

GG: Ah, right! That's what I wanted to know!

AK: Yes, I first called it a "historyeum."

GG: A place that has to do with history; I see.

AK: That was my first thought. Then I said, "See? I can keep doing this!" It doesn't always have to be history. This one is a historyeum; the next one could be a storyeum. So we're going to call the company "Storyeum." All this has happened in the last four months. So I said, "Now why should people go to a museum and take out whatever they want to take out of it, which is: 'This is boring; this is interesting; this is really terrible; this is nice.'" If I tell a story, I can tell it in a tone and manner that I want, and they will leave with the emotions I want to let them leave with. And they will remember it, if I tell it in an interesting way. So I said – and poor Pramod almost *died* when I said this to him, but now he's completely bought into it – "We are going to create a combination of Broadway, theatre, Disneyland, Paramount Studios, and all the new methods of talking to the Internet and television generation. What we're going to create is a series of some twenty mini-theatres, like an auditorium. You walk into the first part, and I want a three-dimensional, animatronics character of Pandit Nehru, Jawaharlal Nehru, who's going to be the storyteller and addresses the audience! Along with that I have footage from BBC, footage from the UK archives, from the Indian archives; it's all audio-visual and sound. Then you move to the next room. I want a hologram of Mahatma Gandhi walking across the room and then going to his final prayer at Rajghat. I want Nathuram Godse, his assassin, as a three-dimensional hologram or animatronics, to come out and fire a bullet, and the room fills with smoke. And everyone there must be completely shocked. Then Godse must be tried and hanged; I want to drop a body with a rope around its neck from the ceiling into the middle of the crowd! So I want to tell the whole story in twenty scenes, and I want to be able to do this using the best techniques in the world, the best equipment in the world, multiple languages, and headphones. Anyone who wants more information can go to the room next door to a touch-screen, and a scholar can find all the information, which he will download and compile. And we'll get all this together!

When Gandhi said, "Jail Bharo," he was telling the Indians to march in the streets and got arrested. "Fill the Jails." How many can the British jail? In that sequence I want prison bars to come down from the ceiling and start squeezing the audience into a smaller space. When General Dyer shoots Indians at the Jallianwallah Baug Tragedy, I want the audience to feel compressed air bullets!

Then we move on to the partition of India. There's a famous book called *The Train to Pakistan* that describes how all the passengers arrived dead at their destination, and how in the massacre only the engine driver was left alive. I want the whole audience to be able to walk in and sit down in a railway compartment. The whole thing should move like a railway train, and on its way, one can see the massacres taking place on a parallel train. I want to juxtapose that, because at the same time Bombay, Delhi and Karachi win their freedom, and there's footage of the celebration and the jubilation with people dancing on the streets and giving out sweets and hoisting flags – while the horrible murder of millions is going on. Then I want to go to the final speech; we have footage of Nehru's "Tryst with Destiny" address.

So that is the story, and when the visitors come out of this audio-visual experience, we must awaken them to a feeling of freedom, like in a big garden, with music and flowers and plants. On the top of a hill, I want to build a memorial, perhaps somewhat like Yad Vashem, the Jewish Holocaust Memorial in Jerusalem, but with candles and lights. I want to build a memorial, and I want a scroll projection of the names of all the freedom fighters who died for India. The names would keep scrolling upwards, continuously, twenty-four hours a day. Then I'd have an auditorium and a theatre, and so on. The audience must experience the event and feel the emotions. People forget what they read, but they remember experiences all their lives!

GG: That's a mammoth project!

AK: A mammoth project! So what have I done since I had the flash? I went to the Apartheid Museum in Africa, then I went to Tel Aviv, and Zipi Roitman introduced me to the woman who is the co-ordinator of the Holocaust Museum. She's got experience; she's done several projects on museums in twenty years. She's a fabulous lady, and I've asked her to come in as an advisor/consultant. We've taken the project through the Ministry, as the University Vice-Chancellor, who's an historian, is backing it. They have land in Delhi. We presented the whole project in three months to the Minister of HRD, who has given us five acres of land in New Delhi worth several million dollars. The land is sanctioned. We have a budget of twenty million dollars to construct and do everything. We've already got the architects' quotations for doing it, and it all works within a budget.

I've gone to one private sponsor whom I spoke to for five minutes. I said, "I'm going to sponsor the project with someone's name because I need another few million or so, and he said, "Stop. I'll contribute as long as you put my name on it." Right now the paperwork, the detailed document with the cost of the whole thing, is being drawn up. I've already got a letter from the government to go ahead. As soon as I go back home, I'm going to fly Orit Hall into India, get her to meet the team – because I need somebody like her to lead it. No one in India has done anything like this. And the maxim is: when it opens in 2009-2010, it must be state-of-the-art so that it'll still be contemporary in 2020. Pramod and I will control the software. We're doing this free for the government. We're not going to make one rupee out of it. But we will create an experience and form a company who can then create twenty of them. I can go to the Indian Armed Forces and create the history of the Indian Armed Forces! I can go to Bollywood and do the Bollywood story. I can do anything!

GG: This is a beautiful example of what I call morpho-evolution: results of a specific creative achievement inspire new creative activities in the same field or some other professional domain.

AK: And I'm doing it for free, but I'll spend three years experiencing how to do it, so I'll become the expert in India for doing this, with an international team and the latest technology. After that I'll have a company, with Pramod and me alone, that can go and do twenty projects like this one.

GG: You can do such projects everywhere in the world!

AK: For me India is big enough! Now, *that* is inspiration!

GG: Yes! What triggers inspiration? What blocks it? Here a trigger occurred, because Kapoor told you, "I want to exhibit photographs." That was the trigger.

AK: And I said, "Who wants to do photographs? Let's just turn it into a big, giant, mega-project, but really make it exciting!" Now wait a minute! If I control the software – which is the whole show, which is twenty rooms – I can go to the Minister of Railways and tell him to give me a railway train and then put this whole exhibition, a second version of it, onto a railway train! A railway train can go to 62,000 stations across India, where a billion people can go to the platform.

GG: People from all of the villages of the rural areas.

AK: Thus the museum will move around the country. The visitors walk in through one end, see each story, and come out of the other end of the train. Then the train moves to the next village or town. I can take this to a billion people!

GG: It sounds very exciting.

AK: It's *very* exciting. What's going to block my inspiration? Nothing! In three months we've already got it signed.

GG: Wonderful.

AK: Everything we did, we did in record time.

GG: Have you ever experienced a block of inspiration – in that project or in some other one?

AK: No. If you have the right partner and the right person with you, and the right team, you just go for it!

GG: Did it ever happen that you had the wrong partner?

AK: Once, with the medical business.

GG: What in your partner's behaviour blocked the inspiration there?

AK: He was a professional manager; he wasn't a charged-up entrepreneur.

GG: And therefore he was a drag rather than an inspiring individual.

AK: Once I experienced a block of inspiration with a dishonest and incompetent events manager. So I've learned never to partner with a professional manager. The wrong people can be a block. And if you've got the wrong team, you're finished!

GG: If somebody does not synchronize with you, but immediately brings seventeen reasons to emphasize why your project might go wrong, this would not be inspiring; it couldn't be!

AK: He might synchronize with me at the beginning, but one year down the line, when things start getting uncomfortable on the market, and he doesn't know how to drive it, he gives up!

GG: But entrepreneurs like you or Mr. Kapoor inspire and drive each other other, fire up your respective imagination so that you have yet another train, a mental train, a team train speeding along.

AK: Yes, that's it. That's why I said the railway train would move. Or at least the passengers would feel like it was moving. And actually it'll vibrate! So right now nothing is blocking my inspiration, but circumstances like a war with Pakistan could block my inspiration. How would I react to it? A few more sleepless nights! What do I do? I pursue it relentlessly. And I think that's what creative leaders do. Pramod – God bless his soul – I don't think really wanted to do anything like this, but now he completely believes in it. The Minister completely buys into it; the Vice-Chancellor of the University believes in it, so I have carried the whole team into faith. We've already taken it through. When the Minister's team saw it, they didn't say, "Good idea, this, that." They didn't discuss anything. They all looked at each other and someone said, "Where should we take the funds from?" Then the discussion became, "We'll get the funds from here." That was it! Seven minutes of discussion after twenty minutes of presentation. Their only reaction was, "Where do we find the money?" What they meant was, "How do we find money without interference?" I don't want anyone interfering with this. What kind of end result does this inspiration lead to? I think it's a contribution to future generations. It's a big contribution! It's a contribution to a history that has been forgotten.

GG: Your mega-project will help to inspire, generate, maintain and further develop a perspective of national identity.

AK: Absolutely! That's a story that must be told and should never be forgotten. There is currently a generation in India that has grown up – and is still growing up on wealth; it's growing up on success; it's growing up on this bright India! People of my generation grew up in the dark ages of India…

GG: … in a world that looked bleak…

AK: …with no hope. We were Gandhian. My father was happy with two shirts. He didn't need the third shirt. We were modest; now everything about us has changed!

GG: You have got a mind-boggling project, and I'm convinced you will succeed in creating it so that it fits your vision.

AK: I think so, yes – unless somebody steals the project from us. A few months later we were duped by Mushirul Hassan, the Vice Chancellor of the Jamia Milia

University. He presented our idea with the entire plan to the President of India – as *his* idea and got presidential permission to be "Project Head for Life! He cheated us and dumped us saying, "Ideas are free!" We had no proof of intellectual property rights – and who wants to fight a politician? You win some, you lose some, so you move on to the next thing. Right now I'm setting up what I hope will be the finest College of Design in Asia – exciting! – and an Adventure Campsite for underprivileged children; also exciting!

GG: Did you have other partners who were a source of inspiration for you? Or other partners with whom you had a working relationship of mutual inspiration and motivation?

AK: I have a great one with Zee—but Elsie Nanji was my first partner. She taught me how to master partnerships, and since, I have managed many.

GG: Could you please give me a concrete example of how this mutual inspiration worked?

AK: I respected her creative talent, and she respected my strategic and marketing judgement. We were both strong on the opposite sides of the coin, which created success value in our work. My maxim was: "Always find a partner whose strength is your weakness, and whose weakness is your strength."

GG: In other words, there was a perfect complementarity of talents between you and Mrs. Nanjing. What did you appreciate most in her?

AK: Elsie had a single-minded creative passion, yet she was mature enough to understand commercial needs and market factors. She never allowed ego to get in the way, which made it reciprocal. She was one of the greatest creative leaders, encouraging and promoting talent rather than hogging the limelight. She had the wisdom of "childlike simplicity," a rarity in today's world. She was "mother" to the office and helped people both in their work and with their personal problems. She was willing to give of her own time, an attitude which made her truly loved. She had a great sense of honesty in both her work and her genuine personal relationships!

GG: What did she appreciate most in you?

AK: Most of all, my passion for great creative work; my willingness to risk financial reward while seeing our work through; and my ability not only to think outside the box, but also to live outside the box.

GG: How and where did the two of you meet for the very first time?

AK: We met a few months after I had started the agency alone. Back then I did freelance projects with many creative directors. Elsie's work appealed to me; it fitted the demands of the new, changing India. It was contemporary and stylish. I offered her a partnership giving her "ownership" of the creative product without wasting her energies on running the business or worrying about strategy.

GG: For how long have the two of you worked together on a more or less daily basis?

AK: For twenty years!

GG: What did the two of you do when you encountered a major obstacle in your creative collaboration, when your imagination stalled? This happens to everybody now and then.

AK: We switched off. I went to her home, relaxed with her family, played with her kids – whom I adore – had a drink and started afresh. The answer usually arrived.

GG: How did the two of you react when you had a major conflict, when contradictions between individual opinions and intentions emerged? Independent, strong-willed individuals clash from time to time; that's quite unavoidable.

AK: We fought, argued, shouted, cried! Then there was a brief mutual sulk, followed by a cooling off time during which I sat down and thought, "Maybe she is right." In all that ranting, raving and arguments, there was some wisdom. That made it easier for me to go back with an open mind, which always results in a better solution.

GG: What kind of professional activities does Mrs. Elsie Nanji pursue today?

AK: Today Elsie runs a very successful design unit known as Red Lion. She also has an interior design partnership and consults for major architects. And she still has time to be my closest friend, sister, family, philosopher and guide.

GG: She must be quite a lady, an extraordinary personality.

AK: Yes, she certainly is.

GG: Okay, that sums it up. You have given me perfect examples of how mutual inspiration and motivation works. Your partnership with Mrs. Elsie Nanji also emphasizes three points that are very crucial in creative leadership. First, autonomous personalities clash from time to time because independent ideas do not always fit, and a misfit of ideas can be a source of positive creative tension. Second, conflict protects against over-adjustment, a frequent cause for the death of inspiration. Third, it is the quality of conflict management that makes all the difference: good conflict management enhances creativity, bad conflict management kills it.

2.33 Phase of Preparation

A cat doesn't proclaim its hunting skills. It catches mice.

Gottlieb Guntern

When an inspired person sets to work on a new project, a phase of preparation begins. Preparatory work consists of many different things. It entails collect-

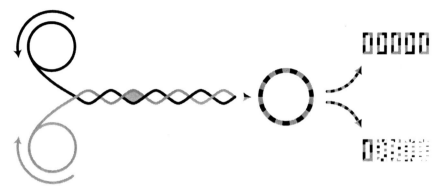

Figure 2.11.   Phase of preparation.

ing and ordering ideas, data, material, methods, techniques, and sometimes the team members needed for the specific creative process in progress. One may talk with experts on the issues to be dealt with, but must study the state-of-the-art in the particular domain in which a creative contribution is intended. It is important to have clear ideas about the purposes and goals of the job at hand. Detailed plans of procedures must be established and polished, and strategies promising successful goal attainment chosen and implemented. It is imperative that the standards and values governing the work to be accomplished be defined along with the yardstick that will be used to measure the quality of the accomplishments.

Now a composer begins to compose; a writer to write; a painter to paint— or at least to prepare a canvas—an inventor begins to tinker; an engineer to calculate the qualities and quantities of materials to be used; an experimental physicist sets about defining the setting, tools and techniques for an experiment; a filmmaker looks for an excellent script and investors; a social scientist thoroughly studies the already existing concepts and theories he aims to improve or replace; and so on and so forth.

If everything goes well, the phase of preparation may move right into a phase of elaboration. Yet such a smooth transition rarely occurs because the gods who hold the crown of success like to see their mortal subjects sweat and swear. Preparation implies going deeply into the topic at hand. Even routine ideas, let alone creative ones, for problem solutions and goal attainment do not fall from the sky as naturally as a rain shower. As the industrial designer George Nelson (Armbruster 1989, 178) once put it, ". . . ideas are a result of a considerable amount of delving into the problem."

What is a problem? In colloquial language a problem is an obstacle, a burden, or some other form of adversity. In the realm of creativity, a problem is

not necessarily anything of the kind. It is a challenge that is often actively
sought, albeit a challenge whose present fascination usually outweighs by far
the future frustrations it is likely to produce. Abstractly speaking, a problem
(P) may be defined as the difference between a desired state (S_d) and a current
state of affairs (S_c):

$$P = S_d - S_c$$

Basically, this formula suggests three possible main strategies for problem
solution:

- Strategy 1: One may diminish the desired state ($S_d\Downarrow$) by renouncing in part
  the quality and quantity of the things desired. For instance, if a mother wants
  her daughter to obey her every order and demand, she may diminish her expectations and thus decrease the compliance problem she has with her child.
- Strategy 2: One may overlook the fact that there is a minus sign (-) between
  a desired state and the current state. The mother may ignore the gap between her expectations and her daughter's obedience from time to time, and
  thus attenuate her problem.
- Strategy 3: One may improve the current state ($S_c\Uparrow$) of affairs in a given domain. Using a clever mix of gratifications and sanctions, mother may insist
  on more compliance from her daughter and thus diminish her problem.

In daily life, the first and second strategies may at times prove to be full of
wisdom. In the realm of creative performance, however, they are likely to lead
directly into the wastelands of mediocrity and defeat. That is why creative
individuals always opt for the third strategy and aim at improving the current
state of affairs. The higher the creative talent and ambitions of a creative individual, the higher on the ladder of success the desired state will be placed
and the more sensitive the creative person will be towards the minus sign
separating the desired and the current state of affairs. The individual will invest all the more effort in climbing from the level of the current state up to the
level of the desired state—and maybe even transcend it!

Some creativity researchers treat creative activity mainly as a specific case
of problem solution. This approach is too narrow to do the facts justice. Of
course, creative individuals are often problem solvers. But they are also continuously on the lookout for new problems, and they may even generate specific problems in order to increase their challenge. A case in point is Galileo
Galilei, the first scientist to pose the problem of how to measure the speed of
light. He failed to come up with a proper solution; with hindsight we may
even say that his approach was rather naive. But to have posed the problem
was in itself a creative act. In 1676, half a century after Galileo's failed at-

tempt, the Danish astronomer Roemer proposed a suitable method, and in the course of time creative experimental physicists have continued to improve the precision of his method.

The greater the difference between a desired future state and a current state, the greater is the problem at hand. The greater the problem, the higher the creative tension driving creative individuals towards their goals. Creative tension needs to be built up, maintained, and then appropriately released. A creative individual must proceed like an archer. When the bow is tightly drawn, the body stance stable, the hand steady, the eye focused on the target, and breathing is calm and regular, that is the moment when the arrow is released and hits the bull's eye of strategic intentions. If, however, creative tension is squandered on activities that have nothing to do with proper training and preparation, then the bow of strategic intention will never be able to release an arrow that will hit the desired target.

A wit once remarked that rich people are not really different from you and me, they only have more money. Creative people *are* different from noncreative ones. They are more ambitious than the average and therefore willing to do what it takes to satisfy their ambitions. They embrace norms, values, attitudes, and behaviors with respect to goals, problems, and problem solutions that are different from those of noncreative people. Like top athletes in pole-vaulting, the farther they progress in their quest for maximum performance, the higher they set their crossbars. Failure will not induce them to give in to resignation or self-pity; it will rather spur them on to train harder and harder until they are able to clear their self-imposed hurdles. Ann Roe (Hayes 1989, 137) studied creative physicists and biologists and concluded, "There is only one thing that seems to characterize the total group and that is absorption in their work, over long years, and frequently to the exclusion of everything else." Perseverance, endurance, stress tolerance, and the ability to cope with frustrations are a sine qua non for every single creative process, not only during the phase of preparation but in other phases as well.

At the very beginning of the phase of preparation, most individuals tend to deal with their creative tensions by means of rituals, repeating highly organized activities to decrease the chaos of ideas, uncertainty, and emotions and increase order. During these rituals, they may sharpen pencils over and over again, wash brushes, line up books and other materials, clean their apartment, answer pending mail, rearrange furniture and objects in the room in which they work, slip into particular clothes, run up and down the stairs twenty-one times, listen to a special piece of music for hours on end, read a specific text over and over again, and so on and so forth. They are as restless as a doe about to drop a fawn and as insistent in their acts as a courtship-minded bowerbird building its sophisticated nest. To take but one example, the poetess Maya

Angelou (Guntern 1997, 50f.) has developed a habit of renting a hotel room in her home town and staying there daily from six in the morning to one in the afternoon. She takes the Bible, Roget's Thesaurus, a dictionary, a deck of cards, and a bottle of Sherry with her. If there are any paintings, photos, or drawings on the walls in the hotel room, she takes them down so as not to be distracted and to avoid impairing her aesthetic sensitivity. And then she concentrates, lays out her cards, and waits for an idea to come. Or she reads the Bible because the musical quality of its texts inspires her. Around nine o'clock she takes a glass of Sherry, only one. Such is her ritual, day in, day out, whenever she wants to write poetry. If she is lucky, that ritual is fruitful and prompts inspiration or illumination.

The writer and literary critic Carol Oates (Parini 1989) said about her phase of preparation: "I take endless notes before I begin writing a novel, often when I travel, I write on the back of envelopes." In the morning she likes to write poems or short stories to prepare for the harder task of novel writing. Similarly, the highly creative French mathematician Jacques S. Hadamard (Hadamard 1945, 45f.), who also investigated the nature of invention in mathematics, emphasized the necessity of preliminary work for facilitating a breakthrough in scientific discovery. Talking about the interaction of chance and necessity, he stated that a scientist has to take aim as precisely as would an artillery gunner, otherwise chance will not favor him. Taking aim is a mental activity of preparation.

Preparation has a lot to do with planning. While some planners may proceed with the discipline and perfection deployed by a chief of staff preparing a decisive battle, others are less systematic in their endeavor. The quality of preparation may already anticipate the fate of the final result of a creative process. Fyodor Dostoevsky (Kjetsaa 1987, 316ff.) confided to beautiful actress Maria Savina his admiration of her perfectionism: "Every single word you utter is as carved from ivory." It is easy to imagine how much preparation it takes for an actress to become such a perfect carver. Dostoevsky, however, despised Savina's friend, writer Ivan Turgenev, whose sloppy style he could not stand. Referring to Turgenev, he told Maria: "But that old fellow of yours just stands there lisping all the time." In contradistinction to Dostoevsky, Turgenev was born into a wealthy family, benefited from early recognition as a highly promising talent, and later enjoyed a gentleman's life of leisure. He did not have to learn the hard way. Such life conditions may breed complacency, and complacency is an archenemy of the discipline necessary for a demanding phase of preparation, elaboration, and evaluation.

Preparation always exists, even in creative individuals who like to posture in the exalted attitudes characteristic of Romantic period artists and pretend that their masterworks swoop down like eagles from the heavens of lofty genius. In this respect, Russian writer Anton Chekhov (Ghiselin 1985a, 6) once stated: "If an artist boasts to me of having written a story without a previously settled design, but by inspiration, I should call him a lunatic." Chekhov is right, but only to a certain extent. Often the design is not settled beforehand at all; it changes its form during the course of preparation and sometimes even later during the phase of elaboration. Preparation tunes the piano and warms up the pianists' fingers for the concert to come. As a general rule, wherever planning is sloppy, the work eventually accomplished is likely to look or sound sloppy, too. But even where planning and preparation run their desired course, the first outcomes of a creative process may be little more than preparatory sketches for better work to come. In a letter addressed to Anton Ridder van Rappard, Vincent van Gogh (Ghiselin 1985a, 47) wrote as follows about his paintings: "The first attempts are absolutely unbearable." As we know, van Gogh was a genius able to transcend the unbearable by means of relentless concentration and continuous hard work.

A guitar must be properly tuned before a guitarist can strum a melody that is on key. Similarly, creative individuals must tune their perceptions, thoughts, and emotions before their minds can be ready to create a harmonious piece of work. Proper tuning may take weeks, months or years. Kandinsky (Herbert 1964, 29) confessed that the notes he took for his essay "Concerning the Spiritual in Art" had "accumulated during a span of at least ten years."

In 1907, Joyce (Ellman 1983, 357) began preparation for his novel *Ulysses*. His wife Nora (Ellman 1983, 524) later reported that he had thought about the book for sixteen years and then took seven years to write it. Hemingway's biographer (Lynn 1987, 311) quotes Walsh, who stated that the first impression a reader gets in reading a story by Hemingway is that the writer had prepared himself "a long time before he began to write." Hemingway, who rarely missed an opportunity for a little braggadocio—especially after having downed a couple of drinks—used to tell everybody around him what he was currently thinking about and what kind of short stories or novels were under preparation. Often he paid a high price for his spontaneous revelations. After talking for years on end to colleagues and other listeners about specific stories he intended to incorporate into a war novel he had in mind, he eventually discovered with dismay (Hotchner 1967, 50) that other writers had stolen his ideas and used them in their own books. Talking about a creative work one intends to produce is a good way of entering a phase of inspiration and of pushing the phase of preparation ahead. Yet too much talk may give rise to two dangers: first, the stories may inspire other individuals and make their creative juices flow—to the detriment of the storyteller; second, too much preparing and talking about ideas produced during the phase of preparation may take the sap out of the whole concept, leaving the creator washed out and the creative process inevitably blocked.

A phase of preparation may begin right after the evaluation of a work that has just been completed, as that evaluation may inspire the creative individual for a new creative performance. This is a common experience shared by all highly creative individuals. Moreover, the phenomenon is an illustration not only of the fact that creative phases do not necessarily follow each other in single file, but also that different creative processes may go on simultaneously in the same individual. A good example is Ibsen (Meyer 1985, 463). Having completed *The Pillars of Society*, he wrote to his publisher Hegel that he intended to create another play in the same genre. But it took a year of mental preparation and incubation before he wrote the first line.

As we have seen, preparation often takes place in a creative individual's head a long time before output activity produces any visible or audible work. Work that is visible from the outside begins once the prepared mind is saturated. The urge to work out conscious ideas on stone, wood, paper, canvas, celluloid, a computer, or some other information carrier or material becomes stronger than the wish to continue to play around mentally with ideas and concepts. Writer and Nobel laureate Toni Morrison (Gower 1992, 4) had the following to say about her phase of preparation: "At some point, after a great deal of dreaming, considering, visualizing, rejecting, and questioning, it's impossible to go any further with that. So you write your first sentence." In a conversation we once had, Gabriel García Márquez told me that sometimes he works for months on end just to write the first sentence of a new novel. If it sounds right with respect to idea, wording, rhythm, melody, and harmony, then he plunges head first into the work of writing sentence after sentence, paragraph after paragraph, and chapter after chapter.

There is no general recipe prescribing the best way to organize a phase of preparation. Arthur Miller's (1987, 590) statement that he usually took years to write a play suggests that not only his phase of elaboration, but also his phase of preparation normally took a long time. The problems popping up during the phase of preparation can be of a conceptual, technical, aesthetic, or ethical order. The reasons for these problems may lie in the topic itself, the methods and tools available, the goals pursued, the creative individual's personality, or specific environmental attitudes and circumstances. A frequent cause blocking the progress of preparation (and subsequently also the phase of elaboration) is the target fixation of a mental action mode that inhibits the mental receptive mode, the ensuing train of mental associations and hence, imagination. This blockage emerges particularly when ambition is very high and patience conspicuously low as, for instance, in high-speed dogfights between enemy aircraft in a war zone. That is why in the nineteenth century, the psychologist Souriau (Hadamard 1945, 48) suggested: "In order to invent, one must think aside." Thinking aside opens the fan of mental associations and thus prevents blockage due to target fixation.

Souriau's statement later inspired intelligence researcher Guilford (Guilford 1988, 200-208) to differentiate between two modes of thinking: convergent and divergent. The dominant brain hemisphere's convergent (strict logical) thinking heads straight for the desired goal. The nondominant brain hemisphere's divergent thinking permits the meandering imagination to take its time in looking for promising ideas, while it slowly slithers towards the desired goal. If convergent and divergent thinking are not properly balanced, then the process of preparation will get stuck, or at best, its quality will suffer. The same balance is likewise needed for other phases of the creative process. I should like to emphasize this fact, because a fashionable misconception pretends that such balance is of no significance whatsoever. There are authors, including self-proclaimed "creativity experts," who equate divergent thinking to creative thinking. Nothing could be farther from the truth. Whenever divergent thinking is not checked by convergent thinking, unfettered imagination will lead to chaos rather than to creative performance. Whenever convergent thinking is not counterbalanced by divergent thinking, the resulting conceptual void will leave no room for creative performance but only for habitual performance and the stereotyped, quite predictable outcome it tends to produce.

One of the consequences of target fixation is that even highly creative scientists fail to see the important implications of their own discoveries. While this may not directly hamper their original phase of preparation, it certainly hinders their chances of getting inspired and entering a new phase of preparation that will in turn lead to another—although thematically linked—creative process; in short, it blocks their chances of making further discoveries. Hadamard (1945, 50) states, for instance, that, "Brücke's mind was too narrowly directed toward his problem." What had happened to Ernst Wilhelm von Brücke? The physician and physiologist had investigated the means of, and found a proper method for, illuminating the retina of the eye. But it was his colleague, Hermann von Helmholtz, who, preparing a lecture on the results of Brücke's research, was struck with the inspiration that Brücke's method might provide a way to produce optical images from the rays reflected by the retina. This idea eventually led to the discovery of the ophthalmoscope and a technique permitting photos to be taken from the retina. Hadamard (1945) was honest enough to confess that, he, too, had often overlooked important implications of his own creative accomplishments in mathematics.

As the process of preparation takes its course, the euphoric mood of the inspired individual may sooner or later give way to disenchantment when the creative process turns out to be more difficult than expected. The individual, whose imagination during the phase of inspiration has been soaring, may now undergo a metamorphosis and find herself or himself painstakingly inching along, much like a beetle caught in the sticky spider web of reality. The poet Shelley (Ghiselin 1985b, 20; Solomon 1988, 126) splendidly worded this disappointing transformation "The mind in creation is as a fading coal . . . " He emphasized that inspiration already declines as the writer begins to compose his poem. Therefore the most glorious ideas for a new poem will never find their way into a poem eventually published. In Shelley's case the glow of the fading coal was often not bright enough for the successful preparation and elaboration of his ideas. Finding himself stuck in the midst of one or the other phase of the creative process, he abandoned many a poetic sketch, because suddenly they seemed lifeless to him.

A creative process may get paralyzed completely during the phase of preparation, as seems to have been the case with Shelley. Individuals who have little experience with their own creativity may panic and insist on breaking through the obstacles blocking their path towards the progress hoped for, come hell or high water. Their efforts are usually vain; exceptionally, they may succeed. Individuals who well know the unpredictable nature of a creative process also respond with dismay whenever preparation gets bogged down. They choose a different coping strategy altogether to deal with the problem. Rather than stubbornly persist in target-fixation, they relax, put their work aside, and move on to something else, letting the unsolved problem drift into the unconscious mind. There it may discretely lie forever. Or, if one is lucky, one day, after a shorter or longer phase of incubation, illumination occurs and the phase of elaboration begins.

An excellent illustration of the above is Leonardo da Vinci (Pochat 1986, 256). Most of his ideas for portraits never went beyond preparatory designs. Nor did his grandiose project for the horse-and-rider sculpture, *il Gran Cavallo,* intended for Ludovico Sforza, the Duke of Milan. The bronze horse carrying a rider was supposed to stand solely on the hoof of one hind leg. Fortunately for his reputation, Leonardo did not have to prove that he was gifted enough to solve a static problem defying the technology of the time. In 1495, the invading French king Charles VIII approached Milan. Ludovico Sforza sent the seventy tons of bronze set aside for the *Gran Cavallo* to Duke Ercole d'Este in Ferrara, who cast the bronze into cannons and cannon balls (Kemp 2004, 35). The French conquered Milan, and five years later the Gascon bowmen of Louis XII, successor of Charles VIII, used the life-size clay model of Leonardo's *Gran Cavallo* for target practice.

Leonardo left more unfinished work behind him than any other creative genius ever did. He was a rather volatile mind with a thousand interests that went from drawing, painting, sculpting, and architecture to engineering and arms production, without forgetting playing Master of Ceremonies in court entertainment, exploring the anatomy of the human body, elaborate flying machines—not to mention mathematics, optics, hydrodynamics, aerodynamics, and many more. The sheer range of his interests increased the probability of his being distracted by continuously emerging inspirations while working through a phase of preparation or elaboration of an idea conceived some time ago. Although Leonardo was very ambitious, his ambivalent character often oscillated between alternative options. Decisions were postponed, procrastination blocked his progress, and his fancy would be captured by yet another new idea. As Walter Benjamin (Der Spiegel 1989, 200) put it, sometimes "the work is the death mask of the conception." It might well be that, beyond the shortcomings described above, Leonardo rejected that death mask; he would not accept but a pale reflection of the glory conceived in his vivid imagination, which had generated his original inspiration.

What can an individual do to support and improve the phase of preparation?

Many things, because the process of preparation is—to quite an extent although by no means completely—a conscious process. Creative individuals can do whatever it takes to improve their concentration, focus, and discipline. They may train their patience and capacity for coping with stress and frustration. They should accept the naturalist Comte de Buffon's often quoted dictum, "*le genie n'est q'une plus grande aptitude à la patience*" (genius is but a higher ability to show patience). They may heed the advice of the great samurai strategist Myamoto Musashi (1974, 91)—"Whatever the Way, the master of strategy does not appear fast"—and continue working stoically, moving forward step by step even when the going gets tough. They may turn on their imagination by searching for ideas, concepts, and methods far beyond the topic of their immediate interest, or even beyond their own professional domain. The missing link connecting what already exists to what should come next is often found in unlikely places. They may relax in order to improve the intuitive judgement that allows one to separate the wheat from the chaff, a mechanism that often offers a clearer view on the next step to be taken. In a nutshell, individuals blocked during a phase of preparation should honor a principle I formulated many years ago: in order to be creative, you have to work intensively and to dream extensively. Without intensive work in the action mode, a phase of preparation leads nowhere; without extensive daydreaming in the relaxed mode, a phase of preparation will lead only to a routine performance and not to a creative accomplishment.

To end this section I should like to state that some creativity researchers seem to believe that the phases of preparation, elaboration, and evaluation are totally conscious processes. This is far from true. In these three phases of the creative process, conscious and unconscious mental activities continuously interact. But while we are able to describe in some detail what happens during conscious work, we can only guess at what happens in the unconscious mind.

Excerpts from an interview with Ashok Kurien (7)

Ashok Kurien spoke about his rebellion as a youngster when he rejected each and every figure of authority. The interviewer told him that in those days he had behaved like the comic strip character Pogo the Possum whose maxim was: "Whatever you say, I'll contradict you; and I will fight to your death for my right to deny you!"

Now Ashok Kurien begins to describe, in his usual candid manner, his very first forays into the world of business, which included renting out porno magazines and stealing a school bell. These forays illustrate that a phase of preparation for future creative performance may originate in dubious circumstances and for some time follow a crooked trail, which is fortunately soon abandoned and left behind. Then one strikes a path that leads towards a promising career and an above board code of conduct. Looking back, Ashok Kurien also understands that his torturous, adolescent experience of repetitive failure prepared him to desire success and to strive for it, until he became the ethically correct businessman and doting father of two daughters that he is today.

In a second section Ashok Kurien tells the interviewer about the phase of preparation he went through, and is still going through right now, for the creation of the STORYEUM, the mega-project he is directing together with his partner, Pramod Kapoor.

GG: In those days you were continuously rebelling against your mother's authority.

AK: I'd rebel against anything! Anything she said, I would disagree with. I would find some reason to get into an argument with her. Today I don't. So I was a failure as a child; in the eyes of my teachers I was a failure as a student. I was a failure as a friend to the people around me, because I used them. But let me tell you, I learned about business when I was twelve or thirteen years old, in school. I went to a very rich school, the St. Thomas Cathedral Boys' High School, created a hundred and fifty years ago by the British. They set up the first Cathedral in Bombay, an Anglican church called the St. Thomas Cathedral, and those ex-pat British people needed a school for their students.

GG: You were born in Mumbai?

AK: I was born in Mumbai. So they set up this school for English students, and later only the very rich Indians and foreigners went there. But if you were a poor

Christian who sang in the St. Thomas Church choir, you could attend Cathedral school for seven rupees a month, which the church gave you as your allowance. All the other students paid a hundred rupees a month in those days. So everyone in Cathedral was very rich, a millionaire, or extremely bright, or the son of a very highly paid, successful executive, or the child of a wealthy foreigner.

GG: How did you get access to that school? Did your mother manage to place you there?

AK: Yes. My mother went to the priest who said, "Make him sing in the church choir; there is a scholarship for poor Christian students in the school." So as a very poor lad, I was up with these very rich people, and my complexes increased. Because I was no good at studying, I had to demonstrate that I was good at other things, whether it was sports or later with girlfriends, using my charm. But I learned something else: I learned the art of trading. That started with a girl I had charmed. She gave me a gold chain, and I sold it. Then I figured I could buy a guitar from one boy and sell it to another one at a profit. Do you remember I said I grew up in this lower middle-class locality, with these street gangs? When I was twelve or thirteen, two eighteen or nineteen-year-old neighbouring boys used to work evenings in a lending library. For four *annas* a day, which was a quarter cent or so, you could borrow a book. The library rented out cheap paperbacks like Mills and Boon, the usual junk. But they also rented out *Playboy* and pornography. So these boys took a big thrill in showing me things which no child that age should have been looking at in those days, and definitely not in India. When I went to school and told some of my friends what I had seen, of course they wanted to see it, too. So I said, "They won't let me take it; you've got to pay." They said, "We'll give you the money." So I figured I could pay four *annas* to the library and run a porn library in school during the lunch break, where several boys would borrow the magazine and pay four *annas* each.

GG: You could make some money by doing so.

AK: The boys would take turns going to the loo and back with the magazine. So I started making money when I was in school. That was my first understanding of business. Then after failing the first year in college, I went off to the village and figured out that if I was charming and clever I could make money. It was all illegal, immoral money-making, but that fundamental, basic concept of business is something that I picked up there and I never had an opportunity to use until I was almost forty years old. Yet once my self-confidence was strong enough, all of a sudden everything fell into place; the simple mathematics of making money emerged. So there was some learning in all that failure. Yet back then, in school, my popularity amongst my peers and my "business" success made me a failure with a lot of the kids, the prefects, and my friends' parents, who held special parent-teacher meetings to discuss my case. They asked: "Why is it that all the kids are running after Ashok?"

GG: It seems that for many people you were the devil incarnate.

AK: They asked: "Why do these boys all talk about this one guy who seems to be teaching the whole school all the wrong things? Including stealing the school bell!"

In the middle of the night, a one hundred and twenty-five-year-old bell, weighing 60 to 80 lbs, donated by the English Worship H.M.S. Victoria to the church, who gave it to the school, just vanished.

GG: It vanished?

AK: It vanished. We stole it!

GG: Did it come to the fore again? Or was it gone forever?

AK: Unfortunately it went into oblivion, although many years later we tried returning it. Because we couldn't be seen giving it back, we gave it to someone to return it to the school for us, but it never made it back. Anyway, that was a long story, one from my earlier years. All in all, I went through a continuous process of failure: failure in the relationship with my mother, failure as a student, failure as a friend, failure to be able to look after myself and to earn a decent living, failure as a husband, and then a firm determination not to fail as a father—because by then my professional success had started. So to make up for all my past failures, I think I went out to become...

GG: ... a very caring father.

AK: Over-caring.

GG: Overprotective too?

AK: I'm not overprotective, there are no double standards; but I'm very liberal, over-caring, over-worrying. In fact I'm surprised I haven't started lactating!

GG: Can you tell me something about the phase of preparation that you went through in the creation of your STORYEUM project?

AK: I went to Israel and South Africa.

GG: What did you study in South Africa?

AK: The Apartheid Museum; it's a wonderful museum in Cape Town. Next week I'm going to visit the Tate Modern Gallery in London and the Imperial War Museum, both recommended by this lady from Tel Aviv. I want to try to meet somebody who manages these places. In a project such as mine, success does not depend upon your plans and intentions but upon how you run it; that's the important thing. Since I don't know how to run our STORYEUM, I have to prepare for it in order to make the right decisions. Remember, when I first thought of that project, I knew nothing. And after having thought about it, I know no more than anyone else. So now I do my homework. And what am I learning? I'm learning the mistakes other people made and deciding not to repeat them. I know what I'm going to do, but I must learn what not to do.

GG: Yes, that's a good strategy, to learn from those who have done something similar before. Now let me move on to a further question. What are frequent obstacles that you encounter in a phase of preparation?

AK: People. It's very difficult to find the right people. I think everything else you can find if you believe in your ideas and if you know how to sell them, and you know how to persuade people. But finding the right collaborators is very difficult.

GG: There are two traps in selecting partners and collaborators: first there are the slick talkers who can easily persuade us that their integrity, competence and goal-oriented performance will match their rhetoric; second, you risk meeting what are known in German as "Bedenkenträger," individuals who pull you back with misgivings, doubts and apprehensions by moaning, "No, this will not work. I don't think we'll ever be able to do this."

AK: Or you find somebody who says, "Yes, yes, yes, yes, yes!" and then you discover he is not able to do it! You also want someone to question you, not just for the sake of questioning you, but in order to make you think. You must say, "Hey! I didn't think of that! Let me give it a thought." Particularly during the early stage: you've thought of it, now you have to mentor it. Once you've mentored it and got your team in place, let it go, and then you'll know where to interfere. I won't interfere in the content of the STORYEUM because I'm not a historian. I don't know the details of the history of our struggle for independence, but I know how I'd like to hear the story! So I will interfere when they interpret that content because it has to be told in a manner which I can understand and which the average Indian will be able to understand. The problem isn't what you're going to put into it; the problem is what are you going to leave out, because there is so much material! So I think that is the preparation. Now I'm going to start reading. I've already picked up books on the mutiny, on freedom. And I will keep visiting museums and shows and places where people tell stories; I think this is important. That's it! It's like boxing; I keep going back to boxing. If you take off your gloves, of course you're going to run into some problems! You're in that ring to win.

GG: Several times you have stressed the value of endurance.

AK: Endurance, yes; it's critical in anything that a creative leader does.

GG: I'm convinced of that.

2.34 Phase of Incubation

A great song matures in the womb of silence.

Gottlieb Guntern

During the phase of preparation, the pattern woven on the enchanted loom begins to develop its textures, shapes, and colors. A more or less complex

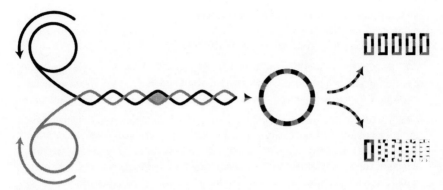

Figure 2.12.   Phase of incubation.

figure with more or less distinct boundary lines gradually emerges from the background of the fabric. The actual pattern woven into the visible tapestry and the virtual pattern designed in the weaver's mind seem to form a single web of interconnected threads. But this unity is treacherous; it exists only as long as the weaving process encounters no major obstacles.

If the weaver runs into minor obstacles, the unconscious mind speedily helps the conscious mind to overcome them. In this case, we may assume that minor incubations have occurred. But if the weaver comes upon a major obstacle completely blocking the desired progress, then the enchanted loom reveals its true magic. The unity between actual and virtual pattern begins to dissolve. Its constituent elements slip farther and farther apart until it ceases to exist altogether.

A weaver with little experience is utterly disappointed when the above occurs and, at a loss to comprehend, tries desperately to hold on to or restore the dissipating unity—to no avail. At this point, the duped weaver is thunderstruck. In the face of the same frustration, however, an experienced weaver will try to mend the cleft between actual and virtual pattern. Recalling Eugene O'Neill's (Gelb and Gelb 1987, xxi) famous statement: "Man is born broken; he lives by mending. The grace of God is glue!" But if the mending is not successful without further ado, the weaver refuses to waste precious energy. After all, there were other clefts before, some of which were eventually woven together again in the unconscious mind while others were not. But the unconscious mind must at least be given a chance to find the right glue and to undertake the mending.

During a creative process, whenever unsolved problems slip into the depths of the unconscious mind, their fate is uncertain. Many problems will lie there forever, definitively putting a stop to the budding creative processes. Other problems, however, will be solved and, by the same token, make their way again into the conscious mind with a perfect proposition for overcoming the obnoxious obstacle. The phase of problem solution occurring in the unconscious mind is called incubation.[6] It may last a few seconds, minutes, hours, days, weeks, months, and sometimes even years. In the section on the phase of illumination more will be said about this time span.

Following is a first example for a phase—or rather several phases—of incubation. For the sake of clarity, I should like to point out that the "periods of gestation" mentioned by the physicist Abraham Pais must have included not only phases of incubation, but also phases of germination and to a certain extent even phases of preparation. Pais (1982, 20), a one-time collaborator of Einstein, writes that, "Long periods of gestation are a marked characteristic in Einstein's scientific development." Einstein's interest in quantum problems appeared in 1900, but it took him five years to write a paper on the subject. In 1895, he had begun to think about problems of central importance to the *Special Theory of Relativity,* eventually published in 1905. Two years later, he began to deal with questions that in 1915 led to the publication of *the General Theory of Relativity.* Three years later, he began to think about the *Unified Field Theory,* yet he did not formulate his first draft until 1928 and continued working on the subject until his death in 1955. Today his *Unified Field Theory,* intended to weld quantum mechanics and general relativity into a single entity, still eludes the grasp of Einstein's followers. It remains an unfulfilled dream bearing witness to the fact that not only many an individual's incubation phase—but also many a collective creative process in cultural evolution—may get stuck for a shorter or longer period of time. In this regard, quantum physicist Steven Weinberg (Interview: DER SPIEGEL 1999, 191-194) stated with tongue-in-cheek: "Theoretical physicists like me spend the major part of their time wasting it. We try out many, many ideas which have but a tiny chance to function."

Nobody really knows what happens during a process of incubation, but on the basis of neurobiological data, concepts of psychology, and general human experience, we can at least make a more or less well-informed guess about these subliminal events. It seems reasonable to assume that during conscious as well as unconscious mental work there is incessant inter-neuronal networking. Quite obviously, mental ideas presuppose the existence of a biological scaffolding for their development: a mind needs a brain in order to function. The generation of ideas implies the existence of specific bioelectrical circuits, biochemical signal transmissions, the construction of new inter-neuronal synapses (protein bridges connecting individual neurons), and the simultaneous firing of interconnected neuronal cell assemblies. If the development of inter-neuronal networking and its concomitant unconscious mental information processing is successful, it produces a specific field gestalt. If this field gestalt corresponds to a problem solution that has unsuccessfully been pursued in the conscious mind during the phase of preparation, then that process of incubation may eventually generate a phase of illumination, which will present a satisfying problem solution to the conscious mind. If, however, inter-neuronal wiring and its concomitant unconscious mental information processing are not successful, then incubation will fail to accomplish its task.

Gwendolyn Brooks (Lanker 1989, 209-225), who won the Pulitzer Prize in 1950 for her poetry, once stated that, "poetry is life distilled." Her formulation is the result of precise observation. Life experience offers fruits. Ambition and desire provide fire. The mind is an alembic distilling a precious liquid, a mental cognac as it were, permitting people to enter altered states of consciousness. In an alembic made of transparent glass, certain aspects of the distillation process may be observed directly, while others remain invisible. The phases of germination and incubation are two invisible aspects of the mental distilling process.

Since incubation cannot be observed directly, some authors have assumed that it does not exist at all. According to Hayes (1989, 142), for instance, there is little evidence for the existence of incubation. He emphasizes that many creative individuals work non-stop at the solution of a problem without ever taking a break, which might permit the intervention of such a phase. Similarly, Perkins (1981, 94) holds that: (a) there is "no evidence at all for extended unconscious thinking;" and that (b) "the work of the unconscious usually concerns routine, entirely uninventive matters." As for Goldberg (1983, 66), he flatly states that most studies on incubation were not able to prove its existence and effect, while those that did have never been replicated.

In my view, these assumptions are quite mistaken. Below are a number of arguments to support my criticism.

Our conscious mind represents but a tiny part of our mental activity. While I am focussed on writing the lines of this paragraph, there are countless processes going on simultaneously in my unconscious mind. There is no evidence to support the assumption that most of those unconscious activities deal with "entirely uninventive matters," although many certainly do. Our unconscious mind is not a programed automaton executing nothing but boring, routine operations. It is an integral part of our brain's activity, continuously weaving new patterns of perceptions, ideas, and emotions.

While a creative person works consciously on a specific problem solution encountered during a phase of preparation, there is still tremendous mental activity going on underground. Ideas for a possible problem solution weave in and out of the conscious mind without the creative person even being fully aware of what is going on. There are countless opportunities for incubation that an unsophisticated observer may overlook. There are, for instance, periods of less concentrated work where the distracted mind is in a no-man's-land, drifting aimlessly between the realms of consciousness and unconsciousness. It is simply impossible for a creative individual to fully, consciously focus on a particular creative process for twenty-four hours nonstop. Creative individuals eat, brush their teeth, daydream, and talk with partners, family members, colleagues, and friends. They commute. They listen to the radio, watch TV, and read books and newspapers. They take walks. They go shopping. They attend parties. During the daytime they take a nap or two, during the night they sleep and dream. All of these activities offer opportunities for the unconscious mind to help the conscious mind to imagine, analyze, and combine possible approaches to problem solutions.

To pretend that the unconscious mind produces only routine operations is totally unjustified. The best proof lies in the testimonies of countless creative individuals, who are by their very nature keen observers with low thresholds of sensitivity to perception. Due to their heightened sensitivity to sensory stimuli, they are able to perceive what less gifted individuals are not able to. Observations made by highly creative individuals suggest that the phase of incubation does indeed exist and that, moreover, it plays a crucial role in the creative process. If contemporary scientific methods fail to cogently prove the existence and function of incubation, we have to assume that these methods are probably as fit for their purpose as a Palaeolithic stone club for playing a Stradivarius. Germination and incubation will be better understood when neurobiology, psychology, and cognitive science have taken great leaps forward. A sine qua non for such understanding will be that we are able to show how developing ideas and inter-neuronal events generate billions of bioelectrical and biochemical signals and are structurally and functionally linked.

To sum up my argument, I entirely agree with the creativity researcher Isaksen (1987, 59) who states very simply, "I doubt that any recognized person would deny the fact that incubation occurs and is frequently helpful."

Let us now mention a few of the observations made by creative individuals with respect to incubation and unconscious mental processes.

Henry James (Ghiselin 1985b, 16) wrote in the preface of his novel, *The American*, that he had dropped his idea "for the time into the deep well of unconscious cerebration," hoping that it might eventually "emerge from that reservoir, as one had already known the buried treasure to come to light, with a firm iridescent surface and a notable increase of weight."

The highly creative mathematician Henri Poincaré (Ghiselin 1985a, 27), one of the first scientists ever to deal with certain aspects of relativity theory and chaos theory, wrote about what he called the "subliminal self" which, in his view, plays an important role in creativity. Poincaré stated that conscious work was "more fruitful because it has been interrupted and the rest has given back to the mind its force and freshness." His scientific efforts, which sometimes seemed sterile, were in fact not sterile at all, for, as he put it, "they have set a-going the unconscious machine." Poincaré added that without the conscious efforts made beforehand, the machine could not have accomplished its task. He also specified (Ghiselin 1985a, 31) that the unconscious mind possesses the ability to select intuitively useful combinations of elements out of the vast array of useless ones. Moreover, he made the interesting observation that liberty reigns in the subliminal self and that this liberty is due to "the simple absence of discipline and to the disorder of chance" giving rise to unexpected combinations. Thus, as his colleague Hadamard (1945, 14) points out, for Poincaré "the role of this unconscious work in mathematical invention appears . . . incontestable." Poincaré also suggested that the thinker can make "a false start" and then get stuck in a groove by wrong assumptions (Hadamard 1945, 33); therefore "incubation would consist in getting rid of false leads and hampering assumption so as to approach the problem with an 'open mind'."

The famous Harvard physiologist Cannon (Cannon 1988, 63)—who introduced the term *homeostasis*[7] into medicine and modern scientific language and who was the first scientist to thoroughly investigate the physiological mechanisms of the fight-flight stress—stated, "As a matter of routine I have long trusted unconscious processes to serve me." As a student in high school, Cannon was repeatedly puzzled by "originals" in algebra. Often, after a night's sleep, he found out to his delight that he was able to solve them. On another occasion he tried to fix a broken mechanical toy in vain, went to sleep, and when he woke up the next morning, he knew exactly how to set the contraption going again. Later, he stated about the unconscious process of problem solution, "The process has been so common and so reliable for me that I have supposed it was at the services of everyone."

Similarly, designer George Nelson observed that often a problem solution "quite possibly won't arrive" unless one turns the active conscious mind off for a while (Armbruster 1989, 179).

Poetess Amy Lowell affirmed about the process of writing poetry (Armbruster 1989, 179): ". . . no power will induce it, if the subconscious mind is not ready." In other words, a phase of conscious preparation presupposes a phase of unconscious germination, and a phase of conscious elaboration presupposes a phase of unconscious incubation.

Lowe (Gerard 1985, 238), in studying the creative process of the poet, critic, and philosopher Coleridge, wrote that the poet's unconscious mind kept working on a problem while his conscious mind was occupied with toothache: ". . . there in the dark moved the phantasms of the fishes and animalcules and serpentine forms of his vicarious voyaging, thrusting out tentacles of association, and interweaving beyond disengagement."

About Hemingway, the biographer Baker (1980, 628) writes that ". . . a good half of his work is done in the subconscious," and that his writing improved whenever the unconscious work could go on in tranquillity. Similar statements emphasizing the importance of quiet and relaxation for the undisturbed operation of the unconscious mind dealing with complex matters have been made by a great number of creative individuals.

"I never try to force an idea," playwright Eugene O'Neill (Gelb and Gelb 1987, 439) once told an interviewer. "I think about it, off and on. If nothing seems to come of it, I put it away and forget it. But apparently my subconscious mind keeps working on it; for, all of a sudden, some day, it comes back to my mind as a pretty well-formed scheme." Once, having written the third draft of *Days Without End* and not being satisfied with his accomplishment, he woke up one early morning and realized that he had dreamt a completely different play, every single scene etched in his mind with utter precision. He sat down (Gelb and Gelb 1987, 761) and by late afternoon he had written a detailed scenario of *Ah, Wilderness!* Then he began to elaborate on the play, and once it was completed, he went back to his work on *Days Without End*. It is quite clear that germination, a (probably) forgotten inspiration, and eventually a phase of incubation had delivered, on the plate as it were, the whole scenario of *Ah, Wilderness!* Waking up generated a phase of illumination that thrust the content worked out by his nocturnal ruminating into his conscious mind.

William Faulkner (Oates 1988, 123), suffering from the sweltering Mississippi summer, once remarked that although he was not writing just then, "I seem to have a novel working in me," and he assumed that he would take pen in hand as soon as the cool weather arrived. We do not know enough about the actual circumstances in which Faulkner made his statement, so it might have implied a phase of germination as well as a phase of incubation.

Hadamard (Burnshaw 1970, 194; Hadamard 1945, 7) the mathematician offers an amazing example of problem solving accomplished during a phase of incubation. The mother and sister of the prominent American mathematician Leonard Eugene Dickson spent an entire evening trying to solve a geometry problem. Although they were in competition and strove to outdo each other, they were unsuccessful. Eventually they went to bed. During the night mother began to talk in her sleep, and her daughter woke up. She took notes while the mother began to develop, in a clear voice and step by step, the whole procedure of the mathematical problem solution. When morning dawned, mother was completely unaware of what she had accomplished during her dream, while her daughter was in possession of a ready-made solution she later presented to her class. *Se non è vero, è ben trovato?*[8] Hadamard states that his colleague Dickson asserted the accuracy of the story.

Fever, drugs (such as alcohol, coffee, psychedelic substances, pain killers, sleeping pills, cocaine, opium, heroin), or unusual experiences made in daily life are able to alter habitual states of consciousness. In altered states of consciousness, our imagination follows different paths from those trodden in habitual states of consciousness and may provide a glimpse into the mysterious underworld of the enchanted loom. Henri Poincaré (Ghiselin 1985a, 25), to give an example, was once working on a mathematical problem dealing with hypergeometric series. In the evening he drank too much coffee, and later, as he lay sleepless in his bed, he had a new and unique experience: "Ideas rose in crowds; I felt them collide until pairs interlocked, so to speak, making a stable combination." When morning came, all he had to do was to write down the results of his nocturnal musings.

Another example of drug-induced altered states of consciousness able to modify the whole creative process and consequently also the phase of incubation are the poets, songwriters, and musicians of the Beat Generation, the free jazz and rock music scene of the 1950s and 1960s. It is fair to assume that the creative breakthroughs in these fields would never have occurred without drug-induced altered states of consciousness affecting every single phase of the creative process. Under the influence of these drugs (heroin, cocaine, psilocybin, LSD), highly conscious concentration is disturbed and a dimming or distortion of normal consciousness favors the expansion of semiconscious and unconscious phases of mental operation. These drugs tend, moreover, to disrupt established inter-neuronal connections and the habitual trains of thought connected to them, thus facilitating the emergence of new and unusual mental associations and ideas.

There seems to be no method available for accelerating the phase of incubation. All the creative mind can do, therefore, is follow Paul Valéry's (Burnshaw 1970, 61) suggestion: "We must simply wait until what we desire appears, because that's all we can do." Similarly, Stéphane Mallarmé (Burnshaw 1970) gave the advice that one must "*céder l'initiative aux mots,*" (leave the initiative to the words) that emerge spontaneously from the unconscious mind. The conscious mind is like a cat waiting in front of a mouse hole. If a lurking cat switches to a frenetic action mode the moment it spies the mouse's whiskers, it will never catch that mouse. But if the cat remains in the relaxed receptive mode, watching motionless while pretending to take no notice of the mouse, then the little rodent will venture out into the open, and chances are the patient hunter will catch its prey. Waiting in the relaxed receptive mode is exactly what, in the course of their life, highly creative individuals learn to do—especially with respect to the phases of germination and incubation.

The next section deals with the phase of illumination. Many statements made therein will further elucidate the mysterious events that occur during the phase of incubation.

Excerpts from an interview with Ashok Kurien (8)

Ashok Kurien often speaks about the cutting-off process he finds so important for his creative work. He emphasizes that he consciously tries to "become zero" in order to overcome an obstacle blocking his way to a desired problem solution.

As we have already treated this subject, the following paragraphs are rather short. The reader is referred to the sections dealing with the phase of germination. What Ashok Kurien said there about germination also applies, to quite an extent, to the phase of incubation.

> GG: Sometimes you get stuck during a phase of preparation, so you drop the topic for a while. If you are lucky, one day you will find a problem solution that just pops into your head—often while you are busy working on quite a different task. Can you tell me something about that phase in your creative work? Something blocks your path to the desired goal, so you quit that path and chose another one until, suddenly, the elusive problem solution pops up in your mind.

> AK: For me it has to do with becoming zero.

> GG: Tell me more about it.

> AK: To become zero is to consciously tell myself, "I don't know the answer." When you become zero and empty, you can be filled. My knowledge and my experience are all up here in my head; they are not in my subconscious mind. The moment I convince myself that I know nothing, I become a zero vacuum. I can fall asleep, and at some point the subconscious mind takes over—whoever or whatever controls that subconscious mind—and invariably, that instinct, or that gut feel, comes into play. I call it a subconscious mind, because there are two distinct minds: my conscious mind, which is always doing things and is beyond gut feel and instinct; it is a mind of its own, a thinking mind; and then there is the subconscious mind.

> GG: If I understand you correctly, you are convinced that if you did not become zero, your subconscious mind would not...

> AK: ... would not come into play because my conscious mind would overrule my subconscious mind, and then the intelligent me would come up with an answer. And because the intelligent me has come up with an answer, I start believing in it and I pursue it, and very often it's wrong.

> GG: Your conscious mind blocks the access to the best resources. Is that your argument?

AK: It blocks the second mind. So you have to truly and genuinely believe you are dumb, stupid, unintelligent, zero: "I do not know the answer. I must let the power of that subconscious mind, or whatever drives and controls that mind, take over." For instance, I have often listened to four hours of mumbo-jumbo about recording devices, a topic which is very complicated and confusing, because everyone who wants to explain it only knows how to demonstrate it by being complicated! And that's where the fog is. When I become zero, I find I cut through the fog. I try not to get answers when I'm listening, although, very often, I do begin to get them. But invariably, when I become zero and cut through the fog, the desired answer comes: it is the solution to the problem. Now, if I have the solution, then I'm working bottoms-up; whereas in every logical problem solution, you work top down. You start off by saying: here is option one, I can go; option two is I cannot go. Sometimes there are several options. If I work only with my conscious mind, then I will come up with a "wonderful" textbook answer; and that answer is rarely original.

GG: That pretty much sums up what I wanted to know from you about the subconscious mind and its importance for producing an original and well-functioning problem solution. Thank you!

2.35 Phase of Illumination

They liked to come especially... while I was gently ascending wooded mountains in sunny weather.
    The physiologist Hermann-Ludwig Ferdinand von Helmholtz on the origin of unexpected insights.

The phase of illumination is an event that strikes with the light of deeper understanding. It marks a breakthrough and represents the happiest moment during a creative process. All of a sudden, a flash of insight brings the eagerly

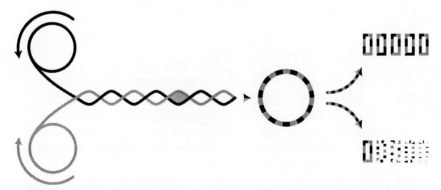

Figure 2.13.   Phase of illumination.

expected solution to a problem that had caused so many headaches during the phase of preparation before it eventually slipped into the unconscious mind, where it entered a phase of incubation.

In authentic illumination, the problem solution revealed by the unconscious mind is sometimes perfect and therefore definitive; nothing has to be added because the illumination presents, as it were, a ready-made fabric emerging from the depths of the enchanted loom. In most illuminations, however, the emerging problem solution is but a piece of a more comprehensive pattern yet to be elaborated. And in a pseudo-illumination, the problem solution that seems perfect at first turns out to be a complete illusion prompted by wishful thinking.

An amusing example of a pseudo-illumination is the following anecdote reported by famous film director Billy Wilder (Karasek 1992b, 160-167). Always on the lookout for a great opening scene for a new movie, Wilder feared that he might miss an idea that came to him during a night dream. So he consciously decided that whenever he dreamed of a promising opening scene, he would wake up immediately and jot it down. One night he dreamed of a grandiose beginning for a movie on whose script he had been working for quite some time. True to his decision he, woke up and jotted down the fantastic idea, then went back to sleep. In the morning he woke up, turned on the light, remembered his dream, grasped the notepad, and read: boy meets girl!

Illumination is often likened to a flash of light. Some creative individuals have spoken of a flash of real light, others, of an event appearing as suddenly as a beam of light cutting through the darkness when somebody turns on a flashlight. Many creative individuals have emphasized the strong conviction of being right about the idea in their illumination; others have ascribed a more hazy character to the same phenomenon. Some individuals have stressed the unexpected suddenness. Others, like Wallace (Hadamard 1945, 38) using the term "intimation," have reported feeling a vague sensation, a kind of foreboding that illumination was about to strike. To take but one example, poet Paul Valéry (Hadamard 1945, 17) once gave a speech to the French Philosophical Society conceding that, in the creative process, such a flash of light is hard to describe; he characterized it as "a gleam of light, not so much illuminating as dazzling."

There are some basic differences between insights produced by logical-deductive reasoning and those acquired in a phase of illumination.

• In logical-deductive reasoning—also called convergent thinking—there is a conclusion drawn from given premises, and to draw it does not require any creativity at all. The conclusion is in fact quite unavoidable provided the right premises exist, rigorous logic is applied, and no mistakes are made in deductive reasoning. When logical-deductive thinking eventually produces a problem solution, the solution causes satisfaction because rational thinking accepts it as being correct.

- In illumination, however, there occurs a leap of imagination transcending the implications contained in the premises. The solution offered by a creative illumination could never have been expected from what was priorly known, or from what was implicitly present in logical premises. Illumination is due to a process of unconscious divergent thinking. When it strikes, it provokes exhilaration of an ecstatic nature because intuition tells us that what we have found is not only an adequate problem solution, but also a very unique and valuable one.

Despite their differences, these two ways of producing a problem solution seem to share a few characteristics:

- There is always a period of prior conscious, disciplined work eventually producing an insight.
- The insight offers a problem solution that had eluded the problem solver for a variable period of time.
- There is a feeling of gratitude and satisfaction following the moment of insight.

There are some major differences between the phase of inspiration and the phase of illumination although both are sudden, unexpected experiences characterized by a discontinuous leap—accompanied by positive emotions—within the context of a continuous incremental process. Inspiration offers an exciting idea that may or may not instigate a successful creative process; illumination offers an exciting problem solution that had been sought in vain for a certain period of time. Inspiration may emerge without prior conscious work; illumination always implies prior conscious thinking during a phase of preparation or even a phase of elaboration. Inspiration is very often, but not always, triggered by an external stimulus. The stimulus for illumination is usually an internal one: the illuminating fulguration stems from the unconscious mind, discharging an inner tension built up over a period of time between a desired future state (successful problem solution) and the current state of affairs (problem to be solved).

When illumination strikes, it is accompanied by a flush of bliss and delirious excitement. These feelings are an integral part of an altered state of consciousness accompanied by heightened alertness and mental awareness. The whole experience is so spectacular that one is almost tempted to speak of a state of hyperconsciousness. Thinking is accelerated and grandiose ideas storm through the pathways of cognition. The enraptured individual is in ec-stasy.[9] Illuminated individuals have the impression that the heavens have be-stowed a precious gift upon them. Surprised and stimulated by illumination, they enter a peak experience where emotions of wonder, gratitude, joy, enthu-siasm, and pride prevail. The self is transported into the realms of grandiosity, and the blessed individuals are filled with the illusion of invulnerability. They seem to partake in a power that transcends them; the epiphany of an illumina-tion lifts them into the welkin, where they drift on cloud nine. Only individu-als of a rather sober nature, who moreover have had former experiences with illuminations, may react with an attitude of ironical detachment described in Bob Dylan's (Shelton 1987, 220) song "I Shall Be Free No 10": The singer is aware of the fact that he is a poet and he hopes not to commit major blun-ders.

Illumination typically occurs while the organism is in a relaxed state, also called a *tropho-tropic* state. In such a state of rest and recovery, creative indi-viduals may be daydreaming, having a night dream, taking an easy walk or a comfortable bus ride, sitting in a bath tub; they may be lost in thought in front of a painting or find themselves in some other similar setting. As a physicist once put it, illuminations often occur in the three B's: bath, bed, or bus. In the very relaxed state of sitting in a bathtub, lying in a comfortable bed, or day-dreaming while riding a bus, an individual switches off the activity of the dominant brain with its rational thinking and instrumental consciousness. Intuitive thinking prevails and with it, there is a consciousness of unity that may at times take on mystical proportions.

As illumination strikes, there occurs a sudden physiological switch from what physiologists call a *tropho-tropic*[10] to an *ergo-tropic* physiological state, in which there is increased awareness, mental alertness, and heightened activ-ity. As mentioned above, in a tropho-tropic state the organism is relaxed, in a state of recovery; in an ergo-tropic state the organism is in a highly active state in which work is accomplished. In an ergo-tropic state the verbal, para-verbal, and nonverbal output[11] rapidly increases in quantity, speed, and inten-sity. An illuminated individual tends to speak non-stop while sketching a picture of formidable achievement and success. The doors to the future stand wide open, and the illuminated hero indulges in a vision of many new hori-zons that will, no doubt, be conquered very soon. Volume, rhythm, and voice intonation increase, shouts of joy may reach a yelling pitch. Gesticulations are lively, rapid, and characterized by large amplitudes. Illuminated individu-als often walk around very fast and to a beat until their surge of energy even-tually ebbs away. They may dance, clap their hands, or pound their fist on the table in a gesture of fascination and triumph. The motto of the hour is, "Look Ma, no hands!"

In Zen Buddhism the phase of illumination suddenly revealing a long searched for spiritual insight is called *satori*. *Satori* is an epiphany able to give sudden significance and deeper meaning even to rather banal daily activities. The lay disciple Ho Koji (Suzuki 1970, 16) must have been in a state of *satori* when he wrote the following poem:

> How wondrous this, how mysterious!
> I carry fuel, I draw water.

As Daisetz Suzuki (1970, 220) states, "Where *satori* flashes, there is the tapping of creative energy." This energy catapults a specific content out of the unconscious mind and into the realm of the conscious mind. Strangely enough there are naive creatures who are fully convinced that creative illumination will strike faster and more effectively if their mind is free of prior learning, discipline, and hard work. For their own benefit they should take into account what Suzuki (1970, 22) wrote about the *satori* experience that an illumination will only strike the well-prepared mind, adding that it is". . . true that genius is born and not made. But it will never be brought out fully unless it goes through stages of serious and severe disciplining."

Physiologists Whitton, Moldofsky, and Lue (1978, 123-133) have stated that a hallucinatory experience resembles somewhat "the sudden internal experience of perceptual resolution in a creative task." That resemblance is confined to the sudden intrusion of sensory (usually acoustic or visual, sometimes sensorimotor) material into the conscious mind and to the vivid emotional experience accompanying it. But apart from these shared features, illumination and hallucinatory experience have nothing in common: they are tapestries woven on two quite different looms. While a hallucinatory experience is often quite frightening, illumination is always accompanied by happy feelings. Although there are exceptions to the general rule, most psychotics would prefer not to be hallucinating, but every single creative individual craves illuminations.

The phase of illumination is also called *heureka* phase.[12] According to legend, the famous Greek mathematician, engineer, and inventor Archimedes (ca. 287-ca. 212 BC) was once presented with a problem that pushed him to the edge of despair. King Hieron of Syracuse, a cruel tyrant, had given a large amount of gold to a goldsmith and commissioned him to make a golden crown. When the crown was delivered, the paranoid tyrant hedged the suspicion that the goldsmith might have stretched the gold with some silver, as the same weight of silver yields more volume than gold. In order to find out whether his suspicion was justified, King Hieron gave the crown to Archimedes requesting that he determine whether or not there was any silver in it. The king also specified that Archimedes was not to destroy the structure of the crown during his investigations. Archimedes pondered and pondered but found no method to solve the problem. The Euclidian geometry available at the time, used to measure flat surfaces bound by straight lines, did not suffice to measure the irregular volume of the crown with its numerous curbs, prongs, spikes, nooks, and crannies. The Riemannian geometry allowing the measurement of geodesic surfaces and lines, and Mandelbrot's fractal geometry allowing that of irregular, indented, and fragmented lines and surfaces would only be invented more than two thousand years after Archimedes' death.

Archimedes was in a fix. If he failed to find the solution to his problem, the irascible king might have him beheaded. Although the ingenious inventor and engineer tried every possible method he could think of, he was unable to produce a reliable answer to the king's question. Then one day, quite exhausted by his painstaking efforts, he strolled to the public baths to relax. As he stepped into the bathtub filled to the brim, he observed that the water overflowed. His intuition told him immediately that the amount of water pushed out of the tub corresponded to the volume of his body that was submerged. Thus the amount of water displaced corresponded to the density of a body. Electrified by his discovery he shouted, "Heureka! Heureka!" and, as legend has it, ran out into the town square stark naked. As he recovered from his ecstatic state he got dressed, ran home, put the crown into a container filled to the brim with water, and measured the amount of water displaced. Then he repeated the experiment with a piece of pure gold of the same weight the king had given the goldsmith. Result? The crown delivered by the goldsmith displaced more water than the piece of pure gold, because the fraudulent goldsmith had stretched the gold with some silver.

Legends often attribute the same events and behaviors to different individuals. A similar story is told about Pythagoras of Samos (ca. 580 BC-ca. 500 BC), who discovered the geometric theorem holding that the square of the hypotenuse of a right triangle is equal to the sum of the squares of the other two sides. According to legend he shouted "Heureka!" when illumination handed him the desired problem solution. Then, in gratitude, he offered the gods a hecatomb of one hundred oxen.

Whatever the origin of the two legends, they both describe a typical phase of illumination. In both cases, long periods of conscious and disciplined preparation followed by a stretch of incubation preceded the highly gratifying phase of illumination.

Illumination can sometimes arrive in two distinct phases. First, there is a picture in the mind of which one is perfectly aware. Second, there comes the verbal formulation of what the picture represents. As my own experience has taught me, the time period between the two phases can sometimes be quite long. When I began to ruminate about the content and form of the present book, and especially about a model representing the stages and phases that, I felt, were necessary for a creative process, I spent a lot of time thinking about the nature of illumination. Eventually, one day a picture came to my mind. It showed a swinging stable door closing with a click of the bolt. After some time this image was replaced by a visual representation of a kind of geodesic dome consisting of myriads of interconnected wire filaments. On top of the wire dome there was a single filament connected only on one side. Suddenly the filament made contact with another one and the whole structure lit up like a Christmas tree with candles and little lamps burning. This picture stayed in my mind for weeks and months before I felt the urge to formulate in words what I had seen in my imagination. When the verbal formulation was accomplished, I wondered why I had not written it down much earlier. The message suggested by the vision of the dome was, of course, the following: During a phase of preparation millions of neurons are connected by synaptic protein bridges, but without "clicking," without producing the light of sudden understanding. Then, during the phase of incubation, the inter-neuronal construction process continues in an inconspicuous manner until one day at last a hitherto missing inter-neuronal link is established. All of a sudden an idea, the mental equivalent of a complex simultaneous inter-neuronal firing, emerges into consciousness and illumination occurs.

Illumination takes place in every single domain where creative processes take place. But the most fascinating testimonies about the existence and true nature of illumination come from science and art, where creative individuals endowed with the gifts of self-examination, meditation, imagination, intuition, and proper verbal formulation have produced an amazing number of revealing statements.

Following are a few observations made by creative scientists with respect to the nature of creative illuminations:

- For years on end, Darwin collected data for his theory of biological evolution. In October 1838, twenty-one years before his great study *On the Origin of Species by Means of Natural Selection* was published, he understood how—given the fact that resources are often scarce—the Malthusian struggle for existence functions in plants and animals. About that happy moment, he stated (Perkins 1981, 53): ". . . it at once struck me that under these circumstances favourable variations tend to be preserved, and unfavourable ones to be destroyed." But he had yet to understand how the differences in species on which natural selection could operate came about. Although after years of hard work, he had all the relevant pieces in hand, he did not know (Cannon 1988, 66f.) how to assemble them. Then one day, he suddenly understood how the various elements fit together. He described his illumination with great precision: "I can remember the very spot in the road, whilst in my carriage, when to my joy, the solution occurred to me." His illumination told him that there were three conditions necessary for biological evolution: hereditary transmission of specific traits; variations due to random changes in the hereditary material transmitted; and subsequent selection by the environment. To put it otherwise: by means of genetic recombination and mutation, nature produces random changes in the genetic material; these changes generate a variation of traits in a species. From then on, there are two possibilities: (1) a mutual fit between the altered species and its environmental conditions occurs, allowing the new species to pass on their genes to new generations; (2) there is a misfit and the new species will be eliminated by the principle of natural selection. Now if we bring the Malthusian struggle and Darwin's theory together, we come upon a competitive fight for vitally relevant resources (food, water, territories, mates) between the different members of a species. The better fit would obviously win and go on to transmit their genes more successfully than the losers.

• The English naturalist Alfred Russel Wallace (Bronowski 1973, 306f.) discovered the principle of natural selection at the same time as Darwin, though quite independently. As he lay ill with malaria on his camp bed in the rain forest on the volcanic island of Ternate, Indonesia, he saw in his feverish dreams the safety valve regulating the pressure of a steam engine. With a leap of imagination, Wallace suddenly understood that natural selection must function like a safety valve. As he put it (Bronowski 1973, 308), "Then I at once saw, that the ever present variability of all living things would furnish the material from which, by the mere weeding out of those less adapted to the actual conditions, the fittest alone would continue the race. There suddenly flashed upon me the *idea* of the survival of the fittest." In 1855, he published his idea in a paper entitled *On the Law Which Has Regulated the Introduction of New Species*. Aware of the fact that Darwin had been working for years on a theory of biological evolution, he sent him his paper. Three years later the two men presented their respective ideas to the Linnean Society in London. This historical example raises the question of simultaneous discoveries and subsequent priority fights that, from time to time, mar the field of human creativity. Cheating excluded, when the time is ripe for a specific idea, it is highly probable that different individuals or teams, whether working together or far apart from each other, will simultaneously draw similar or identical conclusions from given premises. Thus they prepare the cognitive trampoline for the unconscious somersault producing a creative illumination.

- The physicist and physiologist Hermann von Helmholtz (Cannon 1988, 66) reported that his most fruitful insights never arrived "when my mind was fatigued or when I was at my working table." He emphasized (Rubinstein 1973, 207) that his "happy ideas" usually came to him after "one hour of perfect physical freshness and wellbeing . . . in the morning while awakening . . . They liked to come especially . . . while I was gently ascending wooded mountains in sunny weather." Characteristically, an illumination emerges when the organism is in a relaxed state, not involved in hard work, and not thinking at all about the problem to be solved.
- Famed mathematician and astronomer Karl Friedrich Gauss (Rubinstein 1973, 207) observed, "I've had my results already for a long time, but I just don't know how I can reach them." He could grasp them only whenever he got an illumination, as in the following typical example. For years on end, Gauss (Hadamard 1945, 15) had tried in vain to prove a specific mathematical theorem. Then all of a sudden illumination struck, and he later stated that he had succeeded "not on account of my painful efforts, but by the grace of God. Like a sudden flash of lightning, the riddle happened to be solved." He was unable to define "the conducting thread which connected what I previously knew with what made my success possible." There is only one thing wrong with Gauss' statement: the grace of God strikes only those who deserve it. To quite an extent, Gauss' success was also due to his prior conscious efforts to solve the problem although they had not been enough; illumination had to generate the final closure of a conceptual gestalt in his unconscious mind.
- The mathematician Jacques Hadamard (1945, 8) described his illuminations in a similar manner, using almost the same language as Gauss. He reported how, on one occasion, he was awakened from sleep by an external noise, and there it was: ". . . a solution long searched for appeared to me at once without the slightest instant of reflection on my part." He specified (Hadamard 1945, 15) two basic characteristics of the problem solution suddenly presented by illumination emphasizing: "1) (it) was without any relation to my attempts of former days, so that it could not have been elaborated by my previous conscious work; 2) (it) appeared without any time for thought, however brief." We must assume that there was, in fact, a relation between his prior conscious work and the sudden problem solution presented by illumination. But the solution itself did not emerge as a linear extrapolation from conclusions reached during previous conscious work. In his mind there occurred a leap of imagination generating a content-specific discontinuity and a deviation from his original cognitive path.
- The mathematician Henri Poincaré (1985, 26) once participated in a geological excursion. As he stepped onto the bus, he was struck by an illumina-

tion solving a puzzle in the realm of Fuchsian functions. He wrote later that it "came to me, without anything in my former thoughts seeming to have paved the way for it." There again we have an instance of a leap of imagination deviating from the cognitive trails previously tread. Yet such a leap needs a solid foundation, as a trampoline needs a solid metal frame and well functioning coil springs if the jumper is to produce a successful somersault. As Poincaré (Perkins 1981, 49) pointed out on another occasion, a sudden illumination is "a manifest sign of long, unconscious work," which can occur only after a lot of conscious work during a phase of preparation.

- In the chapter on incubation we mentioned the case of the Dickson family, where a mother unwittingly found the right solution for a mathematical problem during a night's dream. This is not as rare an event as it may seem. In daydreams and night dreams, imagination[13] roams freely, unfettered from rational thinking, and thus unusual mental associations and sudden leaps of imagination may occur. If the dreamer wakes up during those moments, a flash of illumination hits the conscious mind. If, however, the dreamer does not wake up to full consciousness, then the solution found by the unconscious mind does not produce an illumination. Therefore, it is fair to assume that creative problem solutions occur more frequently than dreamers are aware of. The following three examples illustrate the occurrence of illuminations during daydreams and night dreams.

- The chemist Kékulé von Stradonitz (Burnshaw 1970, 177), who urged his colleagues "Let us learn to dream, gentlemen!," reported a daydream in which he suddenly understood that the benzene molecule must possess a closed, ring-like structure, which had not yet been discovered. One evening, as he tried to work on a textbook, he got stuck and his attention drifted time and again to other issues. Eventually he turned his chair towards the fireplace and dozed off. In this dreamy state of semiconsciousness, he saw atoms flitting around and forming a pattern of rings. They began to wriggle like snakes until one of them bit its own tail "and the image whirled scornfully before my eyes. As though from a flash of lightning I awoke." He spent the rest of the night trying to work out the consequences of the hypothesis of a ring-like structure.

- Dmitry Ivanovich Mendeleyev (Kedrow 1973, 268) had been working for quite some time on a taxonomy[14] of all the chemical elements discovered at that time. Then, as he later told Inostranzev, one night in his dream he saw what is now known as Mendeleyev's periodic table: all the chemical elements neatly arrayed according to increasing atomic number. When he awoke, he wrote down what he had seen during his dream. Then he began to study his taxonomy and found, to his surprise, that only one correction had to be made where his dream had attributed a wrong position to a specific chemical element. To his utter surprise, his nocturnal illumination had even permitted him to predict the existence of two chemical elements (germanium and scandium) that had not yet been discovered.

• Perhaps the most amazing case of a creative illumination is the one reported by pharmacologist Otto Loewi (Koestler 1989, 205; Cannon 1988, 66). It proves, among other things, that the phase of incubation leading to a stupendous illumination may last a whole seventeen years! Loewi, studying the transmission of nerve impulses on muscles or glands, observed that the same nerve impulse travelling along a nerve axon had an excitatory effect on certain organs and an inhibiting effect on others. In 1903, he concluded that between the nerve impulse and the effectory organ (muscle or gland), a chemical transmitter substance must intervene. For a very long time Loewi sought a suitable experiment to test his hypothesis, but in vain. Eventually he more or less forgot the whole issue—until the night before Easter Sunday in 1920, when he woke up with a very precise idea for an experiment. He switched on the light, jotted down a few notes, then went back to sleep. At six o'clock in the morning he woke up and remembered his notes. To his utter dismay, he was unable to decipher his scrawl. He dressed and went to his laboratory, hoping that in the midst of his equipment he would be able to make sense of the notes or simply remember his nocturnal idea, but to no avail. Yet Loewi was lucky, because the following night he woke up at three o'clock in the morning with the idea for the experiment vividly in mind. This time he immediately got dressed, went to his laboratory, and began to set up an experiment that after a few trials and errors, proved to be, as Cannon (1988) later stated, "one of the neatest, simplest, and most definite experiments in the history of biology." How did the experiment work? Loewi put two beating frog hearts into two separate containers filled with a saline solution. He stimulated electrically the vagus nerve connected to one heart, and it stopped beating. Then he removed that heart and put the other frog's heart into the same solution. It immediately stopped beating without the electrical stimulus! Loewi had witnessed the function of acetylcholine, the first neurotransmitter ever discovered. In 1936, he was awarded the Nobel Prize for his brilliant discovery.

Many creative artists have reported instances of sudden illumination. What they have to say fits nicely with what the scientists have recounted.

William Blake (Martindale 1989, 215) wrote about an illumination that offered him an entire poem on Milton: "I have written this whole poem from immediate dictation, twelve or sometimes twenty or thirty lines at a time without premeditation, and even against my will."

Regarding *Thus Spake Zarathustra,* his rambling treatise on morality and philosophy, Friedrich Nietzsche (Martindale 1989, 215) wrote: "Everything occurs without volition, as if in an eruption of freedom, independence, power and divinity. The spontaneity of the images and similes is most remarkable." As we know, Nietzsche was a rather pathetic fellow; this may explain his exalted formulation.

The above examples need a short commentary. Martindale reports them under the heading "inspiration." In my view this categorization is inadequate for the following reasons:

- First, Martindale refers to Helmholtz, who in 1896 differentiated between four stages of the creative process: preparation, incubation, illumination, and verification. Martindale uses the formulation "illumination or inspiration" thus lumping together what does not belong together at all.
- Second, both instances reported above suggest that phases of prior preparation and incubation had occurred. Blake must have often thought about writing a poem on Milton before illumination unleashed "immediate dictation," as he put it. Nietzsche had had the idea for *Thus Spake Zarathustra* for a long time, then it took more than two years of hard efforts to write the book.
- Third, the finished form in which these texts arrived in the conscious mind (provided that Blake and Nietzsche are reliable sources of information) suggests that in both cases we are faced with a phenomenon of illumination.

For quite some time, Beethoven (Solomon 1988, 17) had been looking for the musical core theme for his "Ode to Joy." First he played around with an adagio but rejected it. When the desired "Joy" theme ("Freude schöner Götterfunken . . .") eventually struck, he wrote: "This is it. Ha! It is now discovered." On another occasion he was travelling in a carriage when he began to slumber and dream. In his dream, he heard a canon but it vanished from his memory before he was completely awake. The next day he travelled along the same route. In a letter dated September 10, 1821 he wrote to Tobias Haslinger (Solomon 1988, 73; Ghiselin 1985a, 42f.) that while sitting in the carriage, this time well awake, he suddenly remembered the canon again.

Poets have made particularly interesting statements about their poems that emerge without warning. It is well known that in poetry, individual phases of the creative process may occur simultaneously or follow each other with lightning speed. It is often therefore not easy to differentiate between inspiration and illumination, especially when we do not know the exact circumstances under which a particular poem was written. Nevertheless, following are three examples that, in my view, bear the hallmarks of typical creative illuminations:

- We have already mentioned Rilke (Sandblom 1987, 117) who, after writing two *Duino Elegies,* endured an excruciating phase of seven years' writer's block. Then, all of a sudden, his creative juices began to flow again and—under the impact of "a hurricane in my spirit"—within a few weeks he completed the elegies and quickly added the *Sonnets to Orpheus,* an ecstatic meditation on death and poetry. With hindsight, it is reasonable to assume that during the seven-year stretch of presumed non-creativity, germination, and incubation must have worked diligently in his unconscious mind.
- The poet Robert Frost (Armbruster 1989, 180) reported how one evening, while leaving his house to get some fresh air, he was suddenly presented, seemingly out of the blue, with the whole poem "Stopping by Woods on a Snowy Evening."
- Similarly, the poet and novelist Conrad Aiken (Armbruster 1989, 180) stated about the creation of a poem, "It seized me at lunch." Whereupon he left the table to write down what had stimulated his mind. As he put it, "Then it finished itself. In a way I had little to do with it."

Although in all three cases we have to take the words of the authors for granted, we should proceed with caution. First, these poets made their statements based upon their subjective recollections, and personal recollections do not always fit what actually happened. Second, poets may tend to have a somewhat exalted attitude towards their own creativity and thus display a tendency to appear more genius-like than they really are. Still, we have to admit that illumination in poetry is known to work in a very rapid fashion since, in a state of high inspiration, all the phases of the creative process can be compressed into a very short period of time.

For about two years, Goethe (Boden 1990, 238; Gérard 1985, 254) had carried the idea of writing a semiautobiographical epistle-novel entitled *The Sorrows of Young Werther.* One day he heard that Jerusalem, a close friend of his, had committed suicide. At that very moment Goethe had an illumination which he described as follows: "At that instant the plan of Werther was found; the whole shot together from all directions and became a solid mass, as the water in a vase, which is just at the freezing point, is changed by the slightest concussion to ice." This is a remarkable observation made by a remarkable man. There is a medium (vase) saturated with matter-energy in a specific state (water near freezing point). A random input (shaking) suddenly changes the field conditions and a new gestalt (ice) emerges. Now let us talk about the parallel. There is a medium (mind) filled with ideas (amongst others, the idea of writing a semiautobiographical novel). A random input (information about Jerusalem's suicide) suddenly changes the mental field conditions and a new gestalt (the precise plan for writing *The Sorrows of Young Werther*) emerges.

The playwright Eugene O'Neill (Gelb and Gelb 1987, 439) was known to be a very honest man, not given to self-indulgence and exaggerated self-admiration. He once told an interviewer that whenever he got stuck (during, let us say, a phase of preparation), he would put his work aside, "but apparently my subconscious mind keeps working on it" until one day, suddenly, there appeared "a pretty well-formed scheme" in his mind. O'Neill seemed to have had quite a congenial relationship with his unconscious mind because he once stated (Gelb and Gelb 1987, 515) with tongue-in-cheek: "Little subconscious mind, say I each night, bring home the bacon!"

The painter Wassily Kandinsky (1964, 39f.) described the development of art as consisting of "sudden illuminations, like lightning, of explosions, which burst like fireworks in the heavens, strewing a whole 'bouquet' of different shining stars about itself." In his view, these discontinuous leaps of illumination were but stages of growth embedded in an organic process of continuous, incremental development. He pointed out that a development in science often wipes out former assumptions and theories, while a development in the arts is of a different kind: "the organic growing of earlier wisdom which is not voided by the latter."

Picasso (Boden 1990, 17) made a more pompous statement about the ready-made contents of his illuminations when he stated, *"Je ne cherche pas, je trouve*—I do not search, I find." Although Picasso's declaration recalls a similar statement by Gauss quoted earlier, it is too grandiose to be true. First, Picasso knew how to play and to please a crowd. Second, great artists who knew him quite well—Georges Braque, Guillaume Apollinaire, and Alberto Giacometti to name a few—were aware of the fact that Picasso often found the things he allegedly did not look for in the work of other artists. He took and copied (some colleagues put it bluntly that he robbed and cannibalized) what he needed without bothering to acknowledge the actual origin of his ideas.

An illumination presents a sudden closure of gestalt. Although the structural components of that gestalt may be of a heterogeneous origin, the event of illumination welds them together into a single entity. A good case in point is playwright Arthur Miller (1987, 338f.). For quite some time he had been looking for a climax scene in *The Crucible*. The play was supposed to faithfully portray the anticommunist witch hunt, characterized by the almost hysterical frenzy of mass psychology provoked by ill-famed 'tail-gunner Joe,' Joseph McCarthy, in the 1950s. In the climax scene, Miller intended to show the blind hatred of an atavistic vendetta where horror, desire for destruction, fear, and piety intermingle in a dance of frantic turmoil. One day, while contemplating a painting depicting a judgement scene during the 1692 Salem witchcraft trials[15]—with the faces of victims and bystanders torn with rage, helplessness, and fake piety—Miller suddenly remembered a scene of dancing men in the Synagogue on

114th street in New York he had witnessed as a child. At that very moment, the two scenes blended into a single entity. As he writes, "Yes, I understood Salem in that flash, it was suddenly my own inheritance."

Illuminations often seem to impose something on the mind—as, for instance, the plan for Goethe's *The Sorrows of Young Werther*, a core scene for Miller's *The Crucible*, the music for Beethoven's "Joy" theme, Kékulé's chemical ring structure of benzene, or the proof of a Gaussian theorem. That is what prompted Paul Valéry (Burnshaw 1970, 52) to speak of ". . . those imperious verbal illuminations, which suddenly impose a particular combination of words." Where does this imperious, imposing quality of illumination stem from? It is due to the unconscious mental work that has discovered, by a series of trials and errors, the form best fitting the content to be conveyed. The intuitive judgment accompanied by strong emotions bestows upon an illumination its imposing character of absolute certainty that may be paraphrased as, "This is it! It's perfect! It couldn't be otherwise!"

Illumination—and its imposing, imperious quality—may be subjectively experienced as coming from the outside, from the environment. But in reality it is born of the inner sea of unconscious mental waves. Illumination may be compared to mythological Aphrodite, the goddess of love and perfect beauty, rising from the sea. In other words, illumination is what one may term an emerging quality. It resembles Anadyomene[16] a colorful epithet of the ancient Greeks to praise beautiful Aphrodite emerging from the foaming sea.

Illumination does not only offer a sudden and often long sought for solution to a problem. In my view it bears all the hallmarks of a creative leadership process whose participants are inter-neuronal cell assemblies rather than human individuals and teams. Its energizing power inspires, thus increasing the number and quality of mental associations. Illumination motivates because the exact definition of creative goals becomes clearer; there are now higher values attached to them, and the creative individual is ready to opt for the long effort and uphill battle that distinguish the phase of elaboration.

Excerpts from an interview with Ashok Kurien (9)

Ashok Kurien offers a lucid report about where, when and how he experienced phases of illumination that enabled him to offer his clients valuable problem solutions. What he tells the interviewer makes clear that he is a truly creative individual able to think "out of the box." He is a long-term strategist shunning micro-tactical problem solutions. His clients ask him for clever advertising campaigns. He offers them marketing campaigns because he understands that an ad is only a tactical element within a comprehensive strategy: the strategy must aim at marketing and selling the product. While talking about an illumination that offered him a perfect solution for an advertising problem presented by a client who sells a cooking oil, he describes details of the subsequent elaboration phase in which the idea presented by the illumination is transformed, step by step, into a concrete application that turns out to be very successful.

As Ashok Kurien emphasizes, his best illuminations come during the "Satvik hours." In the early morning between three and four o'clock when he wakes up from a few hours of deep sleep, the world is still quiet and there is, as he puts it, "silence, silence."

> GG: You have created quite a lot of things that we talked about yesterday. Can you describe the moment when the solution—let's say for the water campaign—hit home, and you knew, "This is it!" You knew that the bottle had to have a different design; that the name had to have a more poetic quality than "spring," which is abstract and mechanical in many people's minds. In the other examples you spoke about how you wanted to establish your own company; the propositions that you made to your clients with your ad agency because you offered them problem solutions. Thus you often lived through moments when a good idea, "That's how I'm doing it!" struck you. Can you give me examples of when and how an illumination, with a ready-made problem solution, pops into your conscious mind?
>
> AK: I think almost all of them come in thirty seconds.
>
> GG: Right! Where do they emerge? In a bar when you try to reach an emotional cut-off from your worries and the exhaustion of a workday?
>
> AK: Usually I'm in bed.
>
> GG: In the morning?
>
> AK: Yes, in the early hours; at 4 o'clock in the morning I'm up.
>
> GG: And then it's there?
>
> AK: It's there. I switch the light on and write it down, five pages, ten pages and I just keep making notes of the whole presentation, the logic. Remember I said, "Bottoms up?" I work the logic, then the whole rationale is written out, and by six or seven in the morning it's there, it's finished. Sometimes I jump up and dance on my bed! And I walk around the room.
>
> GG: Illumination is a state of great exhilaration.
>
> AK: We talked about Archimedes and his Eureka, when he ran out naked into the streets, and I thought it was a funny cartoon. It's not. I actually jump up naked and dance!
>
> GG: Can you give me some more examples of such awakenings? Can you state what kind of ideas for problem solutions you had then and how you reacted to them?

AK: You see, when you are in the advertising business, there's a process. You know the process: you're briefed, and then you discuss it in the office. Sometimes you go back to the client, or they come back to you, and then they leave you with the whole problem. Most people think advertising solutions. I don't often think advertising solutions.

GG: You go beyond that.

AK: I go for a marketing solution because most of my clients were Indian entrepreneurs, people who grew up in the stage of sale: produce and sell. In those days the Indian entrepreneurs didn't understand marketing at all. They knew how to produce a product, and it was sold in what we used to call "the Licence Raj" which meant that there were only three or four manufacturers. Nobody else got licences, so it was about producing, charging a premium, black market, etc. Suddenly the market opened up, and there was competition. So I realized that my strength lay more in inventing a marketing solution, which was very simple to translate subsequently into an advertising solution, which the creative people could interpret in a wonderful way. But the whole thing always worked because there was a great marketing solution, and that marketing solution was translated into great advertising. That's why we were very successful.

GG: Can you give me a concrete example?

AK: There was a company in India that sold a cooking oil called *Saffola* that was good for your health. It was the most expensive cooking oil. For years they had aimed their advertising at men saying, "It's good for your heart." So if you have had a heart attack this is the oil you should buy.

GG: It's healthy because it contains unsaturated fatty acids.

AK: Yes, Saffola is made from the safflower seed. It was sold in small quantities but it wasn't really going anywhere, so they asked me to handle the product. I kept saying that this was a great product and that their ads carried a good message: "It's good for your heart; you should buy it!" But there was a curative ring to that advice, and I thought, "What's the point of selling it in that formulation?"

GG: A formulation which carries the subliminal suggestion that you might die soon.

AK: Right! So I told my client that I went to a couple of stores that sold Saffola and asked, "Do your clients always come back for more Saffola once they have bought it?" He replied, "Some of them don't come back." I asked, "Why?" He said, "Because they passed away." So that is the problem! If you are going to sell it to guys who have had a heart attack, half your customers don't come back. You should be selling it to guys before they have a heart attack! That was the first proposition. Then I told them, "Sell it to forty-five-year-old customers instead of to fifty-five-year-olds. That way your market will grow from 100 customers to 500 customers. You have the opportunity to sell much more than you do now." So great, I came up with a solution. But then I turned around and said,

"I'm that age, but I'm not going to buy this product. Ask me why. I tell you why: (1) I don't buy the cooking oil in the house; (2) I don't cook; (3) I'm a mard. (Mard is the Sanskrit word for male.) Now in India, our mothers – not mine but most Indian mothers – make their sons believe that they are strong and inde- structible and they will live forever. So as a man you don't believe anything is going to happen to you, because the whole concept of health hasn't yet arrived in India. This was fifteen years ago. I told my client, "It's my wife who buys the oil because she's in the kitchen, she does the cooking." So I suggested, "Change your advertising!"

GG: Address the female customers?

AK: Talk to the wife, and say: "Your husband goes to work at 7 o'clock in the morning. He spends his whole day with huge stress. He's got a boss who shouts at him. Things go wrong. He's got targets to meet. And then he comes home. But don't forget: he is doing all this for you and your children. You need to do some- thing for him. Buy Saffola! Cook with Saffola cooking oil. Reduce the health risk that the environment imposes on your husband. Buy Saffola because you love him." So it was a complete turn-around. She gives him a longer life!

GG: So to buy that oil and to cook with it is a token of love.

AK: Right. It's the wife who is doing it for her husband, who is sacrificing his health working to make his family happy. In other words, I proposed they opt for a complete change in their communication; I suggested that they must reach out for another audience. Elsie Nanji and her creative people in the agency translated my marketing strategy into wonderful ads.

GG: So now instead of having a bracket of sixty-year-old men…

AK: … you aim at forty-five-year-old men!

GG: You also have a bracket of twenty to seventy-year-old women you address.

AK: Right. The wife always used to ask, "Why should I buy this expensive oil?" Now she says, "I must buy this oil to protect my husband." And she no longer asks about the price.

GG: Now you are dealing with prevention and rather than with curative medicine.

AK: I'm in prevention. And the whole strategy worked very well. Customers returned every week to buy the oil. One percent of them didn't come back. Maybe that's because they were all living longer and were healthier: their wives were taking care of their health.

Once I had the solution for a new marketing strategy, I called the creative people in my advertising agency together and told them, "Here is what I want : I want you to address my wife and say, 'Look what he goes through every day; he's almost dying. He's got to do this and that and under all that stress!'" Then I give examples of what a stressed man does and thinks: "I've got to catch a flight at five in the morning. I've got to get off the aircraft. I have to rush to that meeting. On the flight I'm reading, because I've got to make that presentation. I come back. I smoke forty cigarettes a day because I can't quit smoking. Then I drink because I just need to unwind. You can't change me, but you can help me. Tell my wife to do whatever she can! I don't want to hear her nagging. I have to work. I smoke, I drink, don't change that. Just tell her to take care of me." So they did many print ads and then translated the whole idea into a TV spot shot at night in dark blue and white. You see an ambulance with its flashing red light and hear its siren screaming. Then you see four guys carrying a man on a stretcher and putting him into the ambulance. You see this simple Indian housewife in a sari, sitting next to him in the ambulance. She's weeping, holding his hand, and praying.

GG: And she's thinking, "If only I had bought that oil!"

AK: Nothing is said. She is holding his hand and crying and you can see she's praying. She's just holding on to him. They reach the hospital – and it's all shot inside the ambulance. You see the ambulance doors open, these guys wheel the stretcher out. She's running behind the stretcher as it is being wheeled into the emergency room, and then the door swings closed. She's standing there, her back to you, and the voice-over says, "There's very little that you can do about the way your husband lives his life"—or some words to that effect. "You can't change the stress, you can't change the strain, you can't change the pressure." And right through this, at the bottom of the TV screen, we have the electrocardiogram, but we do it like in a panel. So it goes "beep-beep-beep," and it's getting weaker as we enter the hospital, and once in the room, it goes flat. And the voice-over says: "But you *can* reduce the chances by making sure his food is cooked in Saffola!" And then the ECG goes "beep-beep" again, getting stronger and stronger. It's a very powerful, very dangerous ad because it's borderline fear; very powerful. This was done fifteen years ago.

GG: It's a little arm-twisting, isn't it?

AK: It is. In real life, don't we twist arms? If I were a salesman sitting opposite to you and talking to your wife, Greta, I would sell it to her in a minute! I am a salesman. And this ad was extremely powerful. The sales of the most expensive oil in India doubled in the first year, doubled in the second year then just exploded; and it's most profitable.

GG: And the breakthrough of that idea came by waking up one day.

AK: Yes, by waking up one morning! I had put the problem aside and gone to sleep, and when I woke up, there I had one answer. But that wasn't good enough. Almost immediately I got the second answer for my problem solution. I understood that I had to switch from curative to preventive, and that I had to address female and not male customers. The question was: how do you talk to the woman, how do you make her love her husband? In the Indian context of sacrifice the wife returns the duty her husband takes on for her sake. Her husband is there to protect her and she, in turn, protects her husband. So the whole thing worked in this wonderful Indian ethos, and the sales grew.

In those days it was the owner who used to take the decisions, and he became very successful. But then he decided to hire professional managers and they said, "You can't scare people like this; you must talk about how the oil is good and healthy and you can have a happy family." That's what they did, and what happened? The sales slowly started to go down. By now I don't have anything to do with the advertising anymore; another agency takes care of that job. They've gone back to my idea in a gentler way, but creating the fear and telling the wife to look out for her husband's health. The awareness of the need to prevent health problems is now gradually increasing. In India, you must remember, we are still fifty years behind the West. We've got to talk to people the way you talked to people in 1950. And if you think about it, this would have worked in Europe in 1950.

GG: Yes, I'm convinced of that. And how did your mind work out this strategic solution? Under what circumstances did you get that phase of illumination?

AK: I honestly believe there is something that runs—and I'll talk about it later—my subconscious mind, which I've learned to switch off. So I go to sleep. Maybe my mind is churning it all around while I'm sleeping. When I wake up at four o'clock in the morning, I've finished with my day's problems and worries. I've rested my mind for four hours, maybe five. So when I get up at four or five in the morning, my mind is completely focussed, open, clear; and almost inevitably somewhere between four and six in the morning, boom! The light comes on.

GG: All of a sudden the solution emerges. So your solutions come to you mainly in bed. Where else do they come? Do they emerge in the morning rather than in the evening, or not necessarily?

AK: The preference is in the Satvik hours. According to the Veda, the Satviks are those who wake up at four in the morning and do their best thinking then. The early morning provides clean, fresh, uncluttered hours of thought. There is silence. There is nobody, there is no distraction, there is nothing.

GG: I know what you are talking about. As a student I used to work hard at night and then sleep until noon. But at the age of thirty my basic biorhythm changed almost overnight. I began to rise every morning between three and five o'clock and enjoy the serenity of the Satvik hours. I still do that today.

2.36 Phase of Elaboration

Creative performance is a domain for long-distance runners, not for sprinters.

Gottlieb Guntern

The energy provided by illumination is like the energy of a great tidal wave. It lifts creative individuals high up towards the heavens then catapults them

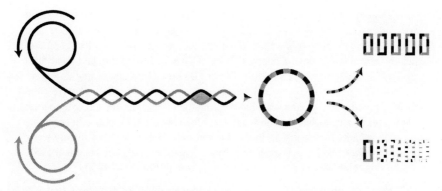

Figure 2.14.   Phase of elaboration.

on the shores of the process of elaboration. On rare occasions, a phase of elaboration may turn out to be short and not demand too much effort. Most of the time, however, such is not the case. As its very name suggests, elaboration usually implies hard labor and requires a lot of time, energy, and efforts. While the phases of inspiration and illumination fit the temperament and predilection of sprinters, the phase of elaboration is a domain for the loneliness of long distance runners: unwavering determination, stubborn endurance, and stoic stress tolerance are indispensable. There is rarely glamour in elaboration, but usually plenty of toil and sweat. The journey of elaboration leads out of the comfort zone and into the desert of stress and frustration. As the prophet Mohammed (Chatwin 1988, 21) once aptly put it, "a journey is a fragment of hell." The journey through the desert of elaboration confronts the wary traveller with a whole array of fragments of hell.

Metaphorically speaking, the days bring the torment of heat, the nights, the agony of cold; there are scorpions, lions, and quicksand; there are desert storms whirling the sand of resistance into the eyes of the traveller; many a *fata morgana* or mirage trick the traveller into believing that he is about to reach the oasis of desired success. All of this may sound somewhat exaggerated, but whoever studies the biographies and autobiographies of great creative personalities cannot help thinking that the journey of elaboration is usually an enormous challenge. The creative pacemakers of cultural evolution tend to pay a heavy toll for their ability to produce an authentic breakthrough that will thrust mankind and his quality of life forward in a significant manner.

As time goes by, the high-energy ergo-tropic excitement of illumination is replaced by a more habitual ergo-tropic daily labor of trial and error, stress, frustration, and pain. Bursts of ergo-tropic overstimulation and goal-oriented frenetic activity will yield from time to time to a tropho-tropic withdrawal to rest and recovery, and the exhausted individual may even show symptoms of resignation, apathy, and depression. Once the depleted energy reservoirs are filled up again, a new sequence of ergo-tropic assault on the task at hand begins. Thus ergo-tropic activity and tropho-tropic restoration tend to follow each other in countless redundant loops.

During elaboration, the deductions of all the preceding phases are worked out in detail. Mental plans give way to observable performance and its results. The various scenes and chapters of a new novel are written and may be worked over time and again. A scientific concept or theory is developed, step-by-step; complexity and degrees of differentiation increase; justified simplification reduces complexity; and qualitative and quantitative predictions are made. The plan for a new building must be polished before it is gradually implemented and the entire structure completed. The sculpture envisioned is hewn from a block of marble or welded together using various pieces of metal. The script for a new motion picture has to be completed, a producer and director found before the casting takes place, and the details of each role have to be discussed and agreed upon. Organizing the stage crew and setting up the technological equipment take time, for making a movie demands the goal-oriented cooperation of hundreds—if not thousands—of individuals. At last the actual shooting can begin, sometimes the same scene must be repeated over and over again. The rushes must be previewed and some scenes reshot until they meet the director's expectations. Then comes a long period of editing in the cutting room. The musical score is composed and revised until it perfectly suits its purpose. Finally the marketing strategy is carefully and minutely described before it is financed and launched.

The above statements might suggest that the process of elaboration boils down to work carried out consciously and with great concentration; but it is not as simple as that. Elaboration occurs also in the unconscious mind and leads, from time to time, to unexpected ideas produced by new phases of inspiration and illumination. In this respect, Jean Renoir (Sarris 1990, 11), filmmaker and son of the painter Auguste Renoir, once stated, "A time comes when you are no longer responsible for your creation, when it escapes you, and yet it still corresponds to the dream you've had and allows you to discover it." During a long phase of elaboration, a work is owned and disowned many times by its author(s), and conscious and unconscious elaboration follow each other in an endless spiral. The rollercoaster does not automatically shoot upwards towards the realm of higher perfection; it also plummets downwards at the risk of being smashed to smithereens in case of failure.

At times, especially in poetry writing, the phase of elaboration may be short. Robert Frost (Burnshaw 1970, 63) reported that the most precious quality of a poem "will remain its having run itself and carried the poet with it." In other fields, however, the phase of elaboration usually turns out to be a time-consuming and rather cumbersome process. It is the hard work demanded during the phase of elaboration that provoked the well-known statement (variously attributed to Edison, Einstein, G. B. Shaw and a few other creative personalities) that genius is ten percent inspiration and ninety percent perspiration. Stress tolerance, tenacity, perseverance, and endurance—qualities termed *sisu* by the Finnish—are essential. So are high concentration and resolute self-discipline. Precision in specific details generates better results than grandiose schemes for the overall quality of creative production. Sober organization will lead farther than high-minded, spontaneous ad hoc improvisation. Solid planning pays better dividends than ambitious daydreaming. Patience and a stoic attitude are of advantage, while impatience, irritation, and the greed for instant success usually bring but new frustrations. The general rule, nevertheless, has its exceptions because there are many roads leading to Rome. The following examples illustrate the attitude and approach to elaboration displayed by two writers of different temperaments and characters.

Playwright August Strindberg (Meyer 1988, 129) hated the detail work required during elaboration, stating that his mind worked incessantly: "It grinds and grinds like a mill and I cannot make it stop." He added, "I write and write and do not even read through what I have written." As he wrote feverishly, the completed pages flew from his desk; new pages were filled with text until he collected the strewn sheets together into a pile—and finished was the new manuscript! Due to his impetuous method of working, Strindberg was very productive in terms of quantity. But the quality of his work suffered; it is irregular and demonstrates how a creative genius can waste a considerable amount of his great gifts.

James Joyce (Ellmann 1982; Parrinder 1984) was carved from another block of wood altogether. His novel *Ulysses* belongs to the master works of all time. Joyce always spent years in writing a novel. When the phase of elaboration and evaluation were finished and the publisher got the manuscript, a new round of fighting for top quality would begin. Joyce used to ask for five proof sheets. To the utter dismay—and even despair—of publishers and printers, he would work those proof sheets over and over again. What was supposed to be a last glance at a finished work and a little polishing here and there usually turned into a marathon session of new elaboration. The volume of his manuscript, newly enriched by endless corrections and insertions, often increased by a third of its original size. But Joyce's patience and meticulous re-elaboration eventually paid off very well. He respected his outstanding talent and gave it what it deserved. With time his readers, acknowledging and admiring his genius, rendered him the recognition he had craved for a lifetime.

The desire to win a gold medal prompts many an athlete to compete in the Olympic Games, though not all of them will be able to satisfy their ambitions. Hemingway (Hotchner 1967, 123) wryly remarked that "greatness is the longest steeplechase ever run; many enter, few survive." This steeplechase, however, does not follow a simple straight line or a well-rounded ellipse. The actual trajectory pursued in the process of elaboration is often rather erratic and includes sudden stops, dead ends, and wide oscillations. There are redundant loops and backtracking that seem to lead nowhere. There is the excitement of an occasional breakthrough, followed by the doubt as to whether it is real or just illusion. Occasionally there emerges the merciless conviction that the whole enterprise is doomed to failure. In short, the phase of elaboration puts a person to the test and separates the wheat from the chaff, the top performer from the mere pretender. "The mind in creation is as a fading coal," lamented Shelley (Solomon 1988, 126). To keep the embers of achievement glowing during the phase of elaboration implies a daily battle against a great number of odds, and only a very determined individual will eventually win it.

The genius cult of the Romantic period was based upon the premise that a creative genius can reap the harvest of success without ploughing the field, sowing the seeds, watering the crops, and fighting off the parasites. People came to believe that a highly creative individual gets pregnant with great performance as easily as a naive maid gets pregnant with child. But a sober observation of reality tells a totally different story. Unlike in inspiration and illumination, nothing comes easily during the phase of elaboration. The high focus on achievement combined with the stress of elaboration can at times be so absorbing and exhausting that individual health and interpersonal relationships may suffer or even be ruined. In contradistinction to high achievers, poor performers tend to preserve their health and the quality of their interpersonal relationships, at the stake of ruining their work during the phase of elaboration. They opt for a premature closure of gestalt usually by accepting the first idea or solution to a problem that enters their conscious mind rather than training their tolerance of ambiguity and considering many possible alternatives before opting for a specific way to proceed. Where utter honesty of judgement should prevail, they deceive themselves, leaving their grandiose goals unaccomplished: the graveyards of creative ambitions are strewn with the tombs of self-cheating cheaters.

During the phase of elaboration there is a continuous, instantaneous evaluation of production; but the actual process is not so simple. As the creative process unfurls its many different folds and dimensions, new germinations, inspirations, preparations, incubations, and illuminations arise. Different creative processes may go on simultaneously in the mind of the productive individual, others will follow in a sequential order, and priorities may change.

Chaos and order, freedom and structural constraints, chance and necessity, rational calculation and instinctive-emotional-intuitive spontaneity embrace each other in a whirlwind. The creator's wheel incessantly spins the threads of invention and discovery. The fabrics woven on the enchanted loom unfold their hues and formal patterns, and the shuttle of associations weaves untiringly back and forth between the unconscious and the conscious mind. The whole, complex process of elaboration may, on occasion, turn into an erratic, discontinuous process with sudden starts and stops, stretches of highly concentrated work, and periods of faltering performance.

Arnheim (Perkins 1981, 19) described in a study on Picasso how the work on the enchanted loom may proceed: "An interplay of inferences, modifications, restrictions, and compensations leads gradually to the unity and complexity of the total composition." Arnheim characterizes that process as an unpredictable jumping backward and forward, from detail to the whole composition and back to the detail again. In other words, a creative process is not like the organic growth of a seed into a seedling and eventually into a plant, It rather resembles the erractic trajectory of a will-o'-the-wisp.

Working on what he intended to be "a simple quick 150 pages whodunit," William Faulkner (Oates 1988, 223) found that during the phase of elaboration his novel "jumped the traces" and turned out to be a rather complex and deeply significant work that he, somewhat disparagingly, qualified as "a mystery story plus a little sociology and psychology." The reader of a Faulkner novel intuitively witnesses how the changing of tracks on the enchanted loom produces a multidimensional tapestry of utter complexity.

Let us now quote a few examples of creative individuals who have made important statements about the phase of elaboration, or whose work highlights important aspects of that phase.

Beethoven (Perkins 1981, 136f.) was much admired by the Viennese society for his creative improvisations on the piano. But he was a painful planner and stickler for perfection when it came to the actual composition of a new score. In his notebooks (Ghiselin 1985a, 115), he focussed time and again on the various elements of a new musical composition. He jotted down fragments of themes and then developed and elaborated them over the years until he was satisfied with their form and content. Brahms (Isaksen 1987, 123), too, was a slow elaborator; it took him a whole twenty years to compose his first symphony.

It has often been stated that Mozart was able to write down fluently a composition he had already completed in his mind. These statements might suggest that with Mozart, elaboration was an ultra-rapid process. Indeed he was faster in elaboration than Beethoven and Brahms, but Mozart carefully composed a new work in his mind before he went for paper, quill, and ink. He was able

(Ghiselin 1985a, 115) to draw up whole symphonies, quartets, and opera scenes mentally before transcribing them on paper. As his biographer Einstein (1983, 149) affirms, writing down a score was for Mozart "a mechanical act" of conveying to the paper what was already completed in his mind. The idea that the actual process of writing a score was an ultra-rapid process has been reported not only by many witness accounts and by Mozart's own statements; it is also suggested by the visual aspect of his manuscripts. Obviously his quills wore down quickly and had to be frequently cut anew to make the writing sharper. His ink changed color because it thickened and had to be diluted in water.

Paul Cézanne (Doran 1978) was known to elaborate endlessly his sketches and paintings, perfectly illustrating de Buffon's statement that *"le génie n'est qu'une plus grande aptitude à la patience"* (genius is but a greater aptitude for patience). For days, weeks, and months on end Cézanne used to change and rearrange the lines, proportions, and hues of his apples and landscapes. His attitude towards art and the creative process is well defined in his assertion (Doran 1978, 14): "Art is a religion; its purpose is to elevate your thinking." It is his never-ending quest for perfection that enabled him to demonstrate the epiphany of his unassuming models, the revelation of their intrinsic beauty and spiritual power. Today, no art lover on earth can see, touch, or eat an apple without thinking of the emotional turmoil that Cézanne went through as he strove for ever-higher perfection in his art. His younger colleague Alberto Giacometti (Lord 1985, 446) paid Cézanne the ultimate compliment when he said: "And yet there is no painter as original as Cézanne."

With reference to the elaboration and ensuing evaluation of his novel *A Farewell to Arms*, Hemingway (Hotchner 1967, 47) stated: "I have rewritten the ending ninety-nine times in manuscript and now I worked it over thirty times in proof, trying to get it right." He also emphasized (Hotchner, 1984, 76) that he wrote each one of his novels "several hundred times," as he would rise early in the morning and first reread what he had written the day before. In that process he would discover formulations he did not like at all and improve them. Hemingway held a deep grudge against writers who shun the hard work of concentrated elaboration and defined his writing technique as follows (Hotchner, 1984): "Most writers slough off the toughest but most important part of their trade—editing their stuff, honing it and honing it until it gets an edge like the bullfighter's killing sword." Hemingway (Hotchner 1967, 221) was well aware of the fact that elaboration and critical evaluation require calm, rational thinking rather than emotional conviction, stating: "You put down the words in hot blood, like an argument, and correct them when your temper has cooled."

Similarly, the playwright Henrik Ibsen (Meyer 1985, 425) wrote: "At the moment of conception one must be on fire, but at the time of writing, cold."

Joseph Conrad (Baines 1986, 178) reported that it took him three years to finish his novel *Almeyer's Folly* and that "there was not a day I did not think of it. Not a day." Vladimir Nabokov (Field 1986, 123) once told an interviewer that he sometimes worked for twelve hours non-stop and that there are short stories on which "I have worked for two months. Sometimes it's necessary to rewrite and change every word."

On the basis of these examples we can easily imagine that a phase of elaboration was quite cumbersome in an epoch when writers had to write several copies of the same piece in order to get it right. Today, computers have made that part of elaboration a good deal easier. But win some, lose some: modern novels often seem to be hastily written. On the one hand, use of the computer allows writers more rapidity; on the other, there is the pressure of publishers and the greed of ambitious authors for instant success. This is a development the famous playwright Eugene O'Neill (Gelb and Gelb 1987, 630) anticipated long ago. He was a genius and a perfectionist who received four Pulitzer Prizes and a Nobel Prize for his plays. Disappointed by contemporary authors of novels, he wrote to a fellow writer that the most applauded modern novels: "... strike me as a dire failure." In his eyes they are all " . . . so padded with the unimportant and insignificant, so obsessed with the trivial meaning of trivialities ." O'Neill accuses these authors of neglecting the task of ruthlessly selecting, deleting and concentrating on the emotional impact ". . . which is the test of an artist—the forcing of significant form upon experience."

As the quote from O'Neill suggests, elaboration is not only a matter of the mere quantity of work; it is the intensity of concentration demanded, the sheer magnitude of problems grappled with, and the frustrations endured while trying to meet standards of excellence that make the process hard work. The higher the ambition of a creative individual, the more thinking, time, energy, and tolerance of frustration must be put into the efforts. As the painter Degas (Sandblom 1987, 27) stated about the art of painting: "It is simple before one knows how, but difficult once one has learned."

After having completed his masterful narration *The Steppe*, Anton Chekhov (Troyat 1984, 108), a physician by training and alluding to the fact that phosphate molecules play a role in the metabolism of the brain, confessed: "I have used much sap, energy and phosphorus; I worked with effort, with tension, tearing out everything from myself, and this has tired me terribly." Similarly, Paul Valéry (Burnshaw 1970, 65) emphasized that, "a work is completed only by some accident, such as exhaustion, satisfaction, the necessity of giving up, or death." He often repeated that a poet should be allowed to dedicate his whole career to writing variations on a single theme. Elaboration never ends in creators with high standards of perfection.

The intensity of ambitious work—Katherine Mansfield (Ghiselin 1985a, 19) spoke aptly of "terrific hard gardening"—transports the creative mind into an altered state of consciousness, where the worlds of imagination and reality intertwine continuously and with ease. Where the trails of those two worlds intersect, problems arise. The creative individual may become highly irritated when mundane claims are made on her or his time and attention. The biographer Benson (1984, 875) gave a beautiful description of how John Steinbeck elaborated *The Winter of our Discontent*: ". . . the process became a matter of trying to discipline the series of detonations that went off, so that the secondary explosions of insight and enthusiasm did not carry the writing process out of control." During that process Steinbeck was like a sleepwalker; he didn't respond when somebody asked him a question; and when they insisted on an answer he exploded in anger." John Steinbeck actually hated the final stages of elaboration and evaluation. He once sarcastically described (Benson 1984, 697) the activities involved in those stages as "dressing a corpse for a real nice funeral," the corpse being the body of his work deserted at that point by the twin souls of inspiration and illumination.

If creative individuals are experiencing severe personal and economic problems, then the process of elaboration is likely to prove very painful. The burdened individual feels like mythological Sisyphus schlepping his huge boulder up a mountain, or like Jesus Christ carrying his cross up the hill of Calvary. In such conditions, the creative process and steady elaboration of ongoing work are marred, and despair looms dangerously in the horizon. Faulkner (Oates 1988, 221f.) once spoke about his "spiritual cowardice" because years of marital problems, struggling with his own alcoholism, the alcoholism and eccentric behavior of his wife, lack of success, and an excruciating financial crisis had left him completely exhausted. He was so beaten and battered that he described himself in the following terms: ". . . all his bottom, reserve strength has to go into physical stamina and there is nothing left to be very concerned with art." But Faulkner, who had originally set out "to leave a scratch on the wall of oblivion," eventually triumphed over adversity. Despite all its shortcomings, the power of his character turned out to be stronger than the number and size of the obstacles fate laid across the path leading towards his desired goals.

It is evident that the process of elaboration must be the hardest in people whose standards of accomplishment are extremely high. Albert Einstein (Regis 1987, 23) once stated that he had thought "a hundred times as much about the quantum problems as I have thought about general relativity theory." Yet the desired goal of creating a coherent theory connecting quantum physics and general relativity theory into one, single, grand, unified field theory continued to elude him. Resignedly he confessed (Regis 1987): "All the fifty years of conscious brooding have brought me no nearer to the answer to the question 'What are light quanta?' Nowadays every Tom, Dick and Harry thinks he knows it, but he is mistaken."

Sometimes the elaboration of different productions appears, as if in the course of a whole lifetim, a creative mind doggedly pursues a single idea whose successful realization never satisfies his standards. Architect Frank Lloyd Wright (Gill 1987, 10) tinkered for over twenty years with the Oak Park house he lived in. He was constantly redesigning or rearranging the furniture in the house and studio, knocking down walls and ceilings, and erecting new ones in order to reach a more satisfying aesthetic effect. It is quite possible that Frank Lloyd Wright (Gill 1987, 461) may have been influenced by the example of President Thomas Jefferson, who had tinkered for over half a century with his buildings in Monticello.

In some cases, the inner elaboration in the creative mind may near perfection while the material elaboration of the creative design in space and time lags far behind. Leonardo da Vinci was a perfectionist when it came to his drawings and paintings. But the "prophet of automation" as he has been called (Galluzzi 1987, 79f.) was less of a perfectionist when it came to testing his technological inventions, although testing implies critical evaluation and is, therefore, an integral part of the careful elaboration of technical inventions. For years Leonardo worked on a mechanical loom that would automate the weaving process, bringing, as the proud inventor promised, huge profits to investors. Yet Leonardo never built a prototype for testing the contraption that functioned beautifully in his mind and in the suggestive power of his perfect-looking drawings. On another occasion Leonardo had promised (Galluzzi 1987, 76) the duke of Milan to cast a "Gran Cavallo" (s. 197) for the equestrian monument to Francesco Sforza, the duke's late father. The gigantic horse was supposed to stand on one of its hindquarters only, a proposition and technical impossibility provoking many nasty remarks from Leonardo's envious competitors. But, quite to the benefit of the inventor, war intervened and, as we have seen before, Leonardo was unable to test his planned technological invention and thus saved from further ridicule.

In the process of elaborating his schemes for flying machines, Leonardo seems to have gone through quite a series of tests, although nobody knows for sure how far these tests actually went. Today we assume that Leonardo never jumped off the roof of the palazzo Sforza in order to test his prototype devices. Yet he mentally conceived, designed, and elaborated on paper clever safety measures to prevent major harm, should such venture ever be undertaken. In his notebooks we read (Galluzzi 1987, 80) the following admonition: "You will try this machine over a lake, and wear a long wineskin around your waist, so that if you should fall you will not drown." As time went by, and as he further elaborated his schemes, he gave up the idea of a man flapping wings attached to his arms and legs and settled for a more realistic technique of "sail flying" like a modern glider. Though this approach was equally unsuccessful, everybody agrees that his investigation into the nature of aerodynamics, hydrodynamics, and turbulence phenomena paved the way for future scientists and technological inventors. It is, by the way, interesting to note that in the course of his research, Leonardo (Galluzzi 1987, 83) made the surprising discovery that aerodynamics and hydrodynamics are governed by similar natural laws and principles. In his notebooks we find the amazing sentence: "Write of swimming underwater and you will have the flight of the birds through the air." Today, if you watch a jumbo jet land at an international airport, you cannot help thinking of Leonardo: the huge plane lowering onto the runway resembles a whale sinking into the ocean.

Independent from the problem of testing hypotheses in real life, Leonardo was often a slow elaborator. While he was painting *The Last Supper* (Payne 1978, 114f.) in the Convent Santa Maria delle Grazie in Milan, he would sit for hours on end in front of his work, pondering and contemplating the forms, colors, proportions, and group configurations of the figures he was creating. From time to time he would slowly get up, climb the scaffolding, seize a brush, and paint a stroke or two. Then he would put the brush aside, sit down again or even leave the room. Taken aback by so much apparent nonchalance, the impatient prior of the convent eventually complained to the Duke of Milan in whose services Leonardo was employed at the time. The prior angrily protested that the master idled his time away instead of doing the work he had been paid to do. When the Duke asked Leonardo why his progress was so slow, Leonardo replied that "men of lofty genius" often work hardest when they seem to do nothing, because in their mind they think things over and over until they know what has to be done next. But men of lofty genius do not only produce sublime ideas, they may also fall prey to not-so-sublime emotions. Leonardo took his revenge. The face of Judas in *The Last Supper* turned out to be the faithful portrait of the nagging prior!

Leonardo's attention during an ongoing phase of elaboration was often distracted by new propositions and interests. He would quit a project, his employer, and even the city where he was working to look after his own interests. At such times he could be lofty enough not to care for the rightful demands and expectations of his patrons, who had paid him huge amounts of money for works commissioned. A typical case in point is the famous painting *The Virgin of the Rocks* (Payne, 1978, 71ff.), often considered as Leonardo's supreme masterpiece. According to the contract he had signed on April 25, 1483 the painting should have been finished by December 8, 1483, the feast of the Immaculate Conception. Yet it was completed only twenty-three years later, and by then the commissioned work had turned into two different paintings, both of which had left Italy. Despite a series of lawsuits filed by the prior, the Chapel of the Conception of the Blessed Virgin in Milan still had no painting.

We like to think of elaboration as a phase of continuous, incremental improvement of ideas, and that is indeed what usually happens. But an ongoing elaboration is sometimes able to destroy the beauty of form and the power of expression, leading downhill where uphill progress is intended. A good case in point is the poet Robert Browning (Burnshaw 1970, 74). His wife Elizabeth, herself a poet, used to persuade him to cancel certain changes made in the process of elaboration. She once told a friend that her husband never altered his lyrics without damaging the original conception of a poem. But this example should not leave us with the impression that poets do not win their uphill battles. In fact, most do.

Working alone in the woods near Pisa, the poet Shelley (Burnshaw 1970, 58) was once visited by Trelawney, who had the opportunity of studying the poet's manuscript of lyrics. It presented, as the amazed visitor remarked, "a frightful scrawl, words smeared out with his fingers, and one upon another, over and over in tires, and all run together." William Butler Yeats (Burnshaw 1970, 64) was called "the greatest remaker" because he heaped one version on top of another until the accomplished poem resembled his original vision. Alexander Pushkin (Briggs 1983, 45), who so eloquently wrote about "that blessed state of the spirit . . . when verses lie down before your pen and ringing rhymes run to meet up with a nicely turned thought," was, in fact, an incorrigible perfectionist, endlessly elaborating and correcting his lyrics and other texts. His biographer Briggs (1983, 98) rightly emphasizes, "Pushkin achieved his apparent spontaneity by hard toil and scrupulous revision."

While elaboration proceeds, evaluation continuously intervenes—as it had already during the phase of preparation. Nevertheless there is one ultimate phase in the creative process which is—with some exceptions, as the example of Joyce mentioned above proves—uniquely dedicated to critical evaluation. It comes after the phase of elaboration is officially terminated. Namely whenever the creative individual is unable to improve the new form any further; whenever the creative individual is satisfied with the new form produced; or whenever the creative individual considers the new form to be a total failure that has to be done away with.

Excerpts from an interview with Ashok Kurien (10)

Ashok Kurien speaks about certain aspects of elaboration. He is so full of passion for his work that he doesn't seem to suffer much frustration as far as his own creative contributions to a specific task are concerned. Yet in his role as head of Ambience Advertising and Zee TV he had to work with teams and hire professional managers, especially during the phases of preparation and elaboration. At times that co-operation turned out to be stressful and frustrating, especially if the co-workers ruined the result of his creative achievements.

GG: Once you have got a phase of illumination, there follows a long phase of elaboration; everything must be worked out in detail. You have had the splendid idea, the moment of bliss and happiness is over, now comes the nitty-gritty work. The saying "genius (or creativity) is ten percent inspiration and ninety percent perspiration" has been attributed to Einstein, to Edison, and to other people. So let's talk about the perspiration part: the ordeal of working out all the details until you have the final product to be delivered. Working out all the details in the planning and implementation of a project is often a long-winded process. Can you tell me more about the phase of elaboration, either in projects you did alone or in those you worked out with teams? Most creative achievements in today's world are made by teams rather than by individuals. Today this is the case even in science. If you look at the CERN (European Research Centre for Nuclear Science), there are teams with up to two hundred engineers, technicians, nuclear physicists, etc. working together. There is a lot of social interaction going on, criticism comes from left and right, there are cockfights between ambitious parties, and so on and so forth.

AK: Let's look at two parallel paths: there's the advertising business and there's the creation of Zee TV. In advertising everything is governed by a deadline, so you almost self-impose your deadline. We don't have the luxury of idly dreaming around.

GG: You are under a lot of external and internal pressure.

AK: Yes, so everything I do tends to have that time aspect. Often you ask yourself or your team, "Can't we cut the time shorter?" The faster you work, the quicker the process and the more work the same team can accomplish. Moreover, things get boring if they stretch out too long. You lose your passion. If I take half an hour to eat my bowl of soup, it doesn't taste as good as the first three spoonfuls. It's the enjoyment that also plays a role in the work. While the high is still there, you have to see the execution through. So I always work with a partner and maybe the two or three collaborators working closely with him; I don't move too far down the hierarchy.

GG: How do you work together with them?

AK: Once I have thought the strategy through, I go to the creative people.[17] I never leave the execution of my ideas with them too long. I want them to come back to me every day and tell me where they are going with it, what they are thinking. I want them to use me as a bouncing board.

GG: You go to the creative people? Are these the collaborators who call themselves the creative people? What do they do exactly?

AK: They do the art and the words; the copywriter and the scriptwriters. As for me, I have to have ownership of my ideas that are executed by them. Not only do I want to own the idea, I want to own the creative work itself. So I interact with that process all the time: "Why do you want to use this picture? Why do you want to use this kind of music? Why do you want to do this? Would it work with this? Can you say this? The sequence planned doesn't communicate properly. Can we look at six other scripts?" In that process I am involved in the actual detail interpretation of the creative process. I may sit with an artist and say, "I think we should paint a sunrise in the middle of the night," for example. So that's the idea. Now, when the artist starts painting, I say, "Why would the sky be mid-dark-blue? Why can't it be black? Would it look nicer in black?" I do think it's very irritating to be like that, but that was my role back then and it made me a very difficult person to work with. Yet each time I saw something good, I recognized it. Remember that many creative people don't know how to sell their ideas; now when I say "creative," I'm talking about the art and the designers. I was their champion, their hero because I led from the front. I went there and stood my ground and sold their wealth for them.

GG: With good arguments.

AK: With very good arguments and because I understood every step of the way!

GG: What about your own perspiration, stress and frustration in that process of elaboration?

AK: You know, when you are passionate about things, there is no perspiration. When I run—I am a sportsman—I perspire, but I don't feel the perspiration. When I box, I don't hear the sound of the crowd. There are five hundred people shouting, yet for me, in the ring, there is silence. When I train, I don't feel the perspiration. When I play rugby, I don't feel the exhaustion. I don't feel the perspiration, because I'm passionate about it. When I work, I don't feel the perspiration.

GG: The fact that you are a sportsman, a very well trained person, certainly helps your endurance, your perseverance, and your stress tolerance.

AK: It does, indeed. When I was doing Zee TV and Ambience at the same time, I worked seven hours a day in three time zones. I would fly to Hong Kong, work there all day, make the presentations, do whatever I had to do, and come back. I would be in advertising in the morning, and in the afternoon I'd be sitting with the television team, briefing the producers. I'd be at the studio at night, watching the shoot, then go back to see what my advertising agency people had done so that I could okay it, then return to the studio, and so on and so forth. On Friday night I would take a flight to Dubai. Friday is a holiday in Islamic countries, but a working day in India. So on Saturday/Sunday I would be working in Dubai, setting up the Zee network, hiring the people, going to clients and selling them advertising. Sometimes I'd go to Saudi Arabia on the week-end. I hated Saudi Arabia; I couldn't bear the corruption there, it was terrible! I'd take a flight back to Bombay at 3 o'clock in the morning India time, and at 9 o'clock I'd be back in the office working. This went on seven days a week, around the clock, for five or six years. I loved it! I'd work on the aircraft. I'd be reading something, watching some show-reels, checking my presentations, switching between four different clients – the advertising, the marketing, the programming – getting those teams together and asking myself, "What do I do when I meet a guy who's a cynic?" I had to convince him and make him a believer! If I couldn't make him a believer, then I'd have to forget the whole thing. But I was determined not to let him go, I was determined to make him a believer. I wanted to convert him and make him feel passionately about my ideas. I still remember we hired the CEO for Zee TV, and we sent him to Unilever, one of the biggest advertisers and clients, telling him to sell advertising space for a specific sum of money. I used to be a space-seller at a time when in my country no one knew how to sell television. So I actually created a method of selling television time in India.

GG: You said a "space-seller"?

AK: Yes, I used to sell advertising space. I forgot to tell you: one of the jobs I did was selling advertising space, and I did that before actually going into advertising. I worked for a girlie magazine called *Debonair*, something like *Playboy*, getting people to put advertisements into it. When you sell television, you do the same thing: you make people put ads on your channel, and I set up a marketing company for that purpose. So when our CEO went to Unilever, he had instructions: "Stick to this price." That's what he did, and they responded, "Nothing doing!" So he called me from another room, saying, "They're not budging. They won't pay us that price." This happened, by the way, in the early days of Zee, so I told him, "Walk back into that meeting room, pick up your papers and walk out." He says, "You can't pick up your papers and walk out on Hindustan Unilever. We need those guys!" I said, "Pick up your papers and walk out and say, 'I'm not going down on that price'." Well, he didn't have the guts to do it. I insisted, "Walk out! I'm telling you, walk out of that meeting!" Finally he walked out, they called him back and agreed to the price. So I actually had to make people believe in themselves. I believed in the product, and I wasn't telling you to believe in me; I wanted you to believe in my product. For this you have to be fearless, because if you fear the outcome, you will never cross the fence. Of course, you have to use good judgement.

GG: As a boxer you were well trained to cope with your own fear.

AK: Yes, I was.

GG: How did the phases of elaboration change as Zee TV and Ambience kept growing?

AK: I was still very close to the three or four key senior people. But the moment you hire a professional manager, he delegates work and the people to whom he delegates, delegate part of that work further down the line. For me it was frustrating no longer to be in close contact with the team members who did the actual work. But then I accepted the reality that I can't personally control everything that is going on in an enterprise which is going to grow so big. I accepted the fact that I couldn't keep doing things hands on myself. You have to let the teams do it. But I created the momentum; I put it there and got the movement. Once I had set it up, for ten years it kept going up to became number one. What is frustrating is when you move out of daily operations, and a new manager comes in and starts messing the whole thing up. You don't want to go back there and fight and argue. You try, but then you back off and just watch somebody destroy it. Eventually you go and find the right person, hire him, bring him on board and watch him take the enterprise back to number one, which is what has just happened again with Zee TV. It's back to number one. That's a tremendous joy.

But let me tell you my theory of "Mini-Me's," which no management book teaches. When you start a company or an organization, you do all the recruiting yourself. You are not aware that you are subconsciously hiring people who in some way are like yourself: Mini Me's! So the culture of the organization is you. It's your personality. It's extremely critical to ensure that this "personality" exists in all the people who work there: that protects the culture. The day you bring in a senior person with a different personality, you will find he cannot be part of your culture. If you make the mistake of letting him recruit people, he will hire his "Mini-Me's," and they won't fit into your company culture.

This is when your organization starts disintegrating, for you have allowed a split personality. Jekyll and Hyde cannot occupy the same space. You must ensure the top management are mini-me's at their core – their values, their passion, their humour, their talent, their craziness all connect with one another. Your culture will create a happy, powerful, creative environment with the strength of a Roman phalanx!

2.37 Phase of Evaluation

They boast that their wine is the finest in France and yet they find fault with every bottle they open.

John Steinbeck on French wine farmers

During the phases of inspiration, preparation, illumination, and elaboration, creators have continuously evaluated their progress. But now begins another ball game altogether. Once the phase of elaboration is officially completed and the new form achieved, there comes the phase of definitive critical evaluation. Paul Klee (Herbert 1964, 87) once remarked that an artist "surveys with penetrating eye the finished forms which nature places before him." During the phase of critical evaluation, the creative individual must examine with

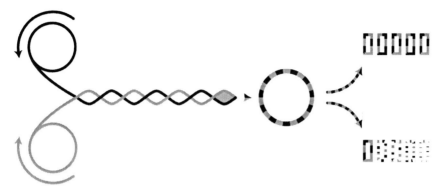

Figure 2.15. Phase of evaluation.

penetrating eye the new form produced by her or his own creative efforts. In cultural evolution, critical evaluation—whether made by the creator at the end of stage II, or later during stage III by professional critics and the general public—plays the same role as natural selection in biological evolution: it checks whether a new form fits the world for which it has been produced. That world is the domain of a creator's own ambitions, purposes, and standards of performance as well as the world of society's expectations and standards of creative performance.

Many questions must be asked during the phase of final evaluation. Does the new form correspond to the original vision that emerged during the phase of inspiration? Does the new form meet the criteria of creative performance and if so, to what extent? Is it unique, is it beautiful, does it function well, and does it generate values for society? If it does not meet these criteria, what is to be done with the new form? Should one try to rescue it through a new phase of elaboration or a whole cycle of germination, inspiration, preparation, etc. Should the new form be stored away for an undetermined time until one can deal with it again? Or should it be immediately physically eliminated so the creator can save face and/or spare the world yet another banality?

During the whole creative process, the creator often found herself or himself in a trance-like state, floating in the cosmos of perceptions, imagination, and meditation. The creator identified with the work in progress, and on the enchanted loom the tapestry of the external and internal worlds were woven together into a single piece of fabric. Creating subject and created object were often experienced as a single entity. The tissue woven by the creator's mental activities and the tissue woven on the loom of observable performance constituted a single, coherent web. During the phase of evaluation, creators must separate themselves from their finished work. They must become autonomous subjects standing outside—and even against—the object or event produced by their own performance, and look at it not with the eyes of a beguiled lover, but with those of a merciless opponent. In the diary of artist Ludwig Kirchner (Piweck 1991, 33), we find under the date August 4, 1919 the following note: "I must draw until I reach a state of frenzy (*'bis zur Raserei'*), only draw. Then, after some time, select the good ones." This remark contains in a nutshell the dynamic interplay between subject and object, imagination and observable performance, fusion and scission, alliance and opposition, admiration and merciless critical attitude.

Throughout the entire creative process, the work in progress has become one with its creator, infiltrating every single cell of her or his organism, vibrating in the cavities and folds of every single tissue. But now, as evaluation begins, a radical separation must occur. The umbilical cord uniting baby and placenta must be cut. Monism gives way to dualism. Identification must yield to alienation. Former 'also-me' must turn into 'no-longer-me.'

The creator-turned-evaluator must intuitively identify with an imaginary critic and visualize that critic's reaction when confronted with the new form. Even better, the creator must enter the mind of a harsh or even obnoxious critic to scrutinize the accomplished work with sharp eyes and a ruthless mind. To take such a critical stance is by no means easy. After all, a mother who has just given birth to the baby she carried for nine months in her womb is happy that the baby is alive. A quick look to check for any malformations in the face, hands, or limbs is easily done. But to ask herself whether the baby is beautiful or ugly, and whether it will later display a pleasant disposition or a quick temper are questions she will postpone for quite some time. Faulkner (Oates 1988, 221) once complained that after a long creative effort it is difficult to take a critical stance and described the situation with the following simile: "It's like standing close to an elephant, after a while you can't see the elephant anymore at all."

The more ordinary the talent, the more it will tend to be lenient in the critical evaluation of its own performance and the results thereof. The readers of the present book have certainly read and/or listened to interviews in which self-styled "creative" actors, actresses, and fashion designers praise their newest accomplishments in the most exaggerated superlatives. But upon discovering what those "creators" have actually accomplished, the public cannot be blamed for their sardonic conclusion: mole hills pathetically gyrating in birth pangs have produced but irrelevant specks of dust—for the umpteenth time! Paul Valéry (Rothenberg and Hausman, 308) once wrote that, "every true poet is necessarily a first-rate critic." This statement applies to great poets. Unfortunately, the majority of poets are lesser scribblers who make a living—and deceive their own selves—by pillaging the work of better poets; they a far cry from first-rate critics.

The greater the creative talent, the more it will tend to be inexorable in critical evaluation. The following two examples illustrate how merciless evaluation may function. They also show how creative individuals were hindered in carrying out their act based upon their evaluations and how, thanks to rescue missions, great creative works were saved from destruction.

As his biographer, Lord (1985, 492) wrote, Alberto Giacometti had developed "a character as strong as the granite in the mountains of the Bregaglia."[18] Giacometti was an adamant evaluator. Seized by a grandiose rage, he would sometimes attack and destroy his new forms with a knife or a hammer because he did not like what he saw. Fortunately he lived together with his brother Diego, who used to hide new drawings, paintings, or sculptures in order to save them. Without Diego, many a great creative work of Alberto's would not exist anymore. Lord (1991, 49) once watched as the artist carried piles of drawings into the courtyard of his Parisian studio and began to tear them to pieces and throw them into a garbage can. Lord tried to stop Giacometti and pleaded with him to look more closely at the drawings before destroying them. But Giacometti would not give in. He pursued his intention with a concentrated fury, betraying his deep frustration with respect to an accomplishment whose results he was unwilling to accept.

In 1945, Vladimir Nabokov (Field 1986, 314) stood in the backyard of his home ready to incinerate the manuscript of *Lolita*, a novel he had been working on for a year. "I think I could destroy this," he said, obviously displeased with the outcome of his efforts. Thankfully, his wife Vera told him to wait another day before throwing the manuscript into the flames, and thus it survived. It was the success of that novel that eventually permitted Nabokov to give up his teaching job and dedicate himself completely to writing.

In a study carried out with art college students, Getzels and Cshikszentmihalyi (Perkins 1981, 159) found that artists rated highest by external evaluators did not think that they had produced a definitive work, but rather admitted that it could still be improved. Lesser talents were more pleased with their own accomplishments. Complacency and self-indulgence breed mediocrity, whereas a pitiless critical stance facilitates the birth of great accomplishments. Paul Cézanne (Doran 1978, 15) once stated: "He who has not the taste for the absolute (perfection) is happy with quiet mediocrity." Cézanne was not of that breed and attacked many a painting with a knife in order to destroy it. He was more critical than anybody else towards his own work, relentlessly searching for the realization of a powerful vision; and when he was unable to meet the yardstick he had set up for himself, he was driven to despair.

Albert Einstein (Regis 1987, 40) was of a more moderate temperament, resorting to humor and irony rather than a knife when taking a critical stance with respect to his own creative accomplishments. Shortly before his death, he finished yet another set of field equations that, according to him, represented the simplest formulation of relativistic field theory that could be constructed. Still, he was not sure whether his newest equations really fit the observable facts and he stated that nature might ". . . obey a more complex field theory." The critical stance Einstein exhibited on this occasion—and on many others as well—reminds us of Claude Bernard's (Hadamard 1945, 48) famous statement, "Those who have excessive faith in their ideas are not well fitted to make discoveries."

Einstein knew how to separate the wheat from the chaff. The den of his creative achievements was more full with ripe grain than that of every other contemporary physicist. But Einstein could be not only humble and wise, he could also be self-confident and assertive in his critical evaluation once intuition and rational thinking had convinced him that his ideas and mathematical formulas fit observable facts. A good case in point is his reaction to the findings of a scientific expedition gathered on the Island of Principe off the northern coast of Brazil. The expedition, led by the British physicist Arthur Eddington, took photographs of a solar eclipse, and the ensuing interpretation of the material gathered proved that Einstein's General Theory of Relativity was correct: it predicted, among other things, that the gravity of a mass bends light beams. On September 27, 1919, Einstein (Clark 1972, 287) received a telegraph from his colleague Hendrik Lorentz, a highly respected physicist, announcing "Eddington found star displacement at rim of sun . . ." Shortly afterwards, when Ilse Rosenthal-Schneider, a disciple of Einstein's, was discussing with him a book attacking his theory, he reached for the telegram and handed it to her. Reading the text she was enthused over the fact that, four years after the publication of The General Theory of Relativity, his calculations had turned out to be correct. He did not seem to share her exuberance, simply stating that he had known all along that he was right. When she asked him how he would have reacted if the findings of the expedition had proved him wrong, he confidently replied, "Then I would have been sorry for the dear Lord—the theory *is* correct."

Like Einstein, playwright Eugene O'Neill adopted a highly critical stance towards his own plays and despised artists who did not. He once formulated his standards of perfection as follows (Gelb and Gelb 1987, 5): The supreme yardstick of creative accomplishment is "that significant beauty which is truth." Writers who didn't move beyond success and push for a abysmal failure were ". . . the spiritual middle-classers. Their stopping at success is the proof of their compromising insignificance. How petty their dreams must have been!" He made this statement right after the Broadway premiere of his play *Beyond the Horizon*. With this attitude solidly anchored in his heart, he went on to write a series of masterpieces that eventually brought him the applause, awards, and recognition mentioned earlier. The above statement is one of the proudest and most courageous I have ever come across with respect to quality control and self-evaluation.

In August 1999, at the *Festspiele* in Salzburg, I watched a solar eclipse in the company of composer and conductor Kent Nagano (former music director of the Los Angeles Opera and now Generalmusikdirektor of the Bayerische Staatsoper), who is well known for his resolute pursuit of perfection. As the sun disappeared behind the moon, the temperature dropped, birds stopped singing, and an eerie light provoked a kind of *Weltuntergangsstimmung*, a mood of impending doom. I quoted the statement by O'Neill, and it impressed Maestro Nagano very much. "This is a beautiful quote, and I shall remember it well and pass it on," he remarked.

At times even great talents may have problems with the phase of evaluation. Thomas Wolfe (1985, 203) confessed that he found cutting the "most difficult and distasteful part of writing." He went on to add that after having erupted like a volcano and having spit out ". . . white heat of his own creative energy, it is very difficult suddenly to become coldly surgical, ruthlessly detached . . ." Wolfe also remarked (Ghiselin 1985a, 203) with respect to the pruning demanded by critical evaluation: "My spirit quivered at the bloody execution. My soul recoiled before the carnage of so many lovely things cut out upon which my heart was set." In fact, Wolfe had been driven to despair in trying to cut and edit his novel *Look Homeward Angel*. His lack of discipline and his inability to clean out and streamline his own work was only partly corrected by the efforts of his editors. This is probably the main reason why today Wolfe is not considered one of the greatest writers of the United States. Just after completing his play, *Strange Interlude* in 1928, Eugene O'Neill (Gelb and Gelb 1987, 630) made the following deprecating statement about contemporary novels stating that they ". . . are all so padded with the unimportant and insignificant, so obsessed with the trivial meaning of trivialities . . ." As Wolfe's novel *Look Homeward Angel* was published in 1929, O'Neill could not have had it in mind when he wrote the above lines, although they do fit certain aspects of the book.

A critical stance towards one's own accomplishment is made easier if there is somebody who helps with the honing, weeding out, and mending. In this case stage II and III of the creative process begin to interact. This interaction can be quite stressful for all concerned, because individual standards, expectations, and purposes tend to vary widely. Vladimir Nabokov, who began to write in Russian, his mother tongue, later switched to English and soon mastered it. Still, he was not a native English speaker and needed help in editing his oeuvre. He knew, however, exactly what kind of help he wanted and what he did not want. In a letter to the editor, Katharine A. White, dated November 10, 1947

(*New York Times Magazine* 1989, 35), he stated that he wanted her to "weed out bad grammar," but made it very clear that he did not want "my longish sentences clipped too close, or those drawbridges lowered which I have taken such pains to erect." He also emphasized that it would not hurt the readers if they had to reread a sentence or two in order to understand it properly.

The critical stance towards one's own accomplishments is made easier if there is a certain time lag between the end of elaboration and the beginning of evaluation. Time becomes the space separating the creator from Faulkner's elephant; the longer the time interval, the larger the critical distance. After a while, one has forgotten not only the labor of performance but, often, also certain parts of its results and is able to look with fresh eyes at a work no longer deeply anchored in one's current emotions. This time-spacing is a technique that many creative individuals use to make sure that no mediocre performance slips through the sieve of their evaluation. To take but one example, poet Stephen Spender (1985, 125) wrote that he usually considers a finished poem to be his "best poem." Yet a few days later, "I relegate it to the past of all my other wasted efforts, all the books I do not wish to open."

In the section on the phase of elaboration, I mentioned that every step of elaboration is accompanied by critical evaluation. But the final evaluation of a work invariably leads to further elaboration, as it may also lead to further germination, inspiration, preparation, incubation, and illumination. Hayes (1989, 42) has collected a series of comments about these interlocking activities:

- Donald M. Murray, writer and Pulitzer Prize laureate, once stated, "Rewriting is the difference between the dilettante and the artist, the amateur and the professional, the unpublished and the published."
- Similarly, writer William Glass emphasized, "I work not by writing but rewriting."
- Dylan Thomas confessed, "Almost any poem is fifty to a hundred revisions—and that's after it's well along."
- Archibald MacLeish spoke about "the endless discipline of writing and rewriting and rewriting."
- Tchaikovsky made the following comments on evaluating and further elaborating a musical sketch: "This phase is of primary importance. What has been set down in a moment of ardour must now be critically examined, improved, extended, or condensed."

In order to improve a critical stance towards one's own accomplishments, some creators have developed a psychological technique resembling the split personality phenomenon often evoked by contemporary mass media, which seems to have fallen in love with the multiple-personality hype. But the technique is only a resemblance, as the evaluating creator is keenly aware of his own unique identity, while a person suffering from split personality is not.

• Charles Baudelaire (Kuspit 1985/86, 30) held that "an artist is only an artist on condition that he is a double man and that there is not one single phenomenon of his double nature of which he is ignorant." Although the statement was made from the perspective of a patriarchal society, it pertains to men and women alike.
• Paul Valéry (Hadamard 1945, 30) similarly maintained that it takes two people to invent anything, "The one makes up combinations; the other one chooses, recognizes what he wishes and what is important to him in the mass of things which the former has imparted on him." And he pointed out that the work of a genius is due more to the second role than to the first because a value judgement is produced by the critical mind. Valéry also emphasized (Hadamard 1945, 57), "You must be your own employee, your own foreman." The foreman plans and gives orders, the employee may have his own opinions and sometimes even offer them, but usually he shuns disputes and executes what the foreman says. The foreman then controls and evaluates what the employee has done.
• John Steinbeck (Benson 1984, 684) wrote about his mode of operation, "I split myself into three people. One speculates and one criticizes and the third tries to correlate. It usually turns out to be a fight but out of it comes the whole week's work."

Another technique to improve the critical stance is to imagine what one's close friends would have to say about the new work. Gabriel García Márquez (Armbruster 1989, 180) thus described his own approach: "In general, I think you usually do write for someone. When I'm writing I'm always aware that this friend is going to like this or that another friend is going to like that paragraph or chapter, always thinking of specific people."

Despite all the techniques to foster critical evaluation, the process can sometimes be hell for the creator and his colleagues. After a long period of hard work, the creative individual's organism is exhausted. It craves relaxation and recovery. Yet stress may be so high in this phase that sleep disorders further burden the individual already under great pressure. Resignation, depression, and apathy may set in. In what is known as helplessness stress, the immune defence system may break down and infections occur. Mental association is sharply decreased or even paralyzed, ideas have vanished into thin air, and there seems to be no chance for further inspiration and illumination. The whole of one's energy is gone in a moment where one would need lots of it to overcome the last obstacles. If high arousal state and low mood coincide, suicidal ideas may even emerge—and sometimes suicide occurs just after a successful accomplishment. The public rarely understands this phenomenon, but the explanation is quite simple. Unless individuals ending the phase of evaluation already have one or more new objectives in mind, after having achieved their goal, they now lose their motivation. Why? A state of motivation has three prerequisites: (a) a specific goal, (b) a value attribution to that goal, (c) serious attempts to reach the goal considered to be valuable. Once the goal is successfully achieved, prerequisite (a) disappears closely followed by (b) and (c). When loss of motivation, high arousal, and low mood coincide, then suicide may seem the best way out for the exhausted individual.

At a meeting of the Société de Philosophie in Paris, Paul Valéry (Hadamard 1945, 60) was asked how he felt after the completion of a new work. He stated frankly that it invariably turned out badly, adding, "*Je divorce.*" A divorce usually entails battles, disillusion, disappointment, separation, grief, and depression.

In December 1894, when Joseph Conrad (Baines 1986, 195) had just finished the eighth chapter of his novel *An Outcast of the Islands* and had yet four chapters to write, he clearly foresaw the stress of finishing the novel. He stated that he faced four centuries of agony and four minutes of bliss: "*...et puis la fin – la tête vide – le découragement et le doute eternel.*" ('. . . and then the end, empty-headed, discouraged and plagued with eternal doubt'). In psychophysiological terms, we would say that based upon his personal experience, Conrad knew that at the end of a long creative effort his organism would switch from the fight stress to the helplessness stress, in which the self-image suffers due to a state of depression caused by exhaustion and doubt as to the value of the accomplishment.

In December 1938, John Steinbeck (Benson 1984, 380ff.) was in the process of evaluating his novel *The Grapes of Wrath*, assisted by his wife Carol and his secretary Elizabeth. The two ladies endeavored to make the changes suggested by the publisher, while Steinbeck fought to defend his artistic integrity. The writer, lying on a couch to relieve his leg suffering from a streptococci infection, railed: "The book was not written for delicate ladies. If they read it at all they're messing in something not their business." But the two women insisted until the manuscript could be sent off for publication. By the end of the month, Carol was ill while John was in a state of near-collapse. In January things got worse. Not only did Steinbeck's leg not heal, he developed two ulcers at the base of one of his teeth and tonsillitis that required a tonsillectomy. As if this were not enough, the stress provoked by the whole experience wreaked havoc on his marriage.

For writers, the very last bit of critical evaluation comes when the proof sheets arrive. We saw in the last section how meticulous—as well as how expansive—James Joyce was when he read proofs. But there are writers who do not even care about proofs at all. Ibsen never read his published books, and referring to his plays said (Meyer 1985, 659) that they "are always better while still unwritten than when they have become reality. So one prefers the unwritten to the finished work." Although he was a very precise and disciplined writer, he stubbornly refused to read proofs, stating proudly (Meyer 1985, 605): "I don't bother about proofs." He had done his meticulous pruning beforehand, and once it was terminated, he could not bear to touch his work anymore.

Whatever the creator's attitude, sooner or later the evaluation is completed. The storm is over. The turbulent waves of moods and emotions settle down, gradually ceding to still waters. But although the organism begins to relax, the slowly emerging serenity may still be disturbed: looming in the distance is the uncertainty as to how the finished work will be judged by critics and the general public. Budding peace of mind may encounter a hint of inner turmoil, and a brief period of happiness, the simmering certainty of future frustration. The same frustration will appear again when the new work leaves the private sector to enter the public sphere, where it will be screened by readers, who may either reject it or give it a lukewarm welcome. It will also return when the germinating ideas and the inspiration experienced during the past creative process lead to a new one.

Whether the phase of evaluation (i.e., the cutting, pruning, and ruthless editing) is easy or difficult, at the end of the process the creator will have made a value judgement with respect to the new form achieved. It can turn out to be right, just as it can turn out to be wrong—independent of how severe the creator is with herself or himself.

The astronomers Nicolaus Copernicus and Johannes Kepler both calculated the orbits of heavenly bodies. Both had the idea that elliptical orbits best fitted their results. Yet both of them rejected their idea; Copernicus did so definitively while Kepler later gave up the concept of circular orbits and accepted the new concept of elliptical orbits. As Boden (1990, 83) wittily remarks, their critical evaluation "exemplifies cosmic irony rather than astronomical creativity." This example also shows that critical evaluation can be marred when a new form does not fit traditional views, established concepts, and the expectations derived there from.

In 1900, Max Planck discovered that heated black bodies emit their radiation not in continuous waves, but in discrete junks he called quanta.[19] Walking one autumn day with his son in the Grunewald Forest outside of Berlin, he proudly exclaimed (Clark 1972, 95): "I have made a discovery as important as that of Newton's." But his critical evaluation was ambiguous towards his own findings. Planck was a rather tradition-oriented man, firmly believing in

Leibniz's credo *"natura non facit saltus"* (nature does not produce jumps). Wary of the idea of discontinuous radiation, he remodelled the description of his historical discovery to make it more palatable for himself and the contemporary scientific community; he emphasized that it pertained only to the relationship between matter and radiation and not at all to the nature of radiation itself. With this opportunistic *Gedankenspiel,* he generated not only confusion, but also what a fellow physicist later called a "scientific scandal."

As Planck's example suggests, the sheer surprise of a totally unexpected discovery may make it very hard for the creator to evaluate it properly. Another example to illustrate the fact concerns quantum physicist Paul Dirac. On the basis of his calculations, Dirac (Lederman and Dick 1993, 275) discovered that for reasons of symmetry, every single electron must have its antielectron (today called positron). Accepting his own findings was rather problematic but, unlike Planck, he eventually did accept them and today his discovery ranks among the greatest in modern quantum physics. Meanwhile the hunt for antiparticles (particles with an opposite electrical charge but the same mass) is on—and so is the hunt for antimatter in outer space.

In the realm of literature, it seems that Hemingway's novel *The Sun Also Rises* was the only one with which he (Baker 1980, 398) was really satisfied. Yet it is by no means his best work. One day, Hemingway was standing in front of a painting by Cézanne. He confessed to a friend (Hotchner 1967, 205) that he had tried all his life to write as perfectly as Cézanne had painted and added: "Haven't made it yet but getting closer all the time." As far as power of vision, parsimony of means, and beauty of style are concerned, he eventually reached his ideal with his novella, *The Old Man and the Sea.* When it was published, the work (Lynn 1987, 565) was hailed as a masterpiece by some critics and torn to bits by others. But whatever the reviews, Hemingway (Baker 1980, 639) understood that with *The Old Man and the Sea* he had accomplished a feat "way past what I thought I could do." In a letter to his publisher, Charles Scribner (Baker 1981, 738), he was more modest stating about the novella: "It is as good prose as I can write as of now."

Excerpts from an interview with Ashok Kurien (11)

Ashok Kurien is known to be a perfectionist. The interviewer wants to know how his self-evaluation works when he looks with a critical eye on the result of a new achievement. Kurien makes clear that there is a positive feedback loop: great performance increases self-confidence, high self-confidence increases the quality of performance. Once again he uses the field of sport to illustrate how that feedback loop works—and how it impacts the client who buys his product. "Believing," "passion" and "winning" are key words in Ashok Kurien's vocabulary. However, he is by no means autistic in his strategy. Quite to the contrary, he emphasizes the importance of empathy, the ability to see the result of his achievement with the eyes of the client. Metaphorically speaking, he enters his client's head, sits in his client's skull, and looks on his achievement with the brain and the eyes of his client. Being a stickler for perfection, he supervises every detail of a specific performance. And if a team member does not measure up to the yardstick of quality he has set up, then he delegates the job of quality enhancement to someone else. Being a very creative entrepreneur, he takes a dim view of managers who do not work with their own money: he certainly does not believe in the manager-myth propagated by business schools singing their own praise. In his experience brand managers are confused creatures who see thousands of trees but no forest; they are detail-centred bureaucrats utterly devoid of the imagination and intuition which are hallmarks of creative individuals. And, last but not least, Ashok Kurien also makes clear that he considers advertising to be a "sick business." That is why he left that sphere and entered greener pastures.

Particularly striking in what Ashok Kurien reports is the following insight: years of striving for perfection have built a huge stock of experience that feeds his intuition. He trusts his intuition more than he trusts market research. But, always being the perfectionist that he is, he probes from time to time and does some after-the-fact market research to check rationally the quality of what his intuition had told him to do.

Although Ashok Kurien is a very successful entrepreneur, he has no room for complacency. As he puts it, "You cannot be a leader of quality if you don't complain." He always finds that the best he has accomplished can still be improved.

GG: So, eventually, once you have elaborated, polished, finished your project, your service, or whatever else you do in a creative manner, comes an ultimate phase: you evaluate. What is it worth? Does it really achieve what it is supposed to achieve? Did I do my best? Can I live with that? Is it good enough? You separate the wheat from the chaff; you decide whether that's it, or no, it's not good enough. John Steinbeck once said that a writer should behave towards the novel he has finished like a good French winegrower towards his wine. Every French wine grower is deeply convinced that he produces the best wine in the country. But with every single bottle he brings up from his cellar, opens and tastes, he finds something that could still be still improved. This should be the attitude.

AK: Absolutely, that's very important!

GG: Let's talk about evaluation: you are a creator. How do you evaluate the result of your creative efforts?

AK: There are two stages. The first is my self-evaluation before I take it to market.

GG: You are talking about your evaluation, the creator's evaluation?

AK: My evaluation; it's not the public evaluation.

GG: No, that comes later.

AK: You have to feel it was the best job you could've done. If it doesn't fit into some number-one rating, it doesn't make sense. You don't want to be number two. At least it's got to be a benchmark of the best; but you evaluate it within the constraints in which you made it. Without finding excuses, the truth is I would love to have a hundred million dollars to do my Storyeum, but I don't. I only have thirty or forty. I will have to tailor that forty to produce the best product I can possibly produce. It won't necessarily be the best product in the world. So there is a limitation. You've got to ask yourself, "Did I do my best?" Invariably I know I've done my best; but when you work with teams, it's vital that the important team players also feel that they've done their best. Now at this stage, before you go to market—for example, if it's a campaign I am selling to a client or before I launch a new product—I have to *believe* it is the best. If I don't, I can't wave that flag and tell all my people to follow me and have them believing it's the best. So sometimes you convince yourself that this is truly the best and that it's number one. When you go forth with that attitude, half the battle is won. You can't always be number one. Maybe I've had the good fortune of pretty much being number one at some stage in many things that I've done; the good fortune of doing five or six "firsts" in a country or playing some part in it is unique. Simply by being first in market, you are number one. If you get that lead and hold on to it, you're still number one. Then you can sell your product with the passion and conviction and faith you have with respect to your achievement. When you are full of conviction that it is going to work, everything you do around it is one hundred percent. I will go to the best guy who can do a specific part of our project. If it doesn't work with him, I'll find someone else, but this time I'll see it through. The crucial thing is to believe you're a winner before you win. How do you win a race? You're down there on your knees, it's a hundred metre sprint, you're only on your marks. You're looking down. You need ten seconds, and in those ten seconds, you have lived every step of that race. You've even seen yourself on the finish line. The gun goes off, you leave. In your head you've won. If you haven't won in your head, how can you win in your body? In other words, first you sell the new product in your head and then you go to sell it to your client. When you go to sell it, the client may tell you, "Oh, no, this is wrong!" Or a customer might say, "I don't think this works," and then you get some feedback. At this point you can either throw the whole thing out, or you can fine-tune it until it is perfect.

GG: What are your own yardsticks for quality? How do you intuitively and analytically measure what you've accomplished before you take it to your client or put it on the market or whatever?

AK: I try not to go into the market unless I am convinced that it is good.

GG: How do you convince yourself that it is good? What are the criteria? What makes something bad, quite good, really fine, or top?

AK: The question you very often have to ask yourself honestly is, "Would I buy it if I were the customer?" If my mother is the customer, I have to ask, "Would she buy it?" If my girlfriend is the customer, I have to ask, "Will she buy it?" I think you need to put yourself in that person's place, and even sometimes talk to them. Too much research is no good. I love using research to tell me whether what I did is right or wrong, but I do it after having finished my task.

I think I have the gift of empathy. I have lived different lives with people of all ages and all incomes – from the poorest in a village to the richest in the country. So I can put myself in that person's head and get a pretty clear picture.

My relatives in small towns would not buy a specific ointment for headaches and another one for backaches. That's for the richer folk. They would buy one tube that deals with both problems and save money. They need a two-in-one, so I wouldn't try selling them two different ones. That's where empathy helps me understand people's needs and arrive at strategic marketing solutions.

GG: You begin to waver?

AK: You waver. You need some knowledge, some data, but you need only what is important.

GG: Can you give me a concrete example?

AK: I'm going to launch a new water product. I say, "I am not going to tell you about it right now because it has got a secret ingredient with a secret benefit which the whole world wants: it's going to make you ten years younger! So you will drink it too, my friend."

GG: I see.

AK: I spoke to the owner of the company, Ramesh Chauhan, my very good friend, and I said, "This one is radical. Do you think we should research it?" He replied, "Ashok, I've known you for twenty-five years, and you've never done any bloody research! You have always told me, 'I know this will work' and you've done it, and it works. Now even I'll get confused! So why don't we do it the same way? Just launch it, man, and we'll research it afterwards." And I thought, "Wow!" How reassuring, when I was beginning to waver. Too many questions had popped up, but his statement gave me back that total confidence: I have a winner. In fact we are now debating the price, and I'm saying that it must meet the same prices as Coca-Cola or anyone else. But he says, "No, I want it to be five rupees more expensive." I am beginning to believe he's right. So this is a concrete example.

When I did the mountain water campaign and changed the colour to green, I didn't research anything. I did a small dipstick, with a few people, showing them a shade of green just to see whether what I believed was true. They said that the colour green suggests health, purity and spirituality, and that was good enough for me. One year after we launched it, we did some market research; about ninety percent of the answers showed that it was right in the middle of the target, perfect. In fact in the periphery there was much more than we expected. There were a couple of errors, and that was good because now we can correct those errors; and that's the fine-tuning.

GG: So this is after the product has left your own private space. It has gone out, and you get some feedback.

AK: You don't need to do the research. But we thought that research might tell us what we did right and what we did wrong." We learned from the feedback; so now we extend the good parts and improve on the bad parts. The important thing is to do your homework and really know your customer by his first name.

GG: What are your yardsticks of evaluation? How do you separate the wheat from the chaff in the things you yourself have created? Have you ever discarded a concept or an idea or a strategy on which you had worked for quite some time, believed in it, and then when you began to evaluate it, all of a sudden you said, "Uh-uh. That's not it!"? And if so, did you decide that it was not good enough?

AK: I had Internet projects with a friend of mine, and for one year we spent a third of a million developing a social network site where people have friends. We hired a CEO who used to work with a big Internet business; that was a mistake! He wasn't an entrepreneur. Once again, it was the mistake of hiring a professional CEO before launching the product. It doesn't work, because you'll get a professional who will ruin it. We let him make decisions. Many of those decisions were wrong, and it set us back six months. So instead of launching our project in four or five months, it took us a year. By that time, the market had changed. Facebook, a social networking website, had suddenly arrived, along with something else: Reliance, the big Indian Ambani family, had launched BigAdda, a youth networking site. Under those circumstances we decided that we had missed the timing. "We'll just burn more money if we try going into that business now, because there's too much competition. We should have gone in six months ago, when we planned it. Let's just close the book, write it off, and put it away." That's what we did.

GG: So this was a case where your self-evaluation had said, "Our idea was good, but we missed the timing. Therefore we have to drop it now."

AK: One year earlier, when we had started the project, it was something that would have worked because it was new and fresh and different. But in the following six months ten other people appeared and launched their products.

GG: In other words, one of the yardsticks of quality for you is: does it fit today's market?

AK: Oh yes, it has to! You have to ask that question: Who is my audience today? Who is my audience tomorrow? It is difficult to predict what will happen tomorrow; but if you don't get it ready by tomorrow, and things have changed by tomorrow, then it's outdated. If I invent a new bullock-cart today, I'll not be able to sell it. Whether I give it pneumatic wheels, whether I make it lightweight or whatever else, I'll not be able to sell it because the market for bullock carts is gone. And then it's not just the timing and the market: when you live with your product for too long, it's dated.

GG: When you live with your product for too long in the construction phase, in the development phase?

AK: In the development phase; then it's already dated. Oh, there are times when I am under pressure in advertising and we have to deliver something on a specific date, and I know we haven't really done our best, and I know it isn't good but because there are professional managers involved and they say, "Just come and show us whatever you've got," I go, but it is half-hearted! Deep down I really don't want to sell it.

GG: Do you tell them, "I don't think we have got it yet" or do you leave it up to them to decide whether the time has come to launch a new product, service or project?

AK: There have been times when I lost interest in the business because I wasn't doing the project myself. It was being managed by professional managers, and they arrived too late with their results – and I knew my creative partner and I could have done it in three days. Yet when you have so-called professional managers, it takes thirty days to accomplish the same thing!

GG: It makes a difference whether you are an entrepreneur or a manager. You are absolutely right. In the fifteen years I worked as a special advisor for multinational corporations, I made my share of observations that fit your own experience.

Now let me switch to another subject. It seems to me that most of the TV spots you watch in various countries are not creative at all. They are *déjà-vu*, produced by copycats who pretend to be highly creative. These people are slick talkers who persuade their clients that their advertising campaigns will be hugely successful in delivering the goods. I'm really convinced that most of these TV spots – I would say eighty percent – are nothing more than a repetition of *The Emperor's New Clothes*.

AK: Ninety percent!

GG: It seems to me that the people working in advertising agencies are suffering from too much freedom. If they had a more critical mind, they would not produce such nonsense.

AK: Not necessarily. Most bad advertising…

GG: …is controlled by managers?

AK: Is controlled by the managers.

GG: The client managers?

AK: Yes, because they insist, and the story is told in the most boring way possible. Most brand managers do not know how to tell a story, how to produce an advertising campaign that really works. Remember I told you, "There is *one* key problem in any project, and you can't find the solution until you get to that *one* key problem." Yet your clients tend to create chaos by telling you that there are ten key problems. You can't have ten key problems! There's *one* key problem, and you have to cut through the fog and say, "The problem lies here." If you've put your finger on the problem, all the rest will fall into place, whether it's the product or the distribution, or the market, or the communication or the trade margin, or the trade support, or the after-sales service. It might be one thing in a million. The trick is to figure out *what* it is. Maybe your price is wrong. Maybe the value you're giving the consumer isn't worth the price your asking! He doesn't see it as value. You can't find a solution before you hit on the key problem! So what happens very often is that the brand manager doesn't tell you what the problem is; he gives you a laundry list of problems. He throws them on the table and insists you solve them all in one single advertisement. What do you do with that? How can you be creative in such a situation? By the time you solve all these problems, you've created some complete rubbish. And that is why that stuff for which multinational companies spend billions of dollars is so boring. Only very rarely are brand managers able to say, "There is *one* core problem. Let's find a solution to that one problem, and solve it with communication." Then you have a problem situation which permits a creative problem solution. You can go to your team in the agency and say, "Don't be boring! Be creative!" And then they are able to do a good job.

GG: In a nutshell your argument is: much of it is sterile and stupid because there are too many structural constraints imposed by your clients who are brand managers. Is that it?

AK: Yes! Occasionally you will see clients who buy some complete rubbish because it is unusual. But that rubbish, for which they pay huge amounts of money, doesn't speak to the customer. It is not functional, has nothing to do with the problem, and therefore doesn't present a problem solution at all. It talks only to the agency that produced it and the client who bought it.

GG: Indeed, there is a lot of publicity, advertising, which speaks only to other advertising agencies. These ads represent a kind of insider joke, and they are a very expensive insider joke. In this incestuous, client-agent nexus the larger interest is completely overlooked. It's like inbreeding, and inbreeding usually generates weak creatures. Lack of vigour makes them candidates for all kinds of dysfunctions and illnesses.

AK: Yes, and that is partly the disease of awards. Very often people create solely for awards and recognition.

GG: You are right. I fully agree with you.

AK: How does a creative person get recognition in the advertising business? It's a sick business! That's why I quit it; I sold it. One big benchmark for recognition of a "creative person" in advertising is to be boring and mundane and work on a big, multinational brand. But because that advertiser spends billions, the sheer power of the money makes it work. So he produces very boring ads and thinks exactly like the client. But the client isn't a creative person, either. As long as the advertiser thinks exactly like the client, the client loves him and keeps his business with that agency. And because he keeps the business with that agency, the advertiser gets paid a lot of money but without going anywhere; all he's doing is understanding the mind of his client.

GG: And over-adapting to it.

AK: And duplicating that mind in a visual, thirty-second spot. Now those are the people who are willing to compromise their own creativity, their values, everything. Very often they're mediocre but financially they do well because they have that exclusive relationship with their client. Other advertisers win awards. The moment you win an award – and it might be for a fake product; at one time it was for products that didn't even exist! — your salary of ten thousand dollars goes up to twenty! If you have won an award, the agency makes you a senior and gives you two or three interesting products. So the award winner manages to pull off another two awards; his salary goes to fifty thousand. Before you know it, he's in a million-dollar bracket because he wins lots of awards. People in Southeast Asia do ads for companies that don't exist – and they win awards! I was in a jury once, and we saw something that was really great, and I said, "Look, this kind of thing can't exist anywhere in Asia." We were all sitting in the room, all the judges, and there was a phone number, so we called it. What did the voice on the other end of the line say? "No, this is a barber shop!" That's how it works! It's great fun to be recognized and to get awards; you're a big name, you're famous, you know you are a star, you come to work at eleven o'clock in the morning, you can drink in the office, you can smoke dope in the office… wonderful!

GG: What a sham! Now, we have been talking about self-evaluation in advertising. Can you tell me something about your self-evaluation when you created Zee TV?

AK: When the television station went up, we were super successful for the first six years while I was there and working hands on. I used to go in every day, take a look, change what had to be changed, and things were moving. In those days we didn't have a CEO, we only had vice-presidents. Then we hired a CEO who was a very brilliant man; but he was a brilliant finance man and a political man and a game player.

GG: Political games?

AK: Right, so he knew politicians, he understood the law, he understood finance.

GG: But not the content of your products, the procedures and values of your company?

AK: No, not at all. Moreover, he also destroyed the teams working in our company. He made sure that all the bright people left.

GG: What did he do to them?

AK: He treated them like idiots. In those days the Indian stock market started going up. The Zee TV share, which as a founder I had bought for one rupee, at one point reached one thousand five hundred rupees.

GG: Was his salary bound to the share value?

AK: Yes, it was, and he also had some equity. At that time shares were going up; his share went from ten rupees or thirty rupees or whatever, to one thousand five hundred rupees.

GG: That's nice – to say the least!

AK: That's nice, but you have to learn to remain yourself. Rather than believing in this imaginary figure, which is more money than I knew existed – I didn't know that that much money existed in the world! I don't know how many zeroes there are in a billion! I just about managed to count a million, and that also took years! At any rate, to cut the story short, the shares went up, and then the whole stock market crashed. At the same time Rupert Murdock's Star TV launched a very successful programme. If our original, bright team had been in place...

GG: ... they could have fought back.

AK: They could have fought back and planned and implemented a good counter-strategy, and we wouldn't have been so weak. We never would have gone down to number two. But by then all the original, bright people had left because this man had made them feel redundant. I used to go to him and say, "We should research these concepts. It's now costing us ten times more per programme, per episode, than it used to do. You can't just allow junior people to decide these things." He didn't understand brands. He didn't understand marketing. He didn't understand teamwork.

GG: But he sure understood the art of ruining teams.

AK: It all happened at a time when people believed in the stock market. All these people who had left our company also had equity, so suddenly all these people were millionaires. Now, when millionaires have been treated badly...

GG: ... they don't take it anymore. They don't have to.

AK: They don't take it, they leave; and they sell their equity. So we had a lot of people who had stopped working because they were millionaires and none of them wanted to cope with that guy's attitude and behaviour.

GG: Then came the crash and the stock fell to ninety. And then?

AK: Then a new team had to come and rebuild and get the company going again. I hired a very bright fellow who used to work at *The Times of India* newspaper.

GG: So you and your partner now decided that you needed a new team, and you fired the old CEO?

AK: Yes, we fired him and he left, but there was no team left. We brought in a person who tried doing something, but he messed it up and spent vast amounts of money without getting anywhere. You see, there's an old strategy: when you're defeated, you can't send a whole army into fifty different places against the other army and win. You've got to find one spearhead, get an entry at one point...

GG: ... breach the wall at one point...

AK: ... then expand your breach and keep expanding it slowly. But you have to have a full strategy of what you'll do after you make the first breach.

GG: You must focus on that one breach and then take it from there.

AK: Exactly. The first CEO we hired attacked fifty different targets and didn't hit a single one, so we lost more money.

GG: He was overreaching instead of concentrating all his power on one, single target.

AK: The new CEO turned out to be very good. We also took Subhash Chandra's son into the company, and he is very good, too. When you're thirty years old, you can feel the pulse of the audience; when you're fifty years old, you can't judge the pulse of the audience. So this young man came in and worked with the new CEO from *Times of India*, who is a great leader. He is a team leader, he hires professional people. He is very bright and helps to change the company's whole image. Gradually over the last three years we've come back to number one position.

GG: And now the shares are up again?

AK: Now the total share must be back to about five hundred rupees.

GG: It was once at one thousand five hundred; how far had it gone down from there?

AK: It went down to ninety rupees.

GG: That far! I have another question for you: have you any examples of a self-evaluation that was very positive, and then later on, when you did a re-evaluation you thought, "Oh, no, that's not it!" Or were you always happy with your result?

AK: No! And my creative partner will sing songs about this, that I am a complainer. I will stand there with passion and faith and belief and go and sell it, and then come back and start telling you everything that's wrong with it. The next day I'll find ten other ways of how to improve it. And I will complain even though the damn thing has been sold to the client and is extremely successful. Everyone loves it, it has won awards, But still I'll complain. You cannot be a leader of quality if you don't complain. The more I look at a concrete result, the more faults I find with it.

GG: Could one say that you are very rarely fully satisfied with your achievements?

AK: Very rarely, and then maybe I'm satisfied for that moment. But anything you look at closely, you can still improve. I'm sure there is a God up there who created this world and on the sixth day, he said, "It's perfect!" On the seventh day he rested because he had done a good job, and the next day, on Monday morning, he said, "What kind of idiot did I make there? Man!"

GG: And he sent a big flood.

AK: Yes, he sent a flood – or rather he sent a woman to ruin the man he had created!

GG: I have a very good friend who is a creative automobile constructor – not a designer. He constructs the whole car, motor, body, everything. He is an Italian, his name is Franco Sbarro and he often repeats, "I am the eternally non-satisfied man." With everything he does, he is not satisfied. He has done great things; he has invented the hubless wheel. Imagine a motorbike, for instance, with no wheel axle; a person could slip right through it. He has put the power transmission and the brakes into the wheel, as the hub is empty. The wheel looks very elegant and its applications are endless: bikes, motorbikes, cars, trains and planes could use it. It looks great and it functions very well. It's more stable than the habitual motorbike. I helped Sbarro when he opened a school for creative automobile construction by teaching there for a year and-a-half, although I don't understand anything about constructing automobiles. But I taught these young people something about creativity, leadership and teamwork.

AK: You can't be a creative leader unless you opt for a rigorous self-evaluation. That's why people like Sbarro and me are never fully satisfied with the results of their creative efforts.

When the phase of evaluation is over, the finished work leaves the private domain of the creator. It now enters the public domain, and stage III of the creative process begins. But before we move on to the discussion of stage III, I should like to say a few words about the interaction of the seven individual phases during stage II of the creative process.

2.38 On the Interaction of the Seven Phases

Before beginning the section on the phase of germination, I stated that the individual phases of a creative process do not follow each other in single file. I should like to expand somewhat on this topic.

The seven phases of a creative process do not follow each other in a simple linear manner; what we actually observe are redundant event trajectories. An individual creative process may suddenly jump or continuously glide forward or backward from one phase to another. It may move, for instance, from illumination to elaboration and back to germination, inspiration and preparation again—and do so several times in a row. As the Nigerian writer and Nobel laureate Wole Soyinka (Soyinka 1994, 64) once sarcastically wrote, some individuals—he aimed at critics—"would make us believe that a writer's creative universe is some straight linear route trodden by only one idea at a time." Similarly, physicist Richard Feynman (Gleick 1993, 380) stated: "We have a habit in writing articles published in scientific journals to make the work as finished as possible, to cover up all the tracks, to not worry about the blind alleys or to describe how you had the wrong idea first."

An individual may jump from one phase of a specific creative process to another phase of a completely different creative process. A painter may be working on a specific painting and then suddenly drop it because he feels inspired to begin another one. A writer may be in a phase of preparation with respect to a novel and suddenly get an illumination for a poem. An inventor may be evaluating the quality of a new machine and suddenly be inspired to continue the elaboration of another machine he had been working on for years. A film director, who during a phase of preparation, gets news of a critic who has demolished (stage III) his latest film that has just reached the box office, may suffer a deep crisis of motivation and interrupt the phase of preparation temporarily or even definitively; then he may enter the cutting room and finish a film he shot years ago. An advertising specialist in a period of total creative sterility may be re-energized and catapulted into new creative performance when he learns that his former campaign, after a period of apparent indifference, has turned out to be a huge success; that it has stimulated a host of other advertising specialists operating in another professional field to improve the quantity and quality of their advertising strategies.

An excellent example to illustrate the fact that different creative processes may go on simultaneously in an individual, and that specific stages and phases interact and overlap not only within the same creative process, but also between various simultaneously running creative processes is Thomas Alva Edison. In 1880 alone, the restless inventor applied for sixty different patents; indeed within the year sixty different inventions had passed his phase of evaluation as well as the cultural selection provided by his collaborators, patrons, and clients. All of these patents had to do with the use of electricity. Five of them covered auxiliary parts, six concerned dynamos, thirty-two furnished improvements in incandescent lamps, while seven covered electrical current distribution. When asked why no other inventor had found a simple but well-functioning problem solution to prevent loss of pressure usually encountered in parallel circuits, English physicist Lord Kelvin wryly stated: "The only answer I can think of is that no one else is Edison" (Josephson 1992, 231). Two years later, in 1882, Edison applied for 141 patents—a unique event in the history of invention and proof for the hypothesis that several creative processes may go on simultaneously in an individual's brain and mutually influence each other (Josephson 1992, 274).

The interplay of phases is, of course, even more complex where whole teams (for instance inventors, engineers, scientists, or managers; film teams; theater groups) are involved in a creative process. Individual members of such a team may find themselves in quite different phases of the creative group process and continuously offering their respective inputs to the group. Moreover, the same team members trying to keep up to date with the leading edge in science may be influenced by the results of stage III or IV of creative processes having occurred in other professional domains. They may be inhibited or stimulated by those results, depending on how the implications of these results feed into their own order and chaos pools.

In other words, the phases of a specific creative process resemble the patterns of tapestries woven on one or several enchanted looms. Such patterns are not stagnant, as the patterns on a normal loom may be at times. They rather behave like the wave patterns in a creek murmuring through an Alpine meadow. The phases of a specific creative process keep dancing and weaving their way through the space-time of mental activities and events, and not even the most sophisticated observer is able to track down their actual trajectories.

Another important point I should like to emphasize once more is that every single phase—whether occurring just once or repeatedly—may last seconds, minutes, hours, days, months, or years. While inspiration and illumination are ultra-rapid events that appear suddenly, evaluation usually lasts weeks or months. Preparation and elaboration often last weeks, months, years, or even decades. We do not know at all, however, how long most phases of germination and incubation last. Moreover, there are specific creative phases for instance, in writing poetry or producing a Zen drawing, where everything following inspiration or illumination may last but seconds or minutes. An inspired or illuminated poet or Zen master works like lightning; there is a tremendous synchronic firing of millions of interconnected neurons leading to ultra-rapid performance. But despite such stupendous variability in the occurrence of phases and stages in a creative process, a basic process pattern does always exist.

This pattern exists everywhere although creative processes in technological invention, science, art, and other domains do have their specific characteristics. In other words, the basic structural pattern of the creative process is universal. As the physicist Kadanoff (Kadanoff 1996, 184) puts it, a process is universal if, independent of concrete microscopic elements, forces and other details, the global macroscopic behavior is, by and large, always the same. Whether creative processes occur in individuals, groups, or whole cultures and whether they occur in the same professional domain or in different ones, there is a trans-scalar self-similarity across the different hierarchical levels of complexity. In nature, such structural self-similarities (Guntern 1995a, 32f.) exist, for instance, in the bifurcation patterns of broccoli plants, trees, flashes of lightning, river estuaries, water whirls in a tube, nerve fibers, arteries and veins, and bronchi. As Cramer (Cramer 1988, 146) puts it: "In principle, a tree[20] is a slowed down lightning. The time scale is approximately 10^{12} slower."

Creative processes are always produced by minds. As minds are complex dynamic systems governed by deterministic chaos, their operations show—as do all complex dynamic systems—the phenomenon of trans-scalar[21] self-similarity. In this respect, the trans-scalar self-similarity of creative processes resembles the *manas* concept of the Hopi Indians; it is the supreme mental pattern connecting all parts and events occurring on the enchanted loom.

In contradistinction to the other phases, which operate in an often slow and usually gradual, incremental, and laborious way, inspiration and illumination occur in a spontaneous, sudden, discontinuous, and rapid manner. That fact has always amazed observers. It has, moreover, given rise to some rather romantic and even naive misconceptions about the true nature of the creative process. One of these misconceptions holds that hard work can be suspended with: the Lord pampers the blessed human creators as he pampers the lilies in the fields; he gives them whatever they need, whenever they need it—and plenty of it. Another misconception is that proper knowledge of facts, procedures, and methods in the field in which one desires to be creative can be dispensed with; such knowledge only hinders the 'divine spontaneity' of the crashing breakthrough. A third misconception is that the ideas offered by creative inspiration and illumination come not from the creator's mind but from the outside; they fly through the atmosphere like invisible humming-birds, and one has only to open the windows of perception to provide them with an opportunity to settle on the window sill of one's own mind. I have even heard this last hypothesis from personalities with a track record of creative performance. They firmly believed that this statement corresponds to observable facts. In my view, they are mistaken because they take their lack of conscious control over these two phases of the creative process as solid proof of an extraorganismic or even transcendental provenience of ideas offered by inspiration and illumination.

And, last but not least, I should like to emphasize that the phase model presented in this chapter is but a map. My map has been constructed on the basis of observable territories. Its construction process has been guided by a grammar of transformation whose rules specify how to get from the directly observable territory of concrete creative activities to the map of the phase model. Whoever reads this map may reach similar or dissimilar conclusions. To make a comparison, the same topographic map showing different details of a specific landscape will stimulate a landscape painter, a collector of mushrooms, a geologist, a scout, an urban developer, or a military strategist to draw quite different conclusions.

In December 1928, Erwin Schrödinger (Moore 1989, 247), a luminary of quantum physics, gave a lecture in Frankfurt on The Epistemological Value of Physical Models. The father of wave mechanics concluded his lecture with the following statement: "We must not forget that pictures and models finally have no other purpose than to serve as a framework for all the observations that are in principle possible." Hopefully, my conceptual map on the stages and phases of the creative process will fit that purpose.

Excerpts from an interview with Ashok Kurien (12)

Asked about experiences made in a specific process of elaboration, Ashok Kurien talks about the creation of a privately-owned machine lottery—and also about the interaction of the various stages and phases of creative processes.

A new lottery game is introduced that uses machines instead of the traditional purchasing of paper tickets, and a CEO is placed in charge of the implementing process. The incompetent CEO fails miserably in achieving set targets. He is fired, and Ashok Kurien is called in to save the project by creating a new strategy. He does so, and his campaign is a winner. The evaluation of a failure leads to inspiration and sets in motion a new creative process which brings rapid success. Yet that success is stopped by power-gamblers who are out fishing for votes in an upcoming election. These light-towers of virtue declare that gambling at a machine lottery impoverishes the already poor—but they fail to attack the illegally operating paper lottery! The privately owned machine lottery is almost ruined. Ashok Kurien has to begin a new creative process in order to save the whole project. During the entire struggle all four stages of a creative process and the seven phases of stage II continuously interact, dashing around in redundant loops like the individual honeybees in a swarm.

> GG: Another one of your creative projects is a privately owned lottery. Can you use that example to say a few words about coping with frustration and stress in the process of elaboration?

AK: What I need to do is talk to you about the creative solution first, and then you will understand the rest of it.

Subhash was again the Zee group partner. He told me he was doing this lottery project and he had a CEO in place. He started with the CEO, and on the day he was launching the project, he discovered that the CEO only had a hundred and twenty-five lottery outlets. Now, the electronic lotto machine consists of an electronic box; you go and type in your number or pay your money and you're allotted an automatic random number. There is a draw every day or every week.

GG: Is the box located in a kiosk?

AK: They're placed in little stores or anywhere that people can easily access them. This is a new concept for India, as we used to have paper lottery, where you went and bought a paper lottery ticket. Indians and people like me are frightened of technology; we don't understand it. I mean, how do you work this machine? Why would a shop take the machine if the owner says, "We don't know if this is going to work?" So on the day of the launch, the advertising agencies spent millions of rupees to make the public aware of the new lottery. Subhash calls me at home and says, "Come and have a drink." And I ask, "What happened?" He responds, "I've sacked the CEO." Now, Subhash had seventy-five machines in operation and it didn't look good. So I said, "Relax. I'll come; I'll help you sort it out." For a long period of time I was again in that ad agency I had once founded. My schedule was back to seven days a week, fourteen to eighteen hours a day, and we moved forward; it was very enjoyable! And here's the challenge: we don't have a distribution, and people don't understand the whole thing. So I went out and tried finding a machine and realized I didn't know where the shops were. (Here, I am describing to you the whole process I went through.) Finally I asked someone in the company, and he said, "Go to such-and-such a place and you'll find a shop which has got a machine." Now, you must know that no customer is going to look for that shop unless there is a very good reason for him to go there. So I go to the shop, and I find out that the guy there hardly knows how to use the machine! I don't know how to use it, I'm frightened to use it, but I don't want him to know that. So I tell him, "I'll go somewhere else." As you can see, there are major problems we are facing. We don't have the machines in place, and you can't do a lottery if you don't have hundreds or thousands of these machines in place. You can spend vast amounts on advertising, educating people, telling them in our ad campaigns how to use these machines; and in our ads we must list the names of all the outlets which have the machines. I thought, "This is too long a process, and it's going to cost lots of money. We've got to climb many mountains and then we don't even know what we are going to do there." Customers had to go to that box, and remember: we are running this lottery on behalf of state governments, because only the government is permitted to run a lottery. So we had a licence from the government, and we made a profit on it.

GG: Why, then, is it called "privately owned"?

AK: Because the operator is privately owned. You know, we are running a government lottery, we pay them a fee, and we make the rest of the money. Now look at the complexity of our problem. For hundred of years they have bought lottery tickets. Suddenly you're telling them to adapt to a new method, a new technology, a new place! So I said, "The first thing we need to do is get into the lottery markets." How do we get in there? Yet another problem!

For it, I came up with a simple, out-of-the-box idea: *The Times of India* is the big newspaper in Bombay and is bought by 700,000 readers. I put a very big ad in that newspaper telling the readers: "This is a free coupon. Cut it out and go to a Playwin lottery outlet from the addresses below; there you can win one *crore*." One *crore* is ten million Indian rupees; that's a quarter of a million US dollars – and that's the price we were offering as a jackpot.

Every person cut that coupon out. Many people bought several newspapers and all their neighbours' newspapers because each one allowed you a free lottery ticket. And the dealer was told, "We are not going to charge you for every coupon you bring back." Many of the dealers must have bought a hundred newspapers, too. So the consumer started looking for where he could go and use this ticket. Then he figured out how to do it. Either hit random and get a ticket, or punch his lucky numbers in and get a ticket. "Wow, this is easy! I hit 1-7-5-3-6-4-2-9-0, go! And when the number is announced the next day, I might be the lucky winner!

GG: Is it announced on TV?

AK: Yes, we do the draw on TV. So you know what happened? In one, single day we had five hundred thousand people going and finding the stores, figuring out how to operate the machine, and there were mile-long queues. Seeing that queue the next-door shop owner said, "Hey, there's a mile long queue there! This guy is making money on this business, I want a machine, too!"

GG: Of course, success observed in other people stimulates one's own desire for success.

AK: So, from seventy-five machines we jumped to five hundred machines. We ran the ad again: free lottery! Within a few months we had six thousand terminals across the country, in the states that allowed the lottery. With a single ad we taught the consumer where to go, how to play it, we educated him completely. With one little ticket, we made the dealer realize that this was a profitable business and every time they saw a queue somebody else bought a machine and said, "Here is your deposit money, give me a machine, I want to be in this business, too." So we created distribution, we created size, scale, education, everything, with one, simple, creative, out-of-the-box solution. This was a strategy that took us to size and scale. After that the whole thing had to be managed. The frustration was that a new political party could suddenly say, "I'm banning this electronic lottery."

GG: With the argument that you are not respecting the existing laws, or what?

AK: No, everything is within the law. The excuse was that people were going to lose all their money in gambling. You see, there was an election coming up and they wanted all the women to vote. So this party pretended to be the good guys and to stop the gambling in order to get the votes. The heads of this party send some hoodlums out to smash some shops and protest with flags: "This is terrible. Poor people are losing all their money to gambling." Rubbish!

GG: Their argument was that gambling is addictive?

AK: They said people became addicted to gambling. The publicity for the political power- gamblers is high, and they get all the women to vote for them. So this is one sort of frustration. There is a lot of corruption involved. Some minister needs more money; he thinks we're not paying enough, so what does he do? He stops our lottery by means of a police raid. Then the next month everything is clean and business starts booming again. It's a turbulent cycle. Business goes up, comes down, goes up, comes down, goes up, comes down. Anybody who starts anything new in a country, every single pioneer, every first mover, pays the price. Eventually the turbulence stops. Six different companies entered this lottery business; four of them lost their money, got wiped out and went home. Only two remained: we and a guy called Martin, who had been in the paper lottery business for thirty years, who understood the whole market, knew all the ministers, knew the police. He was very strong. He stayed, and we stayed. Everybody else went out. So that's the lottery business.

GG: But the politicians can change the law permitting such gambling at any moment, can't they?

AK: It's the state jurisdiction that can do that.

GG: But then the state will lose money because the state received its cut from the gambling in the paper lottery.

AK: The state isn't interested in the money. When they print paper lottery tickets, they can officially print, let's say, a million tickets per draw. But they can unofficially print one million two hundred thousand tickets, two hundred thousand of which are fake. The ministers, the politicians and the policemen get paid a lot by the paper lottery guys; and those two hundred thousand fake tickets also go out into the market. Whereas anything that we do legally is transparent, computerized, audited. We pay the government, and that money is supposed to be used in the fight against underdevelopment.

GG: Do you show the winner on TV?

AK: We show the winners on TV, and we show them in the print media. On TV, there is a live draw; it's all legitimate, no cheating. The money we pay the government is meant to be used for the underprivileged. So the causes are all good, but they can be ruined by greed, corruption, politicians who don't want it to happen because they want to win the elections. At the same time the legal paper lottery still runs in many places; in others, they have banned it completely. But the illegal paper lottery keeps running, which also means somebody is earning some money somewhere.

GG: What was the creative product for which you had to fight the most and the longest? Which gave you the most frustrations, the most stress during the phase of elaboration, until eventually you saw it through? In which was the trail of sweat and tears most frustrating, in that privately owned machine lottery?

AK: I think the frustration was highest in the lottery project. I think the sweat was highest in the Zee TV project – although the excitement was great, too. The lottery in itself may not have given me that excitement, but watching the results of the idea was great excitement. After that it was not really exciting. But the frustration with the lottery was very high, because I hate seeing destroyed something which I built. That, however, is the reality of the environment; it's the reality of the country we live in.

NOTES

1. Since 1981, the International CREANDO Foundation for Creativity and Leadership has organized symposia on creative leadership in economics, arts, and science. Many creative personalities quoted throughout the present book were speakers at these symposia. To find out more about the International CREANDO Symposia, visit the website: www.creando.org

2. 'Organismic state' is a shorter term for "an organism's state of operation".

3. Activated *corpora amygdala* produce a fight-flight stress response; activated *hippocampi* produce a helplessness stress response

4. In a creative process, the phase of inspiration offers one or several new, exciting idea(s). The phase of illumination produces a sudden and very exciting problem solution that may have eluded the creative person for a long time. The context of some of the quotes cited herein does not allow us to differentiate whether the author was referring to inspiration or illumination. In those days, there was no rigorous distinction yet between these two phases of the creative process.

5. Greek: ἐν = in; θέοσ = god; ἐνθουσιάξειν = enthusiasm

6. Lat. *incubare* = to lie, to breed, to herd, to guard

7. Greek: ὅμοιος = equal, similar; στάσιζ = state; a homeostasis is the ability of an organism to keep vitally important physiological variables (for instance, pH, blood pressure, bodily temperature, concentration of blood sugar) in a dynamic equilibrium in order to permit survival and adequate development. The mechanism of homeostasis is regulated by positive and negative feedback loops.

8. Italian proverb: "If it's not true, then it's well invented."

9. Greek ἐκ = out, outside; στάσις = position, standing, staying; ecstasy = a state of mind outside of the normal state, an exalted state of mind

10. Greek τροφή = food, nourishment, τρέπειν = to turn to, ἐργειν = to work

11. *Verbal output*: words, phrases, sentences; *paraverbal output*: volume, speed, frequency, rhythm, quality, and amount of sounds made while speaking; *nonverbal output*: body stance, body movements including mimics and gesticulation.

12. Greek: ἕυρεκα = I've found it

13. We talk here of imagination, although the term *fantasy* would be more adequate. Fantasy is a mental activity generating three types of phenomena: (a) a mental representation of things and events which have once existed or happened; (b) a mental representation of things and events existing or happening at the moment, but not in the same place as the fantasizing person; (c) a mental representation of things and events which do not exist or are not happening at the moment, but might exist or happen one day. The elements of fantasies can be mathematical symbols, words written or spoken, scenes of social encounters, pictures, landscapes, plants, animals, etc. Imagination is a specific form of fantasy characterized by visual-pictorial representations. In today's colloquial language, the term imagination has more or less replaced the term fantasy.

14. Greek: τάξις = order, νόμος =law, science; Taxonomy = ordering scheme, system of categories, table of types

15. Due to mass hysteria in Puritan Massachusetts between June and September 1692, nineteen men and women were convicted of witchcraft and hanged on Gallows Hill near Salem Village. An eighty-year-old man was crushed to death by heavy stones because he refused to submit to trial on witchcraft charges. Hundreds of people were accused of witchcraft, and dozens of them languished in jail for months on end. This event was, by the way, an alarming illustration of the power of destructive leadership, because the mass hysteria was the unfortunate result of mutual inspiration and motivation for extraordinary performance.

16. Greek: ἀνα = up, upwards; δύομαι = to emerge; ἀναδυομενη = the one who has emerged

17. In an advertising agency, team members who write texts and put visual materials (drawings, photos, film, etc.) together are called "the creative people." It's rather a misnomer, as Ashok Kurien's example illustrates. He is actually doing the creative strategy design. What comes afterwards is most of the time routine work governed by established rules and procedures.

18. Val Bregaglia, where Giacometti was born, is a valley in the Southern Swiss Alps bordering on Italy.

19. Lat. *quantum* = how much

20. What is meant here are the similar bifurcation patterns in trees and lightning.

21. Trans-scalar = across different hierarchical levels of dynamic complexity

2.4 STAGE III: CULTURAL SELECTION

A tear of creation on the cheek of eternity

Writer and Nobel laureate Rabindranath Tagore on the Taj Mahal

As soon as an individual or team has finished evaluating the result of her, his, or its own creative achievement and decides that it is satisfying, the new form quits the private sector and enters the public domain. At this point, stage III of the creative process begins.

Stage III consists of a mechanism of cultural selection governed by the social environment. In my view, this mechanism corresponds to that of natural selection, which plays a crucial role in biological evolution. Cultural selection aims at separating the wheat from the chaff; it evaluates the adaptive fit of a new form and thus determines its fate. It leads to a bifurcation and from there, to either recognition or rejection of the new form. Whatever its result, cultural selection does not represent an objective judgement, but a judgement based on an inter-subjective consensus. As Thomas Kuhn (Regis 1987, 216) once put it with respect to the structure of scientific revolutions: "As in political revolutions so in paradigm choice—there is no standard higher than the assent of the relevant community." That assent is not easy to come by; and if it does come easily, then it may well be for the wrong reasons. Moreover, assent and public recognition may change over time.

If cultural evaluation accepts the new form as being of value, morpho-evolution[1] occurs; if cultural evaluation rejects it, morpho-elimination is the consequence. In morpho-evolution, the new form inspires and motivates the creation of other new forms in the same professional discipline or in different professional domains. If morpho-elimination occurs, the new form has no

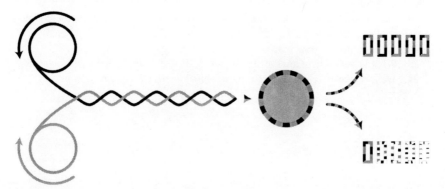

Figure 2.16. Stage III: Cultural selection.

impact; it is rejected by the social environment, forgotten as time goes by, or even physically destroyed.

I should like to discuss but four aspects of the mechanism of cultural evaluation: recognition; rejection; how creative individuals react to the verdict of cultural evaluation; and how the criteria and motives of evaluating persons may change in the course of time.

Excerpts from an interview with Ashok Kurien (13)

Speaking in general terms about cultural selection, Ashok Kurien describes how it worked with entrepreneurs, to whom he sold a strategy or advertising campaign, and how it worked with managers who had only one goal in mind: "to cover their ass," as he puts it. On the other hand he reports a case where an entrepreneur first rejected an idea proposed by Ashok Kurien, only to accept it enthusiastically later on.

> GG: When you were with Ambience, how many times was the original idea accepted by your client, you worked out the details, and when you came back with the final solution, it was rejected?

> AK: For the first ten years my creative partner, Elsie, and I did everything ourselves; very often we just went with one campaign – no alternatives – and it went right through.

> GG: Every time?

> AK: Almost every time.

> GG: Can you give one example where the whole thing stalled? When it was rejected?

> AK: I can't think of many. There were some instances where the client may not have bought the idea on the spot, (the idea may have been to launch a new product), but he might have done it six months or a year later. What happened is, as these clients grew bigger and more successful – the same clients stayed with us for ten, twenty, twenty-five years, all long relationships – they hired professional managers. So suddenly we were dealing with a professional manager, not the entrepreneur.

> GG: Amongst them there are some bloated guys, full of self-importance.

> AK: They are not able to accept a decision or a recommendation which is out-of-the-box, because their career is built on covering their asses. So a manager will do research to cover his ass. On the basis of that research very often he will reject a great idea or a great campaign because nobody has seen it before. He will reject anything which is risky, because he is covering his ass. If you don't take a risk, you will never cross the road. You'll always stand on this side, or

you'll wait for the green light and then take the pedestrian crossing. I like running across the road between the traffic, jumping over the edge.

GG: In the early seventies, my wife Greta did a multi-media project in Philadelphia. For that project she wanted to stage a dialogue between four high-school students wearing bathing suits. The boys wore jeans and a T-shirt, the girls wore bathing suits so that arms, legs and feet were bare. She wanted to show the ballet of nonverbal communication while they talked with each other. She shot the whole scene so that you only saw moving body parts – arms, hands and fingers – and bodies, but no heads. I was dressed like the boys, and my role was to interview these adolescents in order to bring about a lively dialogue. So there was a black girl, a black boy, a white girl, a white boy. They were all beautiful and a joy to be with. I asked them about their attitudes towards life, I asked them all kinds of things; of course we also hit the topic of sex, gender roles and partner relationships, because young people are highly interested in that. The black guy was a bit of a macho, and I asked him, "What is your basic attitude toward girls?" He went into a display posture and said grandiosely, "Defence is the name of the game!" Much later in my career I met managers covering their ass, as you said. I often told them that they were acting according to the maxim: "Defence is the name of the game." That's the main rule that governs them.

AK: Absolutely!

GG: Can you give me an example of rejection? Do you remember a case where your clients said, "You're nuts! Your idea is no good; it will never work!"

AK: There was *Bisleri*, that mineral water, a leader that had fifty percent of the market. The water was sold in a blue bottle, very identifiable; it's very important to have a package which is very identifiable. All the textbooks will tell you that you do not change an identifiable product. You may improve it. You might modernize it, you might contemporize it, but you do not take a brand leader and completely switch it.

GG: The customers wouldn't be able to recognize it immediately anymore.

AK: And I wanted to change everything about *Bisleri* except the name. I wanted to change the shape of the bottle, its colour, its nomenclature, everything! The shape of the bottle is different, the colour is different and the nomenclature is different. I wanted to change mineral water into mountain water. I proposed changing the tone of the communication. In short, I wanted everything to be different.

GG: And the client said, "No, no!"

AK: When I first told him of my idea, it was a "no-no." Then he thought it over and eventually accepted it. By now I have worked with him for twenty-five years, and I've done this to him many, many times.

GG: Then your client put the changed product on the market. Did professional critics write that the whole strategy was completely wrong?

AK: I don't even talk to them.

GG: But did they write negatively about it?

AK: Oh yes. In fact I remember someone saying, "It doesn't look like Bisleri."

2.41 Recognition

When a woman goes wrong, a man goes right after her.

Mae West

Once a new form has cleared the hurdle of the creator's self-criticism, it is hoped or even expected that the result of so much hard labor will be accepted with open arms by contemporary society. A creator desires immediate success and the increase in prestige, status, and financial rewards that go along with it. If such success occurs and if, moreover, it is due to an appraisal delivered by highly competent critics, the self-confidence of the gratified individual receives a boost that fosters her or his motivation to strive towards new creative accomplishments. What is more, an acclaimed creator turns into a social role model inspiring and motivating other individuals and groups for creative performance. Official recognition thus helps to turn the wheel of creative progress.

In many realms, in science and literature for instance, the Nobel Prize is the highest expression of recognition offered by cultural selection. At times, however, it may be awarded to individuals who do not deserve it, for among the motivations and rationals steering the attribution of a Nobel Prize, politics sometimes plays a greater role than it should. Great creative leaders may never receive a Nobel Prize, as the fate of ingenious writers such as Tolstoy, Chekhov, Hardy, Ibsen, Zola, Henry James, Joseph Conrad, Kafka, Joyce, Proust, Brecht, Nabokov, and Jorge Luis Borges amply proves.

As a general rule, recognition by cultural selection begins in the immediate environment of a creative individual. Parents, partners, close friends, and colleagues generate an initial wave of recognition. This wave spreads until its concentric ripples reach more distant shores. Professional critics enter the game; marketing by publishers, gallery owners, and other professionals with vested interests plays a role; so do technical magazines and periodicals. Mass media enhances the power and propagation of the wave, and eventually the general public joins the admiration of a creative accomplishment.

The following examples illustrate how cultural evolution responds positively to the results of creative performance. I should like to emphasize, however, that the choice of the examples presented in the following sections is necessarily a subjective one. For obvious reasons I discuss those cases with which I have become familiar in the course of my scientific research. The samples I choose in no way imply a value judgement against creative personalities or groups not mentioned here. Nor does my selection reflect any particular cultural prejudice. Most of the books and articles I read were published in English, and I had to rely on the data they conveyed.

Let us begin our discussion with the domain of literature. Usually the first few books published by an author are not taken into account at all or are even explicitly rejected, yet history also offers examples of instant recognition. In 1612, Cervantes' *Don Quixote* (Boorstin 1992, 303) was an immediate popular success although its prudent publisher had secured his publishing rights only for Castile. The novel turned into a financial success for clever fellow publishers who had bought the publishing rights for Aragon and Portugal. Today nobody doubts that *Don Quixote* is not only a masterpiece of Spanish literature, but one of the precious literary heirlooms of the world.

In 1774, Johann Wolfgang von Goethe (Boorstin 1992, 599) published *The Sorrows of Young Werther*, a Weltschmerz epistolary in which the lovesick protagonist commits suicide because Lotte, with whom he has fallen in love, marries an older man. Once the book was published, Europe witnessed one of the strangest forms of public recognition ever bestowed upon a creative accomplishment. Across the continent, young people began to wear Werther's frockcoats, buff waistcoats, and yellow breeches. They scented their cheeks with Eau de Werther and showed off their Werther jewellery and Werther gloves. Some of them went even as far as to commit suicide with a copy of *The Sorrows of Young Werther* in their hands and letters of adieu on their bedside tables, in which they referred to parallels between their hero's and their own deep frustrations and disappointments.

On July 21, 1855, a few weeks after the publication of Walt Whitman's *Leaves of Grass*, Ralph Waldo Emerson (Kaplan 1980, 17) paid its author the following compliment: "I find it the most extraordinary piece of wit and wisdom that America has yet contributed." Naturalist Henry David Thoreau (Kaplan 1980, 222), a one-time assistant of Emerson, the author of Walden (a semiautobiographical attack on Western materialistic and consumerist attitudes), and one of the founding fathers of environmentalism, called Whitman "a great fellow." The poet Walt Whitman was thirty-six years old at the time, and such praise from established authorities served to boost his self-confidence.

Russia has produced its share of poets, novelists, and playwrights who have passed the test of cultural selection with flying colors. Among the greatest are Pushkin, Gogol, Turgenev, Dostoyevsky, Tolstoy, Chekhov, and Bulgakov.

Russians place their beloved poet Alexander Pushkin at the top of their rating scale of literature for the scope of his undertakings, his virtuoso style, and his tremendous versatility in literary genres, all of which are unique. Wilson (Wilson 1989, 5), a biographer of Tolstoy's, has called Pushkin ". . . the closest thing that literature has to Mozart." Pushkin's *Bronze Horseman* is a poem praising Tsar Peter the Great, who founded St. Petersburg in order to open Russia to the Western world and its progress. The writer and literary critic John Bayley (Briggs 1983, 118) has praised the *Bronze Horseman* as "the most remarkable of nineteenth-century poems." And Pushkin's long poem *Yevgeny Onegin* is today thought to constitute the very beginning of the Russian novel. Gogol (Kjetsaa 1987, 35) called Pushkin a "revelation of the Russian spirit." Many years later, Dostoyevsky, repeating Gogol's compliment, added that Pushkin was "a prophetic revelation" of the Russian Spirit.

If Pushkin was the Mozart of Russian literature, Tolstoy was its Beethoven. His novels *War and Peace* and *Anna Karenina* are masterpieces. Although ambivalent in his various statements, Ivan Turgenev considered Tolstoy to be a genius of literature. Gustave Flaubert, the author of *Madame Bovary*, saw in Tolstoy another Shakespeare. Anton Chekhov (Wilson 1989, 466) placed Tolstoy higher than Pushkin; for him Tolstoy was the number one creative leader in the Russian literary world.

In 1845, poet Nikolai Nekrasov took Fyodor Dostoyevsky's manuscript of the novel *Poor Folk,* handed it over to critic Vissarion Belinsky (Kjetsaa 1987, 44) and intoned: "We have a new Gogol!" Russia's foremost critic replied with tongue-in-cheek: "With the likes of you, Gogols are springing up like mushrooms." Yet that very evening, after having read the twenty-four-year-old Fyodor's manuscript, Belinsky fully agreed with Nekrasov. Prompted by Belinsky's reaction, Turgenev also began to applaud the new talent and Dostoyevsky soon found himself the center of attention in Moscow's literary circles.

Four years after having been praised as a new Gogol, Dostoyevsky was accused of anti-tsarist activities. He was convicted to forced labor and afterwards served in a Siberian regiment. In 1859, he was permitted to return to St. Petersburg. Three years later, he published his novel *The House of the Dead* in which he portrayed his experiences in a Siberian labor camp. A critic who admired the novel's brilliant style later recalled (Kjetsaa 1987, 136): "One saw in him a new Dante who had descended into the inferno." The literary elite of Moscow and St. Petersburg compared Dostoyevsky to Victor Hugo and Balzac. Tolstoy (Kjetsaa 1987, 366) hailed *The House of the Dead* as "the finest work in all of modern Russian literature."

In 1886, the influential Russian writer Dmitry Grigorovitch wrote to twenty-six-year-old Anton Chekhov (Troyat 1984, 84f.): "You have got real talent, a talent which places you high above the writers of the new generation." For the young physician suffering from tuberculosis and writing in order to financially support his widowed mother and his siblings living in poverty, this compliment was a huge encouragement. A year later Chekhov received the coveted Pushkin Prize for *At Dusk,* his collection of short stories.

In 1899, after the publication of Chekov's love story *The Lady with the Little Dog,* Maxim Gorki (Troyat 1984, 282) wrote to the author: "After the tiniest of your stories, everything appears to be coarse, written not with a plume but with a piece of firewood . . . Your stories are elegantly designed perfume bottles filled with all the aromas of life." Tolstoy, (Troyat 1984, 289) who loved Chekhov's stories as intensely as he rejected his plays, found a comparable image to characterize Chekhov's elegant and featherweight style: "It is as though he throws words into the air haphazardly but, like an impressionist painter, he achieves wonderful results with the strokes of his brush."

Among the Russian writers, Vladimir Nabokov (Field 1986) acquired a unique position—not only because he spoke several languages perfectly and wrote in Russian as well as in English—but also because he developed complex plots and a highly elegant style marked by intricate wordplay and the refined use of alliterations. Nabokov lived in voluntary exile in England, Germany, France, and the United States before the financial success of his novel *Lolita* allowed him to settle in Switzerland in 1960. There he spent the rest of his life, together with his wife Vera, at the Montreux Palace Hotel on the shores of Lake Geneva. *Lolita* was a bestseller both in the United States and in England. The first earnings (Field 1986, 301) came to $250,000; the movie rights sold for $150,000; and film director Stanley Kubrick offered Nabokov another $40,000 to write the screenplay. Nabokov was a stickler for perfection, and his biographer (Field 1986, 174) does not exaggerate when he writes: ". . . it is not too much to say that in all of Russian literature there are really only two prose writers against whose work Nabokov's Russian work may be measured in proper perspective: Gogol and Tolstoy."

If an artist is very lucky because he has got what the Italians call "un amico d'un amico" (a friend of a friend), then he may have even more chances of recognition. The mother of the aspiring French writer Guy de Maupassant (Troyat 1989, 25ff.) cleverly connected her son with her former lover, Gustave Flaubert, well known for *Madame Bovary.* One day, young Guy had the courage to read one of his poems to Flaubert. Flaubert had serious doubts as to whether Guy had real talent or not. Yet he encouraged the young writer, stating that, "Talent, following the words of Buffon, is nothing but a long stretch of patience. Work!" Maupassant took the hint. He worked relentlessly, and in 1880 Flaubert, having read *Boule de Suif* for the second time, wrote to Guy: ". . . I maintain that it is a masterpiece." At the age of thirty-three Guy de Maupassant's pride knew no bounds. To receive such praise from a lion of literature was the best thing that could have happened to him.

The amico principle also worked for Spanish poet and playwright Federico García Lorca. His friends (Gibson 1989, 71)—among them concert guitarist Andrés Segovia and composer Manuel de Falla—persuaded Don Federico García Rodríguez to pay for the publication of his son's collection of poems *Impressions and Landscapes*. Ten years later, Federico García Lorca published *Gypsy Ballads*, which became an instant public and commercial success. The critic of the journal *El Sol* (Gibson 1989, 212) called the book "the most personal and singular instrument of poetic expression in Spanish since the great innovations of Rubén Darío." To be compared with the Nicaraguan poet known as "The Father of Modernism in Spanish literature" was the highest praise Federico could possibly receive. In 1933, three years before he was assassinated by General Franco's Falange militia, Lorca's play *Blood Wedding* (Gibson 1989, 348) premiered in Madrid. At the end of each scene, the curtain rose and fell several times and the play was an instant smash.

The American writer Thomas Wolfe (Donald 1988, 78) was very much impressed by Sinclair Lewis' novel *Main Street* because it offered him a model for his own satire on daily life in a small town. He later told Lewis: "I think you are a man of genius with the most enormous talent for writing." In the summer of 1930, Wolfe published his novel *Look Homeward, Angel*. A critic writing for the *Times* in London (Donald 1988, 243) attributed to the author "a talent of such torrential energy as has not been seen in English literature for a long time." Sinclair Lewis (Donald 1988, 248) agreed that the novel possessed "authentic greatness," and he wished to have "some fresh phrase to express my profound delight." Shortly afterwards, while giving his acceptance speech to the Nobel Prize committee in Stockholm, Sinclair Lewis flatly stated that the novel *Look Homeward, Angel* ". . . is worthy to be compared with the best in our literary production, a Gargantuan creature with great gusto of life."

William Faulkner had a hard time in gaining the recognition he deserved, which included a National Book Award, two Pulitzer Prizes, and, in 1949 the Nobel Prize for Literature. Introverted and a chronic alcoholic (who spent years in Hollywood writing film scripts that were time and again rejected by incompetent directors and producers), he drudged on because it was the only way he could financially survive and support his family. In 1931, his novel *Sanctuary* (Oates 1988, 109) so impressed publishers and editors—who had rejected him until then—that all of a sudden they all wanted to publish him. Overwhelmed by this unexpected recognition, Faulkner wrote to his wife Estelle: "It's just like I was some strange and valuable beast." Five years later, Random House, who also represented James Joyce and Eugene O'Neill, published his novel, *Absalom, Absalom!* Cofounder of Random House Bennet Cerf went even so far as to say that Faulkner was (Oates 1988, 144) "the greatest possible adornment to the Random House list."

Pulitzer Prize-winning author Conrad Aiken (Oates 1988, 173) compared Faulkner to Balzac and praised his persistent search for a new structure and style in writing novels. Aitken's remarks were later echoed by the Swedish Nobel Prize committee when, in 1949, it emphasized that Faulkner (Oates 1988, 245) was being honored "for his powerful and independent artistic contribution in America's new literature of the novel."

In the autumn of 1929, Hemingway's novel *A Farewell to Arms* (Donald 1988, 222) sold 20,000 copies immediately. This commercial success proved that Hemingway's book about the First World War on the Isonzo front in northeastern Italy was accepted by cultural selection as a novel of merit.

In 1940, Hemingway (Lynn 1987, 485) published *For Whom the Bell Tolls,* a novel about the Spanish Civil War, in which he had participated as a war correspondent. *The New York Times Book Review* put the new novel on the front page, and its critic J. Donald Adams hailed the love scenes between the two protagonists, Roberto Jordan and Maria, as "the best in American fiction, period." Hemingway (Lynn 1987, 484) wrote a triumphant telegram to his first wife, Hadley, informing her: "Book selling like frozen Daiquiris in hell." By the end of 1943, the novel had become the biggest bestseller in American fiction since Margaret Mitchell's *Gone with the Wind* (Lynn 1987, 484), and Paramount's film version starring Ingrid Bergman as Maria and Gary Cooper as Robert Jordan became a box office hit, which in turn increased the sale of the novel.

In 1958, *Life Magazine* (Baker 1980, 640) organized a preprint of *The Old Man and the Sea* and sold over 5 million copies within two days. Art critic Bernhard Berenson (Baker 1980, 641), having read Hemingway's *The Old Man and the Sea,* exulted: ". . . a prose as calm and compelling as Homer's verse" and called the new novella a "short but not small masterpiece." The novella won its author the coveted Pulitzer Prize. The following year Hemingway received the Nobel Prize for his literary work.

John Steinbeck (Benson 1984, 120) had a hard life as a young writer. He received one rejection slip after the other, several of his publishers went bankrupt, and he lived on the brink of poverty. Eventually his novel, *The Grapes of Wrath,* about the Okies—the dust bowl migrants of Oklahoma—received the National Book Award, took the Pulitzer Prize in 1940 and became his first bestseller. By then Steinbeck had found his own, unique, and economic style combining poetic landscape portraits with an empathic view on human beings living at the fringes of society. In his strenuous uphill fight for artistic survival, Steinbeck turned out to be a man capable of generosity and able to acknowledge talent wherever he perceived it. He was aware that he had to compete, among others, against a successful Hemingway whom he called, in a letter to his editor, Covici, "the finest writer of our time." Worldwide recognition came in 1962, when Steinbeck was awarded the Nobel Prize in literature.

Ireland has produced more great writers per capita than any other country in the world. Among them are Seán O'Casey, Brendan Behan, Oscar Wilde, Edna O'Brian, James Joyce, and Nobel Prize laureates William Butler Yeats, G. B. Shaw, Samuel Beckett, and Seamus Heaney. Today James Joyce is considered to be the foremost creative innovator of them all. It took him seven years to write his masterpiece, *Ulysses*. In 1922, Hemingway (Ellmann 1983, 529) stated, in a letter to Sherwood Anderson—and in the boyish-casual style he liked to indulge in: "Joyce has a most goddam wonderful book." A year later (Lynn 1987, 161), Hemingway called Joyce "the greatest writer in the world." Despite such praise from a competent colleague, decades went by until Joyce received the worldwide recognition he deserved.

In 1858, the première of *The Vikings at Helgeland* (Meyer 1985, 173) Ibsen's eighth play turned out to be "a triumph," as his biographer writes. It was followed by a wave of rejections until in 1865, his play *Brand* (Meyer 1985, 266), a more popular topic for discussion in Scandinavia than the philosopher Kierkegaard, became a critical and popular success, improving Ibsen's precarious financial situation. *Brand*, together with *Peer Gynt* (Meyer 1985, 331) published in 1867, were so influential that they inspired the development of the modern prose drama, which eventually replaced the traditional verse drama.

In 1873, Ibsen's play *Emperor and Galilean* turned out to be a huge success. His Danish publisher, Frederik Hegel (Meyer 1985, 395), reported that the "large edition . . . was almost entirely subscribed, and the rest were taken by the Copenhagen booksellers on the day of publication." Six years later Ibsen published *A Doll's House*. An eyewitness later reported (Meyer 1985, 476) that the play "exploded like a bomb into contemporary society." Three years later, the publication of *An Enemy of the People* added to Ibsen's growing international acknowledgement. By now he was accepted not only in foreign countries but also by the theater-lovers of Norway.

In 1892, a London critic (Meyer 1985, 688) wrote that Ibsen's influence on English playwrights was tremendous: " . . . It may be said of Ibsen's influence, as Napoleon said of the French Republic, that it is as obvious as the Sun in Heaven, and asks for no recognition." Today Ibsen is considered to be a towering figure whose fellow playwright and Nobel laureate Pirandello (Meyer 1985, 866) simply stated: "*After* Shakespeare I unhesitatingly place Ibsen first." And the four-time Pulitzer Prize winner and Nobel laureate Eugene O'Neill confessed that he found Ibsen "much nearer to me than Shakespeare."

August Strindberg's way to cultural recognition was shorter than Ibsen's. His biographer Meyer (1985, 48) compares the accomplishment of the young dramatist's play, *Master Olof* published in 1872, with the exceptional performance of another young genius: Georg Büchner was twenty-two years old when he wrote *Danton's Death;* two years later he created *Woyzeck.* Seven years after the publication of *Master Olof,* Strindberg published the novel, *The Red Room.* It got mixed reviews in Stockholm, but the press of Copenhagen (Meyer 1985, 80) acknowledged Strindberg as a writer of genius. In December 1883, Ibsen's play, *Lucky Pehr* (Meyer 1988, 122), staged in Sweden, was his first success. The Göteborgsposten was jubilant: "No play at any theatre in human memory has achieved such a triumph." Years later, the Danish critic and scholar Georg Brandes (Meyer 1988, 192) wrote a letter to Nietzsche in which he called Strindberg "Sweden's only genius." In his acceptance speech to the Nobel Prize committee in Stockholm in 1936, Eugene O'Neill (Gelb and Gelb 1987, 234) paid homage to his role model, "that greatest genius of all modern dramatists, your August Strindberg."

As for Eugene O'Neill himself, he now belongs, together with Aeschylus, Sophocles, Euripides, Shakespeare, Ibsen, Strindberg, and Chekhov, to the pantheon of the world's greatest playwrights. In 1920, his first published play *Beyond the Horizon* received the Pulitzer Prize; two years later he was awarded a second Pulitzer Prize for his play *Anna Christie;* in 1928, the play *Strange Interlude* brought him a third Pulitzer Prize. In 1936, he received the Nobel Prize for his creative work and in 1956, three years after his death, he was bestowed with a fourth Pulitzer Prize for *Long Day's Journey into the Night* (Gelb and Gelb 1987, 863). With these five awards, the recognition offered by the process of cultural selection has placed O'Neill in a category shared by none of his fellow playwrights. The highest compliment the jazz composer, bandleader, and pianist Duke Ellington would pay a fellow musician was: "He is beyond category." And that Eugene O'Neill certainly is.

Let us now leave literature and cast a glance upon cultural evaluation in the arts.

In 1334, the city council of Florence named Giotto (Kemp 2004, 205f.; Boorstin 1992, 383f.) capomaestro, surveyor of their cathedral, and first architect of the city. In the following century, Ghiberti and Mantegna reached a higher social status than their contemporary colleagues, although they were unable as yet to climb onto the pedestal of true stardom. Eventually, Leonardo, Michelangelo, and Raphael reached the status of veritable superstars whose services were eagerly solicited by popes, kings, and other dignitaries alike; the creative output of these three artists was highly paid. In 1538, the Portuguese painter Francisco de Hollanda (Boorstin 1992, 408) visited Rome. After having studied the social scene and its status hierarchies, he wrote: "In Italy, one does not care for the renown of great princes; it's a painter only that they call divine."

In the sixteenth century, the multitalented goldsmith Benvenuto Cellini visited France (Kemp 2004, 45). Later he reported that King Francis I admired Leonardo, who lived at his court—where he held the official title of "the first painter, architect and mechanic of the King"—not only as a painter but also as a great sculptor, architect, and outstanding philosopher. Cellini (Payne 1978, 284) forgot to mention that already at the court of Duke Ludovico Sforza in Milano, Leonardo had been a highly appreciated engineer sharing rank with the architect Donato Bramante (Kemp 2004, 116), who would later be chosen by Pope Julius II as the chief architect for the rebuilding of St. Peter's Basilica in Rome. In today's appraisal Leonardo was, as Robert Payne (Payne 1978, xix) writes in the introduction of a carefully researched biography: ". . . one of those rare men who throw shadows which are full of light and full of promise. There is another mountain range called Socrates; another is Dante; a third is Shakespeare."

Flemish painter Peter Paul Rubens (Payne 1978, 307) observed that Leonardo elaborated in a painted object "its most appropriate and most living aspect, and exalted majesty to the point where it becomes divine." Leonardo possessed what he called *saperveder*, the rare talent to look at an object or organism in such a manner that he understood its innermost nature. His curiosity for exploration knew no bounds. Tuscan born mathematical genius Luca Pacioli (Gallluzzi 1987, 132) called his friend Leonardo, whom he mentored in mathematics, a "tireless inventor of new things."

In 1503, Niccolò Machiavelli (Boorstin 1992, 405f.), chancellor of the Signoria in Florence, secured his friend Leonardo the commission to paint in the Council Hall a mural twice as large as *The Last Supper* the artist had created for the refectory of the abbey Santa Maria delle Grazie in Milan. As a topic for the mural, Leonardo chose the Battle of Anghiari where the Florentines had defeated the papal Milanese forces half a century earlier. Leonardo focused on a key scene of this battle representing the moment where the enemy standard was captured. He sketched a prodigious cartoon displaying horses wheeling and kicking, and whose flaring nostrils, bared teeth, and bulging eyes reflected the ferocity deforming the faces of the warring riders.

To Leonardo's utter dismay, the young and highly ambitious sculptor and painter Michelangelo, who had just finished his David (a sculpture judged to be superior to any of Donatello's work), got himself a commission to paint the opposite wall in the same Council Hall. As his topic he chose an episode of the Battle of Cascina where, in 1364, the Pisan enemy had made a surprise attack on Florentine soldiers bathing in the Arno River. Like Leonardo, Michelangelo also made a sketch before he began to paint his fresco.

While the two artists were painting their respective panels, the population of Florence flocked to the Council Hall to watch the ongoing competition; in those eventful days the slowly emerging masterworks were, as Benvenuto Cellini (Boorstin 1992, 406) puts it, "the school of the world." The crowd admired both artists, compared their respective merits, and the degrees of their individual scopes and accomplishments. Unfortunately—and due to particular circumstances—neither one of the two masterpieces has survived. Leonardo, who was experimenting with new methods, applied a binder to the wall that immediately peeled off. Then he had to leave for Milan where, during his service under Duke Ludovico Sforza, he was to paint his masterwork, *Virgin of the Rocks*. It was in this painting that he perfected his sfumato technique, a mysterious haze that enveloped the whole scene in an atmosphere of bucolic enchantment.

As for Michelangelo, he had to leave for Rome where his patron Pope Julius II ordered him to erect a monumental tomb for His Holiness—whose ambition knew no bounds. In both cases, the Signoria of Florence, clever as ever in diplomatic power games, had to give up their commissions in order not to snub Milan's Duke and Rome's Pope.

The competition between Leonardo and Michelangelo went far beyond the question of who was to be the greater painter in the eyes of the Florentine citizens. It was, at the same time, a struggle for the supremacy of one art form over another. The question was: is painting a higher art form than sculpting? In 1436, Leone Battista Alberti, an architect and humanist polymath, had attributed "divine power" to an artist (Boorstin 1992, 408). Later, Leonardo went further and boasted that the result of a painter's creative efforts were "nobler than that of nature" and elevated the painter to "a second god." This ranking relegated a sculptor to a lower status, infuriated young Michelangelo, eager to dethrone Leonardo. Even more irksome for Michelangelo was the sarcastic tone of Leonardo's *Treatise on Painting* in which the latter had maliciously compared the noble gestures of an elegantly dressed master painter with the hard, noisy labor of a sculptor, covered in sweat and marble dust from head to toe.

In 1512, the ceiling of the Sistine Chapel (Boorstin 1992, 417) was revealed, and the beauty and power of expression of Michelangelo's huge painting were overwhelming. So was the fact that he had managed to paint such a gallery of fantastic figures and compositions—nine scenes from the Book of Genesis— not on a flat canvas, but on an irregular curved surface interrupted by protruding edges, lunettes, and triangles. His accomplishment was awe inspiring, not simply beautiful, but sublime. The Romans used the term *terribilità* to characterize the powerful impact his grandiose painting made on the viewers.

As we shall see further on, the public recognition of Michelangelo's masterwork in the Sistine Chapel was tarnished by some ill-advised intrigues. Yet in the end, Michelangelo mastered all the obstacles strewn on his path. On

September 1, 1535, Pope Paul III (Murray 1985, 158; Koch 1991, 163) installed Michelangelo as the Vatican's supreme architect, sculptor, and painter. Such sovereign honor provoked a great deal of envy among the artist's competitors. Yet he prevailed in the face of insidious machinations spun by Bramante and Raphael. In 1546, the seventy-one-year-old artist (Boorstin 1992, 416) was elevated by Pope Paul III to the rank of chief architect and superintendent of the rebuilding of St. Peter's Basilica.

Flemish painter Peter Paul Rubens is probably best known for his erotic paintings of Baroque nudes in all kinds of voluptuous postures. His first successes were portraits of royalties and works of sacral art, and the quantity of his output was as great as its artistic quality. Between 1609 and 1620, Rubens (Schama 1999, 151) painted sixty-three altarpieces: twenty-two for churches and chapels in Antwerp, where he lived; ten for Brussels, and the rest for churches and chapels in Germany and France. In 1611, the committee responsible for the Benedictine Abbey of St. Winnoksberger decided to commission an artist to paint the Abbey's high altar. Merchant Jan le Grand (Schama 1999, 150) recommended Rubens as best choice for that job, naming him "the god of painting." Rubens got the commission and added yet another masterpiece to his already amazing series of creative achievements.

During the 1620s, Rubens went, as Schama (Schama 1999, 179) puts it, "from acclaim as the local Apelles[2] to international recognition as the greatest master of his age." Famous dynasties solicited his services to have their portraits made for posterity. Marie de' Medici, Queen Mother of France, and King Charles I of England were among the principalities vying for his favors. In 1672, the fifty-five-year-old Rubens (Schama 1999, 77) was known throughout Europe under the honorary title "the prince of painters and painter of princes." French painter Delacroix (Butterfield 2005, 14-18) even hailed Rubens as the "Homer of painting." The governments of Flanders, England, France, and Spain competed with each other for Rubens' services as a portraitist and painter of mythical and historical heroic scenes.

Rubens had worked hard to reach the conceptual depth and technical virtuosity underpinning his exalted status. As a young man he had travelled to Italy and studied the art of antiquity and of the Renaissance. He had also read the classic Greek and Roman authors (Butterfield 2005, 14-18) in order to understand topics and techniques used in great art as well as its underlying aesthetic concepts. Between 1600 and 1609, Rubens had served as a court painter to the Duke of Mantua. In those years, he had acquired a mastery of methods and techniques that allowed him to work with great rapidity yet high precision. The biographer of Baroque artists Giovanni Pietro Bellory (Butterfield 2005, 14-18) used the term "*furia del pennello*" (the fury of the brushwork) to characterize Rubens' highly dynamic painting technique.

Simon Schama (Schama 1999, 157) has written an excellent study on Rembrandt and compared the respective merits of Rubens and Rembrandt. He characterizes Rubens' whirlwind attacks on the canvas as a fury of "boiling energy" chasing the brush all over the canvas and discharging its paint in a flurry of turning and twisting lines to create a sophisticated representation of Magdalene, Saint Anne and the Savior.

So great was the fame of Rubens that for the first half of his life, Dutch painter and etcher Rembrandt van Rijn—a generation younger than his great role model—was obsessed with the Flemish genius and did everything he could to reach and bypass Rubens' status and prestige.

In 1629, at the age of twenty-three, Rembrandt (Mee 1988, 80) was already a prodigy who, thanks to the recommendation of the statesman Constantijn Huygens, received an important commission at the court of The Hague. As Schama (1999, 29) points out, back then The Hague was "in its halcyon days:" there was money, there was an aristocratic and merchant clientele able to pay expensive commissions, and there was the public ambition to make of the court city a place able to compete with Amsterdam. Already during the seventeenth century, an expansive overseas shipping trade had made Amsterdam a haven of wealth. Now, two centuries later, the Netherlands was experiencing what historians call the Golden Age of Dutch art, and Rembrandt played a central role in that era.

In 1631, Rembrandt moved to Amsterdam; there he began to etch his *Self-Portrait in a Soft Hat*. Over the years, he seems to have etched eleven versions of that self-portrait until finally he was satisfied with the result of his efforts. His biographer writes (Schama 1999, 37), that etching "was his signature, his claim to be the new Rubens." That work of art already shows all the intimacy and immediacy so typical of Rembrandt's self-portraits and portraits. In 1632, Rembrandt painted the *Portrait of Johannes Wtenbogaert* and *The Anatomy Lesson of Dr. Tulp*. Both paintings reveal a depth of conception and a technical virtuosity rarely achieved by artists.

Ten years after completing the two abovementioned portraits, Rembrandt participated with several colleagues in a commission to paint the great hall of the militia guild, in fact the most spacious room existing in Amsterdam, sixty feet long, thirty feet wide, and fifteen feet high. It was there that he created *The Night Watch* (Schama 1999, 481ff.), a colossal group portrait (363 x 437 cm) that not only relegated his colleagues' paintings to the category of 'also-rans,' but is thought today to be Rembrandt's most important masterpiece. In a treatise on painting, Samuel van Hoogstraten (Schama 1999, 488), a former disciple of Rembrandt, later wrote the following commentary on *The Night Watch*: ". . . the painting . . . will, in my opinion, survive all its rivals because it is so painterly in conception and so powerful that, according to some people, all the other pieces in the *doelen*[3] look like playing cards alongside it."

A contemporary biographer of Rembrandt (Mee 1988, 139f.) characterizes the importance of the fabulous Dutch master in these words: "It may be that the greatest gift art has to give us is to set us free of old limits of perception, thought and feeling; certainly that is what Rembrandt does above all in painting after painting."

In 1866, Claude Monet (Boorstin 1992, 515) exhibited a life-size portrait of his wife Camille. Writer Emile Zola, exulting over the realism of the painter's work, called Monet "a man amid this crowd of eunuchs." Monet's colleagues must have swallowed hard while reading Zola's insulting commentary. Two years later, Monet (Gordon and Forge 1983, 105) returned from a painting trip to Antibes and offered his art dealer Theo van Gogh thirty-six canvases representing landmarks, landscapes, and seascapes. Theo's brother Vincent was very much impressed by the fluency enabling Monet to turn out so many paintings of such high quality. In a letter to Theo, Vincent compared Monet, as Gordon and Forge (1983) put it, to "an old lion able to bring down its quarry with a single blow." The metaphor is an apt one, even for a painter mainly interested in rendering the weightless beauty of light. Vincent van Gogh views Monet as the king of his domain, peerless, and so experienced in his handicraft that he successfully reaches his aims with only minimum effort. Now the lion began to receive recognition, public acclaim, and the accompanying financial success. In 1889, Theo van Gogh (Gordon and Forge 1983, 155) sold one of the Antibes paintings for the then unheard of price of 10,350 francs. Within two years Monet earned over 100,000 francs, which allowed him to buy a house in Giverny that would soon become the center of Monet's private and social life.

Monet and Pissarro were the cofounders of Impressionism, a conceptual revolution that radically changed the outlook of visual arts. Emile Zola helped to prepare Pissarro's (Shikes and Harper 1980, 75) breakthrough by placing him in the category of the "three or four painters of our time . . . A beautiful picture by this artist is the act of an honest man." With the vigorous support of art dealer Durand-Ruell (Shikes and Harper 1980, 102), Pissarro and Monet paved the way for the public acceptance of Sisley, Degas, and Manet—the creative leader in that process being Pissarro. In 1890, Durand-Ruel (Shikes and Harper 1980, 262) paid him 164 francs and just two years later Pissarro pocketed 23,042 francs from the same art dealer. Such a tremendous commercial success beautifully illustrates an artist's recognition by the process of cultural selection. But the best was yet to come. Pissarro's (Shikes and Harper 1980, 315) peak experience occurred in August 1903 when, three months before he died, he was able to write to his son Lucien: "I have been fortunate enough to sell to the Louvre Museum two of my canvases of size 15." Three years later, in the catalogue of his exhibition in Aix, Cézanne (Shikes and Harper 1980, 320; Doran 1978, 98) presented himself as "Paul Cézanne, pupil of Pissarro" and declared: "Monet and Pissarro were the two great masters, the only ones."

The painter and sculptor Alberto Giacometti (Lord 1991, 18) respected and admired authentic individuals, for instance strong personalities such as Cézanne whose work is a bridge between Impressionism and Cubism. Giacometti called the recluse artist, whose creative accomplishments have often been rejected by contemporary experts, "the greatest of them all." In the same vein, Gleizes and Metzinger (Gleizes and Metzinger 1964, 4) flatly stated: "Cézanne is one of the greatest of those who orient history, and it is inappropriate to compare him to van Gogh or Gauguin. He recalls Rembrandt." Today we view Cézanne as a mountain range whose many slopes, caves, and shafts will be explored forever after by miners on the lookout for precious treasures yet to be discovered.

Alberto Giacometti received early though somewhat mitigated recognition in Paris (Lord 1985, 76), where he was known as "the crazy genius." His biographer Lord (1985, 430) points out that many artists—among them Picasso, Matisse, and Degas—expressed themselves in the two domains of painting and sculpting, but that none reached so convincing a synthesis of aesthetic expression in both domains as Giacometti. Writer Jean Genet (Lord 1985, 351) paid the artist the highest tribute by stating: "Giacometti is not working for his contemporaries nor for future generations: he is creating statues to at last delight the dead."

Pablo Picasso (Stassinopoulos 1989; Gilot 1991) was a child prodigy whose career began with acclaim and public triumph. In his early twenties he moved from Spain to Paris. After a few lean years, Picasso's skills in the ruthless manipulation of people and his charismatic showbiz talent paved his way onto the front pages of the tabloid press, into prime time radio shows, and, with the emergence of telecasting, into the news and feature shows of global television.

Picasso's commercial success began to bloom in the autumn of 1909 when the Russian art collector Serge Shchukine (Stassinopoulos 1989, 101) bought fifty of his paintings, partly for motives that Picasso's innate aggressiveness must have relished. Shchukine intended to play a game the French call *épater le bourgeois*: he wanted to shock his aristocratic friends and relatives in Moscow whose appreciation of art was still caught up in a traditional groove. Today Picasso's paintings reach top prices in art auctions. But as a (often overrated) creative artist, his main merit remains that, together with Georges Braque—and highly influenced by the meticulous study of African masks and sculptures—he was the coinventor of Cubism.

Wassily Kandinsky and Paul Klee, sometimes referred to as the "poets of modern painting," both taught at the Bauhaus in Weimar. Klee's (Grohmann 1977, 17) maxim whereby "Art doesn't render the visible, it rather makes visible" has heavily influenced modern art as has Kandinsky's (Kandinsky 1977) contemplation on the spiritual power of art. In 1920, architect Gropius and his colleagues (Grohmann 1977, 19) invited Paul Klee, "unanimously" as they emphasized, to join them. In January 1921, Klee travelled to Weimar and in the same year Kandinsky also joined the Bauhaus group. Today nobody doubts that Kandinsky and Klee were unique figures on the twentieth century art scene. They were innovators, inventors, and visionaries whose theoretical contributions were as important to the evolution of visual art as were their imaginative drawings and paintings.

Let us now turn to the world of classical music[4] and see how recognition by cultural selection works in that realm.

In 1787, Joseph Haydn wrote a letter to Franz Rott (Werner-Jensen 2001, 155) in which he praised the "inimitable works of Mozart" (Amadeus was then thirty-one years old) and suggested that nations should compete with each other in order "to possess such a jewel within their ring walls." Haydn's letter is a typical expression of the genius cult of the eighteenth century that acknowledged a whole series of genius composers ranging from J. S. Bach, to Haydn, Mozart, and Beethoven.

Johann Sebastian Bach (1685-1750) was the first in a row of composers of classical music to be hailed as a genius. His creative output is unique in its depth and breadth of scope. It includes The *Mass in B Minor*, which Boorstin (Boorstin 1992, 433) has described as "the greatest piece of Western music ever composed;" *the Brandenburg Concertos; the St. Matthew Passion; The Musical Offering; The Art of the Fugue; the Cello Suites*; and more than 200 cantatas. Ludwig van Beethoven (1770-1827) indulged in an apt wordplay when he stated with respect to Bach (Boorstin 1992, 437): "Not Bach (brook), but Meer (sea) should be his name." Hofstadter (Hofstadter 1979, 10) sees in *The Musical Offering* "one of Bach's supreme accomplishments in counterpoint" and "a very beautiful creation of the human intellect which we can appreciate forever."

On his seventy-sixth birthday, Joseph Haydn (1732-1809) gave a concert in Vienna. Beethoven (Boorstin 1992, 448) had broken up with his former tutor long before, yet after that concert he knelt before Haydn and kissed his hand—a gesture of deference to acknowledge a genius. Napoleon Bonaparte, who in those days occupied Vienna, also paid his respects to the great composer. He placed a guard of honor in front of Haydn's house, and when the composer died in 1809, a delegation of the French army took part in his funeral procession.

Beethoven (1770-1827) was a rather slow composer, but a virtuoso pianist and a genius when it came to improvisation. In Vienna, a deeply impressed rival pianist (Boorstin 1992, 456) exclaimed: "Ah, he's no man—he's a devil. He will play me and all of us to death." In his mid-twenties, Ludwig van Beethoven began to lose his hearing. Although his acoustic impairment, domestic struggles with his brother, and an unlucky love life drove him to the brink of suicide, he prevailed and created a whole range of piano sonatas, violin concertos and symphonies that boosted him to the status of giant in classical music. In 1849, the Russian anarchist Mikhail Bakunin (Boorstin 1992, 479), an ardent admirer of Beethoven's music, exclaimed: "All, all will perish, not only music, the other arts too . . . only one thing will not perish but last forever: the Ninth Symphony."

The most famous of the geniuses of classical music was Wolfgang Amadeus Mozart (1756-1791). Although his life was rather short and often unhappy due to marital strife and the lack of a steady income, he produced more than 600 compositions and left a legacy that is absolutely unique and still plays a central role in our contemporary concert repertoire worldwide. Mozart was a child prodigy, playing the clavier at the age of three and creating his first compositions at the age of five.

In 1769, 1771, and 1772, Wolfgang Amadeus Mozart made three very successful concert trips to Italy where he received impressive public acclaim, plus commissions to compose three operas in a row. At the end of that decade, in 1777, he created the *Piano Concerto in E flat K.271*, hailed by critics as a major breakthrough. Mozart's biographer Solomon (1996, 296) aptly writes that: ". . . Mozart essentially invented the classical piano concerto." According to Solomon, Mozart explored the concerto's form and expression by composing a ". . . series of highly individual masterpieces. He unveiled a universe and then devoted himself to populating it with the most diverse creations."

In 1781, after having been thrown out of the services of Prince Colloredo Archbishop of Salzburg "with a kick in the arse," as Amadeus specified, the twenty-five-year-old composer left for Vienna, where he was to make his most important breakthrough yet. Promptly looked upon and admired as a great concert pianist, he was often invited to play for Emperor Joseph II. Mozart's opera *The Abduction from the Seraglio* proved to be a huge success and was soon performed in all German-speaking countries of Europe.

In 1783, Mozart's *Mass in C Minor* was premiered in Salzburg and received tremendous acclaim. In February 1785, when three of Mozart's string quartets—K.428, K.464, and K.465—were played for the first time, Joseph Haydn (Einstein 1983, 24) told father Leopold: ". . . your son is the greatest composer, whom I know as a person and by name; he possesses taste and, moreover, the highest science of composition." For once father Leopold, always critical of his son's ideas, efforts, and accomplishments, was more than satisfied. Goethe, who in a conversation with his personal secretary Eckermann (Solomon 1996, 118) stated that Mozart "was altogether in the power of the demonic spirit of his genius, and acted according to his orders," shared Haydn's evaluation.

Mozart's by then famous collaboration with the librettist Lorenzo da Ponte began in the same year in which Haydn had paid him the highest tributes and Mozart had produced three operas (which still belong to the top repertoire of the world's best opera houses): *The Marriage of Figaro, Don Giovanni,* and *Così fan Tutte.* Their success (plus the death of chamber composer C. W. Gluck) may have persuaded Emperor Leopold II to offer Mozart the job of a K. and K. chamber composer. That position demanded no special performances at all and came with the modest salary of 800 Gulden, less than half the salary Gluck had received. Mozart (Einstein 1983, 67) commented on such pay with the sarcastic remark: "Too much for what I do, too little for what I would be able to accomplish!"

In 1791, the last year of his life, Mozart, suffering from depression and what was probably yet another bout of rheumatic fever, composed a series of his most important masterpieces including the opera *The Magic Flute,* the *Piano Concerto in B flat K.595,* the *Clarinet Concerto K.622,* and the unfinished *Requiem K.626,* eventually completed by his disciple and personal friend Franz Xaver Süssmayr.

Mozart died on December 5, 1791. He was buried in an unmarked grave in the St. Marx Cemetery. The weather was so bad—rain, sleet, and snow whipped by a furious wind—that nobody accompanied his remains, not even his wife Constanze. Ten days after Mozart's burial in Vienna, a solemn funeral ceremony was held in Nicolai Church in Prague (Solomon 1996, 499) attended by mourners "in such numbers that neither the church nor the adjacent, so-called Italian Square, could accommodate all of them." Prague had been the stage of Mozart's greatest triumphs, now its population offered the defunct composer an honor which the population of Vienna had withheld.

The huge box office hits of Peter Shaffer's play *Amadeus* and of the film by the same name based on Shaffer's play, directed by Milos Forman and produced by independent film producer Saul Zaentz, bear witness to the fact that the interest in Mozart's music is still as strong today as it had been during the composer's lifetime. The musical structure of Mozart's compositions often reminds me of the forest wasp nests I used to admire during my childhood years in the Southern Swiss Alps: there is a delicate balance of individual structural elements combining formal perfection and a sophisticated, apparently highly vulnerable architecture with amazing stability. The impact of

Mozart's compositions consists of a delicate dynamic equilibrium somewhere between "the unbearable lightness of being" (Milan Kundera) and the melancholic heaviness that makes our heart and our whole being a prey to gravity. Einstein (Einstein 1983, 115), one of Mozart's biographers, pays the composer the ultimate compliment by stating: "He is universal; he is neither a national nor an international musician. He is transnational ('übernational')."

Among the composers following the great classics just discussed, nobody has provoked so much jubilant praise and, at the same time resolute rejection or even outright contempt, as Richard Wagner. In his autobiography the conductor and composer Bruno Walter (Walter 1988, 44) confesses that he was "completely under the spell of Wagner" from the very moment on when he heard for the very first time the opera *Tristan and Isolde*.

On his personal rating scale of greatness, maestro Arturo Toscanini placed Wagner and Verdi as equals on the highest level. In 1884 in his hometown Parma, the then seventeen-year-old Arturo attended a performance of Wagner's *Lohengrin*. Later Toscanini (Sachs 1995, 14), speaking of "Wagner's genius" enthused: ". . . from the first bars of the Prelude, I was overwhelmed by magical, supernatural feelings; the celestial harmonies revealed a new world to me..." In 1899, Toscanini sent a postcard representing Wagner's grave to a friend (Sachs 1995, 72) and wrote: "Here is the tomb of the greatest composer of the century."

In 1887, Toscanini (Sachs 1995, 27) played the second cello while Giuseppe Verdi conducted his own opera *Otello* at Milan's La Scala. At the rehearsals, Verdi exhorted the second cello to play louder a part marked in the score by 'piano' and 'pianissimo.' Toscanini complied and found to his amazement that now the part sounded better. The first performance of *Otello* turned out to be a huge success and, overwhelmed by his emotions, Arturo ran home, woke up his sleeping mother and shouted: "Mamma, Verdi is a genius! Down on your knees to Verdi, down on your knees to Verdi!" For the rest of Toscanini's days, Wagner and Verdi remained his favorite opera composers.

In due time, the creative conductor Toscanini (Sachs 1995, 59) himself passed the test of cultural selection with flying colors. At the age of thirty-one, he was nominated musical director of La Scala, an honor no conductor had received before. Soon the maestro's fame was so great that he was invited all over the world to conduct musical performances.

In science, cultural evaluation plays the same role as in every other creative domain. In the appraisal of their colleagues' accomplishments, scientists are able to deploy great generosity as well as utter meanness. Let us first discuss their generosity; we shall deal with their meanness in a later section.

In 1807, the invading French army approached Göttingen, the home of mathematician Carl Friedrich Gauß (Bernstein 1996, 136). Napoleon, a former artillery officer who loved mathematics, ordered his troops to spare the town "because the greatest mathematician of all times is living here." Still, the French levied heavy punitive fines on the citizens, and Gauß was supposed to pay the equivalent of $5,000 today. He was unable to do so, and the famous French mathematician and astronomer Marquis Pierre Simone de Laplace generously offered to pay the fine, emphasizing that his colleague Gauß was "the greatest mathematician in the world."

Nobel laureate and physicist Eugene Wigner (Gleick 1993, 184) referred to his colleague, experimental physicist Richard Feynman, as "a second Dirac, only this time human." Paul Dirac had, among other accomplishments, predicted the existence of antielectrons. To be compared to such a luminary catapulted Feynman into the realm of geniuses. Dirac (Gleick 1993, 323) in turn hailed Feynman for being "the most original mind of his generation."

Louis de Broglie's (Lederman and Dick 1993, 165) important contribution to wave mechanics elicited Einstein's comment: "He has lifted a corner of the great veil." J. Robert Oppenheimer, leader of the fateful Manhattan Project in Los Alamos, New Mexico, and also known under the sobriquet "Father of the atom bomb," spoke of Erwin Schrödinger's (Lederman and Dick 1993, 169) theory of wave mechanics as "perhaps one of the most perfect, most accurate, and most lovely man has discovered." His colleague Arthur Sommerfeld declared Schrödinger's theory to be "the most astonishing among all the astonishing discoveries of the twentieth century." Nobel laureate and director of the Fermi Lab in Chicago Leon Lederman (Lederman and Dick 1993, 171) characterized Max Born's interpretation of Schrödinger's theory as "the single most dramatic and major change in our worldview since Newton." Biographer Moore (1989, 3) asserts with respect to Schrödinger's four papers on wave mechanics written in 1926 that "there is nothing more beautiful in theoretical physics." And on April 16, 1926, Einstein, who single-handedly founded quantum mechanics (Moore 1989, 209), wrote to Schrödinger: "The idea of your work springs from true genius!"

Italian nuclear physicist Enrico Fermi made numerous major contributions to quantum physics. He has been hailed as a genius, as somebody who stood out of the crowd of highly talented physicists of the first half of the last century. Astrophysicist Chandrasekhar (Wali 1991, 265), who had collaborated with Fermi, described how Fermi's mind functioned. He likened Chandrasekhar's reaction to new problems to the approach of a musician who: ". . . when presented with a new piece of music, at once plays it with a perception and a discernment which one would normally associate only with long practice and study."

India-born Subrahmanyan Chandrasekhar (Wali 1991, 53) was a prodigy in mathematics about whom a childhood friend stated: "He was thought of as a genius by all the people and shown marked deference by all members of the family." In 1928, Chandrasekhar travelled to Calcutta to work with his uncle, physicist Chandrasekhara Venkata Raman. Together with K. S. Krishnan (Wali 1991, 60f.), Raman had made a very exciting discovery: the scattering of light by the molecular structure of a chemical substance. Raman's colleague, famous quantum physicist S. N. Bose, studied that discovery and told Raman: "Professor Raman, you have made a great discovery. It will be called the Raman effect, and you will win the Nobel Prize." His prediction turned out to be correct. Two years later, Raman received the Nobel Prize in physics and the honor made a major impact on Chandrasekhar's own achievement motivation. Chandrasekhar's scientific career began during a meeting presided over by his uncle Raman. The eighteen-year-old undergraduate delivered a lecture on *The Compton Scattering and the New Statistics*, a performance the audience acknowledged with thundering applause. The paper formulated on the basis of that lecture was published the same year in the *Proceedings of the Royal Society*. From that day on and for the next fifty years or so, Chandrasekhar would publish a stream of scientific papers. His biographer Kameshwar C. Wali compares Chandrasekhar's productivity and creative output to that of Sir Walter Raleigh (Wali 1991, 28) who, for a period of more than half a century, published an average of eight to ten papers of high quality every year.

In 1930, Chandrasekhar (Wali 1991, 68) received a Government of India scholarship permitting him to pursue his studies in England. At Trinity College, Cambridge, only one other mathematical genius from India Srinivasa Ramanujan (Wali 1991, 109) had hitherto been admitted—some sixteen years earlier. Chandrasekhar became a research student under Professor R. H. Fowler. Yet the role model who made the most profound impression on him was quantum physicist Paul Dirac, whom Chandrasekhar befriended and whose lectures he adored because Dirac was able to describe and explain complex phenomena in a manner that was simple, precise, and easily understandable for gifted graduates.

In 1934, Chandrasekhar was invited to study for a year with Niels Bohr in Copenhagen. His father received another enthused letter (Wali 1991, 99) expressing the recognition paid by a promising talent to an established, universally recognized genius: "It would be difficult to find Bohr's equal I mean particularly in the greatness of his influence at the moment I can think of only one name Gauss." On December 14, 1932, yet another letter praising Bohr reached Subrahmanyan's father (Wali 1991, 102f.): "He is not one who likes to talk glibly. He is Socratic in his views with the difference that Socrates had time enough but Bohr has not."

Today Chandrasekhar is considered to be the number one creative leader of the Indian quintet of outstanding scientists that includes himself, mathematician Srinivasa Ramanujan, astrophysicist Meghnad Saha, and physicists J. C. Bose and C. V. Raman. He has been honored with many awards (Wali 1991, 296), among them the Royal Astronomical Society Gold Medal in 1953; the National Medal of Sciences given by President Johnson (Chandra was the first astronomer ever to receive that medal) in 1967; the Nobel Prize in 1983 which he shared with William A. Fowler, with whom he had studied and worked at Trinity College in Cambridge; and the Copley Medal in 1984, the highest honor bestowed by the Royal Society.

Let us now move from the realm of physics to that of biology and have a look at a few examples illustrating how the recognition of creative accomplishments works in that field.

Charles Darwin, father of the theory of biological evolution, is as towering a figure in biology as are Newton and Einstein in physics. In the course of time, his trail-blazing book *The Origin of Species* (Darwin 1976) has been hailed and rejected with similar vehemence—the latter mostly by individuals and groups whose emotional convictions have thrown off balance by their professional competence. Mathematician Jacob Bronowski (Bronowski 1973, 308) does justice to Darwin's work by writing that his theory of evolution by natural selection was the most important creative breakthrough in the nineteenth century, adding; " When all the foolish wind and wit that it raised had blown away, the living world was different because it was seen to be a world in movement."

James Watson and Francis Crick (Watson 1969), who received the Nobel Prize for their discovery of the double-helix structure and the decoding of the genetic code, have been praised for having created the most important breakthrough in biology since Darwin. Biologist and Nobel Prize laureate Jacques Monod (Bronowski 1973, 393) once stated that Mendel's discovery of the gene, its chemical identification by Avery and Watson's and Crick's elucidation of the structural basis of the gene's replicative invariance belong to the "most important discoveries ever made in biology." He emphasized that these three breakthroughs eventually established the full significance of Darwin's theory of natural selection.

The mathematician, biologist, and outstanding Greek scholar D'Arcy Thompson is less familiar to the general public than the biologists mentioned above. Yet among the cognoscenti, he is a superstar for he discovered a new and unexpected unity in diversity, a strategic scope pursued by every great scientist. In his book *On Growth and Form* (Thompson 1961), he showed that Darwin's theory does not suffice to explain the origin of new species, emphasizing that mechanical forces governed by natural laws—he spoke of "the deep-seated rhythms of growth"—have a determining impact on new life forms. Biologist and Nobel laureate Sir Peter Medawar (Gleick 1988, 201) even called D'Arcy

Thompson's book "beyond comparison the finest work of literature in all the annals of science that have been recorded in the English tongue." His American colleague, evolutionary biologist and science historian Stephen Jay Gould (Gleick 1988, 202), stated with respect to D'Arcy Thompson's accomplishment: "Few had asked whether all the patterns might be reduced to a single system of forces. And few seemed to sense what significance such a proof of unity might possess for the science of organic form."

In some quarters, outstanding inventors have the double reputation of being somewhat crazy and of having ingenious ideas. There is a kernel of truth in that assumption. Unless you deviate from an established norm, you will never have an ingenious idea; you will only produce or reproduce the ordinary, the already established, but never create the yet unheard of. I should like to emphasize, however, that such norm deviation is not at all pathological; it is, as it were, supernormal or trans-normal.

Inventors bridge the gap between abstract scientific principles and their concrete applications. The prototype of all inventors is Archimedes, who was an astronomer, mathematician, physicist, and engineer. He laid the scientific foundations of hydrostatics and was the first scientist to explain the principle of the lever, applying the latter when he built ingenious catapults to help defend his home city of Syracuse. Hieron II, King of Syracuse, held him in high esteem. The Roman general Marcus Claudius Marcellus, who conquered Syracuse in 212 BC, gave his soldiers the explicit order not to harm Archimedes. As legend has it, however, the unfortunate inventor was accidentally killed by a soldier who encountered him sitting and contemplating a circle he had drawn in the sand, his last words being: "Μη μου τους κύκλους τάραττε!" (don't destroy my circles!) a perfect epitaph for a creative genius working in splendid isolation and totally absorbed by a task at hand.

During the Italian Renaissance, Filippo Brunelleschi and Leonardo da Vinci were inventors with widely recognized engineering skills. Brunelleschi invented, among other things, the first portable clocks. He also played an instrumental role in developing the drawing technique for linear perspective (Bronowski 1973, 179).

In the introduction of the book *Leonardo: Engineer and Architect* (Pedretti 1987), editor Carlo Pedretti qualifies Leonardo as ". . . the father of the airplane, the helicopter, the parachute, the submarine, the automobile, and now even of the bicycle." Leonardo also invented the prototype derived from detailed drawings showing the mechanics and suggesting the dynamics of a specific machine. Pedretti (1987, 4) calls the centrifugal pump for draining marshes "one of Leonardo's most brilliant inventions." Leonardo also (Pedretti 1987, 9) took the first steps towards inventing a fully automated weaving machine. At the service of Medici Pope Leo X in Rome, he experimented with of a machinery of parabolic mirrors (Pedretti 1987, 12) intended to capture solar energy for heating up large boilers in dyeing factories. The weaving industry and the fabric trade had made Florence and the Medici rich. Any invention that could improve the large-scale production of woven fabrics was welcome for a Medici interested in developing a textile industry in Rome.

While working for Duke Ludovico Sforza in Milan and later at the court of the King of France, Leonardo (Pedretti 1987, 14) devised, for the purpose of festive entertainment, mechanical lions with moving parts: this was the beginning of robotics technology. Add to it the invention of sophisticated roller-bearing devices for a bell-holding shaft (Pedretti 1987, 9), a removable axle to fight friction wear in textile machines (Pedretti 1987, 19), a shearing machine, and complex multipurpose screws and pitches to be used in all possible devices and machines, and you have the making of a universal genius in the domain of invention.

In modern times, there have been countless inventors with engineering skills. The two most outstanding ones were Edison and Tesla.

Thomas A. Edison (Josephson 1992, xv) has been called "one of the last great heroes of invention." Recognition came early to Edison because, right from the start, he was not only an ingenious inventor but also a shrewd businessman. Working as a clerk at a Western Union telegraph station, the young Thomas opted for the night shift, which offered him ample opportunity to tinker with his own inventions. At the age of nineteen, Edison obtained his first United States patent for an electric vote recorder.

As an inventor, Edison began by working for Vanderbilt's Western Union, where he developed various new technical innovations for the telegraph. Feeling neglected and exploited by his patrons, he quit and joined their competitor, Jay Gould and his Atlantic & Pacific Telegraph Company. There he invented a duplex telegraph able to send and receive messages simultaneously. He soon added the invention of the quadruplex telegraph considered to be "the masterwork of his youth" (Josephson 1992, 122).

In 1877, thanks to his invention of the phonograph, forty-year-old Edison (Josephson 1992, 165) attained overnight worldwide fame. From then on he was known as "the Wizard of Menlo Park." Menlo Park, New Jersey was home to Edison's laboratories and crew of over a hundred scientists, engineers, technicians, and mechanics. In an editorial of a leading journal, Edison (Josephson 1992, 166) was hailed as "the greatest inventor of the age . . . We are inclined to regard him as one of the wonders of the world." The *American Journal* went on to poke fun at Huxley, Tyndall, Spencer, and other theorists who only talked and talked while Edison "produces accomplished facts, and with his marvellous inventions is pushing the whole world ahead in its march to the highest civilization." More praise came from Paris, where Edison's phonograph was displayed in the International Exhibition of 1878. In those days, an electrical scientist stated that Edison (Josephson 1992, 166) possessed "more genius than a whole scientific senate."

It was the age of electricity and everywhere scientists, engineers, technicians, and entrepreneurs grew interested in the budding industry. In 1880, Edison founded the Edison Electric Light Company and railroad magnate Henry Villard (Josephson 1992, 236) became one of its investors. When Edison showed him the very first incandescent lamp he had just invented, Villard immediately understood that the new electrical industry offered opportunities for making tremendous profits. By then, Edison was already far ahead with his plans to build a whole central-station lighting system with generators for electrical power, transformer stations, power lines, wires, and incandescent lamps. In 1881 (Josephson 1992, 252), at the Paris Electrical Exhibition, Edison showed a model of his central-station lighting system; European engineers and businessmen were enthused by its perfection. Emil Rathenau, politician, entrepreneur, and founder of the German General Electric Company (AEG), purchased most of the Edison patents for Germany. Within a short period of time, electricity was everywhere. It carried elevators up skyscrapers, pulled railway cars across towns, drove streetcars, and brought heat and light into homes. Edison's biographer Josephson (1992, 432) writes: "What James Watt had been to the Age of Steam, Edison was to the new era of technology." From then on newspaper and magazine polls often voted Edison (Josephson 1992, 433) America's "greatest" or "most useful citizen." In 1928, three years before he died, Edison (Josephson 1992, 477) was awarded the Congressional Medal of Honor.

Croatia-born Nikola Tesla is an inventor who has been hailed as a genius and derided as a madman. He lacked the social skills and utter ease with which Edison charmed an audience. Tesla was rather withdrawn, suspicious, erratic, and aggressive—although, at times, he could be quite flamboyant and seductive. Today he is less known than Edison to the general public, but among scientists and engineers he is held in high esteem—and there are even those who believe that he was the greatest inventor of all time.

Tesla's scientific discoveries and technological inventions (Cheney 1993; Commerford Martin 1992) in the domains of the three-phase current, alternating current generator, alternating current motor, poly-phase power distribution systems, radio transmission, and high-tension electricity belong to the great achievements that have heavily influenced the technological progress of the twentieth century. Unlike Edison, who was a hands-on tinkerer, Tesla owed his inventions more to the power of his deductive mind. Gifted with a stupendous eidetic memory, an extraordinary sensorimotor intelligence, and a vivid imagination, Tesla was able to invent machines and control their functioning in his mind without having to resort to their actual construction and experimental testing.

Attending the Polytechnic of Graz, Austria, young Tesla struggled with a direct-current machine that did not function properly. Although he immediately found out what the problem was, his professor was in total disagreement with the problem solution he proposed. Headstrong Tesla (Cheney 1993, 23) paid no heed to Professor Poeschl's criticism and went on to devise a concept and a diagram, which marked the beginning of an invention that would bring its creator fame six years later: a rotating magnetic field produced by two or more alternating currents out of step with each other. As Cheney (1993) writes, Tesla had invented the basic principle of "an induction motor that was the heart of a new system and a quantum leap ahead of the times."

A few years later, Tesla became a collaborator and trouble-shooter of the Continental Edison Company in France and Germany. Its managers were by no means interested in Tesla's alternating current because Edison's insisted on the exclusive use of the direct current system. In 1884, Tesla migrated to the United States and founded the Tesla Electric Light Company, which opened in April 1887 (Cheney 1993, 38). Tesla began to work on his dynamos with tireless energy. Soon he joined forces with Westinghouse and constructed an induction motor that worked with a sixty-cycle current that eventually became the world standard for alternating current. To Edison's utter dismay, Mr. Westinghouse (Cheney 1993, 48ff.) was adamant in his aim to "put the country on an alternating-current." Addressing the American Institute of Electrical Engineers on April 5, 1956, Gardner H. Dales (Cheney 1993, 89) stated: "If there ever was a man who created so much and whose praises were sung so little—it was Nikola Tesla." Dales added that Tesla laid laid the foundation for the power system used throughout the entire world today.

Following in the footsteps of the physicists Faraday, Maxwell, and Hertz, Tesla began his search for new sources of high-frequency currents. In the course of these investigations, he developed the foundations of what later turned into the modern electric clock (Cheney 1993, 61). In 1906, Tesla (Cheney 1993, 188) built the first model of a bladeless turbine, thus realizing a dream he had followed since his boyhood. One month after the burial of J. Pierpont Morgan (Cheney 1993, 190ff.), Tesla met J. Pierpont Morgan Jr. The young banker was immediately taken by the inventor's concept and invested—from then on and for several years in a row—considerable sums in the Tesla turbine.

In 1915, Tesla licensed the use of his patents on the wireless to a German company; he also built a radio station for the United States Naval Radio Service. The First World War was raging, and fast and reliable transmission of information signals often decided on the outcome of military operations. The following year, Tesla (Cheney 1993, 199) took a patent for a valvular conduit that permitted use of his turbine with combustible fuel. Today this conduit plays an important role in fluid diodes.

Tesla died in 1943 at the age of eighty-seven. Less than a year later (Cheney 1993, 267), the United States Supreme Court ruled that he—and not Guglielmo Marconi, who had received the Nobel Prize for his invention of the radio—had been the original inventor of the wireless. Today it is quite evident that Tesla's scientific investigations and technical applications have helped to develop remote control, radar, robotics, ballistics, and nuclear science. In other words, Tesla's track record as an inventor is unique.

Let us now move on to the domain of singers, dancers, and actors in order to see how cultural evaluation attributes recognition to those who deserve it.

At the beginning of the twentieth century, opera critics and the general public elevated tenor Caruso, baritone Titta Ruffo, and bass Chaliapin to the rank of superstars (Lewis 1984, 197). Their counterparts, Joan Sutherland, Renata Tebaldi, and Maria Callas reached similar levels of international fame. Since the days of Caruso, no other opera singer has received as much public acclaim as Maria Callas. She had a powerful voice, a charming personality, and, as the music critic John Ardoin (Stassinopoulos 1982, 70) emphasizes: "Callas was born with an instinct to enjoy the upper hand in a dramatic situation." This instinct served her well the day she made her great breakthrough as a dramatic soprano. At the time she was engaged to sing, at the prestigious La Fenice theater in Venice, Brünnhilde in Wagner's opera *Die Walküre*. At the same, time Margeritha Carosio (Stassinopoulos 1982, 63f.), one of the leading belcanto sopranos of the day, was supposed to sing Elvira in Bellini's opera *I Puritani*. Suddenly she came down with a bad case of influenza and conductor Tullio Serafin urged Maria Callas to take over Carosio's role. Callas refused because there was not enough time to prepare for the difficult role, learn the lines, and exercise her own vocal interpretation. But Maestro Serafin insisted and eventually Callas mustered her courage and gave in to his pleas. January 19, 1949, the opening night of *I Puritani,* turned out to be a tremendous success for Maria Callas. Many years later, film director and opera fan Franco Zeffirelli characterized Maria's performance as follows: "What she did in Venice was really incredible. You need to be familiar with opera to realize the size of her achievement that night." He stated that Maria's challenge was as tremendous as if Birgit Nilsson, a great Wagnerian voice were asked to substitute overnight for the incredible coloratura soprano of Beverly Sills.

From that night in Venice, Maria Callas rushed from success to success. She enlarged her repertoire, and her voice mastered the challenges of dramatic roles with the same ease as it perfected the elaborate embellishments and trills expected from a coloratura soprano. During the 1953-54 season at

La Scala in Milan, Maria Callas sang the main role in Cherubini's opera *Medea* directed by Leonard Bernstein. He later described Maria's impact on the audience (Stassinopoulos 1982, 106) briefly but to the point: "The place was out of its mind. Callas? She was pure electricity." On January 18, 1954, the headlines of the Italian press (Stassinopoulos 1982, 107) discussing her performance in Donizetti's Lucia di Lammermoor conducted by Herbert von Karajan read: LA SCALA IN DELIRIUM   FOUR MINUTES OF AP-PLAUSE FOR THE MAD SCENE   A RAIN OF RED CARNATIONS.

In the world of ballet, quite a few individuals received the highest recognition for their creativity in choreography over the last century. Personalities such as Serge Diaghilev, George Balanchine, Martha Graham, Maurice Bé-jart, and Pina Bausch left their indelible mark and created endless new possibilities for movement that revolutionized classical ballet. In a recent book review, former ballerina Toni Bentley (Bentley 2005, 12) resolutely speaks of George Balanchine as "the greatest dance innovator of the twentieth century, and possibly the most important in all 350 years of classical dance history since the language was codified in the court of Louis XIV." The choreographers mentioned above (Diaghilev was also an impresario, Pina Bausch, a dancer) worked with eminent performers such as Vaslav Nijinsky, Rudolf Nurejev, Mikhail Baryshnikov, Anna Pavlova, Margot Fonteyn, and Alicia Markova. In an inspired teamwork effort, choreographers and dancers would bootstrap each other into an ever-higher position of excellence in performance. Their dance creations existed but for the fleeting moments of a live performance, like a tiny cloud before it evaporates completely. What persisted were the memories of those who were present, bearing witness to the bodies that seemed to defy the laws of physics as the unforgettable beauty and power of their expression unfolded on stage.

The world of theater and film has always been a realm of ruthless competition, where merciless intrigues have been staged on the open scene as well as in the wings. But great actors, actresses, playwrights, directors, critics, and the general public have also paid tribute to great productions and the creative interpretation of difficult roles. A few examples may illustrate how cultural selection has recognized outstanding talent in this field.

In German theater, nobody has ever equalled Max Reinhardt, who at one time directed the Deutsche Theater in Berlin. In his autobiography, conductor Walter Bruno (Walter 1988, 118) remembers fondly how the twenty-two-year-old Reinhardt, who was already a successful actor and lover of music, discussed with him his dream to integrate music into every highly dramatic moment of a play. Reinhardt's vision, intuition, imagination, and critical mind eventually permitted him to create a powerful synthesis of language, acting, music, choreography, and stage design. His brilliant productions of Strindberg's realistic and imaginary plays (Meyers 1988, 572) are legendary; so is his function as a towering role model for countless other actors, directors, producers, and stage designers. After the 1938 Anschluss of Austria, Reinhardt migrated to the United States where his ideas and productions influenced both Broadway and Hollywood. And when we read in Kurosawa's (Kurosawa 1983, 197) autobiographical sketches, "From the moment I begin directing a film, I am thinking about not only the music but the sound effects as well," we are reminded of the fact that Reinhardt's influence reached even across the Pacific.

Director Luc Bondy (Kässens et al. 1987, 12) praises Noelte's stage production of Carl Sternheim's *Der Snob* and Kortner's mise-en-scène of Goethe's *Clavigo* as a "revelation" inspiring his own ideas about what great theater should look like. German theater director Jürgen Flimm (Kässens et al. 1987, 29) sees in his colleague Peter Stein, who brought worldwide fame to the Berliner Schaubühne, "a great master." Similarly, Claus Peymann, a former director of the Berliner Schaubühne and later director of the Vienna Burgtheater, acknowledges in Peter Stein "the only world champion of theatre."

In the mid-1950s, John Osborne (Tynan 1987, 173) wrote an iconoclastic play that was at first rejected by every producer and director. Eventually *Look Back in Anger* was produced, changing the landscape of English theater forever. Osborne's play portrayed the cultural clash between social classes and used a language that was as harsh as it was to the point. Once accepted for production, the play became a planetary success. Within two years, it was staged all over England, in Europe, and on Broadway, where it received three Tony Award nominations. The film based upon the play was equally successful.

Critics must also pass the test of cultural selection. Kenneth Tynan (Tynan 1987, 18), never vacillating when dishing out his often-murderous critiques, has been called the best drama critic since Bernhard Shaw. At Tynan's memorial service, the great playwright Tom Stoppard paid him tribute by stating that Tynan was "the product of his time but . . . the time was of his making."

Actresses and actors are often feared and even loathed for their eccentric behavior. Yet the same hypersensitivity that at times prompts them to act out their inner tensions in the most egocentric and aggressive manner also constitutes a valuable asset for great artistic performance. To take but one example, the two-time Academy-Award-winning actress Glenda Jackson had a bad reputation due to her blunt and even ruthless responses to people who irritated her. But she was also admired worldwide for her perfectionism in playing extremely demanding roles. Mel Frank, who directed her in the film *A Touch of Class* (Woodward 1986, 133), called her "the most magnificent acting instrument of our time" and characterized his collaboration with her as follows: "It's exactly as I expected, like taking the controls of a new Rolls-Royce, gliding effortlessly, smoothly..." *A Touch of Class* (Woodward 1986, 136) brought Glenda Jackson her second Oscar. The film turned out to be a box office hit, grossing $20 million in its first year and providing Glenda with numerous role offers—which she declined because they did not meet her standards of excellence. Joseph Losey, the Harvard-educated film director (Woodward 1986, 161f.), paid her the ultimate tribute by stating that Glenda was "without question the best technical actress I ever knew—and I've worked with hundreds." That was a tall compliment offered by a perfectionist who had directed a string of movie stars such as Elizabeth Taylor, Jeanne Moreau, Sarah Miles, Monica Vitti, and Julie Christie.

If the personalities of actresses and actors and their methods of acting must pass the test of cultural selection, so also must the methods of teaching great acting. In that test, enthused praise and utter contempt are often as close to each other as the feathers on a bird's wing. A good example is the Stanislavski Method of acting. In 1897, Constantin Stanislavski and Vladimir Nenirowich-Danchenko founded the Moscow Art Theater, a company whose declared aim was to get rid of the pathetic melodramatic style of acting then fashionable in Russia and to replace it by a more sober, naturalistic approach.

One of the aims of Stanislavski, himself an accomplished actor and theater director, was to provide access to private emotional memories that would help actors to play their roles in a convincing, authentic manner. In the mid-1920s, a disciple of Stanislavski exported the "Stanislavski system" to the United States, and in 1931 Lee Strasberg, Harold Clurman, and Cheryl Crawford founded The Group Theater in New York. From its very beginning, "the Method" promoted by Strasberg had its adamant opponents as well as its fierce admirers—among the latter were a series of great Hollywood and Broadway actors and actresses that included Marlon Brando, Marilyn Monroe, Shelley Winters, Jessica Lange, Elizabeth Taylor, James Dean, Steve McQueen, Paul Newman, Robert de Niro, Harvey Keitel, Al Pacino, Sean Penn, Anthony Hopkins, and Denzel Washington. They were the best indicators of a process of cultural selection resulting in the recognition of a new form created. Shelley Winters (Winters 1980, 208) praised the so-called affective memory exercise as being "the most powerful tool I ever learned to use in acting."

Film is without any doubt one of the great creative contributions cultural evolution has produced in the last century. The invention of film camera, projector, and screen has produced a whole industry with studios, film theaters, producers, directors, stage designers, camera men, script writers, actresses and actors, agents, different genres (comedies and dramatic films, for instance), movie magazines, film festivals, lowbrow entertainment, and great art. To illustrate how the cultural evaluation of the results of creative efforts operates, we shall discuss principally the work of two of the greatest creative leaders in that field: Ernst Lubitsch and Billy Wilder.

On March 13, 1947, Ernst Lubitsch received an honorary Academy Award for his creative contribution to filmmaking. In his address, director and producer Mervyn LeRoy (Eyman 1993, 14) qualified Lubitsch as "a God-given genius" and a "master of innuendo" who had "advanced the technique of screen comedy as no one else has ever done." Lubitsch, who was suffering from heavy angina and fearing a coronary, was at the zenith of his fame. After a career in European silent movies, he had lived for a quarter of a century in Hollywood. There he had made one great film after the other. Working with the most famous film stars he had enjoyed privileges—last cut and other insignia of total control over creative filmmaking included—that even almighty moguls such as Jack Warner and Darryl Zanuk dared not question.

Like the writer James Joyce, Lubitsch had the gift of epiphany; the Zen-like ability suddenly to recognize the essence of an object, an event, or a living being. Like Joyce he also loved to show the absurdity of life and rejoiced in elevating the trivial into something filled with deep meaning. He was a man beyond category. As his biographer Eyman (1993, 17) writes Lubitsch was a role model for generations of moviemakers to come, although many of his films were not commercial successes at all: ". . . his approach to film, to comedy, and to life was not so much ahead of its time as it was singular, and totally out of any time.."

His first great success came with the premiere of the silent movie *Madame Du Barry* presented on September 18, 1919 at the inauguration of the UFA-Palast in Berlin. An audience of 4,'000 invited guests (Eyman 1993, 60) applauded Lubitsch and his two stars, Pola Negri and Emil Jannings, seated in a special box decorated with flowers. After the show, Max Reinhardt, with whom Lubitsch had worked as a young aspiring actor, remarked to Ernst's father Simon: "Mr. Lubitsch, the student has surpassed the master." For the American market *Madame Du Barry* was renamed *Passion*. When the film hit the screens on December 12, 1920, *The New York Times* hailed it as "the most important film event of the year." The *Times* reviewed it as (Eyman 1993, 74) "One of the pre-eminent motion pictures of the present cinematographic age." Overnight Lubitsch became an American household name, and the intellectuals of New York had a main topic of discussion: Lubitsch and the New Wave of German film directors.

Hollywood star Mary Pickford and her husband Douglas Fairbanks soon belonged to the long list of Lubitsch admirers. In 1923, she wrote to her attorney (Eyman 1993, 93): "Personally, I still believe he is the greatest director in the world and would be willing to back him if I could afford it." Pickford and Lubitsch had just finished making their first movie together. Entitled *The*

Street Singer at first, it was renamed *Rosita. Photoplay* (Eyman 1993, 94) emphasized that Lubitsch had again proved why he "holds his place among the leading directors of the world." A few weeks before the premiere of *Rosita,* Lubitsch (Eyman 1993, 98) had garnered an even higher recognition: in his contract with Warner Brothers he had been granted the right to the final cut, in those days an unheard of privilege for film directors.

While Lubitsch (Eyman 1993, 106) received so much recognition, he was also generous in according the same to his colleagues and friends. He hailed Chaplin's film *Woman of Paris* as "a great step forward . . . It did not, like many plays I see, insult my intelligence." He went on to say that American directors tend to leave nothing to the imagination of the viewer and that the audience "is not allowed to think by the director." In Chaplin, Lubitsch had found a soul mate, and their admiration was mutual.

Meanwhile critics and film lovers began to speak of "The Lubitsch Touch" (Eyman 1993, 127). The term was as vague as it was suggestive. A critic rightly observed: "To speak of Lubitsch in terms of his 'touch' is to reduce feelings to flourishes." Still, the famous Lubitsch Touch enthused critics and audiences alike. In 1930, Lubitsch was the only director to be entered for the fifth time on *Film Daily's* (Eyman 1993, 160) annual list of the ten best directors.

Two years later, Lubitsch's movie *Trouble in Paradise* was enthusiastically received at a preview in Hollywood (Eyman 1993, 200). *Photoplay* hailed it as "one of Lubitsch's best productions." Today it is part of the Lubitsch classics and one of the top film comedies of all time.

When Lubitsch teamed up with Billy Wilder (who was fourteen years younger than him) to write the script for the comedy *Bluebeard's Eighth Wife* (Eyman 1993, 256), he immediately recognized Wilder's great talent as a comedy writer. They hit it off right away and although the movie itself, released in 1938, was not much of a success, the script is great, and movie fans today love the film that its U.S. contemporaries did not much appreciate .

That same year, after the commercial failures of *Angel* and *Bluebeard's Eighth Wife* (Eyman 1993, 270ff.), Lubitsch, under pressure due to comments in the press about his presumably sagging creativity, moved from Paramount to MGM. In 1939 *Ninotchka* with Greta Garbo and Melvyn Douglas proved that the prophets of doom had been too hasty. Already the feedback during the first preview in Hollywood sounded promising. One review card Lubitsch particularly relished read: "Great picture. Funniest film I ever saw. I laughed so hard, I peed into my girlfriend's hand." *The New York Times* praised *Ninotchka* as "one of the sprightliest comedies of the year," while *Variety* acquiesced Ernst Lubitsch's decision ". . . to pilot Garbo in her first light performance in pictures proves a bull's-eye."

The following year Lubitsch's new comedy, *The Shop Around the Corner*, outshone *Ninotchka*. With these two hits, Lubitsch was back in town; he had displayed his ability to snatch success from the brink of impending failure. According to *Variety*, *The Shop Around the Corner* (Eyman 1993, 279)—a slightly melancholic comedy about a leather goods shop in Prague—was "smart and clever . . . with all the vivaciousness and piquant humour" so typical of Lubitsch. His renewed reputation as a great scriptwriter and film director was endorsed by the contract with United Artists for *To Be or Not to Be*, signed in 1941, (Eyman 1993, 293) in which he pulled off writer approval, cast approval, and final cut approval. Once again he was the undisputed leader. Robert Stack, who acted in the film, had this to say about Lubitsch: "He was a Renaissance man. He could do it all. He was an actor, a writer, a cameraman, an art director." When the movie was released, *Variety* (Eyman 1993, 301) praised it as "typically Lubitsch . . . one of his best productions in a number of years" and predicted that it would be "an excellent box-office attraction." Yet for the most part, the movie was rejected for reasons we shall discuss further on.

Heaven Can Wait, released in 1943, was yet another success with Gene Tierny and Don Ameche in the leading roles. Ameche (Eyman 1993, 349) later stated that Lubitsch was the only director he had ever worked with whom he considered to be a genius. The critics praised the sharp-witted comedy, which was a box office smash. Even film director D. W. Griffith, (creator of *The Birth of a Nation*, one of the first feature length movies in the United States), who was always envious of somebody else's success, patronizingly admitted: "I liked the way Lubitsch used colour in *Heaven Can Wait*. And the way he used sound, too."

In 1946, the comedy *Cluny Brown*, directed and produced by Lubitsch (Eyman 1993, 343) and starring Jennifer Jones and Charles Boyer, proved to be yet another success. If the American critics loved the movie, their British counterparts rejected it for the irony with which it depicted English manners. *The New Statesman* let it be understood that the names of the screenwriters, Hoffenstein and Reinhardt, sufficed to explain the lack of cultural knowledge. The chauvinistic, anti-Semitic innuendo of that critique suggested: how could German Jews possibly understand the essence of authentic Englishness? *Cluny Brown* was, by the way, the last movie that Lubitsch finished. On November 30, 1947 he died of a heart attack while shooting *That Lady in Ermine*, later to be completed by Otto Preminger. The circumstances around his death seemed to be drawn directly from one of his frivolous comedies: while making love to a tall blonde, a type of women the short man had admired and desired all his life, he had a coronary and died—while reaching for his pants rather than for the nitroglycerine capsules that might have saved him.

Not only did Lubitsch tower above anybody else, he gave recognition where recognition was due (Eyman 1993, 332). When his friend Anita Loos criticized the perfectionism of film director Eric von Stroheim, Lubitsch replied: "All the rest of us make the equivalent of novellas or short stories . . . Von Stroheim is the only filmmaker who really wrote a novel when he directed." It was Lubitsch who was the first to understand that scriptwriter Joseph L. Mankiewicz had the talent for meeting more complex challenges. When (Eyman 1993, 336) asked to produce *Dragonwyck*, Lubitsch invited Mankiewicz to write the screenplay and direct the movie. Mankiewicz gladly accepted and was thus launched as a successful film director.

Lubitsch had a co-screenwriter, close friend and master disciple who further developed the famous Lubitsch Touch, though with a more sardonic bite, and that was Billy Wilder. In the course of half a century, he (Karasek 1992a, 11) wrote thirty-one screenplays, directed and/or produced sixty films, and received six Oscars, two Academy Awards and an Irving G. Thalberg Memorial Award for his creative contributions to the art of filmmaking. He began his career as a scriptwriter in Berlin and collaborated on fourteen motion pictures, five of them with UFA (Universum Film AG), which was in those days, as Karasek (1992a, 86) puts it, a serious competitor for Hollywood. In 1934, Wilder migrated to the United States and had his first taste of success as a Hollywood screenwriter, co-writing with Lubitsch the script for *Ninotchka*, in which Greta Garbo was said to have laughed on screen for the first time.

There is a nice song by J. J. Cale with a smooth driving rhythm, a gentle guitar intro, and lyrics beginning with "Money talks"—which is also the title of the song. Money is a form of recognition, and in a commercial society it is often even the most cared for form of acknowledgement. In the 1940s, Billy Wilder and his colleague Charles Brackett (Karasek 1992a, 150), known as "the happiest couple" of screenwriters, earned $4,500 per week. They were the best-paid screenwriters in town, and the money they made defined their prestige and market value in Hollywood.

That market value increased as Wilder moved on to become a director-producer who wrote his own scripts. It continued to grow as the Zeitgeist changed during the Second World War and comedies were replaced by the film noir depicting the dark side of human existence. In 1944, the Wilder thriller *Double Indemnity* (Karasek 1992a, 274) received several Oscar nominations: best script, best actress (Barbara Stanwyck), best camera, best music, best sound, and best director. Such recognition proved that Wilder, who had co-written the script with Raymond Chandler, had successfully moved from one film genre to another.

The following year, Wilder's film (Karasek 1992a, 286f.) *The Lost Weekend* described the undignified life of an alcoholic suffering from writer's block who goes on a weekend bender, slides into skid row, and is ready to commit crimes to indulge his craving for intoxication. Despite the disappointing preview, the movie caught on with the audiences and went on to receive four Oscars for Best Actor, Best Picture, Best Screenplay, and Best Director.

At the Academy Awards ceremony of 1951 (Karasek 1992a, 359), there were two films about the fate of aging female stars in competition. *All about Eve*, directed by Joseph L. Mankiewicz with Betty Davis in the starring role, was nominated for fourteen Oscars. Billy Wilder's *Sunset Boulevard*, with Gloria Swanson playing an old movie star who deludes herself into believing that she is still the big star she used to be in the silent movie era, bagged eleven nominations. The Oscar went to Betty Davis, but soon thereafter the National Board of Review attributed the first place to *Sunset Boulevard* and Gloria Swanson, placing *All about Eve* and Betty Davis in second position. The Hollywood Foreign Correspondents Association voted Wilder, his movie, and his star Gloria Swanson number one, relegating Mankiewicz, his movie, and his star Betty Davis to second place.

There is, by the way, an amusing anecdote about peer recognition. Wilder and his co-screenwriter asked Gloria Swanson (Karasek 1992a, 477), a silent movie superstar whose career began to falter when the talkies came along, to undergo a screen test. She asked film director George Cukor whether or not she should accept. His response: "If Wilder and Brackett make the movie, absolutely. They are the most intelligent item Hollywood has to offer. And if you don't do it... I myself will shoot you to death."

In 1959, Wilder released *Some Like It Hot*, a film that successfully combined two genres—screwball comedy and film noir. The script and dialogues were perfect; the acting (Marilyn Monroe, Tony Curtis, and Jack Lemon), fantastic; the gags, hilarious; the speed of action, relentless; the directing, masterful; and the audience response, enthusiastic. Everybody expected it to win several Oscars, although the National Legion of Decency branded it with a C-rating (C standing for condemned). A lascivious Monroe and two men disguised as drag queens eager to escape a group of Chicago gangsters whose crime they had involuntarily witnessed were obviously enough ignition for moral indignation. The film got several nominations but received only one Oscar, for best costume design. Why? Due to the ubiquitous devil of pure chance events, the film *Ben Hur*, a pathetic portrait in Cinemascope of the clash between the corruptness of ancient Rome and the innocence of early Christianity, had also entered the competition. It took ten Oscars. As Billy Wilder sat in the audience and watched the course of the Award ceremony, he recoiled in helpless frustration. Each time " . . . and the winner is . . ." produced another Oscar for *Ben Hur*, Wilder (Karasek 1992a, 277) would throw another double Martini down the hatch. After ten double Martinis, he was so drunk that he tipped over and had to be carried out of the hall. Today, half a century after that fateful ceremony, Wilder and his crew have been given the recognition they so richly deserved. *Some Like It Hot* has become a comedy classic of all times. *Ben Hur,* which had corresponded to the aesthetic and ethic prerogatives of the National League of Decency, today appears outdated, indigestibly pompous, and about as fresh as a fossilized dinosaur.

Wilder's Martini inebriation soon evaporated, and with it his frustration. In 1960 he was back with yet another comedy. *Apartment* starring Jack Lemon and Shirley MacLaine won five Oscars. But once more it became clear that backstage politics and chance events influenced the jury in deciding on whom to bestow the Awards. Jack Lemon, who took the Oscar for Best Actor was furious that Shirley MacLaine did not win Best Actress. That award went to Liz Taylor (Karasek 1992a, 277) for her role as a call girl in *Butterfield Eight,* a movie which Wilder rightly rejected as a "poor movie." During the shooting of *Cleopatra,* Taylor had had to undergo surgery in her trachea, and had almost died in that venture. It was not surprising, then, that the Oscar audience should acclaim her "resurrection" with a standing ovation. Wilder sent Shirley MacLaine a telegram of consolation telling her that he loved her "although you don't have a hole in your bellows."

It is a well-known fact that black actresses and actors have had a hard time making their way into motion pictures in supporting roles, and the road to leading roles was even rockier. As to winning the recognition and awards they deserved, they hardly stood a chance. As had occurred with jazz, racial prejudice and sheer narrow-mindedness combined to prevent equal opportunities for everybody. The very first black faces to be seen on American stages were in minstrel shows of questionable repute where white actors and actresses in blackface makeup appeared in comic skits, variety acts, and song-and-dance numbers. In that context, Afro-Americans were portrayed disparagingly as lazy, ignorant buffoons though joyous and musical.

A *Wikipedia* article on black Academy Award winners and nominees points out how long it took for black actresses and actors to be recognized with an Oscar for their creative performance. The first black person ever to receive one was Hattie McDaniel in 1939 for her supporting role in *Gone with the Wind.* It wasn't until 2001 that Halle Berry became the first black actress to win an Oscar for a leading role in *Monster's Ball.* On the men's side, in 1963, Sidney Poitier was the first Black to take the Oscar for Best Actor for his role in *Lilies of the Field;* and in 2001, the same year as Halle Berry, Denzel Washington won the Oscar for his leading role in *Training Day.* The fact that it took sixty-two years for a second black actress and thirty-eight years for a second black actor to receive an Academy Award is comment enough for the spirit responsible for such gross injustice.

To wind up this section on recognition, let us have a look at a few rather unusual forms of acknowledgement.

After viewing the submarine movie *Morgenrot (Dawn)*, a tale of heroic patriotism released three days after Hitler became *Reichskanzler*, Nazi minister of propaganda Goebbels (Karasek 1992a, 18) confided to his diary: "Maybe we Germans don't know how to live, but we are fabulous when it comes to dying."

Germans knew also how to create beautiful women and great actresses. There is Wilder's *bonmot* about glamorous Marlene Dietrich and her generous character (Karasek 1992a, 345): "Marlene Dietrich was a Mother Teresa, but she had more beautiful legs." Marlene always disposed of her own room in Wilder's Hollywood home and she was, together with Walter Matthau and William Holden, one of the few stars with whom he had a very close personal relationship. Wilder loved her gift for quick-witted replies. During the Second World War, Dietrich often performed at the front to boost the soldiers' morale. In 1945, Wilder met her in Paris and asked her to tell him the truth: did she or did she not make love to General Eisenhower? Her repartee: "How could I? He was never at the front."

Marlene Dietrich (Karasek 1992a, 420) blithely returned Wilder's compliments. When film director Peter Bogdanovich once told her: "You have worked for many great film directors . . ." she interrupted him saying, "Oh no, I have only worked for two great directors, von Sternberg and Billy Wilder."

Billy Wilder had directed Marilyn Monroe in two very successful comedies, *The Seven Year Itch* and *Some Like It Hot*. His rather ambivalent attitude towards the often unpredictable superstar is illustrated by his statement that he had never met a person who could be as "utterly mean" as she was; but he also emphasized that he had never worked with a star—not even Greta Garbo—who had such a marvellous screen presence. He conceded (Karasek 1992a, 397) that Monroe was an "absolute genius as a comic actress. She was gifted." He added that after their last film together he had never again worked with such an actress. He also joked (Karasek 1992a, 402) that there were more books written about Marilyn Monroe than about the Second World War—and he saw some similarities in the comparison. As he put it: "It was hell but it was worth it."

In an interview with Karasek, Billy Wilder (Karasek 1992a, 420) declared that Charles Laughton was the best actor he had ever worked with. Personally, I have my doubts as to the sincerity of that statement. Billy Wilder had worked with stars such as William Holden, Walter Matthau, and Jack Lemon; Holden and Matthau also being two of his rare close friends with whom he shared mutual admiration and respect. Laughton, contrarily, could often be quite a ham.

The movie and theater world also had its circle of writers. Preston Sturges started out as a very successful playwright on Broadway before he was invited as a screenwriter to Hollywood, where he eventually also directed a series of pictures. *The Miracle of Morgan's Creek, The Lady Eve, Sullivan's Travels,* and *The Palm Beach Story* were among his greatest hits. Eventually a movie deal with billionaire Howard Hughes, short-term owner of RKO studios, went sour and Sturges' career began to decline. He wound up a down-and-out drunkard (Karasek 1992a, 237f.), sitting day after day in the bistro Alexandre on Avenue George V in Paris, where he could meet American tourists residing at the Hotel Georges V. Sometimes they paid him a cognac. When Billy Wilder discovered that Sturges was impoverished to the point where he had to beg for drinks, he decided to help and asked the Paramount representative in Paris to get Sturges some work, but to no avail. Sturges eventually died on August 5, 1959 at the Algonquin Hotel in New York while working on his memoirs. Sixteen years later, he received a posthumous Laurel Award, the highest award a scriptwriter can get in Hollywood after the Oscar. Billy Wilder had seen to it that the Writers Guild changed its rules so that the award could be bestowed posthumously. Wilder fully recognized Sturges' unusual talent and accomplishments not only as a writer, but also as a film director. He even stated (Karasek 1992a): "I love most those directors in whose films you forget that there was a director while the movie was being shot. Sturges was one of them."

Last but not least there is another of Billy Wilder's (Karasek 1992a, 20) wry remarks to wrap this section on recognition offered by cultural selection: "Awards and prizes are like hemorrhoids. Earlier or later every asshole gets them."

African-American jazz is a unique art form. Originally created in the United States by the black community of the deep South, it reached its heyday in the city of New Orleans, a melting pot of African, West Indian, Spanish, French, and white American ethnic groups and subcultures. From its very beginnings, jazz was an art form in which the continuous fusions of styles and themes, as well as improvisation, were the desired norm. It was in New Orleans that gospel, work songs, military marches, blues, ragtime, and folksong were interwoven into a new kind of music. From there jazz began to spread throughout the country and eventually to the rest of the world. Often rejected as "slave music" or "Nigger music" and smeared with even worse racial slurs, in time its most important representatives received much acclaim and coveted official honors. Filmmaker Ken Burns, whose documentaries *The Civil War* and *Baseball* met worldwide plaudit, has crowned his epic trilogy on American life with the ingenious documentary *Jazz*. Its ten DVDs (Burns 2000a) give the viewer a fascinating insight into the development of jazz as an art form.

Following are a few examples of how cultural evaluation afforded its recognition to the accomplishments of creative jazz musicians.

After a faltering start, the sheet music of Scott Joplin's *Maple Leaf Rag*
(Gioia 1998, 24) published in 1899 sold over a million copies and the composition turned into the most famous rag of its day.

In the 1920s and 1930s, Bessie Smith (Gioia 1998, 18) was the first female
blues singer to become world-famous. Within a few months, her recording of
Down Hearted Blues sold over half a million copies—in those days an untold
success. With her strong personality and outstanding performances, she paved
the way for other female vocalists who eventually reached international stardom: Billie Holiday, Ella Fitzgerald, Sarah Vaughn, Dina Washington, Carmen
McRae, Etta Jones, Lena Horne, and Alberta Hunter to name a few. Among
them no one captured the public imagination with more zest than did Billie
Holiday. Lady Day's beauty, obvious vulnerability, and delicate behind-the-beat
singing had no counterpart among her competitors. She commanded neither a
powerful voice nor a very wide scale range, yet her personality, style, and
unique phrasing technique (Gleason 1995, 76) combined into what has been
aptly characterized as "sulphur-and-molasses voice—the epitome of sex."

In 1919, Ernest Ansermet, the great Swiss conductor of classical music,
qualified New Orleans-born Sidney Bechet as "an artist of genius" and predicted that his clarinet sound was "perhaps the highway the whole world will
swing along tomorrow." About his solos Ansermet wrote (Gleason 1995, 7):
". . . their form was ripping, abrupt, harsh with a brusque and pitiless ending
like that of Bach's second Brandenburg Concerto."

A few years later Bechet's contemporary Louis Armstrong paid the white
trumpeter Bix Beiderbecke (Gioia 1998, 73) a huge compliment by saying:
"I'm tellin' you, those pretty notes went right through me." Louis 'Satchmo'
Armstrong (Gioia 1998, 69) went on to become the most famous jazz musician of all time for he possessed the rare gift of charisma. With equal ease he
could make his trumpet blare in exuberant triumph or softly whisper and ca-
jole. His rasping voice combined unique phrasing with a guttural growl and a
swinging rhythm imitated, but never achieved by, whole generations of jazz
singers. Drummer Gene Krupa (Gleason 1995, 58) described Armstrong's
electrifying presence with the words: "It was like somebody turned the current on." In the 1960s, when his brand of jazz had lost its popularity, Armstrong's version of the Broadway title song *Hello Dolly* toppled the Beatles
from their fourteen-week-long first position on the Billboard Top 100 chart in
May 1964, and won Armstrong a Grammy Award. In 1972, he was bestowed
posthumously with the Grammy Lifetime Achievement Award. The Rock and
Roll Hall of Fame listed his *West End Blues*, cut in 1928, on its "500 Songs
that Shaped Rock and Roll." Almost a dozen of his recordings were inducted

into the Grammy Hall of Fame. Armstrong's photo (Gleason 1995, 37) made its way to the cover pages of both *Time* and *Life* magazines. And on December 31, 1999, Armstrong's trumpet was included in a series of objects put into a Millennium memorial capsule to be opened in one hundred years. Due to his lifelong masterful performances with illustrious jazz groups, Armstrong became the public icon of jazz admired for his creative genius and deeply loved for his spontaneous, generous, and cordial personality.

Sidney Bechet, Louis Armstrong, Count Basie, Duke Ellington, Charlie Parker, Terence Young, Dizzy Gillespie, Miles Davis, Coleman Hawkins, Sonny Rollins, John Coltrane, Thelonius Monk, and Charlie Mingus all belong to the category of superstars in the firmament of jazz music. All have been recognized by cultural selection as creative mavericks who opened new vistas and deeply influenced the amazingly rapid and radical evolution of jazz music.

Composer, bandleader, and pianist Duke Ellington, of proverbial panache in dressing and behavior, was, along with Armstrong, probably the most influential figure in the history of jazz. Elusive as he was, he was also a very clever operator; his wit and dashing style helped to imbue his fellow jazz musicians and the entire African-American community with solid self-confidence and a sense of pride that had virtually been trod out of their race during centuries of slavery.

In 1943 at Carnegie Hall in New York, Ellington and his band (Gioia 1998, 190) debuted his now-famous composition *Black, Brown and Beige*, whose title alludes to a color and race connection. A critic of The New York Herald Tribune wrote a patronizing verdict: "The whole attempt to fuse jazz as a form with art music should be discouraged." The grandiose and condescending rejection was eventually overcome. Half a century after the historical Carnegie Hall debut, the very competent jazz historian and critic Ted Gioia (1998, 192) compared Ellington's sophisticated composition *Mood Indigo* to Bach's *Goldberg Variations* and Beethoven's *Diabelli Variations*. Such a tribute emphasizes the fact that jazz is as great an art music as is the European classical music. It seems that Ellington composed with the same ease as Mozart. The Duke once told jazz critic Ralph J. Gleason (Gleason 1995, 162) with respect to *Mood Indigo*: "I wrote it in New York in fifteen minutes while I was waiting for my mother to finish cooking dinner." When Ellington died the composer and horn player Gunther Schuller (Gioia 1998, 196) compared him to Bach, Beethoven, and Schoenberg. And the front-page obituary of *The New York Times* hailed him as "America's most important composer."

From its very beginnings, jazz has always been dance music. During the Swing Era, which lasted from the early 1930s to the late 1940s, jazz grew more popular than ever. Almost overnight it became a coast-to-coast craze for countless music fans. The Great Depression caused millions of individuals to lose their jobs, and they craved an escape from their existential nightmare. The pulsating groove of swing produced vibrations full of joy, hope, self-confidence, and exuberance. Its rhythm, tempo, and mood offered dancers an opportunity for every possible form of self-expression. As a result, the American social environment became more favorable to jazz than it had ever been before. Big bands and small bands across the continent brought their music to huge dance halls, medium-sized ballrooms, and small joints everywhere. Clarinettist Benny Goodman, also known as the "King of Swing," and trombonist, trumpeter Tommy Dorsey (Gleason 1995, 14) recorded LPs which turned into box office hits, making the white bandleaders millionaires.

The "King of the Clarinet" and bandleader Artie Shaw could have become as popular an icon as Benny Goodman had he not so hated to play the same compositions over and over again just because his audiences insisted on hearing them. He later confessed when interviewed by the documentary filmmaker Ken Burns (Burns 2000b): "Success is a very big problem, bigger than failure. You can deal with failure; it's tough, it's hard, you fight like hell to get it goin'." Shaw compared success to opium confusing the consumer to a point where he doesn't know anymore what happens to him—nor what he is supposed to do. Artie Shaw was so successful that his version of Cole Porter's composition *Begin the Beguine* relegated Benny Goodman's most famous hits to second position. Yet as a purist, Shaw was not willing to sacrifice the artist he was by nature for the businessman that his role as a bandleader demanded. Keenly aware of the fact that *Begin the Beguine*—the performance of which was requested by his audiences time and again—became "a millstone, an albatross around my neck" he quit the stage, a rather unusual response to cultural recognition.

Charlie Parker and Dizzy Gillespie were the main inventors and pacemakers of bebop, a new jazz form played at breakneck speed and with improvisations whose harmonic structures played a more crucial role than did the melody lines. Drug-addict Parker was a recluse; Dizzy Gillespie, an outgoing, exuberant, and witty personality was utterly at ease with other people. The two musicians formed a complementary duo, and their respect and sympathy for each other helped to spread their music as much as their outstanding performances did. Jazz critic Ross Russell (Shipton 1999, 145f.) stated that: "Parker was the fountainhead of the new music. The flow of musical ideas suggested mysterious, primal forces." While Parker had his roots in blues music, Gillespie had little interest for it. French jazz critic André Hodier (Shipton 1999, 169f.) correctly characterized their cooperation as "the start of a new and valuable aesthetic." Praising Parker's talent as "diabolical," he underlined Dizzy's contribution to bebop and calls him: "More powerful and sure than Armstrong, more rapid than Eldridge." Hodier added: "He seems to laugh at difficulties" and went on to applaud the way in which Dizzy climbed into the highest register "with derisive ease, and his ample tone and heat are something to marvel at." Although the two jazz giants often fought each other, their friendship was staunch. As Dizzy once put it (Shipton 1999, 252): "We loved each other, man. I mean all those stories about the rift . . . there was no question of a rift between Charlie Parker and me." Whatever the truth may be, it is a fact that jazz has always been a highly competitive field; and conflict and tensions fuel the fires of highly creative performance. This is as true for music as it is for every other domain of creative achievement.

In the late 1940s, Charlie Parker's classic quintet—including trumpeter Miles Davis, drummer Max Roach, bass player Tommy Potter, and pianist Bud Powell—produced a series of masterpieces that reached the top of the rating scales. In 1947, Miles Davis won the critics' poll in *Esquire* and, together with Dizzy Gillespie, the critics' *Down Beat* poll. The following year Charlie Parker won his first poll in *Metronome* (Carr 1999, 40). By now the quintet was at the peak of its international fame. But drugs and competitive circumstances generated a rift between Parker and his two acolytes Miles and Roach, and the group disbanded.

At the 1949 Paris Fair, Charlie "Bird" Parker and Sidney Bechet (Carr 1999, 52) were the two main stars, Parker representing the avant-garde and Bechet, New Orleans, the cradle of jazz music. Parker and Miles were, as Ian Carr (1999, 52) writes, "lionized in Paris, fêted everywhere, admired, bombarded with questions." Charlie Parker died young at the age of thirty-five, wasted by drug and alcohol abuse, yet his music will live on forever. The composer, bass player, and bandleader Charlie Mingus (Gleason 1995, 93) characterized the towering influence of the recently deceased Charlie "Bird" Parker on his peers as follows: "Most of the soloists at Birdland had to wait for Parker's next record in order to find out what to play next. What will they do now?"

Saxophone player John Coltrane (Porter 1999, 37) once wrote: "The first time I heard Bird play, it hit me right between the eyes." The compliment he paid Charlie Parker also fits the impact John Coltrane's personality, music style, and inventiveness had on his audience. As a young, very ambitious man he developed a power of concentration so unique that his biographer (Porter 1999, 52) states: "There is absolute agreement that Coltrane practiced maniacally." Soon he was asked to join jazz bands where he could improve both his repertoire and his playing technique. At the age of twenty-nine, Coltrane joined Miles Davis (Porter 1999, 98), who later stated: "The group I had with Coltrane made me and him a legend." Two years later, Coltrane joined Thelonious Monk's group, where he developed a style of shedding rapidly unfolding layers of notes, "sheets of sound" as jazz critic Ira

Gitler (Porter 1999, 111) aptly described them. As for Coltrane, he was happier with Monk than he had been with the moody and narcissistic Davis. As he states in his autobiography, *Coltrane on Coltrane* (Porter 1999, 111), "Working with Monk brought me close to a musical architect of the highest order." Coltrane made a very pertinent observation there. Personally, whenever I listen to Monk's sparse piano playing on his composition *Caravan*, I think of Coltrane's statement; I imagine I am sitting in the Basilica San Marco in Venice watching the honey-colored afternoon light streaming through high-set windows and transforming the manifold spaces of the basilica into a miracle whose enchantment is beyond words. Monk (Gioia 1998, 244) once hinted at the enigma of his sound architecture by stating: "It's not the notes you play; it's those you leave out."

In 1960, pianist Steve Kuhn joined Coltrane at the Jazz Gallery in New York downtown, near Cooper Union. He was so enthused about the experience with Coltrane and his group (Porter 1999, 173) that he later recalled: "It was like electricity. The people in the audience were just going crazy—it was like a revival meeting . . . It was almost hysteria in the audience." Coltrane's composition *Giant Steps*, with its cascades of tumbling sounds, indeed spreads the power of pure electricity.

Imitation has been called the most serious form of flattery. So enormous was Coltrane's influence on other musicians that the British composer, pianist, and jazz critic Leonard Feather (Porter 1999, 205) observed in 1964 that all young sax players kept copying Coltrane. Coltrane's impact on fellow musicians and audiences had by now reached legendary proportions. After attending a concert at the Half Note, jazz historian Dan Morgenstern (Porter 1999, 217) confessed: "If you let yourself be carried by it, it was an absolutely ecstatic feeling. And I think that kind of ecstasy was something that Coltrane was looking for in his music." After years of struggling with heavy drug addiction, John Coltrane was now on a spiritual journey, and ecstasy is a telltale sign of a mystical experience. He described his spiritual search as follows (Porter 1999, 232): "My music is the spiritual expression of what I am—my faith, my knowledge, my being . . . I'd like to point out to people the divine in a musical language that transcends words. I want to speak to their souls."

Biographer Ian Carr (Carr 1999) emphasizes the fact that Miles Davis was a man who combined a lot of contradicting qualities. He possessed great talents, professional perfectionism, and a chameleon-like ability to constantly change musical styles and directions. His influence on jazz music and its continuous creative transformation cannot be overrated. At the same time, Miles displayed an extremely eccentric character: his flashy dress style and often erratic, drug-dictated, flamboyant behavior and mannerisms made him a pain in the neck for a great number of his friends and fellow musicians.

During his long career, Miles was involved, among other things, in the development of bebop and the birth of cool jazz. In the mid-1950s, the Miles Davis Quintet—with tenor saxophonist John Coltrane, drummer Philly Joe Jones, Paul Chambers at the double bass, and pianist Red Garland—began its experimentation with modal jazz. It created a new sound architecture with drawn out melodic lines and smoothly played legatos presenting a radical rupture with the staccato of bebop. In the years to come, Miles Davis worked with a great number of different musicians and eventually ventured into acid rock and funk and became a pacemaker of fusion jazz.

Miles' track record earned him worldwide recognition, even fame, and he received nine Grammy Awards, among them a Grammy Lifetime Achievement Award in 1990, one year before he died. In 1991, Jack Lang (Carr 1999, 542), the French Minister of Culture at the time, made him a Chevalier de la Légion d'Honneur (the highest honorific decoration bestowed in France) addressing him as "the Picasso of jazz" and emphasizing that Davis had "imposed his law on the world of show business: aesthetic intransigence." While Lang's compliment may sound somewhat ambivalent and high-flown, bandleader and drummer Chico Hamilton (Carr 1999, 555) paid Davis a compliment that is very simple and literally down to earth: "Miles Davis is a sound—the whole earth singing!"

In jazz music there are single tunes and specific performances that have met with worldwide renown. Armstrong's *West End Blues*, Billie Holiday's *Strange Fruit*, Artie Shaw's *Begin the Beguine*, Duke Ellington's *The Mooche*, and David Brubeck's *Take Five* fall into this category. So does the composition *Body and Soul* interpreted by sax tenor player Coleman Hawkins (Gioia 1998, 174), hailed as "the most celebrated saxophone solo in the history of jazz." With its intimate phrasing and melody line gently pushing and pulling, releasing and tugging, it weaves a mood of optimistic relaxation.

As mentioned earlier, John Coltrane (Gioia 1998, 245) considered the eccentric pianist Thelonius Monk, who had a special gift for creating wide-open spaces between two subsequent notes, a "musical architect of the highest order." In the foreword to Fitterling's biography of Monk, Steve Lacy (Fitterling 1997, 15) characterizes Monk as "the leading strategist" of the bebop revolution in the 1940s. In those days, Minton's Playhouse in Harlem was a center of progressive jazz and Monk, together with drummer Kenny Clark, formed "the eye of the bebop hurricane" (Fitterling 1997, 31). Soon they were joined by top trumpeter Dizzy Gillespie, and saxophone player Charlie "Bird" Parker. The four musicians (Gleason 1995, 89) played a crucial role in creating modern jazz. Ted Gioia (Gioa 1998, 213) reports that: ". . . pianist Thelonious Monk stood out as one of the most adventurous and clearly the least easy to classify." Monk was the youngest of the Minton players and his conception of improvisation and composition were absolutely unique. Monk was a shy, rather mysterious person and so elusive that in 1955 a concert program described him as the "Greta Garbo of jazz" (Gioia 1998, 245). As time went by he escaped further and further into his inner recesses, and became remote to the point of being looked upon by some people as a lunatic. Yet his music, aided by a contract signed in 1962 with Columbia Records, drew ever more admirers to the point where *Time* magazine dedicated a cover story to him—cultural recognition as good as it comes.

Rock music is a child of the 1960s, born out of a Zeitgeist heavily influenced by a conspicuous antiauthoritarian stance and the use of drugs—marijuana, heroin, cocaine, amphetamines, and psychedelic substances such as LSD and psilocybin (magic mushrooms). Rock music implied a veritable revolution in entertainment, a radical break with the past. Like a hurricane, it swept over the United States and Europe before it reached the Asian borders, where it not only changed the musical taste of audiences, but also their visual outlook and mental orientation. Gone were the bobby socks and clean-cut hair of the Eisenhower era along with all the other emblems of neatness and automatic over-adjustment to society's established values, role expectations, and behavior patterns. To be Mom's beloved boy or Daddy's favorite girl was out; to be outrageous, a rebel with a cause was in. Wildly colored dresses, archaic beards, and primordial hairdos were the insignia of the initiated—an absolute must. Almost overnight, a whole generation was deeply convinced that they were about to invent a new society that would mark an irreversible rupture with the old ways. "Make Love Not War" was the hedonistic maxim. But the most prominent trademark of the new movement was its music. Although drawing heavily on blues, folk, and country, it created its own contents and forms of expression.

Among the famous groups of rock music were the Beatles, the Rolling Stones, The Who, The Eagles, The Beach Boys, The Band, Jefferson Airplane, Pink Floyd, and Genesis. Jimi Hendrix and Janis Joplin reached superstardom with nobody who could match the sheer intensity of their stage performances. Another superstar was charismatic Bob Dylan with his inexhaustible creative output, sophisticated lyrics, and ability to change the phrasing of his singing voice to find, time and again, new forms of expression that nobody was able to match. Dylan, moreover, had a knack for mastering various forms of music—from folksong to acid rock, blues, rhythm & blues, soul, and gospel—and integrating them into a unique sound of his own.

Bob Dylan, whose given name was Robert Allen Zimmerman, was by far the most outstanding poet the rock era has produced. The sources of his inspiration range from the Talmud to the Old Testament; from Western movies and tales about Billy the Kid to anonymous street corner scenes; and from a shoot-out in Durango back in 1849 to a fight in some hamburger joint. Dylan was able to compress a whole world into a simple melody and a string of lyrics as precise as they were full of meaning, earning him the titles "Homer in Denim" and "the Brecht of the juke box" (Shelton 1987, 228f.).

The music critic Ralph J. Gleason (Shelton 1987, 209) described Dylan's knack: ". . . to get poetry into the streets, to the people and on the juke boxes." With that feat Dylan successfully accomplished what the "jazz and poetry guys of the 1950s" had attempted to do in vain. Similarly, poet Allen Ginsberg (Heylin 1991, 144) stated: "Dylan has sold out to God . . . It was an artistic challenge to see if great art can be done on a jukebox. And he proved it can."

In his lyrics, Dylan's mental associations are often surprising, as the second half of a sentence does not lead to where the first half pointed. A good example for that procedure is his description of a woman who never stumbled because she had no place to fall. That characterization not only calls to mind a somewhat puzzling scene, but it prompts one to think about the nature of human predicament. Such is the creative power of Dylan: the poetry of rhythmical word plays and the wisdom of timeless human life experience embrace each other with effortless elegance. The whole thing sounds natural, incredibly simple; it is, in fact, utterly contrived—by a genius.

It is fair to say that Dylan is a creative leader in a class of his own. He has made his contributions as an author, songwriter, singer, composer, musician, bandleader, and role model for generations of musicians—including members and supporters of anti-war and civil rights movements. His regular collaboration with great musicians is legendary. Dylan's recognition includes Grammy, Golden Globe, and Academy Awards. He has been admitted to the Rock and Roll Hall of Fame, the Nashville Songwriters Hall of Fame, and the Songwriters Hall of Fame. In 2000, the Royal Swedish Academy of Music bestowed upon him and violinist Isaac Stern the Polar Music Prize. As different as the two top musicians may have been, they had one thing in common: a relentless striving towards the perfection of their art. In 2007, Dylan was again honored, this time with the Prince of Asturias Award in Arts, often an indicator of a forthcoming Nobel Prize in Literature, for which he has indeed been nominated several times.

Following are a few stepping stones on Dylan's pathway towards international acclaim. In October 1961, A&R executive John Hammond (Sounes 2001, 90) offered the twenty-year-old and still practically unknown Dylan a contract with Columbia Records. This was a surprising and highly promising gesture of recognition because Hammond was the man who had played a major role in the career of three stars on the jazz scene, promoting singer Billie Holiday, clarinettist and bandleader Benny Goodman, and pianist and bandleader Count Basie. In the first half of 1962, Bob Dylan (Sounes 2001,

110) wrote his protest song, *The Ballad of Emmett Till* and John Hammond got Dylan a publishing deal with Duchess Music, Inc. plus $1,000 advance. The well-known folk singer Pete Seeger (Sounes 2001, 111), who would later accuse Dylan of being a traitor to the cause of the American ballad, observed with admiration and a touch of envy: "It looked like every day this genius from out of nowhere had a new song, and a good one, not a pot-boiler, a damn good song. Everybody's talking about him."

In March 1962, Dylan's debut album (Sounes 2001, 113f.) *Bob Dylan* was hailed as an "explosive country-blues debut;" a critic in the *Village Voice* flatly stated: "It's a collector's item already." Dylan, fired up by so much positive feedback, was already sitting in the music studio recording his new song *Blowin' in the Wind*, which would soon make him famous the world over. In October 1962, at the peak of the Cuban missile crisis, many musicians in Greenwich Village played Dylan's anti-war song, *A Hard Rain's A-Gonna Fall*. Arlo Guthrie, son of the legendary folk singer Woody Guthrie, who had been Dylan's first major role model, spoke about the song (Sounes 2001, 122) when describing the aftermath of a nuclear fallout: "The truth rang out so loud in his words, not just for me, but for an entire generation."

The trio Peter, Paul and Mary recorded *Blowin' in the Wind* (Sounes 2001, 135) and on July 13, 1963 their single reached second position on the Billboard chart; sales exceeded one million. By now Bob Dylan had become a household name in the United States, and the Newport Folk Festival of July 26-28, 1963 in the United Kingdom was to spread his fame beyond national borders: Dylan and successful folk singer Joan Baez sang *With God on Our Side* as a duet. Folksinger Tom Paxton (Sounes 2001, 136) later reported: "That was a big breakthrough festival for Bob. The buzz just kept growing exponentially and it was like a coronation of Bob and Joan. They were King and Queen of the festival." Soon the album *The Freewheelin' Bob Dylan* was selling 10 thousand copies per week and this box office hit (Sounes 2001, 138) not only fostered Dylan's self-confidence, it also put him on solid financial feet. The album began to influence The Beatles. Their arrival at Kennedy Airport provoked mass hysteria among their teenage admirers, and when they appeared on The Ed Sullivan Show on February 9, 1964, they triggered the cross-Atlantic mass phenomenon of a fan frenzy quickly baptized "Beatlemania." George Harrison (Sounes 2001, 155) thus described the impact of Dylan's new album on The Beatles: "The content of the song lyrics and just the attitude—it was just incredibly original and wonderful." From then on the Beatles began to replace their simple "I-love-you-yeah-yeah-yeah" lyrics by more sophisticated verse.

In 1964, Dylan published his third album *Another Side of Bob Dylan* followed in 1965 by the album *Bringing It All Back Home,* in which he used an electric guitar for the first time. Folk singers such as Seeger and Baez perceived "going electric" as an offence to the unwritten rules of protest songs; yet the general public greeted the move with enthusiasm. Requests for interviews multiplied. In April 1965, Dylan began his spring tour across the United Kingdom. The highlight of that concert tour came with Dylan's spectacular performance at Royal Albert Hall. The Beatles and The Rolling Stones (Sounes 2001, 175) attended the concert, thus paying tribute to a new superstar who was but twenty-four years old.

In August 1965, Dylan published the album *Highway 61 Revisited,* followed by *Blonde on Blonde,* which, together with *Bringing It All Back Home,* are often considered to be the best LP albums he ever cut. These successes, however, were followed by a radical change in the star's good fortune. On July 29, 1966, he had a motor accident in Woodstock, New York where he lived with his wife Sara Lownds and their children. The accident injured his spine and would cause him severe back pain for years to come. His career took a nosedive as he withdrew from the public eye. Soon thereafter, and hidden from public scrutiny, the recluse artist began to work with Robbie Robertson and his band, a group that later became known under the brand name The Band. They used to record their takes in the basement of a house and the recordings were later released as the *Basement Tapes.* At the end of 1967, Dylan recorded his album *John Wesley Harding* in Nashville, Tennessee. Ever on the lookout for yet another innovation in his music, Dylan frustrated public expectations once again. The formerly opulent instrumentation had become sparse, and Dylan's lyrics betrayed the simultaneous influence of the Bible and the legends of the old American West. The public (Sounes 2001, 229) who had impatiently awaited a new Dylan release eagerly bought the album and made of it yet another success.

In 1970, Dylan released the album *Self-Portrait* containing mostly songs written by other musicians; this ironical tribute to other artists was met by critics and the general public with reluctance, bewilderment, or even outright rejection. That same year *New Morning* came out, and music critic Ralph J. Gleason (Sounes 2001, 261) wrote a favorable review in the magazine *Rolling Stone,* with the jubilant headline: "WE'VE GOT DYLAN BACK!"

Gleason's prediction proved true. In 1973, Bob Dylan composed the score for Sam Peckinpah's movie *Pat Garrett and Billy the Kid,* in which he also played a cameo role. *Knockin' on Heaven's Door*, the theme song, became a super-hit and still ranks as one of the songs most often played all over the world. The following year, Dylan recorded *Planet Waves* while he prepared, together with The Band, a trans-American mega-tour that was to play forty shows in major sport stadiums and theaters. The tour grossed about $5 million with 658,000 tickets sold. Bob Dylan and The Band had become rich, and to top it all, *Planet Waves* (Sounes 2001, 274ff.) was the first Dylan album to make number one on the charts.

By now Sara and Bob had entered a cycle of recurrent fights, separations, reunions, and talk of divorce. This painful experience left its marks on his album *Blood on the Tracks* (Sounes 2001, 285) released in 1975. The LP climbed immediately to first position on the charts and became a worldwide success. Many Dylan fans considered it to contain the most outstanding lyrics Dylan had ever written. Together with *Desire*, released the following year, *Blood on the Tracks* sold several million albums, thus reaching a Multi-Platinum status (Sounes 2001, 298).

After a series of misfortunes and ruptures, including his divorce from Sara and a conversion to born-again Christianity, his album *Slow Train Coming* was another smash in 1979. It included the Grammy-winning song *Gotta Serve Somebody* (Sounes 2001, 333), for which Dylan was acknowledged for the Best Male Rock Vocal Performance.

In the fall of 1985, Columbia Records released *Biograph* (Sounes 2001, 368) a five-record set compilation of Dylan's creative work which grossed $7.5 million, proving once more that cultural evaluation still ranked his kind of music among the best ever produced. In 1989, his record *Oh Mercy* (Sounes 2001, 387) met international acclaim. It was followed by a period of public rejection—which we will discuss later—until *Time Out of Mind* (Sounes 2001, 418) appeared in 1997. It became one of his seven Platinum albums with over a million copies sold. Add to it Dylan's twenty Gold albums (Sounes 2001, 424) —over 500,000 copies sold—and the combined box office successes serve as a yardstick for Dylan's hierarchical position in the pantheon of creative musicians.

Like Thomas A. Edison, who took out 1,300 patents during his long career—an average of one patent every five days—Bob Dylan's case illustrates not only the phenomenon that cultural evaluation offers the highest rewards and the severest punishments to creators whose productions are of outstanding uniqueness, but also the fact that high quality and quantity of creative production are intimately linked. Between 1962 and 2006, Dylan produced thirty-two albums, worked almost day and night with the best musicians in the world, and toured the globe on a gruelling schedule, averaging more than one hundred concerts per year! Such enormous productivity, of course, increased the probability that amid such a great quantity, there was bound to be a good amount of quality.

Simonton (Simonton, 1987) points out that scientific research proves "that a small percentage of workers in any given field of creative activity account for a disproportionate amount of contributions to their discipline." According to him, the top ten percent most productive creators contribute about half of all accomplishments; the fifty percent last productive contributors add but about fifteen percent of the creative output.

These top performers—like Mozart, Edison and Dylan—begin their creative output in early life. Stoically enduring failure and happily relishing success, they keep pushing forward until cumulated achievement eventually reinforces their already high motivation to strive for ever-greater accomplishments. Simonton (1987, 75) compares creative individuals to rats in a Skinner box who receive food pellets for bar pressing: "The first to catch on to the trick and press the lever will get a head start in the rat race for ever more rewards." In my view, it is the great yet still-dormant creative potential that pushes a specific rat to be the first to explore the environment and to press the bar that will bring the very first reward. This then sets a positive feedback loop into motion: motivation begets production that begets success that begets motivation that begets more production that begets further success and so on and so forth. But what happens if the rat pressing a bar for the first time receives an electric shock instead of a food pellet? We shall return to this issue in a later section.

The positive outcome of cultural selection in architecture is also worthy of interest. Hernán Vieco, a Columbian architect and close friend of writer and Nobel laureate Gabriel García Márquez, once told me with a twinkle in his eye: "An architect's handicraft is actually very simple. He builds walls with holes in them. The only problem is: where do you put the holes?" Obviously architects, critics, clients, and the public at large do not always agree about whether the holes have been put in the right places or not.

In the course of time, Charles-Edouard Jeanneret-Gris, who called himself Le Corbusier, has been vigorously condemned and exceedingly praised. Richards (1960, 84) states: "His best work shows a poetic and imaginative use of geometrical forms, inspired originally by Cubism." Le Corbusier's use of geometrical forms is particularly well illustrated in the pilgrimage Chapel of Notre Dame du Haut at Ronchamp in France. The forms, proportions, and colors of its volumes, surfaces, and slanted walls dance in fascinating rhythms and with such harmony that the whole building looks like a primeval sculpture composed of forcefully vibrant biological shapes. Though the chapel does not necessarily pretend to blend in with its natural environment, it nevertheless forms an organic unity with its surroundings while proudly emphasizing its independent identity.

The scholar Kenneth Frampton (1987, 149) attributes to Le Corbusier an "absolutely central and seminal role in the development of 20th century architecture." Unlike Gropius and Mies van der Rohe (Frampton 1987, 154), Le Corbusier was a pacemaker and chief propagandist of modern urbanism in architecture. His influence as a theoretician cannot be overrated; he has inspired and motivated generations of young architects for excellence in performance. His aphorism (Frampton 1987, 155), "a city made for speed is a city made for success," was hailed as a revelation by urban designers, politicians, architects, engineers, and entrepreneurs eager to establish a new architecture for the machine-age civilization.

The new architecture replacing the historicizing style of the nineteenth century aimed to be strictly rational and utilitarian rather than stuffed with multicultural quotations and garnished with a *maquis*[5] of asthma-provoking decorations. Le Corbusier (Richards 1960, 38) formulated the slogan: "*La maison est une machine à habitation*—the house is machine for living." His mechanistic credo derided any sentimental notion of bourgeois coziness or aristocratic pretensions wavering between the gravitas of ostentatious pomposity and the picturesque kitsch of fairytale castles. Yet despite the Calvinistic-Cartesian rigor emphasized in his publications, when it actually came to building machines of habitation, he revealed himself not only as a detail-centered craftsman with a down-to-earth attitude, but also as an artist full of fantasy. Richards (1960, 39) calls him " . . . one of the most imaginative architects of modern times" and adds, "his buildings are remarkable for their freedom from rule-of-thumb designing." Le Corbusier's architecture shows the trademarks of rational design, yet it is at the same time, as Richards (1960) observes, ". . . full of a poetic quality that is pure art and very far from being the product of mechanical thinking."

Le Corbusier was not only a highly successful architect and theoretician of architecture, he was also a highly competent and inventive designer of furniture. His chairs, leather loungers, and black leather and steel sofas belong to the bestsellers of our contemporary furniture industry. His comprehensive approach to architecture and furniture design brought him enduring world-wide recognition.

In 1939 (Gill 1987, 405), Le Corbusier became an honorary member of the Royal Institute of British Architects. Two years, later King George VI awarded him the Gold Medal of the Royal Institute. This was about the highest expression of cultural recognition an architect could get in those days, as the Pritzker Architecture Prize would be established some forty years later. Together with Mies van der Rohe and Walter Gropius, who were both directors of the Bauhaus, and the American architect Frank Lloyd Wright, Le Corbusier was one of the founding fathers of modernist architecture. That movement installed a formal purism clad in steel, concrete, and glass whose progeny still shapes and defines urban landscapes all over the globe.

The Bauhaus, first situated in Weimar, then in Dessau (Germany), lasted only from 1919 to 1933. In that short period of time—which corresponds exactly to the lifespan of the Weimar Republic—the Bauhaus managed to become "the most celebrated art school of modern times" (Whitford 1986, 9). As Wolf von Eckhardt (Whitford 1986, 10) puts it, the Bauhaus "created the patterns and set the standards of present-day industrial design; it helped to invent modern architecture; it altered the look of everything from the chair you are sitting in to the page you are reading now."

Walter Gropius achieved recognition both as a director of the Bauhaus school of architecture and as a creative architect who designed and built private commissions. Convinced that fine arts and crafts were not antithetic but complementary entities, he brought together a staff of excellent teachers including the painters Lyonel Feininger, Johannes Itten, Paul Klee, Wassily Kandinsky, El Muche, and Oskar Schlemmer (who was also a sculptor); the sculptors Gerhard Marcks and Laszlo Mohol-Nagy; and stage producer Lothar Schreyer. With his crew, Gropius radically innovated the traditional teaching approach in architecture: opting for a strategy of interdisciplinary collaboration, he opened wide doors and windows, letting in the gusts of fresh air that would sweep away the dust from the art academies of the past. To this very day, the Bauhaus and what it stood for has had a tremendous impact not only on architecture, but also on the fine arts including painting, sculpture, carving, and many other crafts. Gropius, founder and spiritus rector of the Bauhaus, is viewed worldwide as a creative leader able to inspire and motivate generations of architects, engineers, artists, and craftsmen for extraordinary performance. Critic J. M. Richards (1960, 83) wrote: "Gropius' own architecture, as exemplified in the Bauhaus buildings, is rational to the point of extreme—almost forbidding—severity; but so thoroughly and rhythmically planned, with every part in perfect coordination, as to give the whole a sort of nobility that a more fanciful style seldom achieves."

After a short intermezzo with architect Hannes Meyer on the podium, the Bauhaus was entrusted to a third director: it was Ludwig Mies van der Rohe who conducted the swan song of the influential German school. When the Nazis came to power, he emigrated to the United States, heading the school of architecture at the Illinois Institute of Technology in Chicago, a city in which he built a great number of steel and glass buildings that helped to spread his fame. Together with his disciple Marc Breuer, Walter Gropius also moved to the United States, where he taught at the Harvard Graduate School of Design in Cambridge, Massachusetts.

In the United States, Mies van der Rohe soon became a code name for a very sophisticated style of urban architecture. The houses he built for the Illinois Institute of Technology and the apartment blocks on Lake Shore Drive in Chicago have been hailed (Richards 1960, 109) as "masterpieces of precise engineering, devoid of any ornament . . . They rely for their aesthetic effect on subtlety of proportion and mechanical precision of finish." Mies van der

Rohe played a pace-making role in the industrialization of building methods and thus in bringing together science and business that, in the United States, had hitherto been almost enemies as far as architecture was concerned. His maxim "less is more" echoes Alfred Loos' dictum "ornament is a crime," while his slogan "God is in the details" betrays the spirit of the proverbial German *Gründlichkeit*—a thoroughness and carefulness in the details that rejects any compromise with a sloppy "will do" attitude.

Mies van der Rohe attracted many young followers, and the urban landscape of the United States soon showed and still shows the trademark of his genius: clarity, simplicity bordering on minimalism, sophisticated elegance, and the use of modern building materials such as steel frame, glass panels, and reinforced concrete. Shedding the superfluous, he developed what Furneaux Jordan (Furneaux Jordan 1985, 331) calls the "Miesian tradition" of buildings characterized by an "elegant distinction, the Grecian purity." His conscientiousness in getting every single detail right was nevertheless balanced by a keen sense of historical perspectives and the philosophical implications of great architecture. Mies van der Rohe was well aware of the fact that Gothic cathedrals had expressed the spiritual orientation of a mediaeval society. His aim was to imbue the utilitarian functionalism of modern architecture with a deeper meaning. In his view, modernist architecture was meant to express the Zeitgeist of the industrial age with its unconscious and conscious aspirations and aesthetics. As Frampton (1987, 166) states, it was this philosophical-historical orientation that separated Mies van der Rohe "from the mass-approach of the *Neue Sachlichkeit*."

The support that helped Frank Lloyd Wright to achieve international fame began while he was still in his mother's womb. Convinced that her son should become a famous architect, mother Wright obviously did not expect to give birth to a girl—she plastered the baby's room with engravings of English cathedrals (Gill 1987, 26). Frank Lloyd Wright (Gill 1987, 42) later responded to her pathetic gesture by "inventing a saintly mother bent upon the nurture of a genius." In reality she was an extremely selfish creature given to histrionics marked by outcries of abysmal self-pity.

In 1887, Frank Lloyd Wright (Gill 1987, 75) joined the Adler & Sullivan architecture firm in Chicago, still charred and scarred by the Great Fire of 1871, which had left it devastated. Adler & Sullivan played a major role in rebuilding the destroyed city and modelling its new face. Louis H. Sullivan, the man who had come up with the slogan "form follows function" quickly recognized the excellent drawing ability of his twenty-year-old assistant. There was a deep kinship between their respective talents. As Wright's biographer Brendan Gill (1987, 81) puts it, both of them possessed the rare gift "to move mentally in three dimensions through the volumes of space" and that they were able to set down plan and elevation "in the two dimensions of a sheet of paper."

At the age of twenty-nine, Frank built the Ward W. Willits house in Highland Park, Illinois, which became known as (Gill 1987, 135) "the first masterpiece among the Prairie Houses." The various volumes, structural elements, and elegant proportions of the abode suggest that its architect had been less inspired by the wide-open spaces and rolling slopes of the Western prairies where the buffalo used to roam than by the Japanese prints he had begun to collect, and notably by a half-scale replica of a Japanese temple of the Fujiwara Period (900-1200 AD) he had seen at the Chicago Fair a few years before.

From the days his mother had pampered her "little genius," Frank possessed solid self-confidence. Already as a novice in the profession, he saw himself as (Gill 1987, 164) the greatest living American architect, a characterization soon corrected to "the greatest architect who ever lived." To protect his *délire de grandeur* (Gill 1987, 174), he refused to enter competitions where architectural designs were judged by a jury. For him, the only relevant jury worthy of his prestige and status as an architect was his client. Although he often drove them to despair (Gill 1987, 190), the clients would come back for a second or even a third house. The rapidly increasing demand for his work bolstered his grandiose sense of self, revealed in a letter he wrote to a friend (Gill 1987, 210): "I am cast by nature for the part of the iconoclast. I must strike—tear down—before I can build." And build he did with such a frenzy that his biographer (Gill 1987, 226) muses: "Wright rejoiced at the opportunity to play God in every department: the buildings, the furniture, the lighting fixtures, the crockery, the napery, the glassware."

In December 1916, Wright and his third wife Miriam (Gill 1987, 238) embarked on a venture that would keep him busy for the next six years. From Seattle they sailed west to fulfill the commission he had won to build the Imperial Hotel in Tokyo. His fee for the opulent building was to be more than half a million dollars (Gill 1987, 265), a trophy of recognition of regal proportions. The Imperial Hotel turned into a triumph in Wright's mid-life career. It withstood the great earthquake of 1923, adding to the fame of the architect who later developed his own theory about how he had "outwitted" the seism. The prosaic truth is that the foundations of the hotel had been erected on layers of mud sixty or seventy feet deep (Gill 1987, 258) and able to absorb and withstand the shock of the quake. Nevertheless, Wright (Gill 1987, 264) took great pride in a telegram signed by Baron Okura, Chairman of the Board of Directors of the corporation that had financed the hotel. It read: "HOTEL STANDS UNDAMAGED AS MONUMENT OF YOUR GENIUS HUNDREDS OF HOMELESS PROVIDED BY PERFECTLY MAINTAINED SERVICE CONGRATULATIONS OKURA." What a salute to the architect's genius! Or was it? As Brendan Gill (1987, 264) suggests, we have good reason to assume that Frank Lloyd Wright fabricated the document himself to nurture his voracious self-esteem.

Wright's next undertaking was to develop a new architectural language to replace the Spanish mission style adopted throughout the southwestern United States. His basic idea was to use identical concrete building blocks and combine them with imagination and a proper sense of proportion. The houses would display an array of repeated structural patterns—the surface of each individual block could be molded into a specific form, and come cheap. Always a poet when it came to singing his own praises and luring potential customers, he now christened himself a "weaver" and the blocks were called "textile-blocks" (Gill 1987, 267). The trick worked as it had with his Prairie Houses. Frank Lloyd Wright decided to launch his new building venture in California. *La Miniatura* in Pasadena was the first textile-block house ever realized. According to Wright's biographer (Gill 1987, 268), it is "among the most beautiful houses to be found anywhere in the world, regardless of size."

When "the wizard of Taliesin" reached the age of seventy, his career began to stall. He now lived with his fourth wife Olgivanna and a group of disciples in his former summer home in Spring Green, Wisconsin; the settlement was called Taliesin (Welsh for "shining brow"). Wright's school of architecture was supported by a group of Friends of the Fellowship featuring, among others, Walter Gropius and Mies van der Rohe. Olgivanna, born and raised in Montenegro and a former adept of Gurdjieff's[6] court in Fontainebleau outside of Paris, helped to create an atmosphere fit to impress a cult community: in the center Frank Almighty sitting on a throne, at his feet disciples gaping in speechless devotion before the grand patriarch. That admiration was not necessarily shared by the outside world. Many experts looked upon Wright as a has-been. Yet Wright, cocky as ever, assured reporters and the audiences he used to address throughout the country that his best work was yet to come. His prediction eventually proved true. As Brendan Gill (1987, 339) writes, "History offers few examples of people achieving a deserved success late in life, especially when that success crowns many years of seeming total failure."

In 1934, one year after President Franklin Roosevelt inaugurated the New Deal, Stanley Marcus, later president and chairman of the famous Neiman-Marcus luxury retailer department stores, paid Wright a visit in his Taliesin retreat. He and his wife intended to build a beautiful home and could not decide between Neutra and Lescaze as the better architect to fulfill their dream. Wright (Gill 1987, 341), self-confident and ebullient as ever, taunted them: "Why be satisfied with a substitute when you can get the original?" Their response: "Mr. Wright, we never dreamed that a man of your high reputation would consent to design a house for us." The house was actually never built because the bids offered for the design proposed by Wright turned out to be too high, even for such a wealthy merchant as Stanley Marcus.

That very same year, Edgar J. Kaufmann Jr., the son of a wealthy store-owner in Pittsburgh, showed up in Talisien and became a temporary disciple of Wright's. One day his parents came to visit their son and met the master of the house. Talks began, and eventually Wright designed *Fallingwater* for the Kaufmann family, a house to be built in the wilderness some sixty miles south of Pittsburgh. *Time* magazine put Wright on the cover of its January 1938 issue with a drawing of *Fallingwater* in the background. Overnight it became the symbol of a worldwide Wright revival. Once again, Frank Lloyd Wright had put himself back on the map.

Fallingwater, which straddles the Bear Run in the Appalachians, has by now turned into a destination for pilgrims venerating Wright's architecture. Its free-hanging cantilevers make it look like a fairytale house. As Brendan Gill (1987, 346) puts it, ". . . the house and its series of terraces seem to float in a saucy defiance of gravity above the waterfall." But gravity is pervasive. As time went by, the free-hanging cantilevers began to sag and repairs were needed to uphold the whole structure. Nevertheless, Edgar J. Kaufmann, Jr. remained a staunch supporter of Wright's creative accomplishment, pointing out that the dome of the Hagia Sophia, the belfries of St. Peter's in Rome and the core of the Pantheon in Paris "all threatened the stability of their structures and required drastic repairs." Today these buildings still stand and "add to the glory of their countries and their art." To be compared to the ingenious builders of the Hagia Sophia, St. Peter's, and the Pantheon in Paris is indeed high praise for the architect of *Fallingwater*.

In 1937, in the aftermath of a bout with pneumonia that forced him to move to the southwest, Wright set up winter quarters for himself and his school near Scottsdale, Arizona. The group of buildings erected on a remote mesa overlooking Paradise Valley was baptized Taliesin West. The following year, *Architectural Forum* published a whole issue on Wright's architecture, part of which was dedicated to *Fallingwater* (Gill 1987, 369), prompting a new wave of national and international recognition for its genitor.

In 1939, Wright was invited to lecture on architecture in London (Gill 1987, 40) and became an honorary member of the Royal Institute of British Architects. Two years later, King George VI awarded him the Gold Medal of the Royal Institute, again boosting his self-esteem and eventually catapulting him into a show of recklessness that offended more than only good taste. President Franklin D. Roosevelt invited Wright to Washington, DC to discuss cheap housing needed for the scientists and technicians working at the atom bomb project in Oak Ridge, Tennessee. A witness of the encounter (Gill 1987, 417) could not believe his eyes or ears as the architect—dressed as usual in a cloak, a cane, and a pork-pie hat—did not remove his hat in the presence of the President, whom he was meeting for the first time. Wright addressed President Roosevelt, committed to a wheelchair after poliomyelitis had left him with a permanent paralysis from the waist down, with an impromptu pep-talk: "Frank, you ought to get up out of that chair and look around at what they're doing to your city here, miles and miles of Ionic and Corinthian columns!" Frankly, Frank to Frank, and from one famous authority to another.

Wright's ultimate triumph came with the designing and building of the Manhattan Guggenheim Museum whose spiral, snail-like shape meets Brendan Gill's observation (1987, 429) that "the masterpieces of Wright's old age emanate an air of having always existed, of having been shaped out of the earth itself, by members of a race who have left us no other sign of their existence." The museum housing the collection of non-objective art put together by the industrialist and multi-millionaire Solomon R. Guggenheim opened its doors on October 21, 1959—six months after Wright's death. Immediately hailed as "America's most beautiful building," it has become not only a monument to Wright and Guggenheim, but also a famous landmark for eager visitors from the four corners of the earth. There is no doubt that the Guggenheim Museum in Manhattan is one of the most spectacular buildings ever erected on our planet.

Last but not least, let us have a look at the world of entrepreneurship, where creativity plays a role whenever a completely new and valuable industry, product or service is born.

Alfred Nobel, an industrial tycoon who made his money by producing and selling dynamite and other explosives founded the Nobel Prize for sciences and the arts. Interestingly enough, he did not consider economists or industrialists to be prospective recipients of his award. He must have thought that creative performance might be a rather rare event in these quarters. Indeed there are plenty of hard-working economists and entrepreneurs who mainly reproduce what others have already done. But there are also true creators in economics and creative inventors in the industrial world. By now, scientists in economics have their own Nobel Memorial Prize in Economics established in 1968 by the National Bank of Sweden. Creative inventors and entrepreneurs, however, do not as yet have a Nobel Award or its equivalent. And yet there is no doubt that several individuals—Henry Ford, Walter Rathenau, Werner von Siemens, and Konosuke Matsushita, to name a few—were creative entrepreneurs whose accomplishments not only marked the beginning of the twentieth century, but still heavily influence the present day.

Henry Ford invented and produced cars, "horseless carriages" with gasoline engines, because he understood that the era of horse-drawn coaches was drawing to an end. His vision turned out to be correct and today we cannot begin to imagine a world without automobiles. Henry Ford (Josephson 1992, 406), who worshipped Thomas A. Edison, was certainly encouraged when his idol told him: "Young man, that's the thing! You have it! . . . the self-contained unit carrying its own fuel with it. Keep at it."

Walter Rathenau ran the German AEG (Allgemeine Elektrizitäts-Gesellschaft) founded by his father and became an entrepreneur, politician, and board member of almost a hundred companies that played a fundamental role in the industrial development of the nineteenth century. Werner von Siemens started out with a telegraph he had invented, soon diversified into the production of light bulbs and electrical trains, and eventually built up a conglomerate that belongs today to the major industrial players in the world.

Japan's Konosuke Matsushita made his début by inventing a new electrical lamp socket. At the age of twenty-three, he founded the Matsushita Electrical Appliance factory with his wife Mumeno, her brother Toshio, and Konosuke himself as the only employees of the start-up. Facing bankruptcy, he accomplished an amazing turn around, increased his profits, lowered his prices, improved the marketing, went nation-wide, and became a household name. During the Second World War he embarked, though reluctantly, on the production of airplanes—his contribution to the war effort. In retaliation, the American post-war administration in Japan broke up his conglomerate. After the war, and starting almost from scratch, the creative leader began producing bicycle lamps, a venture which eventually turned into Sanyo Electrics. By the 1970s, Matsushita had become the world's largest producer of electrical goods: all over the globe the trade name Panasonic was a familiar household brand. The brilliant entrepreneur's biographer, Kotter (1997, 2)—who has written a highly interesting leadership study on Matsushita—points him out as "one of the central figures who helped lead the Japanese economic miracle."

Matsushita died in 1989 at the age of ninety-four. In that year, the Matsushita corporation revenues (Kotter 1997, 2) "hit a phenomenal $42 billion . . . . more than the combined sales of Bethlehem Steel, Colgate-Palmolive, Goodrich, Kellogg's, Olivetti, Scott Paper, and Whirlpool." At his funeral services, Matsushita received an honor rarely bestowed upon highly creative individuals: a stream of 20,000 mourners to follow his coffin. The president of the United States sent a telegram to Konosuke's family referring to the industrialist as "an inspiration to people around the world." As for Kotter (1997, 3), the biographer sums up Konosuke Matsushita's track record as follows: ". . . it is difficult to find 20th-century entrepreneurs or executives with a longer list of accomplishments. And as an inspirational role model, he is without peer." What more could be said about a creative leader?

Many of the examples discussed in the present chapter have shown how specific individuals react to recognition. On a more general level I should like to point out that, in my view, there is a trivalent logic of reaction in life: individuals react to an input by embracing it unconditionally, by selectively accepting it, or by totally rejecting it.

Very strong individuals are always encouraged by recognition; some of them even to the point where they lose their heads when success strikes and develop a grandiose self, indulging in such outrageous behavior that they become a nuisance for others. More mature, strong individuals possess a touch of wisdom, like Einstein or Dirac, and never lose their original modesty. The latter category also includes astrophysicist Chandrasekhar (Wali 1991, 239) about whom his colleague, John Wilson, stated: "A genial, modest, and self-effacing individual, Chandra always stood for the very highest level in academic affairs. That is the essence of his being." Despite these tokens of official recognition for his achievements, Chandrasekhar once confessed to his biographer Kameshwar C. Wali (1991, 305): "I don't really have a sense of fulfillment. All I have done seems to be not very much." Such were the words professed by a man of science who was not only one of the most productive scientists ever, but also one of the most creative.

Other good examples of how strong personalities deal with success can be found in the Italian Renaissance. Leonardo da Vinci and Michelangelo were both admired as the greatest artists of their time, and both earned a lot of money; so too did Raphael. Leonardo and Michelangelo coped with their equally great successes in rather different ways. Leonardo spent his wealth on clothes, jewellery, and other beautiful objects for himself and for his male friends and lovers, while frugal Michelangelo was able to set aside quite a fortune. To cite but one example, the completion of his chef d'oeuvre, the ceiling of the Sistine Chapel (Kemp 2004, 28), earned him 2,000 ducats. Although Michelangelo accused him of plagiarism, Raphael had quite some influence on other artists of his day, but he never had the same influence for later generations. Yet in one respect, the reaction of the three artists to recognition was the same: while encountering success after success, they went on working hard and striving towards an ever-higher perfection of their art.

There is a second category of individuals who lack the strong character of the personalities described above. They may react to recognition with ambivalence, display a combination of high sensitivity and vulnerability, and forever doubt whether or not they are really made "of the right stuff." At times, they may exaggerate their own talents, only to denigrate them on other occasions. Ambivalence seems to have influenced Glenda Jackson's reaction (Woodward 1986, 136) to her second Oscar, which she received for her starring role in *A Touch of Class*. She handed the statuette over to her mother, who had already been entrusted with the first one. Glenda's comment: "They'll make a lovely pair of book-ends for my mother's sideboard." Of a generous nature, she shared the recognition received with the other members of the film crew, praising, for instance, her makeup artist and the cameramen who had "done a lot with my tiny eyes and my rotten skin."

Finally, there are weak individuals who are simply overwhelmed by success. They may either fall into the trap of complacency and go on to produce only mediocre results; or they may respond to recognition with a temporary or definitive block of their creative abilities. It is this last reaction that many people do not quite understand. They should heed the observation of the poet William Blake (Ash 1986, 34-41, 40) who wrote: "The strongest poison known came from Caesar's laurel crown." Extreme role expectations are able to block the spontaneous flow of imagination and with it, sophisticated mental operation.

In wrapping up this section on recognition offered by cultural evaluation, I should like to emphasize an important fact: there is a multichannel feedback loop connecting official recognition and the creative individual's reaction to it with the ubiquitous chaos and order of the environment in which recognition and reaction to recognition occur. It was the continuous interplay of chaos and order that originally set off the weaving operation on the enchanted loom, and with it a creative process that produced a result whose value was recognized by cultural evaluation. The same interplay also influenced the creative individual or group's reaction to recognition. And thus we come full circle: beginning and end fuse into one single entity from which new beginnings will sprout anew.

The ultimate recognition of a creative individual or group's accomplishments occurs if one of her, his, or its works becomes an integral part of a people from whose heritage that accomplishment has drawn the chaos and order that went into its making. A wonderful example of such reintegration of an oeuvre into the very belly of the culture from which it arose has been reported by Mexican writer Carlos Fuentes. In his autobiography *Myself with Others* (1990, 9), he describes how one day, on the beach of Lota in Southern Chile, he watched the miners leaving "molelike" their tunnels after having worked many feet below the sea where they had been extracting the coal of the Pacific Ocean. "They sat around a bonfire and sang, to guitar music, a poem from Neruda's Canto General." To his amazement Fuentes discovered that they had no idea the poem had been written by Pablo Neruda, their fellow countryman and Nobel Prize laureate at that. For them the poem was, as Fuentes writes quoting Croce on the Iliad: ". . . 'd'un popolo intero poetante,' of an entire poetizing people."

Excerpts from an interview with Ashok Kurien (14)

Ashok Kurien begins his discussion of recognition by mentioning the years of rejection that eventually ended in an advertising company with a boss who hated and mistreated him. But then his fortune turned, and the boss had to quit the company. From then on Ashok Kurien went from success to success with few exceptions. The cumulative experience was a source of pride, but it also made him aware of his social responsibilities. In that respect he is now working on his mega-project, STORYEUM, already described above. There is little doubt in my mind that this project will bring Ashok Kurien huge recognition from his country, as it will boost Indian self-confidence and promote a solid sense of identity and pride in a culture that is over 5,000 years old.

GG: When did you receive the first recognition for the value of your professional work?

AK: Let me see… I had a boss who was extremely bright and extremely vicious and extremely horrible and made me feel like shit. He hated me. My colleagues thought that I was not good and…

GG: Was this in the first advertising agency where you worked as an employee?

AK: Yes, that was the only ad agency where I was working as an employee, and at one stage I quit, but the owner of the agency said, "Go to South India." The idea was that by moving I could escape the boss. Now he didn't say, "You're good" but, "We don't want you to suffer. Go South". So I went. But then two or three important clients—the sari client, Garden, who gave me my first account; the Lakme client; Mrs. Simone Tata, the Tata family mother, who are still my friends—told our agency that they didn't want my boss to come into their office anymore. They said, "He's dishonest, he's full of hogwash. He plays games with his intellect and we don't want him; we don't like him." At that stage I just got transferred back to Bombay. I had to move back to Bombay because my child was ill. By then that boss in our agency had quit the job or was fired, and I got the position as number two. The two clients I just mentioned said that the only person they wanted to see was Ashok because "he is honest; he has some integrity and he is good." So that gave me some kind of confidence, and I compiled that little book on the basics of placing ads that I already told you about.

GG: And that everybody bought.

AK: Everybody bought it, and I made money with it. So that was another experience of recognition that also increased my self-confidence. Then a client came along who suggested, "Come and start your own agency!" And I thought to myself, "Hell, I'm not as stupid as everybody says I am." So, there you are. Once I had my own agency, I gave my first clients good advice and I earned recognition for it.

GG: Could you give me a concrete example of such advice?

AK: There was a family-owned textile company run by brothers who produced saris. But I predicted that as India was changing, younger people would wear a fabric with stitch-work, an outfit called *salwaar kameez*. It resembles what is worn in Pakistan, a pantsuit with a scarf.

GG: You predicted that a different kind of dress style would become fashionable.

AK: Right. I also predicted that business would grow a lot faster because of the youth of our country. So one of the owners set up a second production unit, where he owned more than his brothers, and in a year that business was almost as big as the sari business, which was about a hundred years old in the family. When his brothers saw him completely changing everything – it was a joint-company – they actually gave him more equity in the mother company, so he controlled it as a whole. Now what I had offered him was not an advertising answer; it was a strategic answer.

GG: Yes, indeed.

AK: Then I gave strategic advice, as I told you, to the owner of Thums Up where I used the "Taste the Thunder!" ad. It became a huge success. I still do work for that man; we are almost like partners. He later sold his soft-drink company Thums Up to Coca-Cola, who used it to fight Pepsi. Well, today that carbonated soft-drink Thums Up still outsells Coca-Cola and Pepsi. That's the power of that brand! Today I help him do bottled water and mineral water, and he has become the water king of India. I have launched three new products for him and done things for him which don't require much advertising. I gave him strategic advice, and his revenues show a thirty percent growth month after month after month. Compared to all the Kinleys and Aquafinas and all the other brands, he is doing much better.

GG: That "Taste the Thunder!" ad must have touched a subliminal dream in men.

AK: It touched deep dreams in the young Indian male because today every Indian wants to prove something. He's now got the confidence. If I were doing that campaign today, I know what I'd do with it. Coca-Cola, that now owns Thums Up, doesn't understand a thing. Thums Up should have a lifetime campaign. You can keep changing it; you just have to understand the mood of India. If you do the right thing with it, that drink can last another hundred years. They tried killing the product; it wouldn't die. In fact in Calcutta, the Coca-Cola Company stopped the production of Thums Up because they thought everyone would then drink Coca-Cola. Do you know what happened? The customers began drinking Pepsi! So Coca-Cola immediately brought Thums Up back. You see, good creative ideas have endurance. If you are able constantly to tune a campaign, tweak it, improve it, add to it, innovate it, that core idea can last and last and last. That's how great brands have been built. Sometimes it's an idea that makes all the difference.

GG: Wonderful example! What was your biggest triumph by way of cultural recognition?

AK: The greatest triumph, I think, would be my role in Zee TV because it's big. You are talking about something that makes a lot of money. A hundred million people all over the world watch the Zee Television channels. We now have nineteen channels. So a hundred million people all over the world are our customers; that's a lot of people. In fact, including the regional channels…hey, wait a minute! What are we talking about? There are a hundred million TV sets; multiply that by four or five to consider how many people watch each TV set. So half a billion people all around the globe watch these channels! And remember, I was the Best Supporting Actor!

GG: What about the private lottery? What kind of recognition did it bring you?

AK: That produced mixed results, as I already told you. The greatest triumph would definitely be Zee TV, and I think now if I do the STORYEUM, it's going to be another very personal great triumph; more so because it is not a commercial enterprise, and in many ways I am going to contribute something which will last fifty years in the country. Fifty years from now, people – my great-grandchildren – will say, "My great-grandfather built that thing!"

GG: They'll be proud of you! And so will the whole Indian population.

2.42 Rejection

"The mind likes a strange idea as little as the body likes a strange protein and resists it with similar energy."

Wilfred Trotter, British pioneer in neurosurgery

More often than not, cultural selection results in a rejection of an individual or group's accomplishment. This is especially true if the creative individual or group is a yet unknown entity; also, the more unique the accomplishment, the more likely it is to be rejected. Individuals coping with a high degree of singularity must adjust to new ways of perceiving, thinking, feeling, physiological functioning, and behaving. Rejection is therefore a shortcut: it permits escape from the hard labor of adjustment to the yet unknown. A typical case in point is Georg Cantor, whose set theory constitutes not only one of the bases of modern mathematics, but also a cornerstone in the architecture of contemporary science. His theory was so unique that it encountered merciless rejection when he published it in the early 1880s. Kronecker, a leading mathematician of the time, was so enraged by set theory (Hadamard 1945, 92) that he staged a ruthless campaign to ruin Cantor's professional career. Cantor was denied new appointments in German universities and his papers were refused publication by German scientific periodicals.

According to psychologist and philosopher William James (Burns 1979, 447), "The deepest principle in human nature is the craving to be appreciated." Quite evidently, rejection deeply frustrates this craving. Rejection comes in many different disguises. Not to be taken into account may be painful, yet it is the most merciful form of rejection dished out by cultural selection. Harder to deal with is criticism formulated in a balanced and convincing way; but by far the worst form of rejection is ridicule ranging from ironic to sarcastic and cynical formulations aimed at disqualifying not only the result of a creative process, but also its producer.

Like a virus, rejection is contagious and contains the potential for destruction. A rejection slip garnished with nasty remarks may discourage a young author to the point where he or she will never write another poem, play, or novel. The content of a vitriolic film review is likely to be copied by other journalists more eager to join the ram leading a herd of bleating sheep than to foster their autonomous evaluation of the quality of the film.

The more prestigious the authority who formulates a rejection, the more the rejection will develop a deleterious impact. In 1724, Peter the Great founded the Academy of Sciences in St. Petersburg. Its official task was to define and control standards of quality in science and other forms of production, including art. Yet quite unavoidably, under a totalitarian regime, the Academy turned into a straightjacket, strangling the imagination and courage of scientists and artists alike. As John Berger (Berger 1969, 25) writes: "Consequently the Academy of Russia was able to conventionalize, inhibit and destroy the potential talent of four or five generations of painters and sculptors." The same could be said with respect to literature, biology, and social sciences. Only mathematics and physics escaped—to some extent—the totalitarian machinery because they were indispensable for technological progress and not suspected to have a negative ideological impact on the post-revolutionary society.

Rejection may imply the physical destruction of the results of creative efforts. In the eighth and ninth centuries AD, the iconoclasm in the Byzantine Empire annihilated countless paintings and sculptures. In the name of the Holy Savior, the Spanish conquistadores destroyed thousands upon thousands of "heathen" paintings, sculptures, temples, precious dresses, and other cult objects in Central and South America. The same spirit of exorcism of destruction also rocked Italy, a cradle of Western culture. In 1497, the fanatic Dominican friar Savonarola (Boorstin 1992, 411), who practically dominated Florence, erected a bonfire of vanities. Boys were sent from house to house to collect all objects supposed to have a negative influence on Christian souls. Items thrown into the fire included not only carnival costumes and masks, but also musical instruments plus countless volumes of "corrupt" Latin and Italian poets, including Boccaccio. In the 1930s, the Nazis burned carloads of paintings, drawings, watercolors, and books they considered to be typical examples of "degenerative art" (*entartete Kunst*); they condemned and forbade jazz on the grounds that it was "non-Aryan nigger music."

In the ninth century AD, Muslim conquerors beheaded the giant statues of Buddha that had been hewn into the rock of a cliff in Bamiyan. The statues were testimonies of an ancient Buddhist culture that had been imported from India across the Silk Road to the heartland of Afghanistan in Central Asia centuries beforehand. In 1997, the fanatical Taliban leader Mullah Wahid threatened to blow them up; a year later the heirlooms were smashed to smithereens by rocket fire. One of the statues towered at fifty-three meters, making it the tallest sculpture in the world. It had been erected in the fifth century AD. Comparable acts of vandalism were committed in the Near and Middle East by medieval bands of greedy Catholic conquerors celebrated by the popes as "Holy Crusaders." They burned, broke, and pillaged, destroying countless works of art and science. Aggression can be a highly destructive emotion; since the dawn of mankind, patriotic and religious fanaticism has bred the most ferocious forms of rejection ever witnessed against creative achievements. It will continue to breed more.

Critics are human beings, and wholesale rejection serves as a shortcut to relieve them of the burden of critical scrutiny. It takes less time and energy to destroy than to construct; with a single sweep of his hand, a child may demolish the sandcastle that had taken imagination and painstaking, concentrated efforts to build. Rejection is also a hobby of many individuals whose original creative ambitions have been thwarted by internal or external circumstances, turning them into critics with a motivation that is all too obvious. In my view, in social hierarchies there reigns a *principle of applied relativity,* which holds that it is easier to reach an up-position by denigrating a competitor's personality and accomplishments rather than by relying on the merits of one's own accomplishments. A lot of ferocious criticism serves the primary purpose of helping the critic feel superior to the criticized individual(s). Writer D. H. Lawrence, for instance, undoubtedly felt quite superior when he wrote to Witter Bynner (Morgan 1980, 276) that fellow writer Somerset Maugham was "a narrow-gutted 'artist' with a stutter." With similar sarcasm American author, critic, and poetess Dorothy Parker (Keats 1988, 247), alluding to Maugham's sexual preferences, once stated: "The old lady is a crashing bore." Katherine Hepburn's performance in a play in which she acted out very much her own role also came under fire when Parker (Keats 1988, 8) sneered that the actress "ran the whole gamut of her emotions, from A to B."

An individual whose work is rejected must muster all the courage it takes to continue to create and not fall prey to resignation. The best attitude is to embrace a motto well known among bullfighters (Hitt 1992, 260): "To fight a bull when you are not scared is nothing; and to not fight a bull when you are scared is nothing; but to fight a bull when you are scared—that is something." One possible trick to help the bullfighter summon up his courage is to resort to his imagination, pretending that the bull is only an ox. Hemingway, who was an *aficionado* of *corridas* (Lynn 1987, 242), defiantly stated at one point when he was battered by rejections: ". . . I have always regarded critics as the eunuchs of literature . . ."

The strong emotions involved in rejecting and rejected individuals are not only connected to our individual psychological makeup, but also to the genetically determined species-specific wiring of our brain (Ledoux 1996, 19). The inter-neuronal structures transporting input from the emotion brain to the neocortex are more powerful than those conveying input from the neocortex to the emotion brain. Godwin (Godwin 2000, 36) compares the direct routes connecting the limbic system to the cortex to "super highways with multiple lanes" and emphasizes that "the traffic from the cortex back to the limbic system has to be content with country lanes, and very few of them at that." Due to phylogenetic causes, therefore, the conscious and voluntary control of our emotion brain by our rational and intuitive thinking is rather weak; emotions, on the contrary, are always able to flood our neocortex and block our intuitive and rational thinking.

I should like to point out that rejection is, per se, by no means a harmful event. First, it is important for a society or culture to separate the wheat from the chaff, and only a critical mind is able to do that. Second, rejection motivates creative individuals whose accomplishment has been disqualified to strive for better performance in future. Young performers especially may profit more from justified rejection than from unjustified recognition, the latter serving only to foster their complacency. If people were rats in a Skinner box, gratification for given performance would increase the probability of it being repeated, while punishment would do the contrary. Such is by far not the case, however, with creative human beings. The mere expectation of rejection may motivate individuals for better performance. As Dr. Samuel Johnson (Boswell and Chapman 1989, 849) once drastically put it: ". . . when a man knows he is to be hanged in a fortnight, it concentrates his mind wonderfully."

There does exist what I call a *trivalent logic of reaction* to an input: individuals may totally agree with an input, they may totally reject it, or they may critically select what they receive as input. Rejection, whether justified or not, may help an individual's future performance just as it may impede it. Recognition, whether justified or not, may decrease the quality of future performance by breeding complacency; but it may also provide the fuel for the rocket of self-confidence, courage, and goal-oriented motivation that help a creative individual to reach the desired destinations.

In the following paragraphs, we shall encounter a great number of cases of massive rejection that have occurred in the course of history. We shall see how individuals and groups have coped with that rejection. If the cases discussed below are known, we have no idea just how many individuals and groups rejection has thrown into the chasm of total oblivion. As Arthur Koestler once emphasized (Boden 1990, 255): "The history of science has its Pantheon of celebrated revolutionaries—and its catacombs, where the unsuccessful rebels lie, anonymous and forgotten."

Young writers are often faced with a never-ending string of rejection slips. Publishers, editors, literary critics, and the general public alike tend to cling to the already established, to whatever is fashionable and sells well at the time. If a new work of literature does not fit the official scheme, it sticks out like a sore thumb only to be rejected. Many critics seem to follow Cardinal Richelieu's (Kjetsaa 1987, 90) cynical devise, "Give me ten words written by the accused and I will find him guilty of an offence that merits the death penalty." Henrik Ibsen and August Strindberg, the Scandinavian playwrights who introduced modern prose drama, are two examples who illustrate perfectly well how critics deal with unique accomplishments.

By 1857, Ibsen had written four full-length plays and rewritten a fifth (Meyer 1985, 156). He had not been particularly successful, for in his realistic plays he attacked the hypocrisy of contemporary Victorian morality, an offence that provoked heavy retribution. Richard Petersen, a civil servant who would later ascend to the honorable position of prison governor, wrote a particularly vitriolic response to Ibsen's sarcastic portraits of bourgeois society, deriding him (Meyer 1985, 171) as "a small-time poet" and "a playwright of gigantic insignificance." Physically Ibsen was small and he was shy to boot, two factors that often provoked comparisons between the respective dimensions of his body and his mind. In 1859, playwright Bjørnstejerne Bjørnson wrote to a friend and called Ibsen a: ". . . rather small and gnomish little chap, with no chest or rump." He deduced from this fact that Ibsen compensated for the lack of size, and he stated rather condescendingly: ". . . as he has no other gifts he has to strain most frightfully when he writes."

The lack of success of his own creative work as a playwright and the lack of success in dealing with incompetent actors and meaningless plays at the National Theater of Christiania (today's Oslo)—where he served as stage instructor and artistic director—were such a stress for Ibsen that he came down with writer's block. Drinking heavily, he neglected his duties at the theater. The public (Meyer 1985, 197) had no craving for serious dramas, preferring appetizers in the form of superficial musical comedies. Ibsen was totally unenthusiastic in delivering that kind of entertainment and was rebuked by the board of the theater. Eventually it went bankrupt, and in 1862 Ibsen was fired.

In January 1863, Ibsen's play *Love's Comedy* was rejected by most critics and theatergoers. In *Morgenbladet,* M. J. Monrad (Meyer 1985, 212) called the play which "denigrates both love and marriage . . . an offence against human decency" and warned its author not to turn into "a mouthpiece for the loose thinking and debilitating nihilism that is now fashionable."

The following year Ibsen, hurt by repetitive rejection and abuse, left Norway (Meyer 1985, 227) and was to live for almost twenty-seven years in self-imposed exile in Italy and Germany. That very year, though, Richard Petersen, chairman of the Christiania Theater, invited him to return and assume the position of artistic director. Repaying rejection with rejection (Meyer 1985, 241) Ibsen declined the "daily abortion" of directing a theater. On December 3, 1865, in a letter to Magdalene Thoresen (Meyer 1985, 250) in which he compared Italy to Norway, he sarcastically wrote that Norwegians speak with enormous complacency of ". . . our Norwegian 'good sense', which really means nothing but a tepidity of spirit which makes it impossible for those honest souls to commit a madness." And he made it clearly understood that in Italy things were quite different.

In 1867, Clemens Petersen, Scandinavia's leading critic at the time, saw some merits in *Peer Gynt* but ultimately rejected the play—as Ibsen's biographer Meyer (Meyer 1985, 285) writes—"on doctrinaire philosophical grounds." Hans Christian Andersen, the Danish poet and author of fairytales, also disliked the play and even confided years later (Meyer 1985, 337) to his diary that *Peer Gynt* was "written by a mad poet."

In 1870, his new play *The League of Youth* was rejected in Norway. In a letter to Jonas Collin (Meyer 1985, 329) written one year after he had been publicly celebrated in Stockholm and honored by the King of Sweden, Ibsen sneered: "It seems that in Norway people regard empty phrase-making, hollowness and mean-mindedness as national characteristics which are therefore sacrosanct. But none of this bothers me in the least." Three years later he wrote another verse drama, *Emperor and Galilean* (an initial failure and subsequent success), but it took him another four years to come up with *The Pillars of Society*, a modern prose drama. In 1872, in the middle of the incubation period that was to produce *The Pillars of Society,* he wrote to his friend Brandes: ". . . my own conviction is that the strongest man is he who stands most alone," a proud hymn on the merits of individual autonomy in the face of adversity.

In 1875, after having lived in Rome and Dresden, Ibsen moved to Munich, a city he immediately liked. Soon he was deeply immersed in writing and elaborating *The Pillars of Society*. Although he loved Bavaria and his creative sap was flowing again after a period of apparent aridity, he had not lost his malicious spirit fed by years of rejection. In a mood of aesthetic revolt he told the composer Grieg (Meyer 1985, 434) who had come to visit him: ". . . a German lady in *grande toilette* always reminds me of a prize cow with gilt trappings and paper flowers between its horns."

A Doll's House, published in Copenhagen on December 4, 1879, was a success (Meyer 1985, 475). Three years later, however, his play *Ghosts* again encountered "violent criticisms and insane attacks," as Ibsen wrote to his publisher Frederik Hegel. The rejection hurt more than he admitted as testified by the lines he wrote on January 28, 1880 to Danish writer Otto Borchsenius (Meyer 1985, 511): "What has most depressed me has been not the attacks themselves, but the lack of guts which had been revealed in the ranks of the so-called liberals in Norway. They are poor stuff with which to man the barricades." In response to that experience, Ibsen published a new play in 1882 *An Enemy of the People* (Meyer 1985, 522), in which Dr. Stockmann scornfully declares: "I think we'd all have to agree that the fools are in a terrifying, overwhelming majority all over the world!"

In 1890, Ibsen published another play, *Hedda Gabler* (Meyer 1985, 675), whose heroine is a feminist attacking the society in which she lives. A critic writing in *Pictorial World* (Meyer 1985, 692) raged: "Hideous nightmare of pessimism . . . the play is simply a bad escape of moral sewage-gas . . . Hedda's soul is a-crawl with the foulest passions of humanity." August Strindberg, on the brink of madness and hoping to inherit the crown of Scandinavia's best dramatist from Ibsen, was convinced that Ibsen had used specific scenes from Strindberg's life in *Hedda Gabler*, prompting him to write (Meyer 1985, 675): ". . . this shit will rebound on him. For I shall survive him and many others, and the day *The Father*[7] kills *Hedda Gabler* I shall stick that gun in the old troll's neck!" The troll never read the statement nor did he know that in another letter Strindberg (Meyer 1985, 676) had given vent to his paranoid conviction: "Do you know that my seed has fallen into Ibsen's brainpan—and fertilized! Now he carries my seed and is my uterus!" But Ibsen was aware that Strindberg's rejection of him was based upon sheer envy, and that envy inspired him to the point that he hung a portrait of Strindberg (Meyer 1985, 770) on the wall of his study. When asked about the purpose of the portrait, he would tell his visitors that he liked "that madman staring at me" and added: "He is my mortal enemy, and shall hang there and watch while I write."

Together with his foe Ibsen, August Strindberg was the cofounder of modern realistic prose drama. Unlike Ibsen, he came from a well-to-do family. His father was a successful entrepreneur who owned (Meyer 1988, 9) forty-one ships, about one third of the fleet of steamships plying their trade out of Stockholm. August was a highly gifted individual who eventually turned into a novel writer, playwright, photographer, and painter and who moreover had scientific interests and dabbled in alchemy. Like Ibsen, he went into voluntary exile, living from 1883 to1889 in France and Switzerland and from 1892 to1898 in Germany and France.

While living in Paris in October 1883, Strindberg had the opportunity to see Sarah Bernhardt perform in *Frou-Frou* (Meyer 1988, 118). With respect to the play he wrote in a missive to Pehr Staaff: "Horrible! Just tricks and mannerisms. For me there is only one yardstick in art—realism." The outright rejection was apparently mutual; the actress dismissed the plays of Strindberg and Ibens with the quip (Meyer 1988 589): "*C'est de la Norderie*—Northern stuff!"

In 1884, Strindberg published *Getting Married*, a collection of short stories depicting "twenty marriages of every variety." It provoked a storm of rejection. The Swedish Ministry of Justice informed the publisher Albert Bonnier (Meyer 1988, 134f.) that the unsold copies of the book were to be confiscated immediately. The official accusation was not of obscenity (including open references to sexual intercourse and venereal disease) but blasphemy in one offensive passage which mocked the ". . . wafers . . which the parson passed of as the body and blood of Jesus of Nazareth, the rabble-rouser who was executed over 1,800 years ago." The maximum sentence for blasphemy was two years of hard labor. The book was condemned not only by the right-wing press, but the liberal press also lashed out with vehemence: "repellent to every healthy mind;" "we doubt if anything more corrupt . . . has appeared in Swedish;" "stinking and repellent rottenness . . . almost worse than Zola," and so on and so forth. Strindberg (Meyer 1988, 139f.) returned to Stockholm to be judged and was acquitted; a nine-man jury found him not guilty. Yet the whole experience left a scar in his soul (Meyer 1988, 154), as he later confessed: "I am an old-fashioned Christian idealist and live in an eternal feud with my former self, a feud which is destroying me. I am split quite in two." The split personality he was alluding to was the yet dormant schizophrenia he would have to fight in the years to come.

In 1886, *The Son of a Servant*, the first volume of his autobiography (Meyer 1988, 156), drew heavy flak from the right-wing press. In Finland the book was banned by the censor. With respect to women he expressed his hatred quite openly (Meyer 1988, 162): "Accuse them, blacken them; abuse them so that they haven't a clean spot—that is dramatic!" With the release of the second volume of *Getting Married*, his marital conflict amplified; his wife Siri withdrew into silent hostility only to explode in a rage whenever he provoked her. He reacted to her rejection with a grandiose attitude confiding to the Danish author and critic Edvard Brandes (Meyer 1988, 170): "Actually, my misogyny is purely theoretical, and I can't live a day without deluding myself that I warm my soul in the glow of their unconscious vegetable existence."

Strindberg continued to rant and accuse his wife of lesbian tendencies. In a letter accompanying the manuscript of his story *A Madman's Defence*

(Meyer 1988, 194), his utter contempt was clear: "Woman, being small and foolish and therefore evil . . . should be suppressed, like barbarians and thieves. She is useful only as ovary and womb, best of all as a cunt."

In the summer of 1888, Strindberg's publisher Karl Otto Bonnier (Meyer 1988, 198) rejected the manuscript of the drama *Miss Julie*. Ibsen was reading Nietzsche at the time, and fascinated by the concept of the Aryan superman, he wrote to Edvard Brandes (Meyer 1988, 198): ". . . my spiritual uterus has found a tremendous fertilizer in Friedrich Nietzsche, so that I feel distended like a bitch in heat. He is the man for me!" As winter approached (Meyer 1988, 203f.), Strindberg was so plagued by financial worries that he wondered how he was to support his children whose clothes were "five years old," as he stated. As if this were not enough, Seligman published *Miss Julie* on November 23 and the critics had yet another field day. Slating reviews hurled abuse at Strindberg: "A heap of ordure," "totally repellent," "repulsive," insinuated that the author must "have been troubled by some affectation of the brain."

On October 20, 1989, Strindberg (Meyer 1988, 224) felt so burned out by rejection, marital strife, financial misery, and his growing paranoia that he hit the trough of creative barrenness. To Ola Hanson, he confided: "Sterility, thoughts of retreat, unsuccessful begging. All doors shut, theatres and newspapers barred to me, envy, abuse, insults." At the beginning of November 1891 (Meyer 1988, 242), he wrote his last will and testament "for I was quite determined to shoot myself . . . Nothing left then but to go to the Hall of Anatomy and sell my corpse!" He survived, and on September 21, 1892 his marriage to Siri von Essen (Meyer 1988, 248) was legally terminated.

Nine days later, Strindberg (Meyer 1988, 250) was in Berlin entering his second period of voluntary exile. On May 2, 1893, he married the young Austrian journalist Frieda Uhl, and at dawn after the wedding night, "brusquely started from a dream" as Frida later stated, grasped her throat, and attempted to throttle her. Later he tried to calm his young wife's nerves blaming his drowsiness for his impulsive act. She tried to believe, him but soon discovered that he was paranoid, superstitious, and crazy enough to believe that by mixing iron sulphate and copper (Meyer 1988, 281) he could create gold and thus relieve their financial burdens. When he published his alchemist ideas in *Antibarbarus* (Meyer 1988, 292), they were met with utter contempt everywhere. His marriage went down the drain and he even developed paranoid ideas about the child Frida had given birth to a few months earlier. Frida left him and was soon pregnant with a child fathered by her new lover, the Austrian writer Frank Wedekind.

Strindberg moved from Austria to Passy in France (Meyer 1988, 303), painted furiously, and begged Frida to come back. She relented and joined him for six weeks then left again when her nurse in Austria gave notice. Frida and August never met again.

Strindberg went on to develop ever more bizarre ideas. One was the theory that the very first gorilla was the offspring of a shipwrecked sailor (Meyer 1988, 317f.) who had had sex with a female chimpanzee! In February 1896, Strindberg moved into the Hôtel Orfila in Paris, where he began to write an *Occult Diary* (Meyer 1988, 329), to which he would confide his innermost ideas for the following twenty-two years. Here he also began to collect material for his semiautobiographical novel *Inferno*, describing his ideas, experiences, interest in alchemy, and occultism, as well as his delusional ideas. Throughout the year, Strindberg teetered on the brink of madness, toppling over more and yet each time succeeding in curbing his descent and climbing uphill again.

In the autumn of the same year, Strindberg went to visit his daughter Kerstin in Austria. Frida's daughter Marie Uhl (Meyer 1988, 354), with whom Kerstin stayed, later reported that he would exchange plates with little Kerstin because he was convinced that Marie wanted to poison him. Wherever he went, he was armed with a Bowie knife and would suddenly slice the air around him to fight off hallucinatory persecutors.

Eventually the storm abated, and the playwright slowly returned to normal. Psychiatrists have put several labels on Strindberg's condition, but whatever the correct label may be, one thing is certain: Strindberg was a highly sensitive person who almost broke under the weight of the rejections he suffered in both his private and professional life. In time he found his way back to a basic equilibrium that enabled him to cope with the rejections met by *Inferno* when it was published in Sweden on November 1, 1897.

Meanwhile, Strindberg's self-confidence had grown, and he decided that he was a scientist rather than a novelist or playwright. To his publisher Geijerstam (Meyer 1988, 372), who begged him to continue writing fiction, he proudly retorted: "I can't write plays and novels, have lost interest and therefore the ability. I have only one book left unwritten and that is my occult natural philosophy." Yet, as the saying goes, nobody is a prophet in his own land: in the four years to follow, Strindberg would publish twenty plays, including the dramatic trilogy *To Damascus* as well as *The Dance of Death, A Dream Play,* and *The Ghost Sonata.*

On May 6, 1901, Strindberg married the not yet twenty-three-year-old actress Harriet Bosse (Meyer 1988, 420), who had learned her craft in Denmark and France and (unlike the declamatory Sarah Bernhardt) acted in a very natural way, fitting Strindberg's conception of realistic theater. The start of that third marriage was, to say the least, not auspicious. Strindberg's distasteful and cruel entry into his diary (Meyer 1988, 421) written three years after-

wards gives goose bumps: "On our first night H___t had a *prolapsus uteri* . .
. Nevertheless I possessed her twice that night, though with distaste." He went
on to specify: "Often at the climax her uterus fell and pushed me out. It felt
as though a hand from within slowly drove me back." That sexual experience
was for him a rejection as painful as those he went on confronting for several
of his new plays. As his biographer Meyer (1988, 434) states, "Strindberg's
fortune as a dramatist had now reached its lowest ebb." His plays disappeared
altogether from the stages of Sweden.

In 1904, Harriet got the divorce she had demanded, and for the third time
Strindberg lost custody of the children he had fathered. Harriet's theatrical
career soon took off, while Strindberg's continued to decline. Things changed
when on November 26, 1907, Strindberg's own *Intimate Theatre*, named after
Max Reinhardt's famous *Kammerspiel-Theater* in Berlin, opened its doors.
But by then Strindberg was beginning to have stomach troubles and was soon
convinced he had stomach cancer—a diagnosis that turned out to be correct.
Strindberg died on May 14, 1912. A few months earlier, he had written to Nils
Andersson (Meyer 1988, 558) that his doctor had not known the cause of his
illness, but that he himself knew it to be "other people's hatred!" Such was
the tragic end of a great creative spirit whose vehemence provoked rejection
and whose own rejections begat further rejections by the social environment
in an endless merry-go-round of denigration and deprecation.

We shall now have a look at a few other cases of rejection.

In the seventeenth century, John Milton (Boorstin 1992, 326), author of the
epic poem *Paradise Lost* and champion of freedom, was imprisoned for his
ideas. With time, Parliament granted him an official pardon, nonetheless ordering the hangman to burn his books and prohibiting all further sales or
publications thereof.

In 1856, Gustave Flaubert (Bernard 1992, 37) received a rejection slip for
his manuscript of *Madame Bovary* that read: "You have buried your novel
underneath a heap of details which are well done but utterly superfluous." The
patronizing statement illustrates the grandiose self of a narrow-minded reviewer. In 1862, a manuscript of poems by Emily Dickinson (Bernard 1992,
30) was rejected with the comment: "Queer—the rhymes were all wrong."
The rejections suffered by Flaubert and Dickinson suggest that many critics
do not at all live up to T. S. Eliot's maxim (Gross 2008, 21-22) that for a critic
"the only method is to be very intelligent."

Tolstoy (Koestler 1989, 34) completely rejected French poets Baudelaire
and Verlaine and wondered "how the French . . . could attribute such importance to these versifiers who were far from skilful in form and most contempt-
ible in subject-matter, is to me incomprehensible." Tolstoy equally decried
Ibsen, Shakespeare, and Dante as being immoral (Meyer 1985, 624) and

therefore bad artists. In 1900, he spurned Ibsen's work as "the poetry and art of the cultural mob." Similarly, he found Chekhov's play *The Seagull* "utterly worthless." Tolstoy (Wilson 1989, 467) loved Chekhov's stories but not his plays. After a production of *Uncle Vanya* he confided to his diary: "There is no real action, no movement towards which the conversation of the neurasthenic intellectuals tends." Once he even put his arm around Chekov gently mocking him: "Shakespeare's plays are bad enough, but yours are even worse!" As for Shakespeare (Wilson 1989, 479), he considered the English poet and playwright "Insignificant and immoral."

In the acknowledgements of his Tolstoy biography, A. N. Wilson (1989) quotes a Jewish proverb: "If God came to live on earth, people would smash his windows." Those who smash windows are often driven by petty jealousy. Turgenev (Wilson 1989, 126) derided the patriarch Tolstoy, who often dressed like a Russian serf, as a "troglodyte" and a fake, stating: "Not one word, not one movement of his is natural! He is eternally posing before us, and I find it difficult to explain in a clever man this impoverished Count's arrogance." In Tolstoy's novel *Anna Karenina* (Wilson 1989, 279), he appreciated only the races, the mowing, and the hunting scenes. As for the rest he claimed: ". . . it's all so sour, it reeks of Moscow, incense, old maids, Slavophilism, the nobility, etc."

Young Dostoyevsky (Kjetsaa 1987, 50f.), whose first novel *Poor Folk* had met immediate recognition, soon had to cope with the envy of his older colleagues within Moscow's literary scene. Turgenev, who had initially shown him much sympathy and respect, began to spearhead a campaign against the young writer, "the new, red pimple on Literature's nose." In 1846, at a meeting of the writers' circle led by Turgenev, Turgenev taunted Dostoyevsky, treating him like a country bumpkin who fancied himself to be a genius. The enraged Dostoyevsky wrote to Mikhail: "These people are scoundrels, envious profit-seekers." A quarter of a century later in his novel *The Possessed*, Dostoyevsky took his revenge by casting Turgenev in the role of the conceited salon radical Karmazinov.

In 1866, Dostoyevsky's novel *Crime and Punishment* (Kjetsaa 1987, 183f.) was published in *The Russian Messenger* in twelve monthly instalments. If it was hailed as a masterwork by some critics, it was furiously rejected by others. Turgenev gave up reading it, writing to a friend: ". . . the whole thing reminds me of an interminable stomach ache. God save us from it during the cholera season!" Grigory Yeliseyev, leading critic at *The Contemporary* considered the novel to be extremely weak and did not hesitate to deride it: "But the author is delighted with the nonsense he has written and apparently deludes himself that he is someone who knows the soul of man—someone in the order of Shakespeare."

Dostoyevsky in turn was not very subtle in his attitude towards the creative accomplishments of other individuals. Travelling in Germany, he and his wife Anna (Kjetsaa 1987, 206) went to listen to a military band playing music by German composers including Beethoven and Mendelssohn-Bartholdy. When the band began to play Wagner, Dostoyevsky got up and left, totally unwilling to listen to "that tiresome German scoundrel in spite of all his fame." According to Anthony Burgess (1987, 116), the rejection of Wagner's music was widespread in those days. After the French premiere of Wagner's opera *Tannhäuser*, the Parisians soon came up with a *bon mot*: "Wagner me tanne aux airs," meaning, "Wagner gets on my nerves."

In 1867, when Ivan Turgenev published his novel *Smoke* (Kjetsaa 1987, 211), Dostoyevsky retaliated by bombastically declaring, "A book like that ought to be burned at the hands of an executioner!" Dostoyevsky (Kjetsaa 1987, 305) also reprobated Emile Zola's novel *Le Ventre de Paris*: "God, what filth! The whole thing is so repulsive that it is only with difficulty that I can bring myself to read it." Last but not least, Dostoyevsky (Kjetsaa 1987, 315) dished out rejection wholesale to the German culture. Not only did he condemn Wagner's music, he sneered Holbein's Darmstadt portrait *Madonna*: "But that is no Madonna! It's a baker's wife! A petit-bourgeois madam! Not an iota more!" But surely Goethe's *Faust*, the pride of every cultivated German, would have seduced Fyodor. His verdict: "It's a mere rehash of the Book of Job; read Job, there you will find everything that is important and valuable in *Faust*." Incidentally, James Joyce seems to have shared Dostoyevsky's judgement in this respect. During his stay in Zurich, where he read German literature and translated the poems of Swiss writer Gottfried Keller, he scoffed at Germany's national hero, referring to Goethe, who was a state officer in Weimar, as "*un noioso funzionario*—a boring civil servant."

In the first decade of the last century, William Saroyan (Bernard 1992, 30), the son of Armenian immigrants, collected several thousand rejection slips, forming a pile about thirty inches high! Later he became one of America's most published authors. In 1940 his play *The Time of Your Life* won him the Pulitzer Prize, which he refused arguing that business people had no business judging the quality of art.

A particularly stressful year for G. B. Shaw was 1881 (Holroyd 1988, 91), during which every single publisher rejected his novels, magazine articles, essays, and short stories. In revenge, Shaw (Bernard 1992, 14) once characterized publishers in the following terms: "They combine commercial rascality with artistic touchiness and pettishness, without being either good businessmen or fine judges of literature." For him, a publisher was nothing else but "an intermediary parasite" between an author and a bookseller.

In 1882, the literary critic Edward Garnett (Holroyd 1988, 97) jeered about two future Nobel laureates: "There is a little genius in Yeats: there is an individuality of mind in Shaw's work, but neither are likely to command much attention." Little wonder that Shaw (Holroyd 1988, 145) showed contempt for critics, persuaded that most of them were "babies at their job, and very corrupt and petulant ones at that." In order to help the babies in their job, he resorted to a trick that the poet Walt Whitman had used before him to good effect. Shaw (Holroyd 1988, 281) began a publicity campaign for his own plays, interviewing himself, writing positive reviews and publishing them in several newspapers. This helped—at least to a point. Even at the peak of Shaw's career, A. B. Walkley (Holroyd 1988, 283) regarded him as "a detestable dramatist" who had made his debut with "a singularly bad piece of work."

In 1911, Marcel Proust proposed the 800-page manuscript of his novel *Remembrance of Things Past* (Bernard 1992, 21) to publishers. Three publishers in a row responded with a rejection slip: one of them was the reviewer André Gide; another was Ollendorf, who commented that it took Proust thirty pages to describe how he turned over in bed. Eventually Proust decided to pay for his own publication. Today Proust and Joyce, both of whom were collectors of countless rejection slips, are acknowledged as two of the most important writers of the twentieth century.

A more comical example of rejection and counter-rejection is to be found in a biography on the Irish poet, dramatist and Nobel laureate William Butler Yeats (Mac Liammóir and Boland 1986, 100). Yeats had been one of the cofounders and early-years director of the Abbey Theatre in Dublin, dedicated to a revival of Irish literature. In 1926, Seán O'Casey's play *The Plough and the Stars* premiered and was hooted from the stage by an irritated audience. An enraged Yeats appeared from behind the wings and lambasted the spectators crying, "You have disgraced yourselves again!"

A flat pebble with smooth surfaces offers the howling wind no angle of attack. A big rock with rough surfaces invites the wind to batter it and to make a lot of noise in the process. In the world of literature, Eugene O'Neill—a four-time Pulitzer Prize winner and Nobel laureate—was such a rock. Before his international fame was solidly established, his plays encountered the machine gun fire of heavy rejection. Fellow playwright Seán O'Casey (Gelb and Gelb 1987, 788) remarked that English critics had no idea how to deal with Eugene O'Neill's work, specifying: ". . . they are, I fear, so nearsighted, looking at the playfulness of the magpies, but with eyes too weak to watch the soar of an eagle in the upper skies." O'Neill had similar experiences in the United States, where many of his masterpieces were at first rebuffed by the critics. Bluntly (Gelb and Gelb 1987, 556) he expressed what he thought: "I hate every bone in their heads."

In 1932, the Irish writer, poet, and dramatist Samuel Beckett (Bernard 1992, 18) wrote the novel *Dream of Fair-to-Middling Women,* but was unable to get it published anywhere. One editor even scoffed: "I wouldn't touch it with a barge-pole," and then went on to denigrate it in the most offensive way. In 1969, Beckett got the Nobel Prize for his outstanding creative accomplishment, but the brandished novel was not published until 1992, sixty years after it had been written.

Mathematician and philosopher Bertrand Russell (Boorstin 1992, 631) attributed to T. S. Eliot impeccable taste in whatever he wrote although he complained that the writer "has no vigour or life—or enthusiasm."

J. D. Salinger's novel *The Catcher in the Rye* (Huddle 1988, 37-38) was rejected by twenty publishing houses before Little, Brown and Company agreed to publish it in 1951. The novel turned out to be a success; its adolescent hero, Holden Caulfield, became a household name among young people, and today Salinger is held in esteem with the most outstanding writers of the twentieth century. His collections of short stories have become classics. As for the author himself, he became quite an enigma. No new work has been published since 1965, and since 1980 the recluse has refused all interviews.

In 1945, George Orwell (Bernard 1992, 72) was given a rejection slip for his manuscript of *Animal Farm*. The publisher claimed: "It is impossible to sell animal stories in the USA." The book turned out to be a bestseller. When Laurence J. Peter (Bernard 1992, 32) submitted his manuscript *The Peter Principle*: *Why Things Always Go Wrong* in 1964 to McGraw-Hill (Bernard 1992, 32), the editor replied: "I can foresee no commercial possibilities for such a book and consequently can offer no encouragement." Peter continued sending his work to other publishers only to receive another thirty rejection slips. Despite the massive shunning in its beginnings, *The Peter Principle* became one of the all-time bestsellers in the category of topic books. Almost two decades later in 1963, John le Carré's (Bernard 1992, 61) bestseller-to-be *The Spy Who Came in From the Cold* met with similar rejection. Its sender predicted arrogantly: "You're welcome to le Carré—he hasn't got any future."

In her discussions with an interviewer in 1981, Belgian novelist Marguerite Yourcenar (Yourcenar 1980, 49) disdained the "openly aggressive" Christianity of her French colleagues Charles Péguy and Paul Claudel. She also showed little sympathy for Jean Cocteau (Yourcenar 1980, 88), whom she saw as a kind of *flaneur* (idler) mainly interested in being and remaining a fashionable French writer. She observed that his attitude often "derailed into futility, the desire to impersonate the Parisian ('*le désir de faire Parisien*')". Her statement on Cocteau echoes what Sir Evelyn Waugh had stated fifty years earlier when he had scorned Cocteau for being "a man in Paris… whose whole life is occupied in trying to be modern."

John Kennedy Toole's (Bernard 1992, 74; Huddle, 1988, 37-38) manuscript of *A Confederacy of Dunces* was turned down by one publisher after another. One of the rejection slips (Bernard 1992, 93) specified that the manuscript was "obsessively foul and grotesque." In 1969, Toole committed suicide. For years his mother tried in vain to have the manuscript published. Finally, with the support and influence of Southern writer Walker Percy, it came out in 1980 and was an instant success. One year later, John Kennedy Toole was posthumously awarded the Pulitzer Prize for his brilliant novel.

Ignorance breeds arrogance, and the arrogant content of rejection slips is able to drive writers into depression, helplessness, despair, and even suicide—as we just saw above. Yet it can also stimulate their rage and disdain. It induced, for instance, the English critic Cyril Connolly (Bernard 1992, 88) to note: "As repressed sadists are supposed to become policemen or butchers, so those with irrational fear of life become publishers."

In 1902, young James Joyce met the already established poet and dramatist W. B. Yeats (Ellmann 1983, 102). They went to a café, and Joyce began to read bits and pieces of his ongoing work. Perceiving that Yeats appeared less than enthused, Joyce defied him: "I really don't care whether you like what I am doing or not. It won't make the least difference to me. Indeed I don't know why I am reading to you." When they parted Joyce (Ellmann, 1983) taunted, "We have met too late. You are too old for me to have any effect on me." In reprisal in 1926, Yeats (Ellmann 1983, 596) compared Joyce to T. S. Eliot, Ezra Pound, and Luigi Pirandello, whose stylistic innovations he deeply abhorred and had this to say about *Ulysses*: ". . . a lunatic among his keepers, a man fishing behind the gas works, the vulgarity of a single Dublin day prolonged through 700 pages—and . . . delirium, the fisher King, Ulysses' wandering."

In 1917, James Joyce (Ellmann 1983, 415) wrote an exasperated letter to his book agent Pinker in which he complained about the rejection slips he had received for his first two novels, *A Portrait of an Artist as a Young Man* and *Dubliners*. About *Dubliners* he stated: ". . . *Dubliners* was refused by forty publishers...," adding that his novel *A Portrait of an Artist as a Young Man* had been refused by every publisher to whom it was offered and, when *The Egoist* eventually decided to publish it, "about twenty printers in England and Scotland refused to print it."

In 1918, James Joyce's novel *Ulysses* (Ellmann 1983, 503ff.) was first published as a serial. Its American editors were punished for distributing obscene material. In 1922, Sylvia Beach, the well-known owner of the Rive-Gauche bookshop Shakespeare and Company, published the whole book. Copies smuggled into England were burned by customs authorities in Folkestone and the book was altogether banned in the United States in 1933.

After the publication of *Ulysses,* T. S. Eliot was invited to tea with Virginia Woolf (Ellmann 1983, 528). If he was enthused over Joyce's accomplishment, she found the novel "underbred . . . the book of a self-taught working man . . . a queasy undergraduate scratching his pimples." In a letter to Louis Gillet, poet and critic Edmund Gosse (Ellmann 1983, 528) likewise condescendingly stated: "He is the perfect type of the Irish *fumiste*[8] . . . He is not, as I say, without talent, but he has prostituted it to the most vulgar uses." Even as late as 1962, when Joyce was already an established authority in modern literature, the much less successful writer Evelyn Waugh (Stannard 1987, 208) derisively commented: "Look at the results of experimentation in the case of a writer like Joyce. He started off writing very well, then you can watch him going mad with vanity. He ends up a lunatic."

In 1931, the Irish novelist and art critic George Moore (Ellmann 1983, 618), whom Joyce had tried to woo for support, wrote a letter to Louis Gillet after reading excerpts from *Finnegan's Wake.* Gillet rejected Joyce's endeavor to develop a new style of writing: "I say metaphysics for Joyce's book has nothing to do with art, nor yet science, so I suppose it must be metaphysics."

American writer Thomas Wolfe (Donald 1988, 236) had originally admired Joyce's *Work in Progress* (later baptized *Finnigan's Wake*), but later suspected that Joyce mistook "the nauseous rumblings of his gut for the trumpet of doom." Joyce was little impressed by these rejections. He always stuck to the self-image he had attributed to his alter ego, Stephen Dedalus in *A Portrait of an Artist as a Young Man* (Parrinder 1984, 31); in his own view he was neither a joker nor a hypochondriac but a "hawk-like man flying sunward above the sea."

Wolfe's novel *Look Homeward Angel* (Donald 1988, 243) was published on July 14, 1930. Swinnerton, writing for the *London Evening News*, condemned Wolfe's "over-excited verbosity" and found it "intolerable" that Wolfe should have indulged in "ecstatic apostrophe" and begun "crying 'O this' and 'O that' as if he were parodying the Greek Anthology." Wolfe was so incensed by the critique that he informed his publisher: "I have stopped writing and do not want ever to write again." And yet he recovered and continued to write. In 1935, he published his novel *Of Time and the River* (Donald 1988, 315), which brought on positive reviews for the most part. Still, Clifton Fadiman of the *New Yorker* was ambivalent. On the one hand he admired the beauty and power of the novel; on the other, he found it "hyperthyroid and afflicted with elephantiasis."

In 1925, Hemingway published *In Our Time* (Lynn 1987, 225), a collection of short stories marking his American debut. His mother and father ordered six copies. In utter horror they read about a war veteran who, rejected by a nurse, had contracted gonorrhoea from a salesgirl while riding in a cab through a Chicago park. Infuriated, Dr. Hemingway, a country physician, decided that did not want such "filth" in his house. The purchased copies were sent back to The Three Mountains Press. This was for Ernest Hemingway the first rebuff in a whole series of rejections yet to come.

Two years later, critic Allen Tate (Lynn 1987, 331) of *The Nation* belittled the "sentimentality" of Hemingway's first novel *The Sun Also Rises*, summarily dismissing Hemingway's scope and ambitions to portray the interactions of a group of vacationers with "He fails . . ." In the same year Hemingway's collection of short stories *Men Without Women* received a couple of rather nasty appraisals. Virginia Woolf (Lynn 1987, 369) found them "a little dry and sterile" adding that Hemingway had a modern style but a not-so-modern vision and that, moreover, lately his talent had shrunk rather than blossomed. Writing in the *New Statesman*, Cyril Connolly (Lynn 1987, 369) characterized the stories as "a blend of Gertrude Stein's manner, Celtic childishness, and the slice of life..." adding that with respect to James Joyce, Hemingway was "more of a dark horse than a white hope." In *The New York Times Book Review,* Percy Hutchinson (Lynn 1987, 370) patronizingly declared that Hemingway's short stories betrayed merely "the art of the reporter, carried to the highest degree."

Hemingway's non-fiction book *Death in the Afternoon* was published in 1932 and brought on mixed reviews. In the *New Yorker* (Baker 1980, 300; Lynn 1987, 397), Robert Coats found the author's he-man posturing boring and criticized his book as being childish "in its small-boy wickedness of vocabulary" and morbid "in its endless preoccupation with fatality." Similarly, H. L. Mencken (Lynn 1987, 398) recognized Hemingway's knowledge of the technical aspects of the Spanish *corrida* but rejected his basic conception of life as a "banality and worse," adding: "The reader he seems to keep in his mind's eye is a sort of common denominator of all the Ladies' Aid Societies of his native Oak Park, Illinois."

Still more merciless was critic Max Eastman (Lynn 1987, 398) whose column *"Bull in the Afternoon"* catcalled the author's he-man attitude by asking why "our full-sized man, our ferocious realist" went blind wrapping himself up "in clouds of juvenile romanticism the moment he crosses the border on his way to a Spanish bullfight?" To his own rhetorical question, Eastman replied: "It is of course a commonplace that Hemingway lacks the serene confidence that he is a full-sized man." Going on to add insult to injury, Eastman (Lynn 1987, 399) maintained that Hemingway's machismo had "begotten a veritable school of fiction-writers—a literary style, you might say, of wearing false hair on his chest." Papa Hemingway got his revenge four years later when he met Eastman in Max Perkin's office. He insisted on showing off his bare chest and demanded that Eastman do the same. Perkins later stated that

Hemingway's chest was "hairy enough for anybody" whereas Eastman's was "as bare as a bald man's head."

In 1934, Ivan Kashkeen wrote an essay entitled *Ernest Hemingway: The Tragedy of Craftsmanship* (Baker 1980, 354) in which he defined Hemingway as "*mens morbida in corpore sano*—a morbid mind in a healthy body;" characterized the author as an individual on the brink of psychotic disintegration; and deplored the "joyless tale of Hemingway's hero, ever the same under his changing names, and you begin to realize that what had seemed the writer's face is but a mask."

That very year, Wyndham Lewis (Lynn 1987, 415) wrote a scathing critique entitled "The Dumb Ox" in which he maintained: "The sort of first-person-singular that Hemingway invariably invokes is a dull-witted, monosyllabic simpleton." Lewis called the I-figure a "lethargic and stuttering dummy." When Sylvia Beach made Hemingway aware of the criticism in her bookstore, in a rage he sent one of her vases of tulips crashing to the floor. In 1937, Hemingway's *To Have and Have Not* (Lynn 1987, 463)—a novel about a fishing boat captain running contraband between Cuba and Florida—was ridiculed by Delmore Schwartz in the *Southern Review*. He called it "a stupid and foolish book, a disgrace to a good writer, a book which should never have been printed." In *The Nation*, Louis Kronenberger (Lynn 1987, 463) chimed in: ". . . a book with neither poise nor integration, and with shocking lapses from professional skill."

In 1950, Hemingway published the novel *Across the River and into the Trees*, describing a romance between the older, war-weary Colonel Cantwell and his young mistress Renata. In the *New Yorker*, E. B. White wrote a parody with the title *Across the Street and into the Grill*. As Hemingway's biographer Lynn so aptly puts it (Lynn 1987, 557): "The gang instincts of literary intellectuals are notorious. In the case of *Across the River*, they smelled blood in the water and instantly swarmed around it like so many killer sharks."

By then Hemingway's patience had worn thin. Moreover, he had acquired an international status and prestige that was a far cry from his humble beginnings in Paris when repetitive rejections had provoked feelings of self-doubt and helplessness rather than outrage. He once confessed to Hotchner, an admirer of his (Hotchner 1967, 61f.), that during that difficult period in his life where he lived in a bare room above a Monmartre sawmill he would daily receive his own manuscripts plus the printed rejection slips he onsidered to be "the most savage of reprimands . . . And I couldn't help crying."

William Faulkner had the gift of creating a literary universe all of his own, namely the legendary Yoknapatawpha County, which was the setting for many of his novels. Yet for decades he had to cope with the rejection of his work. One of the reasons he was spurned was due to the characters that populated his stories and novels; there were also other shortcomings that Thomas Wolfe (Donald 1988, 354) qualified as "pop-eye horrors, pederasts, and macabre distortions." Suffering from severe depression, Faulkner could get himself so intoxicated with alcohol that he barely survived.

In the late 1920s, his third novel *Flags in the Dust* (Oates 1988, 67f.) was turned down by several publishers. Faulkner rebelled: "Nobody dictates to me what I can write and what I can't write." But eventually, mulling over the "fury of denial," he began to see the weakness of some of his constructions and mockingly resigned: "I think now that I'll sell my typewriter and go to work—though God knows, it's sacrilege to waste that talent for idleness which I possess."

Benson, a biographer of American writer John Steinbeck's (Benson 1984, 32), points out that for almost twenty years Steinbeck received little encouragement for his writing and that his financial resources ran often very low: "He endured battles with disappointment and self-doubt, shipwreck after shipwreck of publisher bankruptcy, and rejection after rejection at the gates of nearly every major periodical in the country." In the end his endurance paid off well. In 1939, he received the Pulitzer Prize for his novel *The Grapes of Wrath* and in 1962 the Nobel Prize for his life's work.

The Grapes of Wrath, depicting the life of the Okies who fled the Dust Bowl of the Midwest to work as migrant sharecroppers in California during the Great Depression, also stirred up its share of ferocious rejection. It was accused (Benson 1984, 418) not only of serving as a political crusade against landowners, but also of being full of filth. The novel was burned in several localities from New York to Illinois and California. On October 19, 1939, a dejected Steinbeck (Benson 1984, 424) confided to his journal: "The last two days I have death premonitions so strong that I burned all the correspondence of years." Even the Nobel Prize which had honored Steinbeck also brought with it its lot of hatred, prompting his biographer (Benson 1984, 922) to write: "He was held in virtual paralysis for the rest of his life, not so much by getting the Nobel Prize, as by the outpouring of critical scorn that had accompanied it." To take but one example, in the *The New York Times* the critic Arthur Mizener (Benson 1984, 923) attacked Stockholm's Nobel Prize committee for honoring a writer whose "limited talent is, in his best books, watered down by tenth-rate philosophizing."

On March 22, 1920, Federico García Lorca's first play *The Butterfly's Evil Spell* was premiered in Madrid. Although Lorca (Gibson 1989, 97) had organized a whole claque of friends to support him, the performance of his first dramatic work was a total failure. From the start the audience whistled, booed, and shouted insults. When one of the characters of the play, a scorpion, extolled the taste of a worm he had just eaten, a wit shouted, "Pour

Zotal[9] on him!" inciting the whole theater to roar with laughter. It seems that Lorca's reaction to the offense was well contained. Dissimulating his disappointment, he did no more than poke fun at the audience's negative.

Contrariwise, the 1933 première of Lorca's play *Blood Wedding* was a success. Asked what he thought of the modern Spanish theater, whose fans had dismissed Lorca's plays, the newly self-confident writer (Gibson 1989, 358) replied: "It's theatre by and for swine. Exactly that, a theatre written by swine for swine." The following year Lorca's first production of the play *Yerma* was reprobated by the right-wing press as blasphemous, immoral, and anti-Spanish (Gibson 1989, 398). Conservative Catholics developed a hatred that may well have played a role two years later when he was murdered by the myrmidons of the Nationalist militia.

In 1949, Simone de Beauvoir, author, philosopher, and companion of Jean-Paul Sartre, published two volumes of her treatise *The Second Sex*, in which she offered a thorough analysis of the oppression women suffered in contemporary society. The book soon became a bible of modern feminism. Yet at the time of its appearance, male and female critics alike rejected it heavily. To take but one example, Catholic writer François Mauriac maliciously told a collaborator of de Beauvoir's (Leick 2008, 145-146): "I've learned everything about the vagina of your boss." It would seem that Albert Camus also rejected her, as she once admitted (Leick 2008): "Towards me his tone of voice was usually sarcastic and often enough offensive."

In 1964, writer and philosopher Jean-Paul Sartre (Townes 1999, 153) was offered the Nobel Prize in Literature, which he refused on the grounds that the committee in Stockholm was not competent enough to judge the quality of literature. More discrete than his ostentatious rejection of the Prize was his attempt to receive the Prize money. This time it was the Nobel committee who rejected Sartre's advances. By the way, Sartre seems to have been quite a ruthless expert when it came to rejection. He publicly called his partner Simone de Beauvoir (Lord 1985, 202) a beaver and a "clock in a refrigerator." She paid him back in equivalent currency, painting a less than flattering portrait of Sartre in her roman à clef *Les Mandarins de Paris* and jibed: "Sartre only associates with people who associate with Sartre."

The Caribbean poet, playwright and critic Derek Walcott (Walcott 1998, 190), who received the 1992 Nobel Prize in Literature, scoffed at the dogmatic views held by many American poets and poetry teachers whom he referred to as "Whitman's heirs." He maintained that contemporary American poetics was as "full of its sidewalk hawkers as a modern American city" and he shook his head at "how shrill some of Walt's boys have become."

In his statement, Walcott not only responded to a fashionable trend in American poetry, but also to a deeply rooted nationalist pretension claiming superiority over foreign cultural views. Nigerian poet, playwright, and critic Wole Soyinka, who in 1986 was awarded the Nobel Prize for his creative accomplishments, shared Walcott's perception. In his splendidly written and competently argued book *Art, Dialogue, and Outrage: Essays on Literature and Culture* (Soyinka 1994), he dismisses the patronizing attitude often taken by European critics who deal with non-European—for instance African—art and literature. Soyinka (1994, 7) mocks that brand of European critic as follows: "In some cases he has even undergone a deliberate mental retardation, a sort of 'Takes a simpleton to understand a child.'" Soyinka discovers (1994, 41) an amazing contradiction between claims to high standards and actual performance: "In spite of the exaltation of the individuality of genius, the European artist feels safe within dictated fashion, however temporary." One of those fashions was French structuralism, which in the 1960s was the rage of the town. It did not in the least excite Soyinka (1994, 304), who hated that "structuralist faddism." And when European critics hailed him as an African Shakespeare, he rejected their patronizing label by stating (1994, 254) that he wanted to be a writer, not an *African* writer. He had no desire to be another Shakespeare, either. He insisted on being himself. As Soyinka made clear at an International CREANDO Symposium on Creative Leadership (Soyinka 1997, 307-345, 315), his personal identity is deeply anchored in Yoruba culture and religion about which he proudly states, ". . . unlike many religions, which were taken by the slaves across the Americas, the Yoruba has the distinction of being the most resilient . . ."

In 1994, I published a book (Guntern 1994, 174f.) on the enhancement of creativity. There I formulated, on the basis of my own encounters with structuralist faddism, a *principle of pompous disguise* (*Prinzip der pompösen Verschleierung*) which I defined as follows: ". . . a tendency to misconceive something as being profound only because it is obscure." And I defined its conceptual resonance structure as follows: ". . . a tendency to misconceive something as superficial only because it is transparent." In my view, the principle of pompous disguise is a major force blocking human creativity. It fosters what I call a *créatitude*—a pretension to be creative whereas in fact one simply apes certain attitudes, for instance structuralist faddism, which is intended to make a deep impression on other people.

Although Marie Curie was the first woman ever to receive a Nobel Prize and the first—and up to now only—individual to have received a second Nobel Prize in science, a woman's creative achievement is still less easily recognized than a man's. In literature Simone de Beauvoir is a good case in point. So is the American poet and writer Sylvia Plath. Hypersensitive, vulnerable, high-strung, ambitious, unconsidered, and aggressive, she often fell prey to states of heavy depression. During those periods, Plath's self-esteem was shattered and she often teetered on the brink of suicide, making several serious suicide attempts. Extremely self-centerd, she once confided to her diary (Stevenson 1989, 29): "I do not love; I do not love anybody except myself." Plath's self-centeredness made life with her difficult, to say the least, and explains why she experienced so many rejections.

After a trip to England, where she fell in love with (and soon married) the poet Ted Hughes, and where she had often felt rejected, Plath wrote to publisher Peter Davison (Stevenson 1989, 96) while working for the *Atlantic Monthly Press*: ". . . sick, sick, sick. I have never been so disappointed and disgusted by anything as the London literati, with their outposts in Oxford and Cambridge." Full of narcissistic rage, Plath scorned all young English poets as "incredibly malicious, vain, and with no sense of music, readableness or, for that matter, deep, honest meaning."

In the summer of 1957, the *Saturday Evening Post* and the *Ladies' Home Journal* (Stevenson 1989, 112) turned down the short stories Plath had submitted. *The Yale Series of Younger Poets* sent back her manuscript of *Two Lovers and a Beachcomber*. At first Plath reacted with depression, although she had once sworn to be "stronger" than the English novelist, essayist, and critic Virginia Woolf who, in 1941, had weighted her pockets with stones and waded into a river where she drowned herself. Plath began to thoroughly reread her material, making corrections here and there and establishing plans for future accomplishments. At times her sense of humiliation provoked such a rage in her that her imagination went wild with scenes of carnage. In such a mood she confided to her journal (Stevenson 1989, 124): "I walk around the streets, braced and ready and almost wishing to test my eye and fiber on tragedy—a child crushed by a car, a house on fire, someone thrown into a tree by a horse. Nothing happens: I walk the razor's edge of jeopardy." On another occasion Plath wrote (Stevenson 1989, 193): "I have a violence in me that is hot as death-blood."

That violence lashed out in folly when she erroneously assumed that her husband Ted (Stevenson 1989, 206) was having a fling with an Irish employee at BBC. When he returned to his flat with the good news that BBC would produce the programs he had proposed to them, he found to his utter horror that Sylvia had destroyed all of his notebooks, plays, poems in progress, and even torn to shreds his precious edition of Shakespeare in order to punish him for a misdeed that existed only in her paranoid conviction. The couple separated in late 1962. On February 11, 1963, Sylvia Plath took her life.

In the autumn of 2007, Doris Lessing was awarded the Nobel Prize for literature; she is but the eleventh woman to receive the recognition in the 140 years of its existence. Interestingly enough, Sylvia Plath (Stevenson 1989, 286) had once paid a call on Doris and had been politely declined. Lessing found her alarming in her "incandescent desperation," felt overwhelmed by her "total demand" and was unable to muster much sympathy for her ambitious young colleague. Later she confessed: "I just couldn't cope with her."

Rejection proves to be even more harsh for writers who are politically engaged. Where greed for power, chauvinism, party politics, and art mingle, ugly machinations are likely to occur. When Mario Vargas Llosa (Vargas Llosa 1995, 411f.) ran for president in Peru, incumbent Alan García unleashed a ferocious propaganda war against the challenger. At that time, Vargas Llosa's novel *In Praise of the Stepmother* was being read a chapter at a time on state-controlled Channel 7. García's administration denounced Vargas Llosa as a pervert and pornographer; General Germán Parra even suggested: "According to Freud Doctor Vargas Llosa ought to be under treatment for a mental disorder."

Norman Mailer was never delicate in dishing out merciless comments to the targets of his contempt. But due to his temperament and offensive remarks, he also often found himself on the receiving end. To take but one example, John Leonard (Leonard 2003, 10) wrote a slashing review on Mailer's book *Some Thoughts on Writing*, stating sarcastically that the book felt like a late-night cable commercial for Roy Orbison's Greatest Hits, or Conway Twitty's soliciting the viewer 'act now, call this toll-free number, and we will also send you, at no extra charge, a cool tool to sharpen your knives, whiten your teeth and screw your neighbours.'"

Montaigne described centuries ago how scientists tend to deal with new discoveries made by their colleagues. Whenever scientists hear about a new scientific discovery their first reaction is, "It's probably not correct." If later the accuracy of the findings is confirmed, they admit, "It may be correct but it is not relevant." Eventually, if enough time has passed and the discovery has proved to be relevant, they regret, "Of course, it is correct and relevant, but it isn't new anymore."

In a discussion on the topic of creative thinking, quantum physicist and Nobel laureate Murray Gell-Mann (Gell-Mann 1994, 261) emphasized that, ". . . it is only by breaking away from the excessively restrictive received ideas that progress can be made." In other words, a creative breakthrough is possible only by rebelling against an established idea or paradigm. Since Dirac's discovery of the existence of positronst with an opposite electrical charge, the idea of symmetrical structures, also called resonant structures, has become a leitmotif in our modern worldview. This enables us to understand quite easily that the rejection of an established concept or paradigm will, in turn, be heavily rejected by the adherents of that concept or paradigm. The history of the epistemic process in physics across the centuries is full of examples of rejection and resonant counter-rejection.

Nicolaus Copernicus (1473-1543) placed the sun at the center of our universe and postulated that all planets, including the earth, orbit around it. This was a radical break from the traditional, geocentric Ptolemaic view holding that the earth is at the center of our universe with all the other planets orbiting around it. Copernicus gave his book the title *The Revolution of the Heavenly Orbits*; to this very day authorities dislike the word "revolution" for the threat it implies to their status and prestige.

The first authority to reject Copernicus' new paradigm was the Roman Catholic Church, which still adhered to the Ptolemaic paradigm. As the mathematician Bronowski (1973, 198) puts it, ". . . the Church had made up its mind that the system of Ptolemy was invented not by a Levantine Greek but by the Almighty Himself."

One of Copernicus's contemporaries and the founding father of modern science Galileo Galilei (1564-1642) assumed that scientific proof would be sufficient to do away with the Ptolemaic paradigm once and for all. Obviously he underestimated His Holiness Pope Urban VIII (Bronowski 1973, 208), who grandiosely pontificated: "I know better than all the Cardinals put together! The sentence of a living Pope is worth more than all the decrees of a hundred dead ones." Here was a pope who imperiously rejected established papal ideas, but refused to accept a scientist who rejected established scientific ideas. He ordered the Holy Office of the Inquisition to take care of Galileo, and take care of him they did.

Standing trial before ten judges, all of whom were Domenican Cardinals, Galileo was threatened twice with torture and forced to withdraw his conviction based upon scientific investigation that the earth revolved around the sun and not vice-versa. Galileo was compelled to recant his ideas (Bronowski 1973, 218) and was confined to his villa in Aretri near Florence for the rest of his life. Under strict house arrest, he was not permitted to discuss his ideas with anyone, let alone publish them. As legend has it, Galileo murmured on his deathbed: *"Eppur' si muove*—and yet it (the earth) moves." There were further consequences to the Vatican's victory. Reading the writing on the wall, Descartes (Bronowski 1973, 218) stopped publishing in France and migrated to Sweden. The Protestants of northern Europe soon replaced the southern Catholics by developing into creative pacemakers of the scientific revolution brought about by Copernicus and Galileo.

The rejection of Galileo's heliocentric worldview eventually produced an absurd and hypocritical epilogue. Three-and-a-half centuries after Galileo's death on October 31, 1992, Pope John Paul II admitted that the theologians involved in Galileo's trial had committed some formal errors. He did not, however, go so far as to concede that Galileo's conviction on a charge of heresy had been wrong. For critical minds, there is no doubt that back in 1633 the Dominican Cardinals—*domini canes* is Latin for "the dogs of the Lord—had barked up the wrong tree because their boss had ordered them to do so. The tree of today's scientific knowledge bears many a fruit, and one of its most impressive ones is the Copernican heliocentric paradigm.

Galileo, Kepler, and Descartes disagreed over the nature of the forces that moved the planets along their orbits and the question of how heavenly bodies act when they are not under the impact of external forces. Isaac Newton (1643-1727) was, as Koestler (1977, 496) puts it, "the conductor who pulled the orchestra together and made a new harmony out of caterwauling disorders." The cornerstone of Newton's problem solution was his law of gravity. It holds that the force of attraction between two bodies is proportional to the attracting masses, and that this force diminishes with the square of the distance.

Newton was a man of religious beliefs. In answer to the question of how the forces of gravity governing the motions of heavenly bodies had come into existence, he maintained that the Lord himself had created them. Since the law of gravity implicitly predicted that all bodies attract each other and that, therefore, the whole universe must ultimately collapse, Newton (Koestler 1977, 504) put the Lord in charge of preventing such a catastrophe when he wrote: "Yet would the outside systems descend towards the middle-most, so that this frame of things could not always subsist without a divine power to conserve it . . ." In other words, the Lord was not only the *creator mundi*[10] but also the *conservator mundi* and above all, the *redemptor mundi* of the universe of Newton's theoretical difficulties.

The first rejection of a central part of Newton's new cosmology came from Leibniz (Leibniz 1975, 321). Unlike Newton, Leibniz did not believe that time and space where absolute and stated: "I hold space to be something merely relative, as time is . . . I hold it to be an order of co-existence as time is an order of succession." Leibniz (Koestler 1989, 24) accused Newton of introducing "occult qualities and miracles" into science. Some authors rejected Newton's assumption that the universe was a flat disc. Still others rejected the idea of the Lord playing a role in Newton's framework, or that gravitational forces should act immediately over long distances.

At the end of the nineteenth century, Faraday (Einstein 1976, 253) discovered electromagnetic forces that acted only on electrically charged bodies and did so not instantaneously, but with finite speed. Faraday (Faraday 1975 418f.) observed that magnets create "lines of forces" in the environment, and Maxwell (Maxwell 1975, 432ff.) formalized Faraday's findings into a dynamic theory of the electromagnetic field. Newton's "mass point" was now replaced by the concept of a "field" which, in turn, paved the way for Einstein's General Theory of Relativity, which definitively discarded Newton's idea of absolute space and time.

In 1673, Fermat scribbled a mathematical problem on a page of a copy of a French translation of the famous *Arithmetica* by Diophantus[11] and hinted that he had already found its solution. This formulation entered history under the sobriquet of *Fermat's Last Theorem*. In the following century, Gauss (Bernstein 1996, 137) poked fun at Fermat stating: ". . . I could easily lay down a multitude of such propositions, which one could neither prove nor dispose of." In 1995, mathematician Andrew Wiles falsified the Gaussian rejection by publishing the final proof for Fermat's proposition.

In 1845, the Scottish physicist J. J. Waterston (Koestler 1989, 254), who was living in India at the time, submitted a paper on the molecular theory of gases in which he formulated several laws of the kinetic theory of gases. One of these laws stated that the pressure of a gas is a function of the number of gas molecules per volume. The authority of the Royal Society was intransigent in his verdict: "The paper is nothing but nonsense." Waterston's work fell prey to oblivion, as did its author, who lived in embittered solitude until one day he vanished without a trace.

Gregor Mendel, the father of modern genetics, had to deal with a double rejection. He became a monk in order to get an education. His abbot, obviously aware of the young man's talents, sent him to the University of Vienna (Bronowski 1973, 380f.) where Mendel was supposed to become a teacher. Yet he failed thanks to his examiner's inexorable decision: "lacks insight and the requisite clarity of knowledge." His abbot then sent Mendel to the Augustinian Order of St. Thomas in Brno, where the young monk began to carry out his famous garden experiments with peas. From 1856 to 1864, he worked on his discovery of the basic laws of biological inheritance. Two years later he published his results in the *Journal of the Brno Natural History Society* and, as Bronowski (1973, 385) writes with tongue-in-cheek, Mendel "achieved instant oblivion."

In 1902, German physicist Philipp Lenard (Hoffmann 1973, 52ff.) did some investigations on the nature of the so-called photoelectric effect originally discovered by Heinrich Hertz. Lenard showed that a metal plate bombarded with high-frequency light increased the velocity of electrons ejected by the metal plate but not their number. He stressed the fact that this phenomenon did not at all correspond to what could have been expected on the basis of Maxwell's theory, but was unable to explain what he had discovered. Three years later, Einstein came up with a rather simple explanation: a light beam hurls light quanta against the metal sheet, so electrons are ejected with higher velocities when the sheet is bombarded with high-frequency light. Max Planck, the discoverer of quanta, rejected Einstein's explanation as being wrong. The American experimental physicist Robert Millikan, furthermore, spent a decade trying to prove that Einstein's explanation of the photoelectric effect was wrong—only to find that Einstein had been right from the very beginning.

Lenard (Bernstein 1974, 199), who received the Nobel Prize for his discovery made in 1905, was never able to forget that Einstein had succeeded where he had failed. In 1920, he teamed up with an obscure politician named Weyland plus a well-financed group of supporters in an effort to fight "Jewish physics." They organized anti-Semitic rallies against Einstein's relativity theory. As late as 1933, Lenard (Bernstein 1974, 211), who had meanwhile become a virulent Nazi, still railed against Einstein via the *Völkische Beobachter* bemoaning the influence of Jewis circles on the study of nature and deriding: ". . . Herr Einstein with his mathematically botched-up theories consisting of some ancient knowledge and a few arbitrary additions." Lenard predicted that Einstein's theory would gradually fall to pieces because it was "estranged from nature." What fell to pieces in the end was the irrational hatred that had motivated German anti-Einstein rallies.

In 1905, Einstein (Einstein 1975, 486) published his first paper in a series of four that would rapidly change the face of modern physics. In it he rejected Newton's concept of absolute time and space. It showed that every statement of time was a statement about simultaneity between an event and the hands on a clock placed in the vicinity of that event. Up until that point, statements about time were always relative to a coordinate system, a reference body, or an observer and his motions. Similarly, the length of a body depended upon its motion relative to an observer's coordinate system. Absolute length and dimension and, therefore, absolute space did not exist.

The Special Relativity Theory, integrating Newton's mechanics and the Faraday-Maxwell theory of electromagnetic fields, encountered little resistance that could have been taken seriously. The same holds true for Einstein's General Theory of Relativity published in 1915. It integrated Newton's theory of gravity and the Special Theory of Relativity into one single, conceptual framework. On the basis of this new theory, Einstein made three precise predictions that could not have been deduced from Newton's laws of motion:

- Planets not only revolve in elliptic curves around they sun, they also rotate in the direction of their orbital motions.
- Matter (or its equivalent, its gravitational field) curves space-time.
- The gravitational field of matter produces a red shift in the spectral lines of light coming from a distant star.

Soon experiments proved that Einstein's predictions had been right; so far, so good. By now Einstein was an established authority in physics, a new Newton, one of those rare creative geniuses that appear every 500 years or so within a specific scientific discipline. But despite his genius and fame, Einstein eventually encountered two major types of rejection: the first was handed out by his colleagues in quantum physics; the second, by the very nature of the problem he was grappling with in the forty years between the publication of the General Theory of Relativity and his death.

In 1920, French physicist Louis de Broglie (de Broglie 1975, 512f.) introduced what is known as wave mechanics into atomic theory. A lover of chamber music, he imagined that electrons oscillated in their orbits around the nucleus of an atom as the strings of a harp oscillate when strummed by fingers. He postulated that "a wave must be associated with each corpuscle and only a study of the wave's propagation will yield information on the successive position of the corpuscles in space." At first his idea was ridiculed by his colleagues (Gamow 1966, 81f.), one physicist even denouncing it as yet another vaudeville burlesque presented by the *Comédie Française*. Soon the work of Schrödinger, Born, and Heisenberg proved that de Broglie's intuition had been right.

Born's contribution was to introduce probability theory into quantum physics. According to the new view (Capra 1975, 68f.), matter did not exist with certainty at a definite place, but showed "tendencies to exist" and atomic events showed "tendencies to occur." Bohr and Heisenberg integrated Born's concept into a general quantum theory that was soon called the Copenhagen interpretation because Bohr lived and worked in the Danish capital. One of the results of that synthesis of quantum physics was the discard of the Newtonian-La Place paradigm of total determinism, whereby all events in nature are strictly determined by natural law. According to the new view, all events in nature are due to an incessant interplay of chance and necessity. Or, to expand, all events in nature are caused by a continuous interplay of random events and events determined by natural laws, of freedom and structural constraints, and (whenever human beings are involved) of spontaneity and rational calculation.

Einstein flatly rejected the idea. In 1927, at the sixth Solvay Congress in Brussels, where the luminaries of physics used to meet at regular intervals, a heated dispute arose between two opposite camps. On the one hand, Bohr defended Heisenberg's *Uncertainty Principle,* holding that you can never measure the position of an electron and its momentum at the same time: if you measure its position, its momentum becomes uncertain; and if you measure its momentum, then you do not know where its actual position is. Heisenberg was also supported by Born (Born 1951, 19), who firmly believed that "all laws of nature are really laws of chance in disguise." On the other hand, Einstein, who liked metaphorical language, was convinced that "God does not play dice with the world," leaving no room for chance events in nature. In his view "chance" was just another word for a natural law yet to be discovered. The discussion got so heated that at one point Bohr, usually a rather peaceful fellow, snapped at Einstein: "Stop telling the Lord what he is supposed to do!" Most of the physicists present took sides, and most of them sided against Einstein. And thus the spiral of rejection and counter-rejection moved along—not unlike the probability waves of de Broglie and Born!

Einstein (Hoffmann 1973, 190) never agreed with the Copenhagen interpretation of quantum physics proposed by Niels Bohr and Werner Heisenberg in 1927. A year after its publication, he wrote to Schrödinger, who supported his view: "The Heisenberg-Bohr tranquillizing philosophy—or religion? —is so delicately contrived that, for the time being, it provides a gentle pillow for the true believer from which he cannot be easily aroused." With this statement, he only confirmed his rejection (Regis 1987, 24) already formulated in 1912: "The more success the quantum theory has, the sillier it looks."

Einstein's total rejection of probabilistic determinism—which postulated a continuous interplay of chance and necessity in causing natural events—provoked a symmetrical response. Most of his colleagues found that he, who had single-handedly founded quantum physics with a paper written in 1905, had now lost touch with the new developments. Wolfgang Pauli (Dick 1990, 14) derided Schrödinger's wave theory as "Zurich superstitions." In a letter written in 1926 to Heisenberg, Pauli (Gleick 1993, 242) scoffed: "What Schrödinger writes on the visualizability [*sic*] of his theory . . . I consider trash." Heisenberg originally even called Schrödinger's theory "abominable," although a few years later he began to embrace it. From today's perspective, it would seem that Einstein and Schrödinger were wrong and Bohr, Heisenberg, and Born were right. Chaos theory is the best theory of causality we have in contemporary science. Joseph Ford (Gleick 1988, 314), one of its representatives, sums up nicely the whole Solvay dispute by stating: "God plays dice with the universe. But they're loaded dice. And the main objective of physics now is to find out by what rules they were loaded and how we can use them for our own ends."

The second major rejection for Einstein was due to the sheer complexity of the problems he encountered in his attempt to integrate the General Theory of Relativity and Quantum Mechanics into one, single, conceptual framework called Unified Field Theory. Although he tried time and again to solve the problems he encountered, in the endeavor he always met defeat. Still he remained convinced (Hoffmann 1973, 146; Clark 1972, 650) that "the Lord may be subtle but he is not malicious"—his metaphorical expression for the conviction that nature can, in principle, be understood by man. After his many failures he merely declared: "At least I know 99 ways that don't work." He even insisted on publishing his failures in order to "save another fool from wasting six months on the same idea." The night of his death, Einstein left a piece of paper on his hospital table with an unfinished equation on the Unified Field Theory. Such was his reaction to being rejected by the sheer complexity of a problem he had tried to resolve: stoic acceptance of failure combined with generosity toward his fellow physicians.

Mixing a solution of citric acid, acidified bromate, and a ceric salt, Russian chemist Boris Belousov discovered in the early 1950s an inorganic chemical reaction that oscillated for hours in a lab dish between an initial state and an end state (Thwaites 1990, 136). The editors of a professional journal rejected Belousov's discovery on the grounds that, "Your presumed discovery is impossible." Belousov continued to repeat his experiments and six years later presented a scientific paper on the periodically oscillating chemical reaction for publication. This time it was ruled out with the argument that the paper was too long. In the early 1960s, his younger colleague Anatolij Zhabotinsky refined the experiment by replacing citric acid by malonic acid. The chemical oscillator now switched back and forth between a blue state and a red state. Zhabotinsky eventually succeeded in getting Belousov's paper published. In 1980, ten years after his death, Belousov was awarded the Lenin Prize for his discovery of the periodically oscillating chemical B-Z reaction, which founded the scientific discipline of non-linear chemical dynamics.

In the 1930s, India-born astrophysicist Subrahmanyan Chandrasekhar (Wali 1991, 30) calculated the maximum mass of a non-rotating star able to withstand the pull of gravitational forces. He discovered a fundamental atomic constant, now known as the Chandrasekhar limit, and showed that if the mass of a star exceeded this limit, it would collapse and turn into a black hole. Arthur Eddington, an astrophysicist and the leading luminary in British physics at the time, began to deride Chandrasekhar within the scientific community. He suggested that Chandrasekhar understood neither quantum mechanics nor the General Theory of Relativity. In 1935, Rosenfeld (Wali 1991, 131ff.), a collaborator and close friend of Einstein, read a copy of Eddington's paper. His verdict: "After having courageously read Eddington's paper twice, I have nothing to change in my previous statements; it is the wildest nonsense." Similarly Wolfgang Pauli stated that Eddington did not understand quantum physics. Paul Dirac, too, found Chandrasekhar's paper flawless. In 1983, about fifty years after his ground-breaking discovery, Chandrasekhar received the Nobel Prize in physics for his outstanding creative accomplishment.

Today, lasers are used in a vast array of applications ranging from CD players to aesthetic surgery to guided, target-oriented missiles, and from moving organelles around in living cells to measuring interstellar distances in outer space. Charles Townes (Townes 1999, 65), who together with his colleague Arthur Schawlow discovered the maser principle ("maser" is an acronym for *m*icrowave *a*mplification by *s*timulated *e*mission of *r*adiation) and later the laser principle ("laser" is an acronym for *l*ight *a*mplification by *s*timulated *e*mission of *r*adiation), relates how rejection threatened to kill his scientific research on lasers and how he reacted to it. One day in the 1950s, while Townes was working at Columbia University, two colleagues visited his laboratory. Isidor Isaac Rabi and Polykarp Kusch were the former and current chairmen of the department; both were Nobel laureates and renowned authorities in their field of scientific investigations. They informed Townes that he was wasting the money of research grants urgently needed for other projects. Their rationale: having worked for two years on a project and come up with zero results, he should drop it. Townes and his team of experimental physicists and technicians tenaciously pushed on, however, and within weeks, they had built their first maser. After developing a second one, Townes (1999, 71) visited Niels Bohr in Copenhagen. Bohr asked him what his current field of research was, and Townes described the maser and its performance. "But that is not possible!" Bohr exclaimed. When Townes met John von Neumann at a cocktail party in Princeton and told him about the maser, the mathematical genius's first reaction was that the maser could not possibly function; yet after a drink or two, von Neumann grasped the principle behind it and accepted the accomplishment. In 1964, Townes and Schawlow were awarded a Nobel Prize for their discoveries.

A particular form of mutual rejection seems to hold sway between theoretical and experimental physicists. The former are often convinced that experiments carried out with ultra-expensive machinery only prove what theoreticians found out a long time ago by simply using their brain, a piece of paper, and pencil, or at most an electronic pocket calculator. As for the latter, many seem to share the opinion of their colleague and Nobel laureate, Isidor Isaac Rabi, (Lederman and Dick 1993, 166) who defined a theoretician as a guy who wasn't able "to tie his own shoelaces."

Among the theoretical physicists who had to grapple with various kinds of rejections was Mitchell Feigenbaum (Gleick 1988, 165ff.), one of the founding fathers of chaos theory and discoverer of a law of nature. In the early 1970s, he was studying turbulence in fluids at the Los Alamos National Laboratory in New Mexico. Observing the smoke rising from his own cigarette, the changing shapes of clouds, fluctuating patterns in waterfalls of the Rio Grande gorge, and gurgling vortices in his kitchen sink, he began to grasp intuitively that in a process of self-organization, order is able to produce chaos. In the slow, laminar water flow within a channel for instance, we can observe that somewhere a bifurcation occurs; all of a sudden the flat surface of the water splits apart and a gable-like form appears. After a while, at the end of each branch of the gable-like structure two new bifurcations appear and produce four gable-like structures; the same process repeats itself and yields eight gable-like structures. Suddenly all the structures seem to vanish and give way to the chaotic world of whirls. In other words, due to period-doubling, a dynamic system is able to enter a turbulent state and does so in a self-organizing manner.

With the help of a simple HP-65 calculator, Feigenbaum (Feigenbaum 1995) found out that the ratio of the difference between the values of successive period-doublings is a constant of 4.669. Later, using a more sophisticated computer, he was able to be more precise by extending the three decimals following the period. In 1975, aware of the fact that he had discovered a natural law defining the quantification of a trans-scalar phenomenon[12], he began submitting articles to scientific periodicals. For two years in a row, he received nothing but rejection slips until at last his findings were published. As Gleick (1988, 183) writes, today the scientific community has recognized that Feigenbaum "discovered universality and created a theory to explain it."

The Hungarian physician Ignaz Semmelweis (Koestler 1989, 239) discovered that in Vienna's hospitals a lack of hygiene caused high rates of puerperal fever, which often ended in the death of mothers who had just given birth. He began washing his hands in an antiseptic solution prior to each obstetric intervention. The rate of puerperal fever dropped dramatically. His fellow obstetricians declined to follow his advice; feeling their dignity offended, they fought the Semmelweis method. So much irrational rejection irritated Semmelweis to the point where he openly attacked his fellow physicians, even accusing them of murder. In 1865, he was committed to a mental institution where he was beaten by the guards and died two weeks after his admission. A similar fate befell Robert Mayer (Koestler 1989, 239), one of the founding fathers of thermodynamics. He formulated the law of the conservation of energy that was met with hostility by his fellow physicists, including such luminaries as Helmholtz and Joule. Mayer suffered terribly from that rejection. In 1850, he attempted suicide and was committed to a mental institution. Ten years elapsed before he was released; by then he was a broken man despite the fact that his ideas had won increasing recognition.

Gerd Binning (Binnig 1989, 225) and his colleague Heinrich Rohrer invented the scanning tunnelling microscope, making possible the observation of individual atoms on the surface of molecules. In his book on creativity, Binnig reports that he and his coinventor were at first rejected as being frauds simply because two years after their breakthrough, other physicists had not yet been able to duplicate their device and see an individual atom for themselves. In 1986, Binnig and Rohrer (Binnig 1995a) received the Nobel Prize for their invention.

In the world of technological invention, rejection is often only a means to the end of robbery. Potential customers and producers reject the value of an invention while trying to steal it from the inventor. Moreover, certain entrepreneurs and most top managers are averse to risk-taking and stick to the establish routine rather than venture into new areas; automatically they reject that with which they are not yet familiar. And then there are those who are stuck in their tracks and lack the imagination to recognize a technological revolution when they see one. A typical case in point is that of entrepreneur and engineer George Westinghouse (Josephson 1992, 241). He offered his newly invented air brake to Commodore Vanderbilt, the old railroad magnate who had made his wealth in shipping and railroads. Vanderbilt snubbed the offer with the pretext that he had "not time to waste on fools." In response to the rejection, Westinghouse created a company that produced his air brake, a safety system soon introduced all over the globe.

When young Henry Ford (Josephson 1992, 405f.) was employed as chief engineer at the Detroit Edison Company's powerhouse, he invented a gasoline-powered motorcar he named the "Quadricycle." Alexander Dow, the head of the company, rejected the idea of producing it and demanded instead that Ford invent an electrical car. Ford's concept of the gasoline engine was on the whole rejected until he met Thomas A. Edison. The experienced inventor immediately understood the value of Ford's "horseless carriage" and encouraged him to pursue his ideas. In due time, the gasoline car conquered the world, producing many desired—but also a host of undesired—results.

Nikola Tesla (Cheney 1993, 23ff.) tried so sell his idea of the huge benefits of an alternating current induction motor (AC-dynamo) to the managers of the Continental Edison Company. But because Edison himself was a fervent defender of the advantages of direct current, they rejected it. Later, after having migrated to the United States from what is now Croatia, Tesla met Edison (Cheney 1993, 31) and tried to convince him of the benefits of his invention. Edison replied: "Hold up! Spare me that nonsense. It's dangerous. We're set up for direct current in America." Still, Edison must have recognized Tesla's talent, for he gave him a job on the S. S. Oregon in the maintenance and repair of the ship's lighting plant.

In 1887, Tesla (Cheney 1993, 39f.) formed his own company, the *Tesla Electric Company*, for producing AC-dynamos. He soon joined Westinghouse, only to find that the Westinghouse engineers rejected his invention for a seemingly good reason: conceived for a 60-cycle current, it did not work with the 133-cycle current used by Westinghouse. After much trial and error, the sixty-cycle current was eventually adopted and soon became the worldwide standard for alternating current. Edison, for his part, was infuriated to learn that Tesla and Westinghouse had joined forces.

In 1892, the financier J. P. Morgan organized a merger between the Edison General Electric Company and its rival the Thomas-Houston Electrical Company to form the famous General Electric Company or GE. For years, GE and Westinghouse fought in court over the introduction of the alternative current system; it was Tesla and Westinghouse who won their case.

In 1898 (Cheney 1993, 123f,), Tesla presented the world's first radio-controlled robot boat. He had been able to further develop the wireless, forerunner of our modern radio, and with his robot boat he had introduced automation. Critics and public, however, were not warm to an idea that pointed to a future world of automation, robotics, and guided missiles. During the First World War, the War Department showed interest in Tesla's fantastic turbine that was able to develop 200 horsepower. Yet it was ultimately rejected because the engineers responsible preferred to stick to the established Parsons turbine. A representative of the War Department later declared that they had not sponsored R & D programs on the Tesla turbine (Cheney 1993, 193) because they did not want to pour "money down the rat hole . . ."

Let us note one last example of rejection in the domain of science. In October 1970, the economists Black and Scholes (Bernstein 1996, 315) sent an article to *The Journal of Politics* formulating their ideas about the proper pricing of stock options. The editors rejected the paper with the argument that it was more about politics than economics. Harvard's *Review of Economics and Statistics* also turned it down. Neither of these journals had the paper reviewed by an authority. The paper was eventually published in the May/June 1993 issue of *The Journal of Political Economy*, but only after two influential members of the Chicago faculty had put some pressure on the reluctant editors. The article turned out to be a milestone in the fields of economics and finance. In 1997, Scholes (Black had already died by then) received a Nobel Prize for his contribution to that groundbreaking piece of scientific research.

What about rejection in the realm of art?

Leonardo and Michelangelo, the two greatest geniuses of the Italian Renaissance, were involved in a life-long struggle of mutual rejection. While still working at the court of Duke Ludovico "Il Moro" Sforza in Milan, Leonardo (Payne 1978, 160f.) wrote *Trattato della Pittura*, a treatise on painting in which he declared that painting was a much nobler art than sculpting. He emphasized gleefully that painters worked in noble silence, dressed in silk and velvet while creating masterpieces a sweaty, noisy sculptor was never able to produce. Leonardo maliciously pointed out that sculpting "gives the observer no cause for admiration, as painting does by virtue of the science that enables us on a flat surface, to see vast landscapes and far-off horizons."

In a letter written in 1547, almost thirty years after Leonardo's death, Michelangelo (Payne 1978, 161), still smarting from the offence retaliated: "If he who wrote that painting is nobler than sculpture understood as little about the other things of which he writes—my maidservant could have expressed them better."

Michelangelo—who was not only a painter, sculptor, and architect, but also a highly gifted poet—provoked rejection throughout his long career. Bigger than life itself, he kindled envy and irritation wherever he went. Rome was the place of his greatest triumphs but also of many rejections.

Pope Julius II (Boorstin 1992, 414ff.), known as "The Warrior Pope," was a ruthless master of political intrigue and a power-hungry warmonger, obsessed with expanding the Papal States. Desirous of leaving a scratch on the wall of oblivion, in 1505 he commissioned Michelangelo to build him a gigantic tomb that would include forty sculptures bigger than life-size. The pompous pontifical project utterly displeased Bramante, the architect who had made the designs for rebuilding St. Peter's Basilica, and the painter Raphael, who had hoped to receive some major commissions for vast murals. Both were exceedingly jealous of Michelangelo, who had established a very close relationship with the pope—a private drawbridge connected their respective rooms! Together, the architect and the painter hatched an ingenious plan to eliminate their rival.

First, they told the pope that it would bring bad luck and even premature death to have his tomb built during his lifetime. Second, they suggested that Pope Julius II order Michelangelo to fresco the ceiling of the private chapel built by Pope Sixtus IV and used since then for papal elections. The Sistine Chapel had a tunnel-vaulted ceiling broken up by eight windows, an architectonic structure that produced numerous triangles and lunettes. The two intriguers were convinced that Michelangelo would fail to meet the challenge of painting the complex surface resembling more a fragmented, irregular earthquake zone than a flat canvas.

Their plot failed miserably. In 1512, the ceiling was unveiled and the cardinals, artists, and other visitors who came to see the results of Michelangelo's efforts where overwhelmed by the magnificent painting that smoothly unfurled on the uneven surfaces of the ceiling. Michelangelo had painted the history of our planet from the Creation to the Flood, and from Jesus and his disciples to the resurrection of the dead and the liberation of the souls. Immediately Michelangelo was hailed as a genius and, as a by-product of his masterful achievement, his two opponents suffered a painful defeat. Michelangelo had emerged triumphant from the rejection game and later took further revenge by disparaging Raphael (Murray 1985, 63): "Whatever he is able to do, he has learned it from me."

In the autumn of 1934, Michelangelo returned to Rome from Florence—where he had worked on the façade of the Basilica of San Lorenzo and on a funerary chapel for the Medici—to execute Pope Clement VII's commission for a mural on the huge altar wall of the Sistine Chapel. One month later, His Holiness died. Michelangelo began to make preparations for the enormous mural that would represent *The Last Judgement,* an undertaking that would keep him busy for the next several years.

On September 1, 1535, the newly elected pope Paul III appointed Michelangelo first painter, sculptor, and architect of the Vatican (Murray 1985, 158ff.) and Michelangelo continued his work on the mural. A fall from the scaffolding resulting in a broken leg retarded his progress, but on October 31, 1541 the painting was finally unveiled. The great admiration it aroused was accompanied by equal irritation over the nude figures. According to Christian faith, the *Last Judgement* occurs after the resurrection of the dead. Since the resurrected dead are no longer clothed after so many centuries spent in their tombs, Michelangelo had assumed that, quite naturally, they must be painted naked.

In the years that followed, a war of pro and con raged over the bare bodies of the fresco. Bernardo Cirillo (Murray 1985, 165), a priest and friend of the writer Aretino who, for very personal reasons was furious with Michelangelo, suggested that the nudes would be better off in a garden loggia than in a chapel. Cirillo had connections with the most powerful cardinals in the Vatican, one of whom was Cardinal Caraffa. In 1542, Pope Paul III established the Congregation of the Holy Office of Inquisition and put Cardinal Caraffa in charge of that tribunal aimed at fighting all forms of heresy. The ecclesiastic was determined to get rid of the genitalia shamefully exposed in *The Last Judgement.* In 1555, he was elected Pope, assumed the name Paul IV, and immediately ordered Michelangelo (Murray 1985, 166) to paint some kind of vestment on the naked men and women. Michelangelo's response was clear: "Tell the pope . . . to improve the world, then the paintings will improve by themselves." His Holiness had little choice but to give in until his death in 1559. He was succeeded by Pope Pius IV, and immediately following the Council of Trent and a decree whereby religious art should be protected from "impurity and lasciviousness," it was decided in January 1564 that the nudes in Michelangelo's painting had to be covered. By then the artist was on his deathbed, and the "corrections" would be executed only after his demise.

After Michelangelo's death, Daniele da Volterra was commissioned to conceal the offensive parts of *The Last Judgement.* He completely repainted the figures of Saint Catherine and Saint Blasius and dissimulated the exposed genitals and backsides of the other figures with fig leaves and loincloths. Although he did the job with taste and respect for Michelangelo, he was punished by *vox populi* with the surname "*il Braghettone,*" the painter of breeches. Pius IV died in 1565. His successor, Pius V, hated Michelangelo's masterpiece and schemed to have it destroyed. Thankfully, painter and biographer Giorgio Vasari was able to persuade him not to touch *The Last Judgement*. Over the years, several popes decided to eliminate the chef-d'œuvre but each time its defenders were able to avert the intended iconoclasm. Eventually, under the reign of Pope Clement VIII (1592-1605), the clerics decided (Murray 1985, 167) not to actively destroy the painting but to let time and the gradual decay it brings take its natural course. Fortunately, Michelangelo's great mural survived not only the jealousy of his contemporary colleagues, but also the hypocrisy and aggression of popes and higher clerics as well as the forces of natural deterioration.

More often than not, harsh rejection is but an expression of jealousy, malevolence, or sheer narrow-mindedness. Yet it can at times also be fully justified, as the following case suggests.

At the beginning of the nineteenth century, a group of artists formed a movement in Vienna. Its members, who called themselves the Nazarene painters, intended to restore honesty and Christian spirituality to the world of art. If their movement was short-lived—indeed noble intentions do not always produce the desired results—their paintings turned out to be less than convincing. Aiming at naïve innocence, they produced a kitsch rejected by luminaries—Goethe and Jakob Burckhardt, for instance—as brainless imitations of Raphael and Dürer. The great painter Caspar David Friedrich (Kronsbein 2005, 164), the foremost representative of the German Romantic movement, derided the Nazarenes in rather drastic terms: "If grown up people want to shit in the living room like children, then you would probably not want to believe it."

Let us now return to our main topic, the history of unjustified rejections.

Rejection is the normal fate of artists whose work is so unique that it demands great adjustment on the part of art lovers and the general public trying to cope with unexpected novelty. The latter must change their habitual perceptions, concepts, and criteria of selection in order to deal with the results of an extraordinary performance. Quite naturally, rejection demands less effort in adjustment than acceptance does.

In 1863, the jury of artists who were to select the paintings for exhibition at the annual Paris Salon (Boorstin 1992, 516ff.; Shikes and Harper 1980, 62) rejected sixty percent of the art works submitted. Emperor Napoleon III wanted to give the public a chance to view the paintings that had been eliminated and to judge for themselves whether or not they liked what they saw. A *Salon des Refusés* (exhibition of the rejected) was installed at the Palais de l'Industrie. Courbet, Manet, Cézanne, Pissarro, and Jongkind were among the artists whose paintings were shown. Young Monet did not exhibit any of his work. The emperor dismissed Manet's masterpiece *Le Déjeuner sur l'Herbe* as "immodest," for it portrayed two fully dressed male painters in the company of two completely naked models. Napoleon's rejection of the painting helped to trigger the curiosity of the public, who flocked to the *Salon* only to reject in turn the artwork exhibited. Baudelaire shared the public's attitude (Doran ed 1978, 169); in a letter to Manet he wrote the condescending verdict: "You are number one in the decadence of your art."

In 1866, Claude Monet (Boorstin 1992 515f.) was close to ruin. His creditors threatened to seize all of his possessions, and Monet preferred to slash some two hundred of his canvasses rather than have them taken away by his creditors. In the same year, Cézanne (Shikes and Harper 1980, 70) submitted paintings to the *Salon,* one of them a portrait of Valabrègue. They were not accepted. Valabrègue later reported: "A philistine on the jury exclaimed on seeing my portrait that it was painted not only with a knife but with a pistol as well."

In 1871, Pissarro and Monet (Shikes and Harper 1980, 93), in an attempt to escape the continuous rejection handed out by the jury of the *Salon d'Automne,* submitted their paintings to the Royal Academy of England—and were promptly refused. Monet (Shikes and Harper 1980, 95f.) was so embittered by the continuous rebuff that he left for Holland "in complete discouragement."

In the summer of 1874, the Battignoles Group (Shikes and Harper 1980, 109f.), capitalizing on an idea conceived a decade earlier, organized their first *Salon des Indépendants.* Thirty artists, including Degas, Monet, Renoir, Sisley, Pissarro, and Cézanne, exhibited 165 paintings. Thirty-five hundred visitors attended the opening and displayed every form of aggression short of physical violence. The *Salon des Indépendants* was quickly dubbed "*Salon des Intransigeants*" (Saloon of the Unbending). Some conservative critics decided to punish the artists by ignoring them, others gave them a sound slating. In *Le Charivari,* Louis Leroy satirically labelled the artists "impressionists." The label stuck. Leroy invented a dialogue with a visitor who, put before Pissarro's *Ploughed Field,* exclaimed: "Those are furrows? That is hoar-frost? But those are palette-scrapings placed uniformly on a dirty canvas. It has neither head nor tail, neither top nor bottom, neither front nor back." In *Le Figaro,* the critic Albert Wolff (Shikes and Harper 1980, 132) derided the impressionist painters: ". . . lunatics . . . a frightening spectacle of human vanity gone astray to the point of madness . . ." Then Wolff zoomed in on Pissarro: "Try to make Monsieur Pissarro understand that trees are not violet, that the sky is not the colour of fresh butter, that in no country do we see the things he paints and that no intelligence can accept such aberrations."

All of those cumulated rejections hurt. But there were more to come. In December when the exhibition closed, each of the participants (Shikes and Harper 1980, 113f.) owed the Société des Indépendants 184.50 francs. To make matters worse, their main dealer Durand-Ruel suspended all payments to them. A worldwide economic depression in addition to the ferocious hostility of the Paris critics prevented him from further supporting the painters he loved. The critics' wrath did not subside. Even as late as 1895, when dealer Ambroise Vollard (Shikes and Harper 1980, 274) presented the first one-man show of Cézanne's work, *Le Journal des Artists* denounced the paintings as "atrocities in oil."

Artists were not only rejected by critics and the general public (manipulated by garrulous critics), they also played the rejection game among themselves. In a letter to his colleague Emile Bernard, Cézanne (Cézanne 1978, 63) wrote: "Gauguin was no painter, he produced nothing but Chinese images."

The rejection game among artists reached a new level of vituperation when Pablo Picasso entered the fray. His wife Françoise Gilot (Gilot and Lake 1991, 255) reports Picasso's sentence: "Bonnard is but a neo-impressionist, a decadent, a dusk, not a dawn." When Matisse (Gilot and Lake 1991, 181) got the commission to paint the design for Stravinsky's *Chant du Rossignol*, Picasso exclaimed: "What is a Matisse? A balcony with a big red flower pot falling over it." Talking about Jean Cocteau, Picasso (Stassinopoulos 1989, 186) told a journalist: "He is no poet. Rimbaud is the only one. Jean is only a journalist." Similarly he labelled (Stassinopoulos 1989, 306) the overweight writer Gertrude Stein a "hippopotamus" and to his interviewer James Lord, said about her: "She is as fat as a pig." Similarly, he called her life companion and lover Alice Toklas a "rhinoceros" because she wore bangs to cover her forehead, which—according to Picasso—was marred by a horny outgrowth. Picasso seems to have successfully repressed the memory of the crucial role Gertrude Stein had played in making him famous.

Little wonder that so aggressive a critic as Picasso should also become the target of rejection. Russian émigré Chagall told Mrs. Gilot (Gilot and Lake 1991, 265): "He is a genius, that Picasso. It's a pity that he doesn't create paintings." In 1917, Diaghilev (Stassinopolous 1989, 153) presented the ballet *Parade* with sets designed by Picasso, music by pianist and composer Eric Satie, and a scenario by Jean Cocteau. The première was hooted and booed by an outraged public. The critic of *La Grimace* wrote: "The inharmonious clown Eric Satie has composed his music on typewriters and rattlers . . . His accomplice, the dabbler Picasso, speculating on the eternal stupidity of mankind . . ." To one of these critics an enraged Satie sent a postcard with the following text: "*Monsieur et cher ami*, you are nothing but an asshole and an unmusical one at that."

There was one peer who never took anything that Picasso did as a painter seriously: Alberto Giacometti (Lord 1991, 11ff.), who holds a supreme position on the contemporary rating scale of great artists. Asked what he thought of the portraits Picasso had painted of Apollinaire, Max Jacob, and Stravinsky, he responded: "I detest them, they are vulgar." What about the portraits Picasso had made of Dora Maar? Giacometti (Lord 1991, 21) replied: "They are caricatures of van Gogh." Picasso (Lord 1991, 74) boasted: "Because I wasn't able to reach the top of the scale of values I've broken the scale." Giacometti's sardonic comment: "That doesn't mean a thing. It's like everything Picasso says. At first sight it seems quite ingenious, but in reality it is devoid of meaning."

Giacometti (Lord 1991, 74) had great respect for Cézanne's concept that all objects are spheres, cones, or cylinders, yet he found that cubism was a "stupid enterprise." He emphasized that after his cubist phase Picasso "tried to do Ingres . . . and after that van Gogh." In other words, Giacometti suggested that Picasso, having no sense of direction or solid orientation for an autonomous style, kept imitating other painters who had found their own, unique power of expression. Giacometti (Lord 1985, 325f.) understood that there was no evolution in Picasso's work, only a static hopping around on the same topic of masks: "That is why—without pursuing a single course of work to develop it—Picasso constantly changes his course. There is no progress in the world of objects. It is a closed world."

Giacometti's verdict is echoed by observations made by art critic John Berger (Stassinopoulos 1989, 411), who wrote about the total lack of creativity in Picasso's last period of life that resembled the last days of an aging vaudeville star. He stated rather sarcastically that Picasso was only happy when he could work but that, unfortunately he had no ideas to work on. Berger ended his slating review by stating that Picasso: ". . . takes up the themes of other painters' pictures . . . He decorates pots and plates that other men make for him. He is reduced to playing like a child." Berger added (Stassinopoulos 1989, 422) that Picasso was "condemned to paint with nothing to say."

Alberto Giacometti also had to battle rejection until eventually he was recognized for being a genius able to express himself in two media, painting and sculpture, with the same degree of conceptual depth and technical virtuosity. On December 9, 1934, at an exhibition of Giacometti's abstract sculptures in New York, a critic (Lord 1985, 153) of *The New York Times* confessed that for five minutes he had stared with a blank mind at his typwriter trying to find a statement or two about an abstract sculpture by Giacometti. And he patronized: "If you want the blunt truth of the matter, Mr. Giacometti's objects, as sculpture, strike me as being unqualifiedly silly."

Painter and sculptor Umberto Boccione (Boccione 1964, 52), a founding member of the Italian Futurist movement, dismissed Rodin's realistic sculptures as mere imitations of the sculptures created by Donatello and Michelangelo 400 years earlier. Similarly, Mondrian (Mondrian 1964, 125) rejected surrealism because "limited by individualism it cannot reach the foundation, the universal."

Heinrich Basedow (Whitford 1986, 68), a former disciple of the Bauhaus, dismissed its quality as a creative teaching institution stating that he had "been greatly stimulated but not having learned much." Then he added with condescension (Whitford 1986): "Gropius himself wallowed in his well-meaning, utopian ideas but the entire Bauhaus, apart from making propaganda, never actually did anything at all." In Basedow's view, the most famous members of the Bauhaus were "nothing more than the usual, even though modernistic, rootless painters." A similar rejection was formulated by a former staff member who, in 1920, accused Gropius (Whitford 1986, 44) of "breeding an artistic proletariat." Oskar Schlemmer (Whitford 1986, 49), an associate of the Bauhaus, criticized that there were no architectural classes at the Bauhaus and that none of the Bauhaus disciples tried to become an architec. Schlemmer wondered that: "At the same time the Bauhaus still stands for the idea of architecture's pre-eminence."

A still stronger rejection came on September 30, 1932 (Whitford 1986, 195f.), when the Dessau parliament decided to close down the Bauhaus. Basically, it accused the institution of warped thinking: the Bauhaus promoted an international architectural style rather than a style based upon German values; it was run by a Jewish crew; and it was infested with Bolshevik ideas because Kandinsky was one of the teachers. The Nazis considered the art taught at the Bauhaus as being degenerate because it was "one of the most obvious refugees of the Jewish-Marxist conception of 'art' . . . so far beyond all art that it can only be judged pathological." Nazi hooligans filled to the gills with an emotional brew called "*gesundes Volksempfinden*" ("sound attitude of the people") stormed the school; they broke doors and windows and threw files, tools, and furniture out on the street. Less than a year later on August 10, 1933, director Mies van der Rohe officially closed the school, indicating financial difficulties as the basic reason for his decision.

In 1995, the Russian poet and Nobel laureate Joseph Brodsky (Brodsky 1996, 1997) was a speaker at an annual International CREANDO Symposium on Creative Leadership. In a discussion about the impact of modernist architecture, he repeated what he had written in his book *Watermark* (Brodsky 1992, 17) published three years beforehand, and angrily condemned ". . . that scumbag of an architect, of that ghastly post-war persuasion that has done more harm to the European skyline than any Luftwaffe." His criticism was directed, of course, at epigones, which are the strongest argument against a master.

Frank Lloyd Wright (Gill 1987, 45) used to flout interior decorators as "inferior desecrators." However, he was not disturbed by the fact that his clients considered him to be an inferior designer of office furniture because people trying to sit on his chairs often tumbled to the floor. His response to complaints by his customers: imbalance maintains employees alert and keeps them from taking a discrete nap! DVD portraits and books on the architecture of Frank Lloyd Wright (Burns and Novick 1998; Severns and Mori 2005; A&E, 1996; Brooks Pfeiffer 2007) reveal that he also belonged to the guild of inferior desecrators. There is a stark contradiction between the exterior aspect of his elegantly designed buildings and some of their interiors whose jungle of decorative motifs is likely to provoke an asthma attack in individuals preferring the airiness of a more purist style.

In the middle of the twentieth century, Wright (Gill 1987, 221) got the commission to design the Masieri palazzino on the Canale Grande in Venice. The plans of his modernist design were heavily criticized by most who loved Venice and its unique Renaissance architecture. Hemingway, who used to stay at the Palazzo Gritti whenever he was in Venice but was living in Africa at the time, informed the press that he would rather see Venice burn than have it defaced by a house designed by Wright. Reporters wanted to know how the architect reacted to the famous writer's critique. Wright quipped: "Reaction? Why, none whatsoever. After all, that was nothing but a voice from the jungle."

Wright could not stand Le Corbusier or the architecture he produced. He derided Le Corbusier's Unité d'Habitation in Marseille (Gill 1987, 487) as the "Massacre on the waterfront." As Frampton (1987, 151) points out, that rejection was mutual. Another critic who despised Le Corbusier's architectural designs was writer Evelyn Waugh (Stannard 1987, 466). He stormed at Miss Reynolds from *Harper's* magazine for praising Le Corbusier's design: "Now that at last we are recovering from that swine-fever, the fashionable magazines take it up." Miffed, Miss Reynolds refused to publish his article on architecture.

Frank Lloyd Wright had continuous, and sometimes furious, fights with his clients because the building costs were invariably much higher than originally indicated. As his biographer Brendan Gill (1987, 148) writes with tongue-in-cheek: "He was always to be criticized for the fact that his arithmetic was at the mercy of his desire to create." Some of his clients refused to build the houses he proposed when they checked Wright's estimates and found that they were not realistic at all. Others built with Wright and were enraged to find that their roofs leaked and that building costs were exorbitant. For the leaking roofs, a veritable trademark of Wright's work, the wily architect had a particularly sophisticated excuse (Gill 1987, 270): ". . . the Gods will allow no creative effort of man's to go untested. The Japanese themselves believe them jealous, purposely leaving some glaring fault in a conspicuous place to placate them." And when the Hungarian painter and photographer László Moholy-Nagy (Gill 1987, 438) rejected the concept of a snail shell for the Guggenheim museum in Manhattan, Wright scoffed: "Moholy-Nagy has the nerve to suggest to us what a museum should be like? I never did respect him for brains."

French-American artist Marcel Duchamp (Richter 1961, 88f.) considered many of his contemporaries to be dabbling in a *créatitude* whose behavior and work was governed by the principle of pompous disguise. In response he assumed a radical counter-attitude. In 1913, critics of the New York art world alternatively described his painting *Nude Descending a Staircase* as an "explosion in a shingle factory" and a "masterpiece." In backlash, he invented ready-mades to poke fun at their masquerade as undisputed art experts. Duchamp exhibited a bicycle wheel mounted on a stool, a bottle rack, and a urinal as works of art, honouring the principle of pompous disguise by declaring that the objects were works of art because he had collected them in the context of a trash heap and placed them in the context of an art exhibition.

Duchamp's approach to art and art critics influenced Dadaist artists such as Jean Arp and Kurt Schwitters. The latter made his disdain for art critics amply clear (Richter 1965, 145f.) by stating: "He is a peculiar beast, the critic: a camel before and a window behind." Schwitters emphasized that critics are born, not made, having nothing to learn from experience: "The born critic, thanks to the exceptional sheepness of his wits, finds out exactly what it is not all about." Obviously Bert Brecht (Müller 1987, 29-30) located a similar lack of wits in his fellow writer Thomas Mann when he mused about how it was possible to write such thick books with so little talent. Similarly, and also with respect to Mann, the poet Peter Rümkorf wondered why so many people confused "so many stilted mannerisms" of Mann's with good style.

Let us now see how cultural evaluation produces rejection in the world of filmmaking.

Racial prejudice produced rejection that Ernst Lubitsch shared with celebrities such as tenor Richard Tauber, writer Emil Ludwig-Cohn, and actor and director Charlie Chaplin. According to legend (Eyman 1993, 15), Hitler hated Lubitsch and demanded that a blow-up of his face be mounted in the Berlin train station with a caption reading "The Archetypal Jew." In 1933, an anonymous article in the *Berlin Film Courier* slandered Lubitsch as "an amusingly low-grade entertainer; the sham who created dubious eroticism." After Hitler had become Chancellor, Lubitsch's movies were no longer shown in Germany. In 1940, *The Eternal Jew*, an insidious documentary directed by Fritz Hippler, denounced the "foreign Jew, the deadly enemy of [the German] race." The so-called "documentary" showing film clips with Peter Lorre playing a pedophiliac serial killer in Fritz Lang's film *M – Eine Stadt sucht einen Mörder*, suggested that Jews were depraved, pathologic creatures and a mortal danger for the superior Aryan race. Lubitsch's German citizenship (Eyman 1993, 232) was revoked on January 28, 1935. He and 207 other Russian and Polish Jews were deemed to be "dangerous to the state."

Lubitsch's first masterwork, the costume drama *Madame Du Barry* about the love life of King Louis XV's mistress was a success with audiences and critics when it was released in 1919. Later generations of critics, steeped in Marxist ideology, rejected Lubitsch's films because they neglected the historical, economic, and political context of a story while focusing uniquely on its hedonistic aspects. Critic Lotte Eisner (Eyman 1993, 63), who wrote for the *Cahiers du Cinéma*, emphasized that Lubitsch ignored the radical stance of contemporary plays like Büchner's *Danton's Death*. Indulging in the frivolous life of Madame Du Barry, his interest was "to portray events only as seen from the curtains of an alcove." And since young Ernst had once worked in his father's tailoring firm, she added maliciously that, for Lubitsch history was only a pretext for making films in period costumes because: "Silks and velvets attract the former draper's assistant and delight his connoisseur's eye at the same time as he seeks out the occasion to mingle melodrama and a love affair."

Siegfried Kracauer (Eyman 1993, 63), sociologist, critic, and scientific collaborator of the Museum of Modern Art in New York, went even further than Eisner. In his study *From Caligari to Hitler,* he maintained that Lubitsch's film comedies "sprang from the same nihilism as his historical dramas... The vogue [Lubitsch] helped to create originated in a blend of cynicism and melodramatic sentimentality . . . they characterized history as meaningless . . ."

A different kind of rejection came when *Madame Du Barry,* relabelled *Passion* for its U.S. release, and other German movies became the talk of the town in the United States. *Variety*, one of the messengers of the protectionist trade press, complained about the "dumping" of German films on American screens and about the danger that this influx would cause unemployment in Hollywood. In October 1921, a critic in the *Moving Picture World* (Eyman 1993, 75f.) lamented that most German dramatic features were: ". . . tainted by morbid sexual themes and shriekingly Teutonic in matter of casts... " And he surmised: "American public opinion would never tolerate things of this sort, even if they escaped the censors."

These anti-German feelings, to a certain extent leftovers of the First World War and the role the Germans had played in it, surfaced once more when in 1923, one year after he migrated to the United States, Lubitsch signed a contract with Hollywood star Mary Pickford to film an adaptation of *Faust*.

Lubitsch himself had little sympathy for the movies produced in Germany in the first two decades of the twentieth century. He soon rejected the drama genre and opted for comedies. As he sarcastically put it (Eyman 1993, 45), "the dramatic pictures of that time were so silly, it was much more honest to make comedies." Yet right-wingers rejected his humor, considering it to be a telltale of cultural degeneration.

In December 1926, Jim Tully, a novelist and freelance Hollywood reporter, wrote an unfavorable review in *Vanity Fair* (Eyman 1993, 129f.) disdaining Lubitsch as a director about to degrade into the fabrication of "frothy films for sophisticated chambermaids and cinema critics." Tully maintained that Lubitsch preferred to make yet another comedy instead of creating another *Passion*. To this condescending onslaught, Lubitsch replied facetiously: "Molière was content to do comedy. Chaplin is a genius—he does comedy." Tully was outraged: "Chaplin is merely a clever mimic, hardly to be compared with Molière." When Lubitsch tried to escape the sterile ping-pong match, Tully became downright insulting, denigrating Lubitsch: "Instead of being a great artist, he is merely a merchant like his father. But with this difference . . . his father did not deal in second-hand goods." History has proved Tully's virulent verdict about Lubitsch wrong. It seems that Tully ignored what insiders have known since the days of Aristophanes and Shakespeare: in theater and films, it is much easier to create a heavy drama or a terrible tragedy than to come up with a great comedy.

In 1937, the New York *World Telegram* called the Lubitsch comedy *Angel* with Marlene Dietrich in the main role a "brittle little comedy drama." More than half a century later, Lubitsch biographer Eyman (Eyman 1993, 255) has this to say about the director's attempt to move beyond "polished puppets" and delve into the emotional suffering of real people: "By any standard *Angel* is a failure, but it is nevertheless a key transitional work."

The following year Lubitsch's comedy *Bluebeard's Eighth Wife* (Eyman 1993, 259) with Claudette Colbert and Gary Cooper in the leading roles fared no better. *The New York Times'* critic condescendingly stated: ". . . it's not bad comedy by our current depressed standards . . . it has the dickens of a time trying to pass off Gary Cooper as a multi-marrying millionaire." The New York *Sun* conceded that the picture was "slim but funny." Even biographer Eyman (1993, 260) concedes, "It is the emptiest movie he ever made."

The flops that *Angel* and *Bluebeard's Eighth Wife* proved to be dealt Lubitsch a heavy blow. Lewis Jacob's book *The Rise of the American Film* (Eyman 1993, 262) only added insult to injury by insinuating that the latest Lubitsch pictures "show a significant loss of vitality and timeliness . . . his films seem static . . . his most recent films do not show that he is keeping abreast with the swiftly changing times." The book was widely read, its author respected. All of a sudden Lubitsch was deemed old-fashioned, a death sentence in a culture always feverishly celebrating whatever is young and new. One of the outcomes of so great a lack of success was the split between Paramount and Lubitsch who, during their ten-year collaboration, had written and directed thirteen movies which today are considered classics of film comedies.

In 1939, the Ernst Lubitsch/Ben Hecht movie *Design for Living* (Eyman 1993, 212) got mixed reviews. Richard Watts, Jr. wrote in the New York *Herald Tribune* that the film was even more superficial than Noël Coward's original theater comedy and that one of its stars commented: "You could hardly expect Mr. Cooper to be properly at home as a witty sophisticate, and I fear that he isn't." The misgivings Gary Cooper had had while reading the script were later confirmed in his acting.

To Be or Not to Be, released in 1942, turned out to be another a flop, rejected for similar reasons by critics and the public alike. The New York *Morning Telegraph* (Eyman 1993, 301) spurned the plot that set the Warsaw Ghetto as a place where a group of third-rate theater actors get involved with the Nazis, whom they ridicule. The *New York Times* called the movie "a callous comedy" and questioned: "Where is the point of contact between an utterly artificial plot and the anguish of a nation which is one of the great tragedies of our time?" The audiences were disdainful because three years before the film's release, Hitler had invaded Poland, massacred its population, and established the infamous Warsaw Ghetto. Lubitsch's movie seemed to poke fun at the suffering of a whole nation. The scoff by a Nazi about a bad actor playing *Hamlet*, "What he did to Shakespeare we are doing now to Poland," was ill received. Yet what neither the critics nor the general public had taken into account was the fact that Lubitsch was well aware of the brutality going on in Poland, being himself a Jew of Russian descent, persecuted by the Nazis, and forced to flee to the United States. Today the motion picture is a comedy classic; the Library of Congress has recognized its artistic and cultural value and selected it for preservation in the United States National Film Registry.

Lubitsch not only incurred rejection, he also dished it out whenever his sense of decency was offended. The great German actor, Emil Jannings, played the role of Czar Paul (Eyman 1993, 228) in the Lubitsch silent movie, *The Patriot*. The film won the Academy Award for Best Writing Achievement and several nominations: Best Actor in a Leading Role, Best Art Direction, Best Director, and Best Picture. Jannings' masterful performance met with worldwide acclaim both with the critics and the general public. Years later, Jannings asked the film director Joseph von Sternberg what he thought of his performance as Czar Paul. Von Sternberg snarled: "Shit!" Jannings reported that remark to Lubitsch, who wryly replied: "No man is a genius unless he can deliver honest entertainment." Lubitsch's remark came at a time when von Sternberg's movies with Marlene Dietrich had ceased to be box office hits.

Lubitsch was not the only insider who disliked von Sternberg, known for his arrogant and even insidious behavior and being capable of blocking all creativity in the actresses and actors who worked with him. Cesar Romero had played the male lead in von Sternberg's *The Devil is a Woman*. On one occasion he observed how von Sternberg forced female lead Dietrich to repeat "I love you" more than fifty times—until she broke out in tears. Romero later stated: "Von Sternberg was a son of a bitch." As time went by, the rejection von Sternberg was so eager to dish out provoked a crossfire feedback, terminating his Hollywood career once and for all. Marlene Dietrich, however, who had been humiliated in front of the whole cast, continued to be a star loved and admired worldwide by audiences and critics alike.

One comical anecdote relates how Lubitsch (Eyman 1993, 319f.) dealt with the macho showmanship of Darryl Zanuck, the almighty boss of Fox productions. One day, while working on *Heaven Can Wait*, Lubitsch, Zanuck, and a few other top executives were having lunch together. Zanuck, a pompous Mr. Know-it-all, pontificated: "I've seen the Louvre fifty times and I studied the *Mona Lisa* fifty times; and I have yet to see what's so great about the *Mona Lisa*." Everybody abided in respectful silence. Lubitsch, puffing on his ever-present cigar, quietly said: "There are three pictures I would like to have. One, I would like to have the *Mona Lisa*; two, I would like to have a picture of Darryl Zanuck looking at the *Mona Lisa*; three, I would like to have a picture of the *Mona Lisa* looking at Darryl Zanuck." The master of innuendo proved his courage and mordant wit able to deflate even a producer who had the power to fire him at whim.

Lubitsch and his master disciple Billy Wilder both abhorred camera gags and other artificial effects that had no organic function in a comedy or drama. Wilder (Eyman 1993, 257) rejected experimental shenanigans—for instance a film with no cuts in it or Hitchcock's *Rope*, with only ten setups and a single location—as "exercises in masturbation" and claimed that Lubitsch would have hated such cheap tricks.

At times, rejection came wholesale in the movie industry. In October 1923, New York playwright Edwin Justus Mayer (Eyman 1993, 292) wrote a scathing article in *The New York Times* lambasting Hollywood as "the abode of prosperous failure . . . the retreat of intellectual beachcombers . . . the first refuge of a scoundrel . . . the capital of defeat . . . and outlet of stereotyped forms and sentimental postures." Little did he know that one day his tirade would return to haunt him: Mayer ended up as a Hollywood screenwriter collaborating in forty-seven films for thirty-two years.

French actor Jean Gabin (Eyman 1993, 327) once confessed: "I don't like opera. It's stupid. Nobody sings when he's dying." Unlike Mayer, he did not have to atone for his wholesale rejection by playing opera roles for the rest of his days.

Many silent movie stars were unable to make the transition to the talkies. There were several reasons for the end of their careers. Some stars had squeaking voices; others did not seem to understand that the grimacing and over-acting demanded in silent movies had to be replaced by more moderate interpretation. For directors, the main challenge was that sound movies called not only for convincing plots driving the whole action forward, but also for dialogues increasing the sophistication and entertainment value of films. Charlie Chaplin had celebrated huge triumphs during the silent movie era when his films such as *The Tramp* and *Gold Rush* made him a celebrity all over the globe. In those halcyon days he was his own producer, director, scriptwriter, composer, and starring actor. Yet when he began to write scripts for his sound movies things changed. Billy Wilder (Karasek 1992a, 291), a competent critic, rejected Chaplin's dialogues as flat and banal and emphasized that Chaplin had no relation whatsoever to good literature. Wilder also found that Chaplin speaking his own texts often sounded "like an eight-year-old boy fabricating verses for Beethoven's Ninth Symphony."

In 1951, Wilder created *Ace in the Hole* (Karasek 1992a, 377), the first film in which he was sole writer, director, and producer. The drama won an Academy Award nomination for best story and screenplay, but did not take the Oscar. It bombed with American critics and audiences precisely because of the story dealing with a journalist whose cynical behavior was perceived as amoral and "un-American." In the film, the journalist risks the life of a man trapped in a cave where he was digging for Indian artefacts. In an attempt to save his declining career, the egocentric press writer ruthlessly manipulates the rescue teams and hinders their progress with all kinds of tricks so he can write sensational articles about the dramatic situation—until it is too late. In a literal last-ditch effort, the guilt-ridden journalist tries to rescue the man on his own but fails; the trapped victim dies. The film was better received by critics in Europe. It was nominated for the Golden Lion at the Biennale in Venice, and Billy Wilder received an International Award. Today the picture ranks as a classic.

One of Wilder's romantic comedies, *Kiss Me, Stupid*—the story of two small-town, aspiring songwriters—provoked a huge scandal when it was released in 1964 (Karasek 1992a, 454). In the film, when playboy crooner Dino (parodied by Dean Martin himself) shows up by chance in the wannabes' quaint little town, they engage the services of Polly the Pistol—a beautiful hooker living and operating in a downtrodden trailer—to support their schemes. Due to the unexpected twists of fate occurring in every screwball comedy, the wife of one of the contrivers, who is pathologically jealous, ends up at Polly's place in Dino's arms. The movie caused uproar. If the Hays Office, which ruled the censorship guidelines governing U.S. motion picture production, accepted it, it was immediately rebuked by the Catholic Legion of Decency who gave it a "C" (condemned) rating. *Life* rejected the movie as a "gigantic hogwash." The *New Yorker, New York Daily News, Hollywood Citizens News*, and *Time* all severely lambasted the film in similar terms. Although stunned by such heated rejection, Wilder never lost his sense of humor. To an enraged lady who had written a furious article about the movie, he responded that, having read her article while sitting in a beauty saloon under a hairdryer, he, an "old pornographer," had very much enjoyed her effusion. He signed his missile, "Cheers, Billy Wilder." The course of public moral indignation, however, soon turned and the film was awarded a Golden Lion at the Biennale in Venice. Six years after its release, *Kiss Me, Stupid* was attributed a PG-rating, making it accessible to all age groups.

Another Wilder film *The Private Life of Sherlock Holmes* released in 1970 originally lasted three-and-a-half hours. Film distributor United Artists demanded that it be cut. Wilder (Karasek 1992a, 472) complied, eliminated more than an hour and commented ironically: "Everything is too long, with the exception of one's own life and penis." Despite the cuts the film was no success; shunned by critics and audiences alike, it soon disappeared from the movie theaters. That rejection, however, was eventually replaced by an official rehabilitation: *Halliwell's Film Guide*, first published in 1977, classes the film as a three-star opus.

To wrap up this section on the rejection of new films with a smile, let us have a look at a few funny rejections.

According to Billy Wilder (Karasek 1992a, 20), film mogul Samuel Goldwyn thusly commented Laurence Olivier's performance in *Hamlet*: "I saw *Hamlet* last night. It's full of quotations."

Billy Wilder (Karasek 1992a, 358) had quite a reputation for his courage and sardonic wit. Here are two beautiful examples of what these two character traits were capable of. After the premiere of *Sunset Boulevard*, an infuriated Louis B. Mayer waited for Wilder in the lobby of the movie theater. Mayer roared that Wilder was a bastard who had bitten the hand that fed him and denigrated the whole film industry. He ended his eruption with the proposition that Wilder should be tarred and feathered and driven out of town. Wilder's reply to the incensed mogul was unequivocal: "Fuck you!"

Darryl Zanuck had refused Joseph L. Mankiewicz the last-cut right for *Cleopatra* (Karasek 1992a, 358). When he offered Billy Wilder the opportunity to direct a film for Fox, Wilder wrote back: "Dear Darryl! The sooner the bulldozers raze your studio to the ground, the better for the film industry!"

Humphrey Bogart, who had worked with Wilder in *Casablanca* and *Sabrina*, denounced the director as belonging to the category of the "Prussian dictator with a heavy accent and a horsewhip in his hand." Wilder's friend William Holden (Karasek 1992a, 327) once described him as "a mind full of razor blades." Knowing how Wilder dealt with film moguls Louis B. Mayer and Darryl Zanuck, we can readily believe Holden's characterization. At times Wilder even used these blades to shave his own beard of narcissism. He once confessed to an interviewer (Karasek 1992a, 446) that he had arrived at the "sad conviction that, after *Apartment*, I never again created anything really worthwhile. I'm disappointed in myself."

Wilder's razor-sharp wit could also cut deep into the flesh whenever he applied it to the evaluation of somebody else's accomplishment. He found Barry Levinson's gangster movie *Bugsy* (Karasek 1992a, 493) "over-directed" because he did not appreciate the director's antics, which only flattered his ego without serving the story. About *Bugsy*'s male star Warren Beatty he scoffed: "Evidently he plays the role of a women's hairdresser much better than the role of a macho gangster."

Jazz music and its highly creative artists have often been the target of ferocious rejection, racial slurs included. The main reasons for this rejection are rooted in the demographic, economic, political, and sociocultural environment in which jazz was composed and played. There was yet another reason for rejection: the subculture of jazz itself was highly competitive, focusing on continuous experimentation with new and more sophisticated rhythms, melody lines, harmonies, playing techniques, and combinations of instrument players and vocalists. The trumpeter, composer, and bandleader Terry Clark was a speaker at the 2001 International Symposium on Creative Leadership. He expressed the free spirit of experimentation as we discussed the interplay of trial and error in the creative process: "In Jazz you can't play a wrong note; if you don't like a particular note then the only relevant question is: what is the next note you play? If you choose well, then everything falls into place again."

Jazz underwent a very radical change in the 1940s when its leading artists (Gioia 1998, 205)—Charlie Parker for one—were no longer contented with their role as entertainers; their ambition was to become highly creative leaders in their professional field. Due to the sheer novelty of their approach and its fast and often dramatic development, audiences were at times more than challenged to adjust to these rapid and radical changes. As the French composer Edgar Varèse (Gleason 1995, 142) put it: "An artist is never ahead of his time but most people are far behind theirs." The fabulous pianist and space-time architect Thelonius Monk (Fitterling 1997, 82) shared that conviction: "I say, play your own way. Don't play what the public wants. You play what you want to play and let the public pick up on what you're doing—even if it does take them fifteen, twenty years."

The triple fact that jazz music was born in New Orleans (a city in decline by the end of the nineteenth century), that its cradle was rocked in a red-light district, and that its controverisal black father Buddy Bolden (an aggressive drinker and lunatic) died in a mental asylum made jazz music a prime candidate for rejection by White Protestant Puritanism. Racial prejudice was still so extreme in the first half of the last century that every single black musician suffered from it. In Europe the great black jazz musicians—Louis Armstrong, Sidney Bechet, Charlie Parker, Dizzie Gillespie, and Miles Davis, to name only a few—were celebrated as superstars. Yet as soon as they returned to their native country, they became targets of scorn and abuse. In the segregated South, they were not permitted to sleep in hotels, eat in restaurants, and drink in bars where white patrons held sway. Even in Harlem's Cotton Club, a place where whites and blacks mingled in the audience, the musicians who entertained them were forced to use the back entrance to get on stage.

Within the community of black musicians, however, ferocious competition and macho displays also produced their share of rejection. When trombonist Zue Robertson found his own way of playing a piece of music that pianist and bandleader Jelly Roll Morton had composed, the latter drew a gun and placed it on top of the piano; his way of dealing with rejection produced the desired compliance. A similar incident is reported about young alto sax player Charlie Parker (Gioia 1998, 206). One day he was playing in a jam session run by Jo Jones, the drummer in Count Basie's band. As Parker had trouble keeping up with the tempo, Jones reached for a cymbal and sent it slicing through the air. It crashed at Parker's feet, and the humiliated young musician had to quit in the midst of the bystanders' derisive laughter. Young Dizzie Gillespie (Gioia 1998, 210) prided himself in being the best young trumpeter around Cheraw, South Carolina, although at the time he could only play in one key. His dreams of early fame were shattered when a local trumpeter returned to Cheraw and met the young contender in a cutting contest. That musician started playing in the key of C and Gillespie couldn't find one single note on his trumpet. Gillespie later confessed: "I felt so crushed, I cried, because I was supposed to be the town's best trumpet player."

By then jazz musicians, participating in what has been called the Great Migration, had already moved up North where they found temporary gigs in various dance halls, cabarets, bars, and other places. Between 1908 and 1922, some of the best musicians left New Orleans (Gioia 1998, 45) and headed for better pastures in Kansas City, Chicago, New York, and elsewhere; among them were Jelly Roll Morton, Sidney Bechet, King Oliver, Kid Ory, Johnny Dodds, Baby Dodds, and Louis Armstrong. The invasion of their music had an alarming effect on the guardian spirits protecting the gates of propriety against the influx of Southern barbarians. In the December 1921 issue of *Ladies' Home Journal* (Gleason 1995, 11), the headline read: UNSPEAKABLE JAZZ MUST GO, and jazz was denigrated (pun intended!) as "jungle music." Yet it was not only the WASP culture (Gioia 1998, 200) that rejected the creatures emerging from the jungle. Aspiring members of the black middle class were eager to adapt to the taste and lifestyle of the white community rather than be reminded of their own ethnic and cultural roots.

Sometimes rejection was offered rather jokingly. Banjo player Eddie Condon (Gioia 1998, 78), also known as the founding father of Chicago jazz, once said about a mediocre bandleader: "He made the clarinet talk and it usually said 'please put me back in my case.'" About an incompetent vocalist he jeered: "He once tried to carry a tune across the street and broke both legs." Usually rejection was of a more aggressive sort and able to trigger a counter-rejection in kind. One evening in a nightclub in San Francisco, female singer Carmen "the Queen" McRae (Gleason 1995, 120) was interrupted by a noisy client. She leaned over the microphone and threatened: "Either you're coming up here or I'm going down there!"

Clarinettist Pee Wee Russell (Gioia 1998, 80) had a style of playing that was derided by critic Leonard Feather as being "half B flat, half saliva." He likened Russell's phrasing to "the stammering of woman scared by ghost." Historian, novelist, and jazz critic Nat Hentoff (Gioia 1998, 80) wrote about Russell: "Much of the time, his sound was astringent as if it had taken a long time to find its way out of that long contorted body and was rather exasperated at the rigor of the journey."

In 1941, Duke Ellington chose the prestigious Carnegie Hall in New York as a stage for the première of his ambitious composition *Black, Brown and Beige*. In the *New York Herald Tribune* music critic Paul Bowles (Gioia 1998, 189f.) protested adamantly the bold attempt to ennoble black slave music: "The whole attempt to fuse jazz as a form with art music should be discouraged." In 1965, Duke Ellington (Gleason 1995, 156) suffered an offensive rejection, possibly influenced by racial prejudice. That year the Pulitzer Prize committee was expected to give the Duke a special award in music, but decided not to hand out any award at all in that category. The decision was not unanimous, and two members of the committee walked out in dissent. The sixty-six-year-old Ellington took the decision with a grain of salt: "Fate is being kind to me. Fate doesn't want me to be too famous too young."

Louis Armstrong once suffered a rejection that was due to racial prejudice only. In 1923, after having been celebrated as a star during a triumphant tour in Europe, Armstrong (Gleason 1995, 4) took part in a street parade in New Orleans. After the parade he and his band went to the Suburban Gardens to play music that was to be broadcast. The white announcer took the microphone to introduce the great trumpeter but suddenly turned away exclaiming, "I haven't got the heart to introduce that nigger!"

Cutting contests, as they were known, were originally developed in the realm of stride piano (also called New York ragtime) where, as Gioia (1998, 98) puts it, "a macho, competitive ethos" reigned supreme. These contests of rejection and counter-rejection were social rituals whose merciless competition established hierarchies of status and prestige among the contenders. The rituals were executed while a crowd of connoisseurs watched and listened not only with excitement, but also with a very critical mind. Duke Ellington described how top stride pianist Willie the Lion Smith treated an aspirant to the throne who was ill suited for the ambitions he was hedging. His competitor had a weak left hand and Lion Smith taunted him: "What's the matter, are you a cripple?" Then: "When did you break your left arm?" And finally: "Get up, I will show you how it's supposed to go." To lose such a cutting contest was to lose one's standing with peers and the jazz fans in the audience. Count Basie (Gioia 1998, 99) recalls in his autobiography how he once lost a cutting contest and described his opponent:" He had a left hand like everybody else had a right hand . . . And he dethroned me. Took my crown!"

One of the titans of stride piano was Art Tatum, who hailed from Toledo, Ohio. When the Harlem masters of stride piano—Fats Waller, James P. Johnson, and Willie the Lion Smith—heard that Tatum had arrived in New York, they immediately set up a cutting contest. Each of the competitors gave his best, fighting one round after the other. Art Tatum (Gioia 1998, 103), first caressing sweet arpeggios with his right hand only to blast away with both hands like a whole brass band, won every single round and went on to take the overall contest. His defeated opponent, Johnson, later stated: "When Tatum played *Tea for Two* that night, I guess that was the first time I ever heard it really *played*."

The competitive macho ethos mentioned above is illustrated by the aristocratic titles many jazz musicians paraded with: King, Prince, Duke, Baron, Count, President, Sir; the women's titles included Empress, Queen, and Lady. Musicians and vocalists ennobled with such names were treated like superstars by audiences and usually enjoyed the privileges that came with their status. Yet not every superstar really enjoyed that status, for the special rights it implied also brought on cumbersome duties. A case in point is the King of Clarinet, Artie Shaw (Gioia 1998, 148), who was married eight times—among others to film stars Ava Gardner and Lana Turner. He hated his role as a bandleader, which went far beyond that of a clarinet virtuoso. Nor was he willing to cope with audiences always soliciting him to play his most famous tunes *Begin the Beguine*, for instance. To the never-ending regret of his fans, he eventually rejected both roles and quit the music business altogether.

There are times when the rituals of rejection change scales and reach a higher dimension. This occurred in jazz when the waves of change altered the predilection of the public and with it whole music styles. Under these circumstances representatives of the old style lost their jobs, while the top players of the new style ascended the ladder of success. In the 1930s the end of prohibition wiped out thousands of speakeasies all over the United States. People began to drink at home and listen to the radio, and big band swing replaced the more intimate combos of the New Orleans style jazz. In the 1940s, bebop rebels dethroned swing and put it out of business; as Gioia (1998, 193) points out, in December 1946 alone, eight major swing orchestras disbanded. At first bebop was rejected by great artists whose competence was widely respected. Cab Calloway (Gioia 1998, 217) derided it as "Chinese music." Louis Armstrong scoffed: ". . . all of them weird chords which don't mean nothing . . . you got no melody to remember and no beat to dance to." Benny Goodman accused bebop players of "just faking." And *Down Beat* published a photo showing the traditional cornet player Doc Evans holding a mock funeral for bebop.

In the late 1940s, cool jazz began to seriously compete with bebop. Apart from Stan Getz, Gerry Mulligan, and the Modern Jazz Quartet, Miles Davis was the most innovative leader in the field. Yet he had to fight rejection because his style was too much to chew for audiences and critics. As Davis (Gioia 1998, 293) later confessed: "The club owners just froze me out. Wasn't no gigs happening for me." Davis (Carr 1999, 199f.) did not mince his words when he put down other musicians whose music he did not like. In 1964, the critic Leonard Feather played him a composition by avant-garde musician Eric Dolphy, and Miles angrily spluttered: "That's got to be Eric Dolphy—nobody else could sound that bad!" Feather then played a piece by pianist Cecil Taylor, and Davis jeered: "Is that what the critics are digging? Them critics better stop having coffee. If there ain't nothing to listen to, they might as well admit it." As to the music of Archie Shepp (Carr 1999, 215), he sneered: "No matter how long you listen to it, it doesn't sound any good . . . and people will go for it—especially white people. They go for anything ridiculous like that."

In 1983, twenty-one-year-old trumpeter Wynton Marsalis (Carr 1999, 435f.) bragged in an interview in *Jazz Times* magazine about his vast knowledge of music as he put down Miles Davis. He maintained that Davis gave the whole jazz scene a bad name and that Charlie Parker would "roll over in his grave if he knew what was going on." Picking Davis apart, Marsalis claimed that Davis first imitated Fats Navarro, Clark Terry, Louis Armstrong, Thelonious Monk and Dizzy Gillespie—and he jeered: "Then he sits up and talks about how he listens to Journey and Frank Sinatra. He's just co-signing white boys, just tomming." The "white boys" in question were white saxophonists and guitarists Miles had hired for his band. His reaction to the insults from the trigger-happy young gunslinger? "When he started hitting on me in the press, at first it surprised me and then it made me mad." Davis, who like John Coltrane was always evolving towards new forms of expression, attacked Marsalis' futile attempt to bring jazz music back to its historical roots: "Nostalgia, shit! That's a pitiful concept. Because it's dead, it's safe—that's what that shit is about!" On another occasion (Carr 1999, 465), when Marsalis sought to join Miles Davis on stage, the latter flatly told him to leave; when he didn't follow suite, Davis stopped his band and waited until a humiliated Marsalis had no choice but to trot off.

In the 1960s, free jazz signalled yet another period of revolutionary changes. One of its pacemakers was Ornette Coleman (Gioia 1998, 340). Like every true creative leader, he had to battle rejection. Miles Davis taunted: "Hell, just listen to what he writes and how he plays . . . the man is all screwed up inside." One critic (Gioia 1998, 344) derided Coleman's music by quoting Shakespeare: ". . . sound and fury signifying nothing." But such disdainful disqualification was mild compared to another form of rejection he had received years before in Baton Rouge by a group of thugs. Waiting for him outside a dance hall, they beat him up until he had lost consciousness. The reason behind such brutality was that Coleman's tenor sax solo had stopped the dancers in their tracks.

Another pacemaker of free jazz was poet, composer, and pianist Cecil Taylor (Gioia 1998, 349). In contradistinction to the self-taught Coleman, he had an exhaustive musical education involving not only the study of all the giants of jazz history but also of classical composers such as Igor Stravinsky and Béla Bartók. So unique was his revolutionary approach that he was rejected by critics, the audience, and club owners alike. He once confessed: "Gigs for me have been mostly, like a concert a year, filled in with one or two short nightclub or coffeehouse gigs." To support himself, Taylor had to work as a dishwasher and short-order cook. As Gleason (1995, 150) reports, saxophonists Albert Ayler and Archie Shepp plus pianist Cecil Taylor—three creative leaders of free jazz—were not invited to play at the Monterey Jazz Festival because ". . . such decisions are reached by people in control who are actually not interested in art at all."

On the rock scene, which boomed in the 1960s and soon conquered the planet, rejection and counter-rejection were staged as fiercely as on the jazz scene. The fact that a lot of the leading musicians were into heavy drugs influenced the whole game—as is happening, by the way, on the current rap scene.

At the June 1967 rock festival of Monterey, Janis Joplin appeared as the lead singer of Big Brother and the Holding Company. She was an immediate success. Evolving into a star, she was eager to meet the expectations of audiences, critics, and the media and so she adopted a wild public persona clad in gaudy clothes and accessories—including strings of beads and long, multicolored feathers in her hair. Gulping her ever-present bottle of Southern Comfort on stage, she would indulge, off and on, in her drug addiction ranging from barbiturates to tranquillizers and from amphetamines to heroin. Ill equipped to deal properly with recognition, she was not at all equipped to cope with rejection.

Jon Landau (Friedman 1974, 157), a music critic for *Rolling Stone* magazine, scoffed at her performance at the Newport Festival: "Her melodrama, overstatement and coarseness are not virtues. They are signs of a lack of sophistication and a lack of security with her material." He claimed that Big Brother and the Holding Company was "truly lame . . . the band drags her at every turn." Her second album *Cheap Thrills* (Friedman 1974, 166) released in 1967 was a financial success; nevertheless critics tore to pieces its artistic quality. They derided Janis and her band as a "minstrel show" and accused her of not being "original" but an imitator: "instead of black face, she uses black voice."

On October 4, 1970, Janis Joplin died from an accidental overdose of heroin—less than three weeks after Jimi Hendrix had met the same fate. In July 1971, Jim Morrison, lead singer of The Doors, would also die under the same circumstances. None of the three rock stars had reached the age of thirty. As different as they were in their personalities, they had a few characteristics in common. All were rebels against a post-war society grown stale in its prejudices and petrified in its traditional role expectations. In order to deal with the stress inherent to their rebellion and society's answer to it, they sought freedom in the ecstasies offered by hard drugs—only to find themselves caged in and shackled by their addiction. Jimi Hendrix, the most creative of the three artists, was also the most aggressive. He often worked the strings of his guitar with his teeth and ended many a concert by smashing his instrument to pieces and burning it on a pyre on stage.

The most famous and most creative rock musician of the swinging 1960s was Bob Dylan. While he knew many successes in his long career, he also had to deal continuously with all kinds of rejection. As the musician Dave Van Ronk (Sounes 2001, 84) stated about Dylan's debut in New York: "Nobody wanted to hire Bobby. He was too raw." The young guitarist, harmonica player, and singer from Duluth, Minnesota just did not look the part he wanted to play. His scraggy figure and the yet untrained, nasal, and often shrill voice irritated many music fans. Both Folk Way records and Vanguard refused to sign with him. When folk musician Izzy Young agreed to share the stage with Dylan at the Carnegie Chapter Hall, only fifty-two people showed up (Sounes 2001, 106). Yet as Young observed, Dylan ". . . took it pretty straight."

Things began to change when Dylan composed and delivered the song *Blowin' in the Wind*, today a classic of the post-war era. But at the time, his peers at the Folk Scene rejected the song for various reasons. Dave Van Ronk (Sounes 2001, 114) found it dumb. Pete Seeger, the self-appointed high priest of folksong, claimed that it was "a little easy." Singer-songwriter Tom Paxton sneered: "I hate the song myself. It's what I call a grocery-list song where one line has absolutely no relevance to the next line." *Blowin' in the Wind* survived the assaults to become one of the most popular and admired songs of all times.

On May 12, 1963 (Sounes 2001, 130), Dylan was invited to appear on *The Ed Sullivan Show*. During rehearsals he sang his *Talkin' John Birch Paranoid Blues*, whose lyrics stated that the members of the John Birch Society admired Adolf Hitler. The managers of the show asked him to perform another song. He refused, preferring to leave the prestigious TV show rather than give in to repression.

In 1963, Bob Dylan performed at the Monterey Folk Festival with folksinger Joan Baez, who already had a solid reputation. The critic and later cofounder of *Rolling Stone* magazine, Ralph J. Gleason (Sounes 2001, 150), derided Bob as yet "another New York Jew imitating Woody Guthrie." Gleason would soon regret his rejection and radically change his evaluation of Dylan.

At the 1964 Newport Folk Festival, Dylan premiered his song, *Mr. Tambourine Man* to which the audience responded with enthusiasm. Other songs of his, however, were less welcome as the festival was dedicated to protest songs, then very much in vogue. After the festival, Irwin Silver (Sounes 2001, 160) the editor of *Sing Out!* wrote an open letter to Dylan stating: "I saw at Newport how you had somehow lost contact with people." He pointed out that Bob had collected an entourage of drinking buddies and that his songs were self-indulgent as well as full of sentimentality and unnecessary cruelty.

A very strong wave of rejection hit Dylan during and following the Newport Folk Festival in July 1965. Folk singer Pete Seeger (Sounes 2001, 181f.) introduced the event and emphasized that from then on—just after the United States Marines' ground offensive against North Vietnam—the festival was to be dedicated to social issues and anti-war protest songs. Dylan could have cared less about the context as defined by Seeger. His electrically amplified band threw itself into a roaring version of *Maggie's Farm* that had nothing to do with anti-war protest songs or other connected social issues. The sound mix was awful, the volume too loud. Pete Seeger later stated: "I was absolutely screaming mad. You couldn't understand a goddam word of what they were singing." For many attendants in the audience, an electric guitar was capitalism incarnate rather than a symbol of protest against the war in Vietnam. While Seeger was allegedly backstage trying to cut the cables with an axe and restraining his urge to smash Dylan's electric guitar, Peter Yarrow of the very successful folk trio Peter, Paul and Mary did his best to appease the enraged audience. Backstage, Dylan was stunned and "visibly shaken" by the experience.

In 1979, Dylan (Sounes 2001, 324ff.) quite unexpectedly converted to Christianity and began to compose songs with a spiritual message. In November

1979, he began a two-week performance at the Fox Warfield, an old Vaudeville-type theater in San Francisco, where he and his band were booed every night. The *San Francisco Examiner* was merciless: BORN AGAIN DYLAN BOMBS. As for the *San Francisco Chronicle*, it rebuffed BOB DYLAN'S GOD-AW-FUL GOSPEL. When the crowd again hooted him in Tempe, Arizona, an angry Dylan told them to piss off and attend a concert by the group Kiss, whose members poked out their tongues through their black-and-white facial masks. He added that there they could "rock'n'roll all the way down to the pit!"

The protest against his religious conversion and his new gospel-oriented songs did not abate. Keith Richards (Sounes 2001, 335), Rolling Stones guitarist, dubbed Dylan the "prophet of profit." Rockabilly singer Ronnie Hawkins, whose band The Hawks had worked years before with Dylan, met him on April 20, 1980 when Dylan's concert tour took him to Toronto. He provoked Bob: "After this sells a few, you are gonna be an atheist and sell to all them cats who don't believe nothing." Dylan was not amused at all; his mood worsened when his Christianity-inspired album *Saved* did not do well financially and his concert audiences began to dwindle.

As late as 1986, the release of his new album *Knocked Out Loaded* suffered the drawbacks of the public rejection of his religious conversion. Since his Columbia debut twenty-five years earlier, none of his albums had been as low on the charts. In autumn 1987, Dylan (Sounes 2001, 383) was once again on a world tour. At a concert in London he looked overweight, his face was bloated, and he seemed disinterested in the audience and in what he was doing. After the concert, foremost British rock promoter Harvey Goldsmith told him bluntly, "What you played today was crap." The following year Dylan released the album *Down in the Groove*; it sold even worse than *Knocked Out Loaded*. The decline of his audiences continued although he engaged support groups such as Santana, The Heartbreakers, and The Grateful Dead. It was during a concert in Locarno, Switzerland that he had an epiphany: people came to see *him*, the legendary singer-songwriter, and not his support groups. If he was to retrieve his former success, he had to build up his own little band and play again as he had done during his best years. And that is exactly what he did.

In the course of history, many important exponents of Western classical music have been attacked by colleagues, employers, and other official or self-appointed critics.

When father Leopold Mozart took his two child prodigies Nannerl and Amadeus on a European trip to show them off at the courts of major cities, they also travelled to Paris. On January 1, 1674, they were invited to Versailles and Amadeus (Boorstin 1992, 449) was the center of adulation. Madame de Pompadour, King Louis XV's mistress, however, remained aloof, conspicuous in her lack of interest for the little boy. He responded to her rejection by stating provocatively: "The Empress kisses me. Who is this that does not want to kiss me?" Later his employer Colloredo, Archbishop of Salzburg, showed little respect for the cheeky composer and pianist and relegated him to the servants' instead of inviting Amadeus to share his meals with his Eminence. Amadeus hated him for this humiliation and in 1781, he quit the archbishop's services, but not without taking a last blow. In Amadeus's (Boorstin 1992, 450) own words, his resignation was confirmed "with a kick on my arse . . . by order of our worthy Prince Archbishop."

In July 1791, the last year of his life, Mozart was commissioned to write an *opera seria* for the coronation of Emperor Leopold II in Prague (Solomon 1996, 485f). When it premiered, Empress Maria Luisa who (like her husband) preferred Italian style opera condemned Mozart's German style opera as "*porcheria tedesca*" (German swinery). In a letter she scoffed: "The Gala opera was not much and the music very bad so that almost all of us fell asleep."

In 1794, Ludwig van Beethoven took lessons from Joseph Haydn but the two musicians did not get along well at all. Haydn suggested that Beethoven include the subtitle "Pupil of Haydn" in his first publications, which Beethoven refused to do. Although he did dedicate his first three piano sonatas to Haydn (Boorstin 1992, 456), he emphasized that he had "never learned anything" from him.

In March 1853, Giuseppe Verdi's (Boorstin 1992, 472) opera *La Traviata* premièred at the Teatro La Fenice in Venice and was booed off the stage. Soon thereafter it was celebrated in London, Paris, New York, and St. Petersburg. Today it belongs to the basic repertoire of every major concert hall in the world.

Conductor Bruno Walter (Walter 1988, 120) writes in his autobiography that his friend the composer and conductor Gustav Mahler was for a long time "as undiscovered as the South Pole." Critics denounced Mahler's compositions as an eclectic mix of folk and classical music, an incongruous potpourri of components that did not fit together.

In 1912, Diaghilev's ballet *L'Après-midi d'un Faune* with music by Claude Debussy and choreography by Vaslav Nijinsky provoked a scandal. Viewers (Boorstin 1992, 493) felt offended by the explicit eroticism of Diaghilev's production and let their rejection be heard. The following year, Diaghilev produced Stravinsky's *The Rite of Spring*. It premièred on May 29 with the audience hissing, bellowing, and angrily catcalling in response to the dissonance of the music and Nijinsky's agitated movements. A critic later punned the performance *Le Massacre* (instead of *Sacre*) *du Printemps* (the Massacre of Spring). Today both ballets belong to the mainstay of ballet productions.

Opera composer Gioacchino Rossini (Weeks 1999, 95) stated: "With Wagner you have got beautiful moments, but awful quarter hours." Tchaikovsky (Weeks

1999, 90) confided to his diary: ". . . that scoundrel Brahms. What an untalented bastard!" Dictator Stalin (Weeks 1999, 118), the undisputed master in every single domain of communist Russia, enraged over Shostakovich's *Lady Macbeth von Mzensk,* dictated the editorial of the Pravda that declared: "Confusion instead of music." In 1946, Stalin's camarilla (Boorstin 1992, 509) denounced Shostakovich, who had just created his *Ninth Symphony,* as ". . . an artist without a fatherland and without confidence in advanced ideas."

In 1971, Leonard Bernstein's (Burton 1994, 407) *Mass—A Theatre Piece for Singers, Players and Dancers,* had its premiere. Harold Schonberg, critic of *The New York Times,* gave it a slashing review, deriding "a combination of superficiality and pretentiousness, and the greatest mélange of styles since the ladies' magazine recipe for steak fried in peanut butter and marshmallow sauce."

As the conductor of a philharmonic orchestra, Leonard Bernstein's rather theatrical antics on the podium did little to endear him to critically-minded music lovers. Winthrop Sargeant, former violinist in the Philharmonic turned music critic at the *New Yorker* (Burton 1994, 321), chastised Bernstein's histrionics when conducting a Mahler symphony, scorning the conductor's "fencing, hula-dancing and calling upon the heavens to witness his agonies. I care about Mahler's agonies but I do not care a bit about Mr. Bernstein's." Similarly, a critic from the *Daily Express* (Burton 1994, 311) mocked: "He swayed, stabbed, crouched and leaped in the air, both feet clear of the ground several times, like a pocket-sized Tarzan." Virgil Thomson (Burton 1994, 169) sneered at the "chorybantic choreography" and "the miming of facial expressions of uncontrollable states." Even more sarcastic was a critic in Toledo, Ohio, who considered Bernstein (Burton 1994, 311) to be a charlatan: "He cajoles, he grimaces, he hams outrageously . . . a most profligate waste."

At times critics, sponsors, and the general public join ranks in expressing their total rejection of a new musical composition. According to Burton (1994, 342), the Boston audience attending a concert of John Cage's experimental composition *Music of Chance* in 1964 booed "in some of the noisiest scenes ever witnessed at a Philharmonic concert." As a composer, conductor Bernstein fared no better. In March 1948, Aaron Copland (Burton 1994, 173), whose compositions Bernstein admired, wrote a devastating critique in the *New York Times* that opened: "At its worst, Bernstein's music is conductor's music—eclectic in style and facile in inspiration."

Nikita Khrushchev, notorious for his emotional outbursts, once had a headstrong encounter with sculptor Ernst Iosifovich Neizvestny. In 1962, at the Moscow Manege exhibition (Berger 1969, 83), Khrushchev attacked the sculptor's work as being "degenerative art" and asked him why he disfigured the faces of Soviet citizens. Neizvestny, unimpressed by the attack, replied: "You may be Premier and Chairman but here in front of my works I am Premier and we shall discuss as equals." Two bodyguards seized the sculptor's arm, but unrelenting, he sneered: "You are talking to a man who is perfectly capable of killing himself at any moment. Your threats mean nothing to me." It seems that Khrushchev was quite impressed by the artist's courage. When he died, his family asked the sculptor to build a tomb for the former Soviet leader.

In the world of acting, high-pitched drama is the order of the day. Emotions and words are often expressed in superlatives and tirades; high volume sounds may be shrill; and mimics and gesticulation often prefer maximal amplitudes to the more discreet ones. Critics may be ruthless in their endeavor to make a kill. When theater and film actress Glenda Jackson (Woodward 1986, 237ff.) played Cleopatra in a Peter Brook production in Stratford-on-Avon, a critic of the *Los Angeles Times* coldly stated: "Despite her cheekbones and tigerish grace she never looks a voluptuous, seductive temptress." In *London's Daily Mail* another critic ridiculed her walk ". . . which unfortunately has the suburban waddle of a housewife rushing to the supermarket before it closes." Having been the target of much rejection throughout her career, Glenda Jackson (Woodward 1986, 55) felt continuously insecure. Would she get a next role? If so, would she be a failure in it? Talking about the stress between her engagements, she confessed: "If that goes on for long enough, you get a sense that if you're not in work, you'll never work again; and I don't think I'll ever lose that threat hanging over me."

In the United States, Constantin Stanislavski's method of teaching actors how to act was adopted by Robert Lewis, Harold Clurman, and Lee Strasberg. They soon went their separate ways. Under the influence of Strasberg, Stanislavski's approach—which came to be known as *The Method*—relied more and more on the analysis of an actor's inner states and on speculations about the origin and "true meaning" of his emotions. Analysis of the script, the roles to be played, and their specific function within the whole play were often neglected. Robert Lewis (Lewis 1984, 190) later wrote in his autobiography: "Strasberg's overemphasis on emotion, at the expense of other elements of the craft, had a limiting effect on the style of much American acting." Lewis (1984, 281) denounced "this onanistic school of emotion" with the sarcastic remark: "If crying were the sole object of acting, my Aunt Rivka would have been Duse."

Playwright Arthur Miller (Miller 1987, 420), who was married to Marilyn Monroe, described in some detail how *The Method* of the Actors Studio ruined Marilyn's natural talent. Referring to Paula Strasberg, Lee's second wife and Marilyn's coach, Miller wrote in his autobiography that Marilyn ". . . was being doused by a spurious intellection that was thoroughly useless to her as an acting tool, like a born jazz player being taught to rationalize what he instinctively knows how to do." He stated that Paula was "hip to the Method and knew when to nod sagely as though she understood." Her tutelage only served to fetter Marilyn's natural joyousness and spontaneity, leading the star into depression and paralysing her instinctive acting skills.

Miller's pleas for a change in procedure bore no fruit. Eventually he decided to visit the guru himself in order to remedy the problem. Instead of finding an authentic personality with a solid conceptual view and proper sense of aesthetics, what he came across was a dude posing as a Sunday rancher. Miller (1987, 479) ironically describes the fateful meeting. Miller rang and Strasberg opened the door. Lee's costume made Miller speechless: ". . . in this hundred-degree weather he was dressed in a stiff brand-new cowboy outfit—shiny boots, creased pants, ironed shirt with braided pockets and cuffs—but with the same whitish intellectual face and unexercised body."

In his autobiography, Peter Ustinov (Ustinov 1977, 112f.) also criticizes Lee Strasberg's approach to acting. He does not consider it particularly useful, since much of the straw thrashed in the den of endless discussions does not yield the grain necessary for feeding the meat of great acting. According to Ustinov Strasberg's approach made actors come up with absurd ideas about how to play a specific scene. Thus they kept: ". . . doing incomprehensible things with an aura of self-satisfaction and even authority, which not unnaturally tends to alienate the audience."

The Norwegian actress Liv Ullmann (Ullmann 1995, 188f.) lived many years together with Swedish film director Ingmar Bergmann; the couple had a daughter. In the years with Bergmann, Liv had countless opportunities to meet, watch, and work with great actresses and actors. Later, when the duo separated, she went to live and work in the United States. There she also met colleagues trained in *The Method* and was not overwhelmed by what she saw. In 1994, Liv was invited to be a speaker at the International CREANDO Symposium dedicated to the topic *Imagination and Creativity*. In a discussion I asked her about the experiences she had had with Strasberg's method of acting. She replied: "Actors Studio has ruined many actors." While she attributed to Stanislavski that he was "a brilliant, talented, incredible visionary," she also emphasized that in the hands of his epigones the Stanislavski approach had "degenerated." She recalled that once, on Broadway, she had played Nora in Ibsen's play *A Doll's House*. In one scene the doorbell rang. The housemaid went to receive a caller and bring her on stage. But during the many rehearsals, the maid and the caller never appeared as expected, and Nora and the audience were kept waiting. What lay behind the time lapse? In fact the maid and the caller always acted out what Liv Ullmann characterized as an "Actors Studio-Happening" in order to get their emotions right. They pretended that they had once known each other and that now the housemaid, on opening the door, was amazed to see how Miss

Linde, the visitor, had aged. The maid pulls her into the light to have a closer look at her face, and Miss Linde is ashamed of the fact that she has aged so much. The whole scenario took place in the wings, where nobody could see the two actresses. Meanwhile on stage, Nora was waiting, waiting, and still waiting. . . The sheer silliness of that "out-of-the-pot-plot" is amazing. Not amazing at all, however, is the fact that the unwarranted corridor scene took so long that it completely broke the rhythm of the play.

In operas, such silliness sometimes occurs on the open stage rather than in the privacy of a dark corridor. Conductor Arturo Toscanini (Sachs 1995, 164), who loved Wagner's music, once raged, "Listen to *Siegfried*: You can imagine the leaves rustling in the trees. Then look at the stage: a tree painted on paper. It's ridiculous!" Toscanini scoffed: "In the music there's genius; on the stage you have fat and clumsy singers. It's a travesty!" Toscanini seems to have had more than one emotional outburst while attending an opera performance. At a rehearsal of Alban Berg's *Lulu* (Sachs 1995, 295) at the Teatro La Fenice in Venice, somebody told young Giorgio Strehler (later to become the renowned director of La Scala in Milan) to go and meet Toscanini. As Strehler approached Toscanini's loge, he heard the maestro cursing the music and its composer. Strehler turned on his heels and left. Little wonder that composer and conductor Pierre Boulez (Lewis 1984, 202) once sarcastically demanded: "Bomb the opera houses!"

German theater director Jürgen Flimm (Kässens and Gronius 1987, 31) reports that the writer and Nobel laureate Günter Grass wrote a political diary in the *Süddeutsche Zeitung*. On one occasion, Grass rode a nasty attack on theater director Heinar Kipphardt, which "damaged him to his very death." Now why would Grass do such a thing? Kipphardt supported the anti-Vietnam-war movement and was, moreover, part of a German theater movement, which included Rolf Hochhuth and Peter Weiss. Their declared aim was to write about the guilt feelings connected with the suppressed collective memory of the Nazi atrocities committed under the Third Reich. The collective suppression of memories in which the German theater played a specific role is illustrated, for instance, by the fact that Günter Gründgens—a favorite actor of the Hitler regime years supposed to have entertained close relationships with leading Nazi figures—continued his career after the end of the Second World War. He even became a general director at leading theaters in Düsseldorf and Hamburg, where he strongly influenced the official predilection and taste with respect to topics discussed, plays staged, and actors and actresses put into, or kept off, the limelight. As Flimm (Kässens and Gronius 1987, 46) puts it: "The gentlemen Gründgens and Co. made a theatre which hadn't worked off fascism at all; theirs was a reactionary aesthetics with fascistic remnants. You can prove that."

Two of the leading German theater directors and producers were Erwin Piscator and Bert Brecht. Both were representatives of the epic theater and very much interested in the sociopolitical aspects of the plays they staged. In 1933, Piscator fled to Russia to escape the Hitler regime and in 1939 migrated to the United States. McCarthyism, however, forced him to return to West Berlin where he was appointed manager and director of the Freie Volksbühne in 1951. Similarly Bert Brecht, a convinced Marxist, migrated in 1933 to Denmark, in 1939 to Stockholm, and in 1941 to the United States. Due to his Marxist ideology, he was blacklisted in the Hollywood studios. In 1947 during the McCarthy trials, he was summoned to testify in Washington. The very next day he left for Switzerland, and in 1949 travelled to East Berlin where eventually he got his own theater and directed the *Berlin Ensemble*. Theater director Hansgünther Heyme (Kässens and Gronius 1987, 50), who worked for many years with Piscator and also knew Brecht, reports a dispute between the two who seemed unable to agree on anything. While Brecht favored entertainment and the seduction of the public, Piscator found these aspects of the epic theater rather irrelevant. Brecht was a wily operator who managed to have the critics and the public always on his side, whereas Piscator's life was made hellish by the massive rejections he had to deal with. To this day, German theater directors have not found a proper synthesis of the two distinct views embraced by Brecht and Piscator. Nor have they found an independent pathway leading to an authentic and autonomous modern theater. As the celebrated director Claus Peymann (Kässens and Gronius 1987, 131) put it a few years ago in an interview: "When I look at the theatre in the Bundesrepublik, then I see the same amorphous cheese. Most of the theatres still hibernate."

In 1956, the premiere of John Osborne's play *Look Back in Anger* met with a lot of rejection. One critic (Tynan 1987, 173) advised that the "back street Hamlet" should be "ducked in a horse pond or sentenced to a lifetime of cleaning latrines." In contrast, critic Ken Tynan, who was feared for his sharp tongue, warmly embraced the play that was to change the English theater scene forever (Tynan 1987, 173): "I doubt if I could love anyone who did not wish to see *Look Back in Anger*." Yet while he loved Osborne's harsh realism describing the aimlessly drifting way of life of three young people, Tynan (1987, 233) despised escapist plays and thundered against Broadway's "intricate, stunningly resourceful and brilliantly manned machine for the large-scale utterance of carefully garnished banalities."

In the film industry, rejection comes from all sides. Producers reject the ideas of directors and film editors; directors reject scripts, actors, and actresses, or at least the way in which the latter act out a given scene; critics reject the movies produced and so does the general public. In Hollywood's film industry, countless scriptwriters have suffered from having their scripts snubbed. A typical case is that of William Faulkner, who had been shackled to Warner Brothers by a seven-year contract that made him a slave of the whimsies of other writers, not to mention directors and producers. Faulkner's biographer Stephen B. Oates (1988, 138) writes that usually the final screenplay was impersonal without the stamp of a creative individual. And he emphasizes that joint screenwriting was a torture for a creative artist such as Faulkner: ". . . who needed to work in solitude, to follow his singular vision and inspiration, and to produce something uniquely his own." Movie mogul Jack Warner (Oates 1988, 190) felt nothing but disdain for writers and gibed: "You're all schmucks with Underwoods." Suffering from this rejection, needing the money to support his wife Estelle (a heavy drinker), and daughter, Faulkner fought with depression and would go on drinking binges that often lasted for days or weeks. Such a highly stressful life is emphasized by director Billy Wilder (Der Spiegel 2002, 196), who admitted, "I've become a movie director because I couldn't stand having my scripts ruined any longer."

Life indeed has its serious and sometimes tragic aspects, but happily also its share of absurd events. I should like to finish our section on rejection with two rather diverting anecdotes illustrating how some individuals may react to rejection.

In 1925, young Evelyn Waugh (Stannard 1987, 113), rich in grandiloquence but poor in terms of success, sent the first chapters of his novel *The Temple* to a friend for review and commentary. The reply was sobering: "Too English for my exotic taste. Too much nid-nodding over port." Totally downcast, Waugh, who had already contemplated suicide, decided to end his life. Desirous of departing in style he looked up a Euripides quote, wrote it down on a piece of paper, went to the beach, took off his clothes, put the note on top of the pile, and waded into the water to drown himself. But as his biographer writes with a smile, "He swam into a shoal of jellyfish and was stung back to reason." In his dramatic attempt to reject life and seek out death, Waugh had been rejected by death and whipped back to life by a school of jellyfish!

Another, rather grotesque form of over-adjustment to adverse circumstances is reported with respect to a great philosopher and luminary of the late Age of Enlightenment. On July 9, 1788, the Prussian pastor and minister of justice Johann Christoph von Wöllner released an official *Religionsedikt*. This edict of the fierce enemy of liberal thinking—whom King Friedrich II had once called "a cunning and scheming parson"—prohibited all criticism of the church. Immanuel Kant (Der Spiegel 2007, 150) was ordered explicitly not to deal with the topic of Christian religion any longer. The great philosopher meekly responded: "*Ich ersterbe in devotestem Gehorsam*—I die in most devote obedience."

Excerpts from an interview with Ashok Kurien (15)

Ashok Kurien talks to the interviewer about his creative efforts that were continuously rejected by a boss who headed the ad agency in which he was employed; but the man seems to have been a pathological case. All in all, Ashok Kurien has experienced little rejection of his creative work. Still, he recounts two examples of rejection—the second of which was not devoid of irony. He did an ad for a brand of sneakers called Tuffs. In the interview he made a pun saying that the Tuffs case was a tough case for him. In both cases—the first one, a TV show where sexual topics were discussed, and the second one, a print media advertisement using nude models and causing a public uproar—the rejection was engineered by politicians eager to project a hypocritical image as protectors of virtue.

The following sections take up where Ashok Kurien remembers the boss and the rejections he dished out.

GG: Have you other examples where the environment rejected the results of your creative efforts? Have you been attacked in the media, on the radio, in TV talk shows for instance?

AK: Yes. Zee TV did a show called *Chakravyuh*. It was the first time sex and love affairs were openly discussed; in the cultural context of India it just wasn't done, and there was a lot of protest. People used to say, "How can you talk about things like that? How do you discuss that in public? We don't even discuss it with our families. Our children watch that show!" Our opinion was, "But these are things you should be discussing with your families! These are things you should discuss around your dining table!" Their response was, "No, in our culture we just don't do this."

GG: Who attacked you?

AK: Oh, the media attacked. Sometimes the people attacked. The women attacked.

GG: Did priests attack you?

AK: Well, maybe some association of some religious body did.

GG: Did politicians attack you?

AK: Oh yes, always! There's always somebody who will attack. Anyone who creates radical change has to pay the price of attack. If you are the prime mover, you pay the price.

GG: Yes, that's an experience as old as mankind. So you discussed marital problems on that show, sexual problems.

AK: Yes, and we brought eunuchs on stage. Do you know what a eunuch is?

GG: Yes, at the court of the Chinese emperors all boys who were not members of the imperial family used to be castrated.

AK: There is some old Hindu custom which I don't quite understand in India where they take boys and cut their genitals and offer them to the gods. Those men become eunuchs and dress like women and beg on the streets. But they are auspicious at the time of childbirth and at weddings. At any rate we actually brought some of them on our TV shows. I remember a lot of people saying, "What on earth are you doing?" But the first person always pays the price. The government attacked us. The government didn't attack the second person. The government didn't attack the third person. They attacked us because we were the first to threaten their monopoly. We threatened their power to communicate with the whole country.

GG: Did they reject only your ideas or did they reject only you as a person? Did they insinuate that you might be a creepy kind of human being?

AK: Yes, that happened to me with an advertisement we did eleven years ago for a pair of sneakers. We had a very famous male model who is a bit of a movie star now, and a very beautiful woman who had once been Miss India and was his fiancée at the time. We had them standing naked together, holding each other, and you couldn't see any critical portion of the body except the side profile of the buttocks. They had a genuine python wrapped around them like Adam and Eve.

GG: Was the couple wearing new sneakers?

AK: They were wearing the new sneakers and right under the picture in small letters one could read, "Nice shoes, eh?"

GG: You were heavily attacked for THAT?

AK: I was crazy enough to run that ad.

GG: On TV?

AK: In print.

GG: Please tell me more about it.

AK: We ran big, full-page ads in magazines and papers. The next day the minister for human relationships waves a paper in Parliament of the state of Maharasthra shouting, "Look at the evil that is going on in this country. Look at this!" The two models also happened to be Brahmins, the high caste of Maharashtrians, from Bombay, so they were local people. That added fuel to the fire. By the afternoon hundreds of women, politically motivated by this guy, were standing in front of my office and the homes of the two photo models, burning copies of the magazines and papers.

GG: Were they brandishing posters?

AK: Oh yes, they had posters, and the media was covering the whole story.

GG: Did they say you are the incarnation of the devil or what?

AK: Yes, the whole bit. The next day I get a call telling me that I am going to be arrested together with the whole team who had worked on the project. So I had to say I was the creative director, that I had thought of it, that I owned the company because I didn't want to have my whole office injured. But I couldn't say I was the photographer, too. So I told the photographer, "Listen, I'll take care of you. But tomorrow you and I and the two models are going to be picked up." All the media were there with cameras, the whole lot, because we engineered through some connections to make sure that we were publicly taken in. Once we were in, we just had a cup of tea and they said, "Okay, you are under arrest." Somebody paid some bail, and a little while later, when the crowd disappeared, we were allowed to go home. But publicly we had to be arrested.

GG: Justice was done.

AK: Justice was done. And there was a case by the public and the government against me for the indecent exposure and humiliation of women.

GG: What about the naked man?

AK: There is nothing that says "humiliation of men."

GG: So there is no indecent exposure of men.

AK: No, but I wanted to pose those questions. Then I also had a case from the forest department, because the python is a protected species. I hired the top lawyers and paid them huge amounts of money to make sure that nothing happened to me. So we go to court and the judge says, "They are standing and having sex." I reply, "It's a very difficult position to... you can't stand and...." The judge responds, "How can I believe you? Who would know?"

GG: It's not described in the Kamasutra!

AK: No, you can't stand like that and have sex; you would have to be built very differently. With two people of different heights, it doesn't work. The man is taller, she is shorter. You can't stand straight upright and... We thought the python should also be present because it was involved in the case. Maybe they wanted to ask it whether the two people were having sex. Anyway, I made this big joke about it but they didn't think it was funny. My office closed down for three or four days, and my mother was deeply hurt by the assumption that her son was a pornographer, because all the papers wrote about me as a pornographer.

GG: Quite a story!

AK: My case is treated under the Pornography Act. I had just opened my own ad agency, and this was the beginning of my business: pornography! Yet the ad took the award for the best single ad in India that year, and it won in the New York festivals. The case is still going on eleven years later because I vowed to fight it, defending my right to individual expression because the ad is a work of art. The court doesn't want to hear the case. Every time it comes up, they insist we all go, so every few months we have to go to the court or send a lawyer.

GG: But there is no session?

AK: Yes there is, and if we don't attend it, they issue an arrest warrant to bring us there. So we have to cancel the warrant and appear in the following hearing because the new judge wants to say, "Yes, Milind Soman, Madhu Sapre," and he'll look at the picture, look at her and say, "You did it." And then he looks at the photographer and says, "You are the photographer." He looks at me and says, "You are the creator." Then he adds, "Very good, now we must open this case." And then nothing happens, because they know they can't win. One judge came in and started the session off saying, "All of you should be put in jail." He is a judge, saying this! So I immediately took it to the high court and kept it in there until the judge was changed. Then we took it back to the lower courts because the high court threw it out saying that the lower court should decide. So I have spent tons of money, and for many years I was quite embarrassed and pretty tarnished because people kept saying, "Nobody else but Kurien would do this." In the whole advertising industry only one madman would do this.

GG: But was there a social ostracism towards you; did people move away from you?

AK: No, only my mother, but she was distant from me anyway.

GG: Yes, she apparently was. Tell me, what did the rejection do to the sneakers? Did they sell well?

AK: Every pair of sneakers sold out.

GG: So it was a successful campaign – although it only appeared once.

AK: Very successful, and everybody knew it, because the picture of the ad appeared in other newspapers. Every newspaper reproduced the ad and then the court put a ban on it under the pretext, "You can't publish things like that." So now no one is allowed to carry pictures of the ad.

GG: What about the politician who mobilized the mob against you?

AK: The sneakers were called Tuffs, and that ad was a tough case for me. It was frightening when mobs of people came together, and this was a local affair.

GG: How many people would be in front of your office at worst?

AK: There'd be a crowd of fifty to a hundred people outside the models' homes. Madhu Sapre's mother would call me saying, "What have you done to my daughter? Now nobody will ever marry her!" After the incident nobody wanted to use her as a model anymore because she was associated with this story. So it ruined her career, and she and her fiancé broke up.

GG: That's what some politicians are able to do.

AK: She lost her fiancé, money, her image. But now she is married to an Italian ice-cream maker and she is very happy.

GG: Does he produce a lot of ice cream?

AK: He produces a lot of ice cream!

GG: So she is rich, too?

AK: She is rich, too.

GG: Then all's well that ends well![13]

NOTES

1. Greek μορφή = form, structure, gestalt
2. Apelles of Kos (fourth century BC) was a famous Greek painter.
3. The *doelen* was the building that housed all the commissioned paintings.
4. The term "classical music" as a synonym for a specific form of European traditional music is a Eurocentric misnomer. In the course of time, many a sophisticated culture has developed its own music—from Balinese gamelan to Indian Raga, Persian Mugam, Andalusian Flamenco, and African-American jazz—which fully deserve the epithet "classical."
5. French: *maquis* = a thick scrubby underbrush
6. George Ivanovich Gurdjieff was a Greek-Armenian spiritual teacher, a guru with a large following who, at one time, was a star in France.
7. *The Father*, a play by Strindberg published in 1887
8. French: *fumiste* = pretender, obscene talker
9. Zotal = well-known brand of insecticide.
10. Lat. *mundus* = world
11. Diophantus was a Greek mathematician who lived in the third century BC and is also known as "the father of algebra."
12. Trans-scalar phenomenon = a phenomenon observable across various scales of magnitude, sometimes from the microscopic to the macroscopic and even to the cosmic realm.
13. In December 2009 a judge closed the case. The verdict? The ad had been "obscene" but not "pornographic".

2.5 STAGE IV: MORPHO-EVOLUTION
AND MORPHO-ELIMINATION

Arrogance feeds upon ignorance. It is easier to forget the great creative accomplishments of our ancestors than to honor and celebrate them.

Gottlieb Guntern

Inspired by their own creative achievements, individuals and communities aspire to scale greater heights of excellence. Motivated by their example, others are encouraged and drawn into the world of creativity. Thus the spinning wheel of creative leadership keeps turning until major events such as—war, natural catastrophes, epidemics, gradual sociocultural decline, death—bring it to a standstill.

Throughout the present book, we have seen countless examples of how the spinning wheel of creative leadership functions. We have investigated how cultural evaluation eventually recognizes or rejects the results of creative efforts. If it recognizes their value, they enter a process of morpho-evolution, making way for fresh creative ventures in the same genre or in some other genre. If it rejects them, they fall prey to a process of morpho-elimination, subjecting the results of creative achievements to oblivion or physical destruction.

Excerpts from an interview with Ashok Kurien (16)

Ashok Kurien offers his Zee TV venture as an example of a creative morpho-evolution that he triggered. He mentions the Tuff ad that produced a blend of morpho-evolution and morpho-elimination.

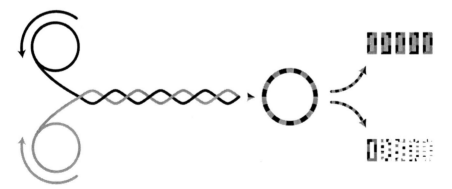

Figure 2.17.   Stage IV: Morpho-Evolution and Morpho-Elimination.

We move on to the creative achievements of Indian culture and how they have influenced the creative morpho-evolution in other parts of the world. In the course of the millennia Indian culture was highly ingenious; in many domains it was a pacemaker of creative morpho-evolution. India's creativity was temporarily blocked by the many invaders who entered the subcontinent, exploiting its population and its many natural resources. Conquerors—from the Mughal Dynasties right up to the British colonizers—hewed a trail of destruction that left its scars not only on the material possessions of the continent but also on the self-confidence of its population. Over the years India has recovered and begun a new strange loop of creative morpho-evolution. Once more it has become a pacesetter of valuable progress, the positive impact of which is felt all over the world. Ashok Kurien is, of course, proud of this turn of events.

GG: Having discussed cultural selection ending with the recognition or rejection of the results of creative achievements, let's move one step further. As a creative achievement is recognized for its true worth by the cultural selection of society, in all probability that recognition will act as an inspiration and motivation for other individuals and groups to emulate that feat of excellence. If you produce a great ad, people will imitate you and try to come up with something similar giving credence to the universal sentiment that imitation is the best tribute to excellence; at times your creative achievement may even inspire and motivate creative pursuits in a completely different professional domain. I call that process of inspiration and motivation leading to new creative accomplishment a "morpho-evolution," from the Greek *Morphê* meaning form, Gestalt, structure, something that has been made. Morphé is a general term for the result of an achievement. Could you provide me with an example from your own experience? Is there a case where your creative achievement has encouraged subsequent creative achievements in your own professional domain or in an altogether different genre?

AK: I once did a couple of projects with a team of eight different people. Two went wrong because I had the wrong partner. Other projects succeeded in which I had some equity. They were successful and they created a momentum. There is an American expression in gambling, "You're on a roll." I win, so I double the money and I go back. Then I double the money again. My luck is there now, so while I'm on the roll, I keep going. I think if you have two failures that roll stops. So that's how it goes. We were the first to enter the market with the direct-to-home dish TV. Now we've got a competitor who is Tata Sky; Rupert Murdoch is in. Now the Ambanis are in. The Bharati group is in. Five of the biggest groups in India have all launched this year because they've all said, "Wow, what a pop! What a pile! Look at the size of it and look how profitably this business is running!"

GG: This is an example where your achievement has inspired and motivated other achievements in the same domain; it illustrates how morpho-evolution works.

AK: Right. Our success made people sit up and see the opportunity in their domain. They said, "You have demonstrated that Mount Everest can be climbed. And if you have demonstrated that Mount Everest can be climbed, then we can all climb Mount Everest because we all want to share in that glory."

GG: Did your Tuff sneaker campaign stimulate similar campaigns by other agencies?

AK: The Tuff sneaker campaign completely reversed things. If someone was going to show a plunging neckline, they immediately made it high. Nobody took any chances after that for many, many years. Even today, the moment any creative person does anything which looks like our ad with the couple and the python, his boss will say, "Are you mad? Do you want me to go to jail? No way!" We were prime movers; we took the risk; we pushed the ladder; we went further than anyone else, and we paid the price for it.

GG: So the Tuff case is an illustration of how morpho-elimination works. Still, the ad won you much acclaim in the international mass media. And it won awards, for instance in the New York Arts Festival.

AK: Yes, we made global news. The ad appeared in *Time* magazine, *Newsweek*, BBC. It appeared in magazines around the world, and what made news was the public's reaction: "Hey, here's a beautiful ad but these guys went to jail for it." Then we won the top award in India for that idea. This was one of Elsie's finest pieces of work.

GG: How did India have the courage to give you the top award when a judge had declared that what you had done was bad?

AK: Creative people make creative judgements; but a judge has to make legal judgements.

GG: Didn't the jury risk being accused of promoting "anti-moral" advertising if they gave you an award for that ad?

AK: No, because there's safety in numbers. When twenty people are in a jury and vote, they know the police are not going to arrest twenty people for giving an award to an ad. But when one guy goes out and does something, he runs a risk. Doing things by yourself is always more dangerous than doing things in a group.

GG: Could you give me examples of other people's creative accomplishments that were recognized by cultural selection and then stimulated further creative achievements in the same line of work?

AK: Globally, there are trends. If someone does an ad for Nike, which says, "Just do it!" in a particular style, it inspires copycats around the world who'll try and do ads in exactly that way. Any great global advertising campaign immediately stimulates copycats. Honda did an ad where a little ball bearing rolls down a slanted surface and hits a part of the car; then that part rolls on and hits another part of the car. The process continues until a rolling part hits the starter and the cart starts. Very brilliant!

Nike did television advertising that set trends which hundreds of other ad agencies imitated. Coca-Cola never did great ads; Pepsi always did. Budweiser beer ran ads with frogs that talked. After that ad agencies produced goats that talked and cows that talked and monkeys that talked and everything that talked!

GG: A Swiss ad agency once produced cows that played football. That TV spot was quite successful.

AK: Yet another follower…

GG: Can you give me examples of cultural recognition in one specific field triggering creative performance in a different field?

AK: People use styles of art, and I use that in advertising. I can't immediately think of a particular one, but there are lots of ads for wine. The background is often painted like a van Gogh. But I think the biggest inspiration for advertising very often is a small snippet from a movie. When you watch a ten-second sequence from a film, you can pull it out and modify it and duplicate it and it lends itself to a product.

GG: At the end of the movie *Casablanca* Humphrey Bogart and a French policeman move through the fog towards an aeroplane. The French policeman says, "I think this is the beginning of a wonderful friendship." I have seen that sequence with similar figures – a man in a trench coat and a police officer – somewhere in ads. This might be an example of reproductive morpho-evolution and not creative morpho-evolution because no genuine creativity was involved there.

AK: Yes, I've seen that in an ad, and there are many such things.

GG: Let's now move from your individual experience to your culture. You are an Indian. In your view, what were the most important creative achievements of Indian culture? What has India offered the world? Which of her contributions do you admire most? What fostered the creativity of the great Indian culture? What blocked it at times?

AK: What was India's major contribution in terms of creative achievements, what fostered them, who tried to block them, and why were they blocked? Let me see. If you remember, I talked about the Vedic system of education. Fundamentally, the 6,000 year-old system put children into a Vedic school, where from ages six to twelve they were taught everything; but, more important, they were observed: their sleeping habits, their eating habits, their attitudes and their responses. This helped the teachers to categorize them; it showed what kind of performance the children were good at. They found that individuals who went to bed earlier, slept fewer hours and woke up at sunrise—which in eastern India is at 4 or 5 o'clock in the morning—were the thinkers. They also found that they couldn't be beaten into learning anything; they couldn't be pressured. They had to be intellectually challenged with a mental task. These children ate less meat and probably less food on the whole—they were more vegetarian—and would never get physically provoked into a battle; but they could be motivated by a mental challenge. That group of boys were categorized as Satviks. At the age of twelve, the boys were separated and trained to be teachers, scientists, artists, poets and priests. The educators figured that this personality type was ideal for a thinking world. The advantage of the Vedic approach was that educators discovered what type of personality you were and taught you what was already inherent in you. They didn't waste their time trying to teach you what wasn't inherent in your potential. So a student didn't struggle with learning; he was involved with what came to him naturally, with what he was good at. In other words, those educators created extremely productive students.

Similarly, there was another group of boys called Rajas. They were physically or commercially aggressive. In both cases they were eager to win. These were youngsters who were born into competing and winning. They tended to eat more meat, they tended to need more sleep, they were physically stronger. So either they went into sports or they became warriors or battlers; or they entered commercial competition and became merchants, traders or ministers responsible for financial matters. Unlike the Satviks, Rajas were challenged by competitors; they had to fight against other people.

And then there were what they called the Tamas — we'd probably call them couch potatoes today — who only responded to the rod; they responded only to orders and fear. So society was actually demarcated into four distinct personality and capability types who were educated in what they were good at. For the boy who was commercially inclined, for instance, it wasn't studying anymore: he just loved what he was doing! The warrior loved what he was doing! The scientist loved what he was doing! The priest loved what he was doing! The poor Tamas had no choice. They'd get whacked and be told, "Stage one is this, stage two is this, stage three is this, stage four is this." Exactly what is taught at McDonald's school – and also at MBA school.

GG: Absolutely.

AK: So it's actually the Tamas who followed...

GG: ...schemes, rules and sanctions.

AK: That's it! I couldn't put it better: schemes, rules and sanctions. Today we call it "process," but in those days they were the lowest of the low because they had to be led. They couldn't be leaders. So I think the Vedic education system is one of the hugest contributions of Indian culture. This was something which must have taken hundreds of years to evolve; hundreds of years of study, of people watching and learning, and it just got destroyed. It was destroyed because of human greed, because parents wanted their children to take after them. It became hereditary; because of the insecurity of losing something we had. And to a great extent, the British contributed to this. I may be wrong, but Lord Macaulay made a statement about the Indian education system which said something to the effect of: "We have to break that system of education and bring in the British system and make them believe that it is superior. Until then we will never dominate this country." So they imposed the white man's method of education and made Indians believe – even today – that it is the better method. "As long as they believe that, they will look up to us and they will feel inferior." Now, just look at the power of that thought in those words! It's amazing: India had water management, from Mohenjadaro and Harappa long before the Roman aqueducts were built.

GG: Your culture is five thousand years old, so your water management must have been invented about three thousand years ago?

AK: Yes, and we had town planning; we had textiles, silks, cottons. We had iron furnaces; the oldest one found dates from 800 B.C., I think. In the third century B.C. King Ashoka erected a series of stone pillars across the Northern Indian continent. His edicts were carved into the stone and many of these pillars still stand today.

GG: Did your parents name you after this famous king?

AK: Yes I was named after him.

GG: Quite a delegation deal!

AK. Yes, indeed… At any rate I was reading up a bit on this. We had civil engineering and ship building. Seafarers followed silk routes going into Southeast Asia for trade. The compass and navigation, before the West learned about it, existed in the Surati Gujarat. Then, of course, India invented the zero. We were leading in mathematics, five hundred years before Europe; we were creative leaders in traditional medicine, which is all coming back today.

GG: Ayurveda?

AK: Ayurveda, yoga, holistic healing. And recently, Mr.Tata has created the Nano, a car which he has produced for two thousand U.S. dollars. It's a four-seater, green, economic, family car. Last month it was on the cover of *Newsweek*.

GG: So it beats the Smart?

AK: Oh, it's much better! In fact, the West has said that this is equivalent to the model T Ford, which revolutionized the way people would use cars. The whole world had said, "You cannot make a car for two thousand dollars." This is the new India! If you look up the cover story in *Newsweek*, it was announced and shown for the first time last month. It's a very stylish, tiny little car which seats four people, looks good, runs well, functions – less metal, more fibre, plastic, more glues than screws – and the darn thing works! Can you imagine what this will do to people all over the world? In fact it bridges the price gap between a car and a motorcycle. In India we have the three-wheeler, what we call an auto-rickshaw, which is almost the same price as the Nano!

GG: Very impressive!

AK: In fact when Tata manufactures it, he has decided to limit the distribution to only five thousand cars for the big cities because he doesn't want to over-crowd them. There you are.

GG: Between Tata's production of the Nano and the invention of the Vedic educational system, Ayurvedic medicine, the invention of the zero, Sanskrit as a language, there were several thousand years. Lots of things have happened in that long period of time. Let's take but one example: what about the invasion of Babur, founder of the Mogul empire; Mogul emperor Shah Jahan who built the Taj Mahal; Mogul emperor Jahangir who had the beautiful gardens in Kashmir installed? What is your opinion about the creative contribution of the Mogul empire? How do you feel about the fusion of Indian mentality and Mogul mentality?

AK: Well, I am not an expert to answer this question, but just from a layman's viewpoint let me say that the original Indian was the Dravidian, the South Indian, from central India downwards. The pure Dravidian in the south is very dark and curly-haired, almost Negroid. The population is fairer-skinned as you go towards the centre and very fair when you reach Kashmir. In the North there is more northern influence in the mix of races, a certain amount in the centre, and pure Dravidian in the South. You will find that the South is extremely non-violent and peaceful. They are creative people who have great literature, art, and so on. They were dominated into submission by these powerful invaders, and all their wealth was taken.

GG: The invaders robbed all the jewels and gold and whatever valuable objects the natives possessed.

AK: The people were robbed by whoever came into power at that time; they were subjugated and taxed. The kings or the emperors lived with no fear of revolution or of any kind of uprising, because they controlled the armies. And all the tremendous wealth allowed them time to fill their boredom with creativity – if they had any aesthetic taste. Every time there was a ruler with some aesthetic taste, he had all the money of that kingdom, which was vast, at his disposal. Once the army was taken care of, he could build palaces, plant gardens and do things for his own pleasure, from jewellery and saris to monuments. You need twenty thousand people to build something? Bring twenty thousand people and build it! "I want it to be the biggest in the world." Okay, we build it the biggest. "I want it to be pure marble; I want to fill it with jewels." Just go out and collect all the jewels all the people have and stick them in there. I think they could indulge in their creativity, which is very different from being creative under pressure or being creative with no money. Correct me if I am wrong: all the creativity of Europe flourished in the years when those states were very well off. Could I be wrong?

GG: Europe was very rich when she robbed her colonies. The British Empire was extremely wealthy when it pillaged India and robbed the Moghul treasury.

AK: Where did the Italians rob from? Where did the Romans rob from?

GG: The Romans robbed from Iran and Mesopotamia to Greece and the Balkans; from Germany to England, France and Spain; and from the Levant to northern Morocco.

AK: Where did France rob from? Where did England rob from? Look at the centres of creativity. Now maybe New York – where did they rob from? I don't know whether there is a centre of creativity…

GG: Why did Bush and his camarilla decide to invade Iraq? There was oil.

AK: It's all a different time and space. Ten years ago I couldn't afford to be creative. Today I can. The project that I'm now doing is going to be extremely creative – to me – and I am doing it for non-profit because it's my pleasure. It's not the same as what I did when I was struggling to win. It's a different kind of victory.

GG: For how many centuries did the South of India live in peace and was able to indulge in creativity? How long were they in power?

AK: I don't know. Remember, the people in the South were originally in the north; they got shoved down.

GG: They were pushed by invaders, from the Aryans to Alexander the Great to the Moghuls.

AK: Then the next lot came and pushed them farther down. These people intermarried and some moved even farther down. So at one time all of India must have been those people who are in the South.

GG: Now Indian culture has many, many influences. One of them is British. What did the British bring to the Indian culture? What did they take away? How much did their impact block Indian creativity? Or did their impact at times foster it? What would you say about that?

AK: They brought a lot to India; they certainly did. I don't know whether we would have done it our own way without them; that, no one can judge today. We can only look at it in the context of history and say, sure, they brought the railways – a fantastic system of railways, without a doubt. They brought our legal system; but is it the best legal system? When I meet lawyers today, they don't seem to believe the British system of law is the best. They think it lacks flexibility. I think there are certain countries which have a far better evolving legal system. They keep modifying the law, changing it. Do the Americans do it? I think they have an evolving form of law, whereas the British left us the old, rigid system. Now that system has bogged itself down, and it only serves the rich and powerful – the lawyers! In India you can keep a case in court for twenty-five years! The average man doesn't understand the law, so the lawyer, like a doctor, is God. It suits the lawyer to keep a case in court for twenty-five years because he earns your money for twenty-five years! I think there is no law in India. There is no justice in India. But here is another interesting angle: would India have ever become a single, unified nation if the British hadn't controlled almost all of the subcontinent? I doubt it. It sounds heretic, but we have to thank the British for India!

GG: What has British dominion done to the self-confidence of the Indian?

AK: After some 400 years of dominion, I think the British[1] took away our confidence. First they took away our money. You must remember that India was one of the greatest exporters of goods. Right down the Silk Road we traded spices, jewellery, wool, textiles…

GG: … and even weapons. Shah Jahan made his money by selling tons of saltpetre to Europe. During the Thirty Years War between the Catholics and the Protestants, there was a tremendous demand for saltpetre to be used in gunpowder. That war lasted from 1618 to 1648. All the major European powers were involved, and the havoc it wrecked in central and northern Europe was terrible.

AK: So for thousands of years India was a great exporter. We had mines, the Golconda mines, the Kohinoor diamond mines; we exported knowledge, we exported learning, we exported everything! We were a rich country!

GG: Indian rubies were in demand everywhere.

AK: Then the British came in, and we stopped exporting. They took everything away; they took away our cotton and we had to import it. They made India importers of everything!

GG: Did you have to import British Indian tea too?

AK: Probably! I don't know. But from a country which exported everything, they turned us into a country of importers. Now for the first time, after sixty years of independence, India is beginning to become an exporter all over again.

GG: Now you have Tata and other global players.

AK: Without forgetting all the other people who are now looking at international markets; we are exporters of minds. Thirty-three percent of the scientists in NASA are Indian. Sixty-five percent of the doctors in the U.K. are Indian. Part of that was a brain drain; because there was no opportunity in India, they went away. Today we are exporting technology, we are exporting software, we are exporting products. We've got a huge manufacturing base in India because for sixty years, the Indian government prevented us from being big importers. We weren't allowed to bring anything in. So we actually evolved our own brands, and that is why we are not affected by this big American bubble burst; because we are not dependent on international trade inwards.

GG: In the nineteenth century you had great scientists: from Ramanujan– a genius – to Raman, a Nobel laureate. Quantum physicist Bose created the foundations for the Bose-Einstein statistics and was several times proposed as a candidate for the Nobel Prize. Chandrasekhar was a Nobel laureate. What enabled them to be creative? Back then they were still under British rule.

AK: It depends on the areas in which they were creative.

GG: Ramanujan in mathematics; Bose and Raman in physics; Chandrasekhar in physics but also in cosmology and astronomy.

AK: These were not things which the British could take away. They would have had to arrest these guys and lock them up! You can't steal thought. You can steal product, you can steal agricultural product, matter, energy; everything that we had was stolen. Everything went into World War I and World War II. We even sent soldiers, Ghurkhas, everything went to the British! But you can't steal the minds. The minds that left the country, left because there was no opportunity in India. Today many of those minds want to come back to India.

GG: You also have a huge export in information technology.

AK: Intellectual property, mind. That's going to be our big strength. China is always going to beat us at production because they have discipline, and that discipline says, "You follow process, and follow it exactly." And you will train people, by the fear of a gun, to produce a world-class product. Whereas Indians just don't have that discipline.

GG: We shall come back to that discipline and the balance between chaos and order. Now, if you look at your society, who were the people who made the most important creative contributions to India? Mahatma Gandhi was certainly one. Are there others that come to mind?

AK: You know, for some reason Gandhi was so vast. Again these things are so personal in terms of your belief and faith. At a national level, when you say India, he was one of the greatest contributors. I think Nehru, in his socialist democracy wisdom, set a pathway for India to be self-sufficient. At the same time he actually encouraged science. He invested in and developed the Homi Bhabha nuclear facility. Today I think Ratan Tata has joined that small club of creative contributors.

GG: That's fine. I have one last question regarding factors which block creativity and factors which foster it. What role did the Hindu caste system play with respect to the fostering or blocking of creativity?

AK: If you look at the Vedic education system, it created great minds; but it wasn't hereditary. Each child was chosen for his personality. But then human greed set in: priests wanted their sons to be priests; a trader's son had to be a trader and keep the money in; the doctor's son had to be a doctor to keep the practice going. I believe it was that greed, actually, that created the caste system. The tragedy is that that amazing educational system became hereditary later on.

GG: It degenerated into a dynastic, hereditary form.

AK: It became dynastic.

GG: And this, if I understand you well, would be a blocking factor in creative development.

AK: Right, because you were no longer picking creative people to be creative.

GG: They were in a box.

AK: The son of a creative individual became creative; the son of a warrior became a warrior. So what is that? Human weakness? Human greed? That actually allowed the growth of the caste system, which lasted for years and years, till Mahatma Gandhi started trying to break it down. Although we've come a long way, it is there still. When you go into the inlands, like I told you, I had to stand outside the cafe to have the food bought out, because of the caste system.

GG: Now let's move to the last bit of chapter three. As I told you, in my view, creativity is the most precious natural resource, which unlike other natural resources such as fresh air, fresh water etc., in principle is absolutely inexhaustible. So for me, it's very important. I would like to ask you first: in your view what role does creativity play generally in societies, in cultures? If you look at your own country for instance, or if you look at Asia more generally speaking, or if you look at the whole world, what, as you see it, is the role that creativity plays?

AK: I don't know if I'm knowledgeable enough to answer that question. It's a big one!

GG: Yes, it is.

AK: And I speak from a small viewpoint.

GG: But you told me, for instance, that Hindu culture had invented the zero, which was a very important step forward; before that it was impossible to manage big numbers. Trying to add together big numbers with Roman numerals is awfully complicated. I studied Latin for eight years, but I still have problems reading a number; I have to decode it. If it is in Arab numbers, it's so simple!

Do you think creativity plays a major role today in India or is India copying what other cultures have done in creativity? For instance, India is now very strong in software development. In your view, is India a creative pacemaker in that domain?

AK: Do you mean are they executors? I'm not too knowledgeable there, either. I know we create, but I have heard lots of people from the West say, "What Indians have created isn't really that great, but they have great capability. What they've created has already been done somewhere else in the world, much better; what we'd like to do is use this talent to help us create. I've heard people talk like this. It's not my field of expertise, but if they really have created, they would patent it. I know that some pharmaceutical companies are actually patenting things.

GG: Ancient medicine, for instance?

AK: No, new medicine.There's a lady called Kiran Mazumdar Shaw, who owns a company called Biocon Limited. I know she is actually locked in some global patents. I think Ranbaxy, the big pharmaceutical company, has done the same.

GG: Do you think Tata is a creative pacemaker or does he reproduce what others have invented? You talked about the Nano car.

AK: I think he's created a process and a method of manufacturing a lowest-cost car, which is acceptable. The car wasn't invented by him. The car wasn't invented by Ford, either, but he created mass production.

GG: So it would be rather an example of what the Japanese call Kaizen, step-by-step, micro innovations.

AK: Only Tata has made a macro innovation! At two thousand dollars…That's what you pay for a dinner if you take six of your friends to a good restaurant. If you have a good bottle of wine, you pay 2,000 dollars! With that money, you can buy a car which can take your family of four; that's a macro-innovation!

GG: Do you think Mittal, the Indian steel magnate, is creative?

AK: You have to consider that there's a difference between resident Indians and Indians who are in the West. Why did a lot of these brilliant Indians emigrate? Because the West could provide opportunity and resources. Why are thirty-three percent of the scientists in NASA Indians? Because Indians at home don't have the laboratories, the facilities or the funding to do the kind of research and developmental work that NASA offers.

GG: Thirty-three percent of the scientists at NASA are Indians?

AK: I think so. That is the figure I've read many times.

GG: Have you read other figures regarding Indian emigrants?

AK: I am told the UK has more doctors from India than from any other country. Look at the number of Indian managers, who in the last ten years have become global leaders of many companies and banks. The West wouldn't accept the Indian as number one for many years; today they are accepting them because of their talent. There is Bose, who invented the speaker systems. He is Indian, but he didn't have a forum in India to create. So when these people end up in a country which provides opportunity and recognition – and resources, they're able to raise funding; all this was very difficult to do in India.

GG: In software development do they produce mostly cheaper material or do they invent?

AK: I think they invent, but many of them do it in the US. If you look at almost every large Internet or software business, there is an Indian partner.

GG: What about Bangalore?

AK: In the US. Bangalore, I think, is used more for outsourcing and development; it is known as the Silicon Valley of India. But the same Indian, when he goes out and works in a software company in the US, actually owns patents himself. We didn't have a concept of patents in India; we first heard the word ten years ago. We didn't know what "intellectual property" meant. Now suddenly we are aware of it.

GG: You've already talked about Bollywood. That is mostly reproduction and production but not really creativity. For songs, it is the same. What about fashion?

AK: We also do western fashion, but we haven't really learned yet, because that product belongs to the West; they've done it for a thousand years. We are just getting into it and trying to do it. We do have a few little sparks, but they are nothing, on the global scene. Indian fashion, however, does very well because nobody else does it except Indians. There is no competition.

GG: Do you think that the British Empire hurt the Indian spirit to the extent that it is taking a long time to recover from a kind of – excuse my term, I don't want to be hurtful in any way, but for the lack of a better word – to escape the "underdog" self-image?

AK: Yes, I think Indians…You see, the white man – and no offence…

GG: You know I come from very poor backgrounds, so please don't feel offended when I say "underdog self-image."

AK: I know, I know, and I am not being offensive when I say "white man." There's always a white man and a black man in India, or a coloured man or whatever. The white man made us feel inferior. I told you about Macaulay's statement[2] saying, "We have to make them believe that the British method of education is the superior method. We have to make them believe that everything we do is superior. Only then will we win in India. First we have to make them feel inferior."

GG: And if we need machine guns for educational purposes, then we need machine guns!

AK: It doesn't matter what method you use. But you did not get a job if you did not have a British education. If you went to an Indian school, they wouldn't give you a job in the government because the government belonged to the British. If you wanted a job in the railways, you had to have a British education. At that time an Indian's whole desire was to become acceptable to the white man. We always felt inferior. We believed we couldn't think. We believed we didn't have the competence; and that's what has changed in the last decade.

GG: Before the British Empire, you had four hundred years of Mogul.

AK: We had Moguls, and it's very difficult to say who's an Indian. Who is an Indian?

GG: You have been invaded so many times over the centuries.

AK: We've been invaded for thousands of years. When did Alexander the Great walk in?

GG: He invaded in 300 B.C. but remained for a very short while.

AK: Yes, but look at the influence he had, too! I think Genghis Khan came in at some stage.

GG: A great creator, yes; and Timur-i-Leng also invaded your country.

AK: Timur-i-Leng came in. Everybody went to India!

GG: Then Babur was a great-grandson of Timur-i-Leng's. Two of your greatest contributions – creative contributions as far as I can understand – were certainly music and certainly Buddhism.

AK: Buddhism?

GG: Buddhism. Emperor Ashoka was the first to go to Buddhism with all his retinue.

AK: Yes, and he created peace. But Hinduism is not a religion; it's a way of life that accepts other religions. Buddhism has no God, Buddha is not a God. Buddhism is a way of living.

GG: That's right: Buddhism has no God, but it is still a philosophical-religious system. What I find beautiful in Daoism and Buddhism – and then in Zen Buddhism, which is a further development – is that never has anything been destroyed in the name of Buddha or in the name of Dao. But wherever Judaism went – and historically Christianity is a sect of the Jewish religion and Islam is a Christian sect of the seventh century – wherever they went, they brought destruction, they killed people, they raped women, they smashed children, they burnt books and left a trail of total destruction. And then Christianity went to Central America, North America, South America, Africa, your country, and left a trail of destruction.

AK: I don't think the Hindus ever went out and created a trail of destruction either.

GG: What about the terrible destruction in 1947?

AK: Or Pakistan, for partition?

GG: Partition; there was a terrible slaughter between Hindus and Muslims.

AK: Yes, but that was a slaughter between them. It wasn't the Hindus going out to destroy another civilisation or a race or anything.

GG: But why did they slaughter each other?

AK: It was a very strange situation, and you never know where it started or who started it. We are talking here about seven million people having to change countries. It meant leaving your home, your belongings, everything, carrying just a suitcase. This happened on both sides. The moment people left, somebody was looting their home. And if they tried to stop them, they would be killed. It all became greed and theft and burglary and grabbing and revenge. If two families had fought and had past enmity, this was a great time to go and wipe each other out. Then there were rumours. One side heard a rumour that their people had been killed, and they exacted revenge. I think it was all these factors that made the entire situation escalate. Remember that these people had lived together in perfect, peaceful harmony. Wherever the British came in and then left, whether it was when they created Israel, or whether they left India and Pakistan...

GG: Oh, absolutely; and they did a poor job in Kenya.

AK: In Africa, wherever they left, they left blood and destruction.

GG: Absolutely.

AK: It was their method of pulling out. If I am leaving, I am going to spoil it for you. It was like this is my plate of food, and now you are telling me I can't have it, so I put my fist in it and mess it up.

GG: Their main power game in India and elsewhere was always *divide et impera*.

AK: Oh yes! Divide and rule. Everywhere they went, they divided and ruled. God help the UK if they pull out of Ireland! But to get back to your point, you're right, that India did create Hinduism, Buddhism, Jainism, which is a different sect.

GG: What about the Hindu caste system? Do you think it was a constructive contribution to cultural evolution or a destructive one?

AK: I can only see it as destructive.

GG: That's what I would see, but I am an outsider, so it's easier to judge.

AK: Maybe there is someone who can tell you what was constructive about it, but to me it was only destructive, because it was built on protecting your own.

GG: And on the scheme of dominance and submission.

AK: Yes, and at the lowest end were the untouchables. So you created a race of people to do only the dirty work that you didn't want to do.

GG: And women had a poor standing.

AK: Women, at one stage, had a great standing. We have women Gods in India. You must remember in Hinduism, there is Durga, Kali ma, Lakshmi, Saraswathi.

GG: They were Goddesses?

AK: Yes. The whole concept of the mother is extremely powerful in India. The mother is a Goddess. We don't say the Fatherland; we say Mother India. I don't know whether any other country says "mother."

GG: No, in the West it's always Fatherland.

AK: In India, we say Motherland: Bharat Ma. We've had women Prime Ministers. We currently have an Italian Roman Catholic woman running the country from behind.

GG: In a strong position, behind the wheels.

AK: We have a woman President right now, Pratibha Patil.

GG: So the gentleman who was a nuclear physicist left in April?

AK: Oh, he's just finished his term and a woman has taken over.

GG: Where did the idea of the burial of widows come from? Is that a Hindu concept?

AK: It's a Hindu concept – or rather an aberration of social customs. It wasn't the burial of women; the widows were meant to jump on their husband's funeral pyre and be burned with him.

GG: Ah, yes, it was a burning.

AK: It's strange; I have no idea where the whole concept came from but if you look at it, it was the man who was saying, "I don't want to leave her behind for anyone else." Also, as a widow, you were treated very badly in society; you had no standing. Even today there are some social outcast taboos about being a widow. In some way they are held responsible that their husband died, so maybe it was better for her to burn herself. All of this usually came out of some selfish, human, male motive.

GG: If you look at the conflict between Islam and Hinduism—for instance the conflict between India and Pakistan or Bangladesh—does this breed creativity, does it breed destruction, does it breed both? What do you think?

AK: It breeds creativity for the politicians, because when you keep people un-educated and then you find a unifying reason to make them focus on hatred, you become a leader for them.

GG: But this would be imagination that is not at all creative, only destructive. It does not generate any value.

AK: I was being sarcastic. It is destructive imagination; but it is produced by politicians. There is no reason for it to stay alive. Sixty years after partition most of the people who existed then are dead. So they foster that hate between their children. They create imaginary fears about what is happening to Muslims in India. People don't really harm Muslims in India, but now there is an unspoken fear and distrust and dislike of Muslims in India. It was never like that. We all lived perfectly well together before partition; partition created this. Ever since then, every time there is a battle in pockets of India, these things are recreated. They are politically created to get the Hindu vote.

The following three sections deal with the influence of medieval Muslim rule, medieval Mongol rule, and the Silk Road on morpho-evolution and morpho-elimination.

2.51 Medieval Muslim Influence on Morpho-evolution and Morpho-elimination

For reasons already mentioned, the present book has so far centered mainly on creative leadership in Europe and its spin-off in the New World. To establish a proper balance between East and West, I shall therefore devote the remainder of my study on human creativity to three topics often neglected in books and articles on Western civilizations and their creative accomplishments. We shall now focus on the influence of Muslim culture, Mongol rule, and the Silk Road on European Renaissance—a Golden Age of Western creativity. These three historical factors constitute chapters in a narrative that Michael Hamilton Morgan (2007) has aptly baptized "lost history." The following section on creative Muslim morpho-evolution is strongly indebted to Morgan and his excellent study excavating precious treasures from the tombs of oblivion.

Lost History is an integral part of our world history. It has been lost for centuries not only, but mainly in the Western world. The ideological blinders of Christian historiographers seriously narrowing down the field of vision have been the main culprit for our collective repressing and forgetting. In their accounts of the Golden Ages of Western creativity in medicine, science, technology, and the arts—from Renaissance to the Age of Enlightenment, and from the Industrial Revolution to the great breakthroughs of the twentieth century—our historians emphasized the impact of ancient Greek and Roman civilizations on Christian civilization. Yet, consciously or unconsciously, they overlooked the impact Japanese, Chinese, Indian, Persian, and Central Asian cultures have had on the Western world. History, as told by Western historians, is by and large a narrative written from the perspective of Western Christian cultural evolution and thus heavily prejudiced by the presumed supremacy of Western imperialism and the Age of Colonialism.

In that skewed history, we are enlightened about the Greco-Roman contribution to European Renaissance, for instance, how Filippo Brunelleschi studied the bold engineering visible in the Pantheon erected in ancient Rome and how his investigations, carried on for many years, eventually permitted him to construct a cupola on top of the basilica Santa Maria del Fiore in Florence. We are told how Galileo and Copernicus investigated the Latin texts of Ptolemy, the great astronomer who lived in ancient Alexandria. We understand how Andreas Vesalius and William Harvey explored the writings of

Hippocrates and Galen in order to make their own scientific contributions, which revolutionized modern medicine. And we are informed about how Roger Bacon and Thomas of Aquinas examined the Latin translations of the ancient Greek philosophers Plato and Aristotle before they made their own creative contributions to philosophy, theology, and science.

In all of these texts celebrating the stupendous leap that connected ancient Greece and Rome with the European Renaissance, we rarely if ever encounter a hint about a rather crucial fact: the acrobats executing that leap were guided, supported, and empowered by the Muslims. For more than a millennium and a half, Muslims ruled the countries crossed by the Silk Road connecting China with Byzanz, Rome, and Andalusia. Traders travelling along the Silk Road—a complex system of interconnected and often parallel pathways— were often preyed upon by bandits and local rulers. In the thirteenth century, Mongols made the Silk Road safe and soon thereafter the Renaissance (1300-1600) began in Italy and then across the whole of Europe. In that process, merchants played a crucial role: they not only accumulated huge wealth for themselves, they also turned into patrons of art and science.

Muslims, rather than Christians, saved ancient Greek and Roman texts from extinction because—unlike many Christians steeped in superstition, intolerance, and religious fanaticism—they had a great respect for human creativity. Over centuries there occurred a tremendous knowledge transfer from the Muslim to the Christian world, a transfer without which the Golden Age of European Renaissance might never have existed at all.

To redress the lopsided record produced by Western historians, we shall now focus on the enormous impact the East had on the West and, more precisely, on how Eastern cultural evolution shaped its Western counterpart.

Muslim Golden Ages

Even if you must go all the way to China, seek knowledge.
    Prophet Muhammad

Muslim civilization which is almost 1,500 years old began with the Hegira— Prophet Muhammad's flight from Mecca to Medina in 622 AD. When he died in 632 AD, his followers established in Damascus the Umayyad Dynasty that lasted from 661 AD to 750 AD. Barely 120 years after Prophet Muhammad's death, a huge empire was set up when Arab Muslim forces in a series of *Blitzkriege* swept through Andalusia, Sicily, and the northern rim of the African Mediterranean coast to Egypt, the Middle East, the Arab Peninsula, Mesopotamia and Persia, and across Central Asia to the Taklamakan Desert, then to Afghanistan and down to the Punjab valley on the Indian subcontinent.

The Umayyads of Damascus met their nemesis when in a bloody revolt they were ousted by the Abbasids, who set up their own dynasty and went on to rule for the next 195 years, from 750 AD to 945 AD. Because recurrent heavy droughts had killed the harvests and made Damascus unfit for nourishing a huge population, the Abbasids moved their capital to Baghdad near the ancient Babylon. Thousands of years before, Mesopotamia had been a cradle of civilization because its fertile soil, fed by the rivers Euphrates and Tigris, had made it a logical choice for major settlements.

In the ruthless killing spree of 750 AD when the Abbasids slaughtered the entire Umayyad clan, the only survivors were the two sons of the royal family and a slave. With the help of friends, the survivors escaped and fled to the west. However, one of the sons, Yahya, was killed in Palestine by Abbasid myrmidons, but his brother Abd al-Rahman and servant Badr survived and made their escape to Andalusia. Within less than a decade, the fugitive prince established a new Umayyad rule that would last from 759 AD to 1031 AD.

By 929 AD, 170 years after the establishment of their domain, the Umayyads of Andalusia felt strong enough to claim the caliphate[3] from a weakened Abbasid rule in Baghdad. But by the end of the eleventh century, the Umayyad Dynasty too degenerated to a point where its princes had to seek the help of the Berber Amoravid Dynasty for military support against Christian foes in northern Spain. The Almoravids, a tribe of fanatical and orthodox Muslims, descended in Andalusia and fought against the Christians; then they ousted the Umayyad princes and began to rule the Iberian Peninsula. They in turn were replaced by the Moroccan Almohad Dynasty whose representatives ruled Spain from 1145 AD to 1232 AD.

Fortune sank on the Almohad dynasty in 1232 AD, when the Nasrid Dynasty who governed the Iberian Peninsula from 1232 AD to 1492 AD threw them out of power. Their rule came to an end when the *reconquista* of queen Isabella of Castile drove them out of their last stronghold in the Alhambra of Granada. Queen Isabella and the Holy Inquisition were responsible for the destruction of many of the architectural monuments built by Andalusia's Arab Muslims. The treasures of huge libraries too were not spared and were consigned to the flames—a destructive morpho-elimination of gigantic proportions.

While the sun of Muslim culture rose and set in the west, the east too went through major changes. In 945 AD, the Persian Buyids drove the Abbasids out of Baghdad and established their own rule. By 1037 they lost out to the Seljuks, a Turkic-Persian[4] Sunni Muslim dynasty that established its capital in Isfahan and ruled over Anatolia and Central Asia for close to 200 years. Their reign came to an end in 1307 when the marauding Mongols swooped down to conquer the empire.

The Mongols were originally a nomad tribe of little influence. But their leader Genghis Khan and his grandson Kublai Khan established one of the grandest empires the world has ever seen. It lasted from 1206 to 1406 and stretched from Korea and China in the east to Anatolia in the west, and from the Baltic Sea in the north to the Persian Gulf in the south. Genghis Khan, a wise ruler despite the terrible reputation he has in Western schoolbooks, divided his empire into four Khanates: The Chagatai Khanate stretched from the Tarim Basin in the East to Uzbekistan in the west; the Golden Horde Khanate ruled the northern landmass from Siberia to eastern Europe; the Ilk Khanate reached from Afghanistan and western Pakistan to Turkey; and the Ögedei Khanate comprised the original heartland Mongolia and later, under the rule of Genghis's grandson Khubilai Khan, also China. Khubilai was the Great Khan, Khan of all Khans, who eventually established the Chinese Yuan Dynasty. Mongol rule brought death and destruction into the Muslim empire—reaching a peak in 1258 when the sack of Baghdad turned that city into a heap of rubble and corpses. Yet Mongol rule also made the Silk Road a safe network for trading goods and information.

Timur-i-leng, also called Tamerlan or Timur the Lame, was a Turkic-speaking military genius of Mongol descent and one of the most vicious mass murderers of all time. In 1363, he founded the Sunni Muslim Timurid Empire that ruled Central Asia and the Middle East until 1506. Its capital was Samarkand, which Timur-i-leng decided to make the centre of the world. For that very purpose, he erected a series of monumental buildings around the Registan, a piazza of tremendous proportions.

On the eastern rim of their empire, the Muslims kept expanding their power and influence. In 1206, the Mamluk[5] dynasty—descendents of Turkish and Circassian prisoners of war whom Genghis Khan sold as slave-soldiers to the sultan of Egypt—established the Islamic Delhi Sultanate. After the end of the Mamluk Dynasty, five different dynasties of Turkic and Pashtun-Afghan descent ruled the Delhi sultanate until eventually they were overthrown by foreign invaders. In 1526 Babur, great-grandson of Timur-i-leng, conquered the Delhi sultanate and established the Mughal Empire that lasted until 1857 when it was conquered and turned into a colony by the British.

In 1291, Osman I, head of a Ghazi emirate that had inherited a part of the old Seljuk Empire, founded the Islamic Ottoman Empire. He began to expand his foothold in western Anatolia towards the frontiers of a slowly decaying Byzantine Empire. His descendants conquered Constantinople in 1453. At the height of its power, the Ottoman Empire spread its reach from the Balkans, the Eastern rim of the Mediterranean Sea, and from Egypt to the Persian Gulf in the east and to the Caucasus in the North.

At the end of the Turkish War of Independence after a period of internal skirmishes, reformations, and gradual downslide, the Ottoman Empire finally disintegrated. In 1922, Kemal Mustafa Atatürk established the modern Turkish nation.

To sum up this section we may say that Muslim rule, from the beginning of Umayyad Dynasty in Damascus in 661 until the end of the Ottoman Empire, lasted more than 1300 years. During the first half of this period—while Europe still slumbered in the stagnant chambers of the 'dark" Middle Ages—it was Golden Ages for Muslim civilization, where creativity bore rich fruits in medicine, science, technology, and the arts. The specifics of these Golden Ages and their stupendous breakthroughs will be discussed in the following sections.

A host of interconnected factors enabled Muslim culture to produce a series of Golden Ages, offering an awe-inspiring volume and quality of creative achievements—from Andalusia to Persia and India, and from and from Cairo to Damascus, Baghdad and Samarkand. The creative proliferation of the Islamic civilization should be credited with filling the spatial and temporal gap that separated the ancient Greek and Roman cultures and the birth of European Renaissance.

The fierce competitive spirit of Arab Muslims and the Prophet's explicit order to conquer the world provided a strong achievement motivation. It also imbued them with a solid self-confidence to jump over the hurdles that blocked the way to their goals. Yet the fierce spirit of conquest bowed graciously to the greater power of knowledge, as acknowledged in a verse in the Holy Qu'ran that reads: "The ink of the scholar is holier than the blood of a martyr" (Morgan 2007, 10). That verse, validating the 'the pen is mightier than the sword' sentiment, prompted a continuous search for knowledge favoring investigations in technology, science, and the arts.

Despite their lust for conquest and their conviction that Islam is the one and only genuine faith on earth, Muslims from the Umayyad Dynasties in the West to the Mughal Empire in the East established a long track record of amazing religious tolerance. For centuries, Muslims, Jews, and Christians have lived in peace with each other—from Andalusia to Cairo, from the Middle East to Central Asia and the Indian subcontinent. Cultural, ethnic, and religious diversity led to a cross-fertilization of ideas that nurtured individuals and groups with tremendous creative propensities and equipped them with a spirit eager to try out concepts, methods, and techniques in different combinations and permutations. Islamic open-mindedness and the explicit focus on the merits of learning also favored the gradual incorporation of ancient Greek and Roman knowledge and technological know-how, providing a mental take-off point for ascending higher levels of creative self-expression.

Fierce competition, genuine self-confidence, assimilation of ancient Greek and Roman knowledge, and cross-cultural exchange among so many nations and ethnic groups laid out a platform for creative pursuits. This process, stretching from 650-1200, was facilitated and promoted by the free flow of trade across the Silk Road. The free trade served two purposes. First, it connected regions far apart—Japan (at least during the Chinese Tang Dynasty), Korea, China, India, Persia, Central Asia, and the Mediterranean Basin including Sicily, the Northern rim of Africa and the Iberian Peninsula—resulting in the germination of a heady brew of ideas and concepts from cross-cultural exchange. Second, free trade along the Silk Road generated stupendous wealth, which in turn motivated ambitious patrons to generously support the creative efforts of craftsmen, inventors, artists, scientists, and theologians.

Following the natural law of development, which postulates what goes up must come down, a combination of forces such as climatic changes, emergence of Mongol power, series of internal conflicts, and intra-systemic clashes induced and finally brought the curtains down on the Golden Ages of Muslim rule. In a tragic culmination, that unfavorable combination of interlinked forces slowed down and eventually killed the spirit of morph-evolution, making way for morpho-elimination.

The gradual decline of Muslim civilization coincided with the gradual ascension of European culture. The ecclesiastic and secular rulers of Europe and the scholars they supported made the Western world forgetful of the Golden Ages and the tremendous debt the West owed to the creative genius of Muslim rule, thereby confirming the universal truth that acknowledging and looking back to the origin is not an easy task when one is on the ascent.

In our brain, memories are not stored like inanimate objects, like hats or gloves in a haberdasher's store. Memories are living, pulsating thought processes that can be shaped and manipulated according to one's current conscious and unconscious desires and intentions. Jewish-Christian society never forgot that its territories had been vandalized, first by Arab Muslims and later by the Ottoman Empire. The memory of that defeat was painful. Thus Western society got retribution by systematically negating, degrading, or even physically eliminating the glories of the multiethnic and multinational Muslim culture that spawned multidimensional creative proliferation—a bouquet of expressions from China, India, Persia, Central Asia, Middle East, Sicily, Egypt, the southern Rim of the Mediterranean Sea, and Andalusia. The Christian West's intended and unintended amnesia did not even spare the truth of the enormous influence that the Muslim culture had on the Italian Renaissance: the enormous knowledge transfer from Muslim culture to the Christian culture triggered a veritable explosion of creative innovations in technology, science, the arts, medicine, and sociocultural organization.

Muslim culture engendered an entire chain of glories for the Christian West. The Italian Renaissance, in its turn, inspired and triggered the emergence of the European Renaissance. That Renaissance was followed by Luther's, Zwingli's and Calvin's Reformations, and Protestant work ethic that played such a crucial role in the industrial revolution and the free spirit giving birth to the Age of Enlightenment. To a certain extent, all of these events owed their origin to the Islamic cultural heritage, although the West denied the contribution of the Muslim civilization. It conveniently overlooked the fact the Muslim era had saved the essence of Greco-Roman culture from oblivion and physical destruction; without its rescue mission, that glorious ancestry might have never been known to the post-medieval Europe.

One does not have to go far to see the acceptance of Greek-Roman influence by the Muslims into the various facets of their culture. The incorporation of ancient Greek and Roman knowledge was visibly demonstrated when Caliph al-Walid, who reigned from 705 to 715, ordered the erection of a splendid Umayyad mosque in Damascus. As Morgan (2007, 37) states, various features of that mosque prove to what degree Muslim culture was able to integrate the architectural know-how of ancient Greece and Rome. Muslim arches resemble Roman triumph arches. Triangular roofs, lintels, and capitella are derived from the gabled roofs, lintels, and capitella of ancient Greece and Rome. Windows high up on the walls echo the windows in Rome's Pantheon. And the courtyard of the Muslim mosque echoes the pagan Pantheon. This morpho-evolution not only connected three different cultures and a time span of 700 years, it also marked the beginning of yet another morpho-evolution: the courtyard of the mosque in Damascus would eventually become a blueprint for sculptor and architect Gian Lorenzo Bernini (1598-1680), commissioned to redesign the Vatican Square in front of St. Peter's Dome. It also influenced the design of the Renaissance piazzas in Venice, Siena, and Florence.

Let's have a closer look at the various Golden Ages of medieval Muslim culture that inspired and motivated Europe to emerge from the dark Middle Ages and to usher in the Renaissance, one of the most creative epochs in human history.

In 750, supported by the Persians (Morgan 2007, 39), the Abbasids defeated the Umayyad army at the tributary of the Tigris River. They overthrew the Umayyad Dynasty, took over the Caliphate, abandoned Damascus, and erected a new capital in Baghdad on the banks of the Tigris River in Mesopotamia. The fall of the Damascus Umayyad Dynasty led to a major morpho-elimination: buildings were razed to the ground; works of art and precious jewels were vandalized and looted. Large numbers of inhabitants were slaughtered; others sought greener pastures and moved on to Baghdad where a new morpho-evolution had begun under Caliph al-Mansur (712-757). He laid the foundations for the first Golden Age of Muslim culture (Morgan 2007, 40), which lasted for half a millennium and heralded great discoveries in medicine, science, technology, and the arts. Baghdad eventually turned into one of the two intellectual hubs of Muslim world—the other one being Qurtuba, ancient Cordoba, where the escaped Umayyad prince Abd al-Rahman erected the capital of a new Umayyad dynasty. Baghdad was now a wealthy metropolis, dotted with marble palaces and splendid mosques. Two hundred years later, historian Yakut (Morgan 2007, 61) praised Baghdad as a city studded with marble palaces several stories high. Palaces and mansions were lavishly equipped, precious tapestry and hangings of brocade and silk established an atmosphere of sophisticated luxury. As the historian wrote: "The rooms were lightly and tastefully furnished with luxurious divans, costly tables, unique Chinese vases and gold and silver ornaments."

Persians, with their rich cultural heritage dating back to the days of Persepolis and Babylon, now shared power with the Arab Muslims of the Abbasid Dynasty and entered high positions in the administration. They played a crucial role in translating ancient texts from Greece and Rome into the Arab language. Pagan Sabians of northern Iraq, who had strong links to Hellenistic astronomy, supported their pursuits (Morgan 2007, 52). Christian physicians and theologians from Constantinople also impacted the culture of the time. Due to their efforts, ideas of Socrates, Plato, Aristotle, Pythagoras, and Euclid entered the domain of Muslim thinking. Such assimilation of ideas and knowledge was, of course, only possible because the rulers of the Abbasid Dynasty practiced an exemplary tolerance towards the adherents of other faiths.

Caliph Haroun al-Rashid (763-809), was of Persian descent and the most famous of Abbasid caliphs. He was an enlightened and therefore open-minded ruler, fascinated by the arts and architecture not less than he was by mathematics and science. A successful military campaigner and a genius in politics and diplomacy, he received pecuniary tributes from the whole Abbasid Empire and even from opponents, such as Byzantium. Thus he strengthened the economic foundations for the first Golden Age of Muslim culture established by al-Mansur. Under his leadership, Abbasid Baghdad reached the height of its glory. He endowed the first public hospital in Baghdad (Morgan 2007, 261f.); generously supported the arts as well as major translations of ancient Hindu and Greek philosophical and mathematical texts; and was a generous patron to the father of chemistry Jabir ibn Haiyan (ca. 721-ca. 815) and other scientists, permitting them to dedicate their time and energies to delve deeply into their ground-breaking investigations.

Profiting from the Silk Road, Haroun al-Rashid entertained good diplomatic relationships with China and the French king Charlemagne (747-814) who reigned from his capital Aix-la-Chapelle, now known as Aachen, a city within West German territory. Charlemagne, his entourage, and his subjects were duly impressed when they received two generous gifts that went beyond their imagination. One such gift was Abul Abbas, the first elephant Europe had seen since the days when Hannibal (247-183 BC) and his troops crossed the Alps in the summer of 218 BC to wage war against the Romans. The other present was a sophisticated water clock. It had ingenious devices indicating the hour of the day: twelve brass balls falling on a cymbal, and twelve carved horsemen parading out of a window. It is quite probable that Haroun al-Rashid's water clock eventually inspired, a millennium later, the construction of the now well-known 'Schwarzwälder Uhren' equipped with a cuckoo whose mechanic voice indicates the time. This is a particular example of morpho-evolution; although it is not a creative one, it is still of value, because kitsch reflects the artistic expression of the time, as it is of value to an individual's emotions and sensibilities.

Caliph al-Mamun (786-833), son of Haroun al-Rashid, made a significant contribution to the morpho-evolution of ideas, methods, and skills. He copied the structure and functioning of the academy of Gundishapur (Morgan 2007, 55f.). That academy was established three centuries earlier at the Gulf of Persia by the Sassanid Empire, with the mission to develop it into a center of learning and innovation. It soon boasted the first teaching hospital of the world, a university, and a well-equipped library. In the course of time, that hospital turned out to be the stimulus for a creative morpho-evolution resulting in a series of hospitals in Baghdad, Cairo and, Cordoba. In the middle of the tenth century, Baghdad (Hunke 1960, 122) boasted of 860 physicians. Around the same time, Qurtuba (Cordoba), the capital of the Western Umayyad Dynasty, already possessed fifty hospitals (Hunke 1960, 117)—indicators of a morpho-evolution that had begun 200 years before with Caliph Haroun al-Rashid in Baghdad.

The academy of Gundishapur involved in scientific and cultural activities received a boost with the arrival of Nestorian Christians, who fled Constantinople because the Council of Ephesus in 431 had condemned them as heretics. This condemnation had produced a schism between the Byzantine Church and the Nestorians who then founded the Assyrian Church of the East. Gundishapur also became a haven for Syriac-speaking Christians and for Greek scholars. Thanks to their activities, ancient Greek and Latin texts were translated into the Fārsi language, and that knowledge was transferred to Baghdad where yet another phase of creative morpho-evolution began.

The following example illustrates particularly well how much al-Mamun (Morgan 2007, 156) cherished the merit of knowledge. After having defeated the Byzantine emperor in battle, al-Mamun demanded no booty of gold and other treasures, but only a copy of the famous *Almagest*, the masterful work on Hellenistic astronomy Ptolemy (83-161 AD) had written in Alexandria. Such a generous gesture, the hallmark of genuine creative leadership, would find its echo in 1187 when sultan Saladin reconquered Jerusalem from the Christian crusaders.

With the help of the academy of Gundishapur, Caliph al-Mamun erected in Baghdad the House of Wisdom, one of the most important interdisciplinary centers of learning the world has ever seen—an inter-neuronal network of information processing, a think tank of unique power which had not existed since the days of ancient Alexandria, founded more than 1,000 years prior by the Macedonian king Alexander the Great. Soon outstanding scientists, inventors, and artists (Morgan 2007, 56f.) flocked to Baghdad, attracted like bees by the sweet scent of honey. Among the great minds entering the House of Wisdom were Mohamed Al-Khwarizmi, father of algebra, inventor of the algorithm, and forerunner of digital computing; and the Banu Musa brothers (Hunke 1960, 83ff.) who were mathematicians, astronomers, and highly gifted engineer-inventors—their book on ingenious devices included valves, automatic controls, float chambers, hurricane lamps, gas masks, fail-save systems, pumps, and many different machines serving the irrigation techniques originally developed by the Persians (Morgan 2007, 38). In time to come, these innovations found their way into Central Asia, the Middle East, the coastal regions of Northern Africa, and Andalusia. In the House of Wisdom, Hunayn ibn Ishak, a Nestorian physician translated the work of Galen and Greek philosophers into Arab language; al-Kindi, a luminary of Arab philosophy, was yet another creative mind working under the same roof.

In the House of Wisdom, a throbbing nerve center of teaching and learning, precious Hindu, Persian, Greek, Latin, and Byzantine texts were translated into Arabic. The getting together of creative individuals and the assimilation of their ideas laid new conceptual foundations for a creative morpho-evolution in medicine, mathematics, astronomy, chemistry, philosophy, and literature. Al-Mamun built *madrasses*, schools for learning (Morgan 2007, 60), which in later time became role models for the first universities established in late medieval Europe. The House of Wisdom and the *madrasses* gave birth to sophisticated intellectual structures, not less dazzling than the exquisite palaces and mosques surrounding that beehive of creativity.

With this explosion of creativity, the first Arabian Golden Age began (Morgan 2007, 45). It was an Age of Enlightenment guided by the conviction that religious faith, rational thinking, and a rigorous empirical approach in the investigation of man and nature are not mutually contradictory, that they can coexist in peace, and that tolerance towards ethnic, and furthermore that cultural diversity is a better teacher of men than fanaticism that plugs all avenues of free expression and heterogeneity of ideas while opting for the monotonous homogeneity of mental and physical violence. This progressive philosophy molded tenth century Baghdad into what Morgan (Morgan 2007, 60) calls "perhaps the most sophisticated city on earth."

It is an irony of history that al-Mamun—the father of an Arab Age of Enlightenment who had a huge observatory built in Baghdad—has but a tiny crater in the moon named after him by contemporary science as an honorific. That European culture has been deeply edified by Muslim civilization can be gauged by the etymology of the language. As Hunke (Hunke 1960, 17-72) writes, there are a host of terms in our language that owe their origin to the Islamic cultural heritage—a gift bestowed upon Europe by the wisdom of Caliph Haroun al-Rashid and his son, Caliph al-Mamun. These terms include names of stars (Vega, Betelgeuze), names of astronomical instruments (Zenith, Azimuth, Nadir, Theodolite), and many other terms: café, mocca, jacket, mattress, carafe, limonade, alcohol, sorbet, artichoke, apricot, banana, conditor, bergamot, orange, ottomane, alcove, mat, galant, damast, musselin, chiffon, carmesine, safran, muscat, estragon benzine, alkali, soda, saccharin, amber, talcum. Moreover, Al-Mamun's observatory initiated a morpho-evolution of structures (Hunke 1960, 81) built for the study of our solar system. Later the Fatimid caliphs al-Asis and al-Hakim erected an observatory in Cairo, Seljuk Malik-Shah built one in Naishpurin in eastern Persia, Mongol Khan Hulagu ordered the construction of an observatory in Maragha in western Persia, and Tartar ruler Ulugh Beg had one built in Samarkand.

While European monks still wrote on parchment, al-Mamun facilitated a technology transfer from China (Morgan 2007, 59ff.) where paper was invented but reserved for the exclusive use by the ruling class. Al-Mamun went a step further and made way for yet another creative morpho-evolution when he ordered the industrial mass production of paper. Paper, in turn, facilitated book publication. Scientific books and literary books were now freely available. Soon there were major public and private libraries to be found in Baghdad. One court scholar is said to have had a library with so many books that it would have taken 400 camels to transport them.

The fusion of cultures creates a new literature. Baghdad became the center of Arab poetry and Scheherazade's *Tales of Thousand and One Nights*, with its fusion of ancient Hindu, Persian, and Arab narratives, found a new literary genre—yet another illustration of creative morpho-evolution, connecting the past with the present and the future. The hugely successful *Tales of Thousand Nights and One Night* was instrumental in inculcating a passion for reading among book lovers, which resulted in the development of a market for scientific and nonscientific literature. By the thirteenth century, Baghdad boasted thirty-six public libraries and 200 booksellers.

While Abbasid Baghdad created the first Arab Golden Age, Umayyad Qurtuba (Cordoba) in far-off Andalusia was in the process of developing yet another Muslim Golden Age. Having escaped the slaughter of his family in Baghdad, Abd al-Rahman I (Morgan 2007, 69ff.) founded in 756 an Umayyad emirate in Andalusia, which by 929 felt strong enough to claim the caliphate from the weakening Abbasid dynasty in Baghdad. Cordoba, originally a settlement of the ancient Romans and later the capital of the Visigoths, evolved into the capital of Muslim Spain. In the eleventh century at the height of the Umayyad caliphate, it grew into a gorgeous city with some 300 baths, 300 mosques, fifty hospitals and a population of half a million whose literacy rate was so high that Cordoba's public and private libraries contained more books than the whole of Christian Europe.

Since the days of Abd al-Rahman I, Mozarabs—Christians, speaking and writing Arabic—and Jews (Morgan 2007, 70) played a role similar to that played by Nestorian Christians and Persians in Baghdad. Mozarabs translated ancient Hebrew, Greek, and Roman classics into Arab language and thus stimulated a creative morpho-evolution in literature, science, and the arts. From the Jewish *diaspora,* Jews flocked to Umayyad Andalusia where *Sefarad*—a Hebrew term for the Jewish homeland—prospered for about 800 years. Jews were not only steeped in a rich Hebrew culture of medicine, literature, science, and the arts, they were also very skilful traders, and their wealth helped to foster a creative morpho-evolution of rare quality and accomplishment.

The highly impressive cultural morpho-evolution of the Umyyad Empire was brutally interrupted in 1090, when the North African fundamentalist Amoravids invaded Andalusia, ransacked Cordoba, and destroyed its splendor. That act of vandalism, perpetrated with sheer ignorance and fanaticism, was a trigger for a morpho-elimination of enormous proportions. The invaders were, however, not strong enough to hold the domains of the former Umayyad caliphate together. Their Muslim state gradually decayed into a great number of so-called *taifas,* city-states coexisting with cities and territories held by Christian rulers.

Morgan (2007, 69) writes, that the *taifas* spurred a new and final era of creative morpho-evolution in Muslim Andalusia. The rulers of the *taifas* Madrid, Seville, Zaragoza, and Toledo competed with each other to foster their strongholds as centers of learning, invention, and cultural excellence. The spirit of tolerance held high by Abd al-Rahman I and his successors survived in the *taifas.* Muslims, Jews, and Christians lived in peaceful *convivencia*: they cooperated with each other and learned from each other. Non-Muslims were forbidden to proselytize, but otherwise they enjoyed more or less the same rights as the Muslims.

In 1492, Isabella of Castile got hold of the Alhambra in Granada thus ending *reconquista* of Muslim Spain. Her reign turned out to be a merciless victory accompanied by murder, rape, and a ruthless morpho-elimination of creative accomplishments. Palaces and libraries went up in flames. Muslims and Jews were tortured and killed; they were forced to convert to Christian faith or to emigrate. From then on the glorious achievements of the Umayyad dynasty and its less creative successors fell prey to an almost total *omertà*[6]: all memories of a highly sophisticated culture were forgotten—at least for centuries. Much later, that chapter in the book of Lost History was rescued from oblivion by open-minded scholars of the twentieth century.

A third medieval Muslim Golden Age occurred in Cairo. In 969 the Fatimids, a Shiite sect of Tunisia (Morgan 2007, 73ff.), invaded the delta of the Nile and conquered the old Muslim fortress al-Quahira. In the decades and centuries to come, they turned Cairo into yet another Muslim center of learning. In 972, they began to build a grandiose mosque and adjacent to that a university, called al-Azhar, destined to become one of the leading universities of the medieval world. Once more, the proverbial Muslim tolerance reigned supreme. Jews, Christians, and Sunni Muslims gained high positions in the administration and elsewhere.

A few decades later, scholars flocked to Cairo to benefit from its liberal atmosphere, to pursue scientific research and teaching activities. They included luminaries such as mathematician and astronomer ibn Yunus (ca. 950-1009) and the Iraqi physicist ibn al-Haytham (965-1039). Ibn Yunus (Morgan 2007, 128) createed the Hakim *ziji*, a star table that was for the next 800 years to become a point of reference for Muslim star-based timekeeping. Ibn al-Haytham was recruited by the mad Fatimid ruler al-Hakim with the explicit order to stop the annual flooding of the Nile delta. Ibn al-Haytham—in the West known under the name Alhazen—failed in that endeavor because the Nile was too big a river and the flow of its enormous mass of water was too powerful for the dams and floodgates created by means of the early eleventh century technology. While Ibn al-Haytham failed to dam the annual flooding of the Nile, he succeeded in his investigations into the nature of light; his *Book on Optics* later influenced European physicists from Copernicus to Galileo, Leeuwenhoek, and Einstein.

On October 18, 1009, the Church of the Holy Sepulchre in Jerusalem built by emperor Constantine in 330 was destroyed on the orders of sultan al-Hakim (reigns 996-1021). This act of vandalism—plus the fact that Byzantium was on the decline while the Seljuks, Fatimids, and Ayyubids (Morgan 2007, 265ff.) struggled for Muslim supremacy—emboldened the Christian Crusaders to recapture Jerusalem and the Holy land in 1099. While the Muslims had ruled in this region for 400 years and had practiced religious tolerance, living

in peace and harmony with Christians and Jews, the Holy Warriors of Chris-
tendom did not display even a hint of chivalry. On their way to Jerusalem,
they harassed and killed members of the Hebrew faith wherever they could
get hold of them. They turned Jerusalem into a slaughterhouse and massacred
all Jews, Muslims, and even Christians who crossed their path. As one French
account (Morgan ib.) put it: "The carnage lasted for a week. The few who
escaped were reduced to horrible servitude."

In 1171, sultan Saladin, of Kurdish descent, conquered Cairo and established a Sunni Ayyubid dynasty (Morgan 2007, 74). Al-Azhar, originally an
Ismaili school, morphed into a Sunni center for learning. In 1187, Saladin
(Morgan 2007, 268ff.) recaptured Jerusalem and the Holy Land. Unlike the
Christian Crusaders who had pillaged Jerusalem and raped and massacred its
population less than a century before, he turned out to be a wise winner, an
epitome of great leadership. Saladin ordered the Christians, who had amassed
great wealth during their time in power, to abandon the city, yet he allowed
them to depart with everything they owned. They simply had to pay a rather
mild tax per capita. When about 30,000 poor Christians were unable to pay
that tax—neither the wealthy Christian Patriarch Heraclius nor any of the rich
Christian administrators and merchants were willing to bail them out—Saladin, his brother, and brother-in-law came to the rescue of the poor Christians
by paying the required tax out of their private pocket.

In 1250, the Seljuks conquered the Ayyubid sultanate and held it until
1512, when they were ousted by the Ottoman Turks. During all these centuries, Cairo remained an important Muslim center of teaching and learning.
(Morgan 2007, 74).

Despite the regime change, al-Azhar university continued to blossom. At
times it gained from events that elsewhere brought death and destruction. In
1258, Baghdad was attacked by the invading Mongols led by Khan Hulegu (ca.
1217-1265), the grandson of Ghengis Khan, and it was levelled to the ground.[7]
Mosques, dazzling palaces, and precious libraries fell prey to a destructive
morpho-elimination of gargantuan dimensions. The invading barabarians from
the Asian steppe slaughtered the inhabitants of Baghdad. The few survivors able
to escape that massacre fled wherever they could. A few scholars arrived in
Cairo where they gave new impetus to the centers of learning. These scholars
included the Syrian-born physician ibn al-Nafis (1213-1288), who taught at the
al-Mansuri Hospital in Cairo. In his scientific investigations (Morgan 2007, 74),
ibn al-Nafis found that Galen (129-200) had been completely wrong in assum-
ing that blood flows from the right heart chamber of human beings through
pores in the wall into the left chamber. Ibn al-Nafis was the first physician ever
to describe how blood flows from the right chamber into the lungs, where it is
enriched with air, and then back into the left chamber.

We have seen already that Persia began to play a major role in Muslim culture in 750 when Persians helped the Abbasids to overthrow the Umayyad caliphate in Baghdad. In the centuries to follow, a great number of Persian scholars and artists made valuable contributions in their respective domains of activity. Persian miniature paintings were, together with poetry, a unique cultural contribution of the time and Persian architects were famous for the sophistication of their work. When the Seljuks invaded Persia, their leader Malik Shah (1072-1092) converted Isfahan into an important center of his new Sunni Muslim empire, which stretched from Anatolia to the Hindu Kush, from Armenia and Georgia to the Persian Gulf and the southern tip of the Arabian peninsula. Architects, poets, painters, and scholars flocked to the new capital (Morgan 2007, 75) and began a new chapter in the book of Persian creative morpho-evolution.

Let's have a look at the contributions of Persian scholars, architects, and artists to the creative morpho-evolution of our world. Since the days of Ajatollah Khomeini, the West has a tendency to look at Iran as a nation run by a clique of fanatical long-bearded clerics. U.S.President George W. Bush—not much of a historian let alone a cultural anthropologist—projected a lopsided image of Iran when he officially declared Iran to be a "rogue state."

Yet—as Morgan (2007) shows in his ground-breaking study *Lost History: The Enduring Legacy of Muslim Scientists, Thinkers, and Artists*—the Persian culture was one of the most sophisticated ones that ever existed on our globe. Steeped in a glorious past reaching back into millennia before the birth of Jesus Christ, Persia has offered the world much more than its famous rugs, exquisite miniature paintings, and the architectural wonders of Isfahan. Persian scholars not only contributed their own knowledge to Muslim culture, they also were instrumental in the significant knowledge transfer from the ancient Hindu culture to Central Asia, the Middle East, and Europe. Through their outstanding efforts they transmitted Hindu-Persian-Muslim thinking to the West where this compound cultural heritage had a major impact on European Renaissance.

Persia has produced a great number of distinguished scholars, poets, and artists, a few of which we shall shortly mention here. Jabir ibn Haiyan (ca. 721-ca. 815), in the West also know as *Geber*, single-handedly founded the discipline of chemistry. He invented the alembic for distilling alcohol. He was known for a strictly empirical approach towards scientific investigations. Mathematician and father of the algorithm al Khwarizmi (ca. 780-ca. 850) worked at the House of Wisdom in Baghdad. The three Banu Musa brothers (ca. 800-873) were astronomers, mathematicians, and engineers who invented ingenious machines. In the ninth century, mathematician and astronomer al-Farghani (dates of birth and death unknown) was a member of al-Mamun's House of Wisdom. Among many other things, he wrote a concise summary of Ptolemy's *Almagest* in Arabic, thus heavily influencing astronomy research in Muslim countries. Physician and polymath Zakaria al-Razi (865-925) published more than 200 books on a wide spectrum of medical topics. Translated into Latin, his work later enriched the Europeans with the medical knowledge of Hippocrates and Galen. Polymath Ibn al-Farabi (870-950) produced five treatises on music and invented several musical instruments. Mathematician and astronomer Abul Wafa (940-997) made fundamental contributions to spherical geometry thus foreshadowing certain aspects of the work of Copernicus.

As a member of the Muslim army (headed by Sultan Mahmud of Ghazna, Afghanistan), when he found seashells in the mountain ranges high above the Kashmir Valley, polymath al-Biruni (973-1048) formulated the amazing geological hypothesis that this mountain range had once been covered by the sea. He later explored the Ganges from its origin in the Himalayas to its outflow into the Bay of Bengal. He also discussed Greek and Muslim philosophies with Hindu philosophers.

Ibn Sina (980-1037), known as Avicenna in the West, was—along with al-Razi—the most famous of Muslim physicians. His books *Canon of Medicine* and *The Book of Healing* strongly influenced European medicine. His hypothesis that contagious diseases could be transferred by means of water droplets or by germs contained in the soil made Ibn Sina the father of microbiology. He painstakingly analyzed more than 400 different drugs for healing purposes and invented a sophisticated instrument to probe the ultra-narrow lacrymal conduit. He also studied the various structures in the human eye and described the chiasma, where the optical nerves intersect. He was the first physician to understand the function of the aorta and the three heart valves. It was Ibn Sina again who concluded that nerves send messages vital to the functioning of all organs. He maintained that tuberculosis was a contagious disease, precious knowledge that the Europeans did not accept for another 400 years. Ibn Sina was a forerunner of systems thinking—which governs our contemporary science (Guntern 1989) in almost every single domain—because he understood that thinking and feeling could cause diseases, an idea Western medicine adopted, although reluctantly, only in the twentieth century.

Omar Khayyám (1048-1122) was not only a highly gifted poet, but also an outstanding mathematician whose pioneering contributions to geometry, the mapping of stars, and the reform of the calendar were legendary. He was supposed to have developed a heliocentric theory—at a time when older heliocentric theories of the Hindus and of the Greek astronomer Aristarchos of Samos (310-230 BC) were forgotten.

Polymath al-Tusi (1201-1274) wrote more than one hundred books on mathematics, astronomy, physics, medicine, and philosophy. His work on spherical trigonometry, to a large extent, was instrumental in preparing the downfall of Ptolemy's geocentric worldview, a breakthrough to be accomplished later by Copernicus.

Poet Jalal ad-Din al-Rumi (1207-1273), spiritual father of the mystical order of the 'Dancing Dervishes' or "Whirling Dervishes,' discovered the spiritual effects of poetry and dancing. He enunciated how the very sound of the poetic rendition and the use of symbolic words impacted the soul in a manner that the scientific method could never accomplish. On the basis of his own experiments, he discovered that an individual dancing continuously for hours on end and spinning around on her or his own axis could free the mind from the fetters of mechanistic thinking and permitted man to enter an altered state of consciousness, also know as mystical ecstasy.

Physician, mathematician, and astronomer al-Shirazi (1236-1311) was the first scientist ever who explained the physical causes of the rainbow. Moreover, he wrote a critique on Ptolemy's *Almagest*.

Al-Futi, thirtheenth-century librarian of the Maragheh observatory in Persia—founded by al-Tusi and in those days the world's foremost observatory—was in charge of a library of about 400,000 science books. In that capacity he played a very critical role for the intercultural knowledge transfer. In 1279, Mongol emperor Khubilai Khan put astronomer Jamal al-Din in charge of building the Beijing observatory. Thus Jamal al-Din helped to connect ancient Chinese astronomy and Persian and Muslim astronomy.

Poet Hafez (born somewhere between 1310 and 1337) was sometimes considered to be the greatest poet of all time. In his *ghazals*—lyrical poetry—he interweaved topics of Sufi mystic experience and the concepts of passionate, romantic love. Although he wasn't aware of it, this accomplishment made him a congenial companion of the medieval French troubadours, who had been heavily influenced by the contacts that Charles Martell (ca. 688-741) and Charlemagne (747-814) made in their southbound military campaigns with Muslim culture. Hafez was, in addition to his other talents, the author of the *Divan*, a work of exquisite poetry that inspired the German poet and writer Johann Wolfgang von Goethe centuries later to create his work *East-West Divan*.

Last but not least, there was Ulugh Beg (ca. 1393-1449), grandson of Timur-i-leng and ruler of the Timurid Dynasty. In 1428 he built in Samarkand a sophisticated observatory called the *Ghurkani Zij*. Using a magnified sextant, he charted the coordinates of a cluster of 1,078 stars and calculated the stellar year—at a time when there were no telescopes and computers were not even in the horizon. Even so, the result of his calculation was, as Thubbron reports (2006, 254) "within seconds of that computed by electronics." Ulugh Beg's performance was one of the most outstanding astronomic achievements of all time.

After this brief section on great Persian minds and their impact on Islamic and other cultures, let us return to the Seljuks. Their empire lasted for about 150 years; inner chaos loosened the cohesion of its various parts and the empire splintered into independent entities. Although some of them survived, with the onslaught of the invading Mongols in the late thirteenth century the Seljuk Empire ceased to exist by the early fourteenth century.

In a later chapter, we shall deal with the impact of the Mongol invasion on Muslim and European civilization and describe the tremendous morpho-elimination and the amazing morpho-evolution produced by that onslaught. For the time being, we will continue our narrative with the influence the Timurid Dynasty had on the Muslim empire and its creative achievements.

In the second half of the fourteenth century, Timur-i-leng founded a new dynasty that lasted until 1506. He was of Turkish-Mongol descent, from the Chagatai Khanate. His main political purpose was to restore the vanished Mongol empire. He adopted Persian language and Persian culture, but in his military campaigns he turned out to be a ruthless killer rather than a cultured ruler. When he conquered Isfahan, he had 70,000 prisoners slaughtered. When he ravaged Damascus, he ordered the rounding up of the inhabitants in front of the mosque: 70,000 again were massacred. On December 17, 1398, just before attacking Delhi, he ordered some 100,000 prisoners, most of them Hindus, to be butchered. According to Thubron (2006, 198), Timur-i-leng massacred about 5 million Hindus in north India. The limping conqueror was eventually killed in a military campaign while invading Ming China.

Although Timur, also known as "The Scourge of God," shared with Attila the Hun and Genghis Khan the reputation of a ruthless slaughterer, he was nevertheless a man interested in architecture and the arts. He erected towers where the skulls of his slain victims were inserted into the walls to announce that, "Timur-i-leng was here." He made Samarkand the capital of his empire and erected the Registan complex (Morgan 2007, 76), which—with its three monumental arches, huge plaza, glittering blue-tiled mosques, and connected madarassas—belongs to the Cultural World Heritage protected by UNESCO.

Timurs successors expanded the Timurid Empire until it stretched from Afghanistan and Pakistan in the east to Mesopotamia in the west and the Caucasus in the north. The steady outpouring of spoils from their vast empire turned Timurid rulers into patrons of the arts whose wealth stimulated new heydays of Persian culture.

After a period of stagnation, Isfahan began to flourish again in the sixteenth century under the reign of the Persian ruler Shah Abbas I (1587-1629), one of the most important rulers of Shiite Safavid Empire founded in 1501 and lasting until 1722. The architecture and civic improvements that followed were stupendous. When the twentieth century travel writer Robert Byron visited

Isfahan (Morgan 2007, 75), he wrote that the huge Imam Square—and the pointed arches and blue-tiled mosques and palaces surrounding it—were more splendid than St. Peter's Basilica in Rome or the palace of Versailles. The Imam square with its surrounding buildings is now also a UNESCO World Heritage site.

West of the Savafid Empire, another empire entered a new phase of expansion and creative cultural morpho-evolution. In 1299, Osman Gazi declared his own little kingdom to be independent from the Seljuk Empire; thus he founded the Ottoman Empire in Anatolia. The Ottoman Empire survived (Morgan 2007, 77) the invasion of the Timurids and outlasted their dynasty. In 1453, sultan Mehmet II conquered Constantinople, turned it into the capital of the Ottoman Turks, and renamed it Istanbul. In the course of time, the Ottoman Turks conquered almost the whole realm of the former Arab Caliphate from Cairo to Central Asia, and from Sudan and Yemen in the south to the Ukraine in the north. They also brought the Balkans under their rule, made forays into Hungary, and laid siege to Vienna, but winter forced them to retreat. In a second onslaught on Vienna, military forces of the Habsburg Dynasty defeated the Ottoman invasion armies. In 1571, the Ottoman Turks, whose naval forces attempted to control the Mediterranean Sea, were defeated in the sea battle at Lepanto by a coalition of Catholic forces led by King Philip II of Spain.

At the peak of the Ottoman Empire, which lasted until 1922, Sultan Suleiman the Magnificent—who reigned from 1520 to 1566—once more demonstrated the religious tolerance we have already encountered with other Muslim rulers such as al-Mamun and Saladin. As Morgan (2007, 77) writes, Suleiman relied on "the use of meritocracy rather than hereditary nobility to administer the empire." A similar open-mindedness and religious tolerance had already been demonstrated in 1492 when one of his predecessors sultan Bayazid II (Morgan 2007, 279) invited the Sephardic Jews from al-Andalus—the *taifas* of Toledo, Madrid, Cordoba, Granada, and Seville—to come to Istanbul and make it their new home. With this influx, the Ottoman Empire received the rich cultural heritage of Arab Muslims, which helped to foster a remarkable creative morpho-evolution in Istanbul and other cities of the Ottoman domains.

There was yet another Muslim empire that emerged later than the Ottoman Empire and ended earlier than it. It gave birth to a stupendous creative morpho-evolution of an advanced culture in which wealthy patrons supported science and the arts, and where religious tolerance permitted the peaceful coexistence of various religious faiths—Muslims, Hindus, Buddhists, and Christians.

In 1526, Babur, a direct descendant of Timur-i-leng (Morgan 2007, 77) and from his mother's side also a descendant of Genghis Khan, invaded the Delhi Sultanate and established in Agra the capital of the Mughal[8] Empire. He was an erudite warrior steeped in Persian culture who wrote the *Baburnama*, considered to be the first authentic autobiography in Muslim culture.

Babur's grandson Akbar (1542-1605) was only fourteen when he inherited the Mughal throne because his father Nasirrudin Humayun died. He turned out to be a polymath and great lover of the arts. Moreover, he was interested in the coexistence of religious faiths and even attempted to lay the foundation for a new religion, integrating Islam and Hinduism (Morgan 2007, 78). In his wisdom, he favored intermarriage between Muslims and Hindus and offered Hindus access to higher posts in his administration. In several campaigns he expanded the influence of Mughal rule on the Indian subcontinent. All of these commending activities made him enter history as Akbar the Great. Today he is considered to have been the most important Mughal ruler of them all.

His son Jahangir (1569-1627) was made of a different stuff. Although he continued to expand the Mughal Empire, he was heavily addicted to opium and alcohol. The adherents of the ancient Hindu Jain religion suffered gravely from his persecution. His favorite wife Nur Jahan seems to have held the reigns of power and, as legend has it, she may even have been involved in the cause of his death.

When Jahangir died, his son Shahbuddin Mohammed Shah Jahan (1592-1666) ascended the Mughal throne. He had already been a favorite of Akbar the Great, who must have sensed the potential of Shah Jahan—the Persian name for 'King of the World'. In fact, Shah Jahan turned out to be a great ruler. In his youth he had shown not only an unusual degree of education and intellectual interests, he had also headed the armies of his intoxicated father and had successfully waged war against the princes of the Deccan, thus increasing the size and importance of the Mughals. Once in power, he continued his military conquests. He also turned out to be a generous patron of architecture and the arts. He built many great palaces, the most famous being the Taj Mahal in Agra and the Red Fort in Delhi.

It seemed that his love for architecture had to do with two quite dissimilar factors—saltpeter and his wife Mumtaz. He sold the warring states of Northern Europe tons of saltpeter (KNO_3), an oxidant used in gunpowder. Between 1618 and 1648, most of the major European powers were involved the so-called Thirty Years' War. Due to religious fanaticism, Protestants and Catholics transformed Germany into a wasteland. In the process of that destruction, Danish, Swedish, and French mercenary armies used tons of gunpowder. What impoverished Europe and its populations made Shah Jahan so rich that he could easily indulge in his obsession with architecture.

And then there was the second factor. At the age of fourteen, he married the Persian princess Arjumand Banu Begum with whom he had fourteen children. She came from a Persian noble family and she invited scores (Morgan 2007,

78) of Persian architects, artists, poets, and scholars to the court in Agra. Once more, Persian culture initiated a new wave of creative morpho-evolution.

Shah Jahan gave Arjuman Banu Begum the name Mumtaz Mahal, a Persian expression meaning 'Beloved Ornament of the Palace.' But she was much more than just an ornament. In fact she became his favorite wife, accompanied him on most of his military campaigns, and was his most trusted adviser. She died on one of his campaigns into the Deccan shortly after having given birth to their fourteenth child. He was inconsolable in his grief and decided to build a grandiose memorial to their love. This was the beginning of the Taj Mahal.

It took twenty-two years to build the monument even though 20,000 artists, architects, engineers, artists, and craftsmen were involved in design and construction. As Morgan (Morgan 2007, 238) writes, thousands of elephants transported blocks of white marble from Rajasthan and expeditions hauled precious stones from the Indian subcontinent and from foreign countries: jade and crystal from China, turquoise from Tibet, lapis lazuli from Afghanistan, sapphire from Sri Lanka, and carnelian from Arabia. When the building was finished, it turned out to be one of the architectonic wonders of the world; a structure of unsurpassed elegance and beauty. Bengal writer and Nobel laureate Rabindranath Tagore later characterized it as "a tear of creation on the cheek of eternity." Today, millions of aesthetic minds all over the globe are in rapture over the mysterious light emitted by the white marble of the Taj Mahal during full moon. Thus Mumtaz Mahal received a memorial of unique beauty that has inspired and keeps inspiring millions of creative individuals to strive for perfection in performance. The Taj Mahal is now a UNESCO World Heritage Site.

Shah Jahan reigned for thirty years, from 1628 to 1658, when his son Aurangzeb led a rebellion and made his spendthrift father a prisoner in the citadel of Agra. Until his death eight years later, Shah Jahan sat in his confinement staring day-in and day-out at the marble palace Taj Mahal.

Aurangzeb (1618-1707) reigned for forty-eight years. Although he is considered to be the last great Mughal ruler, his less than enlightened governance was responsible for the decline of the empire. He lost the cooperation of former Rajput allies as well as the sympathy of his non-Muslim subjects, who were suffering under a massive tax load. When he died, the northwest of the Mughal Empire was gone and the Hindu Maratha Empire had conquered vast territories of the former Mughal domains.

After Aurangzeb's death, the Mughal Empire entered a rapid decline because its rulers got progressively weaker, until the British army eventually disposed of the last. In 1857, Queen Victoria's army quelled a rebellion of the *sepoys*—the native Indian soldiers serving in the army of the British East

Indian Company—and turned the Indian subcontinent into a British colony. Soon a hitherto unheard of exploitation began to plague the Indian subcontinent. The British East India Company, sponsored by the Queen's armies, was the perpetrator of that ruthless venture. On December 31, 1600, the British East India Company was formed by a Royal Charter issued by Queen Elizabeth I. British East India Company was a joint stock company whose main purpose was to get a monopoly on all trade of spices, tea, opium, saltpeter, indigo dye, cotton, and silk. In their mercilessly mercenary policy, the British East India Company and the British military-political administration played a time-honored strategy the ancient Romans called *divide et impera*—divide and rule. They manipulated the various maharajahs and local and regional rulers and turned them against each other. Gradually, the British expanded their power until the whole subcontinent was in their grip—a state of affairs that lasted up to 1947 when India gained independence.

The British East India Company and the British Crown exploited the Indian subcontinent in every possible way—robbing (among other acts of transgression) the timeless crown jewels of the Mughal Empire, including the famous Koh-i-Noor diamond, plus carloads of precious jewellery studded with gold, diamonds, sapphires, rubies, emeralds, and pearls.

But the exploitation went beyond common boundaries. In order to cover its trade deficit with China, the most "Honorable British East India Company" smuggled each year more than 1,000 tons of opium into China against its government's explicit ban on the import of that commodity—an attempt to curb an epidemic drug dependency among the populace. When China tried to squash the drug trafficking by the greedy traders, British armies invaded China and waged two opium wars in order to secure their profits. Other colonizers from Europe joined the cartel. Undermined by wars and internal rebellions, the Qing Dynasty expired in 1911.

Unlike the Mughal Dynasty, whose outstanding creative contributions and (with exceptions) amazing tolerance of other religious faiths we have shortly discussed in the preceding sections, the British Crown and the drug dealers of the British East India Company brought India nothing but a destructive mix of exploitation, humiliation, and misery. British writer Rudyard Kipling's insensitive remark about India being 'the white man's burden' perverted the truth. The British East India Company and its government were in fact the native man's burden, and it was a burden whose manifold consequences Indians were not likely to forget very soon.

The simplicity of the the colonial subjects, which white administrators of the British crown colony interpreted as ignorance and found to their advantage, however reflected the administrator's own abysmal ignorance. In their delusional conviction about their supremacy, the white rulers seem to have considered their subjects to be some sort of twilight-creatures, to be kept beyond the realm of human dignity. The natives responded to condescension, contempt, and repression with a mix of resignation and resentment that eventually led to the independence movements under the enlightened leadership of Mahatma Gandhi and Jawaharlal Nehru.

By now we have discussed the Golden Ages of Muslim rule with its splendid capitals in Cordoba, Cairo, Istanbul, Damascus, Baghdad, Isfahan, Samarkand, and Agra. We have also mentioned the extraordinary creative contributions Persian scholars and artists have made to the morpho-evolution of science, art, medicine, architecture, engineering, and civilization. Now we may delve a little deeper into some of the most dazzling achievements of creative Muslim culture.

Let's begin our inquiry with the topic of music and musical instruments. Our Western culture is teeming with creations whose origin in Muslim culture, of which we are most of the time completely unaware. A good illustration of this fact is to be found in our love songs and musical instruments. Our love songs still carry rhythmical, melodic, and harmonic elements of the rich musical heritage of all the countries medieval Muslims conquered, or came in contact with. Music from China—during the Tang dynasty, even from Japan—Mongolia, Central Asia, India, Persia, Middle East, Egypt, Byzantium, Balkan, Rome, the north of the African continent, Sicily, and Andalusia has had a far reaching impact on Western music.

An inebriated crooner—Dean Martin, for instance—swallowing his consonants while drooling through a washed-out 'I-love-you-dearly' ditty addressed to a buxom damsel represents a far and bawdy echo of an ecstatic poetry originally developed by Muslims (whose Qu'ran forbade the drinking of alcohol!).

When the medieval French rulers Charles Martell and Charlemagne—in prolonged campaigns—fought the Muslims in Spain and drove them back over the Pyrenees, they made prisoners of young Moorish women who had been educated in the long tradition of Muslim love songs celebrating unfulfilled chaste love, chivalry, and mystical experience (Morgan 2007, 241ff.). Together with itinerant musicians from the Iberian Peninsula, these captives inspired French troubadours whose heart-tugging songs of unfulfilled love have ultimately degraded into the anaemic ditties to be found in Western pop song hit lists. And let us not forget that the proverbial white knight in shining armor the troubadours sang about was, of course, a cultural descendant of a black knight galloping on an Arabian steed across the deserts.

In medieval times, there arose a heated dispute among clerics as to whether the melodies played in bawdy houses—melodies which also pleased the ears and souls of listeners who were not familiar with houses of disrepute—could be combined with pious lyrics in order to make church music more attractive. Eventually quite a number of the devil's melodies were adopted to praise the Lord. Yet there is also a more noble source of Western church songs. As Morgan (2007, 241f.) reports, in the thirteenth century King Alfonso the Wise of Castile and Leon ordered and sponsored the creation of more than 400 sacred Christian songs; about 300 of these songs replicated in form and content Andalusian Muslim *al-muwashahat*, strophic songs with a refrain.

The Spanish *flamenco* is a form of music as deep as the African-American blues. The Spanish also call it *cante jondo*, which means 'deep song' or 'song from the depth of one's soul.' The resemblance between flamenco and blues is more than coincidental. Some Arabian slave traders were Muslims, and many of the African natives of the west coast of Africa who were sold into slavery in the United States were also Muslims. Flamenco is a music that demands great artistry in singing as well as in dancing and guitar playing. Arriving at the crescendo, flamenco singers—chanting complex melodies with intricate rhythms in a husky, hoarse voice—pass into *duende*, a state of altered consciousness where instinct and intuition fuse and rational thinking takes a back seat. The term flamenco (Morgan 2007, 243) seems to derive from the Arab words '*fellah mengu*' meaning 'country vagabonds' or 'expelled peasants'—a reminder of the sociopolitical circumstances existing after the end of the *reconquista*.

By the way, the very fact that flamenco is such a refined music emphasizes a point often overlooked: great creative performance does not only occur where generous patrons permit individuals and groups to work in a relatively relaxed setting. Great creative performances also flourish where deep existential pain, grief, and financial problems haunt human beings. In other words, human creativity is stimulated in situations of stress as well as in situations of relaxation. But if these two states reach a maximum, they cease to be stimulating and often block all creativity. We do need optimum states of stress or relaxation in order to be creative (see figure "Windows of Creative Opportunities" in Chapter 2.32 Phase of Inspiration).

In 1492, when Queen Isabella of Castile forced Christians, Muslims, and Sephardic Jews to convert to Christian faith or to emigrate, some went underground and joined Andalusia's gypsies, whose forefathers had migrated from India in the eleventh century and had trekked across Central Asia, the Middle East, the Balkans, and Europe until they reached Spain in the first half of the fifteenth century. Flamenco arose out of this fusion of cultures. Like the blues, it is a creation accomplished by musicians belonging to the lowest stratum of society. Yet flamenco is one of the most sophisticated forms of music that has ever existed, and it has spawned a creative morpho-evolution that has inspired, among others, Manuel de Falla, George Bizet, Carlos Surinach—the latter wrote music for Martha Graham and other choreographers—and many other composers.

After Queen Isabella's conquest of Granada, Spanish conquistadores invading the Americas exported Arab Muslim music. According to Morgan (2007, 243), Brazilian *samba*, Mexican *jarabe*, Chilean *la cueca*, Argentinian *el gato*, and Cuban *la guajira* are all children of the Andalusian Muslim music—and so is, by the way, the *fado* of Portugal.

The movie classic *The Third Man* with Orson Welles, Joseph Cotton, Howard Trevor, and Alida Valli has one of the most unforgettable scores in the history of film music. The main melody is played on an Austrian zither, whose prototype was the Muslim *qanum* instrument (Morgan 2007, 242). The Scottish bagpipe stems from the Arabic *gaita*. The Andalusian guitar on which flamenco virtuoso Paco de Lucia plays his crystalline staccato solos has its forerunner in the Muslim '*ud*. The Broadway musical *Fiddler on the Roof*, in which actor Zero Mostel played the role of the milkman and which received nine Tony Awards, has its share of Arabic connection. The musical instrument that inspired the name of this great musical comedy is derived from the Persian *kamancha* and the Arab *rabab*. And in the unforgettable movie *Alexis Zorbas* where Anthony Quinn dances a wild syrtaki—just after his poorly engineered construction for transporting logs down a steep hill on the island of Crete breaks down—the music is played on the *santur*, an instrument invented by Persian Muslim culture. The *santur* would eventually inspire the construction of European keyboard instruments. And the oboe we hear in a concert of classical Western music owes its existence to the Muslim *zurna*.

The musical notation used by Western composers owes its existence to Arab Muslims and not to Italian musicians as traditional history would have us believe. In his book *Historical Facts for the Arabian Musical Influence*, historian H. G. Farner (Morgan 2007, 241) compares the Italian notes with the Arabian alphabet:

Arabic alphabet:	Mi	Fa	Sad	La	Sin	Dal	Ra
Italian notes:	Mi	Fa	Sol	La	Si	Do	Re

It seems that the Italian notation, which emerged in the eleventh century, came from the Muslims ruling over Sicily. Muslims began to make their first forays into Sicily in the middle of the seventh century. They conquered it step by step between 827 and 902 and then ruled it until 1091, when the Normans ousted the last Arab Muslims from the island. Although between 800 and 840, Calabria and Puglia were also in Muslim hands—Muslims even once advanced to the port of Ostia and entered Rome where they sacked St. Peter's Basilica and St. Paul's Basilica. It is fair to assume that the Italian music notation is the result of a knowledge transfer that occurred between Muslim-governed Sicily and the Italian mainland.

There were a great number of musical geniuses who made landmark contributions to the theory and practice of Muslim music (Morgan 2007, 241). Prominent among them were poets creating lyrics to be sung. Umar ibn Abi Rabi'ah al-Makhzumi (644-712/719) was a poet in Mecca who created poems about his love affairs with noblewoman pilgrims who came to visit the Holy Shrine. Jamil (died 701), from the Udhrah tribe in Hejaz, was another poet who wrote *ghazal* love poems. His topic was the languishing lover pining for the loved-one and dying as martyr of chaste, unrequited love. This mix of chivalric, spiritual-mystic, and passionate earthly love would later become the main theme of French troubadours.

Ziryab (ca. 789-857), a poet and musician of Persian or Kurdish descent (Morgan 2007, 155), was forced to leave Abbassid Baghdad because his teacher became envious of his pupil's talents. A generous offer from the court of Cordoba made his exile easy: he was promised an annual salary of 200 dinars, an annual bonus of 1,000 dinars, some other special bonuses, and eventually a palace and a few villas in the area of Cordoba. He accepted the invitation, left the court of Haroun al-Rashid, and travelled to Andalusia where he set up a music conservatory. Moreover, he soon assumed a role of *maître des cérémonies* who not only played the four-stringed *'ud,* but also an important role as the supreme authority and role model in matters of aesthetics—from fashion in dresses to hair style, perfumes, hygiene, and elegant speaking. It is amazing to note that some 700 years later, Leonardo da Vinci would play a somewhat similar role at the court of Duke Ludovico Sforza in Milan.

Another important contribution to music was made by the polymath al-Kindi (ca. 801-873), a forerunner of Einstein's theory of relativity (Morgan 2007, 165f.). He wrote 361 works on topics as diverse as music, mathematics, astronomy, chemistry, medicine, philosophy, perfumes, and other aromatic substances. Al-Kindi studied the interactions between an organism and ingestion of chemical substances, which made him the founder of pharmacology. His inquiring mind also mused about the relationships between matter, space, and time. He was convinced: "Time exists only with motion; body, with motion; motion, with body . . . if there is motion, there is necessarily body; if there is a body, there is necessarily motion." This is an amazing statement, especially if we consider that 800 years after al-Kindi, Newton (Clark 1972, 103) wrote that space and time are absolute and that space is static while time flows like a laminary stream. Although his contemporary Leibniz (Bronowski 1973, 241) fought Newton's theory of absolute space and time and stated: "I hold space to be something purely relative, as time is," it took another 200 years until Einstein in 1905 came back to al-Kindi's notion of relative space and time. In other words, European physics took 800 and 1,000 years respectively (Leibniz and Einstein) to come to a conclusion that a brilliant Muslim thinker had already conceived a long time before! al-Kindi was not only the most important Muslim philosopher, he was also the first music theoretician and wrote fifteen treatises on music and proposed to add a fifth string to the Arabian *'ud*—a proposition later to be accomplished in the Andalusian guitar.

Ibn al-Farabi (870-950), an important Persian philosopher who published about one hundred works on logics and other topics (including a comment on Aristotle), also wrote five treatises on music (Morgan 2007, 240). He invented (Hunke 1960, 300) musical instruments such as the *rabab*, a precursor of the European violin, (which is plucked like a lute or played with a bow and still in use in Afghanistan today), and the *canum*, a precursor of the Western piano. He wrote about the positive effects of music on human thinking and feeling. Moreover, he created an Arabian tone system still in use in contemporary Arabic music.

The Persian Ibn Sina (980-1037), in the west known as Avicenna, was not only a highly creative contributor to the theory and practice of medicine (Morgan 2007, 191), but also an accomplished music theoretician. In his book on Muslim influence on the occident, Hunke (1960, 301) characterizes him as a "first-rank musical authority." Together with Al-Farabi (ca. 872-ca. 925), he discovered the 5:4 ratio for the major third and the 6:5 ratio for the minor third. Thus the thirds lost their former dissonant character and turned into sounds our contemporary ear perceives as harmonious.

Persian polymath Al-Ghazali (1058-1111) published several treatises on the theory of atomism, on medicine, on psychology, on jurisprudence, and on philosophy. He was also a theologian making major contributions to Sufism (Morgan 2007, 240) by exploring the vast field of mystical music and mystical faith. As we have seen in our discussion on Persian scholars, this was a domain that later Jalal ad-Din al-Rumi (1207-1273) would investigate in more depth.

Ibn Rushd (1126-1198) was yet another representative of that amazing cluster of Muslim polymaths we have mentioned already. In the West, Ibn Rushd—of Andalusian origin and born in Cordoba—was known as Averroes (Morgan 2007, 240). Apart from his comprehensive studies in mathematics, astronomy, physics, medicine, psychology, logic, and philosophy, he was also the main protagonist (Hunke 1960, 263) in a knowledge transfer bringing the wisdom of Aristotle to Thomas of Aquinas and scholastic philosophy. He investigated musical theory and introduced a musical notation based on the Arabian alphabet.

During the dark Middle Ages, European creativity slumbered like the proverbial Sleeping Beauty waking up intermittently on special occasions. The construction of magnificent Gothic cathedrals was one such rousing. Finally, the

Sleeping Beauty opened her eyes when she was kissed by the Prince Charming of Muslim culture. European creativity awakened, soared high, and triggered the Renaissance—a period of time comparable in quality, intensity, and comprehensiveness to the Golden Age in ancient Greece (500-300 BC), the Tang period (618-907) in China, the many Golden Ages of Muslim culture during medieval time, and the Muromachi period (1336-1573) in Japan. Renaissance is the jewel in the crown of European history. The rich Muslim musical knowledge and the instruments invented by them were brought into European civilization by the crusaders returning from the Holy Land via Andalusia, Sicily, and Byzantium. The wealth and sophistication of Muslim culture also had a penetrating impact on European literature and science, thus stimulating yet another creative morpho-evolution that continues to this very day.

Dante Alighieri (1265-1321), author of the *Divina Commedia* and godfather of Italian poetry, was greatly influenced by Muslim culture. His studies of the poetry of French troubadours and their language—the Langue d'Oc of the French Provence—introduced him to the culture and literature of Andalusian Muslims. During his sojourn in Sicily (Morgan 2007, 247), he became acquainted with Muslim folklore, the Qu'ran, and the writings of scholars who had worked in al-Mamun's House of Wisdom in Baghdad. He was also deeply impressed by contemporary Muslim scientists. As Hunke (1960, 332f.) points out, Dante found an Arabian role model in Ibn Arabi (1165-124) whose ideas, metaphors, and choice of words he emulated to quite some extent. Dante's heroine Beatrice, for whom he pines with unrequited love, is the typical female protagonist of the classical Muslim *minnesong*: a spiritual guide of unique beauty and virtue. Beatrice leads her mystical lover on the path of virtue and stimulates his vision, in which he ascends the stairs in paradise towards ever-higher levels of mystical perfection.

Muslim literature not only inspires European poetry, it also impacts its prose. A good case in point is the famous narrative *The Book of Thousand Nights and one Night*. It is the precursor of the great novels of Western culture—from Boccaccio's *Decameron* to Joyce's *Ulysses,* and *One Hundred Years of Solitude* by the Colombian writer and Nobel laureate Gabriel García Márquez.

Constructed not unlike a set Russian *matrioshkas*, the story told in *The Book of Thousand Nights and One Night* is a story about a beautiful Scheherazade (Morgan 2007, 247ff.) who is married to an Indo-Persian king Shahryar. He is a cruel and sadistic fellow who threatens to kill Scheherazade if she is not able anymore to come up with yet another fascinating story. Scheherazade cleverly ends her mesmerizing story every morning with a new cliffhanger, and then stops, thus leaving her husband in a state of suspense where he longs for the next night where Scheherazade will continue spinning her yarn. In the stories, she talks about real and fictional characters such as caliph Haroun al-Rashid, Alibaba and the Thirty Thieves, Sindbad the Sailor, Aladdin and his wonderful oil lamp. Yet this collection of stories, originally published in the tenth century by Baghdad-based editor al-Jahshyari, takes its inspiration also from much older sources including ancient Hindu tales, Homer's *Odyssee*, and a collection of stories called *Hazar Afsana—A Thousand Tales*—attributed to the ancient Persian princess who was a daughter of Shah Artaxerxes II (436-358 BC). In other words, Scheherazade's tales are yet another example of creative morpho-evolution whose origins reach back into folktales several thousand years old, and whose effects on literature are still reverberating today and will continue to do so.

When Christian Crusaders invaded the Holy Land in the eleventh and twelfth centuries, they heard some of these stories and unwittingly served as links in an intercultural knowledge transfer when they brought these tales back into Europe. Giovanni Bocaccio's (1313-1375) *Decameron* and Geoffrey Chaucer's (ca. 1343-ca. 1400) *Canterbury Tales* are strongly inspired by *The Book of Thousand Nights and One Night*.

Spanish writer Miguel de Cervantes (1547-1616) wrote *Don Quixote de la Mancha* (Morgan 2007, 247)—a narrative today considered to be a classic of Western literature and one of the best novels ever written. In 1575, Cervantes was aboard a galley sailing from Naples. On its way to Barcelona it was seized by Algerian corsairs and Miguel de Cervantes was forced to spend five years as a slave in Algeria before he was eventually ransomed and permitted to return to Spain. In Algeria, as well as in his own country, he came into close contact with Muslim folklore. Don Quixote and Sancho Panza, the two heroes of Cervantes's novel, despite their ironical and at times farcical portrayal, are unmistakably descendants of Muslim knights. Don Quixote's chaste love for his heroine Dulcinea del Toboso is a satirical version of the chivalric romance that medieval Muslim poets have celebrated for centuries.

Muslim influence in literature (Morgan 2007, 248) was apparent not only in southern Europe; it was also visible in the northwestern parts. Christopher Marlow (1564-1593), a contemporary of Shakespeare and his most critical competitor, wrote *Tamurlaine*, a play in blank verse about the career of Timur-i-leng, founder of the Timurid Empire. William Shakespeare (1564-1616), the greatest poet and playwright in English language, created *Othello the Moor of Venice*, a tragedy still belonging to the stock and trade of major theaters in the Western world.

Although we shall hear more about the impact of Muslim culture and the Silk Road on the paintings of the Italian Renaissance, we may state here that Muslim literature inspired not only the literature of the European Renaissance, but also its painters and musical composers in the nineteenth and twentieth century. In the eighteenth century, Antoine Galland translated the tales of *The Book of Thousand and One Nights* into French, thus sparking an enduring trend of orientalism. This fad manifested itself (Morgan 2007, 248) in the paintings of Jean-August-Dominique Ingres (1780-1876), Eugène Delacroix (1798-1863), Auguste Renoire (1841-1919), and Henri Matisse (1869-1954). Paul Klee travelled to Tunisia and Egypt and his intricate drawings and polyphone paintings clearly show the influence of Arab decorative patterns. In April 1914 during his trip to Tunisia, Klee happily confided (Gideon-Welcker 1985, 43) in his diary: "Me and the colour have become a unity, I am a painter." Tunisian Muslim architecture and the glowing colors of its landscapes left a deep impression on this very sensitive artist.

The fad of orientalism (Morgan 2007, 248) also inspired the ballet music of composer Pyotr Ilyich Tchaikovsky (1840-1893), while the tales of *The Book of Thousand Nights and One Night* prompted Nicolai Rimsky-Korsakov's (1844-1908) to compose the symphonic suite *Scheherazade*.

By far the most important creative contributions made by medieval Muslim culture occurred in mathematics and science, where technological inventions went hand in hand with breathtaking discoveries. At a time when Europe was still in the fangs of superstition and unenlightened feudal rule, the few literate individuals existing in those times were monks living and working in monasteries. These monks did little more than simply copy ancient texts.

Let's now have a look at a few amazing exploits in medieval Muslim science.

The Qur'an (LXXII: 28) states with respect to Allah (Morgan 2007, 81): ". . . and He has enumerated everything in numbers." This statement echoes a view of the universe formulated by the ingenious Greek mathematician Pythagoras (born between 580-572 and died between 500-490) more than a thousand years before the Qur'an was written. Pythagoras—whose theorem still remains, as Bronowski (1973, 160) puts it, "the most important single theorem in the whole of mathematics"—was convinced that the movements of celestial bodies were strictly ordered, and that this dynamic and harmonious order could and should be expressed in numbers. For Pythagoras, mathematics and music were intimately linked subjects.

Pythagoras discovered that chords pleasing our Western ears correspond to the exact divisions of a string by whole numbers. From that finding (Bronowski 1973, 156f.), Pythagoras and his followers concluded that all regularities, patterns, structures, and order in nature were of a musical kind. The movements of celestial bodies were, as it were, the music of the spheres, a music that could be defined by precise numbers. The idea of encoding nature's mysteries into a set of precise numbers gave an enormous boost to Muslim thinking. The first Muslim mathematician to deal with ancient Greek mathematics and philosophy was the Persian al-Khwarizmi (ca. 780-ca. 850), born in Khwarizm (today Khiva in Uzbekistan).

In 832, Caliph al-Mamun (Morgan 2007, 86) invited the mathematician, astronomer, and geographer Muhammad ibn Musa al-Khwarizmi to join the mathematicians and scientists working in The House of Wisdom in Baghdad. Here al-Khwarizmi met the Assyrian physician and scientist Hunayn ibn Ishaq (809-873), who was involved in a research aimed at finding God in numerals. Huayn ibn Ishaq translated classics of ancient Greek science into the Arabian language. They include Euclid's book on geometry, the *Elements*—still a number one bestseller in mathematics today—plus important writings by Pythagoras, Archimedes, Ptolemy, and the philosophers Socrates and Aristotle. Al-Khwarizmi spoke Greek and helped Hunayn ibn Ishaq in his endeavor; their joint effort strongly influenced Muslim mathematics.

Al-Khwarizmi learned that at the court of Caliph al-Mansur there was an Indian astronomer named Kanka (Morgan 2007, 87f.), who had used formulas developed by an ancient Hindu mathematician named Brahmagupta to calculate the positions of the sun and planets. Al-Khwarizmi sent emissaries to India to find out more about this mathematician. They returned with a whole collection of ancient Sanskrit scriptures, among which was a 200-year-old book called *Brahma Sphuta Siddhanta*. The concept propagated in that book which struck Al-Khwarizmi as the most revolutionary of all mathematical treasures was a dot symbolizing nothingness. Gradually it dawned on him that this dot, the zero of our contemporary mathematics, was the starting point for a total revolution of all of mathematics.

Al-Khwarizmi studied Brahmagupta's decimal system, whose characters represent quantities ranging from zero to nine—which from zero and combined with minus and plus signs can reach up into positive infinity and down into negative infinity. Al-Khwarizmi thus rediscovered the source code that revolutionized the concept of the universe and empowered scientists to describe and define the universe in a precise manner.

The structure of the Hindu method translated into a corresponding Arab notation was of amazing formal elegance. Let's take an example to demonstrate its utter simplicity. In medieval Arabian notation, the year 1488 was defined by only four symbols. Medieval Europeans had to use thirteen symbols to accomplish the same task in Latin capitals: MCCCCLXXXVIII. Even more cumbersome was to jot that year down in English words because we need more than forty abstract characters to do it: one-thousand-four-hundred-and-eighty-eight.

Like a sponge, Al-Khwarizmi absorbed mathematical knowledge from the ancient Hindus and from the works of the ancient Greeks, which he got via Byzantium and through translations done by Huayn ibn Ishaq and himself. He was an outstanding polymath (Morgan 2007, 90f.), publishing books on algebra—his book *Al-Jabr wa al-Muqabala* on astronomy and geography gives the new science of algebra its name. He calculated the latitudes and longitudes of more than 2,400 places on the surface of the earth. He also published studies on the astrolabe, sundials, and the Jewish calendar.

Al-Khwarizmi's decimal system, borrowed from the Hindus and formulated in Arabic symbols, became eventually the foundation for all of modern mathematics. It constituted the very underpinning of the electronic age: Mac, iPod, cell phone, telescope in Palomar, particle accelerator, airplane, rocket, space capsule, digital watch, car, or high-velocity train, would not exist without al-Khwarizmi's ground-breaking innovation. Without al-Khwarizmi, there would be no nuclear physics, genetics, molecular biology, biotechnology, or contemporary economics. He is, in fact, the grandfather of cybernetics and electronics. The term 'algorithm' is a mutilated formulation derived from the name al-Khwarizmi. An algorithm is a set of rules, which applied in rigorous fashion will eventually and in a series of subsequent steps, produce the desired result.

Not a single sophisticated household appliance—from the coffee maker to the dishwasher and the steamer—would exist without al-Khwarizmi.

Unlike other brilliant mathematicians and scientists, al-Khwarizmi did not have to wait a lifetime for his outstanding creative achievements to receive recognition. He was highly respected by his contemporaries and, as Morgan (2007, 91) writes, for centuries European mathematicians and astronomers would end their books with a footnote saying: "*dixit algorithmi*," which means as much as "that is what al-Khwarizmis said." To refer to al-Khwarizmi is to acknowledge the supreme authority on the topics of mathematics and astronomy. With the benediction of his authority (that is the implication), a published work has to be taken very seriously. And since his authority was unquestionable, his work would constitute, right up to the sixteenth century, the very core of the mathematics and astronomy taught in Muslim and European universities.

More than one hundred years after al-Khwarizmi, there came another astronomer and mathematician who believed God existed in the numerals. His name was al-Battani (ca. 868-929) who not only catalogued 489 different stars, but who was also a wizard with numbers. On the basis of his astronomic observations, he calculated the length of one year with utter precision. Using his eye and his mind only, he came to the conclusion that a year lasts 365 days, 5 hours, 48 minutes and 24 seconds. In the twentieth century, astronomers equipped with sophisticated computers and electronic telescopes would find that al-Battani's calculations (Morgan 2007, 94) have been only a few minutes off the mark.

Prophet Muhammad has forbidden the use of physical images as pagan idolatry. In the ninth century, Muslim mathematicians kicked off a creative morpho-evolution in art that continued for about 1,000 years. They organized workshops with artisans and architects and taught them, as Morgan (2007, 96) puts it, "how geometric figures can be easily reproduced and turned into the tiled explosions of infinity that will adorn mosques, palaces, villas and other buildings."

al-Haytham (965-1039), in the West known under the Latinized name Al-hacen, was a gifted polymath who made major contributions to astronomy, mathematics, optics, visual perception, psychology, anatomy, medicine, physics, and philosophy. He was one of the founders of the empirical method, a cornerstone of contemporary science. al-Haytham, whose failure to control the annual flooding of the Nile we have already mentioned, hailed from Basra in Mesopotamia. Basra (the birthplace of the ancient Sumerian civilization) is a port where the confluence of Euphrates and Tigris forms the *Shatt al-Arab* (the waterway of the Arab) flowing into the Persian Gulf. In Basra where sea and sky seems to fuse into a single entity, al-Haytham studied the rays of light during day and night, at dawn, and at sundown, in the clear sky, the hazy mist, and the drifting clouds.

Later, in Cairo, where al-Haytham faked a catatonic stupor to escape the wrath of the mad caliph al-Hakim, he continued his optical studies in a domed building near the al-Azhar university. Eventually, he discovered that Ptolemy's idea (that light beams radiated from the eyes to objects and events, en-ableing an organism to observe them) was totally erroneous. It was in fact vice versa. Light beams reflected by objects and events enter our eye, and they do so under different angles, depending upon the distance between eye and items observed. The cones of the beams of light reflected from external objects and events become wider and wider as an object or event approaches our eye, and they narrow down as an object or event moves away from the eye. This fact is the very base for perspective drawing and painting in art.

The Vatican library (Bronowski 1973, 179) contains a Latin version of al-Haytham's *Optics*. It is heavily annotated by Renaissance sculptor Lorenzo Ghiberti (1378-1455), who created the famous bronze doors of the Baptistery in Florence. If you stand in front of these doors, you are fascinated by the amazing perspective aspect of its figures *en relief*, which represent scenes from the Old Testament. They are so beautiful that Michelangelo has called them "gates of paradise." And they are yet another illustration of how creative morpho-evolution of ideas travels across time and space.

About 200 years before Ghiberti jotted down his comments in the Vatican's Latin translation of al-Haytham's *Optics,* the genius from Basra had already cast his spell on another great European mind. Roger Bacon (ca. 1214-1294), also known as *Doctor mirabilis* (the wonderful teacher), was heavily influenced by Muslim thinkers. He advocated the scientific method and opted for

an empirical approach in the scientific investigations of nature, thus following
the footsteps of Jabir ibn Haiyan (ca. 721-ca. 815) and al-Haytham. In his
Opus Majus published in 1286, Bacon writes "there are two modes of knowing, one is based on argument, the other one on experience." This far-sighted
statement deserves a little comment.

As I have written elsewhere (Guntern 1990, 19; Guntern 1992, 46ff.), with
his idea about the two modes of knowing Bacon has anticipated what contemporary neurobiology has meanwhile spelled out in some detail. Our two brain
hemispheres operate in a different although complementary manner. Our
dominant brain hemisphere thinks in terms of analytical and linguistic argument, while our nondominant brain thinks in terms of intuitive pictures. Our
intuition delivers reliable results of cognition only if it is steeped in experience. And while a lopsided analytical approach to reality may fall into the trap
of idle speculation, intuition is able to see the pattern that connects all the
details and forges diversity into justified unity—a basic goal of all science.

Bronowski (1973, 179) writes that al-Haytham ". . . was the one really
original scientific mind that Arab culture produced." Although al-Haytham
deserves high praise for his creative contributions to science based upon a
rigorous empirical approach, Bronowski's judgment is rather mistaken. It
does not do justice to the scores of great Arab Muslim minds that have shaped
the world of scientific investigation.

By and large, medieval Muslim culture is famous for its religious tolerance.
A philosopher and scientist who benefitted from enlightened Muslim rule and
benevolent Muslim culture was Moses Maimonides (1135-1203), also known
as Musa bin Maimun. Born in Cordoba, he was of Jewish descent and when the
fanatical Almohads took over Andalusia, his family fled persecution and eventually landed in Cairo. There he built a professional career by becoming the
chief physician of sultan Saladin's grand vizier al-Fadil (Morgan 2007, 209f.).
He wrote ten volumes on medicine discussing with great insight health, illness,
and therapeutic methods. Maimonides was not only a physician, he was also a
rabbi and the greatest philosopher of medieval Jewish culture.

Maimonides belonged to the long tradition of Jewish and Catholic scholars who (not hindered by ideological blinders) translated Muslim knowledge and made it accessible to medieval Europe, where ideas were hoarded
in ecclesiastical libraries in the Vatican and various monasteries. Contrary
to the open-minded medieval Muslim culture, in Christian Europe, ideas
were used as tools of power and thus jealously guarded: unlettered folks
were barred from any access that might stimulate their critical thinking. In
the long term, such knowledge hoarding did not function. Under the influence of Muslim culture, the walls of separation and exclusion grew shaky
and a process of inclusion began.

As Morgan (2007, 215f.) explains, the main points of knowledge transfer bringing down the walls that separated Muslim and Christian culture included several cities in Spain, southern France, Sicily, and southern Italy. Toledo, Barcelona, Leon, and Segovia in Spain; Marseilles, Narbonne, and Toulouse in France; Palermo and Syracuse in Sicily; the Benedictine monastery of Monte Cassini near Benevento, and Salerno in southern Italy: they all served as facilitators of knowledge transmission.

Constantine the African (ca. 1020-1087) from Tunisia travelled as far as India, Persia, the Middle East, Egypt, and Ethiopia. He spoke several languages and studied medicine in Salerno, where the first European medical school was founded. There, and also later when he entered the monastery of Monte Cassini, he translateed texts from Greek and Arab into Latin. Robert of Chester (flourished around 1150) translated al-Khwarizmi into Latin. But the most important of those intercultural messengers was Gerard of Cremona (1114-1187). Emperor Friedrich I, called Barbarossa, sent him to Toledo—a famous center of knowledge transfer where Hebrew and Muslim texts were translated into Latin—in order to get hold of Ptolemy's *Almagest* (Hunke 1960, 168).

Fascinated by the treasures he found in that city, he stayed for twenty years before he returned with over eighty books he had translated himself. He translated not only the *Almagest*, but also the classics of Greek science—Archimedes, Hippocrates, Galen, and Euclid (Bronowski 1973, 177). Moreover, he translated from Arabian into Latin works of the Muslim scholars al-Zarqhali, al-Farabi, al-Jabir, al-Razi, al-Khwarizmi, Hunayn ibn Ishak, Banu Musa, al-Haytham, and al-Kindi.

2.52 Medieval Mongol Influence on Morpho-evolution and Morpho-elimination

Temujin, son of a very poor Mongol widow, made one of the most amazing careers in human history. He descended from a restless, marauding Mongol clan whose nomad life consisted mainly of horse and cattle stealing, pillaging the *gers*—domed felt tents mounted on a wooden lattice framework—of neighboring clans, raping and stealing their women, and abducting children to be later used or sold as slaves. From these less than promising beginnings, Temujin developed into Genghis Khan (ca. 1162-1227), a military campaigner the world came to fear and the founder of the Mongol Empire.

His empire was bigger than the domain Alexander the Great had ruled in the fourth century BC. Within a quarter of a century, Genghis Khan conquered more territories than the armies of ancient Rome had taken control of in four centuries. His Empire comprehended a landmass (Weatherford 2004,

XVIIIff.) as big as the African continent; it reached from the Sea of Okotsk in the east to the Black Sea in the west, from Siberia and the Ural in the north to the jungles of Burma and the Gulf of Persia in the south. The thundering hooves of Mongol ponies carried his warriors from the coastal plains of Korea, the "Land of the Morning Calm," and from the rice paddies of Vietnam in the east across the Gobi and Taklamakan deserts and the high plateaus of Central Asia to the *puszta* (steppe) of Hungary and the ragged mountain ranges of the Balkans in the west. His highly mobile armies galloped from the snow-covered tundra of Siberia, the pastures of the Mongolian steppes and the loess-soils of Manchuria in the north to the hot plains of India in the south. Amazingly enough, his nomad Mongol tribe counted a population of about 1 million, out of which he was able to recruit an army consisting of not more than 100,000 warriors. With the help of these troops, he invaded, conquered, and ruled a population of about 3 billion people who mainly lived a sedentary life in the most densely populated areas of those times.

He was loyal in his friendships and alliances, yet merciless against enemies resisting his demands and attacks. He started his conquest of the world with the motto (Tucker 2003, 224): that man's greatest pleasure was to defeat his enemy, to rob his possessions, to make his married women weep and wail, to ride his gelding and ". . . to use the bodies of his women as a nightshirt and support, gazing upon and kissing their rosy breasts, sucking their lips which are as sweet as the berries of their breasts." Yet from this sadistic and hedonistic mental orientation he grew eventually into a personality who earned the respect and deep sympathy of countless people.

Despite the very bad reputation Christian historians have given him, partly for justified reasons (as we have just seen) and partly for ideological motives, Genghis Khan was an enlightened and wise ruler at a time when medieval Europe still chafed under the heavy burden of feudal secular rulers and a Catholic papacy—as narrow-minded and fanatical as it was greedy for money and power.

Mongols created countries—such as China and Korea—that today still have approximately the confines Genghis Khan and his grandson Khubilai Khan had given them. For the first time in its history, Genghis Khan made the Silk Road a safe place, thus creating a reliable international postal system in addition to the largest free trade zone of the medieval world. Genghis Khan's grandson Khubilai Khan introduced the first paper money for international trade, thus getting rid of the cumbersome and expensive transport of bullion and coins.

With the Silk Road protected from highway robbers and greedy regional rulers, Genghis Khan not only fostered an international, bi-directional flow of precious trade, he also pioneered a gigantic inter-cultural knowledge transfer between East and West that was as pivotal for the emergence of European

Renaissance as the knowledge transfer mediated by medieval Muslims. In the fourteenth century, the Silk Road was so safe that Western historians later spoke of a *Pax Mongolica* or *Pax Tatarica*—reminiscent of the *Pax Romana* or *Pax Augustea*, which in the first two centuries AD had brought wealth and peace to the ancient Roman Empire.

In the empire he ruled, Genghis Khan decreed massive tax breaks for everyone and abolished taxes completely for teachers, priests, doctors, and scholars because he was keenly aware of the strategic value of general education and health. His grandson Khubilai Khan created the prototype of contemporary primary schools because he wanted all of his subjects to be literate, this at a time when in Europe only a small elite caste of scholars and monks could read and write. Khubilai Khan introduced a universal alphabet, created by a Tibetan monk, in which all languages could be written. He also offered massive tax reductions to craftsmen and was a generous patron of the arts.

Genghis Khan introduced the first census for all the nations under his rule in order to establish a solid basis for political planning and tax collection. He revolutionized the judicial system by creating a single, comprehensive international law to which national and local laws had to adapt. By that international law, not only poor nomad herders and the population of conquered countries, but also influential administrators and mighty rulers had to abide. Above that international law there was only one authority: the Eternal Blue Sky, the supreme god of the Mongols. Genghis Khan was extremely tolerant, granting complete religious freedom to all nations and ethnic groups living in his empire—as long as they didn't interfere with his politics.

Genghis Khan abolished the time-honored custom of taking hostages and torturing prisoners. He didn't tolerate crime at all and had robbers, thieves, and murderers mercilessly hunted down and killed. He demanded diplomatic immunity for his own ambassadors and granted it for the ambassadors from other nations, even if he was at war with them. When somebody failed to respect that immunity, he and his successors meted out severe punishments.

After the death of Genghis Khan, his successors kept expanding the Mongol Empire for another 150 years. Already under the rule of his four sons, the empire was divided into four more or less independent Khanates—the Golden Horde in Russia, the Il-Khanate in Central Asia, the Khanate of the original Mongol homeland, and the Yuan Dynasty in China. As time went by, these four khanates slowly disintegrated into smaller entities. Some of them were able to continue their existence for many centuries. In 1858, Bahadhur Shah, the last Moghul Emperor of India, was decapitated by the British. And in 1920, Alim Khan II, the last emir of Bukhara, was ousted by the just emerging Soviet Union.

In 1972, the number one hit on the U.S. Top 10 chart was on everybody's lips; people hummed, sang, and whistled its melody on the streets. *The Temp-*

tations sang a funky R&B song about a restless African-American daddy. In the refrain of that song, a widow tells her son what kind of man and husband his just deceased father had been: "Papa was a rolling stone, wherever he laid his hat there was his home." The throbbing, thrusting, forward rhythm of that song sounded like a faraway echo of the thundering hooves of Mongol ponies whose restless riders were continuously on the lookout for new adventures and conquests.

Let's now have a closer look at how the mighty Mongol Empire was established; what it accomplished; how its balance of destructive morpho-elimination and creative morpho-evolution influenced European Renaissance; and with it also our contemporary world.

The original name of Genghis Khan was Temujin. He began his military career as a raider in the service of Ong Khan, ruler of the Kereyids (Weatherford 2004, 40f.), who were the most powerful of the many Mongol tribes. He won the ruler's trust by telling him that he wanted to unite the various Mongol clans under Ong Khan's leadership. Ong Khan liked the idea and accepted Temujin as a vassal. Being a keen observer endowed with the gifts of rational analysis and intuitive synthesis, Temujin not only learned the art of organized warfare, he also noticed how Ong Khan played a power game the ancient Romans called *divide et impera* (divide and rule) by manipulating clan against clan and tribe against tribe. Soon Temujin felt strong enough to become a minor khan ruling his own little Mongol clan. He established a solid power base by distributing roles—from cooks to bodyguards and personal assistants—according to loyalty and merit, and not according to family ties as it was done traditionally. His elite guard consisted of seventy men for the day watch and eighty men for the night watch; they would always protect him.

In the winter of 1196 when Temujin was thirty-three years old, Ong Khan (Weatherford 2004, 42ff.) established a coalition with the Golden Khan of the Jurched tribe that ruled Cathay, today's northern China. The glue temporarily holding these two tribes together was the common goal to attack the much richer Tatars—who had originally settled in the Gobi and then migrated southwards into territories west of Lake Baikal—and to share the spoils made in that venture. The raid was successful, and more lineages of Mongols joined Khan Temujin's clan to profit from the spoils.

A year after the joint venture with Ong Khan, Temujin felt strong enough to attack the Jurkin clan—his relatives who had broken their promise to help him against the Tatars. Now he took his revenge. He defeated them, but triumph did not let him get carried away and muddle his astute mind. He occupied the Jurkin territories and settled the surviving members of that clan into the households of his own clan, instead of killing them off or degrading them as slaves. He even adopted an orphaned Jurkin boy, whom Temujin's mother Hoelun would raise as her son. After organizing the augmentation of his power and the unity with the just-adopted Jurkin relatives, he moved his clan down into former Jurkin territory to a place called Avarga, at the confluence of the Tsenker and Kherlen rivers. Avarga was not only close to Temujin's birthplace in the steppe, but also near the Mongol's sacred mountain Burkhan Khaldun.

In the following years, Khan Temujin was involved in various raids and skirmishes and more often than not he was victorious, leading to the growth of his spoils as well as the number of his followers. In 1202, Ong Khan attacked the Merkid tribe, living east of Lake Baikal and north of Mongol territory, while sending Temujin on a second raid to the Tatars. Temujin's campaign was a success and once more he proved that he was a levelheaded leader rather than a greedy marauder. Against the intention of his followers who wanted to play catch-as-catch-can, he ordered that all the spoils be put into one heap and distributed among those as he thought deserving. He even saw to it that each widow and every child of a killed soldier received the soldier's share. Thus he provoked not only frustration, but also loyalty because his followers realized that he would care for their families if they should be killed during raids or on battlefields. Instead of massacring defeated Tatars or selling them into slavery, he integrated them into the households of his own clan. Male Tatars even had access to higher posts in his administration. Moreover, Temujin began an intermarriage policy that strongly enhanced his image and prestige as a Khan. He not only encouraged his followers to marry Tatar women, he took the aristocratic Tatar Yesugen and her sister Yesui as additional wives although he was already married to Borte. Once more his mother adopted an orphaned Tatar boy. The integration policy was so successful that future historians often confused Tatars with Mongols—in those days the reputation of Tatars was higher than that of Mongols.

In 1203, Temujin introduced a yet more radical innovation in his Mongol army by organizing warriors (Weatherford 2004, 52f.) in so-called *arbans*, squads of ten men. Independent of clan or tribal origin, they now formed a close-knit units, were responsible for each other, and vowed never to abandon each other on the battlefield; if they abandoned each other they were severely punished. Thus time-honored kinship ties gave way to loyalty ties. Moreover, he decreed that their homeland near the sacred Mountain Burkhan Khaldun was now the Holy Land of the Mongols and barred from access by outsiders; that territory was situated at the confluence of the Onon, Kherlen, and Tuul Rivers. In order to make the unity among his followers more cohesive he gave them a new name; they were hitherto referred as the 'People of the Felt Walls' after the *gers* in which they lived.

The People of the Felt Walls soon encountered a major crisis. Temujin wanted to marry Ong Khan's daughter, in order to strengthen his power base. At first the Khan of the Kereyids opposed, then in a bid to kill Temujin set up a trap by pretending to acquiesce to his plan. Temujin (Weatherford 2004, 57ff.) saw through the trick, escaped into the steppe, and all of a sudden he found himself isolated with only a small group of followers, including several Christians and Buddhists plus three Muslims. Soon his career hit a nadir and he faced possible extinction. Yet Temujin managed to snatch success from the brink of total failure—a hallmark of every great leader. He decided to attack and rode back towards Ong Khan's camp. On the way to the Kereyids, his scattered followers began to join him again, thus swelling his ranks. In a surprise attack—when the impetuous Ong Khan was in the midst of celebrating the demise of his would be son-in-law—a humiliated Temujin swooped down with his revenge. The Kereyids were defeated. Ong Khan fled to the desert and died of thirst after his servants abandoned him. Many of the Kereyid troops joined Temujin's victorious army.

In 1204, Temujin (Weatherford 2004, 61ff.) felt strong enough to attack the Naimans, the most populous of all Mongol tribes, who lived south of Tatar territory and west of Kereyid country. He won the battle and incorporated the Naimans into his own army and tribe. In 1206, Temujin organized a *khuriltai* (a political and military council) near the Holy Mountain Burkhan Khaldun. All major tribes of Mongolia attended the mass meeting. He was now officially elected as the Khan of the Great Mongol Nation and adopted the name Genghis Khan. The Mongol word '*chin*' means strong; it is etymologically related to '*chino*' which means wolf. The Mongols claim a mythological descent from the wolf. His choice of a new title (Genghis Khan = Wolf Khan) proved once more that Temujin was a shrewd operator who understood mass psychology: Names have magical power for those who believe in it; and the *khuriltai* sealed a spiritual pact between the Eternal Blue Sky, the Great Mongol Nation and its leader Genghis Khan. From then on, the united Mongols were imbued with self-confidence and a mission that would change the world forever.

Genghis Khan (Weatherford 2004, 67ff.) decreed a Great Law that radically changed the ancient customs of raiding steppe warriors. In order to unite his Mongol forces, he established new rules that would protect the peace within all Mongol tribes. He forbade kidnapping of women from Mongol tribes and the enslavement of children. Animal rustling and stealing became a capital offences punished by execution. Stray animals and lost goods had to be returned to their owners; whoever did not abide by this rule was considered a thief to be punished by execution. In order to avoid mayhem provoked by fanatical adherents of specific religions who claimed to represent 'the only true religion,' Genghis Khan declared that all religions were equivalent and that Buddhists, Manicheists, Muslims, and Christians prayed to the same supreme god, the Eternal Blue Sky.

In order to prevent revolts and an illegitimate usurpation of power, he decreed that every Great Khan must be elected in an official *khuriltai*. Contrary to medieval Europe where feudal rulers were above the law because their power was supposed to be legitimized by the Lord himself, a Mongol ruler had to abide by the Great Law; the same held true for the highest shaman. When Teb Tengeri misused his spiritual powers to enrich himself and his six brothers and defied Genghis Khan's power, the bodyguards of the Khan seized him and broke his spine.

To demonstrate the equality of all tribes under his rule, Genghis Khan nominated Shigi-Khutukhu as supreme judge. This man was the orphaned Tatar boy Temujin had given his own mother for adoption, many years ago. Eventually Genghis Khan introduced other sets of innovations we have already discussed—from tax exemption for individuals in education and health care, to arrow messengers and inter-marriages with Mongols and neighbouring tribes—thus consolidating his power. Now he was ready to take on the world and to build the largest empire on land our planet has ever seen.

In 1210, Genghis Khan was forty-eight years old. A delegation of the Jurched nation that ruled Manchuria, northern China and a large part of southern Mongolia (Weatherford 2004, 81ff.) appeared at the camp of Genghis Khan. They demanded that he submit and become a vassal of the Jurched dynasty. Genghis Khan responded in kind. He allied himself with the Uighur nation living in the Altai mountain range south of Naiman country and with the Tangut nation west of the Jurched territories. In 1211, Genghis Khan decided to attack the Jurcheds, which had a population of 50 million inhabitants. About 65,000 Mongol horsemen crossed the desert Gobi. They travelled light; they did not have an infantry, nor did they care for any supply trains because they relied, as the nomad raiders of the steppes have always done, on hunting and looting.

Once more Genghis Khan proved himself to be a master strategist, gifted in the art of psychological warfare. He openly declared his intent to free the Khitans—a nomadic people roaming the steppes between Manchuria and eastern Mongolia who were vassals of the Jurcheds—and to restore the power of the deposed royal Khitan family. The trick worked (Weatherford 2004, 89ff.). Khitan warriors joined his forces, as did Khitan scholars who spoke, read, and wrote Chinese language. While his forces expanded, there also began a cultural knowledge-transfer that helped Genghis Khan to attract scholars from other nations and thus to improve the level of education and knowledge of the Mongols.

The master of psychological warfare attacked undefended villages whose inhabitants lived from agriculture. The peasants fled and soon over a million fugitives swarmed Jurched cities, clogging the streets, depleting the food and water supply, and telling gruesome tales about the Mongol invaders. Terror psychosis prevailed and produced the desired result. Peasants and Jurched officials rebelled. Jurched engineers defecting to the Mongols thus rolled out yet another knowledge transfer. Mongols accepted a Chinese war technology they hitherto ignored: they adopted the use of catapults and other machines for hurling stones, fire, and explosives over the walls of fortified Jurched cities. In 1214, Genghis Khan besieged the Jurched capital Zhongdu (Beijing). The Golden Khan overwhelmed by the Mongol onslaught gave in. He agreed to become a vassal of Genghis Khan and to seal their pact he paid large amounts of gold, silver, and silk plus 3,000 horses and 500 young men and women.

Satisfied with his victory—and because the warm and humid weather harmed his troops and horses who were accustomed to living in the dry weather of the steppe—Genghis Khan returned with his bounty to Mongolia. Immediately the Golden Khan evacuated his capital and declared his pact with Genghis Khan null and void. After a few months, Genghis Khan returned with his troops, reinforced by Khitan and Chinese defectors, to avenge what he considered to be an act of betrayal. He conquered Zhongdu and then, bothered by the sweltering heat and the odium of sedentary city life, he left again for Mongolia after ordering a Khitan commander to oversee the final sack of the Jurched capital. On their way back to their homeland, Mongol horses trampled the farmland so that peasants could not return to it. Where once rural settlements existed soon a buffer zone of pastures and forests would form a green high-speed lane for further Mongol invasions.

Huge camel caravans (Weatherford 2004, 100ff.) began to transport bales of silk, paper fans, metal armor, bronze knives, iron kettles, jugs of perfume, dyes for makeup, ivory, pearls, precious stones, caskets of wine, sacks full of grain, and tons other goods from the wealthy Chinese civilization to Mongolia. They were accompanied by thousands of prisoners including scholars, engineers, goldsmiths, and other craftsmen. Supply created demand, which in turn stimulated more supply. By then Mongols had become rich to a point where their traditional *gers* were not large enough anymore to store all these goods. Therefore, Genghis Khan ordered the construction of stone buildings to serve as warehouses.

In 1219, when envoys from Kashgar west of the Taklamakan desert appeared at his court complaining about religious persecution of Muslims by the Buddhist Black Khitans, Genghis Khan (Weatherford 2004, 103f.) sent general Jebe and 20,000 warriors on a rescue mission. They rode for thousands of miles west, fought, and defeated the Black Khitans. Genghis Khan now controlled the Silk Road between China and the Muslim states of Central Asia. Clever as he was, he realized that he had now the wherewithal to mediate between, and interfere in, the trade of goods transported back and forth between the extremely wealthy Sung Dynasty in southern China and the equally rich Muslim countries of Central Asia and the Middle East. To strengthen his position, he decided to establish a trading partnership with Turkic sultan Muhammed II, ruler of the Khwarizm Empire reaching from today's Uzbekistan to the shores of the Black Sea and the Persian Gulf. Muslims had a few things to offer which Genghis Khan needed: steel, glass, cotton, and other fine textiles. To impress the sultan, Genghis Khan sent him an expedition of 450 Indian and Muslim merchant traders from Uighur country—the Dzungarai north of the Taklamakan Desert—with a caravan carrying bales of Chinese silk, jade, white camel cloth, and silver bars. When the mission entered northern Khwarizm country, the regional governor massacred the traders and camel drivers to get hold of the spoils. Genghis Khan learned of the carnage of his delegation and was duly outraged. He sent an envoy to the sultan demanding that the greedy governor be severely punished. Here the sultan committed a major blunder. Being the ruler of a highly developed civilization, he publicly demonstrated his disdain for the primitive Mongol delegates by having most of them killed and the faces of others mutilated (he then sent them back to Mongolia). For Genghis Khan this offence meant only one thing: War!

In 1220, Genghis Khan (Weatherford 2004, 108f.) and his troops of about 200,000 men entered the Khwarizim Empire and, although the sultan had about 400,000 men under his command, by the end of that year, Genghis Khan conquered the whole empire. Bukhara, Samarkand, Balkh, Merv, Bamiyan, Ghazni, Peshawar, Margheh, Tabriz, Tbilisis, Astrakhan, and other wealthy cities of Central Asia fell prey to the Mongol armies.

The Arabic, Turkic, and Persian civilizations living in those areas possessed a social organization and a culture more sophisticated than its European counterparts. Its scholars belonged to the creative elite of the world; they excelled in technology, art, science, and healthcare. The whole population was literate and well educated. The Mongol invasion brought the downfall of that highly developed culture, causing a destructive morpho-elimination of enormous dimensions. Muslim soldiers were killed, cities looted, people without professional skills enslaved and used as human shields in the conquest of the next city. Thousands of civilians were slaughtered, yet Genghis Khan spared those whose skills the Mongols needed: craftsmen, merchants, cameleers, individuals with linguistic skills, physicians, apothecaries, astronomers, engineers, musicians, jewellers, imams, Christian priests, rabbis, and all sorts of craftsmen—smiths, carpenters, furniture makers, weavers, skinners, leather makers, miners, glassblowers, tailors, barbers, and cooks.

Meanwhile, the sultan escaped to an island on the Caspian Sea. Since the Tanguts and Jurcheds had betrayed him, Genghis Khan did not trust aristocrats anymore and he divested them of power as vassals who paid annual tributes. He had them all killed, but he spared the life of the sultan's mother and of two-dozen members of her family and sent them into slavery in Mongolian house-holds. Despite that orgy of merciless slaughter, the Mongols stuck to their Law and never tortured or mutilated a prisoner—at a time when popes and kings in Europe introduced ever more sophisticated tools of torture.

Whoever escaped the killing spree of the Mongols fled to the west and spread the reputation of the invaders. Once again psychological warfare prepared the terrain for the Khan's future campaigns. Since he spared those cities that opened their doors and ruthlessly slaughtered those who resisted, more and more cities gave up any attempt to resist. Galloping from victory to victory, Genghis Khan already saw the need to establish order and stabi-lize the future of his rapidly growing empire. He called a *khuriltai* to select his successor and discovered to his utter disappointment that he had ne-glected the emotional needs of his own sons, an oversight that threatened the propagation of his empire.

His wife Borte Khatun bore four sons: Jochi, Chaghatai, Ogodei, and Tolui. Genghis Khan had fathered only three of them, because Borte Khatun was pregnant when he saved her from the Merkids who had abducted her. At the *khuriltai* (Weatherford 2004, 121f.), Genghis Khan permitted Jochi to speak first. This allowance to Jochi, which was only a ritualistic gesture, angered Chaghatai who interrupted Jochi and called him a bastard son. Because of this rude disturbance, Chaghatai lost his chance to be the successor of Genghis Khan. The honor instead was passed on to Ogodei, a heavy drinker. Stunned by the emotional strife among his sons, Genghis Khan was, for once, at a loss of his wits. He resorted to pleading and berating, and even banning them from the court for a while, but to no avail. The fragmentation of blood relationships eventually brought about a fragmentation of the Mongol empire, which soon broke into four different domains relatively independent from each other.

For the time being, though, under the undisputed leadership of Genghis Khan, there were more conquests ahead. In the summer of 1222, the Mongol armies (Weatherford 2004, 125ff.) descended from Kabul via the Khyber Pass into the Indus valley. Genghis Khan's goal was the conquest of the whole northern part of the Indian subcontinent and then to push towards east, paral-lel to the southern Himalayas, into Bengal and across today's Indochina, in order to attack the Sung Empire of southern China. Man proposes but god disposes. The Khan's men and horses fell prey to the hot and humid climate of India. In the damp air, Mongol bows weakened and the deadly accuracy of Mongol sharpshooters wavered. Under these circumstances, Genghis Khan was forced to retreat over the snow-covered mountain passes. That expedition turned out to be no less dramatic than the expedition made by Alexander the

Great more than a thousand years before when his army crossed the snowy Hindu Kush in order to descend into Punjab Valley.

On his return to Central Asia, Genghis Khan decided to head for his homeland. He left behind enough troops to protect the newly conquered territories. Jochi stayed back in Central Asia, still smarting from the humiliation meted out by Chaghatai and from the lack of support by his two half-brothers and Genghis Khan, Soon thereafter he died under rather suspicious circumstances. Meanwhile, Genghis Khan and his troops arrived with their spoils in Mongolia and a huge fiesta celebrated their victories and homecoming.

Mongols were traditionally raiders and hunters shunning all agricultural activities. As a result, the returned warriors and their families became dependant on a continuous flow of traded goods. There were no traders and craftsmen to produce any of the luxury goods to which the Mongols had become accustomed. In order to satisfy the demand of his subjects, Genghis Khan decided to attack the Tanguts—whose territories were wedged between the Uighurs, the Naiman, and the Mongols in the north, and the Jurchen and the Sung dynasty in the south—as a retaliation for their non-cooperation in his Khwarizim campaign. The invasion turned out to be successful, but after six months of war—just a few days before the last victory—the great warrior died. As eighteenth century British historian Edward Gibbon (Weatherford 2004, 131) later put it, Genghis Khan "died in the fullness of years and glory, with his last breath exhorting and instructing his sons to achieve the conquest of the Chinese empire." They were eventually to reach that goal, but only after some fumbling and stumbling.

After the funeral ceremonies of his father, at a *khuriltai* Ogodei (Weatherford 2004, 132ff.) was officially elected the Khan of all Mongols. He began his reign with a ritual that portended little promise for the future. His indulgence in a prolonged drunken binge with his courtiers doomed the future of the empire. Meanwhile, the nations conquered by his father attempted to take advantage of the prolonged mourning for the deceased and the never-ending celebration of Ogodei's ascension—they attempted to break away. Khan Ogodei sent his armies into Central Asia and into northern China to restore the threatened order, but unlike Genghis Khan, he did not lead them into battle. He remained in Mongolia, most of the time drunk. Soon he decided to build a capital worthy of the new Mongol dynasty's great power.

According to ancient custom, the original Mongol homeland now belonged to Tolui, the youngest of the four brothers. Ogodei moved west and built his capital at the banks of the Orkhon River where the early Turkic kingdoms once had their capital. The new capital, called Karakorum, was nothing but a collection of warehouses and workshops. Ogodei's followers continued to live in *gers* in the vicinity of Karakorum. Despite his many shortcomings,

Ogodei turned out to be a tolerant ruler, permitting Christians—he and his brothers had all taken additional Christian wives—Muslims, Buddhists, and Taoists to live in peace together.

Khan Ogodei called for a new *khuriltai* (Weatherford 2004, 138ff.) in order to decide whether to invade Europe or Sung China. Only that would keep the trade routes active and keep the well-oiled wheels of the caravans rolling with their trade goods and tributes from vassals streaming into Karakorum. During the debates at the *khuriltai,* the fateful emotional split between the brothers raised its head once more, threatening to end in an open fight for power. Ogodei, who had just (in a state of heavy drunkenness) annexed the ancient homeland after Tolui died, wanted to invade the Sung Empire in southern China in a bid to expand his personal power base. His brother Chaghatai insisted on moving west, and was supported in his plans by two men who wielded a lot of influence. One was Jochi's son Batu, who now ruled the Golden Horde's territories between Ural and the Caucasus, and who was therefore interested in enlarging his own territories. The other was general Subodei, after Genghis Khan the most impressive military genius of the Mongol generals. A decade earlier, he had pursued the fleeing sultan of Khwarizim and in that campaign, he and his troops reached the Black Sea and conquered one Russian city-state after another. It was at the Black Sea that they befriended Genoese merchants who acted as messengers, informing Europe about the mighty armies of the Mongol Khan. At that time, they had invaded Armenia and Georgia and turned these two Christian countries into faithful vassals of the Mongols. Now, Subodei was eager to go back to the west in order to invade Europe.

After a series of stormy debates, the participants of the *khuriltai* reached a compromise of questionable value. It was decided Ogodei would send three armies headed by his own sons against the Sung Dynasty. Batu would invade Europe and general Subodei would command Batu's armies. The outcome of that decision turned out to be disappointing as far as booties were concerned. The Sung Dynasty fought back the invasion of Ogodei's armies. The European campaign lasted five years and turned out to be a military success, yet the spoils were negligible. Subodei's armies routed Kiev and Nowgorod and killed scores of Russian princes and soldiers; they swept across the Ukraine towards Hungary and in a second prong across Poland toward the cities of the German Hanseatic League. Duke Henry II of Silesia—whose army was reinforced by Christian knights from Poland, Germany, and France—encountered the Mongol invaders on April 9, 1241 at Liegnitz, near today's German-Poland border. The Mongols won the battle and thousands of miners were forced to march east because the Mongols wanted to exploit the rich mineral deposits of Dzungaria. Pillaging and killing, Subodei's armies pushed across Hungary and defeated a Hungarian army on the plains of Mohi. A chronicler writing of 'the Tartar Plague' thus describes the slaughter of the vanquished Hungarians: "The dead fell to the right and left; like leaves in winter, the slain bodies of these miserable men were strewn along the whole route; blood flowed like torrents of rain."

After the victory of Mongol troops over the Poles, Germans, Bulgars, Hungarians, and Serbs, Christian Europe (in a helpless rage because the outcome of the war made them feel impotent against the superior invaders) began a campaign of carnage against its own citizens. Even when their supposedly glorious knights were felled by the tens of thousands, Christan Europeans failed to see the obvious: that their rather clumsy cavalry, infantry, and military technology could be obsolete compared to the highly mobile Mongol armies and their terrifying firepower. Christian Europeans instead looked elsewhere for psychological exoneration. Somebody else surely had to be responsible for the shameful defeat of the once glorious Christian knights. Thus began yet another of the many pogroms against the Jews (Weatherford 2004, 157f.), who were always the preferred scapegoats when something went wrong in medieval Europe. From England to Italy and from Poland to France, Jews were killed by the thousands and—reminiscent of the yellow star that Hitler would one day force upon the Jews—were now ordered to wear special clothes and emblems for easy identification by their perpetrators.

On December 11, 1241, Khan Ogodei died in a drunken stupor (Weatherford 2004, 158f.). At about the same time, Chagatai died, too. Now all four sons of Genghis Khan were gone and the time had come for a *khuriltai* where one of the Great Khan's grandsons would be elected as the new Khan of all Mongols. The armies of Batu and Subodei returned from their campaign, but with less than a fraction of the loot Genghis Khan used to bring home after each of his campaigns. After a lot of dispute at the *khuriltai* held in the fall of 1246, Ogodei's son Guyuk was elected as the new Khan of all Mongols. He turned out to be a cruel and incompetent ruler. After his death two years later, many ruthless power games were played. Eventually Sorkhokhtani, Tolui's widow, called for a *khuriltai*; it elected her oldest son Mongke as the new Khan of all Mongols. Sorkhokhtani was a shrewd operator and two of her other sons also reached very strong power positions: Hulegu would later enlarge the Mongol domains in the Middle East and eventually rule the Ilkhanate of Persia and Iraq; Khubilai would conquer the southern Sung Dynasty and found the Yuan Dynasty of China.

At yet another *khuriltai* in Karakorum in the spring of 1253, Mongke (Weatherford 2004, 176ff.) ordered his brother Hulegu to move with an army westwards in order to attack the extremely wealthy Muslim cities of Baghdad, Damascus, and Cairo. Khubilai received a mandate to invade and conquer the Sung Empire. With these two campaigns, Mongke hoped to achieve the last two goals his grandfather Genghis Khan had set but never reached. Mongke Khan remained in Karakorum and his youngest brother Arik Boke helped him to manage the already vast Mongol Empire.

On the way towards Baghdad, Hulegu conquered several fortresses that were the strongholds where the Nizari Ismailis were holed up; they were a heretical Shiite sect, called the Assassins—a name derived from the Arab word *hashshashin,* meaning 'hashish users.' Their Grand Master had once sworn allegiance to Genghis Khan, but after the demise of the sultan of Khwarizim and the withdrawal of most of the Mongol forces, his roving bands started terrorizing the whole region.

On November 19, 1256, the drug-addicted and perverse Imam (Weatherford 2004, 179ff.) of the Nizari Ismailis was forced to surrender to Hulegu. Soon thereafter, Hulegu reached Baghdad, the most luxurious city of the world. He reprimanded the Caliph for not having supported him in his war against the Assassins, thereby breaking the oath of allegiance once offered to Genghis Khan. Hulegu requested that the Caliph open the doors of Baghdad to the Mongols. The mighty Caliph—assured of the solidarity of Muslim armies from Maghreb to Cairo and Damascus, and the obstacle to the Mongol invasion presented by the two rivers Euphrates and Tigris—haughtily rebuffed Hulegu's demand. Hulegu was incensed. He summoned his Christians allies from Armenia and Geogia and reinforced the Mongol armies now surrounding Baghdad from all sides and besieged it. Christian spies provided Hulegu with crucial intelligence about events within the hostage city. When the expected Muslim armies from the Maghreb and the northern rim of the African continent failed to materialize, the Caliph panicked. He offered to surrender officially, to pay enormous tributes, and to include the name of the Great Khan in his official Friday prayers in the mosque. Hulegu turned down the offer.

After a prolonged assault during which the city was bombarded by the artillery of the time, (ballistic missiles like catapults, mortars and other machines throwing explosives, smoke bombs, grenades, and incendiary rockets), Mongol forces marched into the city on February 15, 1258. The sack of Baghdad turned into a merciless massacre. Only the Christian churches and palaces were spared from looting and vandalizing. Muslim citizens were slaughtered by the thousands; mosques were defiled, palaces pillaged. The orgy of looting and killing continued for seventeen days before the city was set ablaze. The captured Caliph and his male heirs were wrapped in carpets or sewn into sacks and then trampled to death by Mongol horses and warriors. Hulegu then advanced towards Damascus, which, warned by the fate of Baghdad, surrendered. Thus, after seven years of campaigning, Hulegu conquered a domain stretching over 4,000 miles up to the Mediterranean shores. Millions of Arabs, Turks, Kurds, and Persians were now under Mongol rule.

Photo 2.1. Springs of Goliath, Israel (photo by Greta Guntern-Gallati).

Eventually Hulegu's hitherto victorious campaign was stopped in its tracks by an Egyptian Mamluk army. Italian merchants—whom general Subodei had befriended years ago at the ports of the Black Sea—had sold Kipchak and Slavic Russians as slaves to the sultan of Cairo. Now called Mamluks, they had metamorphosed into fierce warriors. On September 3, 1260, the Mamluks routed the Mongols (Weatherford 2004, 185) at the Springs of Goliath in today's Israel. This Mamluk victory put an end, once and for all, to the westward expansion of the Mongol Empire.

Meanwhile, Khubilai (Weatherford 2004, 185ff.) failed to make any progress in his campaign against the Sung Empire. Khubilai, who loved a life of indulgent luxury, turned out to be a poor military strategist. Being obese and suffering from gout, he did not like to ride horses. Khan Mongke, exasperated by Kublai's performance, summoned him to Karakorum. Khubilai returned and threw himself on the mercy of his brother. In 1257, one year before the sack of Baghdad, Mongke decided to take command of the troops invading the Sung Dynasty. He was an experienced campaigner trained by general Subodei. In May 1258, three months after the demolition of Baghdad, Mongke's armies crossed the Yellow River and began the invasion of Sichuan to the west and Yunnan to the southwest of the Sung Empire. Once again the hot and humid climate of the south foiled the success of the campaign. Soldiers fell prey to malaria and dysentery and on August 11, 1259, Khan Mongke succumbed to illness. This brought a temporary end to the planned conquest of the Sung Empire.

Neither Hulegu, who now owned Central Asia, nor Berke, the successor of Batu who ruled the domains of the Golden Horde, attended the *khuriltai* planned to elect a new Mongol Khan. They preferred to stay where they were and to hold on to their territories. Arik Boke (Weatherford 2004, 189ff.), supported by Mongke Khan's widow and sons, held his *khuriltai* in Karakorum. He was elected Great Khan of all Mongols. However, that election lacked legitimacy because Hulegu and Khubilai didn't accept the procedure. The latter called for a *khuriltai* in his southern territory and was proclaimed Great Khan by his followers—yet another election that lacked the general support of the Golden Family. Khubilai, not bothered by the lack of recognition, declared himself emperor in 1260 by adopting the title of *Zhontong*, "central rule." Now he had total control not only of his Chinese and his own Mongol troops, but also of the flow of trade from China towards Karakorum. The soil of Mongol homeland did not lend itself to cultivation, and the hard to please Mongols of Karakorum, too accustomed to luxury, found life tough without an uninterrupted flow of goods brought by trade caravans. Khubilai decided to turn the situation to his advantage. He moved north, conquered Karakorum, looted, and destroyed it. Once more the climate played an important role—as it had done for the demise of the Umayyad Dynasty in Damascus. Between 1250 and 1270, temperatures dropped in Mongolia and animals died from starvation. The winter of 1263 was so harsh that in 1264, a resigned Arik Boke arrived in Shangdu to surrender to Khubilai.

Khubila summoned a *khuriltai* to legitimize his position as Great Khan. But the Golden Family refused to attend. Khubilai banned his brother Arik Boke from the court and had his closest supporters killed. Two years later, Arik Boke died under suspicious circumstances. Now Khubilai was the Great Khan, heading the largest army in the world and ruling over a nation with the biggest population in the world. He was the sovereign of Korea, Manchuria, China (minus the Sung Empire), eastern Mongolia, and Tibet—which already in 1246 had become an official vassal state of the Mongols. Still, Hulegu and Berke, the rulers of the Golden Horde, refused to acknowledge him as Great Khan of all Mongols.

Khubilai was not a gifted military campaigner, yet he was a genius when it came to political strategy. He created a new Chinese Dynasty and, like grandfather Genghis Khan, he was very clever with respect to mass psychology. On the suggestion of his Chinese advisor Liu Ping-chung (Rossabi 1988, 136), he gave the new imperial line the name Yuan Dynasty. In the *I Ching*, the so-called *Book of Changes*—one of the oldest classical Chinese texts—*yuan* means 'origin of the universe' or 'primal force.' With this etymological anchoring, Khubilai Khan's new dynasty won an immense prestige among the Chinese population.

Khubilai Khan established a Chinese administration, adopted a Chinese name, in 1272 built a Chinese capital in Zhongdu (today's Beijing) also known as Khanbalik, and indulgeed in the luxurious lifestyle for which Chinese emperors had always been famous. Fully aware of the traditional Chinese ritual worship of ancestors (Rossabi 1988, 133), he decided to turn ancestor reverence to his advantage by adopting that custom in order to better embed his dynasty into ancient local value systems and role expectations. He ordered the consecration of ancestral temples in honor of Genghis Khan and all of his direct descendants. In 1277, he posthumously bestowed all of them with Chinese names. Painters who created their portraits made them look like ancient Chinese sages rather than uneducated Mongol conquerors. Khubilai Khan morphed into a wise ruler and fostered friendly relations between Mongols and the conquered Han Chinese. In order to better integrate the various ethnic groups in his vast empire, his administration employed not only Chinese mandarins but also Tibetan, Armenian, Khitan, Arab, Tajik, Uighur, Tangut, Turk, Persian, and European officials—including the Venetian trader Marco Polo[9] who supposedly served seventeen years in Khubilai Khan's administration. Khubilai Khan brought about social upward-mobility by continuously promoting individuals from the lower strata of society. Emulating his grandfather Genghis Khan, he employed mostly Uighurs (Rossabi 1988, 16) and other Muslims from Central Asia as his main advisors in military matters.

From his grandfather Genghis Khan he learned the psychological power of propaganda, without which the best armies of the world would never be able to sustain their victories. He reduced taxes, softened the hard penal code of the (still not conquered) Sung Dynasty, reduced the number of capital offences by almost fifty percent, and replaced torture by the use of canes for lashing the culprits—at a time when European ecclesiastic and secular rulers and their fanatic henchmen invented ever new modes of torturing their helpless victims. Khubilai also improved the roads in order to facilitate trade and communication. Since transport via waterways was much cheaper than surface transport, he built a canal that connected his capital to the Yellow River. He also expanded the Grand Canal connecting the Yellow River with the Yangtze River, increasing the transport of grain and other agricultural products from the south to the north. He introduced the use of paper money throughout his empire, a major factor for facilitating trade.

In order to improve general education and literacy, he set up a Mongolian Language School in 1269 and the Mongolian National University in Zhongdu in 1271 (Weatherford 2004, 205). During his reign, a total of 20,166 public schools were to be founded and children attended them during wintertime (when farmers had less work to do). The Tibetan Buddhist lama Phags-pa (Rossabi 1988, 155f.) created a set of forty-one letters derived from the Tibetan alphabet, which Khubilai introduced as the official script in his Empire. Han Chinese and other ethnic groups were permitted to use their own traditional script, and thus the Tibetan script eventually did not have the impact Khubilai Khan had hoped for.

In his capital Zhongdu, various ethnic groups lived together in peace. The Forbidden City, a kind of miniature steppe in the middle of the capital, was reserved for Mongols and the imperial clan. For the entertainment of Mongols and Chinese, a fusion of Mongol music and traditional Chinese drama formed a new hybrid trend—the very basis for the future Peking Opera.

Khubilai Khan preferred painting to literature, and the Yuan Empire (Rossabi 1988, 165f.) produced masterpieces that have been hailed as "revolution" in painting. Since Mongols loved horses, the new paintings depicted masterful portraits of noble Arabian stallions and steeds set in a landscape whose geological formations, trees, bushes, and birds were reminiscent of traditional Chinese paintings. Chao, a famous painter descendent from the Sung royal family, liberated the artists' imagination, which had been fettered by the Confucian bureaucracy of the Sung Dynasty. With his brilliant paintings, Chao bolstered the legitimacy of Mongols amongst the Chinese Han.

Since the days of Genghis Khan, Mongols have been interested in crafts-manship. On their many campaigns they brought all kinds of craftsmen back to China. Khubilai Khan (Rossabi 1988, 169f.) exempted craftsmen from most taxes. Potters, whose creativity had been paralyzed by the dogmatic rules of the Sung Dynasty, unleashed their talents. They upgraded the kilns for baking ceramics and brought about innovation in forms, colors, and patterns of decoration. The delicate blue and white glazes for which the pottery of the Ming Dynasty would be immortalized actually have their origin in the Yuan Dynasty. Yuan pottery was much in demand across the Mongol Empire and was exported in huge quantities. 'China' became a worldwide English generic for porcelain. A similar creative morpho-evolution as existed in pottery began in the writing of novels and in the weaving and designing of silk robes, as well as in the production of lacquer-ware, in paper fabrication, in jade sculpture, in Buddhist rock and stone sculpture, in the design of jewellery, and in architecture. The Nepalese architect A-niko made such an impression on Khubilai Khan that the emperor elevated him to the rank of supervisor of all Chinese craftsmen and showered him with gifts and privileges. Khubilai Khan's wife Chabi arranged a marriage with a descendant from the Sung royal family for the young architect.

Khubilai Khan continued the tradition of religious tolerance instituted by his grandfather Genghis Khan. The various religious groups enjoyed privileges in his capital Zhongdu as well as in his summer residence Shangdu, also called K'ai-p'ing. To honor the sentiment of his Chinese scholars (Rossabi 1988, 141), he respected the Confucian system of education. He embraced Buddhism, an attitude that pleased the Tibetan and Chinese Buddhists. Tibetan lamas have a long tradition of spiritual and secular power: Khubilai learned from them how to combine these two powers. Christians, as well as Muslims, ascended high positions in his administration. The latter were exempted from regular taxation.

The reputation of Khubilai Khan's empire (Weatherford 2004, 208f.) grew to a point where more and more subjects of the Sung Dynasty defected and joined the Mongols. The gradually eroding Sung Dynasty eventually collapsed in 1276 under the onslaught of Mongol armies headed by general Bayan, a military commander as ingenious as Subodei had been. Khubilai, ever the wise ruler, permitted the dowager empress to continue to live a luxurious life in her palace. He sent the young emperor to Tibet where he became a Buddhist monk in 1296. Empress Ch'üan (Rossabi 1988, 91) entered Buddhist nunnery in China.

Having taken over the Sung navy, Khubilai now set his eyes on distant goals. He wanted to conquer the spice-islands in the south—Java and Ceylon—plus the island of Japan. Thus the peninsula of Korea was turned into a gigantic shipyard and a launching pad (Weatherford 2004, 210f.) for the conquest of the Empire of the Rising Sun, which had good trading relationships with China since the opening of the Silk Road in the second century BC. In 1274, an armada of about 900 ships entered the treacherous strait separating the Korean Peninsula from Kyushu, the southernmost island of Japan. But the invasion failed for three reasons. First, the Korean vassals built the ships of the armada with little enthusiasm, realizing they wouldn't gain much from the spoils of the invasion. Second, Khubilai Khan had commissioned the shipbuilders for bulk delivery, causing the ships to have shallow keels, a fact which severely endangered their stability in a churning sea. Third, for reasons unknown, the Chinese-Mongol troops did not pursue their initial attack on Kyushu Island, but reloaded the ships and on their way back, during the night, the fleet was destroyed by a terrible storm—later baptized *Kamikaze*, Divine Wind, by the Japanese. The greatest armada in history and some 30,000 warriors drowned in the turbulent sea.

Undeterred by the bad news, Khubilai Khan (Weatherford 2004, 211f.) did not scrap his plans to subdue the Japanese. The following year, (Rossabi 1988, 100) he sent his envoys to Kamakura, southwest of today's Tokyo—the residence of the Shogun and his Bakufu, or military government—and demanded that the Japanese emperor stationed in Kyoto should travel to Zhongdu to present his formal submission. To a rather stunned shogun, Khubilai Khan's emissaries also offered Khubilai Khan's solemn pledge that, after the ritual submission, the emperor would be reinstated as the ruler of Japan but only as a vassal. The shogun, supreme commander of the proud samurai caste, committed the same folly that had cost the sultan of Khwarizim his life and empire a few years before. He had the envoys decapitated by samurais and had their heads displayed for public mockery.

Khubilai Khan was outraged by this insolence, which offended the Mongol Eternal Law instituted by Genghis Khan that guaranteed the diplomatic immunity of ambassadors. Seven years later in 1281, he sent two fleets against the Japanese. The Korean fleet (Rossabi 1988, 209) manned with 40,000 warriors entered Hakata Bay and waited for the support of the Chinese fleet consisting of 100,000 warriors, who approached from the south. However, the southern fleet did not materialize until two weeks later. Once more, heavy gales and a stormy sea came to the rescue of the Japanese. The two battle fleets were smashed by the storm and about 1,000 warriors drowned.

Following these dramatic events, Japan turned its back on the West and opted for splendid isolation. Khubilai Khan (Weatherford 2004, 212f.) now focused his interests on conquests on land. His armies entered Burma, Vietnam, and Laos. Although, like the problems faced by the Mongol army in the sweltering Indian subcontinent, this campaign too fell prey to climatic severity. Several Southeast Asian kingdoms were conquered and their rulers became vassals of the Yuan Empire. Khubilai Khan's armada reached Malabar, the paradise of spices on the southwest coast of India. In 1292, a Mongol invasion fleet landed on the island of Java where, after an initial success, many of their troops were ambushed and decimated. The Java defeat occurred thirty-two years after Hulegu's westward advance had been thwarted at the Springs of Goliath. Failures of the campaigns in Japan and Java put a halt to the further expansion of Khubilai Khan's Empire. Ominously, rebellions in Tibet (Rossabi 1988, 221f.) and Manchuria were the first indicators of the impending decline of the Mongol Empire. By now, Khubilai Khan was an old man. Due to political events and personal mishaps, he was bogged down with depression (Rossabi 1988, 227) and the consumption of excessive quantities of *koumiss*[10] and wine failed to lift his spirits and willpower. He died on February 18, 1294 at the age of eighty.

We have already summarized a few of the most important innovations and impacts the Mongol Empire has had on the world. They include the unification of countless civilizations, nations, and tribes; a system of significant values shared by many different ethnic and linguistic groups; the tolerance towards all religions; the Eternal Law subsuming all local and regional laws and by which not only subjects, but also all rulers must abide; diplomatic immunity; the integration of technologies stemming from various nations and cultures; the abolishment of torture; significant tax reductions for everybody; a high-speed arrow postal system; improved road and water transport, plus a Pax Mongolica that made the Silk Road a safe place and triggered a bi-directional flow of free trade, information, and intercultural knowledge transfer (eventually providing the platform for wealth generation and the emergence of the European Renaissance).

European Renaissance would never have happened without a solid basis of very rich European traders who became patrons of the arts and science in order to consolidate their own status and prestige. The generation of their wealth began with the improvement of regional and national methods of production by means of technologies imported via the Silk Road from the Mongol Empire, which in turn had incorporated the sophisticated know-how of the Muslim empires of Middle East and Central Asia. These new technologies (Weatherford 2004, 235f.) paved the way for mechanization of production that diminished the need for human and animal labor. They included new ways of harnessing water and wind power; blast furnaces producing very high temperatures needed for sophisticated metal work; specialized tools for working wood; cranes and hoists for construction sites; new crops and foods improving the health and general well-being of the population; trousers and jackets replacing tunics and skirts; catapults, cannons, and guns for more effective warfare; paper replacing parchment and vellum; printing technology stimulating mass production and distribution of valuable information; and scientific knowledge from mathematics to astronomy, physics, medicine, art, history, and religion.

As a specific example of that vast knowledge transfer, we shall take the amazing impact the Mongol Empire had on the father of Italian Renaissance art. In our textbooks, we usually learn that Giotto di Bondone (ca. 1267-1337) marks the beginning of Renaissance painting in Europe. Little or nothing is said about the sources of his inspiration, which radically changed the conceptual and technical outlook of his art. Was it divine inspiration or the parthenogenesis of ideas often attributed to a genius that differentiated Giotto so radically from his predecessors and colleagues? In his biographies on the great artists of the Italian Renaissance, painter and architect Giorgio Vasari (1511-1574) seems to suggest a combination of these two alternatives. He offers a highly speculative account on the origin of Giotto's art (Vasari 1988, 133), that revolutionized painting and initiated the creative morpho-evolution of Renaissance art. Vasari states that—due to Heaven's grace— Giotto had been able, ". . . to bring to life the almost dead art and to elevate it to a point, where we may call it excellent." He wondered how it was possible that a historical context of clumsy masters was able to give rise to a wunderkind, a stupendous virtuoso of drawing.

Time-honored experience shows that the actual truth is generally more prosaic than the exalted lyrics of legends and romantic speculations. What Vasari attributed to "heaven's grace" and what he considered to have been "a rare wonder" was in fact due to the influence of the heathen Mongols, whose supreme God was not the Christian Lord in heaven but the Eternal Blue Sky. Once more, the historian Weatherford (2004, 237f.) puts the record straight. What actually triggered Giotto's revolution of traditional concepts and techniques in painting was the following sequence of events.

In 1288, Pope Nicholas IV—a former Franciscan monk who had just received a letter and rich gifts from an envoy he had sent to the Mongol court—decreed the building of a new mother church in Assisi. Already twice before, the Franciscans had sent envoys to the Mongols where they had encountered the highly sophisticated art of Chinese and Persian painters. To celebrate their own importance and their good relationships to the mighty Mongols, the dignitaries of the Franciscan order now commissioned artists to paint frescoes celebrating Franciscan superiority with respect to other Christian orders. Little wonder that these artists now painted scenes of ancient Christian life in Palestine where various figures had Mongol faces, were clad in Mongol dresses and headgears, rode Mongol horses, and boasted Mongol bows. St. Francis—who had always preached and honored the virtue of a very modest life—was represented as an opulent saint wrapped in luxurious Mongol silks and brocades. Landscapes showed the rocky crags and trees of ancient Chinese paintings, which 200 years later Leonardo da Vinci would depict in his drawing and painting. Moreover, the Assisi frescoes were not flat as had been typical for the medieval European style; they showed a beginning of perspectivistic representation.

Cimabue (ca. 1240-ca. 1302) created quite a number of the frescoes painted in the church of Assisi, and Giotto was one of his disciples. It is not clear whether Giotto, who was in his twenties when the Assisi frescoes were painted, was actually assisting his master Cimabue. What is clear, however, is that he painted frescoes in the famous Scrovegni Chapel in Padua, also called the Arena Chapel according to the territory on which it was built. Enrico Scrovegni was the son of a usurer whom Dante Allighieri in his *Divina Commedia* had relegated to eternal condemnation in hell. Enrico's intention was to build a unique chapel in order to redeem his father's and his own soul.

The Scrovegni Chapel, dedicated on March 16, 1305, is a highly impressing work of art. The color of its barrel vaulting reminds us of the Eternal Blue Sky of the Mongols. In Giotto's frescoes, the robe of Christ shows fabric and style of a Mongol emperor. The golden trim is painted in Mongol letters using the square Tibetan Phagspa script we have mentioned before. The Vice of Infidelity is represented as a woman wearing the pith helmet Khubilai Khan loved to wear. In their hands, Old Testament prophets hold scrolls whose text is written in Mongol script. As Weatherford (2004, 238) puts it, "The direct allusions to the writing and clothing from the court of Khubilai Khan showed an undeniable connection between Italian Renaissance art and the Mongol Empire." This is indeed the case, and I should like to add that the vivid color pigments used by Giotto are reminiscent of those encountered in ancient Chinese and Persian paintings.

Less than three decades after the construction of the Scrovegni Chapel in Padua, the Mongol Empire began to crumble. The causes for its downfall were twofold. Like any other dynasty in human history, the Mongol dynasty also degenerated into a nadir of incompetence. After the death of Khubilai Khan in 1294, his successors indulged in an even more luxurious life than the founder of the Yuan Dynasty had done. Yet unlike him, they neglected their duties as rulers. Inner strife and palace intrigues quickly eliminated several members of the Golden Family on the Khan's throne. And then a second disaster struck. The plague, also called the Black Death, wiped out vast numbers of China's population.

The pest bacterium is transmitted by fleas settling in the fur of rats, marmots, dogs, and other animals. In 1331, about ninety percent of the population of Hopei Province fell prey to the plague (Weatherford 2004, 243f.). Twenty years later, more than one-half of China's population had been wiped out by the pandemic. The death of so many human beings caused a destructive morpho-elimination of gigantic proportions. The caravans of the Silk Road spread the fleas and thus the plague westward. In 1345, the Black Death reached the Crimean port of Kaffa and the Genoese merchants who then shipped it into Europe. Once it reached the crowded and filthy European cities and its equally packed and polluted monasteries, the pandemic exploded, ravaging the whole continent from Sicily to Ireland and even crossing the North Atlantic. In the winter of 1350, it killed more than half of the settlers in Iceland and it brought about the final extinction of the already weakened Viking colony in Greenland.

It is estimated that in the sixty years between 1340 and 1400, the plague wiped out up to 80 million inhabitants on the African continent; it killed about 200 million people in Asia and about 25 million in Europe—almost half of its population. All in all, the plague may have killed about 400 million or more people. Mass death wiped out not only most of the labor force, but also countless scholars, artists, and skilled craftsmen. It killed all international trade and communication. Once more, superstitious Europe was on the lookout for a scapegoat. Pogroms caused the death of thousands of Jews between Russia and Spain.

The demographic, economic, and political impact on the global Mongol Empire was enormous. The Ilkhanate of Central Asia disappeared. The Golden Horde of Russia decayed into little fragments. Mongol China (Weatherford 2004, 251f.) fell prey to a Han Chinese rebellion, whose rulers established the Ming Dynasty[11] and expelled all Muslim, Christian, and Jewish traders—as well as the Buddhist Tibetan lamas—from their territories.

Yet the plague and the gradual decay of the Mongol Empire, which interrupted the flow of trade goods on the by now unsafe Silk Road, caused more than an intercultural destructive morpho-evolution. It also had a positive impact on Europe, because these events motivated the fifteenth-century European explorations of maritime routes in order to get a safer access to the riches of Asia. That motivation was further increased when the Ottoman Empire conquered Constantinople on May 29, 1453. Now Sultan Mehmed controlled all by-land accesses to the Silk Road, his monopoly was total. Europe, smarting from the definitive demise of the Christian Byzantine Empire, had no interest in dealing with its archenemy and paying him exorbitant tolls and taxes. It didn't help that Sultan Mehmed had the insolence to re-baptize Constantinople (the once glorious capital of the former Christian Byzantine Empire), to call it Istanbul, and to turn it into the new capital of the Muslim Ottoman Empire.

On October 12, 1492, the Genoese Christopher Columbus—employed in the service of Queen Isabella of Spain, who was eager to control the highly lucrative spice trade—reached land in the Caribbean Sea. Catching sight of the colored natives, he erroneously assumed that he had landed in India south of Cathay (today's China) as he had intended. Thus he gave the natives the name 'Indians,' a misnomer still used to this very day.

In 1497, Portuguese explorer Vasco de Gama sailed around the Cape of Good Hope in South Africa and eventually reached Goa and Calicut on the southwest coast of India. In these ports, Arabian ships had bought spices for centuries, and the Ming admiral Zheng Ho had already landed here in the first decade of the fifteenth century in order to initiate a flourishing spice trade with China.

In 1519, Spanish explorer Ferdinand Magellan sailed with five ships southwest to find a sea route to the Asian Spice Islands. Having reached the southern tip of the Tierra del Fuego, admiral Magellan entered the Pacific Ocean on November 28, turned northwest, and reached the Marianas and Guam on March 6, 1921.

The successful ventures of these three explorers prepared the stage for the rise of the Portuguese and Spanish colonial powers, thus setting an example that other nations, for instance England, would soon emulate. Between 1577 and 1580, Sir Francis Drake's expedition sailed around the world. Via the Magellan strait at the southern tip of Tierra del Fuego, he entered the Pacific, turned northwest, crossed the equator, reached the Spice Islands of the Moluccas in Indonesia, sailed west across the Indian Ocean and the Cape of Good Hope, and returned via the Atlantic Sea to England.

From the viewpoint of today's globalization, there is yet another revolution the Mongols have introduced, and whose consequences still influence our contemporary world. In feudal Japan, samurais where on top of the social ladder—merchants and traders were almost at its bottom. Similar social hierarchies existed in ancient China and in medieval Europe where inherited aristocratic titles and privileges were by far more important than an individual's personal merits and track record. Under Khubilai Khan, the social status and prestige of traders and merchants ranked high, just below government officials. Originally, Mongols were herders, hunters, and raiders. Their territory offered pastures for nomad herds, but it was unfit for agriculture. As the Mongol Empire grew and Mongols were not interested in becoming peasants or craftsmen, they depended on imports. And since they amassed a lot of power and wealth, their tastes and demands soon increased in sophistication and quantity. For that very reason, merchants catering to Mongol taste for living a luxurious life climbed the social ladder and turned trading into a very respectable profession.

A traveller visiting medieval Europe would certainly have admired the palaces of emperors, popes, kings, cardinals, and condottieri—or the gothic cathedrals whose majesty also indicated where wealth and power resided. Today, if you visit Europe's cities, you will find that the headquarters of governments and multinational corporations are the most stupendous buildings; they suggest where real power resides—and in case of doubt, multinational corporations have more money and wield more power than most governments do. But who will remember that our plutocratic social hierarchy and focus on international trade were born in an empire whose cradle was rocked, almost a millennium ago, in a dirty and smoke-infested *ger* in the Mongolian steppe?

We have stated that Mongols did not want to become peasants and merchants, although they were stockholders of caravans transporting everyday goods and luxury items. Mongol authorities played a wise role in improving the crops of the countries they governed. In his excellent study on Genghis Khan, Weatherford (2004, 228) gives a fascinating overview about the impact of these policies on international agriculture. Mongols introduced tea and rice from China into Persia and the Middle East. Profiting from the superior technology of Muslims and the know-how of Southeast Asia, the Mongols imported a better triangular plough into China. In order to improve the soils of Persia—exhausted and eroded by centuries of agriculture to feed a growing population—Mongols brought seeds from China and planted bushes and trees to serve as windbreakers. They also imported new varieties of rice and millet as well as fruit trees and root crops into Persia. They increased the varieties of citrus trees. In their vast empire, they transplanted all possible varieties of peas, beans, grapes, lentils, nuts, carrots, turnips, melons, and leaf vegetables from one country to the next one. New hybrids increased biodiversity and thus improved the ecological environment in which people could live a healthy life. Apart from food crops, cotton, silk, and other crops for making textiles and ropes were introduced into new areas; so were dyes, oils, ink, paper, medicine, and all kinds of peace-time technologies and therapeutic methods. Together with the new crops came new technologies, methods, and instruments for ploughing, planting, irrigating, pruning, harvesting, drying, grinding, threshing, brewing, distilling, and cooking. These advancements were either invented or transplanted from one region to the next one.

Since the administration of war and peace demanded mathematical skills and methods, Mongols learned from Muslims the use of the Arabic decimal system and of algebra and geometry. Paper production and printing facilities where single characters were combined to words were innovated and spread across the whole empire. Thanks to these innovations and improvements, the price of paper fell in the Mongol Empire at a time when Europe still used parchment or vellum (whose production was much more cumbersome and time-consuming than the Chinese method of paper production). With the help of these new technologies, printed materials such as government decisions, medical and science text books, pamphlets and almanacs on agricultural methods, historical studies, mathematical theories, songs, novels, and poems were distributed from Korea to Moscow, from the Black Sea to the Mediterranean Sea, and from Siberian tundra to the Persian Gulf.

In other words, the Mongol Empire was not only a juggernaut of global destruction (as often depicted by European historians), it was also a haven for creative morpho-evolution. The rulers and armies of the Mongol Empire provoked chaos, but also order, and the balance between these two factors eventually became so good that it motivated one of the most revolutionary and most comprehensive creative processes the world has ever seen. In this respect, the Golden Age of the Mongol Empire can be duly compared to the medieval Muslim Golden Ages and the European Renaissance: all of them began with chaos and destructive morpho-elimination and then they moved towards a proper balance of chaos and order, freedom and structural constraint, spontaneity, and rational calculation fostering an amazing creative morpho-evolution.

2.53 Influence of the Silk Road on Morpho-evolution and Morpho-elimination

> *"Meditation in the midst of action is a billion times superior to meditation in stillness."*
> Japanese Zen-master Hakuin Ekaku (1686-1768)

A culture is defined by the values, codes of conduct, and tales it hands down from generation to generation. It shapes its identity by what it loves to remember and prefers to forget. The collective consciousness thus constructed is more important for the mind of human beings than the physical events that have shaped the history and character of the time.

In the course of time, East and West have tended to emphasize what separates them rather than what connects them. Yet what unites them intimately is the exchange of ideas, religious convictions, scientific discoveries, technical inventions, artworks, trade goods, myths and legends, strategically important military and diplomatic information, and gossip carried across the Silk Road—the very lifeline of an intercultural dialogue that has lasted for millennia.

For thousands of years caravans, with jingling bells—often counting up to 1,000 double-humped Bactrian camels—have trekked across deserts and endured sweltering heat during daytime and bitter cold at night. They have climbed windswept mountain passes, journeyed past snow-capped mountain peaks 7,000 meters high, trotted across arid plateaus strewn with boulders and pebbles, forded rivers and creeks, crossed fertile valleys studded with vines and fruit trees, and entered the shelter of oases filled with the banter of kids

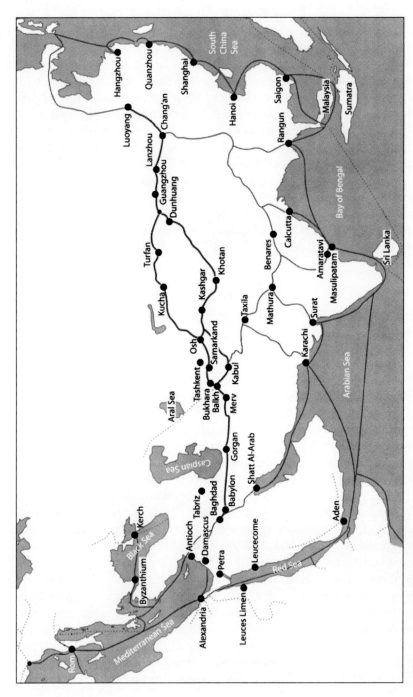

Figure 2.18. Main land routes and maritime routes of the Silk Road.

and the noise of bustling markets, until they have eventually reached their ultimate destinations in East and West.

Camel drivers, merchants, missionaries, explorers, and troops accompanied caravans to protect precious cargo from roving bandits and nomadic war tribes eager to pillage and kill. Although in its halcyon days the Silk Road reached from Cordoba, Rome, and Constantinople in the West to Beijing, Nara, and Kyoto in the East, a caravan never travelled the whole stretch. From China to the shores of the Mediterranean Sea, the Silk Road was more than 10,000 km long. Thus traders walked, for example, from Samarkand to Buchara (a journey lasting seven days), or from Chang'an, the ancient capital of the Middle Kingdom of China, to Kashgar at the western end of the Taklamakan desert (a trip that took a whole year). Then another caravan would take over the cargo and transport it over a certain stretch of the route to the next caravan, until traders eventually reached their intended goal.

The Silk Road, the oldest network of international routes on earth, has been travelled for millennia and by myriads of travellers. Its heydays lasted about 1,500 years, from the second century BC—when Han emperor Wudi (reigned 140-87 BC) sent an envoy into the Ferghana Valley to buy 'heavenly horses'—to the fifteenth century, when the Ming Dynasty closed its borders towards Central Asia and maritime routes became ever more important for the East-West trade. In the course of its history, the Silk Road boasted four Golden Ages: during the Han Dynasty (206 BC-220 AD), the Tang Dynasty (618-907 AD), the Muslim Dynasties (eighth century-early thirteenth century), and the Mongol Dynasty (thirteenth century-fifteenth century).

The Silk Road was never one single route connecting east and west. It was a complex lattice of trails spreading across the Eurasian continent and branching off at many different places in order to connect north and south—from the Siberian tundra to the jungles of Burma, from Lake Baikal to the Indian subcontinent, and from the Caucasus to Yemen. The Silk Road skirted the northern and western seams of the Taklamakan desert; it embraced the Mediterranean Sea by means of two main trails. The northern trail consisted of the Via Egnatia and the Via Appia. The former connected Byzantium with Dyrrachium (Durazzo) at the Albanian west coast, where ships carried the trade goods across the Adriatic Sea to Brindisi, the latter connected Brindisi with Rome. And then there was the southern trail, leading from Antioch to Palestine and Cairo, and from there across the northern rim of the African continent to Gibraltar and, eventually, to Cordoba and other Muslim strongholds in Andalusia.

In order to get a picture of the overall structure and functional importance of the Silk Road, let's imagine the Eurasian mega-continent as a giant lying on his belly and planning where and how to get his next meal. That giant has a brain, a dorsal spine, and an aorta. The brain is connected to the spinal chord in the dorsal spine, from which nerve fibers exit at each vertebra, to the left and right, running in cascades of multiple bifurcations across the whole body. Similarly, from the aorta, arteries spread out to the left and right forming cascades of branching-off blood vessels, which grow smaller and smaller until they end in capillaries nourishing the tissues of the whole body. The brain plans and controls all activities going on in the giant's organism. Nerve fibers carry vitally important information from the center to the periphery and back again to the center. Arteries feed the organism with oxygen and hormones, without which no life can exist. As long as brain, nerves, and blood vessels function well, the giant's organism is healthy and develops in an optimal manner. But as soon as one of these three structural components doesn't function properly anymore, the organism succumbs to illness. Depending on where information flow and matter-energy flow are disturbed, specific organs or whole organ systems will decline and may even die.

Our giant is the hypothetical (and fantastic) representation of a complex social mechanism particular to any period of time. Therefore it doesn't amaze us at all that, in the course of time, our Eurasian giant has produced many different brains—the capitals of tribes, nations, empires, or whole civilizations where vitally relevant information was pooled, strategic decisions were made, orders were given, and their proper execution was controlled. The giant's blood vessels were the complex lattice of highways ways—including ancient maritime routes[12] long before European naval expeditions of the fifteenth century explored new ones—transporting vitally important information and materials that the Eurasian continent needed for its well-being and prosperity. And since hypothesis brooks fantasy, it doesn't strike us as absurd that our giant had a very turbulent life story. The giant did not only develop new brains and lose old ones. There were also nerves interrupted and blood vessels clogged by unexpected events: regional raids, internal strife, wars, climate changes, and pandemics.

In the course of time, settlements—from small towns to big cities and metropolitan areas—situated along the Silk Road have been a gigantic international laboratory in whose sociocultural crucible different languages, ethnic groups, nations, regional and imperial dynasties, forms of government, myths and legends, religions, values and beliefs, rituals and codes of conduct, customs and costumes, scientific disciplines and art forms, food and drinks, and countless crafts were mixed together in continuously changing combinations. So much requisite variety combined with structural constraints (imposed by urgent needs and goal-oriented intentions) constituted propitious field conditions under which human creativity blossomed. A laboratory bustling with activities is continuously threatened by human actions and environmental events, producing not only intended but also unintended consequences. Sometimes crucibles and alembics explode and wreak havoc. When such a mishap occurs, destructive morpho-elimination prevails over creative morpho-evolution.

However, the multiple chapters in the huge diary of the Silk Road are but a part of lost history. What we know today are bits and pieces of an ancient palimpsest whose texts have been written, scraped off, and written time and again in the course of millennia. Only a few phrases and single letters of that gigantic text have survived to this day, yet the meaning we are able to decode from these fading symbols helps us to better understand the timeless interplay of destructive morpho-elimination and creative morpho-evolution, which still impacts our present world and will also impact the future of our planet.

Let's now have a closer look at some aspects of the Silk Road relevant for the topic of the present book. These include the Silk Road's very name, geographic and climatic conditions, destinations along the main land trails and maritime routes, major historical events influencing trade and communication, types of cargo transported, sericulture and other important creative inventions and discoveries, and their distribution along the Silk Road.

'Silk Road' is a name much younger than the geographical and historical realities it denotes. It was coined by the nineteenth century German explorer Baron von Richthofen (ten Grotenhuis 2002a, 15). Silk was one of the most precious and sought-after cargos transported between East and West. There were other high-quality trade goods exchanged in huge quantities which also could have suggested names for the gigantic lattice of trade routes: horses, jade, glass, gold, cotton, spices, porcelain, and lacquer ware.

Due to the huge extension of the Silk Road, travellers crossed different kinds of climatic and geographical conditions while travelling from destination to destination. The jungles of Indochina were hot and humid. The plains of the Indian subcontinent oscillated between weltering heat and heavy monsoon rains. The Chinese heartland enjoyed a rather moderate climate. Its alluvial soil was covered with loess, silt blown in from the Gobi Desert for millions of years (Tucker 2003, 76) and covering an area of approximately 300,000 km^2. The climate of the deserts and oases of Central Asia was extreme, with temperatures reaching at times 40 degrees Celsius during the day and minus 40 degrees during the night. In the Gobi Desert and Taklamakan Desert, suddenly erupting sandstorms threatened the very survival of man and beast. An eighteenth century report (Wood 2003, 75) thus describes the impact of these storms on traders and Bactrian camels: "This wind moves swiftly, and passes in a moment, and is gone, but if they did not so protect themselves, they would be in danger of sudden death." Bactrian camels with their broad pads were perfectly adapted for treading on shifting sands, and their inborn ability to close their nostrils completely during sand storms made them perfect cargo carriers for the Silk Road.

Towering sand dunes could be up to one hundred meters high and change their position continuously, a fact that made a proper navigation difficult in an era when a precise electronic global positioning system was still a far-off dream. Wandering dunes presented a perfect metaphor for the uncertainties and risks threatening trade caravans. In contrast to shifting dunes, there were vast but highly stable mountain ranges. The Taklamakan Desert forms a huge oval, about 1,000 km long and 400 km wide, covering about 270,000 km^2 of the Tarim Basin. It is surrounded by snow-capped mountain peaks between 7,000 and 8,000 meters high: the 'celestial mountains' of the Tian Shan ranges to the north, the Altun Shan ranges to the south, and the Pamirs, Hindu Kush, and Karakoram ranges to the west.

Geographical and climatic conditions became more agreeable as soon as caravans arriving from China reached the Ferghana Valley of Eastern Uzbekistan and the fertile plains of central Uzbekistan. These plains were watered by the two rivers Syr Darya and Amu Darya, known to the ancient Greeks under the names of Jaxartes and Oxus rivers. On the land between these two imposing rivers there were Bukhara and Samarkand, two of the most famous trading centers of the Silk Road. In the seventh century, Chinese Buddhist monk Yuanzhang (Wood 2003, 68) visited Central Asia. In his report *Record of the Western Regions* addressed to Tang emperor Taizong (reigned 626-649 AD), Yuanzhang had this to say about Samarkand: "The climate is agreeable and temperate and the people brave and energetic."

Similar climatic conditions reigned in the Middle East from Mesopotomia to Anatolia, into the Levant, across the Balkans, and into Italy. The trade routes leading from Cairo across the deserts at the northern rim of the African continent had a dry and hot climate, yet not as extreme as that of the Tarim Basin. Andalusia, the end station of that trail, boasted a hot and dry, yet rather moderate climate.

The Silk Road reached its longest extension during the Chinese Tang Dynasty (618-907 AD). In those days, Japan was involved in intensive trade and communication with China and thus Kamakura, Nara, and Kyoto were the easternmost destinations of the Silk Road. Cordoba and other Muslim strongholds in Andalusia formed its westernmost destinations. From Japan's coast, traders travelled by ship to South Korea and then over land across the Korean Peninsula into Manchuria, and south again until they reached Luoyang (Tang capital from 904 to 907) and Chang'an (Tang capital from 618 to 904), today called Xi'an.

Wishful thinking was the guardian spirit baptizing the Tang capital: Chang'an means "forever peace" (Sheng 2002, 42f.). The geographical situation for Chang'an (Thubron 2006, 13f.) was indeed propitious, because the city—founded by Shi Huangi (259-210 BC), emperor of the Qin Dynasty

(221-206 BC)—was situated on the loess-covered fertile soil between the Wei and Yellow rivers. As Tucker (2003, 76) reports, that region has attracted settlers since the Paleolithic age and has played a crucial role in the past 3,500 years of Chinese civilization. Amazingly enough, the founder of Chang'an must have had little faith in the magic power of names because he felt that control is better than trust: in his tomb he later had a huge terracotta army watching over his mortal remains.

Chang'an (Wood 2003, 11) remained a capital not only during the Qin Dynasty (221-206 BC), but also during the Han Dynasty (206 BC-220 AD) and the Tang Dynasty (618-907 AD). At the time of the Tang Dynasty, Chang'an in Shaangxi boasted a population of about 2 million inhabitants. In those days, it was the cosmopolitan center of the most sophisticated civilization of the world, the very first hub of a spinning wheel we call today globalization. Chang'an was protected (Thubron 2006, 19) against invasions from northern nomad warriors by twenty-two miles of ramparts.

The metropolis boasted two main gates, the Eastern Gate and the Western Gate. The latter was the starting point for caravans leaving for the Gansu corridor, Vietnam, Tibet, and Central Asia—and the destination of caravans arriving from those regions. At the Western Gate, there was a bustling market studded with about 3,000 bazaars and workshops. All in all, there were about 200 guilds of merchants (Thubron 2006, 20; Tucker 2003, 88) whose members hailed from the most diverse ethnic and linguistic groups: Koreans; Chinese; Tibetans; Javanese; Malays; Singhalese; Chams from Vietnam and Thailand; Indians; Jews; Arabs; Khorezmians; Persians; Tokharians; Uighurs and other members of the Turkic people settled around the Tarim Basin and farther west in Central Asia; Sogdians from Samarkand; Bactrians from the fertile plains between the Pamir range and the Hindu Kush; Syrians; traders from the Caucasus region; and many more. While Sogdians—their language was the *lingua franca* of the Silk Road—dominated all trade, the Uighurs were moneylenders and usurers demanding exorbitant interests on the sums they lended.

The Chinese government controlled trade and movement of caravans as well as it could. Chinese traders (Wood 2003, 59) carried passports indicating the cargo of their caravans as well as the destination and purpose of their journey. Custom posts in and outside of Chang'an checked smuggling and collected taxes. Arab trader Abu Zaid Al-Hasan (Tucker 2003, 88), for instance, was indignant because he had to deliver one third of his cargo to the imperial warehouse before he was allowed to do business in the country.

At the time of the Tang Dynasty, religious tolerance in China was as great as it was in the Muslim dynasties to the West. Various types of temples in Chang'an proved that adherents of Chinese Taoism and Confucianism lived in peace with the followers of imported Jewish religion, Islam, Zoroastrism,

Manichaeism, Christian Nestorianism, and Tibetan and Indian Buddhism. The latter's importance increased after pilgrim-monk Xuanzang (Thubron 2006, 21; Tucker 2003, 87) returned in 645 AD from India with a caravan carrying 600 Buddhist scriptures. For the rest of his days, Xuanzang translated them in the Great Goose Pagoda, which still stands today.

Emperor Yangdi (reigned 604-617 AD), the second emperor of the Sui Dynasty (581-618 AD) founded by his father Emperor Wendi (541-604 AD), had a knack for grandiose building projects. He ordered to rebuild Luoyang, once the capital of the Eastern Han Dynasty (25-220 AD). He embarked on a reconstruction of the Great Wall, an adventure costing the life of 6 million workers. And he built a network of canals (Tucker 2003, 75) linking the Yellow River with the Huai and Yangtze River, a water route eventually 2,000 km long.

During the Tang Dynasty, tributes arriving via canals from the south of the country plus income from international trade and taxes imposed upon merchants made Chang'an a very wealthy city, and its inhabitants enjoyed the pleasures of life. Wealthy patrons supported painters, calligraphers, poets, and musicians. During the Tang Dynasty, the melting pot Chang'an boasted sometimes up to 20,000 foreigners (Sheng 2002, 43; Thubron 2006, 20). That group included priests, merchants, diplomats, sages, pilgrims, musicians, poets, architects, craftsmen, dancers, acrobats, jugglers, and trapeze artists. So-called 'Sogdian whirling girls' clad in crimson robes and green damask pantaloons were the rage of the town. Tucker (2003, 92) reports that in 777 AD, eleven Japanese dancing girls entertained the Tang court, as did Burmese orchestras and Vietnamese musicians visiting Chang'an. Quite a number of foreigners got access to high posts in the Tang administration; even the elite bodyguards at the Tang court were of foreign origin.

Poets are sensitive antennae, perceiving the most delicate, subliminal changes in a society's soul. At the same time they are senders, transmitting their perceptions, experiences, and thoughts in a subtly encoded mode of communication. Poems are to culture what butterflies are to nature; they offer one of the most sophisticated forms of expression produced by creative morpho-evolution and although they are ephemeral creatures, they are able to give birth to an enduring legacy of precious values. During the Tang Dynasty, Chinese poetry flourished in a way that reminds us of the heyday of Arabian poetry during medieval Muslim Golden Ages. A scholar who wanted to pass the civil service examinations in order to become a highly placed official of the imperial Tang administration had to be able to write good poetry. If we compare this requirement to the fact that most of our contemporary governmental bureaucrats seem to be unable to write decent prose, we are forced to admit that our present *mediocratic society* (Guntern 2000, 27ff.) is a rather poor substitute for the highly sophisticated meritocracy of the Tang Period.

The most famous Tang poets were Li Bai (701-762), also known as Li Po, and his close friend Du Fu. Li Bai became a protégé of Emperor Xuanzong (reigned 712-756) and even held a position in the imperial administration, which he quickly surrendered (Tucker 2003, 107). A romantic at heart, he got involved in the unsuccessful An Lushan rebellion[13] of 755 and was exiled to southern China. Though he was pardoned before arriving there, he kept wandering throughout the whole country. Li Bai (Cooper 1973) was a hedonist and in his Dionysian states an enfant terrible, openly venting his scorn against the Confucian value system (Cooper 1973, 27). He wrote about 900 poems, many of which were set to music. They either described scenes seen in his nocturnal dreams or they celebrated the beauty of women, the splendor of nature, the simple pleasures of life, the merits of good friendships, and his own hopes and desires. He loved drinking and carousing and, as legend has it, he died by falling in a drunken state from his boat into the Yangtze River because he attempted to embrace the full moon reflected in the water.

Du Fu (712-770), also called Tu Fu, held a minor government position and—like his close friend Li Bai (Cooper 1973, 42) with whom he stayed for a while in 744 or 745—got involved in the An Lushan Rebellion, was imprisoned, and exiled, spending the last decade of his life in Sechuan Province. He has been called a poet-sage and poet-historian, and about 1400 of his poems have survived (Tucker 2003, 107). After loosing his youngest child, he compared his own sorrow to the sorrow of Chinese society gravely disrupted by the An Lushan Rebellion. The following verse suggests the deep empathy enabling him to transcend personal grief by contemplating the grief of a society gone haywire: "Brooding on what I have lived through, if even I know such suffering, the common man must surely be rattled by the winds."

Tang poetry was the culmination of Chinese literature. As Tucker (Tucker 2003, 107) reports, an anthology of Tang poetry compiled during the Qing Dynasty (1644-1911 AD) listed about 50,000 poems created by 2,200 poets—more poems than had been written in the 2,000 years preceding the Tang Dynasty.

Apart from its Western Gate, Chang'an also boasted an Eastern Gate, which played its most significant role during the Tang Dynasty. From here traders travelled via Manchuria to Korea and from there by ship to Japan. Japan is often thought of having been totally isolated from the outside world—notwithstanding the two unsuccessful Mongol invasions we have already discussed—until Portuguese sailing ships blown off course entered the ports of its southern islands in 1542. Yet the truth of the matter is quite different.

During the Tang Dynasty, trade and exchange of ideas between Chang'an and the imperial city of Nara in Japan reached a point of culmination prompting author Ryoichi Hayashi to call Nara's imperial Shosoin repository "the final destination of the Silk Road." That repository contains 2,794 complete items (Tucker 2003, 106; Ma and Levin 2002, 25-39) plus thousands of fragments from various countries from Korea, China, Central Asia, India, Persia, and the Mediterranean area. The whole collection bears witness to the splendor and sophisticated aesthetic taste of the Tang Dynasty, and those countries with which it had trade connections. There are, among other artifacts, mirrors, paintings and ceramics from China; rugs and silk textiles with Chinese and Persian motifs; glass and silver vessels from Persia; the world's only surviving relic of an ancient Indian Lute; several expensively decorated Chinese pear-shaped *pipas*; about 170 grotesquely shaped dance masks used in *gigaku* plays, originally imported from China; and a great number of paintings, sculptures, lacquer ware, ceramics, calligraphies, swords, tools, furniture, Buddhist altar fittings, perfumes, medicines, and dance costumes. As the cello virtuoso Yo-Yo Ma (2002) states, in the Shosoin repository there are several four-stringed lutes similar to those still played today.

Apart from the trade of goods there, was also an exchange of concepts that strongly influenced Japanese civilization and culture. Among other things, Buddhism and style of government were imported. The Nara Period (710-784), also known as Tempyo Period, was strongly influenced by the Tang Dynasty (Tucker 2003, 106). Emperor Shomu (reigned 724-749) was a Buddhist who founded monasteries in all the provinces of Japan, thus elevating Buddhism to the rank of a state religion.

Many Japanese envoys spent years in Chang'an (Tucker 2003, 91ff.) to pursue subjects in which they were interested. The outcome of their studies shaped the imperial cities Nara and Kyoto according to the architectural model of Chang'an. Scholar Kibina Makibi spent eighteen years in Chang'an. He used signs and symbols of Chinese writing to create the Japanese syllabic Katakana script. His colleague Kobo Daishi (Kukai) left Japan in 804 AD to study tantric practices in Chang'an. Upon his return, he not only founded the Buddhist Shinton sect, but also invented the Hiragana script. It was much simpler than the formerly used Kanji script adopted during the time of the Chinese Han Dynasty (206 BC-220 AD). Japanese women, too, learned the Hiragana script and that very fact radically changed the writing of literature during Japan's Heian period (794-1185 AD). *Genji monogatari—The Tale of Genji*—written by noble-woman Murasaki Shikibu in the early eleventh century became a classic of Japanese literature. In 1968, in his Nobel Prize acceptance speech, novelist Yasunari Kawabata praised *The Tale of Genji* as "the highest pinnacle of Japanese literature."

During the Tang Dynasty, monk Min travelled in 608 to Chang'an where he lived for twenty-six years while studying Buddhist doctrine. Takamuko no Kuromaro stayed even longer, for a whole thirty-four years, in Chang'an to study the process of well-organized government. After having returned to Japan, he became involved in the Taika Reform Movement headed by emperor Kotoku Tenno (645-655). With that reform, the formerly loosely affiliated states were changed into provinces ruled by a central imperial administration headed by the emperor. From that point on, government officials were required to qualify in service examination comparable to those their Chinese counterparts were required to. The imperial court became the supreme place of appeal for all demands and complaints made by the population.

Scholar and poet Abe no Nakamaro (701-770) spent a total of fifty-four years in Chang'an, where he eventually died. He became an administrator at the imperial court and was a close friend of the Chinese poets Li Bai and Wang Wei. When Li Bai heard that Abe no Nabakamaro, on his visit to Japan to see his ailing parents, had met with a tragic end in a ship wreck—fortunately wrong information as it later turned out—he wrote an elegy *Mourning Chao*, a masterpiece of Tang poetry (Tucker 2003, 91).

All in all, we may say that the Tang Dynasty has had a considerable impact on Japan, ushering in—by the exchange along the Eastern end of the Silk Road—a creative morpho-evolution whose imprint on architecture, art, poetry, and government we still admire today. Far from aping a foreign culture, Japanese ingenuity streamlined and refined the opulence of Chinese artwork, from architecture to ceramics, painting, sculpture, and other domains. Japanese aesthetic preferences opted for simplicity, purism, and refinement—for the combination of *wabi* and *sabi* already discussed in an earlier chapter of the present book.

Let's now return to the Chang'an and its Southern and Western Gates.

From the Southern Gate, a trade route[14] led to Guangzhou, a port at the Pearl River connecting that city to the southern Chinese Sea. From here, maritime routes went further south to the spice islands of Indonesia.

The main land route of the Silk Road left Chang'an at the Western Gate, went west, and after a week's travel, caravans had two options. They could turn south in order to reach—via Chengdou and Kunming, and after many weeks of journey—Hanoi, situated at the right bank of the Red River. From here a sea route went south to Indonesia. The main branch of the Silk Road, however, went from Chang'an westward to Tianshui and Lanzhou. In Lanzhou, a southern branch went via Xining to Lhasa in Tibet, and from there to the Mouth of the Ganges River in Bengal. From the ports of the Ganges River delta, two major maritime routes took over the transport of trade goods. One route led from the Gulf of Bengal via the Malacca strait southeast to Indonesia. The other maritime route went from the Gulf of Bengal around the southern tip of the Indian subcontinent to the spice coast of Malabar, to the mouth of the Indus River and—via the Strait of Hormuz—to Basra in the Persian Gulf.

From Lanzhou, the main land route headed northwest via Wuwei to Anxi where yet another bifurcation occurred. A northern branch led to a wide arc via Turfan and Yining to Balasagun west of Lake Issy K-Kul, and from there, northwest to Taskhent and Otrar at the Syr Darya River. From Otrar, that land route bent southwest, again leading towards Khiva and Kunya Urgench at the Amu Darya River. From Urgench, a northern branch continued to Astrakhan north of the Caspian Sea, to the cities at the banks of the Wolga River, and to the Krim on the shores of the Black Sea.

The main land route from Anxi led into Dunhuang in the Gansu Corridor. Dunhuang and the nearby cliff of Qianfodong (Wood 2003, 88)—both sitting at the eastern edge of the Tarim Basin—were, together with Kashgar at the basin's western edge, the most important of all oases surrounding the Takla-makan Desert. In Dunhuang, caravans rested before travelling further west or further east. Dunhuang was protected by the Great Wall against invasions by northern nomad warriors, especially by the westernmost watchtower, which stood in the nearby Lop Nor region. Due to its strategically important posi-tion, Dunhuang became a very rich oasis attracting not only traders, but also artists and Buddhist monks.

In the fourth century AD, Buddhist monks had begun to hollow out the cliffs and fill the caves they created in the course of seven centuries with sculptures of Buddhist deities (whose style was influenced by earlier Bud-dhist centers of Bamyian and Gandhara), splendid wall paintings, and count-less piles of precious scripts. These 492 Mogao Caves (Sheng 2002, 39-57; Tucker 2003, 126; Thubron 2006, 93f.; Wood 2003, 88ff.) contain, among others, some 45 thousand wall paintings covering 45,000 square meters, plus more than 2,000 sculptures. The murals represent, among others, groups of musicians with all kinds of instruments, including thirty-five different kinds of drums. Unfortunately, in the twentieth century, foreign explorers and ad-venturers looted the most precious treasures of these caves.

In 1900, an earthquake shook Dunhuang and cracked open a sealed chamber. Guardian Abbot Wang peered into the cleft, got a glimpse of the chamber's content, and locked it up again. In 1907, the Anglo-Hungarian explorer Aurel Stein investigated relics of the nearby Great Wall. When he heard stories about the cave and its contents, he persuaded the abbot to let him have a look at that chamber. Eventually, the abbot gave in to Stein's glib talking and opened the cave. To his utter amazement, Stein faced a wall of documents piled up almost ten feet high; the dry air had perfectly conserved the manuscripts.

What Wood (2003, 90f.) calls "the world's earliest paper archive" con-tained texts dating between 400 AD and about 1,000 AD. Most of the texts and the paintings were Buddhist and of Chinese origin. There were also texts in Sanskrit, Tibetan, Hebrew, Uighur, Khotanese, Kuchean, and Sogdian. The content of the texts dealt with Taoist, Confucian, Hebrew, Manichean, and Christian Nestorian topics. Some of the texts dealt with economic, historical, and social topics of the area.

After some clever negotiations, Stein loaded his camels with 20,000 documents and silk paintings. The most precious booty he got hold of was a woodblock-printed paper scroll over twenty feet long and equipped with a delicately carved frontispiece. The scroll was a copy of the diamond sutra that had been woodblock printed during the Tang Dynasty in 868. It is today considered to be the oldest 'book' of the world. Later, Stein returned and departed with five more crates filled with manuscripts.

Other adventurers followed, among them men of French, Russian, and Japanese origin. The most destructive robber of them all was the American historian and Harvard professor Langdon Warner, who pried out some murals in such a clumsy manner that he destroyed more than he could steal. He also departed with two precious Tang statues. He later made amends for his barbarism by advising, at the end of the Second World War, the American government against bombing Kamakura, Kyoto, and Nara.

The looting of the Mogao caves occurred a long time after the heyday of Dunhuang. When the Ming Dynasty replaced the Mongol Yuan Dynasty, China turned its back on the Silk Road and opened maritime routes to the south where trading was safer. Dunhuang declined and was, for centuries, almost completely deserted. Today, the Mogao Caves are a UNESCO World Heritage site.

Let's return to the first millennium of our era, when caravans left the Jade Gate at Dunhuang. There were three branches of the Silk Road they could take: a north-south route connecting Siberia with Tibet (Thubron 2006, 88), a northwestern route crossing the salt crusts of the former Lop Nor lake (Wood 2003, 75) in order to reach Turfana, or one of the two branches of the Silk Road skirting the rims of the Taklamakan desert. The northern branch ran at the foot of the Tian Shan ranges, along the northern rim of the Tarim Basin from Loulan to Kuqa and southwest to Kashgar at the foot of the Pamir ranges. The southern branch looped between the foot of the Kunlun Shan range and the southern rim of the Taklamakan desert, reaching Miran and Khotan, and then bent northwest to Kashgar. The most important desert oases in the Tarim Basin were Loulan and Kuqa to the north, Khotan in the south branch, and Kashgar in the west where the two branches met.

Extremely well-preserved mummies found under the sand dunes near Loulan prove that the earliest settlers in this area were Caucasians (Wood 2003, 64). These people, also known as Tokharians, were big, had blond-reddish hair, and probably blue eyes. They wore woollen cloth with tartan patterns strongly resembling the patterns still seen in modern Scottish kilts. It is assumed that the Tokharians must have emigrated from the region of the Caspian Sea and that they may even have been members of a migrating Celtic tribe. A famous mummy called 'Beauty of Loulan' (Tucker 2003, 171) is clad in woollen clothes and fur. Radiocarbon dating of her bones and some artefacts indicate that she has been buried around 2000 BC. At the time of the Tang Dynasty, Tokharian ladies (Tucker 2003, 95) were known for their proverbial beauty. Ladies of the imperial court of Chang'an eagerly copied the Tokharian Beauties makeup, hairstyle, and fashion.

Kuqa, also called Kucha, was a Buddhist kingdom ruled probably by clans of Indian descent during the Tang Dynasty, and was the largest of the so-called 'Thirty-Six Kingdoms of the Western Regions' (that is, of Central Asia). It was famous for its musicians (Tucker 2003, 92f.) who played *pipa* (four-stringed lute), lacquered drum, and flute. Musical instruments and compositions from Kuqa were in high demand in Chang'an. When monk Xuanzang visited Kuqa in the seventh century AD he wrote, "The musicians of this land outshine those of other kingdoms by their talent on the flute and lute."

The desert oasis Khotan was famous for the role it played in the transmission of the secrets of sericulture, which we shall discuss later, and as the most important place in Central Asia where jade was found. Moreover, it was reputed for its sophisticated painters.

As early as the third millennium BC, jade was traded from Khotan to China in the east and westwards to several countries including Mesopotamia. Boulders of nephrite jade (Tucker 2003, 180) were washed down from the Kunlun range by two rivers, the Karakash (Black Jade River) and the Kurungkash (White Jade River). Jade, considered to be 'crystallized moonlight' (Thubron 2006, 127f.), was harvested from the river and later craftsmen carved it into all kinds of objects and figurines. In Chinese lore and traditions, jade played a role maybe even more crucial than silk. Jade came in all possible colors from black to green, deep red and a particularly treasured milky 'mutton-fat'. The shapes and smooth surfaces of nephrite jade suggested different things to different people.

Tang emperor Xuanzong (685-762) had one hundred dancing horses (Wood 2003, 80) trained to perform the most amazing tricks. Their attendants wore white shirts and jade belts which must have been transported from Khotan via the Jade Gate of Dunhuang to Chang'an. Poet Li Bai sang about saffron-spiced wine offered in "brimful cups of jade." In those days, every household of wealthy patrons in China boasted jade objects representing horses, dragons, Buddha figurines, female dancers, and other figures.

For Confucius, jade represented the virtues of the perfect man. For many Chinese people, the luminosity of white and yellow jade symbolized the purity of a beautiful woman's skin. As Thubron (Thubron 2006, 128) reports, "old handbooks of sexuality exalted the jade stalk entering the jade garden until jade fountains overflowed." Emperors, kings, princes, and rich merchants drank powdered jade with rice and dew not only as an aphrodisiac, but also in order to gain immortality. Jade amulets covered the corpses of princes, including their eyes, lips, and penis. Sculptures of reptiles in their tombs were covered with jade plates sewn together with threads of gold. Around 1200 BC, Fu Hao, a queen of Shan Dynasty, died and her tomb (Wood 2003, 26) boasted more than 700 jade objects, some were thousands of years old.

During the Sui Dynasty (589 AD-618 AD) and Tang Dynasty, Khotanese painters (Tucker 2003, 183) were in high demand not only in Chang'an, but also at the Tibetan court. Weichi Boqina and his son Weichi Yiseng were famous for their sophisticated 'relief' style. They used to put layers upon layers of color one on top of the other to get the desired shapes and colors of faces, bodies, and objects.

From Khotan, the southern branch of the Silk Road ran westward to Kashgar, where it converged with the northern branch coming from Kuqa. In ancient times, the journey from Chang'an to Kashgar lasted a whole year. Kashgar was once the desert oasis marking the western frontier of China. In 78 AD, Han emperor Zhang Di (reigned 76-88) established a Chinese garrison in Kashgar (Wood 2003, 153) that was soon ousted by the Western Turks. In the early years of the Tang Dynasty, Kashgar was reconquered and soon lost again to invading Arabs. In 747 AD, a Chinese army crossed the Hindu Kush to drive off these invaders, and in 751, the Arabs won a decisive battle at the Talas River northeast of Tashkent. Central Asia and the oases around the Tarim Basin fell into the hands of Muslims who not only gained control over the Silk Road, but also captured papermakers and silk workers (Thubron 2006, 181). The craft they brought with them was now introduced into all the countries under Muslim influence—from Kashgar to Samarkand, Baghdad, Cairo, and Cordoba. The last heyday of Kashgar occurred under Mongol rule. After the crash of the Yuan Dynasty, Kashgar and the two branches of the Silk Road skirting the Tarim Basin went into decline. Until the eighteenth century, Kashgar would not be anymore under Chinese control.

In the nineteenth century, Kashgar became one of the many battlegrounds in the 'Great Game' played by Russia and England over the control of Central Asia. That so-called Great Game was a wrestling match between Russians and England, both bent on expanding their imperial grip on foreign countries from Tibet to Afghanistan and Uzbekistan (Wood 2003, 147). Already in the seventeenth century, Russia had begun to colonize southern Siberia, pushing towards the Amur River—which today forms the borderline between Russian Far East and northwestern China. In the eighteenth century, Russian Empress Catherine the Great (reigned 1762-1796) played with the idea (Wood 2003, 149) of wrestling India from the British Empire. Soon thereafter,in 1807,

Napoleon tried to motivate Tsar Alexander I for a joint military campaign on
the Indian subcontinent, yet those ambitious Russian dreams of expansion
never materialized. In the first half of the nineteenth century, (Wood 2003,
149) Russian troops conquered the Moslem khanates of Bukhara, Khiva (former capital of Khwarezmia), and Khokand at the southwestern end of Ferghana Valley. Tashkent, Samarkand, and Khiva fell into Russian hands between 1865 and 1873. In the middle of the nineteenth century, Britain
conquered India and tried to increase its domains north of the Himalayan
range by establishing a consulate in Kashgar to mark its presence while getting hold of vitally important information. At times, the corridor separating
the two empires involved in the Great Game was a few hundred miles wide,
and in the Pamir range even less than twenty. Today Kashgar is once more
under Chinese rule, and the native Uighurs are more and more pushed aside
by Han Chinese settlers sent by the government in Beijing.

In the course of the millennia, Kashgar has been a place from where traders, devotees, and conquerors started out to cross the Pamirs and the Hindu
Kush in order to reach Taxila, where the Silk Road forked into three branches.
A western branch led to Kabul. An eastern branch ran through the Kashmir
valley to Mathura in today's Uttar Pradesh state—a holy city for Hindus because it was believed to be Krishna's birthplace. From Mathura, that branch
of the Silk Road continued southwest to the seaport of Barygaza in Gujarat
state. From here, ships left to cross the Indian Ocean in order to reach the
Arabian Peninsula or the Gulf of Persia, while another maritime route led
around the southern tip of the Indian subcontinent to the Spice Islands of Indonesia. And in the middle of the western and eastern branch leaving Taxila,
there was a trail leading into the Punjab valley and to the mouth of the Indus
River—from where several maritime routes left for their eastbound, southbound, and westbound journeys.

Due to its strategically located position, Taxila, a former vassal state of
Alexander the Great and now capital of a Buddhist kingdom, played a major
role for centuries. For almost 1,000 years—between the sixth century BC and
the fifth century AD—Taxila was not only a rich trading place but also a major center of learning where Vedic-Hindu and Buddhist scholars exchanged
and refined their ideas.

From Kashgar, a westbound branch of the Silk Road led to Osh and Ku-
jand, there it then bifurcated to the north to reach Tashkent and to the southwest to join Samarkand and Bukhara. We have already discussed the importance of these wealthy trading cities during the Golden Ages of Muslim rule,
during Mongol times, and when Timur-i-leng built his capital in Samarkand.

Samarkand—the ancient Greeks called it Maracanda—was once the capital
of the Sogdians, a people of Iranian descent (Thubron 2006, 196f.) and, as al-

ready stated, for centuries the master traders on the Silk Road. As Thubron (2006) puts it, Sogdian traders were so clever and successful that Chinese people believed that "their mothers fed them sugar in the cradle to honey their voices, and their baby palms were daubed with paste to attract profitable things." The Sogdians were not only clever traders, they were also fierce warriors and skilled in forging strong armor; operated a well-functioning chain mail system; were experts in winemaking; and in establishing underground irrigation systems for the waters drawn from the Syr Darya and the Amu Darya rivers. The purpose of underground irrigation systems, which had been invented in Persia (Wood 2003, 16) thousands of years before, was to diminish evaporation in a region where annual rainfall was but 200 mm or less. During the era of the Kushan Empire, the Sogdians (Tucker 2003, 257) even built a leaden aqueduct.

Founded ca. 700 BC, Samarkand is one of the oldest cities in the world. During the Persian Achaemenid Empire (550-330 BC), it was the capital of the Sogdian satrapy. In 329 BC, when Alexander the Great conquered Samarkand, it was already a very wealthy city. Later Samarkand was conquered by the Yuezhi, an Indo-German tribe driven away by the Xiongnus (Turkic-Huns) from its settlements at the eastern Tarim Basin and first wandering west and then south, where they eventually founded the Kushan Empire (1th century BC – fourth century AD) with capitals in Peshawar, Mathura, and Taxila. In the following centuries, Samarkand was ruled by Turks, Huns, Arabian Muslims, Mongols (Wood 2003, 86), Timur-i-leng, Uzbek Turks, Persians, and eventually Russians. In the course of its turbulent history, and as a result of its strategically important location, Samarkand was alternately destroyed and built up a number of times.

Within all that chaos marked by destructive morpho-elimination, there was also much order introduced by creative morpho-evolution. Being at the crossroad of so many different civilizations and empires, Samarkand was famous for its artists (Tucker 2003, 257), whose styles and themes were influenced by Byzantine, Arabian, Persian, Indian, and Chinese art.

The road connecting Samarkand and Bukhara has been called the *Shah Rah* (the Royal Road). Bukhara was founded around 3000 BC. In the fifth century BC, Bukhara was already a very important trading center and an extremely wealthy city with beautiful mosques and palaces. That evolution was mainly due to two reasons. First, sitting between the Syr Darya and Amu Darya, the oasis of Bukhara was embedded in a land made very fertile by the highly sophisticated irrigation system built in the first millennium BC by Iranian Sogdians. Second, the oasis of Bukhara sat literally at a crossroads of the Silk Road. From here, a northern branch went to Samarkand, a western branch to Khiva and Kunya Urgench (Old Gurgench, Gurganj), a southern branch to Merv and Nishapur, and an eastern branch to Balkh.

Around 500 BC, Bukhara became a vassal state of the Persian Empire. Then it passed into the hands of Alexander the Great, the Seleucid Empire of his successors, and the Greco-Bactrian kingdom, which reached down into the Punjab Valley and westward to the Caspian Sea. Later, Bukhara became a part of the Kushan Empire until it was conquered (Tucker 2003, 247f.) in 709 AD by invading Arabian armies. In 892, Bukhara was chosen as its capital by the Persian Samanid dynasty. Their rulers became generous patrons of scholars and craftsmen, whose know-how boosted the wealth and reputation of Bukhara as an intellectual center and a place of great handicrafts.

From its capital Bukhara, the Samanid dynasty ruled over Khwarezm (Khwarizm, Chorasam), a collection of little states. Within Khwarezm there was the city of Khiva, birthplace of polymath al-Kwharizmi, and Kath, birthplace of polymath al-Biruni. The latter was a colleague of polymath Ibn Sina who was born in Bukhara (or born in Balkh and educated in Bukhara according to some sources). Both worked together (Tucker 2003, 239) at the famous Muslim al-Mamun academy of Gurgench. It is, by the way, quite interesting to read what these two outstanding scholars thought about the relationship between wealth and science, and religion and science. Asked why scholars always knocked at the doors of the rich while the opposite didn't occur (Tucker 2003, 240), al-Biruni quipped: "The scholars are well aware of the use of money, but the rich are ignorant of the nobility of science." And Ibn Sina, alias Avicenna, once sarcastically stated (Tucker 2003, 251): "The world is divided into men who have wit and no religion and men who have religion and no wit." If we look at our contemporary world haunted by commercial greed and sectarian fanaticism, then we easily agree with these two great creative minds who lived and worked in the area of Bukhara. As for al-Khawarizmi, al-Biruni, and Ibn Sina: these three men illustrate that creative minds belonged to the most precious treasures to be found along the Silk Road. During millennia, their discoveries and ideas shaped the course of creative morpho-evolution and with it major progress made in technology, science, the arts, and other aspects of various civilizations.

As mentioned earlier, an eastern branch of the Silk Road connected Bukhara with Balkh. Like Bukhara, Balkh was situated at a crossroads where branches coming from all four points of the compass met. Balkh was a settlement originally established by Indian-Iranian tribes arriving from the Amur Darya region. Arabs called Balkh *Umm Al-Belaad* (Mother of Cities) because of its origin, dating back to the second millennium BC. At the time of the ancient Persian Empire, Balkh was conquered by Cyrus the Great (ca. 530-ca. 590 BC). Later it was taken by Alexander the Great—who married Roxane, the beautiful daughter of Sogdian ruler Oxyarte (Tucker 2003, 204), there in 329 BC—and then it became the capital of a Greco-Bactrian kingdom. That kingdom was very wealthy: its land was made fertile by the waters of the Amu Darya; it was situated at a crossroads of international trade; and it was rich in precious minerals. Gold, silver, and rubies were mined here, and farther east in the hills of Badakshan, there was, as Tucker (Tucker 2003, 204ff.) states, "the only source of lapis lazuli known to the ancient world."

Due to its wealth, the whole area was an irresistible magnet for ambitious settlers. That's why the ancient Greeks called that region "land of a thousand cities." As a result of this great wealth, Balk shared the fate of Samarkand: it was built, destroyed, and rebuilt many times in the course of history. In the fourth century AD, an invasion of the Sassanian army destroyed the northern part of the city. Yet in 630 AD, during the Tang Dynasty, when Chinese Buddhist monk Xuanzang travelled to India to get hold of sacred Buddhist scriptures, he reported that Balk boasted a hundred Buddhist monasteries with about 3,000 monks. Soon thereafter, the city fell into the hands of invading Arab Muslims who called Balkh—which soon turned into a center of Muslim scholarship—"the dome of Islam" and "paradise on earth."

In 1221, that paradise on earth was levelled to the ground by the armies of Genghis Khan because it had resisted his demands for opening its doors to the Mongols. This is how an ancient source (Tucker 2003, 206) described the sack of Balkh: Genghis Khan ordered that the whole population of Balkh be driven out onto the plain ". . . and divided up according to their usual custom into hundreds and thousands to be put to the sword." Obviously Balkh was soon rebuilt again, because in the fourteenth century Timur-i-leng once more destroyed the city. His successors, the Timurids, built it up again. According to an Arab source (Tucker 2003, 204), by the sixteenth century Balkh had been built, destroyed, and rebuilt again more than twenty times. In the following century, young Moghul emperor Aurangzeb made Balkh his government seat. In 1736 AD, Balkh was conquered by Nadir Shah the founder of the Persian Afsharid Dynasty, and in the nineteenth century, it fell under the rule of the Muslim Bukhara emirate. Today it is a deserted place situated about fifteen miles northwest of the Afghanistan city Mazar-e Sharif, and heaps of rubble lying in the sand still bear witness to a once glorious culture.

Similar to Bukhara, Balkh was the birthplace of great minds. Zoroaster, founder of a religion, was born in Balkh—the dates of his birth vary widely, from 6000 BC to 100 BC. Another great son of that famous city was Sufi poet Mawlana Jalaluddin Blakhi (1207-73), better known as Rumi, spiritual father of the 'Whirling Dervishes.' When the Mongols approached the city, Rumi fled with his family (Tucker 2003, 206) to Konya in Anatolia where he wrote his masterpiece the 26,000 verses epic *Mathnavi*, which many scholars consider to be the most outstanding creative achievement of Persian poetry. Apart from Rumi, Balkh also produced a host of other Persian poets of renown.

From Balkh, a northwestern branch of the Silk Road led to Termez and Samarkand; a western branch joined a place near Chardzhou, from where a northwestern branch went to Khiva, Kunya Urgench, and further northwest to Astrakhan; a southern branch connected Balkh with Herat where it met the Silk Road leading from Kandahar to Nishapur and, across the Caspian Sea to Baku in Azerbeijan; and a southwestern branch connected Balkh with Bamiyan and Kabul. In other words, Balkh sat like a spider in the center of a web whose threads run in all directions of the compass thus forming a center of attraction where many a desired prey was caught.

Let's now shortly mention the western part of that huge Silk Road lattice connecting Central Asia with the Middle East and the shores of the Mediterranean Sea in order to get a complete picture of the extent and importance of the Silk Road. Since we have already discussed—in the chapters on the Muslim Golden Ages and on Mongol rule—the main trade destination within that lattice, we shall not enter into too many details here.

From Nishapur, a southwestern branch of the Silk Road lead to Ray in Iran Persian Empire, and from there northwest to Tabriz, Trabzon at the Black Sea, or (at a bifurcation in Erzerum, in western Armenia) to Ankara, Byzantium and via the Via Egnatia across the Balkans to the seaport of Durres (Durrazzo in today's Albania) where ships left for Brindisi. In Brindisi, there began the Via Appia that connected the seaport at the Tyrrhenian Sea with Rome.

A southwestern branch connected Ray to Hamadan—former Ekbatana, capital of the Median Empire founded in the seventh century BC—and Ctesiphon situated at the east bank of the Tigris River. From Ctesiphon, one branch of the Silk Road ran to the Shatt el Arab, the delta in the Persian Gulf formed by the Euphrates and Tigris rivers. Western branches of the Silk Road connected Ctesiphon via Mosul with Antioch or via Baghdad with Palmyra, Damascus, and Petra in Jordan.

We have already discussed the fate of Baghdad and Damascus during the Muslim Golden Ages and the time of Mongol invasion. To round up our general picture of the Silk Road, a few words are about about Antioch, Palmyra, and the city of Tyre at the Mediterranean coast.

After Alexander the Great died in Babylon on July 14, 323 BC, the *Diadochoi*[15] entered an embittered power struggle to secure a slice of the huge empire that the not yet thirty-three-year-old Macedonian king had left behind. One of the victors of that merciless power grab was Seleucus I Nicanor, one of Alexander's most gifted generals. He took hold of the eastern domains of Alexander's empire and made Babylon the capital of his newly founded Seleucid Empire (312-60 BC). Expanding his empire westwards, he established at the end of the fourth century BC, a western capital at Antioch in the Orontes River Valley—Antioch has today morphed into Antakya situated at the southernmost tip of Turkey near the frontier to Syria. Antioch soon developed into a powerful trading center whose wealth made it, apart from Rome and Alexandria (Thubron 2006, 336f.), one of the wealthiest cities of the Middle East. Seleucus I Nicanor ordered the construction of avenues lined with fields of wheat and designed in such a manner that it would be able to catch the summer breeze and the winter sun. At the watchtowers of the fortified city, Seleucus I Nicanor had some of the 500 elephants tethered; these impressive giants were a part of the prize a local ruler had paid after Seleucus I Nicanor had ceded his territories in the Indus Valley in 305 BC.

The land routes of the Silk Road connecting Baghdad and Ctesiphon with Byzantium and Rome passed through Antioch. Moreover, maritime routes connected Antioch directly with Byzantium and Rome. Due to this strategic location, the city of Antioch turned quickly into a major trading center. From the Levant arrived precious woods, feathers, animal skins, and gold plus—via the Incense Road connecting Egypt with the Arabian Peninsula and India—frankincense, myrrh, and Indian spices. Soon Antioch was very wealthy boasting a population of half a million. The inhabitants of Antioch wore exquisite Chinese silk dresses and enjoyed a hedonistic life. So lascivious were Antioch's festivals and erotic ballets that Roman writer Juvenal (born in the first century, died in the second century AD) feared that the lascivious life style of that Seleucid capital was undermining solid Roman values and the code of conduct.

Palmyra is an oasis situated 215 km northeast of Damascus and in ancient time that caravan station was known under the lovely name *Bride of the Desert*. According to Hebrew sources, in the second millennium BC king Solomon of Judea, son of king David, built that desert city. When the Seleucids took over Syria, Palmyra became a part of the Seleucid Empire. Palmyra's career culminated eventually under Roman rule. Syria was annexed by Tiberius (42 BC - 37 AD), successor of Augustus, the first Roman Emperor. In 106 AD, Roman Emperor Trajan (53-117) turned Palmyra into the most important trade center in the whole region. Most of the caravans (Tucker 2003, 328ff.) transporting cargo destined for Rome, Arabia, Persia, and India passed through the Bride of the Desert. In about 129, Emperor Hadrian visited Palmyra and was so impressed by its beauty and wealth that he baptized it *Palmyra Hadriana* and made it a free city, permitted to collect taxes and to decide its own financial affairs. Wealthy citizens of that oasis soon led a lifestyle parallel to that of the conspicuous consumption of Antioch. Under the reign of Emperor Septimius Severus (145-211), Palmyra grew so big that its diameter was about 12 km. Emperor Caracalla (188-217), who coreigned with his father Septimius Severus between 198 and 211, made Palmyra a Roman Colony, freed it from having to pay taxes to Rome, and thus boosted its economic growth even further.

In the third century AD, the Roman Empire founded in 509 BC entered a phase of successive crises; on its fringes, provinces began to rebel and break away from Rome. The Goths, having migrated from the Baltic Sea to the shores of the Black Sea, ravaged Asia Minor. Shapur I, king of the Persian Sassanian (also called Sassanid) Dynasty, invaded Mesopotamia and Syria. Around 251 AD, Odainat, leader of an Arabian clan and profiting from the general unrest on the eastern borders of the Roman Empire, began to carve out his own kingdom (Tucker 2003, 330) and made Palmyra its capital. In 259, Shapur I captured Roman Emperor Valerian (reigned 253-260) in the battle of Edessa, Mesopotomia. Now Odainat launched his own campaign against Shapur's capital Ctesiphon. During a battle in Cappadocia, 'The Land of Beautiful Horses,' Odainat and his crown prince were killed and in 268, his wife Zenobia ascended the throne. Contemporary sources describe her as an exquisitely beautiful and courageous warrior queen whose armies conquered Syria and invaded Anatolia and Egypt. Roman Emperor Aurelian (reigned 270-275) put an end to her expansionist policies and in 272, he presented her and her sons in golden chains to the masses attending his triumphal procession in Rome. When the city of Palmyra rose and massacred Aurelian's garrison, the Roman emperor ordered Palmyra's sack in 273; it never recovered again.

The last three destinations in the Levant were Petra, Tyre, and Sidon. Petra, whose buildings are cut into the rocks of Mount Hor in Jordan, must have been an ancient caravan station. It had probably been established in the middle of the first millennium BC by Nebataean Arabs, and its tombs betray a Greco-Roman influence. Yet as Palmyra rose, Petra went into decline and was eventually abandoned.

Tyre and Sidon (Tucker 2003, 334ff.) were two very important Phoenician port cities situated on the eastern shores of the Mediterranean Sea, on the coast of today's Lebanon. From here, the Silk Road connecting the Levant with Rome entered maritime routes leading to the seaports of Brindisi, Ostia, and Civitavecchia.

In the third millennium BC, ships leaving these ports exported olive oil, wine, and cedarwood to Egypt while importing gold, copper, and turquoise. Phoenician scholars are credited with the invention of an alphabet consisting of consonant phonemes. That was not only a major step towards the invention of the Greek alphabet, which eventually also included vowel phonemes. The Phoenician alphabet also boosted trade and diplomatic relationships with other countries.

Like the Sogdians of Central Asia, Phoenicians were extremely skilled traders and fierce warriors. Between 1500 and 300 BC, their galleys (man-powered sail-ships) roamed the Mediterranean Sea and their political, religious, and sociocultural influence spread to Cyprus, Rhodes, Crete, Malta,

Sardinia, Spain, Portugal, and Tunisia. In the ninth century, they founded Carthage in Tunisia, whose armies conquered Spain and became a serious threat to the Roman Empire when Hannibal (247-183 BC), one of the greatest military leaders of all time, crossed the Alps with his troops and elephants and invaded the Italian Peninsula.

Phoenicians were also highly skilled craftsmen and jewellers, and thus their military campaigns were not only motivated by their quest for power, but also by the need to procure gold, silver, tin, copper, and precious stones for their workshops. Sidon manufactured glass—the art of glass blowing was actually invented by Sidon—and purple dye. The latter was secreted by the mucus of the shellfish *murex trunculus* and sold to emperors and kings for whose insignia of power purple was a sine qua non. Apart from Alexandria, Tyre was for centuries a main center for the production of Byzantine silk. By the seventh century AD, silk production became a state monopoly centered in Constantinople. With that shift, the importance of Tyre declined.

Having discussed the main destinations within the Eurasian lattice of Silk Roads, we may now have a look at the cargo transported by camel caravans and ships across the countless land and maritime routes between East and West.

Let's begin our overview with silk, the very fabric to which the Silk Road owes its poetic name. The invention of sericulture is shrouded in the mist of myths and legends. According to orally transmitted ancient tales, sericulture began during the reign of the Yellow Emperor, the father of the Han Chinese people, who died in 2579 BC after having ruled for a hundred years. He is credited with all the major inventions of ancient China—from music, to the calendar and the basic principles of Chinese medicine, including acupuncture and moxybustion (the burning of dried leaves of *artemisia vulgaris* on or near acupuncture points). His wife Lei-tzu 'The Lady of the Silk Worms' (Thubron 2006, 4) is said to have initiated sericulture. Like every truly creative process, her inspiration began with a chance event. One day she watched a silk worm breaking its cocoon. She began playing around with the broken cocoon and by mistake—yet another chance event—it fell into her cup of tea. The hot tea softened the cocoon and Lei-tzu grasped a filament and began to unwind it. In utter amazement, she looked at the beautiful, glistening thread of silk. And in due time, she began to teach her female entourage the art of silk weaving. *Se non è vero, è ben trovato.*

So far the legend. Historically, it seems to be established (ten Grotenhuis 2002, 15-23) that sericulture was invented in China about 4,000 years ago. Women were mainly responsible for feeding silk worms with fresh mulberry leaves and to see to it that the hypersensitive creatures—who hated noises, strong scents, and vibrations—were protected from environmental molesta- tions. Women watched how caterpillars began to spin their cocoons and waited while the metamorphosis from caterpillar to chrysalis and silk moth took place. But just before the hairy moths could break their shrouds, the cocoons were thrown into hot water. The hot water softened the sticky *sericin* glue holding together the *fibroin* fibers. Once unwound, the fibers yielded filaments up to 1,000 or, as Thubron (Thubron 2006, 126) reports, even up to 1,600 meters long. Silk has an amazing tensile strength, and a silk rope is even stronger than a steel cable of the same diameter! Chinese ingeniousness soon discovered all kinds of practical applications: silk (Thubron 2006, 30) was not only used for fabrics, but also as strings on bows and lutes, as fishing lines, as waterproof silk bags for carrying liquids, and as lacquered silk cups. Moreover, silk fabric lent itself as a material that could be written, drawn, or painted on.

Apart from its character as a multi-use-material, silk was also decay-resistant. In a Neolithic village (Thubron 2006, 5), archaeologists discovered a silkworm carved on an ivory cup more than 6,000 years ago and an artificially broken cocoon. In a Neolithic site at Hemudu in Zhejiang province, they unearthed (Wood 2003, 28) dyed silk gauzes and weaving tools dated to 3600 BC. In a site in Turkmenistan, they discovered silk fabric dated to the late third millennium BC. In other early sites, spinning tools and red-dyed silk ribbons have been found.

Chinese silk from about 1500 BC was found in a tomb in north Afghanistan (Thubron 2006, 24); on a tenth-century BC Egyptian mummy, investigators came across strands of hair interwoven with strands of silk. In the tomb of a sixth-century BC German prince, archaeologists have found Chinese silk; and the horse blanket of a fourth-century BC Scythian chief also contains a framed piece of brilliant silk fabric. In the permafrost of the Altai Mountains, about 800 kilometers north of the Silk Road, archaeologists (Barber 2002, 57-73) dug out a saddlecloth dated to about 300 BC. Its silk was, as Barber (2002) reports, "embroidered with colourful, pheasant-like phoenixes roosting in delicate scrolls of greenery." All of these finds prove that Chinese sericulture is older than the legendary Yellow Emperor and his wife Lei-tzu, they also suggest that in ancient times silk must have been much in demand even outside of China.

In Chinese sericulture, silk filaments were wound around a reel and then spun into silk fabric. Already during the Shang Dynasty (ca. 1600-1050 BC), women working in the imperial household (Barber 2002, 57-73) mastered the art of dying silk—which easily absorbs colors applied to it—and of weaving it into delicately patterned fabrics.

Silk was not only a commodity fetching high prices on the market, it was also used as a money-ersatz for paying taxes or—throwing in at times also a couple of princess brides—for bribing nomad warriors from the northern steppes to prevent them from invading the Middle Kingdom. (ten Grotenhuis

2002, 15-23). Originally a privilege of the imperial family (Barber 2002, 57-73), as time went by silk production became a family business and eventually the craft of silk production reached industrial proportions. The Yangtze delta area, once a producer of fish and rice, became one gigantic silk producing facility (Wood 2003, 31)—a process changing the landscape and economy of the whole region. The delta was now dotted with narrow water lanes whose banks were lined with stunted mulberry trees.

The more sericulture thrived in China, the better imperial and common families lived from producing and selling silk. For quite obvious reasons, they were keen not to divulge the methods of sericulture and to keep their crafts-manship in producing, dyeing, spinning, and weaving silk a top secret. An imperial edict imposed the death penalty on whoever dared to export mul-berry seeds or live silkworms.

But to no avail. Greed and cunning have always helped thieves and other gangsters to get the better of the lawmaker's decree. Legend has it that in 430 AD, a Chinese princess (Thubron 2006, 126; Wood 2003, 151; Tucker 2003, 181) was sent westward to marry the king Vijaya Jaya of Khotan. Hidden in her piled up hairdo, she smuggled mulberry seeds and silkworms across the Gansu corridor and the Jade Gate at Dunhuang to the oasis at the southern rim of the Tarim Basin. And around 552 AD, two Nestorian monks (Tucker 2003, 182) arriving from Khotan brought silkworm eggs they had hidden in their staffs to the Emperor Justinian of Constantinople. Now the secret was out, the Chinese monopoly broken. Soon avenues of mulberry trees as well as instal-lations and tools for sericulture began to appear along the Silk Road of Cen-tral Asia, in Persia around the southern shores of the Black Sea and Caspian Sea, and on the eastern shores of the Mediterranean Sea. Alexandria and Tyre (Tucker 2003, 357) became centers of Byzantine silk production. A millen-nium later in the seventeenth century and under the reign of the Ottoman Empire, silk production became a state monopoly and the whole silk industry was centralized in Constantinople.

Around 400 BC, silk fabrics (Barber 2002, 57-73) began to appear in Eu-rope. They were brought by nomads wandering across the grass belts of the steppes, from China all the way to the Hungarian Puszta. Three hundred years later, silk coming from India emerged on the markets of western Asia. West-ern weavers began making a living by unravelling heavy Chinese brocades and weaving silk thread into light and luminous fabrics. Soon the Greeks fell in love with the new fabric. A wit even pronounced that wily ladies clad in silk were pretending to be modestly dressed whereas in fact they looked as if they were naked.

While silk trade via maritime routes from India to Persia seems to have preceded land-based trade, the latter began to increase due to an initiative taken by a Han emperor. Around 105 BC, Emperor Wudi (reigned 140-87 BC) sent an envoy to Mithradates II (reigned 123-88), ruler of the Parthian Empire of Persia (Tucker 2003, 15). Emperor Wudi was not only interested in fast horses from the Ferghana Valley in order to reinforce the power of his armies, he also looked for major trade opportunities with the countries west of the Taklamakan Desert in order to boost the wealth of his empire.

The Parthian Empire (238 BC-226 AD) was a powerful trade partner for China because it reached from today's Pakistan, Afghanistan, Turkmenistan, and Armenia to Iran, Bahrein, Iraq, Syria, and Anatolia. Silk was traded between China and Parthia for half a century before the Roman Empire (Tucker 2003, 82; Thubron 2006, 283) got in touch with that precious commodity. That fateful encounter emphasized that the sublime combines beauty and terror and fills human beings with a strange blend of enchantment and fear. In 53 BC at Carrhae in southeast Turkey, a Parthian army clashed with an army led by general Marcus Licinius Crassus, governor of the Roman province Syria. As the Parthian horsemen entered at a gallop, the wind unfurled their colorful, glittering silk banners, the Roman legions turned heel to escape the frightful sight of their enemies. The defeat of the habitually victorious Roman army—whose panicked troops even lost their legion standards during their tumultuous flight—was as total as it was humiliating. Ancient Rome's interest in silk originated right there and then.

Eight years after the defeat at Carrhae, in his triumph procession in Rome, Julius Caesar displayed the dazzling Parthian silk banners (Thubron 2006, 339) that had frightened the Roman legions at Carrhae. The luminous, beautifully colored silk fascinated the Roman masses. Silk was seen as the epitome of beauty and triumph. First, wealthy Romans began to wear patches of silk, dyed with Phoenician purple and scarlet colors, sewed like brooches on their woollen or linen togas. Then wealthy women began to wear clothes made of silk and soon everybody was craving silk fabrics. The hunger for precious silk was so tremendous that its import soon threatened to ruin the state finances— in an empire whose armies had fought against the Parthians in order to acquire gold to finance future Roman military campaigns.

In 14 BC, Rome's Senate (Tucker 2003, 15) decreed that it was dishonorable to wear silken cloths, and men were explicitly banned to wear silk because they were "disgracing themselves with the effeminate delicacy of silk apparel." Obviously, the Senate feared a population indulging in a luxurious lifestyle would undermine Rome's military power and thus its wealth and political influence. Philosopher Seneca (ca. 54 BC-ca. 39 AD)—always on the lookout for a new topic able to kindle the flames of his rhetoric and boost his public image—thundered (Wood 2003, 30): "Wretched flocks of maids labour so that the adulteress may be visible through her thin dress, so that her husband has no more acquaintance than any outsider or foreigner with his wife's body." And in his treatise *On Benefits* (Tucker 2003, 15) he lambasted: "Silk garments provide no protection for the body, or indeed modesty, so that when a woman wears them she can scarcely . . . swear that she is not naked."

Quite obviously, Seneca's masterfully crafted rhetoric didn't curb Roman demand for silk supply. Naturalist Pliny the Elder (23-79 AD) decried the negative trade balance because Rome had to pay gold and silver for the imported silk. According to his estimates (ten Grotenhuis 2002, 15-23), Rome shelled out a hundred million *sesterces* a year for silk. Pliny's warnings had no impact whatsoever. In 273, Emperor Aurelian (214-275) warned (Thubron 2006, 339): "Let us not exchange Roman gold for spiders' webs." Yet that exchange continued. A century later, even the poorer classes wore silk dresses and the drain on the state finances hastened the decline and eventual fall of the Roman Empire.

Between the fourth and the sixth centuries, the western half of the impoverished Roman Empire was annihilated by successive waves of barbarian invasions (Goths, Huns, Goths, Visigoths, Vandals, and other tribes). In 408, Alarich king of the Visigoths (reigned 395-410) besieged Rome, controlling all passages into the famine-stricken city. To relieve the citizens' misery, the Senate decided to pay a ransom of 5,000 pounds of gold, 30,000 pounds of silver, 4,000 silken tunics, 3,000 hides dyed scarlet red, and 3,000 pounds of pepper.

The Eastern Roman Empire survived longer, but by the eleventh century, its territories were reduced to Asia Minor, the Balkans, and southernmost parts of the Italian boot. Parallel to the decline of the Eastern Roman Empire, the Muslims established their empires from Andalusia to the Tarim Basin. While controlling all trade on the Silk Road, they soon faced problems comparable to ancient Rome. At the battle on the bank of the Talas River (Thubron 2006, 190), situated in today's Kyrgyzstan, Abbasid Muslim troops routed a Chinese army and the humiliated Tang Dynasty turned its back on the land route of the Silk Road. At that battle, the victorious Muslims captured Chinese silk workers. Their handicraft boosted sericulture and the production of refined silk fabrics in Persia and Syria. Persian silk fabrics, characterized by the opulent designs of an ancient culture imbued with a highly refined aesthetic taste, were so splendid that they even dazzled the hard to please emperors of the Tang Dynasty—yet another example illustrating the power of creative morpho-evolution.

Moors established their own sericulture and silk production in Andalusia. Palaces and mansions of caliphs, sultans, emirs, and wealthy merchants glittered in silk fabrics as dazzling as a peacock's tail. Turbans, dresses, and slippers were made of silk and, as Thubron (Thubron 2006, 190) puts it, the retinues of the noble and wealthy "glittered like water." Bales of woven silk fabrics and bolts of silk cloths were lavished on influential figures to express loyalty or to buy favor. Thus the austerity decreed by the Qu'ran was replaced by conspicuous consumption and indulgence in a luxurious life.

As a rejoinder to the history of silk and its origins, it is interesting to note that originally Rome was as ignorant (Thubron 2006, 86) about the true nature of silk as the Chinese were misinformed about the origin of cotton. The Chinese assumed that cotton was a kind of hair produced by animals—maybe because it resembled in texture and color to the Kashmir wool produced by kids. Romans believed that silk grew on trees. Greek philosopher, geographer, and historian Strabo (ca. 63 BC-24 AD) maintained that silk (Wood 2003, 30) came from India where it was "dried out of certain barks." About 70 AD, Roman naturalist Pliny the Elder (ten Grotenhuis 2002, 15-23,16) described silk as a pale floss growing on leaves in the forests inhabitated by people (Thubron 2006, 338) called Seres who lived at the eastern edge of the world. In the second century AD, Romans heard tales about eight-legged Seres spiders who spun silk around their feet.

Although silk was very expensive, dazzling, and therefore much in demand, there was other cargo transported by camel caravans on land routes and by ships on maritime routes of the Silk Road. That cargo was supplied from countless countries and it was carried into all directions of the compass. Various authors (ten Grotenhuis 2002, 15-23; Barber 2002, 57-73; Thubron 2006; Wood 2003; Tucker 2003) have compiled the vast array of trade goods transported during centuries over shorter or longer distances on the Silk Road. The following summary of items is based upon their accounts.

China produced and sold diaphanous silk fabrics in all colors of the rainbow, opulent silk brocades, satins, ornamented lacquer-ware, diamonds, tortoise shells and pearls from the South China Sea, carved jade objects in various hues, raw silver and all kinds of objects made of silver, copper coins and the technique of copper coinage; the latter was, for instance, adopted by the Persians. China produced iron, bronze, precious ornamented ceramics in various colors, musk, and perfumes. China (Thubron 2006, 24) grew and traded westward tea, oranges, apricots, mulberries, peaches, roses, camellias, peonies, azaleas, chrysanthemums, and rhubarb—the latter being used as a purgative and, as we have seen before, even withheld in the vain effort to force the British Empire to its knees. China invented and exported gunpowder, weapons, and mechanical clocks to the west. It also traded princesses to Central Asian kings: they became brides and served, together with other hostages also traded on the Silk Road, as a guarantee for the stability of political alliances.

Pants were an invention of nomadic horse warriors roaming the grass belt of the steppes from Siberia and Mongolia westward to the Hungarian Puszta. In the fifth century BC, when China had a hard time fighting off roving bands crossing the Gobi Desert in order to rob and vandalize the sedentary peasantry of northern China, the Chinese not only began looking for better horses, they also began to wear pants that were more practical for horsemen than skirts.

In 751 AD, when Muslim forces—composed of Arab, Kyrgyz, and Nepali warriors—routed a Tang army at the banks of the Talas River in northern Kyrghisztan near the border of Kasakhstan, they captured Chinese silk workers and papermakers and sent them into Central Asia. Samarkand became a new center of silk production and paper production. From there both techniques spread westwards.

Mongols invented the *morin khuur*, a horse-head fiddle, and the bow to strum its two strings. The male string consisted of hairs from a stallion's tail, the female string of hairs from a mare's tail. From Mongolia, the fiddle spread south and west and, as time went by, successive new inventions changed its form, number of strings, and sound. Who would have thought that Niccolò Paganini (1782-1840), who enthused his contemporaries with his virtuoso technique on the violin, was playing an instrument whose origin dated back to a far off day when the first barbarian in the wind-swept Asiatic steppe fiddled his melancholic melodies on a simple *morin khuur*? Once more we witness here the vagaries of creative morpho-evolution.

Central Asia traded gold, precious stones, and Yak hair from Tibet to China. It produced carpets, grapes, cotton, donkeys, jade, and horses—the latter two commodities were very much in demand in China. It seems that Ukraine was the region where the domestication of horses began around 4000 BC. These horses pulled ploughs, sleds, and chariots and carried riders. In the following two millennia, horse breeding became ever more sophisticated until noble mares and stallions developed into one of the most desired trade goods that China imported from Ferghana Valley and Valley of Ili south of Lake Balkash.

The fertile Ferghana valley (Thubron 2006, 188; Tucker 2003, 27ff.) encompassed a vast region situated in Kyrgyzstan, eastern Uzbekistan, and northeastern Tajikistan—and it was the breeding ground for what the Chinese called "heavenly horses." Their exalted denomination was due to the nefarious impact of nomad warriors who plagued China for centuries. The Siberian Xiongnu marauders rode horses that were much faster than their Chinese counterparts—a serious drawback in cavalry battles. Chinese horses were little, shaggy *tarpan* or Wild Asian Horse of the Asian steppe, which the nineteenth century Russian explorer Przewalski was later the first to describe scientifically. Already Shi Huang Di (reigned 247-210 BC), the first emperor of the Qin Dynasty, understood the superiority of cavalry over infantry in open field battles. A famous underground terracotta army guarded his burial grounds to secure eternal piece for the mighty architect of a unified China.

Unfortunately, the presumed magical power of those terracotta horses didn't enhance the military strength of warriors still alive. In 201 BC (Wood 2003, 54), when Gao Zu (reigned 206-195 BC) the first emperor of the Han Dynasty, sent an army mostly consisting of infantry against the raiding Xiongnu, that army was meted out a humiliating defeat.

In 139 BC, Han Emperor Wudi (reigned 141-87 BC) sent an envoy consisting of palace courtier Zhan Qian, a Xiongnu slave named Ganfu, and hundred troops to the Yuezhi king—whose people had been driven westward to Bactria by the Xiongnu—to solicit his aid against the Xiongnu. On his way to the west Zhan Qian was captured by the Xiongnu. While their prisoner, he took a Xiongnu wife who gave birth to a son. After more than ten years, Zhan Qian was able to escape; yet when he reached Bactria, the Yuezhi king wasn't willing to enter a coalition with the Chinese emperor. On his way back, Zhan Qian was once more captured by the Xiongnu, but after one year he, his wife, and slave Ganfu eventually returned to Chang'an. Emperor Wudi was enthused by Zhan Qian's report about the swift horses of Ferghana Valley that, according to legend, were foaled from mares in heaven and were, as the Chinese believed, half dragon. In reality, these swift horses were descendents of Turkoman and Caspian horses (Tucker 2003, 334) that, together with Arabian horses, seem to have formed the original breeding stock for all noble Asian and Western horses.

Apart from the people of the Ferghana Valley, the Yuezhi in Bactria and the Wusun nomads of the Ili Valley north of the Tian Shan range and south of Lake Balkash (Wood 2003, 54) were famous for their horse breeding. Since Zhan Qian had returned from Bactria without having received any good will from the Yuezhi, Emperor Wudi now set his eyes on the horses of the Ferghana Valley. In 119 BC, he lost more than 100,000 Chinese horses (Tucker 2003, 82) in his campaign against the raiding Xiongnu. With that debacle, the time had come for the emperor to radically improve his own strategic position. In 102 BC, he sent general Guangli with an army and the declared mission to invade the Ferghana Valley. After four years of embittered fighting, the ruler of Ferghana Valley was beheaded by his own followers. The latter agreed to send 3,000 horses to China. The following year, Emperor Wudi (Wood 2003, 55), waiting at his court in Chang'an for the herds of noble horses to appear at the horizon, composed a hymn whose jubilant verses praise the Heavenly Horses that, after the conquest of the barbarians of the West, are now arriving after having "crossed the Flowing Sands".

From then on, the people of Ferghana Valley every year sent at least two 'heavenly horses' to China. China also received alfalfa grass seeds (Lucerne grass seeds). The import of alfalfa was crucial because that perennial legume is able to fix nitrogen even in nitrogen-poor soil, and thus to yield a protein-rich feed. Alfalfa grass also improved the lactation of the mares, an important factor in an agriculture whose loess soil was notorious for its calcium deficiency. Now the Chinese had the wherewithal to develop their own livestock and to breed swift horses able to pursue the Xiognu bands of raiding warriors. As for Emperor Wudi, he built the Jianzhang Palace and the Shanglin Gardens to celebrate his victory over the barbarians. As Tucker (2003, 81) reports, the Shanglin Gardens boasted 3,000 varieties of flowers and fruits trees, rare birds from West Asia, rhinoceroses from India and, of course, some 'heavenly horses' from the Ferghana Valley.

Central Asia also exported musicians and dancers—including the 'Sogdian whirling girls'—who were entertainers much admired in Tang China. Musicians and dancers brought new musical compositions, instruments, techniques, and styles of performing. Moreover, Central Asia sent trapeze artists, jugglers, and acrobats to China. Central Asia also produced flutes, but their invention seems to be much older than the Silk Road. Archaeologists have found a flute in Slovenia that was made as early as 40,000 BC. Another flute excavated in the Svabian Alps in southern Germany dates its creation around 30,000 BC. Due to its basically simple construction, it is assumed that in the course of the millennia the flute has been invented independently in many different countries.

Another instrument that has travelled east from Central Asia—a kind of switchboard for the distribution of trade goods to all directions of the compass—was the harp. Very popular in ancient times, it has survived as the Chinese *guqin*, Japanese *koto*, Indian-Persian *santur*, and Austrian *zither* to this very day.

Central Asia was a main transmitter of religious faiths finding their way from western regions into China: Christian Nestorianism from Constantinople; Zoroastrianism and Manicheism from Persia; Hinduism from India; Buddhism from India and Tibet; Hebrew religion from the Levante—Jewish craftsmen (Tucker 2003, 91) were skilled in producing, dyeing, and trading silk textiles in their shops in Chang'an.

When the Sassanian Empire broke down, fleeing traders and craftsmen imported Islam into China, but although there were mosques in Chang'an during the Tang Dynasty, Islam never really caught on. To this very day, the oases around the Tarim Basin remain Islam's easternmost bastions. In the seventeenth century, Roman Catholic Jesuits established themselves in China where they soon wielded quite some influence. Kangxi (1654-1722) emperor of the Manchu Qing Dynasty (Wood 2003, 148) whose sixty-one-year-long reign brought China much prosperity, employed Jesuits to survey and map his newly conquered territories. His grandson, Emperor Qianlong (1711-1799) who again extended the Chinese Empire to the west, twice invaded the Turkic

domains around the Tarim Basin and conquered the Gurkha state in Nepal in
order to increase his empire. Jesuits at his court had massive engravings produced in Paris to celebrate these military conquests.

Central Asia supplied China with Bactrian camels. They were not only
much in demand as beasts of burden, they were also fast carriers of messages
for diplomatic and military purposes. So-called 'Emissaries of the Bright
Camels' used "Flying Dragon Camels' (Wood 2003, 76) from the imperial
stables for their high-speed postal delivery system—comparable to the later
Mongol postal express system and the mid-nineteenth century Pony Express
connecting St. Louis Missouri with Sacramento, California. Camel hair was
used to weave cloth and camel meat was reputed for its high quality. Tang
Poet Du Fu (712-770) wrote enthused verses about "the hump of a purple
camel emerging from the blue cauldron."

From Persia and Central Asia, seedlings of vines and fig trees, flax, pome-
granates, jasmine, saffron, walnuts, dates, olives, sesame, peas, onions, cu-
cumber, coriander, and different kinds of vegetables and herbs were traded to
China where they improved the variety and quality of food and medicines.
From the same regions also came the skills of winemaking and building underground irrigation systems, improving Chinese agriculture. Afghanistan
was a source of lapis lazuli, while Persia traded supposedly aphrodisiac rhinoceros horns from South Asia and Africa, plus ivory from African and Syrian elephants—in that process the latter were hunted to extinction. Craftsmen
in China carved ivory into effigies of Buddhist deities, and into combs, opium
pipes, and many other objects. Persia's exquisite silver handicrafts very much
influenced Chinese craftsmanship in producing silverware. Persian cobalt
enabled Chinese potters to produce their beautiful blue and white porcelain.
The Persian polo game was so fashionable at the Chang'an court that even
ladies rode horseback, swinging their long-handled mallets to drive the ball
into their opponents' goal.

Persia was the home of a highly sophisticated Islamic art—miniature
paintings (Tucker 2003, 225), poetry, and historical literature—emerging in
the fourteenth century and strongly supported under the patronage of Mongol Il-Khans. Persian miniaturist Kamal al-Din Bihzad (ca. 1450-1536)
painted indigo colored fabrics decorating the walls of interiors. Indigo, also
applied in European Renaissance paintings, was so precious in China that
only the empress was permitted to use it as a makeup for her eyelids. This
is a rather curious twist of fate, and yet another demonstration of the power
of creative morpho-evolution, because in India indigo cloths were originally
worn only by the untouchables and if a member of a higher caste touched
an indigo cloth, rituals of purification and atonement purged that violation
of social etiquette.

While Chinese emperors refused to accept sheep as a tribute from Central Asian vassals, they were willing to accept wool. According to Berger (Barber 2002, 57-73), sheep were domesticated around 4000 BC in the Zagros range separating Iran and Iraq. As time went by, crossbreeding turned the originally almost hairless sheep into woollen sheep. Later, this new breed spread in all directions of the compass. As we have seen before, "The Beauty of Loulan" (the Tokharian mummy buried around 2000 BC in the Eastern Tarim Basin) wore pieces of woollen fabric.

Central Asia supplied China with Tibetan mastiffs and hunting dogs from Persia, Samarkand, and Kucha. Much in demand were also lap dogs from Kucha, generally known as 'Roman dogs.' As Tucker (Tucker 2003, 97f.) puts it, "the pulchritudinous" Yang Guifei, celebrated concubine of the Tang Emperor Xuanzong (reigned 712-756), was regarded as the ideal of feminine beauty by the ladies of Tang. Her baroque body and her towering 'cloud-tresses' became the role model followed by countless women at the court. The emperor liked to watch her bathe naked in the hot springs outside Chang'an, which he had built especially for that purpose. She returned his favors by providing him a means of saving face during board games: when His Majesty was about to lose, she released her Samarkand lapdog or her parakeet to overturn the pieces on the board.

When Timur-i-leng erected his capital in Samarkand (Wood 2003,137ff.), he imported not only elephants from India, but also architects, craftsman-builders, tile-makers, gem cutters, glass-makers, and painters from India, Persia, and Syria. One of the gems of Timur-i-leng's capital was the Bibi Khanum Mosque dedicated to his favorite wife, a Mongol princess of exquisite beauty. Another architectural gem was his own tomb. About 500 stonemasons (Tucker 2003, 262) from Azerbaijan, Persia, Syria, and India worked to construct that mosque; ninety-five elephants transported building materials to the construction site. Twentith-century Islamic scholar Sharaf al-Din held that the mosque "would rank supreme were it not for the sky itself."

Timur-i-leng's tomb received not less praise. The twentieth-century British travel writer Robert Byron was stunned by the gold and glittering turquoise tiles of the dome of Timur's mausoleum, whose ribs were "scattered with black and white diamonds." Timur-i-leng was one of the most merciless destroyers of human beings and their creative achievements our planet has ever seen. Once more we witness the fact that destructive morpho-elimination and creative morpho-evolution go often hand in hand; sometimes the former quite evidently facilitates the latter. As Timur-i-leng's case suggests, human ambition is able to drive both processes with the same zest.

Arabia traded frankincense and myrrh. It delivered slaves to the Roman Empire, to Central Asian traders, and later, via maritime routes, to the Americas. Slaves were also used and traded by Mongols to China and other countries. As late as the nineteenth century, Bukhara and Khiva were centers of slave trade and the Russians (Wood 2003, 161) used the ignominy of that trade as a pretext in their Great Game against the British to move further south and to conquer the last Muslim khanates.

India offered whole elephant tusks and delicately carved ivory objects such as combs, fans, and boxes for cosmetics. It produced gold jewellery, diamonds, rubies, sapphires, semi-precious gemstones in various colors, tea, ebony—fine-grained black heartwood—and spices. The latter were in demand since ancient times. For centuries before our common era, Arabian traders had crossed the Indian Ocean to reach the coast of Malabar, the heartland of pepper and other precious spices. In the second century BC, Roman and Greek ships sailed from Red Sea ports to India (ten Grotenhuis 2002, 15-23, 21) to trade for spices.

Originally, cotton was produced in the Indus Valley around 3000 BC (Barber 2002, 57-73). Later, cotton seedlings were imported to Egypt, Persia, Central Asia, and China. India also produced fine woollen and linen fabrics.

Nepal and India saw the origins of Buddhism, which was modified by scholars of the Indo-German Yuezhi people who founded the Kushan Empire (ca. 1th-third century AD). The Kushan Empire comprised today's Tajikistan, Afghanistan, Pakistan, and the Indian Ganges river valley. Kushan rulers entertained diplomatic and trade relationships with Rome, Persia, and China. Kushan's flexible brand of Buddhist religion eventually found its way to China and Japan. So did Kushan Buddhist's artwork—Hellenistic paintings, sculptures, and Corinthian capitals ornamented with acanthus leaves. Kushan's art had been influenced by the Greco-Bactrian Empire (250-125 BC), founded by the successors of Alexander the Great. It reached from the Pamirs in the east to today's Pakistan in the south, the Caspian Sea in the west, and the Aral Sea in the north.

The Roman Empire was a main supplier for the trade along the Silk Road. It offered purple woollen cloth, Mediterranean coral, brass for Buddha effigies, and glass products that spread as far as China. Already in 166 AD (Tucker 2003, 329), a merchant arrived at the Indochinese port of Tonkin and presented himself as an envoy of the Roman Emperor Marcus Aurelius. He carried glass with him, but Chinese officials were very much disappointed that he had "no precious stones whatsoever" to offer.

Glass production technology (Barber 2002, 57-73) was invented by Sumerians in southern Mesopotamia around 3000 BC. Originally, quartz sand was melted in open pits at temperatures above 1,600 degrees Celsius and then slowly cooled over weeks. Around 250 BC, the invention of blowpipes permitted the blowing of glass into all possible shapes instead of simply melting and cutting it. The process of making glass was eventually accelerated by inserting pieces of old glass into melting silicates. Adding metallic oxides into the melt generated an array of dazzling colors, making glass as attractive to China as its luminous silk fabrics were to Western eyes.

The Roman Empire produced linen made of flax fibers, a very agreeable fabric to wear in hot climates. The invention of linen must be very old; it was found, for instance, in Egyptian mummies and in a Swiss lake (in the remains of a dwelling on stilts dated to 8000 BC). The Roman Empire produced cameo and intaglio carving, products also in demand in China. It also invented chairs that changed the Chinese and Japanese customs of sitting on mats. Flanders and Italy manufactured fabrics traded along the Silk Road. Turkey delivered falcons very much in demand by Central Asian hunters. And amber from the Baltic Sea was yet another trade good travelling along the Silk Road.

Today we often use the number of patents issued per unit of time as a yardstick for the creative achievements of a country. At the time of the Silk Road, there were no patents, but great inventions and innovations were made and their impact changed the outlook of Western and Eastern civilizations. We have already seen that and how sericulture and the art of silk weaving invented in China spread to the west while the art of glass manufacturing invented in the eastern Mediterranean countries spread east until it reached China. Now we shall have a look at a few other inventions, their creative morpho-evolution and gradual distribution in all directions of the compass.

In 332 BC, Alexander the Great (Wilcken 1967, 108ff.; Green 1992, 251ff.) was waging war against Persian king Darius and set about to conquer the Phoenician city-state of Tyre, situated on an off-shore island separated from the mainland by a narrow arm of sea. While his siege engines kept hurling rocks at the strong fortifications of the city, Alexander had a mole built from the mainland to the walls of Tyre. After seven months of embittered resistance, siege-engines placed on ships were eventually able to breach the southern ramparts and in the bloody struggle that followed, Macedonian crossbows wreaked havoc in the lines of their enemies.

Crossbows had already been in use for about 200 years in China and simultaneously, or so it seems, in Greece. They were the result of a long morpho-evolution that had begun between the fourth and third millennium in the Eurasian steppes, somewhere between Ukraine and the regions north of the Tian Shan ranges. Nomads invented simple bows and, as time went by, they improved the bows' operational range and accuracy. In that process (Barber 2002, 57-73), they learned how to bend wood permanently. Eventually, their creativity enabled them to curve wooden strips full-circle around a set of radial struts and thus they invented the spoked wheel. It could be used for transporting goods or human beings. War chariots were one of the many devices using the spoked wheel. That invention spread westwards and between 1800-1600 BC, the Hittites riding chariots conquered Anatolia, while the Myceneans using the same technique took over Greece. From these two countries, warfare chariots spread to the Levant and Egypt. Half a millennium later, China also began to use warfare chariots. This example illustrates once more how creative morpho-evolution and destructive morpho-elimination are often intimately linked.

Around 1475 BC, Egyptian warriors on horse chariots drove the Asian Hyksos Dynasty out of Egypt and invaded Syria. They returned to their homeland with Syrian weavers and their tapestry looms, plus methods of weaving. Almost a millennium later, the handicraft and art of weaving tapestry reached the Tarim Basin. As everything else in the course of cultural evolution, Syrian art of weaving started from humbler beginnings—the oldest fabric of woven tissue found in the city of Fayum north of Cairo dates back to about 5,000 BC.

Copper smelting was invented in the fourth millennium BC in West Asia (Flemings 2002, 107-121). Excavations made in the Euphrates-Tigris delta prove that the invention of bronze—an alloy consisting of copper and a few percent tin—dates back to the early third millennium. That technology then spread eastwards along the Silk Road—copper alloys appear in Central Asia in the late third and early second millennium BC—and still later into northern China.

The use of meteoritic iron in the eastern Mediterranean areas dates back to about 5000 BC, but the smelting of iron seems to have been invented in eastern Anatolia around the middle of the second millennium BC. Eventually, up to one percent of carbon was added to the smelted iron in order to produce steel. Steel turned into a very hard metal when it was properly heated and then rapidly cooled in water or oil. In east Africa, archaeologists have found steel dating back to 1400 BC.

Scythian nomads roamed domains reaching from the Caspian Sea to the Tian Shan ranges, skirting the northern rim of the Tarim Basin, and from the Ural to the Punjab Valley. It is assumed that these nomads imported the technology of iron smelting into China around the eighth century BC. Around the fourth century BC, ingenuous Chinese craftsmen invented blast furnaces—a quantum leap in the evolution of metallurgic technology. Bellows blew air into the bloom consisting of iron, three to four percent carbon, and a little silicon and produced temperatures of above 1,100 degrees Celsius, at which iron bloom became liquid. Liquid iron was cast into molds and, depending upon the form of the molds, all kinds of utilitarian objects were created in foundries—from cooking pots to agricultural instruments, armor, weapons, and sculptures. By reducing the carbon in a mix of wrought and cast iron bloom, Chinese metallurgists produced steel in the second century BC. After a long time lag, this new technology began to travel west along the Silk Road. Only around 1380 AD did the first blast furnaces appear in the German Rhine Valley.

Paper was invented in China. In the caves of Dunhuang, explorer Aurel Stein (Wood 2003, 107) discovered a fragment of paper that dates back to about 200 BC. This find proves that the invention of paper must have occurred earlier than eunuch Chai Lun (died 121 AD) had written in his 105 AD report to the emperor, describing the production of paper from "the bark of trees, remnants of hemp, rags of cloth and fishing nets." Paper (Thubron 2006, 26) found many practical applications, from clothes to armor, handkerchiefs, kites, belts, and money. After the battle at the Talas River in 751 AD, captured Chinese paper workers (Wood 2003, 67) brought paper production to Samarkand, and from there it spread gradually to the west and eventually to Europe.

Paper production inspired yet another process of creative morpho-evolution that began with woodblock printing around 200 AD in China. Movable type printing was invented much later, around 1040 AD, also in China. The handicraft then gradually spread west until it eventually reached Europe in the late thirteenth century AD. Around 1439, Johann Gutenberg began to develop the first printing press with movable types.

Arab chemists seem to have invented gunpowder in the seventh century AD. In the ninth century, it was also discovered—maybe influenced by Arab knowledge, maybe independently—by Chinese alchemists who were actually searching for an elixir of immortality (Flemings 2002, 107-121). As we stated in the chapter on Muslim Golden Ages, Muslims developed all kinds of weapons and explosive devices, and Mongols later further refined the techniques of explosives they used in their invasions in the west and in their attacks on the Kyushu island of Japan. In the seventeenth century, Mogul emperor Sha Jahan sold tons of saltpeter, used for the production of gunpowder, to the warring European nations involved in the highly destructive Thirty Years War.

According to Thubron (2006, 15), gunpowder pounding the ramparts of castles and fortresses to smithereens caused the end of the feudal era in Europe, an era that had begun when Charles Martell and his infantry army first encountered a Muslim cavalry at the battle of Tours in 732 AD. After that fateful victory over the Muslims, Europe began to develop not only castles and fortresses; it also produced battalions of mounted and ironclad knights. These knights were stabilized on horseback by metal stirrups invented in the fourth century AD by Chinese metallurgy. The seventeenth century, philosopher Francis Bacon (Thubron 2006, 78) maintained that three inventions have transformed his contemporary world: printing, gunpowder, and the magnetic compass—all of them invented by Chinese ingenuity.

Water clocks seem to have been invented in China and India as early as around 4,000 BC. Approximately in 800 AD, Caliph Haroun al-Rashid sent the French emperor Charlemagne a mechanical clock. By the eleventh century, Chinese craftsmen had created mechanical clocks (Flemings 2006, 107-121). In 1292, one of the first European mechanical clocks was installed in the Cathedral of Canterbury.

Often inventions took many centuries to be transmitted from China to the West. Tucker (2003, 19) reports that cross bows, porcelain and iron suspension bridges were invented in Chine thirteen centuries before they emerged in the West. It took the magnetic compass (loadstone spoon) eleven centries, paper ten centuries, gunpowder up to six centuries, wood movable type printing four centuries and metal movable type printing one century to travel from China to the West.

In the present section, we have emphasized several times that the Silk Road consisted not only of a vast, international lattice of land routes, but also of maritime routes. At the end of the section on Mongol creative morpho-evolution and destructive morpho-elimination, we have described the European naval explorers who began to discover maritime routes by the end of the fifteenth century. They did so in order to overcome the Ottoman Empire's blockade of the land-based Silk Road after the decline and fall of the various Mongol empires of China, Russia, and Central Asia. Yet European marittime explorers were by no means the first ones to launch major naval expeditions to get access to the riches of Asia. A Chinese explorer who had engineered his amazing exploits almost a century earlier than the Europeans preceded them.

Admiral Zheng He (1371-1433 AD), also known under the name Cheng Ho, was probably the most important maritime explorer of all time. Born into a Muslim family whose forefathers had moved east with the Mongols, he grew up with in the province of Yuan. His grandfather, governor of province Yuan, and his father had made the obligatory *Hadjj* to Mecca and told young Zhen He stories about their long sea voyage to the Arabian Peninsula, and about their encounter with foreign people and their customs. These tales fuelled the boy's imagination, planting the seeds for his later professional career. In 1381, when he was but ten years old, soldiers from the neighboring Ming Empire invaded his hometown, killed his family, and captured him. He was abducted to the Ming capital Nanjing and there he was castrated, a barbarian custom practiced since time immemorial in China on male prisoners to be employed at the court. His fortune changed in 1390 when he was transferred to the court of the Ming crown prince in Beijing. He soon won the favors of crown prince Zhu Di, who eventually usurped the throne in 1402 and adopted the name Emperor Yongle (1360-1424), 'Emperor of Perpetual Happiness.' The mandarins at the court were not at all pleased with their new emperor, who in 1421 transferred the Ming capital from Nanjing to Beijing. With his legitimacy questioned by the mandarins, Emperor Yongle put his trust in several eunuchs and nominated Zhang He as the first master-builder of the imperial palace.

Emperor Yongle (reigned 1402-1424) was as cruel as he was ambitious. He set himself three major goals: to increase his powerbase and gain legitimacy by making foreign rulers paying him tribute; to extend the reach and upgrade the structure of the Great Wall in order to protect the Ming Empire from northern intruders; to boost the image and significance of Chinese culture. In the pursuit of the first of these three goals, he gave Zhang He a key role and named him admiral of a yet to be built armada. Legend has it that half of China was deforested to supply the wood needed for building huge ships in the dry docks of Nanjing's Dragon Bay.

Between 1405-1433, Zheng He (Wood 2003, 130; Tucker 2003, 166f.) undertook seven naval expeditions visiting more than thirty foreign countries. His main mission was to coax foreign rulers into paying tribute to the 'Emperor of Perpetual Happiness' in order to increase her Highness' legitimacy, and to barter silk and porcelain against pepper and other precious trade goods.

On the first expedition, Admiral Zheng He commanded a flotilla of 300 ships and 28,000 crewmen, many of them troops to protect men, horses, and trade goods. His flagship is said to have been up to 130 meters long and 56 meters wide, although today's experts opt for smaller sizes. Nevertheless, Zheng He's flagship carrying 1,000 men was much larger than Christopher Columbus' flagship St. Maria almost a century later.

Exploiting the monsoon winds and sailing along the coastline of southern China, the flotilla reached Guangzhou in Southern China, a port where many Arabian Muslims lived. Here Zheng He hired Arabian navigators. Arabians were the first seafarers who had mastered sailing the open oceans between the Arabian Peninsula and southeast China. And although the Chinese invented the magnetic compass needle, it was the Arabians who had adapted it to be used for naval navigations. Already during the Song Dynasty (960-1279), Chinese traders (Tucker 2003, 229), cut off from the land routes of the Silk Road by Muslim conquests, had begun to compete with Arabian seafarers. They began to build big ships with six masts and up to forty meters long and four stories high to transport huge amounts of cargo.

With the help of the instruments and the know-how of the recruited Arab navigators, Zheng He then sailed southwest to Java, through the Malacca strait to Ceylon, eventually reaching the coast of Malabar. Here Zheng He, not only a cunning trader but also a highly skilled diplomat, was able to exchange silk, porcelain, and other Chinese trade goods against pepper, gold, pearls, and precious stones. Pepper was a rare commodity in China and in much demand as a spice and medicine. Pepper was so expensive that Chinese merchants and families used it, like silk, as a particular form of money to pay taxes and debts.

On his following expeditions, Zheng He also employed Arabian navigators and their star maps, permitting him to quit the coastline and to sail right across the Indian Ocean, a feat that drastically reduced the time needed to arrive in Aden at the southern tip of today's Yemen. Here, at the port from which trade caravans crossed the Arabian Peninsula to reach the Mediterranean shore lines, Zheng He traded for frankincense, an aromatic commodity much in demand in China. From Aden, he proceeded along the African coastline until he reached the port of Malindi in today's Kenya. This was an important place for Zheng He because Emperor Jongle had his eyes fixed on precious African gold.

After years of being at sea, in 1415 Zheng He returned home from his first mission. His ships carried envoys from more than thirty different countries ready to pay homage and offer gifts to the Chinese Emperor. The admiral's cargo contained tons of precious trade goods, plus a giraffe and some zebras for the imperial zoo in Beijing. Emperor Jongle was as impressed by that African giraffe as Emperor Charlemagne had been when he had received an Indian elephant from Haroun al-Rashid some 600 years earlier.

After seven more missions, Zheng He's fortunes changed once more. The mighty mandarins at the imperial court were irritated because the naval expeditions cost tremendous sums of money. Contemporary economist have calculated that under the rule of Emperor Jongle Ming, China paid as much as $6 billion per year for his naval adventures, a sum which threatened to ruin imperial finances.

In 1421, lightening struck the Forbidden City of Beijing, by now the new capital of the Ming Empire. Emperor Jongle and the mandarins saw this event as a bad omen; they interpreted the event as a sign from heaven indicating that the Gods had began the countdown for the stage exit of the Emperor of Perpetual Happiness and his irresponsible power games. Emperor Jongle died four years after the Heavens had signalled their ire and the impending withdrawal of the Heavenly Mandate. The mandarins decreed by law that it was now forever forbidden to build ships with more than two masts and Zheng He's mighty armada was destroyed. Once more, creative morpho-evolution had been replaced by destructive morpho-elimination. Zheng He died in 1433, finishing his stupendous professional career as lonesome a creature as he had begun it.

NOTES

1. The British exploited India for about 350 years; they ruled the subcontinent for about 200 years.

2. Lord Macaulay was a Victorian historian and colonial administrator. He was a member of the Supreme Council of India, and Secretary of War. In 1835 he wrote the statement Ashok Kurien refers to: "The languages of Western Europe civilised Russia. I cannot doubt that they will do for the Hindu what they have done for the Tartar ... We must at present do our best to form a class who may be interpreters between us and the millions whom we govern; a class of persons, Indian in blood and colour, but English in taste, in opinions, in morals, and in intellect."

3. Caliph = supreme spiritual leader of Islam

4. Turkic people share a common (Turkic) language, but they belong to quite different ethnic groups. They are a Eurasian people whose original domains reached from the Caspian Sea to northeastern Siberia. Later they also moved west into Anatolia.

5. In 1250, Mamluks also established a sultanate in Egypt; it lasted until 1811 when Muhammad Ali Pasha, a military leader of the Ottomans, had the Mamluk leaders killed in the 'massacre of the Cairo citadel'.

6. Italian: *omertà* = code of silence respected by members of the Sicilian mafia.

7. The next invader reducing Baghdad to a heap of rubble was to be a fumbling and stumbling American president giving order to his troops to invade the city in the early twenty-first century, presumably to capture Al-Qaeda terrorists who had masterminded—on September 11, 2001— the destruction of the twin towers in Manhattan. In one of the many subsequent versions of his motives, he pretended to have ordered the invasion "to find weapons of mass destruction" aimed at the "free world."

8. *Mughal* = Persian word for Mongol

9. Marco Polo's sojourn (Rossabi 1988, 147) at Khubilai Khan's court has raised some questions. He never mentions the Great Wall, yet if he was in northern China he must have seen it. In his autobiography *Il Milione*, he reports that he was present at the siege of Hsiang-yang, yet this battle occurred two years before he arrived in China. He claims to have been governor of Yang-chou for three years, but Chinese sources don't mention him at all. He claims to have been in Khotan (Wood 2003, 151) yet doesn't mention that it was a center for jade and silk—he mentions only wheat, flax, hemp, and wine. In a Genoese prison cell, Marco Polo and Rustichello of Pisa are supposed to have produced a report—*Divisament du Monde*—about Polo's adventures, yet the first manuscripts handed down were written in medieval French provençal language (Wood 2003, 121ff.).

10. *Koumiss* = fermented mare's milk, a traditional Mongol drink.

11. The Ming Dynasty (Thubbron 2006, 280) would eventually unrig its entire merchant fleet of 3,500 ships, forgo all international trade by land and sea, and thus isolate itself from the outside world. The fact that Timur-i-leng prepared a campaign in 1404 to conquer the Ming and to forcibly convert the Chinese to Muslim faith further convinced the Ming to lock their doors to the Silk Road—although Timur-i-leng died in that endeavor at Otrar, north of Tashkent.

12. Originally, ancient maritime routes skirted the coastlines, for instance of India, Persia, and the Arabian Peninsula. By first century AD, seafarers discovered (Tucker 2003, 329) that the monsoon winds blow southwest across the Indian Ocean from March to September, and northeast from November to January. Sailing across the Indian Ocean drastically shortened the duration of naval trips.

13. That rebellion was caused by general An Lushan of Turkic descent. Supported by the imperial concubine Yang Guifei, his scheming paramour, An Lushan was installed as commander of three northern garrisons. Lusting for the imperial laurel, he instigated a coup d'état against Tang Emperor Xuanzong (reigned 712-756). Wars and famine produced by that rebellion—lasting from 755-763—cost the lives of 36 million people. Eventually, An Lushan was killed by his own son and Yang Guifei was strangled with a silk cord.

14. The Eurasian lattice of the Silk Road was of such complexity that it is difficult to describe it in a satisfying manner. Readers who are not particularly interested in the extent of that spatial network are advised to skip the sections describing it in some detail.

15. διάδοχοι = Greek term for successors

Chapter Three

Strange Loops

Reaching a destination is but the beginning of a new journey.
Gottlieb Guntern

Threads woven on the enchanted loom of human creativity run along many different trails while creating patterns of breathtaking beauty and power of expression.

Some of these trails form strange loops: specific threads return, along visible or invisible pathways, to their original point of departure. When they reach that destination, the point of origin looks quite different from what it had been at the time they left it to venture into unknown territories.

In other words, the results of creative morpho-evolution and destructive morpho-elimination feed back into the twin pools of chaos and order, the primordial womb where every single creative process begins. To put it simply: the creative process of human beings—individuals, teams, ethnicities, nations, cultures, and whole civilizations—is one gigantic strange loop. In the pages of the present book, we have delved into the various aspects of that loop's structures and functions. Like the traders on the ancient Silk Road, we have crossed deserts of dynamic complexity in order to find temporary comfort in oases of justified simplicity.

Now we have reached the end of our journey. The mystery of the creative process has divulged some of its secrets while holding back others. I sincerely hope that readers will be inspired by the present book to begin or intensify their own search into the magic orb of the enchanted loom.

As stated before, human creativity is one of the most precious natural resources on our planet. Unlike other natural resources, it does not diminish with mining. It propagates, nurtured by its own vitality. It is a virtually inex-

haustible resource because the results of specific creative achievements always inspire and motivate new creative processes, producing yet another set
of creative accomplishments. As long as human beings exist on our planet, the
enchanted loom will not grind to a halt. As long as mankind strides this planet
of ours, the whirr of the enchanted loom will never fall into silence. It will
continue to weave sheer magic, bringing the seven colors of the rainbow in
every weft and warp of man's dreams and aspirations. It will continue to give
birth to new fabrics whose sophistication will fill the hearts of human beings
with gratitude, awe, and the sensation of joyful puzzlement.

Excerpts from an interview with Ashok Kurien (17)

Our interview ends with a contemplation of hybris, the trap of the grandiose
self that creative individuals have to avoid in order not to paralyse their creativity. Ashok Kurien, a wise man by now, talks about the illusion of total
control over objects, events, other people, and ourselves.

GG: Ashok, you have achieved so much in life. How do you avoid the pitfall of
complacency?

AK: It's so important to remind myself what I am and who I am. I have a couple
of tricks to do that. I used to put a black spot on my right hand with a felt pen
every morning. The black spot would tell me, "Stay humble, stay humble, stay
humble!" Every night when I go to sleep I am so grateful that I have such a
wonderful soft bed and wonderful soft pillows. I sleep in this luxurious comfort
and I say, "My God look at people around the world...I am so blessed that I can
come home and lie down in this bed." Every once in a while it's good to sleep
in a bed that isn't so great, because it reminds you of certain realities.

GG: It reminds you of the difference between your past and your present.

AK: I see the difference, and when I wake up, the firSt thing I do is I take one
breath to remind myself of what I am worth. One breath is all I am worth. If I
didn't have the next breath, I would be worth zero. So I'll never mix up money
with my value, with what I'm really worth. Because what are we worth? You are
worth your next breath, that's all you are worth. You are worth what you leave
behind for other people. I hope one day I will figure out how to write a book that
will inspire other people to do something similar to what I did. But if I can't
inspire other people with my book, then it will be of no worth whatsoever. We
must inspire and encourage other people. This is what I try to do and what I
teach my children. We have no control over the moment we enter this world. We
have no control over the moment we exit this world. So how can we control
anything in between our entrance and our exit? Yet we have this illusion of being
in charge, of being in control of events, people and things. Yet most of the time,
we can't even control ourselves!

GG: This is the general delusion of all the power gamblers; they always fancy themselves to be in total control. For twenty years I was very much involved in couple therapy and family therapy. I met parents obsessed with the idea of having total control over their children. I met adolescents who wanted to subdue their parents. I encountered husbands and wives who wanted to have total control over their partner. And all of these control freaks failed in their pathetic endeavour. I used to tell them a little story to make them aware of their illusion. It went like this: "Imagine it is a very hot day in August. You are walking a trail leading up a steep mountain. You are very thirsty and eventually you come across a spring with ice-cold water gushing out. You cup your hands and scoop some water. As you lift your hands to your lips, you see that water drips from them down to the ground. Your immediate impulse is to control that loss of precious water, so you roll your hands into fists. And what happens? You squeeze all of the water out of your hands. Unless you learn your lesson, you will never be able to satisfy your thirst." In other words, individuals who want to control everything ultimately control nothing at all. It is they who are totally controlled by their obsession to control everything. It's a paradox, but that's the way it is.

AK: That's the way it is. That's part of the human condition.

GG: Thank you, Ashok, very much for this interview. It was a great experience; I loved every minute of it.

Bibliography

Ackermann, D. "O Muse! You Do Make Things Difficult!" In *The New York Times Book Review*. November 12, 1989.

A&E Home Video. *America's Castles: The Homes of Frank Lloyd Wright*. A&E Home Video, 1996.

Armbruster, Bonnie B. "Metacognition in Creativity." In *Handbook of Creativity (Perspectives on Individual Differences)*, edited by John A Glover et al. New York: Plenum Press, 1989.

Ash, Timothy Garton. "Prague: Intellectuals & Politicians." In *The New York Times Book Review*. June 1, 1986: 34-41.

Astre, Georges-Albert. *Ernest Hemingway in Selbstzeugnissen und Bilddokumenten*. Reinbek bei Hamburg: Rowohlt Taschenbuch Verlag, 1961.

Baines, Jocelyn. *Joseph Conrad: A Critical Biography*. Harmondsworth, UK: Penguin Books, 1986.

Baker, Carlos, ed. *Ernest Hemingway: A Life Story*. New York: Avon Books, 1980.

Barber, Elizabeth. "Fashioned from Fiber." In *Along the Silk Road: Asian Art and Culture*, edited by Elizabeth ten Grotenhuis, 57-73. Seattle: University of Washington Press, 2002.

Bateson, Gregory. *Steps to an Ecology of Mind*. New York: Ballantine Books, 1976.

Bayley, John. "The Complete Poems of Anna Akhmatova." In *The New York Times Book Review*. May 13, 1990.

Benson, Jackson J. *The True Adventures of John Steinbeck, Writer: A Biography*. New York: The Viking Press, 1984.

Bentley, Toni. "The Master." *The New York Review of Books* 52, no. 4, March 10, 2005.

Berger, John. *Art and Revolution: Ernst Neizvestny and the Role of the Artist in the U.S.S.R.* New York: Pantheon Books/Random House, 1969.

Bernard, André. *Rotten Rejections: The Letters That Publishers Wish They'd Never Sent*. London: Robson Books, Ltd., 1992.

Bernstein, Jeremy. *Einstein*. New York: The Viking Press, 1974.

Bernstein, Peter L. *Against the Gods. The Remarkable Story of Risk.* New York: John Wiley & Sons, Inc., 1996.

Berry, Chuck. *Chuck Berry: The Autobiography.* New York: Harmony Books, 1987.

Binnig, Gerd. *Aus dem Nichts: Über die Kreativität von Natur und Mensch.* München, Zürich: Piper, 1989.

————. "Kreativität – die Fähigkeit zur Evolution." In *Chaos und Kreativität. Rigorous Chaos* edited by Gottlieb Guntern, 303-338. Zürich: Scalo Verlag AG, 1995a.

Boccione, Umberto: "Futurist Sculpture." In *Modern Artists On Art: Ten Unabridged Essays,* edited by Robert L Herbert. Englewood Cliffs, NJ: Prentice-Hall, Inc., 1964.

Boden, Margaret A. *The Creative Mind: Myths & Mechanisms.* London: Weidenfeld and Nicolson, 1990.

Boorstin, Daniel J. *The Creators: A History of Heros and the Imagination.* New York: Random House, 1992.

Born, Max. *The Restless Universe.* New York: Dover Publications, Inc., 1951.

Bornstein, Eli. *"On the Artist." The Structurist.* no. 25/26, Saskatoon: University of Saskatchewan, 1985/86.

Boswell, James and Chapman, R. W. eds. *Life of Johnson.* Oxford: Oxford University Press, 1989.

Briggs, A. D. P. *Alexander Pushkin: A Critical Study.* Totowa, NJ: Barnes & Noble Books, 1983.

Briggs, John and F. David Peat. *Die Entdeckung des Chaos: Eine Reise durch die Chaos-Theorie.* Wien: Carl Hanser Verlag, 1990.

Brodsky, Joseph. *Watermark.* London: Hamish Hamilton, 1992.

————. "Aesthetik – die Mutter der Ethik." In *Intuition und Kreativität,* edited by Gottlieb Guntern, 71-130. Zürich: Scalo Verlag, 1996.

————. In *The Challenge of Creative Leadership,* edited by Gottlieb Guntern, 65-105. London: Shepheard-Walwyn Publishers Ltd., 1997.

Bronowski, Jacob. *The Ascent of Man.* Boston: Little, Brown and Company, 1973.

Brooks Pfeiffer, Bruce. *Frank Lloyd Wright.* Köln: TASCHEN GmbH, 2007.

Brown, Robert T. "Creativity: What Are We Able to Measure?" In *Handbook of Creativity (Perspectives on Individual Differences),* edited by John A. Glover et al., 3-32. New York: Plenum Press, 1989.

Burgess, Anthony. *Little Wilson and Big God: Being the First Part of the Confessions.* London: Heinemann, 1987.

Burns, James MacGregor. *Leadership.* New York: Harper & Row Publishers, 1979.

Burns, Ken and Novick Lynn. *Frank Lloyd Wright.* PBS Home Video, 1998.

Burns, Ken. *Jazz.* Box Set of 10 DVDs. Florentine Films, PBS Home Video, 2000a.

Burns, Ken. "Episode 5 (Swing, Pure Pleasure)." *Jazz.* Florentine Films, PBS Home Video, 2000b

Burnshaw, Stanley. *The Seamless Web: Language-Thinking; Creature-Knowledge; Art-Experience.* New York: George Braziller, 1970.

Burton, Humphrey. *Leonard Bernstein.* New York: Bantam Doubleday Dell Publishing Group, Inc., 1994.

Butterfield, Andrew. *The Homer of Painting: The New York Review of Books.* April 7, 2005: 14-18.

Cannon, Walter Bradford. "The Role of Hunches in Scientific Thought." In *The Creativity Question*, edited by A. Rothenberg and C. R. Hausman, 63-69. Durham, NC: Duke University Press Inc., 1988

Capra, Fritjof. *The Tao of Physics: An Exploration of the Parallels Between Modern Physics and Eastern Mysticism.* Berkeley: Shambhala Publications, Inc., 1975.

Carr, Ian. *Miles Davis: The Definitive Biography.* New York: Thunder's Mouth Press, 1999.

Cezanne, Paul. "Lettres à Emile Bernard." In *Conversation avec Cézanne*, edited by Michael Doran.Collection Macula, 1978.

Chatwin, Bruce. *The Songlines.* London: Pan Books, 1988.

Chekov, Anton. *The Steppe and Other Stories.* Oxford: Oxford University Press, 1991.

Cheney, Margaret. *Tesla: Man Out of Time.* New York: Barnes & Noble, 1993.

Clark, Ronald William. *Einstein. The Life and Times.* New York: Avon Books, 1972.

Commerford Martin, Thomas. *The Inventions, Researches and Writings of Nikola Tesla.* New York: Barnes & Noble Books, 1992.

Cooper, Arthur: *Li Po and Tu Fu: Poems.* London: Penguin Books, 1973.

Cramer, Friedrich. *Chaos und Ordnung: Die komplexe Struktur des Lebendigen.* Stuttgart: Verlas-Anstalt, 1988.

Darwin, Charles. *The Origin of Species by Means of Natural Selection or The Preservation of Favoured Races in the Struggle for Life*, edited by J. W. Burrow. Harmondsworth, UK: Penguin Books, 1976.

De Broglie, Louis-Victor. "The Wave Nature of the Electron." In *Physical Thought from the Presocratics to the Quantum Physicists: An Anthology*, edited by Shmuel Sambursky. New York: Pica Press, 1975.

Der Spiegel. "Der Philosoph, Walter Benjamin." nr. 7, 43. Jahrgang, 13.2.1989: 200.

———. "Du sollst Dich Nicht Langweilen – Billy Wilder Zitate aus drei Spiegel Jahrzehnten." 8.4.2002: 15/196-197.

———. "Der okkulte König." 50/2007: 148-150.

Dias De Sousa Ribeiro, Agostino and Anna Bonboir. "A la recherche des moyens de stimuler la créativité." In *Bulletin de Psychologie*. Tome XXXVIII, no. 18, 1985.

Dick, Teresi. "The Lone Ranger of Quantum Mechanics." In *The New York Times Book Review.* January 7, 1990: 14-15.

Donald, David Herbert. *Look Homeward: A Life of Thomas Wolfe.* New York: Fawcett Columbine, 1988.

Doran, Michael. *Conversations avec Cézanne.* Collection Macula, 1978.

Edwards, Mark R. and J. Routh Sproull. "Creativity: Productivity Gold Mine?" In *Journal of Creative Behaviour* 18, no. 3, 1984.

Einstein, Albert. "On the Electrodynamics of Moving Bodies." In *Physical Thought from the Presocratics to the Quantum Physicists: An Anthology*, edited by Shmuel Sambursky. New York: Pica Press, 1975.

———. *Ideas and Opinions.* New York: Dell Publishing Co., Inc., 1976.

Einstein, Alfred. *Mozart: Sein Charakter - Sein Werk.* Frankfurt: Fischer Taschenbuch Verlag, 1983.

Eliot, T.S.: „Little Gidding", The Four Quartets. In *Selected Poems.* London: Faber and Faber, 1962.

Elliot, Jeffrey. *Conversations with Maya Angelou.* Jackson: University Press of Mississippi, 1989.

Ellmann, Richard. *James Joyce: New and Revised Edition.* Oxford: Oxford University Press, 1983.

Eyman, Scott. *Ernst Lubitsch: Laughter in Paradise, A Biography.* New York: Simon & Schuster, 1993.

Faraday, Michael. "On the Physical Lines of Moving Bodies." In *Physical Thought from the Presocratics to the Quantum Physicists: An Anthology,* edited by Shmuel Sambursky. New York: Pica Press, 1975.

Feigenbaum, Mitchell. "Die Feigenbaumroute ins Chaos." In *Chaos und Kreativität: Rigorous Chaos,* edited by Gottlieb Guntern, 111-164. Zürich: Scalo Verlag AG, 1995.

Field, Andrew. *The Life and Art of Vladimir Nabokov.* New York: Crown Publishers, Inc., 1986.

Fitterling, Thomas. *Thelonious Monk: His Life and Music.* Berkeley, CA: Berkeley Hills Books, 1997.

Flemings, Merton C. "Travelling Technologies." In *Along the Silk Road: Asian Art and Culture,* edited by Elizabeth ten Grotenhuis, 107-121. Seattle: University of Washington Press, 2002.

Frampton, Kenneth. *Modern Architecture: A Critical History.* London: Thames and Hudson, 1987.

Friedman, Myra. *Buried Alive: The Biography of Janis Joplin.* New York: Bantam Books, 1974.

Fuentes, Carlos. *Myself with Others: Selected Essays.* New York: Farrar, Straus, and Giroux, 1990.

Furneaux Jordan, Robert. *Western Architecture: A Concise History.* London: Thames and Hudson, 1985.

Galluzzi, Paolo. *Leonardo da Vinci: Engineer and Architect* . The Montreal Museum of Fine Arts Catalog: May 22 to November 8, 1987.

Gamow, George. *Thirty Years That Shook Physics: The Story of Quantum Theory.* Garden City, NY: Anchor Books/Doubleday & Company, 1966.

García Márquez, Gabriel. *Chronicle of a Death Foretold.* London: Pan Books/Picador, 1983.

———. *Love in the Time of Cholera.* London: Penguin Books, 1989.

———. In *Irritation und Kreativität,* edited by Gottlieb Guntern. Martigny und Zürich: Creando Stiftung und Scalo Verlag, 1993.

Gelb, Arthur and Barbara: *O'Neill.* New York: Harper & Row, Publishers Perennial Library, 1987.

Gell-Mann, Murray. *The Quark and the Jaguar: Adventures in the Simple and the Complex.* London: Abacus, 1994.

Gerard, R. W. "The Biological Basis of Imagination." In *The Creative Process: A Symposium,* edited by Brewster Ghiselin, 236-259. Berkely: University of California Press, 1985.

Ghiselin, Brewster, ed. *The Creative Process: A Symposium.* Berkeley: University of California Press, 1985a.

————. "Introduction." In *The Creative Process: A Symposium,* edited by Brewster Ghiselin, 1-21. Berkeley: University of California Press, 1985b.

Gibson, Ian. *Federico García Lorca: A Life.* New York: Pantheon Books, 1989.

Giedion-Welcker, Carola. *Paul Klee: mit Selbstzeugnissen und Bilddokumenten.* Hamburg: Rowohlt Taschenbuch Verlag GmbH, 1985.

Gill, Brendan. *Many Masks: A Life of Frank Lloyd Wright.* New York: G. P. Putnam's Sons, 1987.

Gilot, Françoise and Carlton Lake. *Vivre avec Picasso.* Paris: Calmann-Lévy, 1991.

Gioia, Ted. *The History of Jazz.* New York: Oxford University Press, 1998.

Gleason, Ralph J. *Celebrating the Duke, and Louis, Bessie, Billie, Bird, Carmen, Miles, Dizzy, and Other Heroes.* New York: Da Capo Press, 1995.

Gleick, James. *Chaos: Making a New Science.* New York: Viking Penguin Inc., 1988.

————. *Genius: Richard Feynman and Modern Physics.* London: Abacus, 1993.

Gleizes and Metzinger. "Cubism." In *Modern Artists On Art: Ten Unabridged Essays,* edited by Robert L. Herbert. Englewood Cliffs, NJ: Prentice Hall, Inc., 1964.

Godwin, Malcolm. *Who Are You? 101 Ways of Seeing Yourself.* New York: Penguin Books, 2000.

Goertzel, Victor and Mildred George Goertzel. *Cradles of Eminence.* Boston: Little, Brown and Company, 1962.

Goldberg, Philip. *The Intuitive Edge. Understanding Intuition and Applying it in Everyday Life.* Los Angeles: Jeremy P. Tarcher, Inc., 1983.

Gordon, Robert and Andrew Forge. *Monet.* New York: Harry N. Abrams, 1983.

Gower, Timothy. "Do Great Minds Think Alike?" In *The Boston Phoenix,* section 2, May 15, 1992: 4-6.

Green, Peter. *Alexander of Macedon, 356-323 B.C.* Berkeley: University of California Press, 1992.

Greenfield, Susan A. *The Human Mind Explained.* New York: Henry Holt and Company, Inc., 1996.

Grohmann, Will. *Der Maler Paul Klee.* Köln: DuMont Buchverlag, 1977.

Gross, John. "Something Marvelous to Tell." *The New York Book Review.* May 15, 2008: 21-22.

Guilford, J. P. "Factor Analysis, Intellect and Creativity." In *The Creativity Question,* edited by A. Rohtenberg and C. R. Hausman, 200-208. Durham, NC: Duke University Press, 1988.

Guntern, Gottlieb. *Social Change, Stress and Mental Health in the Pearl of the Alps.* Berlin: Springer-Verlag, 1979.

————. "Die Auto-Organisation in Humansystemen, 157ff. " In *Der blinde Tanz zur lautlosen Musik,* edited by Gottlieb Guntern. Brig: ISO-Stiftung, 1987.

————. *Therápodos – La via del terapeuta. Lineamenti di eccoantropologia e di terapia sistemica.* Milano: Hoepli, 1989.

————, hrsg. *Der Gesang des Schamanen.* Martigny: ISO-Stiftung, 1990.

————, hrsg. *Der kreative Weg.* Zürich: Verlag Moderne Industrie AG & Co., 1991a.

————. "Kreativität und Kreativitätsforschung." In *Der kreative Weg,* edited by G. Guntern. Zürich: Verlag Moderne Industrie, 1991b.

————. *Im Zeichen des Schmetterlings: Vom Powerplay zum sanften Spiel der Kräfte: Leadership in der Metamorphose.* Bern: Scherz Verlag, 1992.

————, hrsg. *Irritation und Kreativität.* Zürich: Scalo Verlag AG, 1993.

————. *Sieben goldene Regeln der Kreativitätsförderung.* Zürich: Scalo Verlag AG, 1994.

————. hrsg. *Chaos und Kreativität. Rigorous Chaos.* Zürich: Scalo Verlag AG, 1995a.

————. hrsg. *Imagination und Kreativität.* Zürich: Scalo Verlag, 1995b.

————. hrsg. *Intuition und Kreativität.* Zürich: Scalo Verlag, 1996.

————. ed. *The Challenge of Creative Leadership.* London: Shepheard-Walwyn Publishers Ltd., 1997.

————. ed. *Risk-Taking & Creative Leadership.* London: Shepheard-Walwyn Publishers Ltd., 1998.

————. *Maskentanz der Mediokratie. Kreative Leadership versus Mittelmass.* Zürich: Orell Füssli Verlag AG, 2000.

————. *Götter, Helden und Schamanen. Archetypen der kreativen Eliten.* Zürich: Orell Füssli Verlag AG, 2001.

————. *Mit den Schwingen des Adlers. Wege zur kreativen Leadership.* Zürich: Orell Füssli Verlag AG, 2003.

Gurko, Leo. *Ernest Hemingway and the Pursuit of Heroism.* New York: Thomas Y. Crowell Company/Apollo Editions, 1969.

Hadamard, Jacques. *The Psychology of Invention in the Mathematical Field.* New York: Dover Publications Inc., 1945.

Hayes, J. R. "Cognitive Processes in Creativity." In *Handbook of Creativity: Perspectives on Individual Differences,* edited by John A. Glover et al., 135-145. New York: Plenum Press, 1989.

Hemingway, Ernest. *Death in the Afternoon.* Harmondsworth, UK: Penguin Books, 1974.

————. *A Farewell to Arms.* London: Granada Publishing, 1984.

Hemingway, Ernest. *Selected Letters 1917-1961.* Edited by Carlos Baker. London: Granada Publishing, 1981.

Hemingway, Gregory H. *Papa: A Personal Memoir.* Boston: Houghton Mifflin Company, 1976.

Herbert, Robert L. *Modern Artists on Art: Ten Unabridged Essays.* Englewood Cliffs, NJ: Prentice Hall, Inc., 1964.

Heylin, Clinton. *Bob Dylan: Behind the Shades.* London: Penguin Books, 1991.

Hitt, William D. *Thoughts on Leadership. A Treasury of Quotations.* Columbus: Battelle Press, 1992.

Hoffmann, Banesh in collaboration with Helen Duka. *Albert Einstein: Creator and Rebel.* New York: New American Library, 1973.

Hofstadter, Douglas R. *Gödel, Escher, Bach: An Eternal Golden Braid.* London: Basic Books Inc., 1979.

Holmes, Richard. "The Romantic Cycle." *The New York Review,* April 10, 1997.

Holroyd, Michael. *Bernard Shaw: Volume I: 1856-1898, The Search for Love.* New York: Random House, 1988

Hotchner, A. E. *Papa Hemingway: A Personal Memoir.* New York: Bantam Books, 1967.

———. *Choice People: The Greats, Near-Greats and Ingrates I Have Known.* New York: William Morrow and Company, Inc., 1984.

Housman, Edward. "The Name and Nature of Poetry." In *The Creative Process: A Symposium,* edited by Brewster Ghiselin. Berkely: University of California Press, 1985.

Huddle, David. "Let's Say You Wrote Badly This Morning." In *The New York Review of Books,* January 31, 1988: 37-38.

Hunke, Sigrid. *Allahs Sonne über dem Abendland, Unser arabisches Erbe.* Stuttgart: Deutsche Verlags-Anstalt GmbH, 1960.

Isaksen, Scott G. *Frontiers of Creativity Research: Beyond the Basics.* Buffalo, NY: Bearly Limited, 1987.

Josephson, Matthew. *Edison: A Biography.* New York: John Wiley & Sons, 1992.

Joyce, James. *Ulysses.* New York: Vintage Books/Random House, 1961.

Kadanoff, Leo P. "Tanz mit dem Computer." In *Intuition und Kreativität,* edited by Gottlieb Guntern, 169-215. Zürich: Scalo Verlag, 1996.

Kafka, Franz: *Metamorphosis.*Vanguard Press, 1946.

Kandinsky, Wassily. "Reminiscences." In *Modern Artists on Art: Ten Unabridged Essays,* edited by Robert. L. Herbert, 19-44. Englewood Cliffs, NJ: Prentice Hall, Inc., 1964.

———. *Concerning the Spiritual in Art.* New York: Dover Publications, Inc., 1977.

Kandinsky, Wassily and Franz Marc, eds. *The Blaue Reiter Almanac.* New York: The Viking Press, 1974.

Kaplan, Justin. *Walt Whitman: A Life.* New York: Simon & Schuster, 1980.

Karasek, Hellmuth. *Billy Wilder: Eine Nahaufnahme.* Hamburg: Hoffmann und Campe, 1992a.

———. "Salto mortale vom sechsten Stock". In *Der Spiegel,* 31/1992, 27.07.1992b, 160-167.

Kässens, Wend and Jörg W. Gronius. *Theatermacher: Gespräche mit Luc Bondy, Jürgen Flimm, Hansgünther Heyne, Hans Neuenfels, Peter Palitzsch, Claus Peymann, Frank-Patrick Steckel, George Tabori, Peter Zadek.* Frankfurt: Athenäum Verlag, 1987.

Keats, John. *You Might as Well Live: The Life and Times of Dorothy Parker.* London: Penguin Books, 1988.

Kedrow, B. M. "Zur Frage der Psychologie der wissenschaftlichen schöpferischen Arbeit (anlässlich der Entdeckung des periodischen Systems der Elemente durch Medelejew)." In *Kreativitätsforschung,* edited by Gisela Ulmann, 249-278. Köln: Kiepenheuer & Witsch, 1973.

Kemp, Martin. *Leonardo.* Oxford: Oxford University Press, 2004.

Kert, Bernice. *The Hemingway Women.* New York: W. W. Norton & Company, 1983.

Kjetsaa, Geir. *Fyodor Dostoyevsky: A Writer's Life.* New York: Fawcett Columbine, 1987.

Koch, Heinrich. *Michelangelo: Mit Selbstzeugnissen und Bilddokumenten.* Reinbek bei Hamburg: Rowohlt Taschenbuch Verlag GmbH, 1991.

Koestler, Arthur. *The Sleepwalkers: A History of Man's Changing Vision of the Universe.* New York: The Universal Library/Grosset & Dunlap, 1977.

————. *The Act of Creation.* London: Arkana/Penguin Group, 1989

Kotter, John P. *Matsushita Leadership: Lessons from 20ᵗʰ Century's Most Remarkable Entrepreneur.* New York: The Free Press, 1997: 302.

Kronsbein, Joachim. "Club der malenden Mönche". In *Der Spiegel,* 15/2005, 11.04.2005: 162-164.

Krupp, Alfred. "Ein paar Knochen, der Rest ist Gas". In *Der Spiegel,* nr. 21, 43 Jg., 22.05.1989.

Kurosawa, Akira. *Akira Kurosawa: Something Like an Autobiography.* Translated by Audie E. Bock. New York: Vintage Books/Random House, 1983.

Kuspit, D. "Artist and Critic: Never the Twain Shall Meet." In *The Structurist,* no. 25/26 (1986/86): 30-36.

Lanker, Brian. "I Dream the World." *National Geographic* 176, no. 2 (August 1989): 209-225, 223.

Lankheit, Klaus. In *The Blaue Reiter Almanac,* edited by Wassily Kandinsky and Franz Marc, 38. New York: The Viking Press, 1974.

Lederman, Leon and Teresi Dick. *The God Particle: If the Universe is the Answer, What is the Question?* New York: Bantam Doubleday Dell Publishing Group, Inc., 1993.

LeDoux, Joseph. *The Emotional Brain: The Mysterious Underpinnings of Emotional Life.* New York: Simon & Schuster, 1996.

Leibniz, Gottfried Wilhelm. "Relative Space and Relative Time." In *Physical Thought from the Presocratics to the Quantum Physicists: An Anthology,* edited by Shmuel Sambursky. New York: Pica Press, 1975.

Leonard, John. "Don Quixote at Eighty." *The New York Review of Books* 50, no. 4, (March 13, 2003): 10-12.

Lewis, Robert. *Slings and Arrows: Theater in My Life.* New York: Stein and Day, 1984.

Lombroso, Cesare. "Genius and Insanity." In *The Creativity Question,* edited by A. Rothenberg and Carl R. Hausman. Durham, NC: Duke University Press, 1988.

Lord, James. *Giacometti: A Biography.* New York: Farrar Straus Giroux, 1985.

————. *Un Portrait par Giacometti, Suivi de Où étaient les Tableaux: Mémoire sur Gertrude Stein et Alice Toklas.* Paris: Gallimard, 1991.

Lynn, Kenneth S. *Hemingway.* New York: Simon & Schuster, 1987.

Ma, Yo-Yo and Theodore Levin. "A conversation with Yo-Yo Ma." In *Along the Silk Road: Asian Art and Culture,* edited by Elizabeth ten Grotenhuis, 25-39. Seattle: University of Washington Press, 2002.

Mac Liammóir, Micheál and Eavan Boland. *W.B. Yeats.* London: Thames and Hudson, 1986.

Mansfield, Richard S. and Thomas V. Busse. *The Psychology of Creativity and Discovery. Scientists and Their Work.* Chicago: Nelson-Hall, 1981.

Martindale, Colin. "Personality, Situation, and Creativity." In *Handbook of Creativity (Perspectives on Individual Differences),* edited by John A. Glover et al., 211-232. New York: Plenum Press, 1989.

Maxwell, James Clerk. "A Dynamical Theory of the Electromagnetic Field." In *Physical Thought from the Presocratics to the Quantum Physicists: An Anthology*, edited by Shmuel Sambursky. New York: Pica Press, 1975.

Mee, Charles. *Rembrandt's Portrait: A Biography*. New York: Simon & Schuster, 1988

Meyer, Michael. *Ibsen: A Biography*. Harmondsworth, UK: Penguin Books, 1985 (reprint).

————. *Strindberg: A Biography*. Oxford: Oxford University Press, 1988.

Miller, Arthur. *Timebends: A Life*. New York: Grove Press, 1987.

Mondrian, Piet. "Plastic Art & Pure Plastic Art." In *Modern Artists on Art: Ten Unabridged Essays*, edited by Robert L. Herbert. Englewood Cliffs, NJ: Prentice Hall, Inc., 1964.

Moore, Henry: "On Sculpture & Primitive Art." In *Modern Artists on Art: Ten Unabridged Essays,* edited by Robert L. Herbert. Englewood Cliffs, NJ: Prentice Hall, Inc., 1964.

Moore, Walter. *Schrödinger: Life and Thought*. Cambridge: Cambridge University Press, 1989.

Morgan, Michael Hamilton. *Lost History: The Enduring Legacy of Muslim Scientists, Thinkers, and Artists*. Washington, DC: National Geographic Society, 2007.

Morgan, Ted. *Maugham: A Biography*. New York: Simon & Schuster, 1980.

Mueller, André. "Dichter müssen dumm sein": "Ein Gespräch mit Heiner Müller." In *Die Zeit*, nr. 34, August 14, 1987: 29-30.

Murray, Linda. *Michelangelo: Sein Leben - sein Werk - seine Zeit*. Stuttgart: Klett-Cotta, 1985.

Musashi, Miyamoto: *A Book of Five Rings: The Classic Guide to Strategy*. Woodstock, NY: The Overlook Press, 1974.

New York Times Magazine. "Nabokov's Letters: 'Let me explain a few things.'" Sept. 17, 1989, New York edition.

Newman, Cathy. *The Wonderland of Lewis Carroll*. National Geographic, 179. no. 6, June, 1991.

O'Neill, Eugene. *Eines langen Tages Reise in die Nacht*. Schauspiel in vier Akten. Basel: Grosse Bühne, Theater, 1989.

Oates, Stephen B. *William Faulkner: The Man and the Artist. A Biography*. New York: Perennial Library/Harper & Row, 1988.

Pais, Abraham. *Subtle is the Lord....:The Science and the Life of Albert Einstein*. Oxford: Clarendon Press/Oxford University Press, 1982.

Parini, Jay. "The More They Write, the More They Write." *The New York Times Book Review*, July, 1989.

Parrinder, Patrick. *James Joyce*. Cambridge: Cambridge University Press, 1984.

Payne, Robert. *Leonardo*. Garden City, NY: Doubleday & Company, 1978.

Pedretti, Carlo. "Introduction." In *Leonardo da Vinci: Engineer and Architect,* edited by Paolo Galluzzi, 1-21. Montreal: The Montreal Museum of Fine Arts, 1987.

Perkins, David N. *The Mind's Best Work*. Cambridge, MA: Harvard University Press, 1981.

Piweck, Kristina. "Zeichnen bis zur Raserei". In *Handelszeitung* nr. 32, 8.8.1991, 33.

Po, Li and Tu Fu. *Li Po and Tu Fu: Poems*. Translated and edited by Arthur Cooper. London: Penguin Classics, 1973.

Pochat, Götz. *Geschichte der Ästhetik und Kunsttheorie: Von der Antike bis zum 19. Jahrhundert*. Köln: DuMont Buchverlag, 1986.

Poincare, Henri. "Mathematical Creation." In *The Creative Process: A Symposium*, edited by Brewster Ghiselin, 22-31. Berkely: University of California Press, 1985.

Porter, Lewis. *John Coltrane: His Life and Music*. Ann Arbor: The University of Michigan Press, 1999.

Preiser, Siegfried. *Kreativitätsforschung*. Darmstadt: Wissenschaftliche Buchgesellschaft, 1976.

Regis, Ed. *Who Got Einstein's Office? Eccentricity and Genius at the Institute for Advanced Study*. Reading, MA: Addision-Wesley Publishing Company, Inc., 1987.

Reid, Robert. *Marie Curie: derrière la Légende*. Paris: Editions du Seuil, 1974.

Richards, J. M. *An Introduction to Modern Architecture*. Baltimore: Penguin Books, 1960.

Richter, Hans. *Dada. Art and Anti-Art*. New York and Toronto: Oxford University Press, 1965.

Ridler, Vivian: *The Holy Bible, Containing the Old and New Testaments and the Books Called Apocrypha*. Oxford: Oxford University Press, 1960.

Rossabi, Morris. *Khubilai Khan: His Life and Times*. Berkeley: University of California Press, 1988.

Rothbart, H. A. *Cybernetic Creativity*. New York: Robert Speller & Sons, Publishers, Inc., 1972.

Rothenberg, Albert and Carl R. Hausman, eds. *The Creativity Question*. Durham, NC: Duke University Press, 1988.

Rubinstein, S. L. "Die Arbeit." In *Kreativitätsforschung*, edited by Gisela Ulmann, 196-218. Köln: Kiepenheuer & Witsch, 1973.

Sachs, Harvey. *Toscanini*. Roseville, CA: Prima Publishing, 1995.

Sambursky, Shmuel. *Physical Thought from the Presocratics to the Quantum Physicists: An Anthology*. New York: Pica Press, 1975.

Sandblom, Philip. *Creativity and Disease: How Illness Affects Literature, Art and Music*. Philadelphia: George F. Stickley Company, 1987.

Sarris, Andrew "The Magnificent Child." In *The New York Times Book Review*, March 25, 1990.

Severns, Karen and Koichi Mori. *Magnificent Obsessions: Frank Lloyd Wright's Buildings and Legacy in Japan*. DVD. Chicago, IL. Facets Multimedia, 2005.

Schama, Simon. *Rembrandt's Eyes*. London: Penguin Books, 1999.

Schregenberger, Johann W. "Methodenbewusstes Problemlösen. Ein Beitrag zur Ausbildung von Konstrukteuren, Beratern und Führungskräften." Zürich: Institut für Bauplanung und Baubetrieb ETH, Publikation nr. 15, Dezember, 1981.

Shelton, Robert. *No Direction Home: The Life and Music of Bob Dylan*. London: Penguin Books, 1987.

Sheng, Bright. "Melodic Migration in Northwest China." In *Along the Silk Road: Asian Art and Culture*, edited by Elizabeth ten Grotenhuisn, 39-57. Seattle: University of Washington Press, 2002.

Shikes, Ralph E. and Paula Harper. *Pissarro: His life and Work*. New York: Horizon Press, 1980.

Shipton, Alyn. *Groovin' High: Phe Life of Dizzy Gillespie*. New York: Oxford University Press, 1999.

Simonton, Dean K. "Genius: The Lessons of Historiometry." In *Frontiers of Creativity Research: Beyond The Basics*, edited by Scott G. Isaksen, 66-87. Buffalo, NY: Bearly Limited, 1987.

Sochen, June. *Mae West: She Who Laughs, Lasts*. Arlington Heights: Harlan Davidson Inc., 1992.

Solomon, Maynard. *Beethoven Essays*. Cambridge, MA : Harvard University Press, 1988.

———. *Mozart: A Life*. New York: Harper Perennial, 1996.

Sounes, Howard. *Down the Highway. The Life of Bob Dylan*. New York: Grove Press, 2001.

Soyinka, Wole. *Art, Dialogue and Outrage: Essays on Literature and Culture*. New York: Pantheon Books, 1994.

———. "Kultur und Ueberleben." In *Intuition und Kreativität*, edited by Gottlieb Guntern, 307-345. Zürich: Scalo Verlag, 1996.

———. In *The Challenge of Creative Leadership*, edited by Gottlieb Guntern: London: Shepheard-Walwyn Publishers, Ltd., 1997.

Spender, Stephen. "The Making of a Poem." In *The Creative Process: A Symposium*, edited by Brewster Ghiselin, 113-126. Berkely: University of California Press, 1985.

Stannard, Martin. *Evelyn Waugh: The Early Years, 1903-1939*. New York: W. W. Norton & Company, 1987.

Stassinopoulos, Arianna. *Maria Callas: The Woman Behind the Legend*. New York: Ballantin Books, 1982.

———. *Picasso: Creator and Destroyer*. London: Pan Books, 1989.

Stevenson, Anne. *Bitter Fame: A Life of Sylvia Plath*. Boston: Houghton Mifflin, 1989.

Suzuki, Daisetz Teitaro. *Zen and Japanese Culture*. Princeton: Princeton University Press, 1970.

ten Grotenhuis Elizabeth, ed. *Along the Silk Road: Asian Art and Culture*. Seattle: University of Washington Press, 2002a.

———. "Introduction: The Silk Road, Ancient and Temporary." In *Along the Silk Road: Asian Art and Culture*, edited by Elizabeth ten Grotenhuis, 15-23. Seattle: University of Washington Press, 2002b.

Thompson, D'Arcy. *On Growth and Form*. Cambridge: Cambridge University Press, 1961.

Thubron, Colin. *Shadow of the Silk Road*. London: Chatto & Windus, 2006.

Thwaites, Barnabas. "Das Ballett der Moleküle." In *GEO*, nr. 2, 07.05.1990: 136-139.

Townes, Charles H. *How the Laser Happened: Adventures of a Scientist*. New York: Oxford University Press, Inc., 1999.

Troyat, Henri. *Tchekhov*. Paris: Flammarion, 1984.

———. *Maupassant*. Paris: Flammarion, 1989.

Tucker, Jonathan. *The Silk Road: Art and History*. London: Philip Wilson Publishers, Ltd., 2003.

Tynan, Kathleen: *The Life of Kenneth Tynan*. New York: William Morrow and Company, 1987.

Ullmann, Liv. "Inspiration fängt erst mitten im Schaffen an." In *Imagination und Kreativität,* edited by Gottlieb Guntern, 205-268. Zürich: Scalo Verlag, 1995.

Ustinov, Peter. *Dear Me*. Harmondsworth, UK: Penguin Books, 1977.

Vargas Llosa, Mario. *A Fish in the Water: A Memoir*. London: Faber and Faber, 1995.

Vasari, Giorgio. *Leben der ausgezeichnetsten Maler, Bildhauer und Baumeister von Cimabue bis zum Jahre 1567: Band I*. Worms: Wernersche Verlagsgesellschaft, 1988: Band I, 132-173.

Walcott, Derek. *What the Twilight Says*. New York: Farrar, Straus, and Giroux, 1998.

Wali, Kameshwar C. *Chandra: A Biography of S. Chandrasekhar*. Chicago: The University of Chicago Press, 1991.

Walter, Bruno. *Thema und Variationen: Erinnerungen und Gedanken*. Frankfurt am Main: S. Fischer Verlag, 1988.

Waters, Frank. *Book of the Hopi*. New York: Ballantine Books, 1974.

Watson, James D. *The Double Helix: A Personal Account of the Discovery of the Structure of DNA*. New York: A Mentor Book/New American Library, 1969.

Weatherford, Jack. *Genghis Khan and the Making of the Modern World*. New York: Random House, 2004.

Weeks, Marcus. *Musik: Klassisches von der Gregorianik bis zur Moderne*. München: Prestel, 1999.

Weinberg, Steven. "Die Welt ist kalt und unpersönlich." Spiegel-Gespräch, *DER SPIEGEL,* 30/1999: 191-194, 191.

Werner-Jensen, Arnold. *Das Reclam-Buch der Musik*. Stuttgart: Reclam, 2001.

Whitford, Frank. *Bauhaus*. London: Thames and Hudson, 1986.

Whitton, Joel L, Harvey Moldofsky, and Franc Lue. "EEG Frequency." In *Biological Psychiatry* 13, no. 1, 1978: 123-133.

Wilcken, Ulrich. *Alexander the Great*. New York: W. W. Norton & Company, Inc., 1967.

Wilson, A. N. *Tolstoy*. New York: Fawcett Columbine/Ballantine Books, 1989.

Winters, Shelley. *Shelley: Also Known as Shirley*. New York: William Morrow and Company, 1980.

Wolfe, Thomas "The Story of a Novel." In *The Creative Process: A Symposium,* edited by Brewster Ghiselin, 192-205. Berkely: University of California Press, 1985.

Wood, Frances. *The Silk Road: Two Thousand Years in the Heart of Asia*. Berkeley: University of California Press, 2003.

Woodward, Ian. *Glenda Jackson: A Study in Fire and Ice*. London: Coronet Books/ Hodder and Stoughton, 1986.

Wordsworth, William. Preface to Second Edition of Lyrical Balllads. In *The Creative Process: A Symposium*, edited by Brewster Ghiselin, 81-82. Berkely: University of California Press, 1985.

Yourcenar, Marguerite. *Les yeux ouverts: Entretiens avec Matthieu Galey*. Paris: Editions Le Centurion, 1980.

Name Index

Breinigsville, PA USA
14 March 2011
257532BV00002B/17/P

0 1341 1365285 0

RECEIVED

MAY 3 1 2011

GUELPH HUMBER LIBRARY
205 Humber College Blvd
Toronto, ON   M9W 5L7